Brief Contents

Thematic Table of Contents   xiii
Preface   xv
Real Support for Instructors and Students   xxx
A Note to Students from Susan Anker   xxxiii

Part 1 How to Write Paragraphs and Essays   1

1. Critical Thinking, Reading, and Writing   3
2. Writing Basics   27
3. Finding, Narrowing, and Exploring Your Topic   42
4. Writing Your Topic Sentence or Thesis Statement   52
5. Supporting Your Point   68
6. Drafting   77
7. Revising   96

Part 2 Writing Different Kinds of Paragraphs and Essays   111

8. Narration   113
9. Illustration   132
10. Description   152
11. Process Analysis   170
12. Classification   188
13. Definition   207
14. Comparison and Contrast   225
15. Cause and Effect   246
16. Argument   265

Part 3 Special College Writing Projects   289

17. Writing Summaries, Reports, and Essay Exams   291
18. Writing the Research Essay   302

Part 4 The Four Most Serious Errors   327

19. The Basic Sentence ✓   329
20. Fragments ✓   341
21. Run-Ons ✓   359
22. Problems with Subject-Verb Agreement ✓   377
23. Verb Tense ✓   397

Part 5 Other Grammar Concerns   423

24. Pronouns ✓   425
25. Adjectives and Adverbs   448
26. Misplaced and Dangling Modifiers   458
27. Coordination and Subordination   465
28. Parallelism ✓   478
29. Sentence Variety   486
30. Formal English and ESL Concerns   499

Part 6 Word Use   533

31. Word Choice   535
32. Commonly Confused Words   545
33. Spelling   557

Part 7 Punctuation and Capitalization   565

34. Commas ✓   567
35. Apostrophes ✓   582
36. Quotation Marks   590
37. Other Punctuation   598
38. Capitalization ✓   604

EDITING REVIEW TESTS 1–10   609

Part 8 Readings for Writers   619

39. Narration   621
40. Illustration   629
41. Description   638
42. Process Analysis   648
43. Classification   657
44. Definition   667
45. Comparison and Contrast   675
46. Cause and Effect   687
47. Argument   696

Index   I-1
Real Take-Away Points
Editing and Proofreading Marks
For Easy Reference: Selected Lists and Charts

✓ LearningCurve activity available for this topic. Visit bedfordstmartins.com/realwriting/LC

SIXTH EDITION

Real Writing
with Readings

Paragraphs and Essays for College, Work, and Everyday Life

Susan Anker

Bedford / St. Martin's
Boston ◆ New York

In memory of Dominic Deiro, 1990–2011

For Bedford/St. Martin's

Senior Executive Editor, College Success and Developmental Studies: Edwin Hill
Executive Editor, Developmental Studies: Alexis Walker
Senior Developmental Editor: Martha Bustin
Senior Production Editor: Deborah Baker
Senior Production Supervisor: Jennifer Peterson
Senior Marketing Manager: Christina Shea
Editorial Assistants: Amanda Legee, Regina Tavani
Copy Editor: Kathleen Lafferty
Indexer: Mary White
Photo Researcher: Naomi Kornhauser
Permissions Manager: Kalina K. Ingham
Senior Art Director: Anna Palchik
Cover Design: Billy Boardman
Cover Photos: Front: © Sam Bloomberg-Rissman/Getty Images. *Back:* Joel Beaman
Composition: Graphic World Inc.
Printing and Binding: RR Donnelley and Sons

President, Bedford/St. Martin's: Denise B. Wydra
Presidents, Macmillan Higher Education: Joan E. Feinberg and Tom Scotty
Editor in Chief: Karen S. Henry
Director of Marketing: Karen R. Soeltz
Production Director: Susan W. Brown
Associate Production Director: Elise S. Kaiser
Managing Editor: Elizabeth M. Schaaf

Library of Congress Control Number: 2012935726

Copyright © 2013, 2010, 2007, 2004 by Bedford/St. Martin's

All rights reserved. No part of this book may be reproduced, stored in a retrieval system, or transmitted in any form or by any means, electronic, mechanical, photocopying, recording, or otherwise, except as may be expressly permitted by the applicable copyright statutes or in writing by the Publisher.

Manufactured in the United States of America.

7   6   5   4   3
f   e   d   c

For information, write: Bedford/St. Martin's, 75 Arlington Street, Boston, MA 02116 (617-399-4000)

ISBN 978-1-4576-0199-6 (Student Edition)
ISBN 978-1-4576-2425-4 (Loose-leaf Edition)

Acknowledgments

Acknowledgments and copyrights are continued at the back of the book on pages 717–18, which constitute an extension of the copyright page. It is a violation of the law to reproduce these selections by any means whatsoever without the written permission of the copyright holder.

Contents

Thematic Table of Contents   xiii
Preface   xv
Real Support for Instructors and Students   xxx
A Note to Students from Susan Anker   xxxiii

Part 1
How to Write Paragraphs and Essays   1

1. **Critical Thinking, Reading, and Writing: Making Connections**   3

   What Is Critical Thinking?   6
   - FOUR BASICS OF CRITICAL THINKING   7
   What Is Critical Reading?   9
   - 2PR: The Critical Reading Process   9
     Amanda Jacobowitz, *A Ban on Water Bottles: A Way to Bolster the University's Image*   12
   What Is Writing Critically about Readings?   16
   - Reading and Writing Critically   16
   What Is Writing Critically about Visuals?   21
   What Is Problem Solving?   24
   Chapter Review   26

2. **Writing Basics: Audience, Purpose, and Process**   27

   - FOUR BASICS OF GOOD WRITING   27
   Understand Audience and Purpose   27
       DIAGRAM: Relationship between Paragraphs and Essays   32
   Understand the Writing Process   34
   Understand Grading Criteria   35
   Chapter Review   41

3. **Finding, Narrowing, and Exploring Your Topic: Choosing Something to Write About**   42

   Understand What a Topic Is   42
   Practice Narrowing a Topic   43
   Practice Exploring Your Topic   46
   Write Your Own Topic and Ideas   50
   Chapter Review   50

4. **Writing Your Topic Sentence or Thesis Statement: Making Your Point**   52

   Understand What a Topic Sentence and a Thesis Statement Are   52
   Practice Developing a Good Topic Sentence or Thesis Statement   55
       DIAGRAM: Relationship between Paragraphs and Essays   56
   Write Your Own Topic Sentence or Thesis Statement   64
   Chapter Review   66

5. **Supporting Your Point: Finding Details, Examples, and Facts**   68

   Understand What Support Is   68
   Practice Supporting a Main Point   71
   Write Your Own Support   73
   Chapter Review   75

6. **Drafting: Putting Your Ideas Together**   77

   Understand What a Draft Is   77
   Arrange Your Ideas   78
   Make a Plan   80

v

Practice Writing a Draft Paragraph 82

Practice Writing a Draft Essay 84

Write Your Own Draft Paragraph or Essay 91

Chapter Review 94

7. Revising: Improving Your Paragraph or Essay 96

Understand What Revision Is 96

Understand What Peer Review Is 97

Practice Revising for Unity, Detail, and Coherence 98

Revise Your Own Paragraph 105

Revise Your Own Essay 107

Chapter Review 109

Part 2
Writing Different Kinds of Paragraphs and Essays 111

8. Narration: Writing That Tells Important Stories 113

Understand What Narration Is 113

FOUR BASICS OF GOOD NARRATION 113

Main Point in Narration 115

Support in Narration 116

DIAGRAM: Paragraphs vs. Essays in Narration 118

Organization in Narration 121

Read and Analyze Narration 123

PROFILE OF SUCCESS: Kelly Layland, Registered Nurse 123

Student Paragraph: Jelani Lynch: *My Turnaround* 124

Professional Essay: Amy Tan, *Fish Cheeks* 126

Write Your Own Narration (Assignments) 128

Writing about College, Work, and Everyday Life 128

Reading and Writing Critically 128

Writing Critically about Readings 129

Writing about Images 129

Writing to Solve a Problem 130

Checklist and Chapter Review 130

9. Illustration: Writing That Gives Examples 132

Understand What Illustration Is 132

FOUR BASICS OF GOOD ILLUSTRATION 132

Main Point in Illustration 134

Support in Illustration 135

DIAGRAM: Paragraphs vs. Essays in Illustration 136

Organization in Illustration 139

Read and Analyze Illustration 140

PROFILE OF SUCCESS: Karen Upright, Systems Manager 140

Student Paragraph: Casandra Palmer, *Gifts from the Heart* 142

Professional Essay: Susan Adams, *The Weirdest Job Interview Questions and How to Handle Them* 144

Write Your Own Illustration (Assignments) 147

Writing about College, Work, and Everyday Life 147

Reading and Writing Critically 148

Writing Critically about Readings 148

Writing about Images 149

Writing to Solve a Problem 150

Checklist and Chapter Review 150

10. Description: Writing That Creates Pictures in Words 152

Understand What Description Is 152

FOUR BASICS OF GOOD DESCRIPTION 152

Main Point in Description 154

Support in Description 156

DIAGRAM: Paragraphs vs. Essays in Description 158

Organization in Description 160

Read and Analyze Description 161

PROFILE OF SUCCESS: Celia Hyde, Chief of Police 161

Student Paragraph: Alessandra Cepeda, *Bird Rescue* 163

Professional Essay: Oscar Hijuelos, *Memories of New York City Snow* 164

Write Your Own Description (Assignments) 166

Writing about College, Work, and Everyday Life 166

Contents   **vii**

    Reading and Writing Critically   167
        Writing Critically about Readings   167
        Writing about Images   167
        Writing to Solve a Problem   168
   Checklist and Chapter Review   169

11. Process Analysis: Writing That Explains How Things Happen   170

Understand What Process Analysis Is   170
■ FOUR BASICS OF GOOD PROCESS ANALYSIS   170
   Main Point in Process Analysis   172
   Support in Process Analysis   172
      DIAGRAM: Paragraphs vs. Essays in Process Analysis   174
   Organization in Process Analysis   176

Read and Analyze Process Analysis   176
   PROFILE OF SUCCESS: Jeremy Graham, Youth Pastor and Motivational Speaker   177
   Student Paragraph: Charlton Brown, *Buying a Car at an Auction*   178
   Professional Essay: Ian Frazier, *How to Operate the Shower Curtain*   179

Write Your Own Process Analysis (Assignments)   183
   Writing about College, Work, and Everyday Life   183
   Reading and Writing Critically   184
      Writing Critically about Readings   184
      Writing about Images   184
      Writing to Solve a Problem   185
Checklist and Chapter Review   186

12. Classification: Writing That Sorts Things into Groups   188

Understand What Classification Is   188
■ FOUR BASICS OF GOOD CLASSIFICATION   188
   Main Point in Classification   190
   Support in Classification   193
      DIAGRAM: Paragraphs vs. Essays in Classification   194
   Organization in Classification   196

Read and Analyze Classification   197
   PROFILE OF SUCCESS: Leigh King, Fashion Writer / Blogger   197
   Student Paragraph: Lorenza Mattazi, *All My Music*   198

   Professional Essay: Frances Cole Jones, *Don't Work in a Goat's Stomach*   199

Write Your Own Classification (Assignments)   202
   Writing about College, Work, and Everyday Life   202
   Reading and Writing Critically   203
      Writing Critically about Readings   203
      Writing about Images   204
      Writing to Solve a Problem   204
Checklist and Chapter Review   205

13. Definition: Writing That Tells What Something Means   207

Understand What Definition Is   207
■ FOUR BASICS OF GOOD DEFINITION   207
   Main Point in Definition   209
   Support in Definition   210
      DIAGRAM: Paragraphs vs. Essays in Definition   212
   Organization in Definition   214

Read and Analyze Definition   214
   PROFILE OF SUCCESS: Walter Scanlon, Program and Workplace Consultant   215
   Student Paragraph: Corin Costas, *What Community Involvement Means to Me*   216
   Professional Essay: Janice E. Castro with Dan Cook and Cristina Garcia, *Spanglish*   218

Write Your Own Definition (Assignments)   220
   Writing about College, Work, and Everyday Life   221
   Reading and Writing Critically   221
      Writing Critically about Readings   222
      Writing about Images   222
      Writing to Solve a Problem   223
Checklist and Chapter Review   223

14. Comparison and Contrast: Writing That Shows Similarities and Differences   225

Understand What Comparison and Contrast Are   225
■ FOUR BASICS OF GOOD COMPARISON AND CONTRAST   225
   Main Point in Comparison and Contrast   228
   Support in Comparison and Contrast   229

viii Contents

    DIAGRAM: Paragraphs vs. Essays in Comparison and Contrast 230

    Organization in Comparison and Contrast 232

Read and Analyze Comparison and Contrast 235

    PROFILE OF SUCCESS: Brad Leibov, President, New Chicago Fund, Inc. 236

    Student Paragraph: Said Ibrahim, *Eyeglasses vs. Laser Surgery: Benefits and Drawbacks* 237

    Professional Essay: Mark Twain, *Two Ways of Seeing a River* 238

Write Your Own Comparison and Contrast (Assignments) 240

    Writing about College, Work, and Everyday Life 240

    Reading and Writing Critically 241

        Writing Critically about Readings 241

        Writing about Images 242

        Writing to Solve a Problem 243

Checklist and Chapter Review 244

15. Cause and Effect: Writing That Explains Reasons or Results 246

Understand What Cause and Effect Are 246

    FOUR BASICS OF GOOD CAUSE AND EFFECT 246

    Main Point in Cause and Effect 250

    Support in Cause and Effect 251

    DIAGRAM: Paragraphs vs. Essays in Cause and Effect 252

    Organization in Cause and Effect 254

Read and Analyze Cause and Effect 255

    PROFILE OF SUCCESS: Mary LaCue Booker, Singer, Actor 256

    Student Paragraph: Caitlin Prokop, *A Difficult Decision with a Positive Outcome* 257

    Professional Essay: Kristen Ziman, *Bad Attitudes and Glowworms* 259

Write Your Own Cause and Effect (Assignments) 261

    Writing about College, Work, and Everyday Life 261

    Reading and Writing Critically 262

        Writing Critically about Readings 262

        Writing about Images 263

        Writing to Solve a Problem 263

Checklist and Chapter Review 264

16. Argument: Writing That Persuades 265

Understand What Argument Is 265

    FOUR BASICS OF GOOD ARGUMENT 265

    Main Point in Argument 267

    Support in Argument 268

    DIAGRAM: Paragraphs vs. Essays in Argument 270

    Organization in Argument 276

Read and Analyze Argument 278

    PROFILE OF SUCCESS: Diane Melancon, Oncologist 279

    Student Essay 1: "Yes" to Social Media in Education: Jason Yilmaz, *A Learning Tool Whose Time Has Come* 281

    Student Essay 2: "No" to Social Media in Education: Shari Beck, *A Classroom Distraction—and Worse* 282

Write Your Own Argument (Assignments) 284

    Writing about College, Work, and Everyday Life 284

    Reading and Writing Critically 285

        Writing Critically about Readings 285

        Writing about Images 286

        Writing to Solve a Problem 287

Checklist and Chapter Review 287

Part 3
Special College Writing Projects 289

17. Writing Summaries, Reports, and Essay Exams: Showing What You Have Learned 291

Write a Summary 291

    FOUR BASICS OF A GOOD SUMMARY 291

Write a Report 295

    FOUR BASICS OF A GOOD REPORT 295

Write a Response to an Essay Exam Question 298

    FOUR BASICS OF A GOOD RESPONSE TO AN ESSAY QUESTION 299

Chapter Review 301

18. Writing the Research Essay: Using Sources in Your Writing 302

   Make a Schedule 302
   Choose a Topic 303
   Find Sources 304
   Evaluate Sources 307
   Avoid Plagiarism 310
   Cite and Document Your Sources 313
   DIRECTORY OF MLA IN-TEXT CITATIONS 314
   DIRECTORY OF MLA WORKS CITED 316
      Student Research Essay: Dara Riesler, *Service Dogs Help Heal the Mental Wounds of War* 319

Part 4
The Four Most Serious Errors 327

19. The Basic Sentence: An Overview ✓ 329

   The Four Most Serious Errors 329
   The Parts of Speech 329
   The Basic Sentence 331
   Chapter Review and Test 339

20. Fragments: Incomplete Sentences ✓ 341

   Understand What Fragments Are 341
   Find and Correct Fragments 342
   Edit for Fragments 353
   Chapter Review and Test 356

21. Run-Ons: Two Sentences Joined Incorrectly ✓ 359

   Understand What Run-Ons Are 359
   Find and Correct Run-Ons 361
   Edit for Run-Ons 371
   Chapter Review and Test 373

22. Problems with Subject-Verb Agreement: When Subjects and Verbs Don't Match ✓ 377

   Understand What Subject-Verb Agreement Is 377
   Find and Correct Errors in Subject-Verb Agreement 379
   Edit for Subject-Verb Agreement 391
   Chapter Review and Test 393

23. Verb Tense: Using Verbs to Express Different Times ✓ 397

   Understand What Verb Tense Is 397
   Practice Using Correct Verbs 398
   Edit for Verb Problems 416
   Chapter Review and Test 418

Part 5
Other Grammar Concerns 423

24. Pronouns: Using Substitutes for Nouns ✓ 425

   Understand What Pronouns Are 425
   Practice Using Pronouns Correctly 425
   Edit for Pronoun Problems 442
   Chapter Review and Test 444

25. Adjectives and Adverbs: Using Descriptive Words 448

   Understand What Adjectives and Adverbs Are 448
   Practice Using Adjectives and Adverbs Correctly 449
   Edit for Adjective and Adverb Problems 454
   Chapter Review and Test 455

26. Misplaced and Dangling Modifiers: Avoiding Confusing Descriptions 458

   Understand What Misplaced Modifiers Are 458
   Practice Correcting Misplaced Modifiers 459
   Understand What Dangling Modifiers Are 460
   Practice Correcting Dangling Modifiers 460
   Edit for Misplaced and Dangling Modifiers 461
   Chapter Review and Test 462

✓ **LearningCurve** activity available for this topic. Visit **bedfordstmartins.com/realwriting/LC**.

x   Contents

27. Coordination and Subordination: Joining Sentences with Related Ideas 465

    Understand What Coordination Is   465
    Practice Using Coordination   465
    Understand What Subordination Is   471
    Practice Using Subordination   471
    Edit for Coordination and Subordination   474
    Chapter Review and Test   475

28. Parallelism: Balancing Ideas ✓ 478

    Understand What Parallelism Is   478
    Practice Writing Parallel Sentences   479
    Edit for Parallelism Problems   483
    Chapter Review and Test   484

29. Sentence Variety: Putting Rhythm in Your Writing 486

    Understand What Sentence Variety Is   486
    Practice Creating Sentence Variety   487
    Edit for Sentence Variety   496
    Chapter Review and Test   497

30. Formal English and ESL Concerns: Grammar Trouble Spots for Multilingual Students 499

    Basic Sentence Patterns   499
    Pronouns   505
    Verbs   507
    Articles   524
    Prepositions   527
    Chapter Review and Test   530

Part 6
Word Use   533

31. Word Choice: Using the Right Words 535

    Understand the Importance of Choosing Words Carefully   535
    Practice Avoiding Four Common Word-Choice Problems   536
    Edit for Word Choice   542
    Chapter Review and Test   542

32. Commonly Confused Words: Avoiding Mistakes with Soundalike Words 545

    Understand Why Certain Words Are Commonly Confused   545
    Practice Using Commonly Confused Words Correctly   545
    Edit for Commonly Confused Words   555
    Chapter Review and Test   556

33. Spelling: Using the Right Letters 557

    Finding and Correcting Spelling Mistakes   557
    Strategies for Becoming a Better Speller   558
    Chapter Review and Test   563

Part 7
Punctuation and Capitalization   565

34. Commas (,) ✓ 567

    Understand What Commas Do   567
    Practice Using Commas Correctly   567
    Edit for Commas   578
    Chapter Review and Test   579

35. Apostrophes (') ✓ 582

    Understand What Apostrophes Do   582
    Practice Using Apostrophes Correctly   582
    Edit for Apostrophes   587
    Chapter Review and Test   588

36. Quotation Marks (" ") 590

    Understand What Quotation Marks Do   590
    Practice Using Quotation Marks Correctly   590
    Edit for Quotation Marks   595
    Chapter Review and Test   596

37. Other Punctuation (; : ( ) -- -) 598

    Understand What Punctuation Does   598
    Practice Using Punctuation Correctly   598
    Edit for Other Punctuation Marks   601
    Chapter Review and Test   602

✓ **LearningCurve** activity available for this topic. Visit **bedfordstmartins.com/realwriting/LC**.

38. Capitalization: Using Capital Letters ☑ 604

    Understand Three Rules of Capitalization 604

    Practice Capitalization 604

    Chapter Review and Test 607

    EDITING REVIEW TESTS 1–10 609

Part 8
Readings for Writers 619

39. Narration 621

    Lauren Mack, *Gel Pens* 622

    Pat Conroy, *Chili Cheese Dogs, My Father, and Me* 625

40. Illustration 629

    True Shields, *To Stand in Giants' Shadows* 629

    Dianne Hales, *Why Are We So Angry?* 634

41. Description 638

    Brian Healy, *First Day in Fallujah* 638

    Eric Liu, *Po-Po in Chinatown* 642

42. Process Analysis 648

    Jasen Beverly, *My Pilgrimage* 648

    Sherman Alexie, *The Joy of Reading and Writing: Superman and Me* 652

43. Classification 657

    Kelly Hultgren, *Pick Up the Phone to Call, Not Text* 657

    Stephanie Ericsson, *The Ways We Lie* 661

44. Definition 667

    John Around Him, *Free Money* 667

    Michael Thompson, *Passage into Manhood* 671

45. Comparison and Contrast 675

    Courtney Stoker, *The Great Debate: Essentialism vs. Dominance* 675

    Judith Ortiz Cofer, *Don't Misread My Signals* 682

46. Cause and Effect 687

    Holly Moeller, *Say, Don't Spray* 687

    John Tierney, *Yes, Money Can Buy Happiness* 692

47. Argument 696

    SNITCHING 696

    Robert Phansalkar, *Stop Snitchin' Won't Stop Crime* 697

    Bill Maxwell, *Start Snitching* 700

    Alexandra Natapoff, *Bait and Snitch: The High Cost of Snitching for Law Enforcement* 703

    RIGHTS FOR ILLEGAL IMMIGRANTS 708

    Heather Rushall, *Dream Act Is Finance Fantasy* 708

    Dominic Deiro, *I Have a DREAM* 712

Index I-1
Real Take-Away Points
Editing and Proofreading Marks
For Easy Reference: Selected Lists and Charts

☑ **LearningCurve** activity available for this topic. Visit **bedfordstmartins.com/realwriting/LC**.

Thematic Table of Contents

Education

Jason Yilmaz, *A Learning Tool Whose Time Has Come* (argument)   281

Shari Beck, *A Classroom Distraction—and Worse* (argument)   282

Jasen Beverly, *My Pilgrimage* (process analysis)   648

Sherman Alexie, *The Joy of Reading and Writing: Superman and Me* (process analysis)   652

John Around Him, *Free Money* (definition)   667

Heather Rushall, *Dream Act Is Finance Fantasy* (argument)   708

Dominic Deiro, *I Have a DREAM* (argument)   712

Humor

Amy Tan, *Fish Cheeks* (narration)   126

Susan Adams, *The Weirdest Job Interview Questions and How to Handle Them* (illustration)   144

Ian Frazier, *How to Operate the Shower Curtain* (process analysis)   179

Frances Cole Jones, *Don't Work in a Goat's Stomach* (classification)   199

Language and Communication

Susan Adams, *The Weirdest Job Interview Questions and How to Handle Them* (illustration)   144

Janice E. Castro with Dan Cook and Cristina Garcia, *Spanglish* (definition)   218

Kelly Hultgren, *Pick Up the Phone to Call, Not Text* (classification)   657

Stephanie Ericsson, *The Ways We Lie* (classification)   661

Courtney Stoker, *The Great Debate: Essentialism vs. Dominance* (comparison/contrast)   675

Personal Stories

Amy Tan, *Fish Cheeks* (narration)   126

Oscar Hijuelos, *Memories of New York City Snow* (description)   164

Mark Twain, *Two Ways of Seeing a River* (comparison/contrast)   238

Lauren Mack, *Gel Pens* (narration)   622

Pat Conroy, *Chili Cheese Dogs, My Father, and Me* (narration)   625

True Shields, *To Stand in Giants' Shadows* (illustration)   629

Brian Healy, *First Day in Fallujah* (description)   638

Eric Liu, *Po-Po in Chinatown* (description)   642

Jasen Beverly, *My Pilgrimage* (process analysis)   648

Sherman Alexie, *The Joy of Reading and Writing: Superman and Me* (process analysis)   657

Judith Ortiz Cofer, *Don't Misread My Signals* (comparison/contrast)   682

Psychology: Behavior and the Mind

Kristen Ziman, *Bad Attitudes and Glowworms* (cause/effect)   259

Dara Riesler, *Service Dogs Help Heal the Mental Wounds of War* (argument)   320

Dianne Hales, *Why Are We So Angry?* (illustration)   634

Brian Healy, *First Day in Fallujah* (description)   638

Stephanie Ericsson, *The Ways We Lie* (classification) 661

Michael Thompson, *Passage into Manhood* (definition) 671

Courtney Stoker, *The Great Debate: Essentialism vs. Dominance* (comparison/contrast) 675

John Tierney, *Yes, Money Can Buy Happiness* (cause/effect) 692

Social Issues and Challenges

Amanda Jacobowitz, *A Ban on Water Bottles: A Way to Bolster the University's Image* (argument) 12

Jason Yilmaz, *A Learning Tool Whose Time Has Come* (argument) 281

Shari Beck, *A Classroom Distraction—and Worse* (argument) 282

Dara Riesler, *Service Dogs Help Heal the Mental Wounds of War* (argument) 320

Brian Healy, *First Day in Fallujah* (description) 638

Stephanie Ericsson, *The Ways We Lie* (classification) 661

Michael Thompson, *Passage into Manhood* (definition) 671

Holly Moeller, *Say, Don't Spray* (cause/effect) 687

Courtney Stoker, *The Great Debate: Essentialism vs. Dominance* (comparison/contrast) 675

Robert Phansalkar, *Stop Snitchin' Won't Stop Crime* (argument) 697

Bill Maxwell, *Start Snitching* (argument) 700

Alexandra Natapoff, *Bait and Snitch: The High Cost of Snitching for Law Enforcement* (argument) 703

Heather Rushall, *Dream Act Is Finance Fantasy* (argument) 708

Dominic Deiro, *I Have a DREAM* (argument) 712

Trends

Amanda Jacobowitz, *A Ban on Water Bottles: A Way to Bolster the University's Image* (argument) 12

Janice E. Castro with Dan Cook and Cristina Garcia, *Spanglish* (definition) 218

Jason Yilmaz, *A Learning Tool Whose Time Has Come* (argument) 281

Shari Beck, *A Classroom Distraction—and Worse* (argument) 282

Dianne Hales, *Why Are We So Angry?* (illustration) 634

Kelly Hultgren, *Pick Up the Phone to Call, Not Text* (classification) 657

Holly Moeller, *Say, Don't Spray* (cause/effect) 687

John Tierney, *Yes, Money Can Buy Happiness* (cause/effect) 692

Work

Susan Adams, *The Weirdest Job Interview Questions and How to Handle Them* (illustration) 144

Frances Cole Jones, *Don't Work in a Goat's Stomach* (classification) 199

Mark Twain, *Two Ways of Seeing a River* (comparison/contrast) 238

Kristen Ziman, *Bad Attitudes and Glowworms* (cause/effect) 259

Brian Healy, *First Day in Fallujah* (description) 638

Preface

From its first edition to the present, *Real Writing*'s central message to students has been that good writing is not only *essential* but also *achievable*. In support of this message, the book provides both an engaging real-world context for writing and an abundance of engaging exercises and activities that will help students write strong sentences, paragraphs, and essays.

Real Writing reframes writing for students who view it as irrelevant, impossible, as an activity that only other people do, or as an arbitrary requirement, externally imposed. Instead, the text presents writing and the work of the writing class as potentially life-altering: eminently learnable and worthy of students' own best efforts. In small and large ways, *Real Writing* is designed to help students connect the writing course to their other courses, to their real lives, and to the expectations of the larger world.

Core Features

The core features that have worked so well for so many instructors and students in previous editions of *Real Writing* continue to anchor this edition.

MOTIVATES STUDENTS WITH A REAL-WORLD EMPHASIS

- **Profiles of Success** showcase former students who have overcome challenges to succeed in college and in life. Now employed in a range of professions, these inspiring individuals give examples of their workplace writing, explaining why writing skills are important in their jobs, and helping students connect those skills with their own long-term goals. New profiles in this edition showcase a youth pastor and motivational speaker, a fashion writer and blogger, and a doctor.

PROFILE OF SUCCESS

Narration in the Real World

Background In high school, I was not a good student. I had a lot of other things to do, like having fun. I am a very social person; I loved my friends, and we had a great time. But when I decided I wanted to go to college, I had to pay the price. I had to take lots of noncredit courses to get my skills up to college level because I had fooled around during high school. The noncredit English course I took was very beneficial to me. After I passed it, I took English 101 and felt prepared for it.

Degrees/Colleges A.S., Monroe Community College; LPN, Isabella Graham Hart School of Nursing; RN, Monroe Community College

Employer Rochester General Hospital

Writing at work I write nursing notes that are narratives of patients' changing conditions and the level of care required. When I describe physical conditions, I have to support my descriptions with detailed examples. When I recommend medication for treatment, I have to justify it by explaining the patient's condition and the reasons I am making the recommendation. I also

Kelly Layland
Registered Nurse

- **"Community Connections"** sidebars offer mini-profiles of students whose engagement in college and community activities has helped them forge connections, stay in school, and build a path to future success.

- **Numerous models of student and professional writing** address such real-world issues and concerns as answering challenging job-interview questions, buying a car at an auction, and staying organized at work.

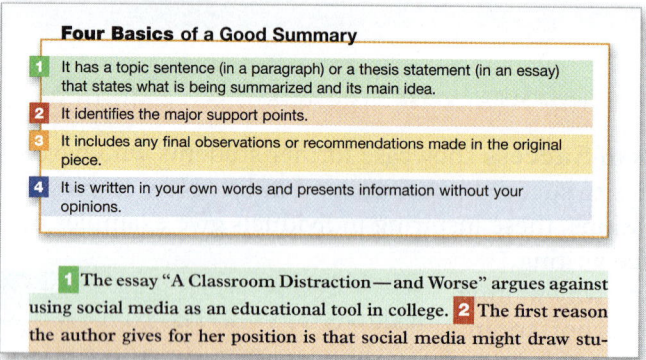

PRESENTS WRITING SKILLS IN MANAGEABLE INCREMENTS

- **Four Basics boxes** guide students to focus first on the most important elements of writing. For example, the "Four Basics of Good Writing" stresses audience; purpose; a clear, definite main point; and support. In addition, each chapter in Part 2, "Writing Different Kinds of Paragraphs and Essays," begins with the four key points to remember about the particular type of writing being discussed, followed by models that are color-coded to show the four basics at work. ▼

> **Four Basics** of a Good Summary
> 1. It has a topic sentence (in a paragraph) or a thesis statement (in an essay) that states what is being summarized and its main idea.
> 2. It identifies the major support points.
> 3. It includes any final observations or recommendations made in the original piece.
> 4. It is written in your own words and presents information without your opinions.

> 1 The essay "A Classroom Distraction—and Worse" argues against using social media as an educational tool in college. 2 The first reason the author gives for her position is that social media might draw stu-

- **End-of-chapter writing guides** give students step-by-step advice as they write and revise their papers.

MAKES GRAMMAR LESS OVERWHELMING

- **A focus, initially, on the four most serious errors**—fragments, run-ons, subject-verb agreement problems, and verb-tense problems—helps students avoid or fix the grammar mistakes that count against them most in college and the real world. Once students master these four topics and start building their editing skills, they are better prepared to tackle the grammar errors treated in later chapters.

- **"Find and Fix" boxes and end-of-chapter review charts** visually summarize key information and make excellent review and reference tools. ▼

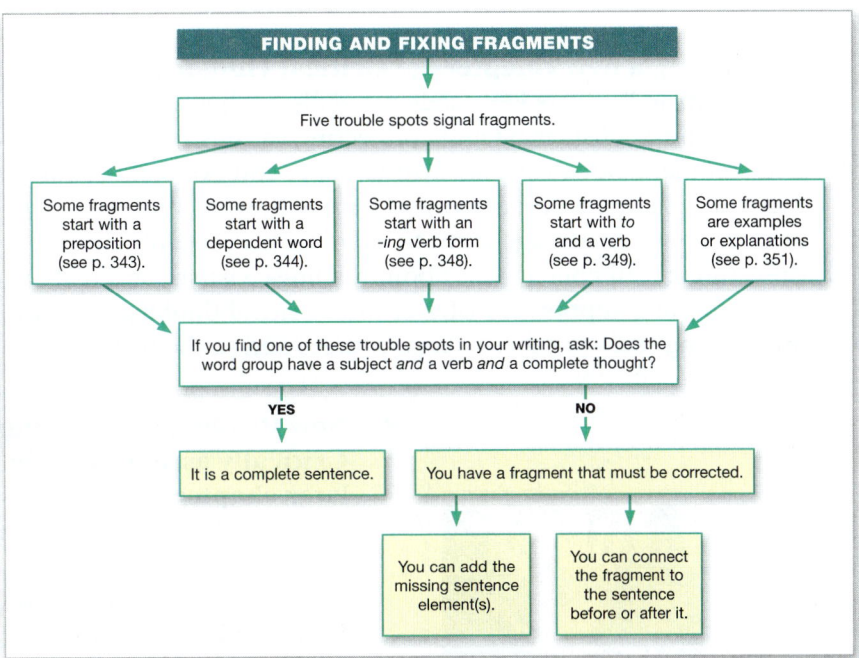

New Features

Helpful input from many instructors and students guided us in making the following changes in this edition.

NEW INTEGRATED MEDIA: LEARNINGCURVE ACTIVITIES

✓ **LearningCurve, innovative online quizzing, lets students learn at their own pace**. Each new copy of *Real Writing* now comes with access to LearningCurve, featuring a game-like interface that encourages them to keep at it. Quizzes are keyed to grammar instruction in the book, so what is taught in class gets reinforced at home. Instructors can also check in on each student's activity in a grade book.

A student access code is printed in every new student copy of *Real Writing* and *Real Writing with Readings*. Students who do not purchase a new print book can purchase access by going to bedfordstmartins.com/realwriting/LC. Instructors can also get access at this site.

NOTE: LearningCurve is also available in *WritingClass* and *SkillsClass* (see p. xxii), so if you are using either of these, encourage your students to access it there.

MORE HELP WITH CRITICAL THINKING, READING, AND WRITING

As we sought feedback from instructors, a major point of consensus emerged: Educators want to do more to build students' critical thinking skills, and with good reason. These skills are crucial not only for academic success but also for success in the workplace. According to the *2010 Critical Skills Survey* of the American Management Association, the ability to think critically is one of the most in-demand competencies in the workplace.

▼ Accordingly, **a new Chapter 1, "Critical Thinking, Reading, and Writing,"** covers key academic skills, such as questioning assumptions; considering and connecting various points of view; and summarizing, analyzing, synthesizing, and evaluating source material. Examples and activities begin with what students already know; encourage them to examine preconceptions and draw thoughtful conclusions about readings, visuals, and real-life problems; and support transfer of these critical thinking, reading, and writing skills to other college courses and to the workplace.

- **New Reading and Writing Critically assignments in later chapters** ask students to apply what they learned in Chapter 1. Additionally, the popular "College, Work, and Everyday Life" assignments have been revised to support transfer of critical thinking skills to multiple contexts.

- **An expanded argument chapter** (Chapter 16) also builds on the critical thinking skills students learned in Chapter 1, encouraging them to question assumptions as they search for evidence, a strategy that will help them create sound, well-supported arguments.

Preface xix

MORE EFFICIENT, VISUAL PRESENTATION OF INSTRUCTION

- **New color-coded charts** give students a quick, at-a-glance understanding of the similarities and differences between writing paragraphs and writing essays. ▼

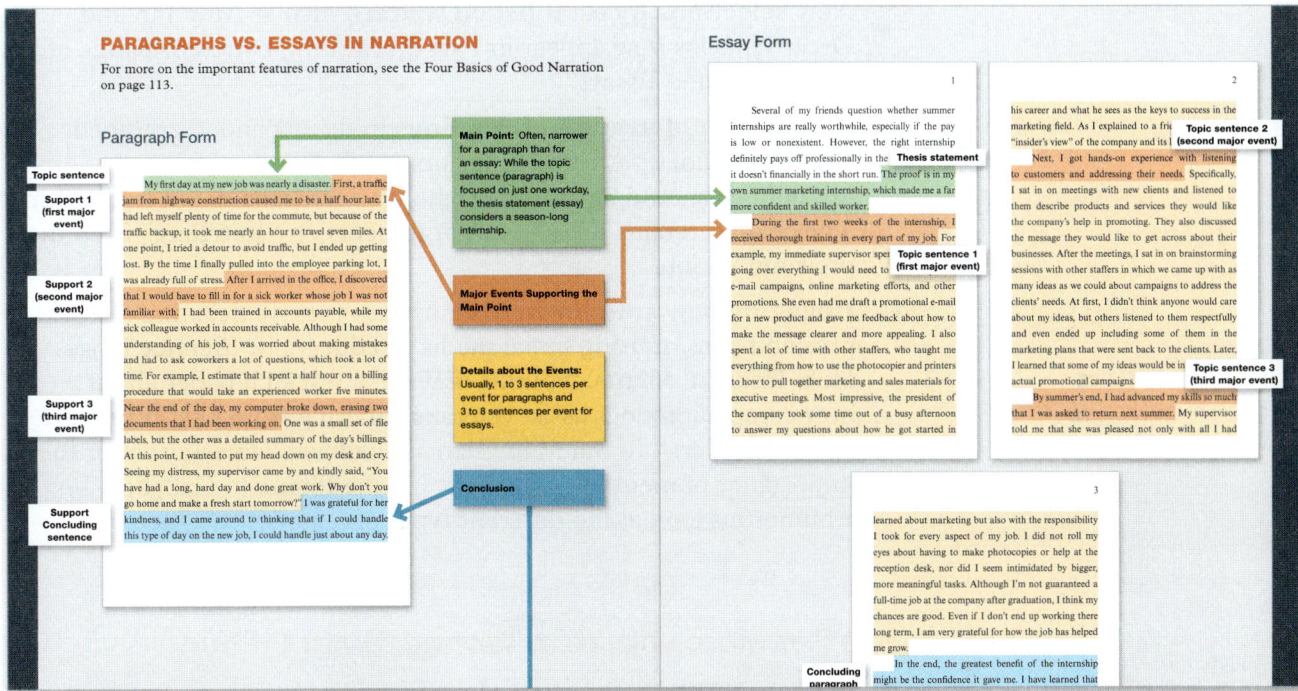

- **New, carefully selected images,** many drawn from photojournalism and the world of contemporary photography, form the basis of two activity threads: writing prompts that help students visualize and understand the various rhetorical modes ("Seeing Narration," "Seeing Illustration," and so on) and "Writing about an Image" assignments, which ask students to apply the critical thinking skills introduced in Chapter 1. ▶

Writing about Images

Study the photograph below, and complete the following steps.

1. **Read the image** You could explain to a friend what a sinkhole is, or you could show your friend the picture below. What makes this photograph such a striking visual definition? (For more on reading images, see Chapter 1.)

MANY NEW READINGS, WITH A BROADER RANGE OF AUTHORS AND TOPICS

- **Forty-six new readings** comprise more than half of the book's seventy-eight readings and provide an abundance of fresh, thought-provoking material for discussion and writing.

- **New selections by established writers** such as Amy Tan and Oscar Hijuelos now appear in Part 2, "Writing Different Kinds of Paragraphs and Essays."

- **A larger set of argument readings** in the expanded argument chapter includes paired readings on whether undocumented immigrants should be granted rights to financial aid and citizenship. The chapter retains the popular arguments on "snitching" from the previous edition.

- **Engaging new student writing** includes essays debating the pros and cons of using social media in education; "Service Dogs Help Heal the Mental Wounds of War," a research paper about how companion dogs assist veterans suffering from post-traumatic stress disorder; "To Stand in Giants' Shadows," an essay about the importance of mentors; and "Pick Up the Phone to Call, Not Text," a humorous look at the different types of texters.

You Get More with *Real Writing*, Sixth Edition

Real Writing does not stop with a book. Online and in print, you will find both free and affordable premium resources to help students get even more out of the book and your course. You will also find free, convenient instructor resources, such as a downloadable instructor's manual, additional exercises, and PowerPoint slides.

For information on ordering and to get ISBNs for packaging these resources with your students' books, see pages xxiv–xxv. You can also contact your Bedford/St. Martin's sales representative, e-mail sales support (**sales_support@bfwpub.com**), or visit **bedfordstmartins.com /realwriting/catalog**.

In the descriptions of resources below, the icon showing a book indicates a print ancillary. The icon showing a computer screen or disk indicates a media option.

STUDENT RESOURCES

Free and Open

- *Real Writing*'s free companion Web site, *The Student Site for Real Writing,* at **bedfordstmartins.com/realwriting**, provides students with supplemental exercises from *Exercise Central*, helpful guidelines on avoiding plagiarism and doing research, annotated model essays, advice on writing for the workplace, graphic organizers and peer review forms for all modes of writing covered in the book, and links to other useful resources from Bedford/St. Martin's.

- *Exercise Central* at **bedfordstmartins.com/exercisecentral** is the largest database of editing exercises on the Internet — and it is completely **free**. This comprehensive resource contains over 9,000 exercises that offer immediate feedback; the program also recommends personalized study plans and provides tutorials for common problems. Best of all, students' work reports to a grade book, allowing instructors to track students' progress quickly and easily.

Free with the Print Text

- **Supplemental Exercises for *Real Writing with Readings*, Sixth Edition,** offers more than one hundred additional practices to accompany the editing and research chapters of *Real Writing*. ISBN: 978-1-4576-2431-5

- **Quick Reference Card.** Students can prop this handy three-panel card up next to their computers for easy reference while they are writing and researching. It gives students, in concise form, the Four Basics of Good Writing, the structure of paragraphs and essays; a checklist for effective writing; the Four Most Serious Errors; tips for writing on the computer; and advice on evaluating sources, avoiding plagiarism, and documenting sources using MLA style. ISBN: 978-1-4576-2422-3

- *Exercise Central to Go: Writing and Grammar Practices for Basic Writers* **CD-ROM** provides hundreds of practice items to help students build their writing and editing skills. No Internet connection is necessary. ISBN: 978-0-312-44652-9

- *The Bedford/St. Martin's ESL Workbook* includes a broad range of exercises covering grammatical issues for multilingual students of varying language skills and backgrounds. Answers are at the back. ISBN: 978-0-312-54034-0

- The *Make-a-Paragraph Kit* is a fun, interactive CD-ROM that teaches students about paragraph development. It also contains exercises to help students build their own paragraphs, audio-visual tutorials on four of the most common errors for basic writers, and the content from *Exercise Central to Go: Writing and Grammar Practices for Basic Writers*. ISBN: 978-0-312-45332-9

- The *Bedford/St. Martin's Planner* includes everything that students need to plan and use their time effectively, with advice on preparing schedules and to-do lists plus blank schedules and calendars (monthly and weekly). The planner fits easily into a backpack or purse, so students can take it anywhere. ISBN: 978-0-312-57447-5

- *Journal Writing: A Beginning* is designed to give students an opportunity to use writing as a way to explore their thoughts and feelings. This writing journal includes a generous supply of inspirational quotations placed throughout the pages, tips for journaling, and suggested journal topics. ISBN: 978-0-312-59027-7
- *From Practice to Mastery* (study guide for the Florida Basic Skills Exit Tests) gives students all the resources they need to practice for—and pass—the Florida tests in reading and writing. It includes pre- and post-tests, abundant practices, many examples, and clear instruction in all the skills covered on the exams. ISBN: 978-0-312-41908-0

Premium

- *WritingClass* provides students with a dynamic, interactive online course space preloaded with exercises, diagnostics, video tutorials, writing and commenting tools, and more. *WritingClass* helps students stay focused and lets instructors see how they are progressing. It is available at a significant discount when packaged with the print text. To learn more about *WritingClass*, visit **yourwritingclass.com**. For access card: ISBN: 978-1-4576-2426-1
- *SkillsClass* offers all that *WritingClass* offers, plus guidance and practice in reading and study skills. This interactive online course space comes preloaded with exercises, diagnostics, video tutorials, writing and commenting tools, and more. It is available at a significant discount when packaged with the print text. To learn more about *SkillsClass*, visit **yourskillsclass.com**. ISBN: 978-1-4576-2346-2
- *Re:Writing Plus,* **now with VideoCentral,** gathers all of our premium digital content for the writing class into one online collection. This impressive resource includes innovative and interactive help with writing a paragraph; tutorials and practices that show how writing works in students' real-world experience; VideoCentral, with over 140 brief videos for the writing classroom; the first-ever peer review game, *Peer Factor*; *i-cite: visualizing sources*; plus hundreds of models of writing and hundreds of readings. *Re:Writing Plus* can be purchased separately or packaged with *Real Writing with Readings* at a significant discount. ISBN: 978-0-312-48849-9

E-BOOK OPTIONS

- *Real Writing with Readings* **e-book**. Available for the first time as a value-priced e-book, available either as a CourseSmart e-book or in formats for use with computers, tablets, and e-readers—visit **bedfordstmartins/realwriting/formats** for more information.

FREE INSTRUCTOR RESOURCES

- **The *Instructor's Annotated Edition of Real Writing with Readings*** gives practical page-by-page advice on teaching with *Real Writing with Readings*, Sixth Edition, and answers to exercises. It includes discussion prompts, strategies for teaching ESL students, ideas for additional classroom activities, suggestions for using other print and media resources, and cross-references useful to teachers at all levels of experience. ISBN: 978-1-4576-2396-7

- ***Practical Suggestions for Teaching Real Writing with Readings,* Sixth Edition,** provides helpful information and advice on teaching developmental writing. It includes sample syllabi, reading levels scores, tips on building students' critical thinking skills, resources for teaching non-native speakers and speakers of nonstandard dialects, ideas for assessing students' writing and progress, and up-to-date suggestions for using technology in the writing classroom and lab. Chapter 7, "Facilitating Cooperative Learning," suggests specific activities for using the cooperative, group-oriented approach to foster students' positive interdependence and personal accountability as well as improved writing skills. Available for download; see **bedfordstmartins.com/realwriting/catalog**.

- ***Additional Resources for Teaching Real Writing with Readings,* Sixth Edition.** This collection of resources supplements the instructional materials in the text with a variety of extra exercises and tests, transparency masters, essay planning forms, and other reproducibles for classroom use. Available for download; see **bedfordstmartins.com/realwriting/catalog**.

- ***Bedford Coursepacks*** allow you to plug *Real Writing with Readings* content into your own course management system. For details, visit **bedfordstmartins.com/coursepacks**.

- ***Testing Tool Kit: Writing and Grammar Test Bank* CD-ROM** allows instructors to create secure, customized tests and quizzes from a pool of nearly 2,000 questions covering 47 topics. It also includes 10 prebuilt diagnostic tests. ISBN: 978-0-312-43032-0

- ***Teaching Developmental Writing: Background Readings,* Fourth Edition,** is a professional resource edited by Susan Naomi Bernstein, former co-chair of the Conference on Basic Writing. It offers essays on topics of interest to basic writing instructors, along with editorial apparatus pointing out practical applications for the classroom. ISBN: 978-0-312-60251-2

- ***The Bedford Bibliography for Teachers of Basic Writing,* Third Edition** (also available online at **bedfordstmartins.com/basicbib**) has been compiled by members of the Conference on Basic Writing under the general editorship of Gregory R. Glau and Chitralekha Duttagupta. This annotated list of books, articles, and periodicals was created specifically to help teachers of basic writing find valuable resources. ISBN: 978-0-312-58154-1

- *TeachingCentral* at **bedfordstmartins.com/teachingcentral** offers the entire list of Bedford/St. Martin's print and online professional resources in one place. You will find landmark reference works, sourcebooks on pedagogical issues, award-winning collections, and practical advice for the classroom.

- **Answers to all grammar exercises** in *Real Writing,* Sixth Edition, are now available for download to instructors at **bedfordstmartins.com/realwriting/catalog**.

ORDERING INFORMATION

To order any of these ancillaries for *Real Writing with Readings*, Sixth Edition, contact your local Bedford/St. Martin's sales representative; send an e-mail to **sales_support@bfwpub.com**; or visit our Web site at **bedfordstmartins.com**.

Use these package ISBNs to order the following supplements packaged with your students' books:

REAL WRITING WITH READINGS, SIXTH EDITION, PACKAGED WITH:		
WritingClass (access card)	978-1-4576-4353-8	Premium
SkillsClass (access card)	978-1-4576-4358-3	Premium
Re:Writing Plus (access card)	978-1-4576-4351-4	Premium
Quick Reference Card for *Real Writing*	978-1-4576-5402-4	Free with print text
Journal Writing: A Beginning	978-1-4576-4354-5	Free with print text
Merriam-Webster's Dictionary	978-1-4576-4350-7	Free with print text
Bedford/St. Martin's ESL Workbook	978-1-4576-4356-9	Free with print text
Exercise Central to Go CD-ROM	978-1-4576-4355-2	Free with print text
Make-a-Paragraph Kit CD-ROM	978-1-4576-4349-1	Free with print text
Bedford/St. Martin's Planner	978-1-4576-4357-6	Free with print text
From Practice to Mastery	978-1-4576-4348-4	Free with print text
REAL WRITING, SIXTH EDITION, PACKAGED WITH:		
WritingClass (access card)	978-1-4576-4443-6	Premium
SkillsClass (access card)	978-1-4576-4442-9	Premium

Re:Writing Plus (access card)	978-1-4576-4441-2	Premium
Quick Reference Card for Real Writing	978-1-4576-5401-6	Free with print text
Journal Writing: A Beginning	978-1-4576-4445-0	Free with print text
Merriam-Webster's Dictionary	978-1-4576-4449-8	Free with print text
Bedford/St. Martin's ESL Workbook	978-1-4576-4450-4	Free with print text
Make-a-Paragraph Kit CD-ROM	978-1-4576-4436-8	Free with print text
Exercise Central to Go CD-ROM	978-1-4576-4434-4	Free with print text
Bedford/St. Martin's Planner	978-1-4576-4448-1	Free with print text
From Practice to Mastery	978-1-4576-4435-1	Free with print text

Acknowledgments

Like every edition that preceded it, this revision of *Real Writing* grew out of a collaboration with teachers and students across the country and with the talented staff of Bedford/St. Martin's. I am grateful for everyone's thoughtful contributions.

REVIEWERS

I would like to thank the following instructors for their many good ideas and suggestions for this edition. Their insights were invaluable.

Nikki Aitken, Illinois Central College
Debbie Benson, Northwest-Shoals Community College
Jan Bishop, Greenville Technical College
Candace Boeck, San Diego State University
Delmar Brewington, Piedmont Technical College
Judy D. Covington, Trident Technical College
Deborah DeVries, Oxnard College
Karen Eisenhauer, Brevard Community College
Lindsay Estes, Howard College
Toni Fellela, Community College of Rhode Island
Wendy Galgan, St. Francis College
Lynn Gold, Bergen Community College
Anissa Graham, University of North Alabama
Judy Haberman, Phoenix College
Donna Hogarty, Edinboro University of Pennsylvania
Laura Jeffries, Florida State College at Jacksonville
Eric Johnson, Grossmont College
Theresa Johnson, Troy University
Billy P. Jones, Miami Dade College

Raven L. Jones, Lansing Community College
Timothy Jones, Oklahoma City Community College
Kristyl Kepley, Georgia Military College
Jan Lauten, College of The Albemarle
Ginger Long, Northwest-Shoals Community College
Paulette Longmore, Essex County College
Rosalind Manning, Atlanta Technical College
Applewhite Minyard, College of the Desert
Virginia Nugent, Miami Dade College
Robin Ozz, Phoenix College
Charles Porter, Wor-Wic Community College
Anne Marie Prendergast, Bergen Community College
Marion Ruminski, Belmont Technical College
Tamara Shue, Georgia Perimeter College
Julia Simpson-Urrutia, Fresno City College
Marvin Spiegelman, Miami Dade College
Karen Taylor, Belmont Technical College
Elizabeth L. Teagarden, Central Piedmont Community College
Terri Wells, University of Arkansas–Fort Smith
Patrick Williams, Chandler-Gilbert Community College
Elizabeth Wurz, College of Coastal Georgia

I also want to acknowledge the invaluable help provided by reviewers of the previous edition. Space does not permit listing all reviewers who have provided advice for previous editions. I would just like to say that the book and the series would not be what they are without their help and advice.

Désiré Baloubi, Shaw University; Elizabeth Barnes, Daytona State College; Renee Bell, DeVry University; Randy L. Boone, Northampton Community College; Cynthia Bowden, Las Positas College; Michael Boyd, Illinois Central College; Cathy Brostrand, Mt. San Jacinto Community College; Dawn Copeland, Motlow State Community College; Claudia Edwards, Piedmont Technical College; Deb Fuller, Bunker Hill Community College; Tatiana Gorbunova, Owens Community College; Frank Gunshanan, Daytona State College; Vivian Hoskins, Phillips Community College of the University of Arkansas; Blaine Hunt, Tacoma Community College; Brenda J. Hunt, Western Piedmont Community College; Peggy Karsten, Ridgewater College; Merle K. Koury, College of Southern Maryland; Cathy Lally, Brevard Community College; Tricia Lord, Sierra College; Monique N. Matthews, Santa Monica College; Aubrey Moncrieffe, Housatonic Community College; Matthew Petti, PsyD, MFA, Instructor of English, University of the District of Columbia; Sandra Provence, Arkansas State University; Rick P. Rivera, Columbia College; Neal Roche, Adjunct Professor, Essex County College; Bill Shute, San Antonio College; Ann Smith, Modesto Junior College; Catherine Whitley, Edinboro University of Pennsylvania; Lisa Yanover, Napa Valley College; Rose Yesu, Massasoit Community College; and Guixia Yin, Bunker Hill Community College.

STUDENTS

Many current and former students have helped shape each edition of *Real Writing*, and I am grateful for all their contributions.

Among the students who provided paragraphs and essays for the book are Jess Murphy, John Around Him, Shari Beck, Jasen Beverly, Charlton Brown, Dominic Deiro, Brian Healy, Kelly Hultgren, Said Ibrahim, Amanda Jacobowitz, Jelani Lynch, Lauren Mack, Lorenza Mattazi, Holly Moeller, Casandra Palmer, Robert Phansalkar, Caitlin Prokop, Dara Riesler, Heather Rushall, True Shields, Courtney Stoker, and Jason Yilmaz.

The eight students featured in the new part opener portraits contributed their candid and thought-provoking answers to the question *What do you write?* and in so doing, helped us all to be aware of the deep usefulness of writing. My sincere thanks go to Daniel Brown, Tate Brown-Smith, Chris Eatmon, Jade Ellison, Katie Figueroa, John Fuqua, Ali Kellett, and Sam Malone.

Additionally, I would like to thank the students we profiled for the "Community Connections" sidebars. Some of them also contributed writings for exercises and examples. The students featured are Alessandra Cepeda, Corin Costas, Shawn Elswick, Jenny Haun, Caroline Powers, Evelka Rankins, Jorge Roque, Lynze Schiller, and Robin Wyant.

Last, but certainly not least, I would like to thank the nine former students who are included as "Profiles of Success." They are an inspiration to other students, and their words of advice and examples of workplace writing are central to the book. The Profiles of Success are Mary LaCue Booker, Jeremy Graham, Celia Hyde, Leigh King, Kelly Layland, Brad Leibov, Diane Melancon, Walter Scanlon, and Karen Upright.

CONTRIBUTORS

I gratefully acknowledge the invaluable help of Beth Castrodale, who was a tremendous font of energy, ideas, art, and words of wisdom. In addition to contributing to the reading and photo programs, critical thinking initiatives, and the new "Paragraph vs. Essay" charts, Beth was a brilliant adviser and sounding board from beginning to end. As I have noted in the past, I am truly blessed to work with Beth and to have had this chance to get to know her — as a creative and tireless contributor, an ever-delightful and insightful team member, and treasured friend.

In addition to the reviewers and students already mentioned, I would like to thank several others whose efforts were essential to producing this new edition of *Real Writing*. Michelle McSweeney and Valerie Duff helped to locate a variety of interesting new readings, and Michelle was extremely helpful in weighing in as we decided which of the many possible selections to include.

Art researcher Naomi Kornhauser, working with Martha Friedman, assisted with finding and obtaining permission for the many new, thought-provoking images included in the book.

Kathleen Karcher, working with Kalina Ingham, successfully completed the large and essential task of clearing text permissions.

I am also deeply grateful to designer Claire Seng-Niemoeller, who not only freshened the look of the book's interior but also helped us translate our ideas for the paragraph-essay charts into a vivid reality.

Photographer Joel Beaman contributed the eight striking new student portraits that appear in the "I Write" series of part openers. Working with students at Florida State College at Jacksonville and the University of North Florida, he made this series come to life. I thank him for his dedication, talent, skill, and infectious cheerfulness.

Finally, I would like to thank copyeditor Kathleen Lafferty for her careful attention to detail, good questions, and varied contributions to this book. She is a truly valuable team member.

BEDFORD / ST. MARTIN'S

Since undertaking the first edition of *Real Writing*, I have been extremely fortunate to work with the incredibly talented staff of Bedford/St. Martin's, whose perceptiveness, hard work, and dedication to everything they do are without parallel.

Alexis Walker, executive editor for Developmental Studies, has provided valuable insights from the start of the revision, helping to keep us on top of teaching trends and classroom needs. Thanks also to Edwin Hill, senior executive editor for College Success and Developmental Studies. Editorial assistants Amanda Legee, Mallory Moore, Karen Sikola, and Regina Tavani have helped with innumerable tasks, from running review programs to assisting with manuscript preparation to revising the book's companion Web site. Once again, we were very fortunate to have Deborah Baker, senior production editor, shepherding *Real Writing* through production. With her creativity, careful eye, project-management skills, and sense of humor, she made the path to publication seem as smooth as fresh blacktop despite the inevitable bumps in the road. Overseeing and thoughtfully contributing to all aspects of the design was Anna Palchik, senior art director. Like Claire, she was instrumental in making the new paragraph-essay charts a reality. Thanks to Billy Boardman for his work on the cover design. Pelle Cass consulted on the development of the photo program and brought his expert design sense to the book's brochure, both significant contributions that I gratefully acknowledge.

I must also extend tremendous gratitude to the sales and marketing team. Christina Shea, senior marketing manager, has been a great advocate for all my books and has helped me to forge greater connections with the developmental market and to stay up to date on its needs. I am also grateful to Jim Camp, senior specialist, Developmental Studies and College Skills, and to Dennis Adams and his team of humanities specialists, all of whom share so much valuable information from the field. And I continue to be deeply thankful for the hard work and smarts of all the sales managers and representatives.

The New Media group continues to develop great new teaching tools that respond to the needs of students and instructors. Many thanks especially to Harriet Wald, director of Digital Product Development, and to Marissa Zanetti, New Media editor. Many thanks also to

Barbara Flanagan for all her work on the LearningCurve activities for *Real Writing*.

Like all the previous editions of *Real Writing*, this edition would not have reached its fullest potential without the input and attention it received, from the earliest stages of development, from executives and long-time friends in the Boston office: Joan Feinberg, former president of Bedford/St. Martin's and now co-president of Macmillan Higher Education; Denise Wydra, president, Bedford/St. Martin's; Karen Henry, editor in chief; Karen Soeltz, director of marketing; and Jane Helms, associate director of marketing. I value all of them more than I can say.

Finally, the greatest share of the thanks for this edition of *Real Writing* must go to my editor and valued friend, Martha Bustin, whose countless good ideas for the revision, keen visual sense, attention to design, and endless well of patience and good humor both inspired and sustained me. Thank you so much, Martha.

As he has in the past, to my great good fortune, my husband Jim Anker provides assurance, confidence, steadiness, and the best companionship throughout the projects and the years. His surname is supremely fitting.

—*Susan Anker*

Real Support for Instructors and Students

GOALS AND LEARNING OUTCOMES	SUPPORT IN *REAL WRITING*	SUPPORT IN STUDENT ANCILLARIES	SUPPORT IN INSTRUCTOR ANCILLARIES
Students will connect the writing class with their goals in other courses and the larger world.	■ Part 1: Chapter 1, "Critical Thinking, Reading, and Writing: Making Connections" ■ Part 2: "Profiles of Success" and "Community Connections" sidebars ■ Part 4: "Why Is It Important?" feature ■ Part 8: Student writing with biographical notes and photos	■ **Quick Reference Card:** Portable guide to the basics of writing, editing, using sources, and more ■ **Student Site for Real Writing:** Advice on finding a job (**bedfordstmartins.com/realwriting**) ■ *The Bedford/St. Martin's Planner:* Helps students to plan and use their time effectively ■ *WritingClass, SkillsClass:* Online course spaces with activities that help students apply what they have learned	■ **Instructor's Annotated Edition:** Marginal notes and tips suggest activities and discussion topics to help students see the context and relevance of what they are learning ■ *Practical Suggestions:* Chapters 4, "Bringing the Real World into the Classroom," and 5, "Building Community in the English Class"
Students will write well-developed, organized paragraphs and essays.	■ Part 1: Thorough coverage of critical thinking, reading, and writing process for paragraphs and essays ■ Part 2: Coverage of rhetorical strategies, with detailed writing checklists; a focus on the "Four Basics" of each type of writing; and a special emphasis on main point, support, and organization ■ Part 3: Focus on writing summaries, reports, essay exams, and research essays ■ Parts 2 and 8: Models of different kinds of essays by students and professional writers	■ **Quick Reference Card:** Portable advice on understanding the structure of paragraphs and essays and a checklist for effective writing ■ *Student Site for Real Writing:* Additional model readings and writing advice (**bedfordstmartins.com/realwriting**) ■ *Make-a-Paragraph Kit* CD-ROM: Paragraph development advice and exercises ■ *Exercise Central to Go* CD-ROM: Writing exercises (with more available at **bedfordstmartins.com/exercisecentral**) ■ *Re:Writing Plus:* Additional writing support at **bedfordstmartins.com/rewriting** ■ *WritingClass, SkillsClass:* Online course spaces with activities that help students apply what they have learned	■ **Instructor's Annotated Edition:** Marginal notes suggest activities and questions for use in teaching development, organization, and support ■ *Practical Suggestions:* Advice on helping students develop critical thinking skills (Chapter 6), implementing a group approach to improve students' paragraphs and essays (Chapter 7), and using writing portfolios (Chapter 12) ■ *Additional Resources:* Reproducible planning forms for writing ■ *Testing Tool Kit* CD-ROM: Tests on topic sentences, thesis statements, support, organization, and more
Students will build grammar and editing skills.	■ Parts 4 through 7: Thorough grammar coverage and many opportunities for practice, with a focus on the "Four Most Serious Errors" (Part 4) ■ Editing Review Tests: Ten realistic cumulative tests follow the last grammar and punctuation part (Part 7, "Punctuation and Capitalization")	■ ✓ **LearningCurve Activities:** Bedford/St. Martin's innovative online grammar quizzing system with adaptive technology and a game-like interface ■ **Quick Reference Card:** Portable advice on avoiding the "Four Most Serious Errors" ■ *Supplemental Exercises for Real Writing:* Offers more practices to accompany the editing chapters	■ **Instructor's Annotated Edition:** Marginal suggestions to help students learn and review grammar ■ *Additional Resources:* Reproducible exercises and transparencies for modeling correction of the "Four Most Serious Errors" ■ *Student Site for Real Writing:* For instructors, downloadable answer key for all exercises in the text

GOALS AND LEARNING OUTCOMES	SUPPORT IN *REAL WRITING*	SUPPORT IN STUDENT ANCILLARIES	SUPPORT IN INSTRUCTOR ANCILLARIES
Students will build grammar and editing skills. (continued)		■ *Student Site for Real Writing:* More grammar exercises through *Exercise Central,* with instant scoring and feedback (**bedfordstmartins.com /realwriting**) ■ *Make-a-Paragraph Kit* CD-ROM: Tutorials on finding and fixing the "Four Most Serious Errors" ■ *Exercise Central to Go* CD-ROM: Editing exercises (with more available at **bedfordstmartins .com/exercisecentral**) ■ *WritingClass, SkillsClass:* Online course spaces with activities that help students apply what they have learned	■ *Testing Tool Kit* CD-ROM: Test items on every grammar topic ■ *Re:Writing Plus:* Additional instructional support at **bedfordstmartins.com /rewriting**
Students will build research skills.	■ Chapter 18, "Writing a Research Essay," helps students choose a topic, find and evaluate sources, use summary and paraphrase, avoid plagiarism, and cite sources. Includes a sample student paper	■ *Quick Reference Card:* Portable research and documentation advice ■ *Supplemental Exercises for Real Writing:* Offers many additional practices to accompany the research chapter in *Real Writing* ■ *Student Site for Real Writing:* Additional resources for students on evaluating and integrating sources, avoiding plagiarism, and more (**bedfordstmartins.com /realwriting**) ■ *Re:Writing Plus:* Research and documentation advice at **bedfordstmartins.com/rewriting** ■ *WritingClass, SkillsClass:* Online course spaces with activities that help students apply what they have learned	■ *Instructor's Annotated Edition:* Marginal notes on helping students explore and become comfortable with the research process ■ *Additional Resources:* Reproducible research exercises and other handouts
Students will read closely and critically.	■ Chapter 1, "Critical Thinking, Reading, and Writing," helps students to preview, read, pause to reflect, and review and respond. The critical reading process is then covered throughout the book. ■ Parts 1, 2, and 8: Integrated coverage of the critical reading process, with reinforcement on the need, when reading critically, to preview, read, pause, and review	■ *Student Site for Real Writing:* Provides annotated model essays and vocabulary help (**bedfordstmartins.com /realwriting**) ■ *WritingClass, SkillsClass:* Online course spaces with reading skills instruction and activities	■ *Instructor's Annotated Edition:* Marginal tips for improving students' critical reading abilities ■ *Practical Suggestions:* Advice on helping students bring in content from the real world and see connections in what they read (Chapter 4) and develop critical thinking and reading skills (Chapter 6)

Continued >

GOALS AND LEARNING OUTCOMES	SUPPORT IN *REAL WRITING*	SUPPORT IN STUDENT ANCILLARIES	SUPPORT IN INSTRUCTOR ANCILLARIES
Students will think critically.	■ Chapter 1: Step-by-step critical thinking and reading advice ■ Parts 1, 2, and 8: Critical thinking components—summary, analysis, synthesis, and evaluation—are reinforced with questions	■ *Student Site for Real Writing:* Provides peer review forms, helpful checklists, and annotated model essays (**bedfordstmartins.com /realwriting**) ■ *WritingClass, SkillsClass:* Online course spaces with activities that help students apply what they have learned	■ *Instructor's Annotated Edition:* Marginal critical thinking prompts ■ *Practical Suggestions:* Advice on helping students bring in content from the real world and see connections in what they read (Chapter 4) and develop critical thinking and reading skills (Chapter 6)
Students will prepare for and pass tests.	■ Chapter 17: Advice on writing essay exams ■ Parts 4–7: Tests at the ends of grammar chapters ■ Editing Review Tests: Ten realistic cumulative tests follow the last grammar and punctuation part (Part 7, "Punctuation and Capitalization")	■ *Student Site for Real Writing:* Includes section on test-taking and, in *Exercise Central,* grammar exercises, with instant scoring and feedback (**bedfordstmartins.com /realwriting**) ■ *From Practice to Mastery:* Study guide for the Florida Basic Skills Exit Test ■ *WritingClass, SkillsClass:* Online course spaces with activities that help students apply what they have learned	■ *Additional Resources:* General diagnostic tests as well as tests on specific grammar topics ■ *Practical Suggestions:* Advice on assessing student writing, with model rubrics, advice on marking difficult papers, and more (Chapter 11) ■ *Testing Tool Kit* CD-ROM: Tests on all writing and grammar issues covered in *Real Writing*
ESL and multilingual students will improve their proficiency in English grammar and usage.	■ "Language Notes" throughout the grammar instruction ■ ESL chapter (Chapter 30) with special attention to sentence patterns, pronouns, verbs, articles, and prepositions	■ *Student Site for Real Writing:* ESL exercises in *Exercise Central,* with instant scoring and feedback (**bedfordstmartins.com /realwriting**) ■ *The Bedford / St. Martin's ESL Workbook:* Special instruction and exercises for ESL students ■ *Exercise Central to Go* CD-ROM: Includes ESL exercises (even more exercises available at **bedfordstmartins.com /exercisecentral**) ■ *WritingClass, SkillsClass:* Online course spaces with activities that help students apply what they have learned	■ *Instructor's Annotated Edition:* Tips for teaching ESL students ■ *Practical Suggestions:* Advice on teaching ESL students and speakers of nonstandard English (Chapter 10) ■ *Testing Tool Kit* CD-ROM: Test items on ESL issues

To order any of these ancillaries for *Real Writing with Readings* or *Real Writing,* Sixth Edition, please contact your Bedford/St. Martin's sales representative, e-mail sales support at **sales_support@bfwpub.com**, or visit our Web site at **bedfordstmartins.com**.

A note to students from Susan Anker

For the last twenty years or so, I have traveled the country talking to students about their goals and, more important, about the challenges they face on the way to achieving those goals. Students always tell me that they want good jobs and that they need a college degree to get those jobs. I designed *Real Writing* with those goals in mind— strengthening the writing, reading, and editing skills needed for success in college, at work, and in everyday life.

Here is something else: Good jobs require not only a college degree but also a college education: knowing not only how to read and write but how to think critically and learn effectively. So that is what I stress here, too. It is worth facing the challenges. All my best wishes to you, in this course and in all your future endeavors.

"I write ideas and summaries. Writing is a tool in my creative process."
—Tate Brown-S., student

Part 1

How to Write Paragraphs and Essays

1	Critical Thinking, Reading, and Writing	3
2	Writing Basics	27
3	Finding, Narrowing, and Exploring Your Topic	42
4	Writing Your Topic Sentence or Thesis Statement	52
5	Supporting Your Point	68
6	Drafting	77
7	Revising	96

YOU KNOW THIS

You have experience thinking critically.

- You figure out what is going on in a situation.
- You analyze how people act.
- You ask yourself if you believe what you hear or see.

think What do you think *critical thinking* is?

Critical Thinking, Reading, and Writing

Making Connections

"To be successful, be a critical thinker." This statement is becoming more and more common, and it is true. College courses require critical thinking. Workplaces require it. Life requires it. The good news is, you already practice critical thinking, and it is a skill you can strengthen, as you will learn in this chapter.

Take a closer look at a type of critical thinking you are already familiar with: making judgments about what to buy, or not to buy, based on product labels and advertising. First, **study** the picture to the right. **Ask yourself:**

- Why do you think the designers of this label chose to make it appear as it does?
- What textual and visual elements of the label suggest health and purity?
- **Make a connection** to your daily life: Does this label make it any more likely that you will purchase Pure Health Water or any other type of bottled water? Why or why not?

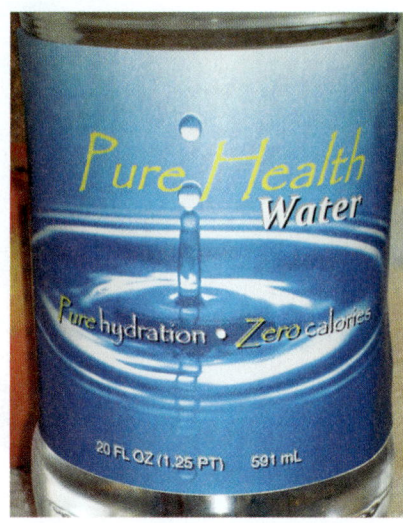

Now, **study** this advertisement from Tappening, an environmental group. **Ask yourself:**

- What is this ad's main message?
- What is the message behind the **boldface** note in the lower left corner of the ad?
- **Make a connection** to the previous label: How would the creator of the Tappening ad respond to the way the bottled-water company presents its product?
- **Make a connection** to your daily life: Does the Tappening ad make bottled water any less appealing to you? Why or why not?

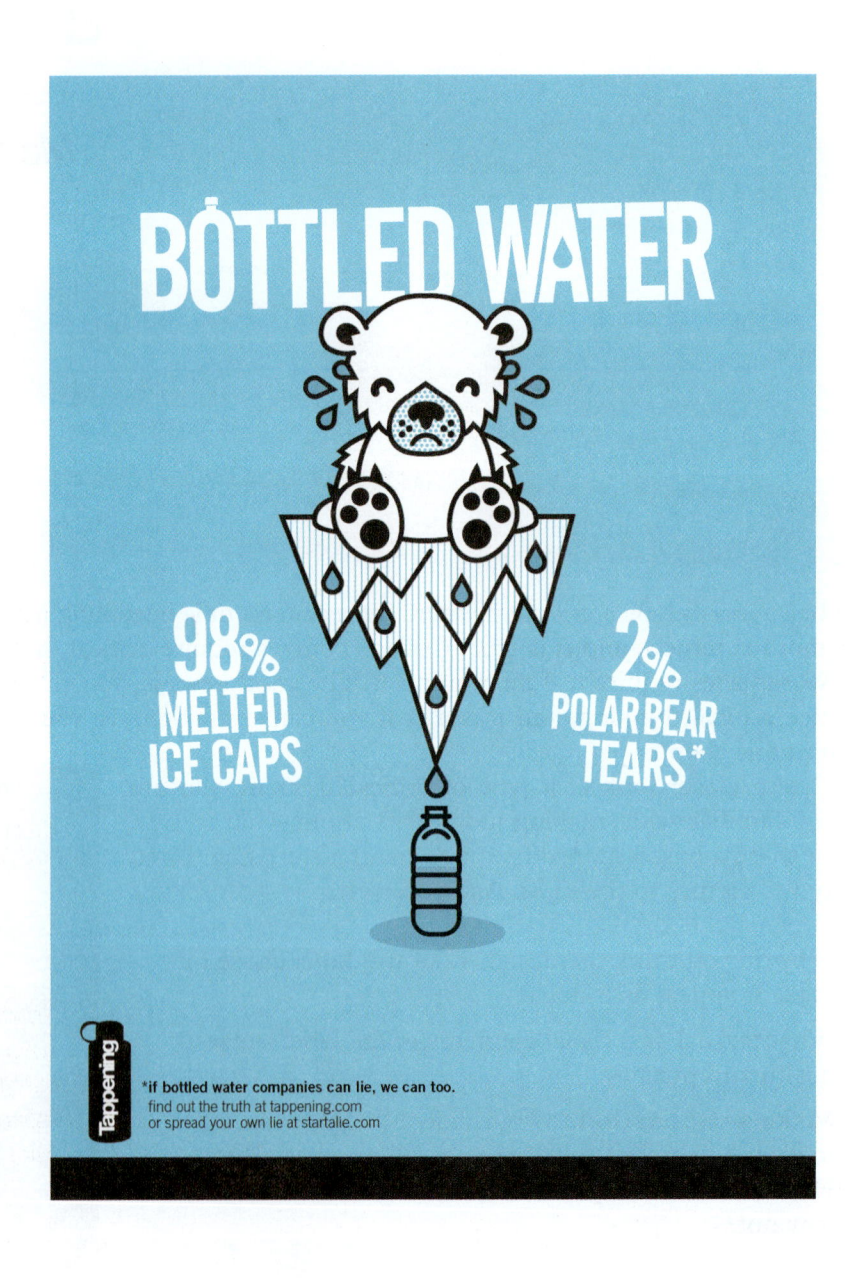

BOTTLED WATER

98% MELTED ICE CAPS

2% POLAR BEAR TEARS*

*if bottled water companies can lie, we can too.
find out the truth at tappening.com
or spread your own lie at startalie.com

Finally, **study** these labels. **Ask yourself:**

- What do these bottled-water labels say about the companies that produced them?
- **Make a connection** to the previous advertisement: How do these labels respond to the main message of the Tappening advertisement?
- **Make a connection** to your daily life: Reflect on all the previous images—the labels and the Tappening ad. Do they make you think differently about what kind of bottled water to purchase or about whether to buy bottled water at all? In what ways have product labels, your own experiences, and other information contributed to your decision?

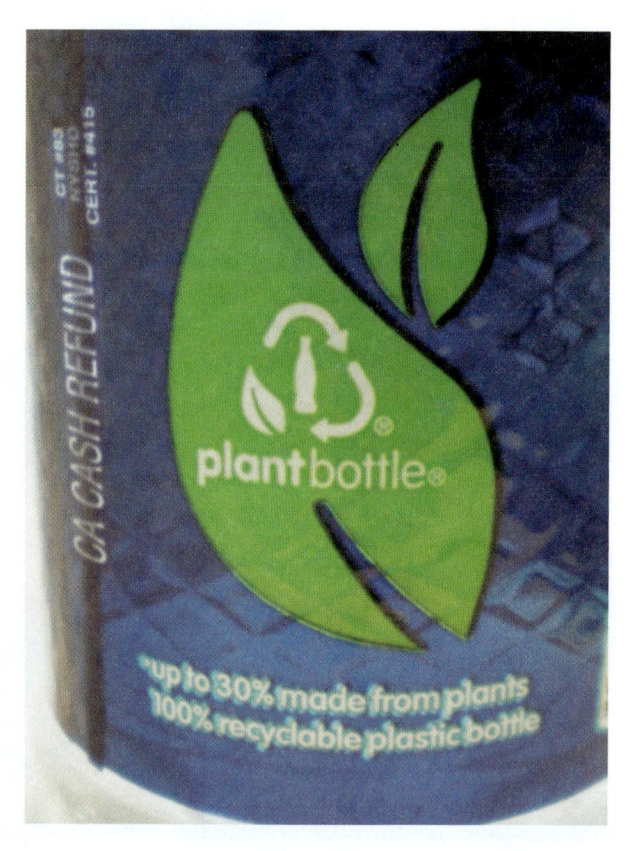

The previous activities took you beneath the surface of the product labeling and beyond quick reactions to it. In other words, they encouraged **critical thinking**, actively questioning what you see, hear, and read to come to thoughtful conclusions about it. Building your critical thinking skills is one of the most important things you can do to succeed in college, at work, and in everyday situations.

As the previous activities show, critical thinking also involves **making connections**

- between existing impressions and new ones
- among various beliefs, claims, and bits of information

In the following sections, we will take a closer look at critical thinking strategies. Also, we will explore the connections among critical thinking, reading, and writing.

What Is Critical Thinking?

Jess: I've been thinking about it a lot, Mar, and I really need to quit school.

Maryn: Really? You were so excited about it last summer.

Jess: I know, I know. But I'm working, like, thirty hours a week now. And I'm just too burned out to study.

Maryn: Could you cut back your hours?

Jess: I can't afford to. Not now, anyway.

Maryn: What about cutting your course load some?

Jess: Yeah, I guess that's a possibility, but . . .

Maryn: But what?

Jess: I know it sounds weird, Mar, but I feel like I'm defying the odds to stay in school. I mean, nobody in my family has ever finished college, so what makes me think I can?

Maryn: You're not them. You're you.

Jess (laughing): For better or worse.

Maryn: Seriously. Where's the Jess who told me a few weeks ago that she was loving her design class? The Jess who has some really amazing stuff in her portfolio?

Jess: She's still here. Just tired.

Maryn: OK. How can we keep her going?

The conversation between Jess and Maryn illustrates some important processes behind critical thinking.

Four Basics of Critical Thinking

1. Be alert to assumptions made by you and others.
2. Question those assumptions.
3. Consider and connect various points of view, even those different from your own.
4. Do not rush to conclusions, but instead remain patient with yourself and others and keep an open mind.

Assumptions—ideas or opinions that we do not question and that we automatically accept as true—can get in the way of clear, critical thinking. Here are some of Jess's assumptions:

She has no alternative but to quit school.

Because nobody in her family has ever finished college, she should not expect to either.

Because she has gotten fatigued and overwhelmed from all she is doing, it is a sign to give up on her dreams.

In college, work, and everyday life, we often hold assumptions that we are not even aware of. By identifying these assumptions, stating them, and questioning them, we stand a better chance of seeing reality and acting more effectively. Also, as in Jess's case, we can open up new possibilities for ourselves.

When questioning assumptions, try to get a bit of distance from them. Imagine what people with entirely different points of view might say. You might even try disagreeing with your own assumptions. Take a look at the following examples.

Questioning Assumptions

SITUATION	ASSUMPTION	QUESTIONS
COLLEGE: I saw from the syllabus that I need to write five essays for this course.	I am never going to pass this course.	Other students have passed this course; what makes me think I cannot? What obstacles might be getting in my way? What might be some ways around those obstacles? What have others done in this situation?
WORK: Two of my coworkers just got raises.	My own raise is just around the corner.	Did my coworkers accomplish anything I did not? When was their last raise, and when was mine?
EVERYDAY LIFE: My neighbor has been cool to me lately.	I must have done something wrong.	Is it possible it has nothing to do with me? Maybe he is going through something really difficult in his life?

TIP In every situation, try to be open to different points of view. Listen and think before responding or coming to any conclusions. Although you may not agree with other points of view, you can learn from them.

You need to be aware not only of your own assumptions, but also of those in what you read, see, and hear. For example, bottled-water labels and advertising might suggest directly or indirectly that bottled water is better than tap water. What evidence do they provide for this assumption? What other sources of information could be consulted to either support, disprove, or call into question this assumption? However confidently a claim is made, never assume it cannot be questioned.

PRACTICE 1 Thinking Critically

What assumptions are behind each of the images on pages 3–5? Write down as many as you can identify. Then, write down questions about these assumptions, considering different points of view.

In addition to assumptions, be aware of **biases**, one-sided and sometimes prejudiced views that may blind you to the truth of a situation. Here is just one example:

> No one older than fifty can pick up new skills quickly.

Others could contradict this extreme statement with their own experiences, exceptions, and insights or with additional information that could show reality is more nuanced or complicated than this statement allows.

Be on the lookout for bias in your own views and in whatever you read, see, and hear. When a statement seems one-sided or extreme, ask yourself what facts or points of view might have been omitted.

What Is Critical Reading?

Critical reading is paying close attention as you read and asking yourself questions about the author's purpose, his or her main point, the support he or she gives, and how good that support is. It is important to think critically as you read, looking out for assumptions and biases (both the writer's and your own). You should also consider whether you agree or disagree with the points being made.

Here are the four steps of the critical reading process:

2PR The Critical Reading Process

- **P**review the reading.
- **R**ead the piece, double-underlining the thesis statement and underlining the major support. Consider the quality of the support.
- **P**ause to think during reading. Take notes and ask questions about what you are reading. Talk to the author.
- **R**eview the reading, your guiding question, your marginal notes, and your questions.

2PR Preview the Reading

Before reading any piece of writing, skim the whole thing, using the following steps.

READ THE TITLE, HEADNOTE, AND INTRODUCTORY PARAGRAPHS

The title of a chapter, an article, or any other document usually gives you some idea of what the topic is. Some documents are introduced by headnotes, which summarize or provide background about the selection. If there is a headnote, read it. Whether or not there is a headnote, writers often introduce their topic and main point in the first paragraphs, so read those and make a note stating what you think is the main point.

READ HEADINGS, KEY WORDS, AND DEFINITIONS

Textbooks and magazine articles often include headings to help readers follow the author's ideas. These headings (such as "Preview the Reading" above) tell you what the important subjects are within the larger piece of writing.

Any terms in **boldface** type are especially important. In textbooks, writers often use boldface for key words that are important to the topic.

CRITICAL READING
- Preview
- Read
- Pause
- Review

LOOK FOR SUMMARIES, CHECKLISTS, AND CHAPTER REVIEWS

Many textbooks (such as this one) include features that summarize or list main points. Review summaries, checklists, or chapter reviews to make sure you have understood the main points.

READ THE CONCLUSION

Writers usually review their main point in their concluding paragraphs. Read the conclusion, and compare it with the note you made after you read the introduction and thought about what the main idea might be.

ASK A GUIDING QUESTION

As the final step in your preview of a reading, ask yourself a **guiding question**—a question you think the reading might answer. This question will give you a purpose for reading and help keep you focused. Sometimes, you can turn the title into a guiding question. For example, read the title of this chapter, and write a possible guiding question.

2PR   Read the Piece: Find the Main Point and the Support

CRITICAL READING
- Preview
- **Read**
- Pause
- Review

After previewing, begin reading carefully for meaning, trying especially to identify a writer's main point and the support for that point.

MAIN POINT AND PURPOSE

For more on main points, see Chapter 4.

The **main point** of a reading is the central idea the author wants to communicate. The main point is related to the writer's **purpose**, which can be to explain, to demonstrate, to persuade, or to entertain. Writers often introduce their main point early, so read the first few paragraphs with special care. After reading the first paragraph (or more, depending on the length of the reading selection), stop and write down—in your own words—what you think the main idea is. If the writer has stated the main point in a single sentence, double-underline it.

PRACTICE 2   Finding the Main Point

Read each of the following paragraphs. Then, write the main point in your own words in the spaces provided.

1. Making a plan for your college studies is a good way to reach your academic goals. The first step to planning is answering this question: "What do I want to be?" If you have only a general idea—for example, "I would like to work in the health-care field"—break this large area into smaller, more specific subfields. These subfields might include

working as a registered nurse, a nurse practitioner, or a physical therapist. The second step to planning is to meet with an academic adviser to talk about the classes you will need to take to get a degree or certificate in your chosen field. Then, map out the courses you will be taking over the next couple of semesters. Throughout the whole process, bear in mind the words of student mentor Ed Powell: "Those who fail to plan, plan to fail." A good plan boosts your chances of success in college and beyond.

MAIN POINT: _____

2. Networking is a way businesspeople build connections with others to get ahead. Building connections in college also is well worth the effort. One way to build connections is to get to know some of your classmates and to exchange names, phone numbers, and e-mail addresses with them. That way, if you cannot make it to a class, you will know someone who can tell you what you missed. You can also form study groups with these other students. Another way to build connections is to get to know your instructor. Make an appointment to visit your instructor during his or her office hours. When you go, ask questions about material you are not sure you understood in class or problems you have with other course material. You and your instructor will get the most out of these sessions if you bring examples of specific assignments that you are having trouble with.

MAIN POINT: _____

SUPPORT

Support is the details that show, explain, or prove the main point. The author might use statistics, facts, definitions, and scientific results for support. Or he or she might use memories, stories, comparisons, quotations from experts, and personal observations.

For more on support, see Chapter 5.

PRACTICE 3 Identifying Support

Go back to Practice 2 (p. 10), and underline the support for the main ideas of each passage in the practice.

Not all support that an author offers in a piece of writing is good support. When you are reading, ask yourself: What information is the author including to help me understand or agree with the main point? Is the support (evidence) valid and convincing? If not, why not?

For online exercises on support, visit *Exercise Central* at bedfordstmartins.com/realwriting.

CRITICAL READING
- Preview
- Read
- **Pause**
- Review

2PR Pause to Think

Taking notes and asking questions as you read will help you understand the author's points and develop a thoughtful response. As you read:

- Double-underline or write the main idea in the margin.
- Note the major support points by underlining them.
- Note ideas that you agree with by placing a check mark next to them (✓).
- Note ideas that you do not agree with or that surprise you with an **X** or **!**, and ideas you do not understand with a question mark **?**.
- Note any examples of an author's or expert's bias.
- Jot any additional notes or questions in the margin.
- Consider how parts of the reading relate to the main point.

CRITICAL READING
- Preview
- Read
- Pause
- **Review**

2PR Review and Respond

After reading, it is important to take a few minutes to look back and review. Go over your guiding question, your marginal notes, and your questions—and *connect yourself to what you have read*. Consider, "What interested me? What did I learn? How does it fit with what I know from other sources?" When you have reviewed your reading in this way and fixed it well in your mind and memory, it is much easier to respond in class discussion and writing assignments. To write about a reading, you need to generate and organize your ideas, draft and revise your response, and above all, use your critical thinking skills (see p. 7).

A Critical Reader at Work

Read the following piece. The notes in the margins show how one student applied the process of critical reading to an essay on bottled water.

Amanda Jacobowitz

A Ban on Water Bottles: A Way to Bolster the University's Image

Amanda Jacobowitz is a student at Washington University and a columnist for the university's publication *Student Life*, in which the following essay appeared.

Guiding Question: What does the author think about the ban on bottled water?

1 Lately, I am always thirsty. Always! I could not figure out why until I realized that the bottled water I had purchased continuously throughout my day had disappeared. At first I was just confused. Where did all the

water bottles go? Then I learned the simple explanation: The University banned water bottles in an effort to be environmentally friendly.

Ideally, given the ban on selling water bottles, every student on campus should now take the initiative to carry a water bottle, filling it up throughout the day at the water fountains on campus. Realistically, we know this has not and will not happen. I have tried to bring a water bottle with me to classes—I do consider myself somewhat environmentally conscious—but have rarely succeeded in this effort. Instead, although I have never been too much of a soda drinker, I find myself reaching for a bottle of Coke out of pure convenience. We can't buy bottled water, but we can buy soda, juice, and other drinks, many of which come in plastic bottles. I am sure that for most people—particularly those who give very little thought to being environmentally conscientious—convenience prevails and they purchase a drink other than water. Wonderful result. The University can pride itself on being more environmentally friendly, with the fallback that its students will be less healthy!

Even if students are not buying unhealthy drinks, any benefit from the reduction of plastic water bottles could easily be offset by its alternatives. Students are not using their hands to drink water during meals. They are using plastic cups—cups provided by the University at every eatery on campus. Presumably no person picks up a cup, drinks their glass of water, and then saves that same cup for later in the day. That being said, how many plastic cups are used by a single student, in a single day? How many cups are used by the total campus-wide population daily, yearly? This plastic cup use must equate to an exorbitant amount of waste as well.

My intent is not to have the University completely roll back the water bottle ban, nor is my intent for the University to level the playing field by banning all plastic drink bottles. I'm simply questioning the reasons for specifically banning bottled water of all things? Why not start with soda bottles—decreasing the environmental impact, as well as the health risks. There are also many other ways to help the environment that seem to be so easily overlooked.

Have you ever noticed a patch of grass on campus that's not perfectly green? I can't say that I have. The reason: the sprinklers. Now, I admit that I harbor some animosity when it comes to the campus sprinklers; I somehow always manage to mistakenly and inadvertently walk right in their path, the spray of water generously dousing my feet. However, my real problem with the sprinklers is the waste of water they represent. Do we really need our grass to be green at all times?

The landscaping around our beloved Danforth University Center (Gold LEED Certified) is irrigated with the use of rainwater. There is a

50,000-gallon rainwater tank below the building to collect rain! I admit, this is pretty impressive, but what about the rest of the campus? What water is used to irrigate and keep green the rest of our 169 acres on the Danforth campus?

Town/city water, I assume.

I understand that being environmentally conscious is difficult to do, particularly at an institutional level. I applaud the Danforth University Center and other environmental efforts the University has initiated. However, I can't help but wonder if the University's ban on the sale of water bottles is more about appearance and less about decreasing the environmental impact of our student body. The water bottle ban has become a way to build the school's public image: we banned water bottles, we are working hard to be environmentally friendly! In reality, given the switch to plastic cups and the switch to other drinks sold in plastic bottles, is the environmental impact of the ban that significant? Now that the ban has been implemented, I certainly don't see the University retracting it. However, I hope that in the future the University focuses less on its public image and more on the environment itself when instituting such dramatic changes.

Is it really about public image? What would a university administrator say?

7

PRACTICE 4 Making Connections

Look back at the images on pages 3–5. Then, review the reading by Amanda Jacobowitz. What assumptions does she make about bottled water? What evidence, if any, is provided to support these assumptions? Based on your observations, would you like to see bottled water not banned or banned at your college? Why or why not?

Read Real-World Documents Critically

Careless reading in your everyday life can cause minor problems such as a ruined recipe, but it can also have more serious consequences. For example, if you overlook the fine print in a loan offer, you might end up agreeing to a high interest rate and, therefore, more debt.

To read real-world documents closely and carefully, try the **2PR** strategy, especially for longer documents. Also, when you see a document or sign that makes a claim, ask yourself: Does this claim look too good to be true? If so, why?

PRACTICE 5 Reading Real-World Documents

Working by yourself or with other students, read the following documents from college, work, and everyday life, and answer the critical reading questions.

1. What is the writer's purpose? _____

2. Is the writer biased? _____

3. What are the key words or major claims? _____
   _____

4. What is in the fine print? _____
   _____
   _____

5. What do you think of what you have read? Why? Does anything seem odd, unrealistic, or unreliable? Give specific examples. _____
   _____
   _____
   _____

COLLEGE: AN E-MAILED ADVERTISEMENT

GET A COLLEGE DEGREE IN *TWO* WEEKS!

Are a few letters after your name the only thing that's keeping you from your dream job? Degree Services International will grant you a B.A., M.A., M.S., M.B.A., or Ph.D. from a prestigious nonaccredited institution based on what you already know!

NO CLASSES, EXAMS, OR TEXTBOOKS ARE REQUIRED
for those who qualify

If you order now, you'll receive your degree within two weeks.

CALL 1-800-555-0021

HURRY! Qualified institutions can grant these diplomas only because of a legal loophole that may be closed within weeks.

WORK: A POSTING ON A TELEPHONE POLE

Earn Thousands of Dollars a Week Working at Home!

Flexible Hours ♦ No Experience Needed

The health-care system is in crisis because of the millions of medical claims that have to be processed each day. You can benefit from this situation now by becoming an at-home medical claims processor. Work as much or as little as you like for great pay!

CALL 1-800-555-5831
for your starter kit

Some supply purchases may be required.

EVERYDAY LIFE: ADVERTISEMENT

Gift Certificate — Redeem this Certificate for a **FREE** *GENUINE FAUX 9 CARAT SAPPHIRE PENDANT*

...show you the quality and low prices of our merchandise. ...pphire pendant: Print your name and address below, and ...te, along with $9.95 cash, check, or money order to cover

EVERYDAY LIFE: PART OF A DRUG LABEL

TIP Pay attention to the dosage for adults.

Drug Facts

Directions

■ Do not take more than directed.

Adults and children 12 years and over	■ Take 4 to 6 caplets every 2 hours as needed. ■ Do not take more than 8 caplets in 24 hours.
Children under 12 years	Do not use this product in children under 12 years of age. This could cause serious health problems.

What Is Writing Critically about Readings?

Being able to write critically about what you read is a key college skill because it shows your deep understanding of course content. When you write critically about readings you summarize, analyze, synthesize, and evaluate, and in doing so, you answer the following questions.

Reading and Writing Critically

Summarize
- What is important about the text?
- What is the purpose, the big picture?
- What are the main points and key support?

Analyze
- What elements have been used to convey the main point?
- Do any elements raise questions? Do any key points seem missing or undeveloped?

> ■ **Synthesize**
> - What do other sources say about the topic of the text?
> - How does your own (or others') experience affect how you see the topic?
> - What new point(s) might you make by bringing together all the different sources and experiences?
>
> ■ **Evaluate**
> - Based on your application of summary, analysis, and synthesis, what do you think about the material you have read?
> - Is the work successful? Does it achieve its purpose?
> - Does the author show any biases? If so, do they make the piece more effective or less effective?

Summary

A **summary** is a condensed, or shortened, version of something—often, a longer piece of writing, a movie or television show, a situation, or an event. In writing a summary, you give the main points and key support in your own words.

The following is an excerpt from the *Textbook of Basic Nursing* by Caroline Bunker Rosdahl and Mary T. Kowalski. It comes from a chapter that discusses some of the stresses that families can face, including divorce.

> Adults who are facing separation from their partners—and a return to single life—may feel overwhelmed. They may become preoccupied with their own feelings, thereby limiting their ability to handle the situation effectively or to be strong for their children. The breakdown of the family system may require a restructuring of responsibilities, employment, childcare, and housing arrangements. Animosity between adults may expose children to uncontrolled emotions, arguments, anger, and depression.
>
> Children may feel guilt and anxiety over their parents' divorce, believing the situation to be their fault. They may be unable to channel their conflicting emotions effectively. Their school performance may suffer, or they may engage in misbehavior. Even when a divorce is handled amicably, children may experience conflicts about their loyalties and may have difficulties making the transition from one household to another during visitation periods. . . .
>
> Experts estimate that approximately 50% of all children whose parents divorce will experience another major life change within 3 years: remarriage. The arrival of a stepparent in the home presents additional stressors for children. Adapting to new rules of behavior, adjusting to a new person's habits, and sharing parents with new family members can cause resentment and anger. When families blend children, rivalries and competition for parental attention can lead to repeated conflicts.

TIP For more information on summarizing, see Chapter 17.

Now, here is a summary of the textbook excerpt. The main point is double-underlined, and the support points are underlined.

> Although divorce seriously affects the people who are splitting up, Rosdahl and Kowalski point out that the couple's children face equally difficult consequences, both immediately and in the longer term. In the short term, according to the authors, children may blame themselves for the split or feel that their loyalty to both parents is divided. These negative emotions can affect their behavior at school and elsewhere. Later on, if one or both of the parents remarry, the children may have trouble adjusting to the new family structure.

Analysis

An **analysis** breaks down the points or parts of something and considers how they work together to make an impression or convey a main point. When writing an analysis, you might also consider points or parts that seem to be missing or that raise questions in your mind.

Here is an analysis of the excerpt from the *Textbook of Basic Nursing*. The main point is double-underlined, and the support points are underlined.

> We all know that divorce is difficult for the people who are splitting up, but Rosdahl and Kowalski pay special attention to the problems faced by children of divorce, both right after the split and later on. The authors mention several possible outcomes of divorce on children, including emotional and behavioral difficulties and trouble in school. They also discuss the stresses that remarriage can create for children.
>
> The authors rightly emphasize the negative effects that divorce can have on children. However, I found myself wondering what a divorcing couple could do to help their children through the process. Also, how might parents and stepparents help children adjust to a remarriage? I would like to examine these questions in a future paper.

[Note how the writer raises questions about the textbook excerpt.]

Synthesis

A **synthesis** pulls together information from additional sources or experiences to make a new point. Here is a synthesis of the textbook material on divorce. Because the writer wanted to address some of the questions she raised in her analysis, she incorporated additional details from published sources and from people she interviewed. Her synthesis of this information helped her arrive at a fresh conclusion.

In the *Textbook of Basic Nursing*, Rosdahl and Kowalski focus on the problems faced by children of divorce, both right after the split and later on. According to the authors, immediate problems can include emotional and behavioral difficulties and trouble in school. Later on, parents' remarriage can create additional stresses for children. Although the authors discuss the impact of divorce on all parties, they do not suggest ways in which parents or stepparents might help children through the process of divorce or remarriage. However, other sources, as well as original research on friends who have experienced divorce as children or adults, provide some additional insights into these questions.

A Web site produced by the staff at the Mayo Clinic recommends that parents come together to break the news about their divorce to their children. The Web site also suggests that parents keep the discussion brief and free of "ugly details." In addition, parents should emphasize that the children are in no way to blame for the divorce and that they are deeply loved. As the divorce proceeds, neither parent should speak negatively about the other parent in the child's presence or otherwise try to turn the child against the ex-spouse. Finally, parents should consider counseling for themselves or their children if any problems around the divorce persist.

The Web site of the University of Missouri Extension addresses the problems that can arise for children after their parents remarry. Specifically, the Web site describes several things that stepparents can do to make their stepchildren feel more comfortable with them and the new family situation. One strategy is to try to establish a friendship with the children before assuming the role of a parent. Later, once stepparents have assumed a more parental role, they should make sure they and their spouse stand by the same household rules and means of discipline. With time, the stepparents might also add new traditions for holidays and other family gatherings to help build new family bonds while respecting the old ones.

To these sources, I added interviews with three friends—two who are children of divorce and one who is both a divorced parent and a stepparent. The children of divorce said that they experienced many of the same difficulties and stresses that Rosdahl and Kowalski described. Interestingly, though, they also reported that they felt guilty, even though their parents told them not to, just as the Mayo Clinic experts recommend. As my friend Kris said, "For a long time after the divorce, every time me and my dad were together, he seemed distracted, like he wished I wasn't there. I felt bad that I couldn't just vanish." Dale, the stepparent I interviewed, liked the strategies suggested by the University of Missouri Extension, and he had actually tried some of these approaches with his own stepchildren. However, as Dale told me, "When you're as busy as most parents and kids are these days, you can let important things fall by the wayside—even time together. That's not good for anyone."

Thinking back on Kris's and Dale's words and everything I've learned from the other sources, I have come to conclude that divorced parents and stepparents need to make sure they build "together time" with their own children and/or stepchildren into every day. Even if this time is just a discussion over a meal or a quick bedtime story, children will remember it and appreciate it. This approach would help with some of the relationship building that the University of Missouri Extension recommends. It would also improve communication, help children understand that they are truly loved by *all* their parents, and assist with the process of postdivorce healing.

Fresh conclusion

TIP For more on finding reliable sources of information for your writing, see Chapter 18.

Works Cited

Leigh, Sharon, Maridith Jackson, and Janet A. Clark. "Foundations for a Successful Stepfamily." U of Missouri Extension, Apr. 2007. Web. 13 Oct. 2011.

Mayo Clinic Staff. "Children and Divorce: Helping Kids after a Breakup." *Mayo Clinic*. Mayo Clinic, 14 May 2011. Web. 12 Oct. 2011.

Rosdahl, Caroline Bunker, and Mary T. Kowalski. *Textbook of Basic Nursing*. 9th ed. Philadelphia: Lippincott Williams & Wilkins, 2008. 92. Print.

Evaluation

An **evaluation** is your *thoughtful* judgment about something based on what you have discovered through your summary, analysis, and synthesis. To evaluate something effectively, apply the questions from the Reading and Writing Critically box on pages 16–17. You will want to refer to these questions as you work through later chapters of this book and through readings from other college courses.

Here is an evaluation of the excerpt from the *Textbook of Basic Nursing:*

In just a few paragraphs, Rosdahl and Kowalski give a good description of the effects of divorce, not only on the former spouses but also on their children. The details that the authors provide help to clearly communicate the difficulties that such children face. In the short term, these difficulties can include emotional and behavioral problems and trouble in school. In the longer term, if one or both of a child's parents remarry, the child faces the stress of dealing with a new and different family. Although the authors do not specifically address ways that parents and stepparents can ease children into divorce and/or new families, other sources—such as the Web sites of the University of Missouri Extension and the Mayo Clinic, as well as people I interviewed—do get into these issues. In the end, I think that Rosdahl and Kowalski present a good overview of their subject in a short piece of writing that was part of a larger discussion on family stresses.

PRACTICE 6 **Making Connections**

As you work through this exercise, refer to the Reading and Writing Critically box on pages 16–17 and to your responses to Practice 4 (if you completed it).

1. **Summary:** Summarize Amanda Jacobowitz's essay on pages 12–14.

2. **Analysis:** Whether you agree or disagree with Jacobowitz, write a paragraph analyzing the points she presents.

3. **Synthesis:** Read additional opinion pieces or blog postings about bottled water. In one paragraph, state your position on the subject according to your reading of these materials. Also, explain the range of opinions on the subject.

4. **Evaluation:** Write a paragraph that evaluates Jacobowitz's essay.

What Is Writing Critically about Visuals?

Images play a huge role in our lives today, and it is important to think critically about them just as you would about what you read or hear. Whether the image is a Web site, a photograph or illustration, a graphic, or an advertisement, you need to be able to "read" it. You can apply the same critical reading skills of summary, analysis, synthesis, and evaluation to read a visual.

Look carefully at the advertisement from Tappening on page 4. Then, consider how to read a visual using the critical thinking skills you have learned.

Summary

To summarize a visual, ask yourself what the big picture is: What is going on? What is the main impression or message (the main point)? What is the purpose? How is this purpose achieved (the support)? To answer these questions, consider some strategies used in visuals.

DOMINANT ELEMENTS

Artists, illustrators, and advertisers may place the most important object in the center of an image. Or, they may design visuals using a **Z pattern**, with the most important object in the top left and the second most important object in the bottom right. In English and many other languages, people read printed material from left to right and from top to bottom, and the Z pattern takes advantage of that pattern. Because of these design strategies, the main point of a visual can often be determined by looking at the center of the image or at the top left or bottom right.

FIGURES AND OBJECTS

The person who creates an image has a purpose (main point) and uses visual details to achieve (or support) that purpose. In a photograph, illustration, or painting, details about the figures and objects help create the impression the artist wants to convey. (Here, the term *figures* refers to people, animals, or other forms that can show action or emotion.) When studying any image, ask yourself:

- Are the figures from a certain period in history?
- What kind of clothes are they wearing?
- What are the expressions on their faces? How would I describe their attitudes?
- Are the figures shown realistically, or are they shown as sketches or cartoons?
- What important details about the figures does the creator of the image want me to focus on?

PRACTICE 7   Summarizing a Visual

Focus on the Tappening advertisement on page 4, and answer the following questions.

1. What is the big picture? What is going on? _____
   _____

2. What is at the center of the ad? _____

3. What is the ad's purpose? _____

4. What details do you notice about the figure in the ad? Include as many as you can. _____
   _____
   _____

Analysis

To analyze a visual, focus on the parts of it (figures, objects, type), and ask yourself how they contribute to the message or main impression. Consider the background, the use of light and dark, and the various elements' colors, contrasts, textures, and sizes.

PRACTICE 8 Analyzing a Visual

Focus on the Tappening advertisement on page 4, and answer the following questions.

1. What color is the background? What colors are used in other elements? What impressions do the different colors suggest? _____
   _____
   _____
   _____
   _____
   _____

2. What elements are placed in large type? Why? _____
   _____
   _____

3. How do all these features contribute to the main impression? _____
   _____
   _____

Synthesis

To synthesize your impressions of a visual, ask yourself what the message seems to be, using your summary and analysis skills. Consider how this message relates to what else you know from experience and observation.

PRACTICE 9 Synthesizing Your Impressions of a Visual

Focus on the Tappening advertisement on page 4, and answer the following questions.

1. What is the ad's central message? _____
   _____
   _____

2. How does this message relate to what you already know or have heard or experienced? _____

Evaluation

To evaluate an image, ask yourself how effective it is in achieving its purpose and conveying its main point or message. What do you think of the image, using your summary, analysis, and synthesis skills? Consider any biases or assumptions that may be working in the image.

PRACTICE 10 Evaluating a Visual

Focus on the Tappening advertisement on page 4, and answer the following questions.

1. What do you think about the ad, especially its visual elements?
   _____

2. Does the creator of the ad seem to have any biases? Why or why not?
   _____

3. Is the ad effective, given its purpose and the main point it is trying to make? Why or why not? _____
   _____

What Is Problem Solving?

In college, at work, and in everyday life, we often need to "read" situations to make important decisions about them. This process, known as problem solving, can also involve summarizing, analyzing, synthesizing, and evaluating. Let's look at key steps in the process.

1. **Summarize the problem.**

   Try to describe it in a brief statement or question.

   EXAMPLE: My ten-year-old car needs a new transmission, which will cost at least $750. Should I keep the car or buy a new one?

2. **Analyze the problem.**

   Consider possible ways to solve it, examining any questions or assumptions you might have.

   > **EXAMPLES:**
   >
   > *Assumption:* I need to have a reliable car.
   >
   > *Question:* Is this assumption truly justified?

Answer: Yes. I can't get to school or work without a reliable car. I live more than fifteen miles from each location, and there is no regular public transportation to either place from my home.

POSSIBLE SOLUTIONS:

- Pay for the transmission repair.
- Buy a new car.

3. **Synthesize information about the problem.**

   Consult various information sources to get opinions about the possible solutions.

EXAMPLES:

- My mechanic
- Friends who have had similar car problems
- Car advice from print or Web sources
- My past experience with car repairs and expenses

4. **Evaluate the possible solutions, and make a decision.**

   You might consider the advantages and disadvantages of each possible solution. Also, when you make your decision, you should be able to give reasons for your choice.

EXAMPLES (CONSIDERING ONLY ADVANTAGES AND DISADVANTAGES):

- Pay for the transmission repair.

   Advantage: This option would be cheaper than buying a new car.

   Disadvantage: The car might not last much longer, even with the new transmission.

- Buy a new car.

  Advantage: I will have a reliable car.

  Disadvantage: This option is much more expensive than paying for the repair.

  FINAL DECISION: Pay for the transmission repair.

  REASONS: I do not have money for a new car, and I do not want to take on more debt. Also, two mechanics told me that my car should run for three to five more years with the new transmission. At that point, I will be in a better position to buy a new car.

PRACTICE 11 Solving a Problem

Think of a problem you are facing now — in college, at work, or in your everyday life. On a separate sheet of paper, summarize the problem. Next, referring to the previous steps, write down and analyze possible solutions, considering different sources of information. Then, write down your final decision or preferred solution, giving reasons for your choice.

Chapter Review

1. What are the four basics of critical thinking? _____
   _____
   _____

2. What are the four major steps of the critical reading process? _____
   _____

3. Why is it important to read real-world documents critically? _____
   _____

4. What are the four major steps of writing critically about readings and visuals? _____

5. Without looking back in the chapter, define the task of synthesizing in your own words. _____
   _____

> **reflect** Using what you have learned in this chapter, revise your response to the "think" question on page 3.

YOU KNOW THIS

You write almost every day, for many reasons.

- You write a note to explain your child's absence from school.
- You e-mail a friend or coworker to ask a favor.

think How does the way you communicate change with different people (for example, a friend and a teacher)?

Writing Basics

Audience, Purpose, and Process

Four elements are key to good writing. Keep them in mind whenever you write.

Four Basics of Good Writing

1. It considers what the audience knows and needs.
2. It fulfills the writer's purpose.
3. It includes a clear, definite point.
4. It provides support that shows, explains, or proves the main point.

This chapter discusses the four basics in more detail. It also outlines the writing process, previewing steps that will be covered more thoroughly in the next five chapters. Finally, it gives you some typical grading criteria and shows how they are applied to assess unsatisfactory, satisfactory, and excellent paragraphs.

Understand Audience and Purpose

Your **audience** is the person or people who will read what you write. In college, your audience is usually your instructors. Whenever you write, always have at least one real person in mind as a reader. Think about what that person already knows and what he or she will need to know to understand your main point.

Your **purpose** is your reason for writing. Let's take a look at some different audiences and purposes.

Audience and Purpose

TYPE OF WRITING	AUDIENCE	PURPOSE	TIPS
COLLEGE: A research essay about the environmental effects of "fracking": fracturing rock layers to extract oil or natural gas	The professor of your environmental science class	• To complete an assignment according to your professor's instructions and any research methods discussed in class • To show what you have learned about the topic	When writing to fulfill a course assignment, never make assumptions like, "My instructor already knows this fact, so what's the point of mentioning it?" By providing plenty of relevant examples and details, you demonstrate your knowledge of a subject and make your writing more effective.
WORK: An e-mail to coworkers about your company's new insurance provider	Fellow workers	To make sure that coworkers understand all the important details about the new provider	Define or explain any terminology or concepts that will not be familiar to your audience.
EVERYDAY LIFE: An electronic comment about an online newspaper editorial that you disagree with	• The editorial writer • Other readers of the editorial	To make the editorial writer and other readers aware of your views	Keep all correspondence with others as polite as possible, even if you disagree with their views.

The tone and content of your writing will vary depending on your audiences and purposes. Read the following two notes, which describe the same situation but are written for different audiences and purposes.

SITUATION: Marta woke up one morning feeling strange, and her face was swollen and red. Marta immediately called her doctor's office and got an appointment. Marta's mother was coming to stay with Marta's children in a few minutes, so Marta asked a neighbor to watch her children until her mother got there. Marta then left a note for her mother telling her why she had already left. When she got to the doctor's office, she was feeling better, and since the doctor was running late, she decided not to wait. The nurse asked her to write a brief description of her symptoms for the doctor to read later.

MARTA'S NOTE TO HER MOTHER

Ma,
Not feeling well this morning. Stopping by doctor's office before work. Don't worry, I'm okay, just checking it out. Can't miss any more work. See you after. Thanks for watching the kids.

MARTA'S NOTE TO THE DOCTOR

When I woke up this morning, my face was swollen, especially around the eyes, which were almost shut. My lips and skin were red and dry, and my face was itchy. However, the swelling seemed to go down quickly.

PRACTICE 1   Comparing Marta's Notes

Read Marta's two notes, and answer the following questions.

1. How does Marta's note to her mother differ from the one to the doctor? _____

2. How do the different audiences and purposes affect what the notes say (the content) and how they say it (the tone)? _____
   _____
   _____
   _____

3. Which note has more detail, and why? _____
   _____

As these examples show, we communicate with family members and friends differently than we communicate with people in authority (like employers, instructors, or other professionals) — or we should. Marta's note to her mother uses informal English and incomplete sentences because the two women know each other well and are used to speaking casually to each other. Because Marta's purpose is to get quick information to her mother and to reassure her, she does not need to provide a lot of details. On the other hand, Marta's note to her doctor is more formal, with complete sentences, because the relationship is more formal. Also, the note to the doctor is more detailed because the doctor will be making treatment decisions based on it.

In college, at work, and in your everyday life, when you are speaking or writing to someone in authority for a serious purpose, use formal English; people will take you seriously.

TIP For more practice with writing for a formal audience, see the Using Formal English practices in Chapters 20–23. Or, visit *Exercise Central* at **bedfordstmartins.com/ realwriting**.

PRACTICE 2   Writing for a Formal Audience

A student, Terri Travers, sent the following e-mail to a friend to complain about not getting into a criminal justice course. Rewrite the e-mail as if you were Terri and you were writing to Professor Widener. The purpose is to ask whether the professor would consider allowing you into the class given that you signed up early and have the necessary grades.

> To: Miles Rona
> Fr: Terri Travers
> Subject: Bummin
>
> Seriously bummin that I didn't get into Prof Widener's CJ class. U and Luis said it's the best ever, lol. Wonder why I didn't . . . I signed up early and I have the grades. Sup w/that?
>
> C ya,
>
> TT

Understand Paragraph and Essay Form

In this course (and in the rest of college), you will write paragraphs and essays. Each kind of writing has a basic structure.

PARAGRAPH FORM

A **paragraph** has three necessary parts: the topic sentence, the body, and the concluding sentence.

PARAGRAPH PART	PURPOSE OF THE PARAGRAPH PART
1. The **topic sentence**	states the **main point**. The topic sentence is often the first sentence of the paragraph.
2. The **body**	supports (shows, explains, or proves) the main point with **support sentences** that contain facts and details.
3. The **concluding sentence**	reminds readers of the main point and often makes an observation.

Read the paragraph that follows with the paragraph parts labeled.

Topic sentence ──────────── Following a few basic strategies can help you take better notes, an important skill for succeeding in any course. First, start the notes for each class session on a fresh page of your course notebook, and record the date at the top of the page. Next, to improve the speed of your note taking, abbreviate certain words, especially ones your instructor uses regularly. For example, abbreviations for a business course might

Body ──────── include *fncl* for *financial*, *svc* for *service*, and *mgt* for *management*. How-
(with support sentences) ever, don't try to write down every word your instructor says. Instead, look for ways to boil extended explanations down into short phrases. For instance, imagine that a business instructor says the following: "A profit-and-loss statement is a report of an organization's revenue and expenses over a specific financial period. Often, P-and-L's are used to

determine ways to boost revenue or cut costs, with the goal of increasing profitability." The note taker might write down something like, "P&L: rpt of revenue + expenses over a specific period. Used to boost rev or cut costs." Although you do not need to record every word of a lecture, listen for clues that indicate that your instructor is making a point important enough to write down. At such times, the instructor might raise his or her voice. Or, he or she might introduce key information with such phrases as "It's important to remember" or "Bear in mind." In addition, if the instructor has made a certain point more than once, it is a good indication that this point is important. By carefully listening to and recording information from your instructor, you are not just getting good notes to study later; you are already beginning to seal this information into your memory. — Concluding sentence

ESSAY FORM

An **essay** is a piece of writing that examines a topic in more depth than a paragraph. A short essay may have four or five paragraphs, totaling three hundred to six hundred words. A long essay may be many pages long, depending on what the essay needs to accomplish, such as persuading someone to do something, using research to make a point, or explaining a complex concept.

An essay has three necessary parts: the introduction, the body, and the conclusion.

ESSAY PART	PURPOSE OF THE ESSAY PART
1. The **introduction**	states the **main point**, or **thesis**, generally in a single, strong statement. The introduction may be a single paragraph or multiple paragraphs.
2. The **body**	supports (shows, explains, or proves) the main point. It generally has at least three **support paragraphs**, each containing facts and details that develop the main point. Each support paragraph has a **topic sentence** that supports the thesis statement.
3. The **conclusion**	reminds readers of the main point and makes an observation. Often, it also summarizes and reinforces the support.

PARAGRAPH		ESSAY
Topic sentence	→	Thesis statement
Support sentences	→	Support paragraphs
Concluding sentence	→	Conclusion

The diagram on pages 32–33 shows how the parts of an essay correspond to the parts of a paragraph.

RELATIONSHIP BETWEEN PARAGRAPHS AND ESSAYS

For more on the important features of writing, see the Four Basics of Good Writing on page 27.

Paragraph Form

Topic sentence

Although they are entering the job market in tough economic times, Millennials (those born between 1981 and 2000) have some important advantages in the workplace. **Support 1:** First, having grown up in a fast-changing world, they value flexibility, independence, and collaboration. According to a report from the Boston College Center for Work and Family's Executive Briefing Series, Millennials seek flexibility in the workplace; meaning, for one thing, that they want the independence to find the most effective way to work. Additionally, younger people generally prefer to work collaboratively and to motivate others on their team; therefore, they hold the promise of being inspiring leaders. **Support 2:** Second, Millennials are smart about using technology to make connections and succeed on the job. Most are accustomed to being in nearly constant contact with others via phones, laptops, or other devices. Millennials who use their electronic communication skills wisely will be comfortable keeping managers and colleagues up to date about projects. Also, Millennials' social media skills can be put to good use by employers looking for new ways to market products. **Support 3:** Finally, the economy is creating more jobs that demand the flexibility, independence, and technological skills that Millennials are acquiring. For example, many jobs are being created in the health care field, where workers must not only exercise independence in decision making but must also be able to collaborate effectively. Additionally, many more companies need employees who know how to use social media and other electronic tools. **Concluding sentence:** As long as they remain determined, Millennials have every reason to believe that they will achieve success.

Main Point: May be the same for a paragraph and an essay (as in this case). Or, the main point of a paragraph may be narrower than one for an essay (see pp. 30–31).

Support for the Main Point

Facts, Details, or Examples to Back Up the Support Points: Usually, 1 to 3 sentences per support point for paragraphs and 3 to 8 sentences per support point for essays.

Conclusion

Essay Form

1 — *Introductory paragraph*

Fairly often, I hear older people saying that Millennials (those born between 1981 and 2000) are spoiled, self-centered individuals who have much less to contribute to the workplace than previous generations did. Based on my own experiences and r— *Thesis statement* — disagree. Although they are entering the job market in tough economic times, Millennials have some important advantages in the workplace. — *Topic sentence 1*

First, having grown up in a fast-changing world, they value flexibility, independence, and collaboration. Unlike their parents and grandparents, Millennials never knew a world without personal computers, and the youngest of them never knew a world without the Internet or ever-changing models of smart phones. They are used to rapid change, and most of them have learned to adapt to it. Consequently, Millennials, for the most part, expect workplaces to adapt to them. According to a report from the Boston College Center for Work and Family's Executive Briefing Series (EBS), Millennials seek flexibility in the workplace—for example, in when and where they work. This attitude does not mean that

2

they are looking out for themselves alone. Instead, they want the independence to find the most effective and productive way to work. Additionally, according to the EBS report, Millennials are more likely than older workers to reject old-fashioned business hierarchies in which managers tell lower-ranking employees what to do, and there is no give-and-take. In general, younger people prefer to work collaboratively and to do what they can to motivate others on their team; therefore, they hold the promise of being inspiring leaders. — *Topic sentence 2*

Second, Millennials are smart about using technology to make connections and succeed on the job. Most of them are accustomed to being in nearly constant contact with others via phones, laptops, or other devices. Although some people fear that such connectedness can be a distraction in the workplace, these technologies can be used productively and allow effective multitask— — *Support paragraphs* — For instance, over the course of a day, Millennials who have learned to use their electronic communication skills wisely will be comfortable keeping managers and colleagues up to date about projects and responding

3

to questions and requests as they arise. Furthermore, most Millennials are open to continuing such electronic exchanges during evenings and weekends if they feel they are collaborating with colleagues to meet an important goal. Also, many Millennials are skilled in using social media to reach out to and remain connected with others; in fact, some people refer to them as "the Facebook generation." Employers can put these skills to good use as they look for new ways to market their products and find new customers. — *Topic sentence 3*

Finally, the economy is creating more jobs that demand the flexibility, independence, and technological skills that Millennials are acquiring. For example, many jobs are being created in the health care field, where workers, such as nurses and physician assistants, must not only exercise independence in decision making but must also be able to collaborate effectively. Additionally, many more companies need employees who know how to use social media and other electronic tools for marketing purposes. Similarly, Millennials with social media skills may have an advantage in finding work in the marketing

4

and advertising industries specifically. There is also always a need for independent-minded people to create new businesses and innovations. Thus, Millennials play a valuable role in helping the economy grow. — *Concluding paragraph*

As long as they remain determined and confident, Millennials have every reason to believe that they will achieve career success. According to the EBS report and other sources, meaningful, challenging work is more important to this generation than having a high salary. In the long term, workers with those types of values will always be in demand.

33

Understand the Writing Process

The chart that follows shows the four stages of the **writing process**, all steps you will follow to write well. The rest of the chapters in Part 1 cover every stage except editing (presented later in the book). You will practice each stage, see how another student completed the process, and write your own paragraph or essay. Keep in mind that you may not always go in a straight line through the four stages; instead, you might circle back to earlier steps to further improve your writing.

THE WRITING PROCESS

Generate ideas

CONSIDER: What is my purpose in writing? Given this purpose, what interests me? Who will read this paper? What do they need to know?

- Find and explore your topic (Chapter 3).
- Make your point (Chapter 4).
- Support your point (Chapter 5).

Draft

CONSIDER: How can I organize my ideas effectively and show my readers what I mean?

- Arrange your ideas, and make an outline (Chapter 6).
- Write a draft, including an introduction that will interest your readers, a strong conclusion, and a title (Chapter 6).

Revise

CONSIDER: How can I make my draft clearer or more convincing to my readers?

- Look for ideas that do not fit (Chapter 7).
- Look for ideas that could use more detailed support (Chapter 7).
- Connect ideas with transitional words and sentences (Chapter 7).

Edit

CONSIDER: What errors could confuse my readers and weaken my point?

- Find and correct errors in grammar (Chapters 19–30).
- Look for errors in word use (Chapters 31 and 32), spelling (Chapter 33), and punctuation and capitalization (Chapters 34–38).

Some writing strategies—such as finding and exploring a topic, coming up with a main point, and revising—are similar for both paragraphs and essays. In these cases, this book discusses the strategies for paragraphs and essays together. (See Chapters 3, 4, and 7.) However, other activities, such as supporting main points or drafting individual parts of paragraphs or essays, are somewhat different for the two types of writing. (See Chapters 5 and 6.) In those cases, this book makes greater distinctions between paragraphs and essays.

NOTE: AVOIDING PLAGIARISM

In all the writing you do, it is important to avoid plagiarism—using other people's words as your own or handing in information you gather from another source as your own. Your instructors are aware of plagiarism and know how to look for it. Writers who plagiarize, either on purpose or by accident, risk failing a course or losing their jobs and damaging their reputations.

To avoid plagiarism, take careful notes on every source (books, interviews, television shows, Web sites, and so on) you might use in your writing. When recording information from sources, take notes in your own words, unless you plan to use direct quotations. In that case, make sure to record the quotation word for word. Also, include quotation marks around it, both in your notes and in your paper. When you use material from other sources—whether you directly quote or put information in your own words (paraphrase)—you must name and give citation information about these sources.

TIP For more on avoiding plagiarism, and citing and documenting outside sources, see Chapter 18. Visit the Bedford/St. Martin's Workshop on Plagiarism at **http://bcs.bedfordstmartins.com/plagiarism** for online resources on avoiding plagiarism.

Understand Grading Criteria

Your instructor may use a **rubric**—a list of the elements that your papers will be graded on. If your instructor uses a rubric, it may be included in the course syllabus, and you should refer to it each time you write. Also, use the rubric to revise your writing.

The following sample rubric shows you some of the elements you may be graded on. Many rubrics include how each element is weighted; because that practice differs among instructors and courses, the example does not specify percentages of importance or points.

Sample Rubric

ELEMENT	GRADING CRITERIA	POINT RANGE
Appropriateness	• Did the student follow the assignment directions?	0–5
Main idea	• Does the paper clearly state a strong main point in a complete sentence?	0–10

(continued)

ELEMENT	GRADING CRITERIA	POINT RANGE
Support	• Is the main idea developed with specific support, including specific details and examples? • Is enough support presented to make the main point evident to the reader? • Is all the support directly related to the main point?	0–10
Organization	• Is the writing logically organized? • Does the student use transitions (*also, for example, sometimes,* and so on) to move the reader from one point to another?	0–10
Conclusion	• Does the conclusion remind the reader of the main point? • Does it make an observation based on the support?	0–5
Grammar	• Is the writing free of the four most serious errors? (See Chapters 20–23.) • Is the sentence structure clear? • Does the student choose words that clearly express his or her meaning? • Are the words spelled correctly? • Is the punctuation correct?	0–10

The paragraphs that follow show how rubrics are applied to a piece of writing. For a key to the correction symbols used, see the Useful Editing and Proofreading Marks chart at the back of this book.

ASSIGNMENT: Write a paragraph about something you enjoy doing. Make sure you give enough details about the activity so that a reader who knows little about it will have an idea of why you enjoy it.

PARAGRAPH 1

In my spare time, enjoy talking with friends. Talk about everything like problems fun things we have to do or nothing important. One friend Karen especial. She really understands me we been frends since ten. Without her, I need a shrink to help me thru tings.

ANALYSIS OF PARAGRAPH 1: This paragraph would receive a low grade, for these reasons.

Sample Rubric

ELEMENT	GRADING CRITERIA	POINT: COMMENT
Appropriateness	• Did the student follow the assignment directions?	2/5: Generally, yes, although without providing the details the assignment required.
Main idea	• Does the paper clearly state a strong main point in a complete sentence?	0/10: No. The topic sentence is not a complete sentence (it is missing a subject).
Support	• Is the main idea developed with specific support, including specific details and examples? • Is enough support presented to make the main point evident to the reader? • Is all the support directly related to the main point?	0/10: No. The major problem with the paragraph is that it includes few details.
Organization	• Is the writing logically organized? • Does the student use transitions (*also, for example, sometimes,* and so on) to move the reader from one point to another?	2/10: The writing is not logically organized, although there are transitions.
Conclusion	• Does the conclusion remind the reader of the main point? • Does it make an observation based on the support?	3/5: No reminder of the main point, but the last sentence has the start of an observation.
Grammar	• Is the writing free of the four most serious errors? (See Chapters 20–23.) • Is the sentence structure clear? • Does the student choose words that clearly express his or her meaning? • Are the words spelled correctly? • Is the punctuation correct?	2/10: No. The writing has many errors of all kinds. **TOTAL POINTS: 9/50**

PRACTICE 3 Adding Detail

Rewrite Paragraph 1, adding detail about the second and fourth sentences. If you know how to correct the grammar (including spelling and punctuation), make the corrections.

Now, look at Paragraph 2.

PARAGRAPH 2

In my spare time, I enjoy talking with my friend Karen. I know (tense) Karen since we ten, so we have growed up together and been (tense) (tense) through many things. Like a sister. [frag] We can talk about anything. Sometimes we talk about problems. Money problems, problems with men. [frag] When I was in a difficult relationship, for example. [frag] Now we both have children and we talk about how to raise them. Things are diffrent [sp] then [sp] when we [tense] kids. Talking with a good friend helps me make good decisions and patience [wc]. Especially now that my son is a teenager. [frag] We also talk about fun things, like what were [punc] going to do on the weekend, what [run-on] clothes we buy. We tell each other good jokes and make each other laugh. These conversations are as important as talking about problems.

ANALYSIS OF PARAGRAPH 2: This paragraph would receive a higher grade (but still not an A or B), for the following reasons.

Sample Rubric

ELEMENT	GRADING CRITERIA	POINT: COMMENT
Appropriateness	• Did the student follow the assignment directions?	**5/5**: Yes.
Main idea	• Does the paper clearly state a strong main point in a complete sentence?	**10/10**: Yes.
Support	• Is the main idea developed with specific support, including specific details and examples? • Is there enough support to make the main point evident to the reader? • Is all the support directly related to the main point?	**5/10**: The paragraph has more support and detail than Paragraph 1 does, but it could use more.
Organization	• Is the writing logically organized? • Does the student use transitions (*also, for example, sometimes,* and so on) to move the reader from one point to another?	**6/10**: The student uses a few transitions (*sometimes, when, for example, now*).
Conclusion	• Does the conclusion remind the reader of the main point? • Does it make an observation based on the support?	**3/5**: The conclusion is better than the one in Paragraph 1. It relates back to the main point, but the observation is weak.

ELEMENT	GRADING CRITERIA	POINT: COMMENT
Grammar	• Is the writing free of the four most serious errors? (See Chapters 20–23.) • Is the sentence structure clear? • Does the student choose words that clearly express his or her meaning? • Are the words spelled correctly? • Is the punctuation correct?	6/10: Compared with Paragraph 1, the writing has fewer grammar errors, but it still has some major ones. **TOTAL POINTS: 37/50**

PRACTICE 4 Making Corrections

Correct any of the errors in Paragraph 2 that you can.

PRACTICE 5 Writing a Concluding Sentence

Try writing a concluding sentence to Paragraph 2. (Several answers are possible.)

Now, look at Paragraph 3.

PARAGRAPH 3

In my spare time, I enjoy talking with my friend Karen. We have been friends since we were ten, so we have grown up together. We have been through many things, both good and bad, in our lives, and we understand each other without having to explain the background of any situation. We have talked about our various problems throughout the years. Long ago, most of our problems were with our parents, who tried to control us too much. We would plan how to get around the rules we didn't like. Over the years, we have often talked about our relationships with men, which we call "the good, the bad, and the ugly." When I discovered that a man I was dating was cheating on me, Karen helped me see that the relationship wasn't good for me. She helped me get out of and over it. She helped me move on and value myself when I felt low. Now we talk often about our children and how to raise them right. For example, my son is now a teenager, and sometimes I can't control him, just as my parents couldn't control me. Karen helps me think of ways to get through to him without losing my temper. Also, we have always been able to make each other see the humor in whatever is going on. We tell each other good jokes, we make fun of people who are unfair to us, and we have a whole language of fun. These conversations are as important as the ones that help solve problems. Throughout my life, talking with Karen has helped keep me on a good path, and I truly enjoy talking with her.

HOW TO WRITE PARAGRAPHS AND ESSAYS

Chapter 2 • Writing Basics

ANALYSIS OF PARAGRAPH 3: This is an excellent paragraph, for the following reasons.

Sample Rubric

ELEMENT	GRADING CRITERIA	POINT: COMMENT
Appropriateness	• Did the student follow the assignment directions?	5/5: Yes.
Main idea	• Does the paper clearly state a strong main point in a complete sentence?	10/10: Yes.
Support	• Is the main idea developed with specific support, including specific details and examples? • Is there enough support to make the main point evident to the reader? • Is all the support directly related to the main point?	10/10: Good support with lots of details.
Organization	• Is the writing logically organized? • Does the student use transitions (*also, for example, sometimes,* and so on) to move the reader from one point to another?	10/10: Good use of transitions (*long ago, over the years, when, now, for example, also, throughout*).
Conclusion	• Does the conclusion remind the reader of the main point? • Does it make an observation based on the support?	5/5: Strong concluding sentence with a good observation.
Grammar	• Is the writing free of the four most serious errors? (See Chapters 20–23.) • Is the sentence structure clear? • Does the student choose words that clearly express his or her meaning? • Are the words spelled correctly? • Is the punctuation correct?	10/10: No errors. **TOTAL POINTS: 50/50**

PRACTICE 6 Analyzing the Paragraph

Referring to Paragraph 3, answer the following questions.

1. Which sentence is the topic sentence? _____

2. Underline some of the added details that make Paragraph 3 stronger than the first two paragraphs, and note those details here. _____
_____

HOW TO WRITE PARAGRAPHS AND ESSAYS
Chapter Review

3. Circle the transitions, and write them here. _____
   _____

4. In what way is the last sentence a good concluding sentence? _____
   _____
   _____

Chapter Review

1. Highlight important terms in this chapter. Make a list of them, noting what page they appear on.

2. In your own words, define *audience*. _____
   _____

3. In college, who is your audience likely to be? _____

4. What are the stages of the writing process? _____
   _____

5. Think of other courses in which you have written papers or taken tests. What purposes has that writing had? _____
   _____

6. What are four of the elements often evaluated in rubrics?
   _____
   _____

> **reflect** Having read this chapter, would you change your response to the "think" question on p. 27?

3

Finding, Narrowing, and Exploring Your Topic

Choosing Something to Write About

YOU KNOW THIS

You already know what a topic is:

- What was the topic of a movie you saw recently?
- What topic is in the headlines this week?
- What was the topic of an interesting conversation you had recently?

STUDENT VOICES

Chelsea Wilson exchanged messages with her friend Nick Brown about an assignment she had received. Nick had taken the same writing course a semester earlier.

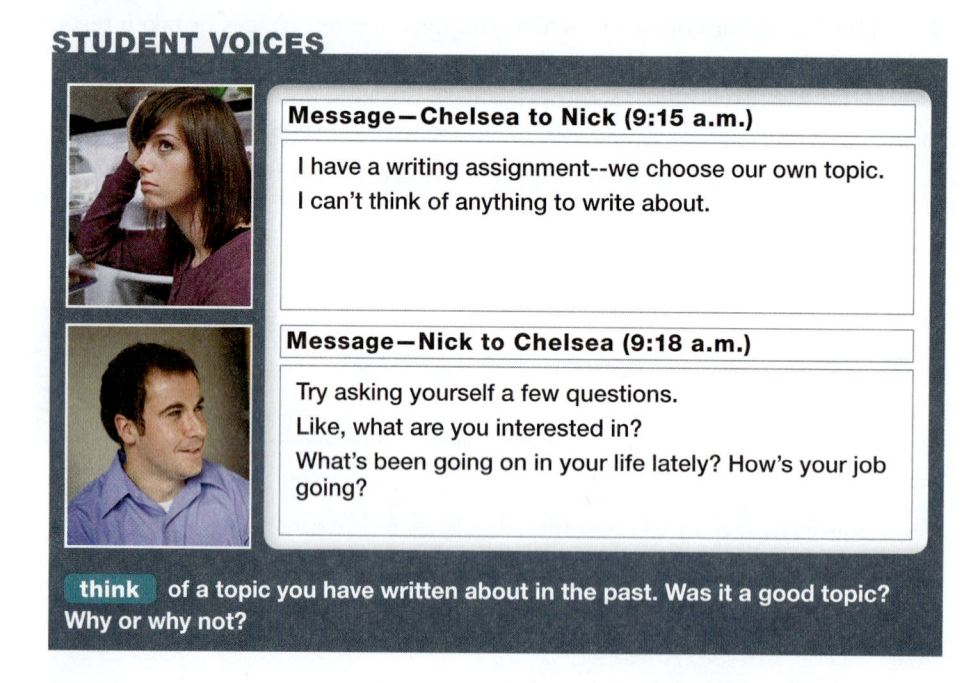

Message—Chelsea to Nick (9:15 a.m.)

I have a writing assignment--we choose our own topic. I can't think of anything to write about.

Message—Nick to Chelsea (9:18 a.m.)

Try asking yourself a few questions.
Like, what are you interested in?
What's been going on in your life lately? How's your job going?

think of a topic you have written about in the past. Was it a good topic? Why or why not?

Understand What a Topic Is

A **topic** is who or what you are writing about. It is the subject of your paragraph or essay.

QUESTIONS FOR FINDING A GOOD TOPIC

- Does this topic interest me? If so, why do I care about it?
- Do I know something about the topic? Do I want to know more?
- Can I get involved with some part of the topic? Is it relevant to my life in some way?
- Is the topic specific enough for the assignment (a paragraph or a short essay)?

TIP For help finding topic ideas, visit www.plinky.com.

Choose one of the following topics or one of your own and focus on one part of it that you are familiar with. (For example, focus on one personal goal or a specific problem of working students that interests you.)

Music/group I like	Sports
Problems of working students	An essential survival skill
An activity/group I am involved in	A personal goal
Something I can do well	A time when I took a big risk
An issue in the news	My ideal job
Relationships	A current trend

PRACTICE 1   Finding a Good Topic

Ask the Questions for Finding a Good Topic about the topic you have chosen. If you answer "no" to any of them, keep looking for another topic or modify the topic.

MY TOPIC: _____

With the general topic you have chosen in mind, read this chapter and complete all the practices. When you finish the chapter, you will have found a good topic to write about and explored ideas related to it.

Practice Narrowing a Topic

If your instructor assigns a general topic, it may at first seem uninteresting, unfamiliar, or too general. It is up to you to find a good, specific topic based on the general one. Whether the topic is your own or assigned, you next need to narrow and explore it. To **narrow** a general topic, focus on the smaller parts of it until you find one that is interesting and specific.

Here are some ways to narrow a general topic.

DIVIDE IT INTO SMALLER CATEGORIES

A PERSONAL GOAL
- Lose weight
- Get a degree
- Make more money

THINK OF SPECIFIC EXAMPLES FROM YOUR LIFE

GENERAL TOPIC **Crime**
Stolen identities (how does it happen?)
When I had my wallet stolen by two kids (how? what happened?)
The e-mail scam that my grandmother lost money in (how did it work?)

GENERAL TOPIC **Social media**
Twitter (which feeds do I follow regularly? what do I get from them?)
Facebook (what features are fun or useful? what feels like a waste of time?)
Google+ (is it just another Facebook, or is it truly different?)

THINK OF SPECIFIC EXAMPLES FROM CURRENT EVENTS

GENERAL TOPIC **Job-creation ideas**
Tax breaks for businesses
Training of future entrepreneurs in growth areas, like solar or wind energy
A special fund for public projects that will employ many people

GENERAL TOPIC **Heroism**
The guy who pulled a stranger from a burning car
The people who stopped a robbery downtown

QUESTION YOUR ASSUMPTIONS

Questioning assumptions—an important part of critical thinking (see Chapter 1)—can be a good way to narrow a topic. First, identify any assumptions you have about your topic. Then, question them, playing "devil's advocate"; in other words, imagine what someone with a different point of view might say. For example, imagine that your general topic is the pros or cons of letting kids play video games.

HOW TO WRITE PARAGRAPHS AND ESSAYS
Practice Narrowing a Topic

POSSIBLE ASSUMPTIONS	QUESTIONS
Video game pros: Kids get rewarded with good scores for staying focused. →	Does staying focused on a video game mean that a kid will stay focused on homework or in class?
Video games can teach some useful skills. →	Like what? How am I defining "useful"?
Video game cons: They make kids more violent. →	Is there really any proof for that? What do experts say?
They have no real educational value. →	Didn't my niece say that some video game helped her learn to read?

Next, ask yourself what assumptions and questions interest you the most. Then, focus on those interests.

When you have found a promising topic for a paragraph or essay, be sure to test it by using the Questions for Finding a Good Topic at the beginning of this chapter. You may need to narrow and test your ideas several times before you find a topic that will work for the assignment.

A topic for an essay can be a little broader than one for a paragraph because essays are longer than paragraphs and allow you to develop more ideas. But be careful: Most of the extra length in an essay should come from developing ideas in more depth (giving more examples and details, explaining what you mean), not from covering a broader topic.

Read the following examples of how a general topic was narrowed to a more specific topic for an essay and an even more specific topic for a paragraph.

GENERAL TOPIC	NARROWED ESSAY TOPIC	NARROWED PARAGRAPH TOPIC
Internships	→ How internships can help you get a job	→ One or two important things you can learn from an internship
Public service opportunities	→ Volunteering at a homeless shelter	→ My first impression of the homeless shelter
A personal goal	→ Getting healthy	→ Eating the right foods
A great vacation	→ A family camping trip	→ What I learned on our family camping trip to Michigan

PRACTICE 2 Narrowing a General Topic

Use one of the four methods above to narrow your topic. Then, ask yourself the Questions for Finding a Good Topic. Write your narrowed topic below.

MY NARROWED TOPIC: _____

Practice Exploring Your Topic

TIP Scholar and writer Mina Shaughnessy said that a writer "gets below the surface of a topic." When it comes to exploring a topic, what do you think getting "below the surface" means?

Prewriting techniques can give you ideas at any time during your writing: to find a topic, to get ideas for what you want to say about it, and to support your ideas. Ask yourself: What interests me about this topic? What do I know? What do I want to say? Then, use one or more of the prewriting techniques to find the answers. No one uses all those techniques; writers choose the ones that work best for them.

PREWRITING TECHNIQUES

- Freewriting
- Listing/brainstorming
- Discussing
- Clustering/mapping
- Using the Internet
- Keeping a journal

When prewriting, your goal is to come up with as many ideas as possible. Do not say, "Oh, that's stupid" or "That won't work." Just get your brain working by writing down all the possibilities.

A student, Chelsea Wilson, was assigned to write a short essay. She chose to write on the general topic of a personal goal, which she narrowed to "Getting a college degree." The following pages show how she used the first five prewriting techniques to explore her topic.

Freewriting

TIP If you are writing on a computer, try a kind of freewriting called "invisible writing." Turn the monitor off, or adjust the screen so that you cannot see what you are typing. Then, write quickly for five minutes without stopping. After five minutes, read what you have written. You may be surprised by the ideas that you can generate this way.

Freewriting is like having a conversation with yourself, on paper. To freewrite, just start writing everything you can think of about your topic. Write nonstop for five minutes. Do not go back and cross anything out, and do not worry about using correct grammar or spelling; just write. Here is Chelsea's freewriting:

> So I know I want to get a college degree even though sometimes I wonder if I ever can make it because it's so hard with work and my two-year-old daughter and no money and a car that needs work. I can't take more than two courses at a time and even then I hardly get a chance to sleep if I want to do any of the assignments or study. But I have to think I'll get a better job because this one at the restaurant is driving me nuts and doesn't pay much so I have to work a lot with a boss I can't stand and still wonder how I'm gonna pay the bills. I know life can be better if I can just manage to become a nurse. I'll make more money and can live anywhere I want because everyplace needs nurses. I won't have to work at a job where I am not respected by anyone. I want respect, I know I'm hardworking and smart and good with people and deserve better than this. So does my daughter. No one in my family has ever graduated from college even though my sister took two courses, but then she stopped. I know I can do this, I just have to make a commitment to do it and not look away.

Listing / Brainstorming

List all the ideas about your topic that you can think of. Write as many as you can in five minutes without stopping.

> GETTING A COLLEGE DEGREE
>
> want a better life for myself and my daughter
> want to be a nurse and help care for people
> make more money
> not have to work so many hours
> could live where I want in a nicer place
> good future and benefits like health insurance
> get respect
> proud of myself, achieve, show everyone
> be a professional, work in a clean place

Discussing

Many people find it helpful to discuss ideas with another person before they write. As they talk, they get more ideas and immediate feedback.

If you and your discussion partner both have writing assignments, first explore one person's topic and then explore the other's. The person whose topic is being explored is the interviewee; the other person is the interviewer. The interviewer should ask questions about anything that seems unclear and should let the interviewee know what sounds interesting. In addition, the interviewer should identify and try to question any assumptions the interviewee seems to be making (see page 44). The interviewee should give thoughtful answers and keep an open mind. He or she should also take notes. Here is Chelsea's discussion with Nick, a friend who had taken this writing course a semester before:

TIP If you find that talking about your ideas with someone is a good way to get going, you might want to ask another student to be your regular partner and discuss ideas before beginning any paragraph or essay assignment.

Nick: How's work?

Chelsea: It's OK except for lots of hours, a sleazy, stingy boss, and dirty conditions. Actually, I can't stand it. I want better.

Nick: Like what?

Chelsea: Getting a degree and becoming a nurse. Nurses make good money and can live wherever they want because everyone needs nurses.

Nick: Isn't a personal goal one of the topics the instructor gave you to choose from? How about "getting a degree and becoming a nurse"?

Chelsea: Yeah, I could write about getting a nursing degree, but I'm not sure I know enough about it. And I didn't leave lots of time to find out. The draft is due in two days, and I have to work.

Nick: So, other than wanting to become a nurse, why else do you want a degree? Write about that.

HOW TO WRITE PARAGRAPHS AND ESSAYS

Chapter 3 • Finding, Narrowing, and Exploring Your Topic

PRACTICE 3 Exploring Your Narrowed Topic

Use two or three prewriting techniques to explore your narrowed topic.

Clustering / Mapping

TIP For online mapping tools, visit **http://bubbl.us**.

Clustering, also called mapping, is like listing except that you arrange your ideas visually. Start by writing your narrowed topic in the center. Then, write the questions Why? What interests me? and What do I want to say? around the narrowed topic. Using Chelsea's clustering below as a model, write three answers to these questions. Keep branching out from the ideas until you feel you have fully explored your topic. Note that when Chelsea filled in "Why?" "What interests me?" and "What do I want to say?" she had lots of reasons and ideas that she could use in her writing assignment.

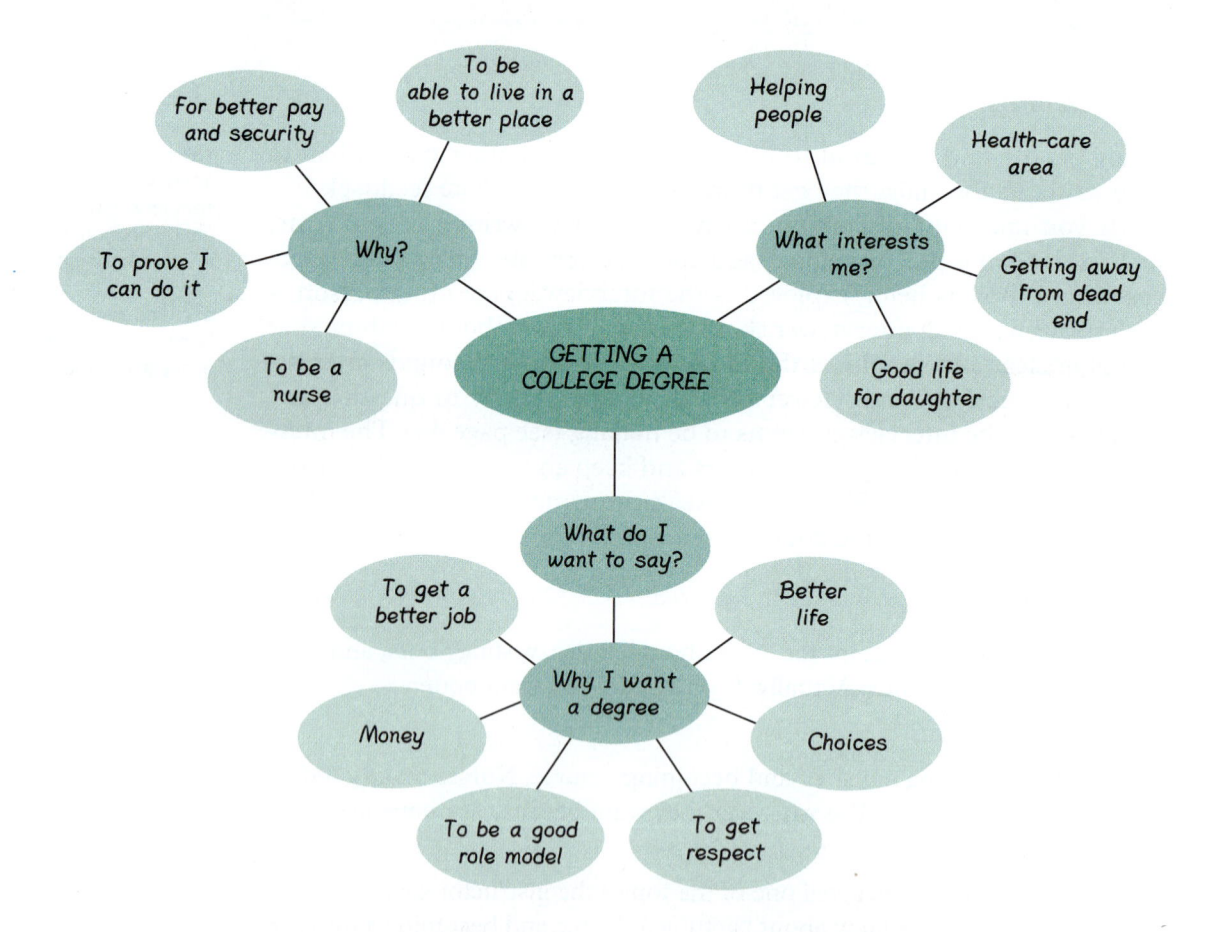

Using the Internet

Go to www.google.com, and type in specific key words about your topic. The search will provide more results than you can use, but it will help you with ideas for your paper. For example, Chelsea typed in "reasons to get a college degree" and got lots of information about aspects of her topic that she did not know much about, such as what a college degree is worth. Make notes about important or useful ideas you get from the Internet.

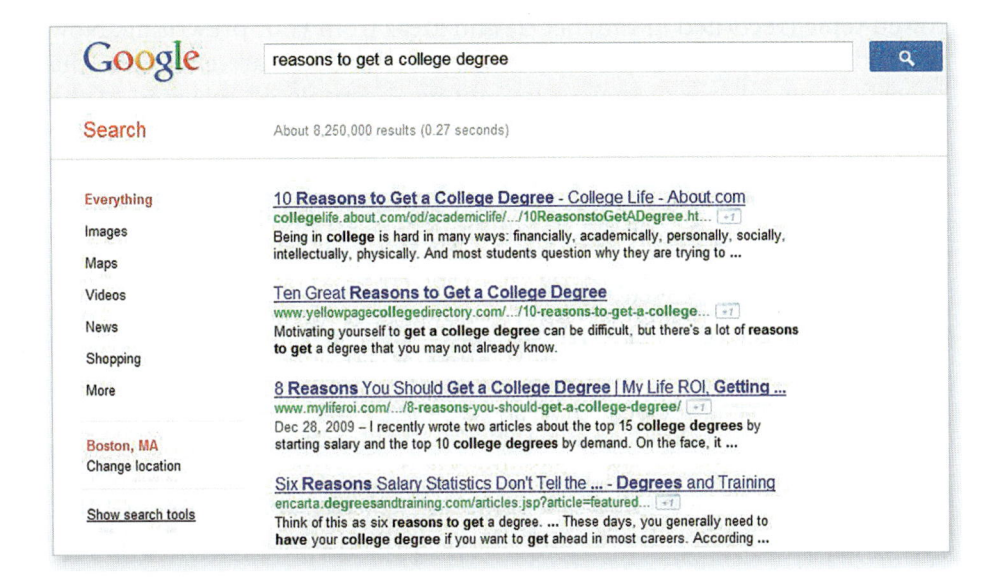

Keeping a Journal

Setting aside a few minutes on a regular schedule to write in a journal will give you a great source of ideas when you need them. What you write does not need to be long or formal. You can use a journal in several ways:

- To record and explore your personal thoughts and feelings
- To comment on things that happen, to you personally or in politics, in your neighborhood, at work, in college, and so on
- To explore situations you do not understand (as you write, you may figure them out)

One student, Jack, did all these things in the following journal entry.

TIP Look for the Idea Journal and Learning Journal assignments throughout this book.

> Been feeling a little confused about school lately. Doing OK in my classes and still liking the construction tech program. But having some doubts. Elena, another student in my English class, is studying to be a solar tech in a new program at the school. She's going to learn how to install and repair solar energy systems at a facility near campus, and that's pretty cool. Solar seems kind of sci-fi, and I love sci-fi movies. But seriously I'm truly interested in the technology, and some of the skills I've been learning in construction tech would probably transfer. And maybe I'd have a better chance of getting a job in solar energy since it's a field that seems to be growing? Not sure, but something to investigate. Bottom line: I can't get this new idea out of my mind, even though I thought I was sure about construction tech. I guess I'll keep talking with Elena about the solar tech program. And maybe I should meet with one of the instructors in the program? Or visit the solar facility?

TIP If you start keeping a journal, you might use some of the strategies described by writer Joan Didion. She says, "I write entirely to find out what I'm thinking, what I'm looking at, what I see and what it means. What I want and what I fear."

Write Your Own Topic and Ideas

If you have worked through this chapter, you should have both your narrowed topic (recorded in Practice 2) and ideas from your prewriting. Now is the time to make sure your topic and ideas about it are clear. Use the checklist that follows to make sure you have completed this step of the writing process.

> **CHECKLIST**
>
> **Evaluating Your Narrowed Topic**
> ☐ This topic interests me.
> ☐ My narrowed topic is specific.
> ☐ I can write about it in a paragraph or an essay (whichever you have been assigned).
> ☐ I have generated some things to say about this topic.

Now that you know what you are going to write about, you are ready to move on. Chapter 4 shows you how to express what is important to you about your narrowed topic.

Chapter Review

1. Highlight important terms from this chapter (for example, *topic, narrow,* and *prewriting techniques*), and list them with their page numbers.

2. What are four questions that can help you find a good topic? _____
   _____
   _____

3. How can you narrow a topic that is too broad or general? _____
   _____
   _____

4. What are some prewriting techniques? _____
   _____

5. Write for one minute on "Topics I would like to know more about."

6. Write for one minute about "What questions I should ask my instructor."

STUDENT VOICES

Message—Chelsea to Nick (11:37 a.m.)

OK, I'm going to write about a personal goal: why I want to get a college degree.

That's something I've thought a lot about.

Message—Nick to Chelsea (12:15 p.m.)

Sounds good!
What's your next move?

reflect What prewriting technique was best for you? Do you have something to write about? What?

4

Writing Your Topic Sentence or Thesis Statement

Making Your Point

YOU KNOW THIS

You already have experience in making your point:

- You explain the point of a movie to someone who has not seen it.
- When a friend asks you, "What's your point?" you explain it.
- When you persuade someone to do something you want, you make your point about why he or she should.

STUDENT VOICES

Chelsea Wilson exchanged messages with her friend Nick Brown about an assignment she had received. Nick had taken the same writing course a semester earlier.

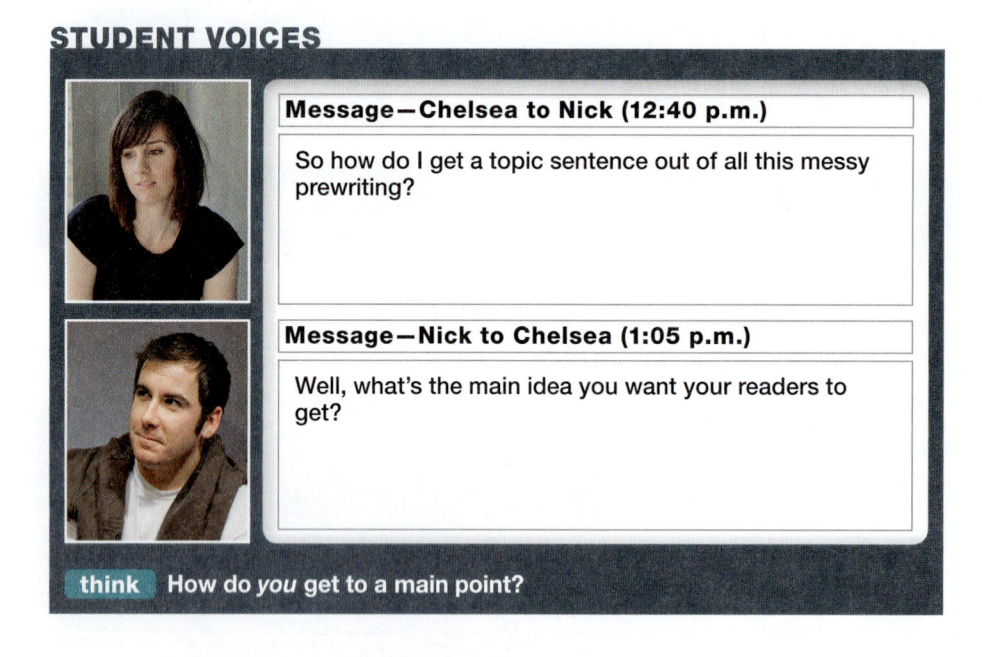

Message — Chelsea to Nick (12:40 p.m.)

So how do I get a topic sentence out of all this messy prewriting?

Message — Nick to Chelsea (1:05 p.m.)

Well, what's the main idea you want your readers to get?

think How do *you* get to a main point?

Understand What a Topic Sentence and a Thesis Statement Are

Every good piece of writing has a **main point**—what the writer wants to get across to the readers about the topic or the writer's position on that topic. A **topic sentence** (for a paragraph) and a **thesis statement** (for an essay) express the writer's main point. To see the relationship between the thesis statement of an essay and the topic sentences of paragraphs that support a thesis statement, see the diagram on pages 56–57.

In many paragraphs, the main point is expressed in either the first or last sentence. In essays, the thesis statement is usually one sentence (often the first or last) in an introductory paragraph that contains several other sentences related to the main point.

A good topic sentence or thesis statement has several basic features.

BASICS OF A GOOD TOPIC SENTENCE OR THESIS STATEMENT

- It fits the size of the assignment.
- It states a single main point or position about a topic.
- It is specific.
- It is something you can show, explain, or prove.
- It is forceful.

WEAK	Giving children chores teaches them responsibility, and I think doing chores as a kid made me a better adult.
	[This statement has more than one point (how chores teach responsibility and how they made the writer a better adult); it is not specific (what is "responsibility"? what does it mean to be a "better adult"?); and it is not forceful (the writer says, "I think").]
GOOD	Giving children chores teaches them the responsibilities of taking care of things and completing assigned tasks.
	Being assigned chores as a child helped teach me the important adult skills of teamwork and attention to detail.

IDEA JOURNAL What are your strongest communication skills? What other skills or talents do you have?

One way to write a topic sentence for a paragraph or a thesis statement for an essay is to use this basic formula as a start:

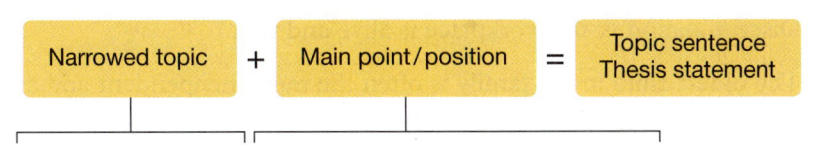

Narrowed topic + Main point/position = Topic sentence / Thesis statement

The tutoring center has helped me improve my writing.

If you have trouble coming up with a main point or position, look back over the prewriting you did. For example, when the student Chelsea Wilson looked over her prewriting about getting a college degree (see p. 46), she realized that several times she had mentioned the idea of more options for employment, living places, and chances to go on and be a nurse. She could also have chosen to focus on the topic of respect or on issues relating to her young daughter, but she was most drawn to write about the idea of *options*. Here is how she stated her main point:

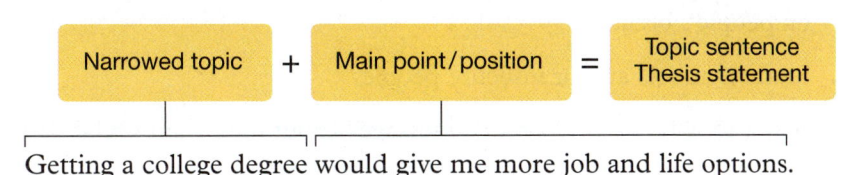

Narrowed topic + Main point/position = Topic sentence / Thesis statement

Getting a college degree would give me more job and life options.

HOW TO WRITE PARAGRAPHS AND ESSAYS

54 Chapter 4 • Writing Your Topic Sentence or Thesis Statement

PRACTICE 1 Finding the Topic Sentence and Main Point

Read the paragraph that follows, and underline the topic sentence. In the spaces below the paragraph, identify the narrowed topic and the main point.

> A recent survey reported that employers consider communication skills more critical to success than technical skills. Employees can learn technical skills on the job and practice them every day. But they need to bring well-developed communication skills to the job. They need to be able to make themselves understood to colleagues, both in speech and in writing. They need to be able to work cooperatively as part of a team. Employers cannot take time to teach communication skills, but without them an employee will have a hard time.

NARROWED TOPIC: _____

MAIN POINT: _____

_____

PRACTICE 2 Identifying Topics and Main Points

In each of the following sentences, underline the topic and double-underline the main point about the topic.

> **EXAMPLE:** Rosie the Riveter was the symbol of working women during World War II.

1. Discrimination in the workplace is alive and well.
2. The oldest child in the family is often the most independent and ambitious child.
3. Gadgets created for left-handed people are sometimes poorly designed.
4. Presidential campaigns bring out dirty politics.
5. Walking away from a mortgage has become a financial survival strategy for some homeowners.
6. The magazine *Consumer Reports* can help you decide which brands or models are the best value.
7. According to one study, dogs might be trained to detect signs of cancer on people's breath.
8. Status symbols are for insecure people.
9. Some song lyrics have serious messages about important social issues.

10. The Puritans came to America to escape religious intolerance, but they were intolerant themselves.

....

As you get further along in your writing, you may go back several times to revise the topic sentence or thesis statement based on what you learn as you develop your ideas. Look at how one student revised the example sentence on page 53 to make it more detailed:

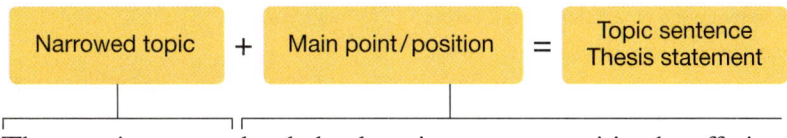

Narrowed topic + Main point/position = Topic sentence Thesis statement

The tutoring center has helped me improve my writing by offering friendly, one-on-one guidance.

Practice Developing a Good Topic Sentence or Thesis Statement

The explanations and practices in this section, organized according to the "basics" described previously, will help you write good topic sentences and thesis statements.

It Fits the Size of the Assignment

As you develop a topic sentence or thesis statement, think carefully about the length of the assignment.

Sometimes, a main-point statement can be the same for a paragraph or essay.

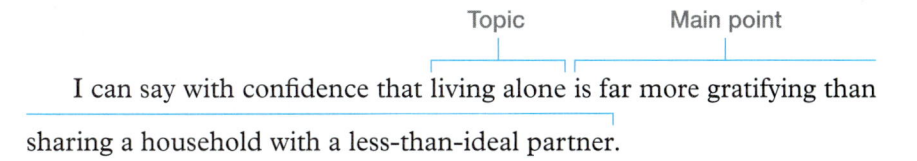

Topic   Main point

I can say with confidence that living alone is far more gratifying than sharing a household with a less-than-ideal partner.

If the writer had been assigned a paragraph, she might follow the main point with support sentences and a concluding sentence like those in the "paragraph" diagram on pages 56–57.

If the writer had been assigned an essay, she might develop the same support, but instead of writing single sentences to support her main idea, she would develop each support point into a paragraph. The support sentences she wrote in a paragraph might be topic sentences for support paragraphs. (For more on providing support, see Chapter 5.)

Often, however, a topic sentence for a paragraph is much narrower than a thesis statement for an essay, simply because a paragraph is shorter and allows less development of ideas.

RELATIONSHIP BETWEEN PARAGRAPHS AND ESSAYS

For more on the important features of writing, see the Four Basics of Good Writing on page 27.

Paragraph Form

Topic sentence

    I can say with confidence that living alone is far more gratifying than sharing a household with a less-than-ideal partner. One advantage of living alone is that I can spend my free time as I choose. If I want to sleep in past noon on a Saturday and devote the rest of the day to listening to music or watching movies, no one is there to make me feel guilty or to try to convince me that my time could be better spent. If I decide to take a night class during the week, no one questions my choice or says that building new skills is a "waste of time," as my ex did. Another advantage of living alone is that I am free to make my own life decisions, big and small, without push-back. On the small side, there is no one to complain about the financial consequences if I decide that I would like to sign up for a gym membership or buy a nice pair of jeans. On the big side, I can now take the step of adopting a child—something my husband was opposed to. The final, and perhaps greatest, advantage of living alone is that it has strengthened my social connections. When I was married, I spent little time going out with existing friends, making new friends, or getting involved in community activities. Now, however, I am able to accommodate a busy social life and also volunteer work. As a result, my life is more fulfilling than ever. Although a strong romantic partnership can be rewarding, I strongly believe that the advantages of being single are underrated.

- Topic sentence
- Support 1
- Support 2
- Support 3
- Concluding sentence

Main Point: May be the same for a paragraph and an essay (as in this case). Or, the main point of a paragraph may be narrower than one for an essay (see pp. 30–31).

Support for the Main Point

Facts, Details, or Examples to Back Up the Support Points: Usually, 1 to 3 sentences per support point for paragraphs and 3 to 8 sentences per support point for essays.

Conclusion

56

Essay Form

1

Introductory paragraph

As a young woman, I saw being single as a temporary—and undesirable—condition. When, at twenty-four, I married, I considered myself extremely lucky. That was until I spent years in an increasingly unsatisfying relationship that ultimately ended in divorce. Since the divorce, however, my life has changed for the better in many ways. **I can now say with confidence that living alone is far more gratifying than sharing a household with a less-than-ideal partner.** *Thesis statement*

Topic sentence 1

One advantage of living alone is that I can spend my free time as I choose. If I want to sleep in past noon on a Saturday and devote the rest of the day to listening to music or watching movies, no one is there to make me feel guilty or to try to convince me that my time could be better spent. If I decide to take a night class during the week, no one questions my choice or says that building new skills is a "waste of time," as my ex did. Also, when I am able to take vacation days, I can spend them relaxing at home, visiting out-of-state family members, or doing something more adventurous. In other words, I can set my own agenda, all the time.

2

Topic sentence 2

Another advantage of living alone is that I am free to make my own life decisions, big and small, without push-back. On the small side, there is no one to complain about the financial consequences if I decide that I would like to sign up for a gym membership or buy a nice pair of jeans. On the big side, I can now take the step of adopting a child—something my husband was opposed to. I realize that making all my own decisions requires personal responsibility and the ability to take some risks. But, to me, the benefits of independence far outweigh the challenges. *Support paragraphs*

Topic sentence 3

The final, and perhaps greatest, advantage of living alone is that it has strengthened my social connections. When I was married, I spent little time going out with existing friends, making new friends, or getting involved in community activities. If I did not spend nearly all of my free time with my husband, he would complain. Now, however, I am able to accommodate a busy social life and also volunteer work in my community. As a result, my life is more fulfilling than ever.

3

Concluding paragraph

Although a strong romantic partnership can be rewarding, I strongly believe that the advantages of being single are underrated. Consequently, I would like to offer one piece of advice to partnered people: Do not feel sorry for your single friends. One day, you may join their ranks and find that you have never been happier.

Consider how one general topic could be narrowed into an essay topic and into an even more specific paragraph topic.

GENERAL TOPIC	NARROWED ESSAY TOPIC	NARROWED PARAGRAPH TOPIC
Internships	→ How internships can help you get a job	→ One or two important things you can learn from an internship

POSSIBLE THESIS STATEMENT (ESSAY)	The skills and connections you gain through a summer internship can help you get a good job after graduation.
	[The essay would discuss several benefits of internships, describing the various skills they can teach and the professional connections they can offer to interns.]
POSSIBLE TOPIC SENTENCE (PARAGRAPH)	A summer internship is a good way to test whether a particular career is right for you.
	[The paragraph would focus on one benefit of internships: They are a way to test out a career. The paragraph might go on to discuss signs that a certain type of work is or is not passing the test.]

PRACTICE 3 Writing Sentences to Fit the Assignment

Using the following example as a guide, write a thesis statement for the narrowed essay topic and a topic sentence for the narrowed paragraph topic.

EXAMPLE:

TOPIC: Sports

NARROWED FOR AN ESSAY: Competition in school sports

NARROWED FOR A PARAGRAPH: User fees for school sports

POSSIBLE THESIS STATEMENT (essay): *Competition in school sports has reached dangerous levels.*

POSSIBLE TOPIC SENTENCE (paragraph): *This year's user fees for participation in school sports are too high.*

1. **TOPIC:** Public service opportunities

    NARROWED FOR AN ESSAY: Volunteering at a homeless shelter

    NARROWED FOR A PARAGRAPH: My first impression of the homeless shelter

    POSSIBLE THESIS STATEMENT (essay): _____

    _____

    POSSIBLE TOPIC SENTENCE (paragraph): _____

    _____

2. **TOPIC:** A personal goal

   NARROWED FOR AN ESSAY: Getting healthy

   NARROWED FOR A PARAGRAPH: Eating the right foods

   POSSIBLE THESIS STATEMENT (essay): _____

   _____

   POSSIBLE TOPIC SENTENCE (paragraph): _____

   _____

3. **TOPIC:** A great vacation

   NARROWED FOR AN ESSAY: A family camping trip

   NARROWED FOR A PARAGRAPH: A lesson I learned on our family camping trip

   POSSIBLE THESIS STATEMENT (essay): _____

   _____

   POSSIBLE TOPIC SENTENCE (paragraph): _____

   _____

Some topic sentences or thesis statements are too broad for either a short essay or a paragraph. A main idea that is too broad is impossible to show, explain, or prove within the space of a paragraph or short essay.

TOO BROAD	Art is important.
	[How could a writer possibly support such a broad concept in a paragraph or essay?]
NARROWER	Art instruction for young children has surprising benefits.

A topic sentence or thesis statement that is too narrow leaves the writer with little to write about. There is little to show, explain, or prove.

TOO NARROW	Buy rechargeable batteries.
	[OK, so now what?]
BROADER	Choosing rechargeable batteries over conventional batteries is one action you can take to reduce your effect on the environment.

PRACTICE 4 Writing Topic Sentences That Are Neither Too Broad Nor Too Narrow

In the following five practice items, three of the topic sentences are either too broad or too narrow, and two of them are OK. In the space to the left of each item, write "B" for too broad, "N" for too narrow, or "OK" for just right. Rewrite the three weak sentences to make them broader or narrower as needed.

EXAMPLE: _B_ Life can be tough for soldiers when they come home.
We are not providing our returning soldiers with enough help in readjusting to civilian life.

1. ___ I take public transportation to work.

2. ___ Because of state and national education budget cuts, schools are having to lay off teachers and cut important programs.

3. ___ College is challenging.

4. ___ I would like to be successful in life.

5. ___ Having a positive attitude improves people's ability to function, improves their interactions with others, and reduces stress.

It Contains a Single Main Point

Your topic sentence or thesis statement should focus on only one main point. Two main points can split and weaken the focus of the writing.

MAIN IDEA WITH TWO MAIN POINTS

High schools should sell healthy food instead of junk food, and they should start later in the morning.

The two main points are underlined. Although both are good main points, together they split both the writer's and the readers' focus. The writer would need to give reasons to support each point, and the ideas are completely different.

MAIN IDEA WITH A SINGLE MAIN POINT

High schools should sell healthy food instead of junk food.

OR

High schools should start later in the morning.

PRACTICE 5 Writing Sentences with a Single Main Point

In each of the following sentences, underline the main point(s). Identify the sentences that have more than a single main point by marking an X in the space provided to the left of that item. Put a check mark (✓) next to sentences that have a single main point.

EXAMPLE: _X_ Shopping at secondhand stores is a fun way to save money, and you can meet all kinds of interesting people as you shop.

1. ___ My younger sister, the baby of the family, was the most adventurous of my four siblings.

2. ___ Servicing hybrid cars is a growing part of automotive technology education, and dealers cannot keep enough hybrids in stock.

3. ___ My brother, Bobby, is incredibly creative, and he takes in stray animals.

4. ___ Pets can actually bring families together, and they require lots of care.

5. ___ Unless people conserve voluntarily, we will deplete our water supply.

It Is Specific

A good topic sentence or thesis statement gives readers specific information so that they know exactly what the writer's main point is.

GENERAL   Students are often overwhelmed.
                 [How are students overwhelmed?]

SPECIFIC   Working college students have to learn how to juggle many responsibilities.

One way to make sure your topic sentence or thesis statement is specific is to make it a preview of what you are planning to say in the rest of the paragraph or essay. Just be certain that every point you preview is closely related to your main idea.

PREVIEW: Working college students have to learn how to juggle many responsibilities: doing a good job at work, getting to class regularly and on time, being alert in class, and doing the homework assignments.

PREVIEW: I have a set routine every Saturday morning that includes sleeping late, going to the gym, and shopping for food.

PRACTICE 6   Writing Sentences That Are Specific

In the space below each item, revise the sentence to make it more specific. There is no one correct answer. As you read the sentences, think about what would make them more understandable to you if you were about to read a paragraph or essay on the topic.

EXAMPLE: Marriage can be a wonderful thing.

Marriage to the right person can add love, companionship, and support to life.

1. My job is horrible.

2. Working with others is rewarding.

3. I am a good worker.

4. This place could use a lot of improvement.

5. Getting my driver's license was challenging.

It Is an Idea You Can Show, Explain, or Prove

If a main point is so obvious that it does not need support or if it states a simple fact, you will not have much to say about it.

OBVIOUS   The Toyota Prius is a top-selling car.

Many people like to take vacations in the summer.

REVISED	Because of rising gas costs and concerns about the environmental impact of carbon emissions, the Toyota Prius is a top-selling car.
	The vast and incredible beauty of the Grand Canyon draws crowds of visitors each summer.
FACT	Employment of medical lab technicians is projected to increase by 14 percent between 2008 and 2018.
	Three hundred cities worldwide have bicycle-sharing programs.
REVISED	Population growth and the creation of new types of medical tests mean the employment of lab technicians should increase by 14 percent between 2008 and 2018.
	Bicycle-sharing programs are popular, but funding them long-term can be challenging for cities with tight budgets.

PRACTICE 7 Writing Sentences with Ideas You Can Show, Explain, or Prove

Revise the following sentences so that they contain an idea you could show, explain, or prove.

EXAMPLE: Leasing a car is popular.
Leasing a car has many advantages over buying one.

1. Texting while driving is dangerous.

   _____

2. My monthly rent is $750.

   _____

3. Health insurance rates rise every year.

   _____

4. Many people in this country work for minimum wage.

   _____

5. Technology is becoming increasingly important.

   _____

It Is Forceful

A good topic sentence or thesis statement is forceful. Do not say you *will* make a point; just make it. Do not say "I think." Just state your point.

WEAK	In my opinion, everyone should exercise.
FORCEFUL	Everyone should exercise to reduce stress, maintain a healthy weight, and feel better overall.
WEAK	I think student fees are much too high.
FORCEFUL	Student fees need to be explained and justified.

PRACTICE 8 Writing Forceful Sentences

Rewrite each of the following sentences to make them more forceful. Also, add details to make the sentences more specific.

EXAMPLE: Jason's Market is the best. *Jason's Market is clean, organized, and filled with quality products.*

1. I will prove that drug testing in the workplace is an invasion of privacy. _____

2. This school does not allow cell phones in class. _____

3. I strongly think I deserve a raise. _____

4. Nancy should be the head of the Students' Association. _____

5. I think my neighborhood is nice. _____

Write Your Own Topic Sentence or Thesis Statement

If you have worked through this chapter, you should have a good sense of how to write a topic sentence or thesis statement that includes the five features of a good one (see p. 53).

Before writing your own topic sentence or thesis statement, consider the process that Chelsea Wilson used. First, she narrowed her topic.

> **GENERAL TOPIC:** *a personal goal*
>
> **NARROWED TOPIC (FOR A PARAGRAPH):** *why I want to get a nursing degree*
>
> **NARROWED TOPIC (FOR AN ESSAY):** *the many benefits of getting a college degree*

Then, she did prewriting (see Chapter 3) to get ideas about her topic.

> **FOR A PARAGRAPH:** *why I want to get a nursing degree*
> *make more money*
> *get a better job*
> *become a respected professional*
> *live where I want*
>
> **FOR AN ESSAY:** *the many benefits of getting a college degree*
> *get a job as a nurse*
> *make more money*
> *be a good role model for my daughter*
> *be proud of myself*

Next, she was ready to write the statement of her main point.

> **TOPIC SENTENCE (PARAGRAPH):** *My goal is to get a nursing degree.*
>
> **THESIS STATEMENT (ESSAY):** *My goal is to get a college degree.*

Finally, Chelsea revised this statement to make it more forceful.

> **TOPIC SENTENCE:** *My goal is to become a registered nurse.*
>
> **THESIS STATEMENT:** *I am committed to getting a college degree because it will give me many good job and life options.*

TIP For tools to use in getting a job, visit the *Student Site for Real Writing* at **bedfordstmartins.com/ realwriting**.

You may want to change the wording of your topic sentence or thesis statement later, but following a sequence like Chelsea's should start you off with a good basic statement of your main point.

WRITING ASSIGNMENT

Write a topic sentence or thesis statement using the narrowed topic you developed in Chapter 3, your response to the idea journal prompt on page 53, or one of the following topics (which you will have to narrow).

Community service	Holiday traditions
A controversial issue	A strong belief
Dressing for success	Snitching
Movies	Exciting experiences
Saving money	Juggling many responsibilities
Interviewing for jobs	Friendship
Music	Learning/teaching cooking skills

After writing your topic sentence or thesis statement, complete the checklist that follows.

CHECKLIST

Evaluating Your Main Point
- ☐ It is a complete sentence.
- ☐ It fits the assignment.
- ☐ It includes my topic and the main point I want to make about it.
- ☐ It states a single main point.
- ☐ It is specific.
- ☐ It is something I can show, explain, or prove.
- ☐ It is forceful.

LEARNING JOURNAL How would you help someone who asked, "I have some ideas about my topic, but how do I write a good topic sentence or thesis statement?"

Coming up with a good working topic sentence or thesis statement is the foundation of the writing you will do. Now that you know what you want to say, you are ready to learn more about how to show, explain, and prove your main point to others. The next chapter, Supporting Your Point, helps you make a strong case, consider what your readers need to know, and provide sufficient details and examples in your paragraph or essay.

Chapter Review

1. Highlight important terms from this chapter (for example, *topic sentence*, *thesis statement*, and *main point*), and list them with their page numbers.

2. The **main point** of a piece of writing is _____
_____

3. One way to write a **topic sentence** or a **thesis statement** is to include the narrowed topic and _____

4. The basics of a good topic sentence or thesis statement are

   _____

   _____

   _____

   _____

   _____

5. Write for one minute about "What questions I should ask my instructor."

STUDENT VOICES

Message—Chelsea to Nick (2:33 p.m.)

I feel good about my topic sentence!
It's specific, I know about the topic, AND it could be interesting to readers.

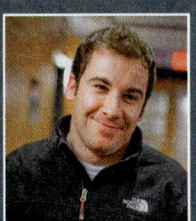

Message—Nick to Chelsea (2:48 p.m.)

Hey, you've got me wanting to read it!
That's something!

reflect What do you think of Chelsea's topic sentence? Does it fit the basics of a good topic sentence?

5

Supporting Your Point

Finding Details, Examples, and Facts

YOU KNOW THIS

You have lots of experience in supporting your point:

- You explain why you think a movie was boring.
- You explain to a child why locking the door is important.
- In a job interview, you list specific qualifications to persuade an employer to hire you.

STUDENT VOICES

Chelsea Wilson exchanged messages with her friend Nick Brown about an assignment she had received. Nick had taken the same writing course a semester earlier.

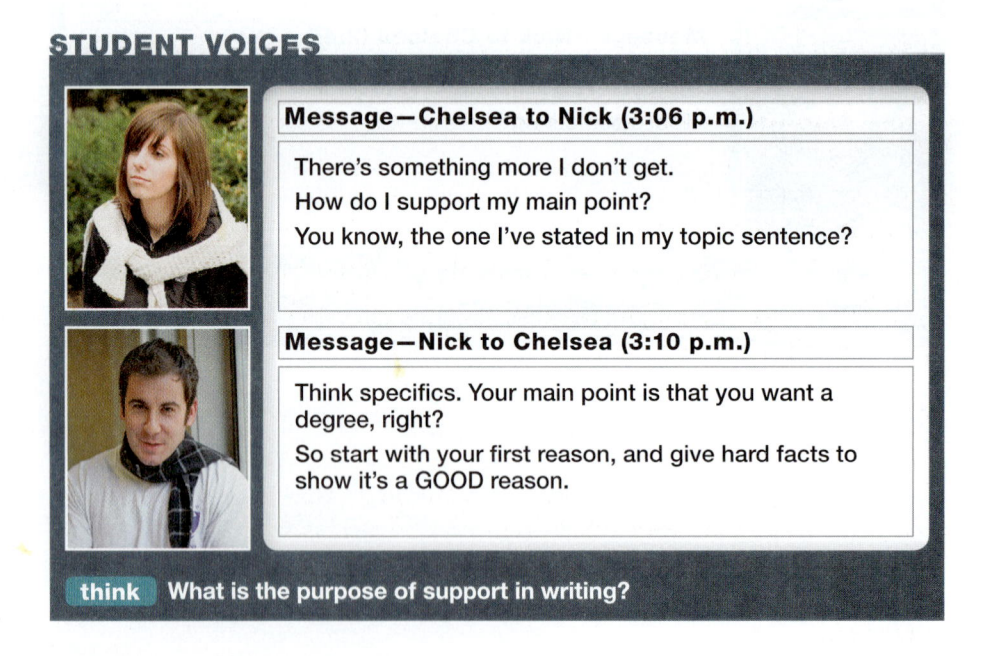

Message — Chelsea to Nick (3:06 p.m.)

There's something more I don't get.
How do I support my main point?
You know, the one I've stated in my topic sentence?

Message — Nick to Chelsea (3:10 p.m.)

Think specifics. Your main point is that you want a degree, right?
So start with your first reason, and give hard facts to show it's a GOOD reason.

think What is the purpose of support in writing?

Understand What Support Is

Support is the collection of examples, facts, or evidence that shows, explains, or proves your main point. **Primary support points** are the major ideas that back up your main point, and **secondary support** gives details to back up your primary support.

Key Features of Good Support

Without support, you *state* the main point, but you do not *make* the main point. Consider these unsupported statements:

The amount shown on my bill is incorrect.
I deserve a raise.
I am innocent of the crime.

The statements may be true, but without good support, they are not convincing. If you sometimes get papers back with the comment "You need to support/develop your ideas," the suggestions in this chapter will help you.

Also, keep in mind that the same point repeated several times is not support. It is just repetition.

REPETITION, NOT SUPPORT	The amount shown on my bill is incorrect. You overcharged me. It didn't cost that much. The total is wrong.
SUPPORT	The amount shown on my bill is incorrect. I ordered the bacon-cheeseburger plate, which is $6.99 on the menu. On the bill, the order is correct, but the amount is $16.99.

As you develop support for your main point, make sure it has these three features.

IDEA JOURNAL Write about a time you were overcharged for something. How did you handle it?

BASICS OF GOOD SUPPORT

- It relates directly to your main point. Remember that the purpose of support is to show, explain, or prove your main point.
- It considers your readers and what they will need to know.
- It gives readers enough specific details, particularly through examples, so that they can see what you mean.

TIP Showing involves providing visual details or other supporting observations. Explaining involves offering specific examples or illustrating aspects of the main point. Proving involves providing specific evidence, sometimes from outside sources.

Support in Paragraphs versus Essays

Again, primary support points are the major ideas that back up your main point. In paragraphs, your main point is expressed in a topic sentence. In both paragraphs and essays, it is important to add enough details (secondary support) about the primary support to make the main point clear to readers.

In the following paragraph, the topic sentence is underlined twice, the primary support is underlined once, and the details for each primary support point are in italics.

When I first enrolled in college, I thought that studying history was a waste of time. But after taking two world history classes, I have come to the conclusion that these courses count for far more than some credit hours in my college record. First, learning about historical events has helped me put important current events in perspective. *For instance, by studying the history of migration around the world, I have learned that immigration has been going on for hundreds of years. In addition, it is common in many countries, not just the United States. I have also learned about ways in which various societies have debated immigration, just as Americans are doing today.* Second, history courses have taught me about the power that individual people can have, even under very challenging circumstances. *I was especially inspired by the story of Toussaint L'Ouverture, a former slave who, in the 1790s, led uprisings in the French colony of Saint-Domingue, transforming it into the independent nation of Haiti. Although L'Ouverture faced difficult odds, he persisted and achieved great things.* The biggest benefit of taking history courses is that they have encouraged me to dig more deeply into subjects than I ever have before. *For a paper about the lasting influence of Anne Frank,[1] I drew on quotations from her famous diary, on biographies about her, and on essays written by noted historians. The research was fascinating, and I loved piecing together the various facts and insights to come to my own conclusions.* To sum up, I have become hooked on history, and I have a feeling that the lessons it teaches me will be relevant far beyond college.

In an essay, each primary support point, along with its supporting details, is developed into a separate paragraph. (See the diagram on pages 56–57.) Specifically, each underlined point in the previous paragraph could be turned into a topic sentence that would be supported by the italicized details. However, in preparing an essay on the preceding topic, the writer would want to add more details and examples for each primary support point. Here are some possible additions:

- **For primary support point 1:** more connections between history and current events (one idea: the rise and fall of dictators in past societies and in the modern Middle East)

- **For primary support point 2:** more examples of influential historical figures (one idea: the story of Joan of Arc, who in the fifteenth century led the French to victories over English armies)

- **For primary support point 3:** more examples of becoming deeply engaged in historical subjects (one idea: fascination with reprinted diaries or letters of World War II soldiers)

---

1. **Anne Frank** (1929–1945): a German Jewish girl who fled to the Netherlands with her family after Adolf Hitler, leader of the Nazi Party, became chancellor of Germany. In 1944, Anne and her family were arrested by the Nazis, and she died in a concentration camp the following year.

Practice Supporting a Main Point

Generate Support

To generate support for the main point of a paragraph or essay, try one or more of the following strategies.

THREE QUICK STRATEGIES FOR GENERATING SUPPORT

1. *Circle an important word or phrase* in your topic sentence (for a paragraph) or thesis statement (for an essay), and write about it for a few minutes. As you work, refer back to your main point to make sure you're on the right track.

2. *Reread your topic sentence or thesis statement, and write down the first thought you have.* Then, write down your next thought. Keep going.

3. *Use a prewriting technique* (freewriting, listing, discussing, clustering, and so on) while thinking about your main point and your audience. Write for three to five minutes without stopping.

PRACTICE 1   Generating Supporting Ideas

Choose one of the following sentences, or your own topic sentence or thesis statement, and use one of the three strategies to generate support just mentioned. Because you will need a good supply of ideas to support your main point, try to find at least a dozen possible supporting ideas. Keep your answers because you will use them in later practices in this chapter.

1. Some television shows stir my mind instead of numbing it.
2. Today there is no such thing as a "typical" college student.
3. Learning happens not only in school but throughout a person's life.
4. Practical intelligence can't be measured by grades.
5. I deserve a raise.

IDEA JOURNAL Write about any of the sentences you don't choose for Practice 1.

Select the Best Primary Support

After you have generated possible support, review your ideas; then, select the best ones to use as primary support. Here you take control of your topic, shaping the way readers will see it and the main point you are making about it. These ideas are *yours*, and you need to sell them to your audience.

The following steps can help.

1. Carefully read the ideas you have generated.
2. Select three to five primary support points that will be clearest and most convincing to your readers, providing the best examples, facts,

TIP For a diagram showing the relationship between topic sentences and support in paragraphs, and thesis statements and support in essays, see pages 56–57 of Chapter 4.

and observations to support your main point. If you are writing a paragraph, these points will become the primary support for your topic sentence. If you are writing an essay, they will become topic sentences of the individual paragraphs that support your thesis statement.

3. Cross out ideas that are not closely related to your main point.
4. If you find that you have crossed out most of your ideas and do not have enough left to support your main point, use one of the three strategies from page 71 to find more.

PRACTICE 2 Selecting the Best Support

Refer to your response to Practice 1 (p. 71). Of your possible primary support points, choose three to five that you think will best show, explain, or prove your main point to your readers. Write your three to five points in the space provided.

_____

_____

_____

_____

Add Secondary Support

Once you have selected your best primary support points, you need to flesh them out for your readers. Do this by adding **secondary support**, specific examples, facts, and observations to back up your primary support points.

PRACTICE 3 Adding Secondary Support

Using your answers to Practice 2, choose three primary support points, and write them in the spaces indicated below. Then, read each of them carefully, and write down at least three supporting details (secondary support) for each one. For examples of secondary support, see the example paragraph on pages 69–70.

PRIMARY SUPPORT POINT 1:

_____

SUPPORTING DETAILS: _____

_____

_____

PRIMARY SUPPORT POINT 2: _____

    SUPPORTING DETAILS: _____

    _____

    _____

PRIMARY SUPPORT POINT 3: _____

    SUPPORTING DETAILS: _____

    _____

    _____

Write Your Own Support

Before developing your own support for a main point, look at how Chelsea developed support for her paragraph.

> **TOPIC SENTENCE:** *My goal is to get a nursing degree.*

First, she did some prewriting (using the listing technique) and selected the best primary support points, while eliminating ones she didn't think she would use.

PRIMARY SUPPORT POINTS

> GETTING AN L.P.N. DEGREE
>
> nurses help people and I want to do that
> jobs all over the country
> good jobs with decent pay
> ~~good setting, clean~~
> a profession, not just a job
> opportunity, like R.N.
> bigger place, more money
> treated with respect
> role model
> pride in myself and my work, what I've done
> ~~good benefits~~
> ~~nice people to work with~~
> may get paid to take more classes—chance for further professional development
> ~~uniform so not lots of money for clothes~~
> ~~I'll be something~~

Chelsea noticed that some of her notes were related to the same subject, so she arranged them into related clusters, with the smaller points indented under the larger ones.

ORGANIZED LIST OF SUPPORT POINTS

> good job
>   decent pay
>   jobs all over the country
> a profession, not just a job
>   treated with respect
>   opportunity for the future (like R.N.)
>   maybe get paid to take more classes?
> pride/achievement
>   a job that helps people
>   I would take pride in my hard work
>   I'd be a role model

Then, she took the notes she made and organized them into primary support and supporting details. Notice how she changed and reorganized some of her smaller points.

> **PRIMARY SUPPORT:** Being an L.P.N. is an excellent job.
>   **SUPPORTING DETAILS:** The pay is regular and averages about $40,000 a year.
>   I could afford to move to a bigger and better place with more room for my daughter and work fewer hours.
>
> **PRIMARY SUPPORT:** Nursing is a profession, not just a job.
>   **SUPPORTING DETAILS:** Nurses help care for people, an important job, giving to the world.
>   Future opportunities, like becoming an R.N. with more money and responsibility.
>   People respect nurses.
>
> **PRIMARY SUPPORT:** Being a nurse will be a great achievement for me.
>   **SUPPORTING DETAILS:** I will have worked hard and met my goal.
>   I will respect myself and be proud of what I do.
>   I will be a good role model for my daughter.

WRITING ASSIGNMENT

Develop primary support points and supporting details using your topic sentence or thesis statement from Chapter 4, your response to the idea journal prompt on page 71, or one of the following topic sentences/thesis statements.

Same-sex marriages should/should not be legal in all fifty states.

The drinking age should/should not be lowered.

All families have some unique family traditions.

People who do not speak "proper" English are discriminated against.

Many movies have important messages for viewers.

After developing your support, complete the following checklist.

CHECKLIST
Evaluating Your Support
- ☐ It is directly related to my main point.
- ☐ It uses examples, facts, and observations that will make sense to my readers.
- ☐ It includes enough specific details to show my readers exactly what I mean.

LEARNING JOURNAL In your own words, explain what good support points are and why they are important.

Once you have pulled together your primary support points and secondary supporting details, you are ready for the next step: drafting a paragraph or essay based on a plan. For more information, go on to the next chapter.

Chapter Review

1. Highlight important terms from this chapter (such as *support*, *primary support*, and *secondary support*), and list them with their page numbers.

2. Support points are examples, facts, or evidence that _____, _____, or _____ your main point.

3. Three basics of good support are: _____
_____
_____
_____

4. To generate support, try these three strategies:
_____
_____
_____
_____
_____

5. When you have selected your primary support points, what should you then add? _____

6. Write for one minute about "What questions I should ask my instructor."

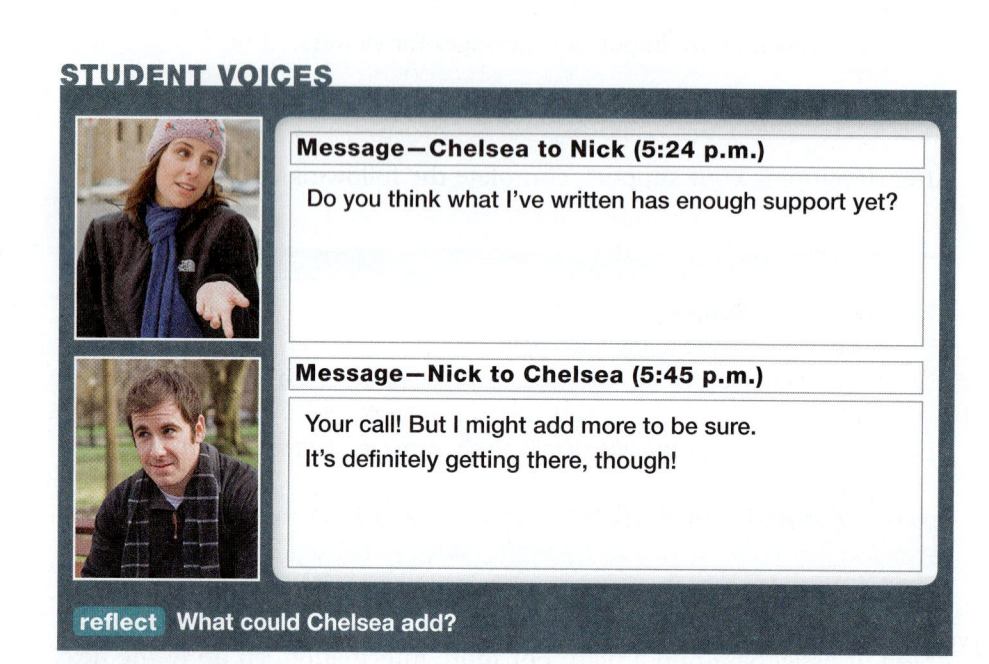

STUDENT VOICES

Message—Chelsea to Nick (5:24 p.m.)

Do you think what I've written has enough support yet?

Message—Nick to Chelsea (5:45 p.m.)

Your call! But I might add more to be sure. It's definitely getting there, though!

reflect What could Chelsea add?

YOU KNOW THIS

You often "give something a try," knowing you might not get it just right the first time:

- You rehearse in your head something you want to say to someone.
- You rehearse for a big event or play.
- You put out clothes you want to wear to an important event.

6

Drafting

Putting Your Ideas Together

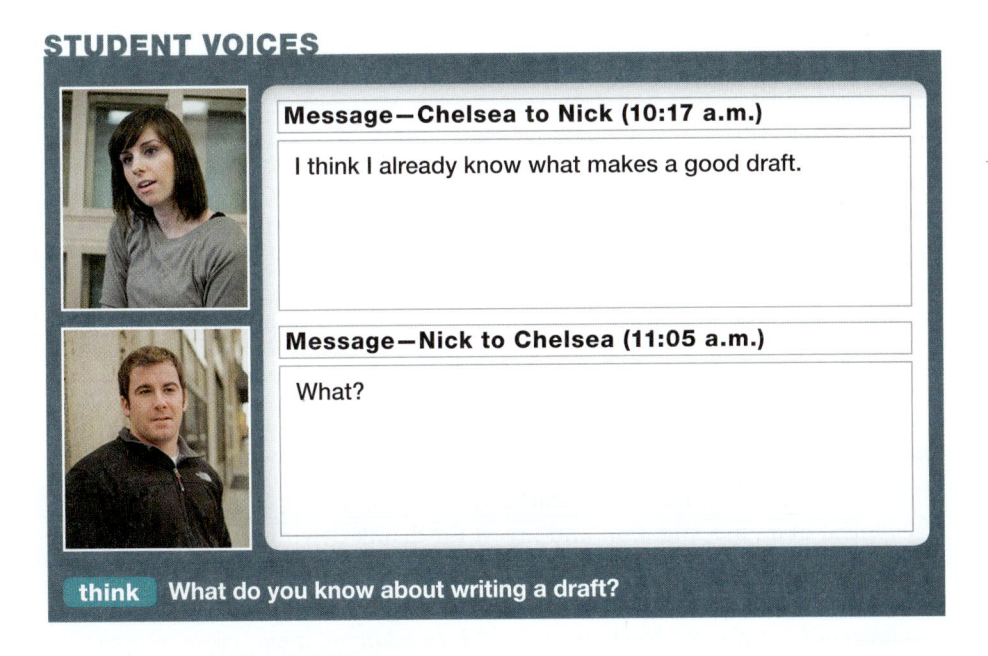

STUDENT VOICES

Message—Chelsea to Nick (10:17 a.m.)

I think I already know what makes a good draft.

Message—Nick to Chelsea (11:05 a.m.)

What?

think What do you know about writing a draft?

Chelsea Wilson exchanged messages with her friend Nick Brown about an assignment she had received. Nick had taken the same writing course a semester earlier.

Understand What a Draft Is

A **draft** is the first whole version of all your ideas put together in a piece of writing. Do the best job you can in drafting, but know that you can make changes later.

IDEA JOURNAL Write about a time when you had a trial run before doing something.

BASICS OF A GOOD DRAFT

- It has a topic sentence (for a paragraph) and a thesis statement (for an essay) that makes a clear main point.
- It has a logical organization of ideas.
- It has primary and secondary support that shows, explains, or proves the main point.

- It has a conclusion that makes an observation about the main point.
- It follows standard paragraph form (see pages 91–92) or standard essay form (see page 93).

Two good first steps to drafting a paragraph or essay are (1) to arrange the ideas that you have generated in an order that makes sense and (2) to write out a plan for your draft. We will look at these steps next.

Arrange Your Ideas

In writing, **order** means the sequence in which you present your ideas: What comes first, what comes next, and so on. There are three common ways of ordering—arranging—your ideas: **time order** (also called chronological order), **space order**, and **order of importance**.

Read the paragraph examples that follow. In each paragraph, the topic sentences are underlined twice, the primary support points are underlined once, and the secondary support is in italics.

IDEA JOURNAL Write about a plan you came up with recently. How well did it work?

Use Time Order to Write about Events

Use **time order** (chronological order) to arrange points according to when they happened. Time order works best when you are writing about events. You can go from

- First to last / last to first
- Most recent to least recent / least recent to most recent

EXAMPLE USING TIME ORDER

Officer Meredith Pavlovic's traffic stop of August 23, 2011, was fairly typical of an investigation and arrest for drunk driving. First, at around 12:15 a.m. that day, she noticed that the driver of a blue Honda Civic was acting suspiciously. *The car was weaving between the fast and center lanes of Interstate 93 North near exit 12. In addition, it was proceeding at approximately 45 mph in a 55 mph zone.* Therefore, Officer Pavlovic took the second step of pulling the driver over for a closer investigation. *The driver's license told Officer Pavlovic that the driver was twenty-six-year-old Paul Brownwell. Brownwell's red eyes, slurred speech, and alcohol-tainted breath told Officer Pavlovic that Brownwell was very drunk. But she had to be absolutely sure.* Thus, as a next step, she tested his balance and blood alcohol level. *The results were that Brownwell could barely get out of the car, let alone stand on one foot. Also, a breathalyzer test showed that his blood alcohol level was 0.13, well over the legal limit of 0.08.* These results meant an arrest for Brownwell, an unfortunate outcome for him, but a lucky one for other people on the road at that time.

What kind of time order does the author use? _____

Use Space Order to Describe Objects, Places, or People

Use **space order** to arrange ideas so that your readers picture your topic the way you see it. Space order usually works best when you are writing about a physical object or place, or a person's appearance. You can move from

- Top to bottom/bottom to top
- Near to far/far to near
- Left to right/right to left
- Back to front/front to back

EXAMPLE USING SPACE ORDER

Donna looked professional for her interview. Her long, dark, curly hair was held back with a gold clip. No stray wisps escaped. Normally wild and unruly, her hair was smooth, shiny, and neat. She wore a white silk blouse with just the top button open at her throat. Donna had made sure to leave time to iron it so that it wouldn't be wrinkled. The blouse was neatly tucked into her black A-line skirt, which came just to the top of her knee. She wore black stockings that she had checked for runs and black low-heeled shoes. Altogether, her appearance marked her as serious and professional, and she was sure to make a good first impression.

What type of space order does the example use? _____

IDEA JOURNAL What would you wear to look professional?

Use Order of Importance to Emphasize a Particular Point

Use **order of importance** to arrange points according to their significance, interest, or surprise value. Usually, save the most important point for last.

EXAMPLE USING ORDER OF IMPORTANCE

People who keep guns in their homes risk endangering both themselves and others. Many accidental injuries occur when a weapon is improperly stored or handled. For example, someone cleaning a closet where a loaded gun is stored may handle the gun in a way that causes it to go off and injure him or her. Guns also feature in many reports of "crimes of passion." A couple with a violent history has a fight, and, in a fit of rage, one gets the gun and shoots the other, wounding or killing the other person. Most common and most tragic are incidents in which children find loaded guns and play with them, accidentally killing themselves or their playmates. Considering these factors, the risks of keeping guns in the home outweigh the advantages, for many people.

What is the writer's most important point? _____

_____

IDEA JOURNAL What do you think about keeping guns in your home? Does it guard against robberies? Is there risk involved?

Make a Plan

TIP Try using the cut-and-paste function on your computer to experiment with different ways to order support for your main point. Doing so will give you a good sense of how your final paragraph or final essay will look.

When you have decided how to order your primary support points, it is time to make a more detailed plan for your paragraph or essay. A good, visual way to plan a draft is to arrange your ideas in an outline. An **outline** lists the topic sentence (for a paragraph) or thesis statement (for an essay), the primary support points for the topic sentence or thesis statement, and secondary supporting details for each of the support points. It provides a map of your ideas that you can follow as you write.

Outlining Paragraphs

Look at the outline Chelsea Wilson created with the support she wrote. She had already grouped together similar points and put the more specific details under the primary support (see p. 74). When she thought about how to order her ideas, the only way that made sense to her was by importance. If she had been telling the steps she would take to become a nurse, time order would have worked well. If she had been describing a setting where nurses work, space order would have been a good choice. But because she was writing about why she wanted to get a college degree and become a nurse, she decided to arrange her reasons in order of importance. Notice that Chelsea also strengthened her topic sentence and made changes in her primary support and secondary support. At each stage, her ideas and the way she expressed them changed as she got closer to what she wanted to say.

SAMPLE OUTLINE FOR A PARAGRAPH

> **TOPIC SENTENCE:** Becoming a nurse is a goal of mine because it offers so much that I value.
>
> **PRIMARY SUPPORT 1:** It is a good and practical job.
>
> **SUPPORTING DETAILS:** Licensed practical nurses make an average of $40,000 per year. That amount is much more than I make now. With that salary, I could move to a better place with my daughter and give her more, including more time.
>
> **PRIMARY SUPPORT 2:** Nursing is a profession, not just a job.
>
> **SUPPORTING DETAILS:** It helps people who are sick and in need. Being an L.P.N. offers great opportunities, like the chance to go on to become a registered nurse, with more money and responsibility. People respect nurses.
>
> **PRIMARY SUPPORT 3:** I will respect and be proud of myself for achieving my goal through hard work.
>
> **SUPPORTING DETAILS:** I will be a good role model for my daughter. I will help her and others, but I will also be helping myself by knowing that I can accomplish good things.
>
> **CONCLUSION:** Reaching my goal is important to me and worth the work.

Outlining Essays

The outline below is for a typical five-paragraph essay, in which three body paragraphs (built around three topic sentences) support a thesis statement. The thesis statement is included in an introductory paragraph; the fifth paragraph is the conclusion. However, essays may include more or fewer than five paragraphs, depending on the size and complexity of the topic.

The example below is a "formal" outline form, with letters and numbers to distinguish between primary supporting and secondary supporting details. Some instructors require this format. If you are making an outline just for yourself, you might choose to write a less formal outline, simply indenting the secondary supporting details under the primary support rather than using numbers and letters.

TIP For an example of a five-paragraph essay, see Chapter 7.

SAMPLE OUTLINE FOR A FIVE-PARAGRAPH ESSAY

Thesis statement (part of introductory paragraph 1)

   A. **Topic sentence for support point 1** (paragraph 2)

      1. Supporting detail 1 for support point 1

      2. Supporting detail 2 for support point 1 (and so on)

   B. **Topic sentence for support point 2** (paragraph 3)

      1. Supporting detail 1 for support point 2

      2. Supporting detail 2 for support point 2 (and so on)

   C. **Topic sentence for support point 3** (paragraph 4)

      1. Supporting detail 1 for support point 3

      2. Supporting detail 2 for support point 3 (and so on)

Concluding paragraph (paragraph 5)

PRACTICE 1 Making an Outline

Reread the paragraph on page 78 that illustrates time order of organization. Then, make an outline for it in the space provided.

   TOPIC SENTENCE: _____

   _____

      PRIMARY SUPPORT 1: _____

      _____

         1. SUPPORTING DETAIL: _____

         _____

         2. SUPPORTING DETAIL: _____

         _____

PRIMARY SUPPORT 2: _____

_____

1. SUPPORTING DETAIL: _____

_____

2. SUPPORTING DETAIL: _____

_____

PRIMARY SUPPORT 3: _____

_____

1. SUPPORTING DETAIL: _____

_____

2. SUPPORTING DETAIL: _____

_____

Practice Writing a Draft Paragraph

As you write your paragraph, you will need to go through the steps in the following sections. Also, refer to the Basics of a Good Draft on pages 77–78.

Write a Draft Using Complete Sentences

Write your draft with your outline in front of you. Be sure to include your topic sentence, and express each point in a complete sentence. As you write, you may want to add support or change the order. It is OK to make changes from your outline as you write.

Read the following paragraph, annotated to show the various parts of the paragraph.

Title — **Parabens: Widely Used Chemicals Spark New Cautions**

Topic sentence — Parabens, preservatives used in many cosmetics and personal-care products, are raising concerns with more and more consumers. In some people, parabens cause allergic reactions, but the effects of these chemicals may be more than skin deep. After being applied to the face or body, parabens can enter the bloodstream, where they have been found to mimic the hormone estrogen. Because long-term exposure to

Support — estrogen can increase the risk of breast cancer, researchers have tried to determine whether there is any link between parabens and breast cancer. So far, the findings have been inconclusive. One study found parabens in the breast cancer tissue of some research subjects. However, the study was small, and based on its results, it cannot be said that parabens actually cause cancer. Nevertheless, some consumers wish to reduce their use of paraben-containing products or to avoid them altogether. To do so, they carefully read the labels of personal-care products, looking out for ingredients like butylparaben, ethylparaben, methylparaben, isopropyl, and propylparaben. All these chemicals are parabens. Consumers who do not wish to give up parabens entirely might consider avoiding only those paraben-containing products, like lotions and makeup, that stay on the skin for an extended period. Products that are rinsed away quickly, like shampoos and soaps, do not have as much time to be absorbed through the skin.

— Support

Although paragraphs typically begin with topic sentences, they may also begin with a quote, an example, or a surprising fact or idea. The topic sentence is then presented later in the paragraph. For examples of various introductory techniques, see pages 86–88.

TIP For more on topic sentences, see Chapter 4.

Write a Concluding Sentence

A **concluding sentence** refers back to the main point and makes an observation based on what you have written. The concluding sentence does not just repeat the topic sentence.

In the paragraph above, the main point, expressed in the topic sentence, is "Parabens, preservatives used in many cosmetics and personal-care products, are raising concerns with more and more consumers."

A good conclusion might be, "Given the growing concerns about parabens and uncertainties about their potential dangers, more research is clearly needed." This sentence **refers back to the main point** by repeating the words *parabens* and *concerns*. It **makes an observation** by stating, "more research is clearly needed."

Concluding paragraphs for essays are discussed on pages 89–90.

PRACTICE 2 Writing Concluding Sentences

Read the following paragraphs, and write a concluding sentence for each one.

1. One of the most valuable ways parents can help children is to read to them. Reading together is a good way for parents and children to relax, and it is sometimes the only "quality" time they spend together during a busy day. Reading develops children's vocabulary. They understand more words and are likely to learn new words more easily than children who are not read to. Also, hearing the words aloud helps children's pronunciation and makes them more confident with oral language. In addition, reading at home increases children's chances of success in school because reading is required in every course in every grade.

Possible Concluding Sentence: _____

_____

_____

2. Almost everyone uses certain memory devices, called *mnemonics*. One of them is the alphabet song. If you want to remember what letter comes after *j*, you will probably sing the alphabet song in your head. Another is the "Thirty days hath September" rhyme that people use when they want to know how many days are in a certain month. Another mnemonic device is the rhyme "In 1492, Columbus sailed the ocean blue."

Possible Concluding Sentence: _____
_____
_____

Title Your Paragraph

The title is the first thing readers see, so it should give them a good idea of what your paragraph is about. Decide on a title by rereading your draft, especially your topic sentence. A paragraph title should not repeat your topic sentence.

Look at the title of the paragraph on pages 82–83. It includes the topic (parabens) and the main point (that these chemicals are sparking concerns). It lets readers know what the paragraph is about, but it does not repeat the topic sentence.

Titles for essays are discussed on page 91.

PRACTICE 3 Writing Titles

Write possible titles for the paragraphs in Practice 2.

1. _____
2. _____

Practice Writing a Draft Essay

The basics of a good essay draft are all listed on pages 77–78. In addition,

- The essay should include an introductory paragraph that draws readers in and includes the thesis statement.
- The topic sentences for the paragraphs that follow the introduction should directly support the thesis statement. In turn, each topic sentence should be backed by enough support.
- The conclusion should be a full paragraph rather than a single sentence.

Let's start by looking at topic sentences and support for them.

Write Topic Sentences, and Draft the Body of the Essay

When you start to draft your essay, use your outline to write complete sentences for your primary support points. These sentences will serve as the topic sentences for the body paragraphs of your essay.

PRACTICE 4 Writing Topic Sentences

Each thesis statement that follows has support points that could be topic sentences for the body paragraphs of an essay. For each support point, write a topic sentence.

> **EXAMPLE**
>
> **THESIS STATEMENT:** My daughter is showing definite signs of becoming a teenager.
>
> **SUPPORT POINT:** constantly texting friends
>
> **TOPIC SENTENCE:** *She texts friends constantly, even when they are sitting with her while I'm driving them.*
>
> **SUPPORT POINT:** a new style of clothes
>
> **TOPIC SENTENCE:** *She used to like really cute clothing, but now she wants to wear more grown-up-looking outfits.*
>
> **SUPPORT POINT:** doesn't want me to know what's going on
>
> **TOPIC SENTENCE:** *She used to tell me everything, but now she is secretive and private.*
>
> **SUPPORT POINT:** developing an "attitude"
>
> **TOPIC SENTENCE:** *The surest and most annoying sign that she is becoming a teenager is that she has developed a definite "attitude."*

1. **THESIS STATEMENT:** Rhonda is doing everything she can to pass this course.

   SUPPORT POINT: attends most classes

   TOPIC SENTENCE: _____

   SUPPORT POINT: always has her book and does her homework

   TOPIC SENTENCE: _____

   SUPPORT POINT: is part of a study group to prepare for tests

   TOPIC SENTENCE: _____

2. **THESIS STATEMENT:** The Latin American influence is evident in many areas of U.S. culture.

   SUPPORT POINT: Spanish language used in lots of places

   TOPIC SENTENCE: _____

SUPPORT POINT: lots of different kinds of foods

TOPIC SENTENCE: _____

SUPPORT POINT: new kinds of music and popular musicians

TOPIC SENTENCE: _____

Drafting topic sentences for your essay is a good way to start drafting the body of the essay (the paragraphs that support each of these topic sentences). As you write support for your topic sentences, refer back to your outline, where you listed supporting details. (For an example, see Chelsea Wilson's outline on page 80.) Turn these supporting details into complete sentences, and add additional support if necessary. (Prewriting techniques can help here; see Chapter 3.) Don't let yourself get stalled if you are having trouble with one word or sentence. Just keep writing. Remember that a draft is a first try; you will have time later to improve it.

Write an Introduction

The introduction to your essay captures your readers' interest and presents the main point. Ask yourself: How can I sell my essay to readers? You need to market your main point.

IDEA JOURNAL Write about the ways that advertising attracts people's attention.

BASICS OF A GOOD INTRODUCTION

- It should catch readers' attention.
- It should present the thesis statement of the essay, usually in the first or the last sentence of an introductory paragraph.
- It should give readers a clear idea of what the essay will cover.

Here are some common kinds of introductions that spark readers' interest. In each one, the introductory technique is in boldface. These introductions are not the only ways to start essays, but they should give you some useful models.

OPEN WITH A QUOTATION

A good, short quotation definitely gets people interested. It must lead naturally into your main point, however, and not be there just for effect. If you start with a quotation, make sure you tell the reader who the speaker is.

> **George Farquhar once said that necessity was the mother of invention, but we know that to be nonsense, really:** Who needs an iPod that holds 10,000 songs? There is, however, one area of life in which technology keeps step with nature—the size of things. As we Americans are getting bigger (the Centers for Disease Control and Prevention in

Atlanta estimate that roughly a third of Americans are overweight, with 20 percent of us qualifying as obese), so, too, is our stuff.

—James Verini, "Supersize It"

GIVE AN EXAMPLE, OR TELL A STORY

People like stories, so opening an essay with a brief story or example often draws readers in.

> **Something snapped inside Jerry Sola during his evening commute through the Chicago suburbs two years ago.** When the driver in front of the fifty-one-year-old salesman suddenly slammed on his brakes, Sola got so incensed that he gunned his engine to cut in front of the man. Still steaming when both cars stopped at a red light, Sola grabbed a golf club from the backseat and got out.
>
> —Dianne Hales, "Why Are We So Angry?"

START WITH A SURPRISING FACT OR IDEA

Surprises capture people's interest. The more unexpected and surprising something is, the more likely people are to notice it.

> **I learned to read with a Superman comic book.** Simple enough, I suppose. I cannot recall which particular Superman comic book I read, nor can I remember which villain he fought in that issue. I cannot remember the plot, nor the means by which I obtained the comic book. What I can remember is this: I was 3 years old, a Spokane Indian boy living with his family on the Spokane Indian Reservation in eastern Washington state. We were poor by most standards, but one of my parents usually managed to find some minimum-wage job or another, which made us middle-class by reservation standards. I had a brother and three sisters. We lived on a combination of irregular paychecks, hope, fear, and government surplus food.
>
> —Sherman Alexie, "The Joy of Reading and Writing: Superman and Me"

OFFER A STRONG OPINION OR POSITION

The stronger the opinion, the more likely it is that your readers will pay attention. Don't write wimpy introductions. Make your point and shout it!

> Cedric "C. J." Mills. Isaiah Brooks. Tedric Maynor. Felicia Hines. Vinson Phillips. Kurt Anthony Bryant. Amuel Murph. Alfonso Williams. These names are forever inscribed on my private "Wall of Black Death." My wall contains the names of black people killed by other black people, along with those believed to have been killed by fellow blacks, in the Tampa Bay area since May. I will update the roster as new deaths are reported. More are sure to follow. I do not have

answers as to how to stop blacks from killing their brethren. **But I do have an answer for catching some, if not all, of these murderers. Snitch.**

—Bill Maxwell, "Start Snitching"

ASK A QUESTION

A question needs an answer, so if you start your introduction with a question, your readers will need to read on to get the answer.

> **Have you ever noticed how many gym membership advertisements appear on television right after the New Year?** Many people overindulge through the holiday season, beginning with Halloween candy and ending with the last sip of eggnog on Christmas evening. On average, Americans gain seven pounds in that six-week period. That weight gain does not include the other forty-six weeks of the year when people typically overeat and quit going to the gym. Do not despair; there is hope! Instead of dreading the inevitable holiday weight gain and spending money on expensive exercise clubs, you can instead resign yourself to starting a new exercise routine at home. Exercise is the best way to combat the "battle of the bulge." One of the most effective ways to lose weight and get into shape is aerobic exercise. I am living proof that beginning a home workout regimen will become a positive, life-altering experience that quickly balances your physical and emotional health, has a maximum gain for minimum pain, and can lead you to improve other aspects of your life as well.
>
> —Michele Wood, "My Home Exercise Program"

TIP If you get stuck while writing your introductory statement, try one or more of the prewriting techniques described in Chapter 3 on pages 46–49.

PRACTICE 5 Marketing Your Main Point

As you know from advertisements, a good writer can make just about anything sound interesting. For each of the following topics, write an introductory statement using the technique indicated. Some of these topics are purposely dull to show you that you can make an interesting statement about almost any subject, if you put your mind to it.

> **EXAMPLE**
>
> **TOPIC:** Reality TV
>
> **TECHNIQUE:** Question
>
> *Exactly how many recent top-selling songs have been recorded by former contestants of reality TV singing contests?*

1. **TOPIC:** Credit cards

    TECHNIQUE: Surprising fact or idea

    _____

2. **TOPIC:** Role of the elderly in society

   TECHNIQUE: Question

   _____

3. **TOPIC:** Stress

   TECHNIQUE: Quote (You can make up a good one.)

   _____

PRACTICE 6 Identifying Strong Introductions

In a newspaper or magazine, an online news site, an advertising flier—or anything written—find a strong introduction. Bring it to class to explain why you chose it as an example.

Write a Conclusion

When they have finished the body of their essay, some writers believe their work is done—but it isn't *quite* finished. Remember that people usually remember best what they see, hear, or read last. Use your concluding paragraph to drive your main point home one final time. Make sure your conclusion has the same energy as the rest of the essay, if not more.

BASICS OF A GOOD ESSAY CONCLUSION

- It refers back to the main point.
- It sums up what has been covered in the essay.
- It makes a further observation or point.

In general, a good conclusion creates a sense of completion. It brings readers back to where they started, but it also shows them how far they have come.

One of the best ways to end an essay is to refer directly to something in the introduction. If you asked a question, re-ask and answer it. If you started a story, finish it. If you used a quote, use another one—maybe a quote by the same person or maybe one by another person on the same topic. Or, use some of the same words you used in your introduction. Look again at two of the introductions you read earlier, and notice how the writers conclude their essays. Pay special attention to the text in boldface.

HALES'S INTRODUCTION

> **Something snapped inside Jerry Sola during his evening commute through the Chicago suburbs two years ago.** When the driver in front of the fifty-one-year-old salesman suddenly slammed on his brakes, Sola got so incensed that he gunned his engine to cut in front of the man. Still steaming when both cars stopped at a red light, Sola grabbed a golf club from the backseat and got out.
>
> —Dianne Hales, "Why Are We So Angry?"

HALES'S CONCLUSION

Since his roadside epiphany, Jerry Sola has conscientiously worked to rein in his rage. "I am a changed person," he says, "especially behind the wheel. I don't have to listen to the news on the car radio. Instead, I put on nice, soothing music. I force myself to smile at rude drivers. And if I feel myself getting angry, I ask a simple question: 'Why should I let a person I'm never going to see again control my mood and ruin my whole day?'"

—Dianne Hales, "Why Are We So Angry?"

MAXWELL'S INTRODUCTION

Cedric "C. J." Mills. Isaiah Brooks. Tedric Maynor. Felicia Hines. Vinson Phillips. Kurt Anthony Bryant. Amuel Murph. Alfonso Williams. These names are forever inscribed on my private "Wall of Black Death." My wall contains the names of black people killed by other black people, along with those believed to have been killed by fellow blacks, in the Tampa Bay area since May. I will update the roster as new deaths are reported. More are sure to follow. I do not have answers as to how to stop blacks from killing their brethren. **But I do have an answer for catching some, if not all, of these murderers. Snitch.**

—Bill Maxwell, "Start Snitching"

MAXWELL'S CONCLUSION

Because I regularly write about this issue, I receive a lot of hate mail from both blacks and whites. White letter-writers remind me that blacks are "animals" and "cause all of America's social problems." Black letter-writers see me as the "enemy of people" and a "sell-out" because I condemn blacks for killing one another without taking into account the nation's history of racism. To whites, I have nothing to say. **To blacks, I have one message: We need to start snitching. Only we can stop black-on-black murders. Until then, I will be adding names to the Wall of Black Death.**

—Bill Maxwell, "Start Snitching"

PRACTICE 7 Finding Good Introductions and Conclusions

In a newspaper or magazine or anything written, find a piece of writing that has a strong introduction and conclusion. (You may want to use what you found for Practice 6.) Answer the questions that follow.

1. What method of introduction is used? _____

2. What does the conclusion do? Restate the main idea? Sum up the support? Make a further observation? _____

3. How are the introduction and the conclusion linked? _____

Title Your Essay

Even if your title is the *last* part of the essay you write, it is the *first* thing readers read. Use your title to get your readers' attention and to tell them, in a brief way, what your paper is about. Use vivid, strong, specific words.

BASICS OF A GOOD ESSAY TITLE

- It makes people want to read the essay.
- It hints at the main point (thesis statement), but it does not repeat it.

One way to find a good title is to consider the type of essay you are writing. If you are writing an argument (as you will in Chapter 16), state your position in your title. If you are telling your readers how to do something (as you will in Chapter 11), try using the term *steps* or *how to* in the title. This way, your readers will know immediately not only what you are writing about but how you will discuss it.

TIP Center your title at the top of the page before the first paragraph. Do not put quotation marks around it or underline it.

PRACTICE 8   Titling an Essay

Reread the paired paragraphs on pages 89–90, and write alternate titles for the essays that they belong to.

Hales's introduction/conclusion: _____

Maxwell's introduction/conclusion: _____

Write Your Own Draft Paragraph or Essay

Before you draft your own paragraph, read Chelsea Wilson's annotated draft below. It is based on her outline from page 80.

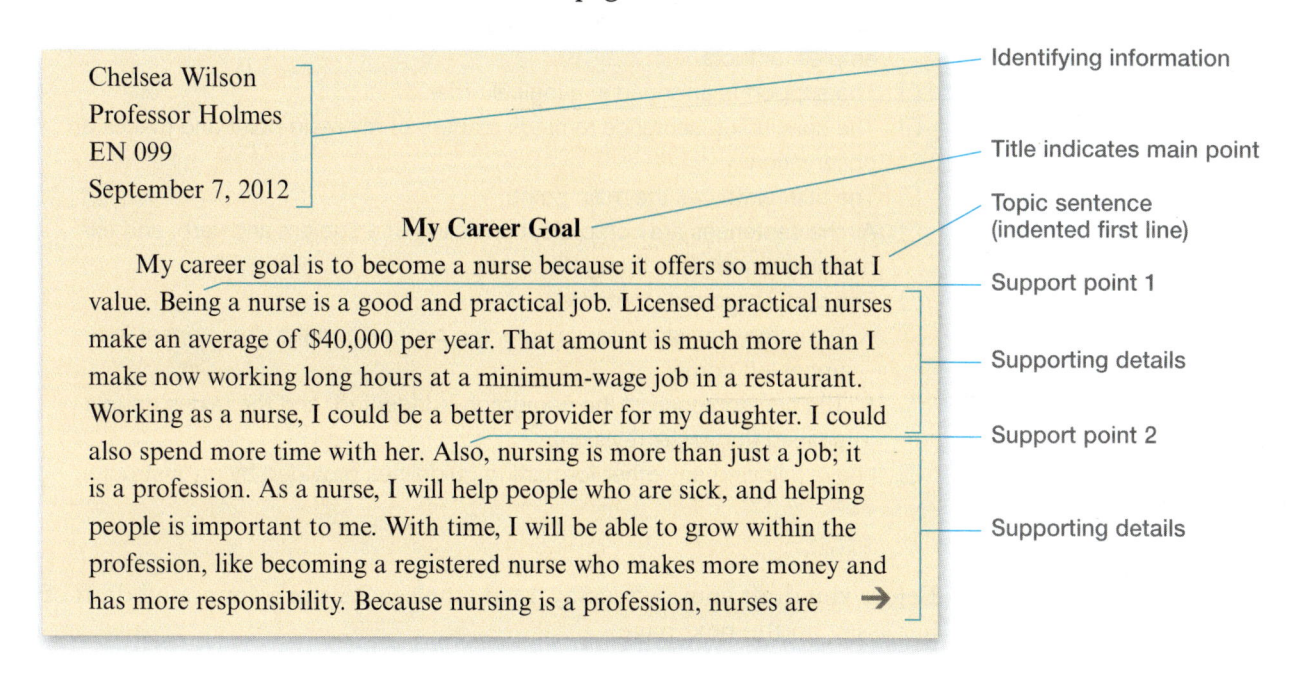

Chelsea Wilson
Professor Holmes
EN 099
September 7, 2012 — *Identifying information*

My Career Goal — *Title indicates main point*

   My career goal is to become a nurse because it offers so much that I value. *— Topic sentence (indented first line)* Being a nurse is a good and practical job. *— Support point 1* Licensed practical nurses make an average of $40,000 per year. That amount is much more than I make now working long hours at a minimum-wage job in a restaurant. *— Supporting details* Working as a nurse, I could be a better provider for my daughter. I could also spend more time with her. Also, nursing is more than just a job; it is a profession. *— Support point 2* As a nurse, I will help people who are sick, and helping people is important to me. With time, I will be able to grow within the profession, like becoming a registered nurse who makes more money and has more responsibility. *— Supporting details* Because nursing is a profession, nurses are →

92 Chapter 6 • Drafting

Support point 3 ──────┐
Supporting details ────┤
Concluding sentence (refers back to main point) ─┘

> respected. When I become a nurse, I will respect myself and be proud of myself for reaching my goal, even though I know it will take a lot of hard work. The most important thing about becoming a nurse is that it will be good for my young daughter. I will be a good role model for her. For all of these reasons, my goal is to become a nurse. Reaching this goal is important to me and worth the work.

WRITING ASSIGNMENT Paragraph

Write a draft paragraph, using what you have developed in previous chapters, your response to the idea journal prompt on page 77, or one of the following topic sentences. If you use one of the topic sentences below, you may want to revise it to fit what you want to say.

Being a good _____ requires _____.

I can find any number of ways to waste my time.

People tell me I am _____, and I guess I have to agree.

So many decisions are involved in going to college.

The most important thing to me in life is _____.

After writing your draft paragraph, complete the following checklist.

CHECKLIST

Evaluating Your Draft Paragraph

☐ It has a clear, confident topic sentence that states my main point.
☐ Each primary support point is backed up with supporting details, examples, or facts.
☐ The support is arranged in a logical order.
☐ The concluding sentence reminds readers of my main point and makes an observation.
☐ The title reinforces the main point.
☐ All the sentences are complete, consisting of a subject and verb, and expressing a complete thought.
☐ The draft is properly formatted:
  • My name, my instructor's name, the course, and the date appear in the upper left corner.
  • The first sentence of the paragraph is indented, and the text is double-spaced (for easier revision).
☐ I have followed any other formatting guidelines provided by my instructor.

Before you draft your own essay, read Chelsea Wilson's annotated draft of her essay on the next page.

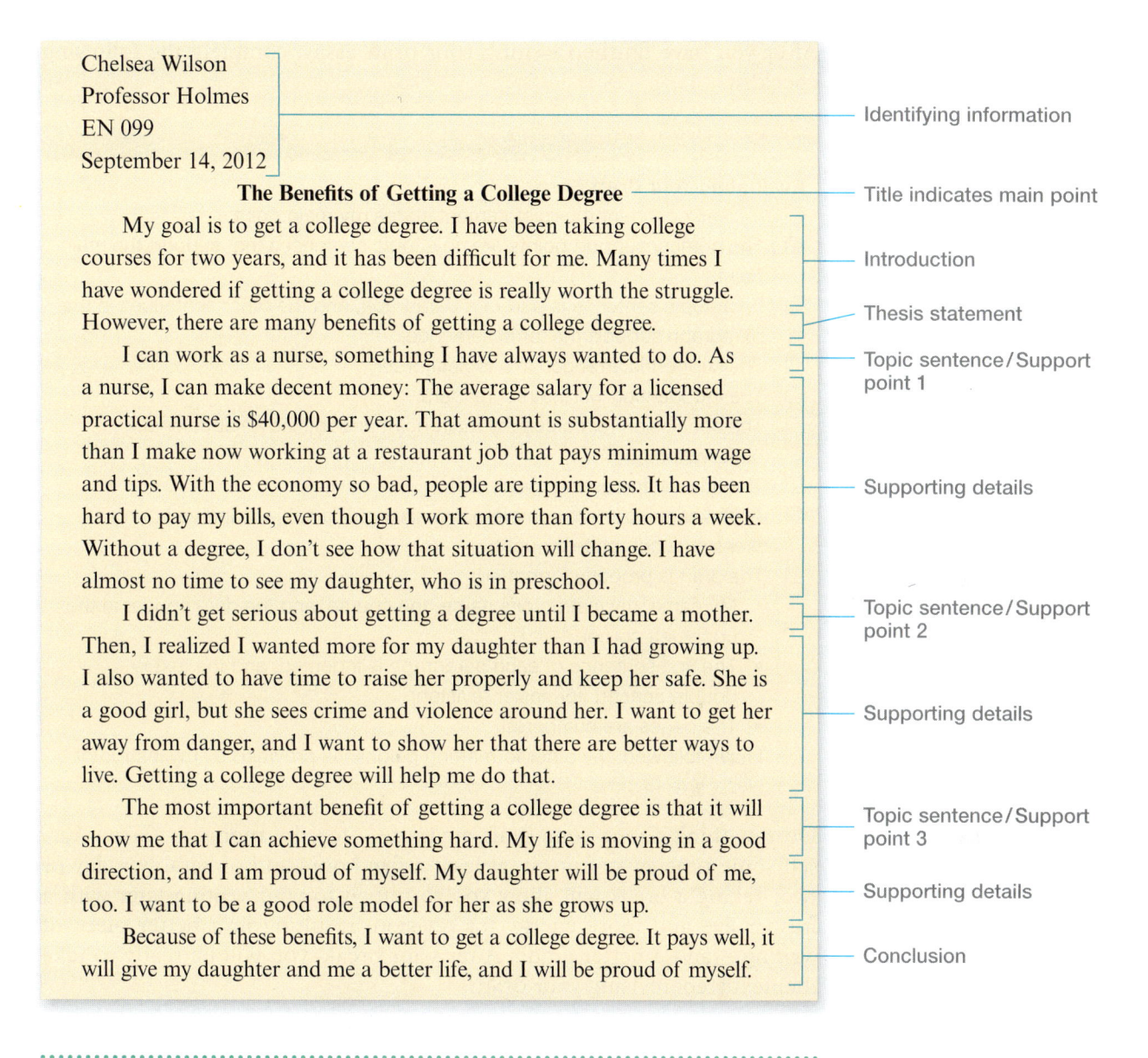

Chelsea Wilson
Professor Holmes
EN 099
September 14, 2012

The Benefits of Getting a College Degree

My goal is to get a college degree. I have been taking college courses for two years, and it has been difficult for me. Many times I have wondered if getting a college degree is really worth the struggle. However, there are many benefits of getting a college degree.

I can work as a nurse, something I have always wanted to do. As a nurse, I can make decent money: The average salary for a licensed practical nurse is $40,000 per year. That amount is substantially more than I make now working at a restaurant job that pays minimum wage and tips. With the economy so bad, people are tipping less. It has been hard to pay my bills, even though I work more than forty hours a week. Without a degree, I don't see how that situation will change. I have almost no time to see my daughter, who is in preschool.

I didn't get serious about getting a degree until I became a mother. Then, I realized I wanted more for my daughter than I had growing up. I also wanted to have time to raise her properly and keep her safe. She is a good girl, but she sees crime and violence around her. I want to get her away from danger, and I want to show her that there are better ways to live. Getting a college degree will help me do that.

The most important benefit of getting a college degree is that it will show me that I can achieve something hard. My life is moving in a good direction, and I am proud of myself. My daughter will be proud of me, too. I want to be a good role model for her as she grows up.

Because of these benefits, I want to get a college degree. It pays well, it will give my daughter and me a better life, and I will be proud of myself.

WRITING ASSIGNMENT   Essay

Write a draft essay using what you have developed in previous chapters, your response to the idea journal prompt on page 77, or one of the following thesis statements. If you choose one of the thesis statements below, you may want to modify it to fit what you want to say.

Taking care of a sick (child/parent/spouse/friend) can test even the most patient person.

Being a good _____ requires _____.

Doing _____ gave me a great deal of pride in myself.

A good long-term relationship involves flexibility and compromise.

Some of the differences between men and women create misunderstandings.

After you have finished writing your draft essay, complete the following checklist.

> **CHECKLIST**
>
> **Evaluating Your Draft Essay**
> - ☐ A clear, confident thesis statement states my main point.
> - ☐ The primary support points are now topic sentences that support the main point.
> - ☐ Each topic sentence is part of a paragraph, and the other sentences in the paragraph support the topic sentence.
> - ☐ The support is arranged in a logical order.
> - ☐ The introduction will interest readers.
> - ☐ The conclusion reinforces my main point and makes an additional observation.
> - ☐ The title reinforces the main point.
> - ☐ All the sentences are complete, consisting of a subject and verb, and expressing a complete thought.
> - ☐ The draft is properly formatted:
>   - My name, my instructor's name, the course, and the date appear in the upper left corner.
>   - The first sentence of each paragraph is indented, and the text is double-spaced (for easier revision).
>   - The pages are numbered.
> - ☐ I have followed any other formatting guidelines provided by my instructor.

LEARNING JOURNAL In your own words, explain how you write a draft.

Do not think about your draft anymore—for the moment. Give yourself some time away from it, at least a few hours and preferably a day or two. Taking a break will allow you to return to your writing later with a fresher eye and more energy for revision, resulting in a better piece of writing—and a better grade. After your break, you will be ready to take the next step: revising your draft.

Chapter Review

1. Highlight important terms from this chapter (such as *draft*, *concluding sentence*, and *title*), and list them with their page numbers.

2. A draft is _____
   _____

3. List the basic features of a good draft paragraph or essay: _____
   _____
   _____
   _____
   _____
   _____

HOW TO WRITE PARAGRAPHS AND ESSAYS
Chapter Review

4. Three ways to order ideas are _____, _____, and _____.

5. Making an _____ is a useful way to plan your draft.

6. Five ways to start an essay are

_____

_____

_____

_____

_____

7. Three features of a good essay conclusion are

_____

_____

_____

8. Two basic features of a good essay title are

_____

_____

9. Write for one minute about "What questions I should ask my instructor."

STUDENT VOICES

Message—Chelsea to Nick (5:38 p.m.)

OK, I think I'm done!

Message—Nick to Chelsea (5:50 p.m.)

Are you totally sure?
I used to think I was done with a paper, but then I would set it down for a while and come back to it.
And I always found things I wanted to fix!

reflect What two changes could Chelsea make to improve her paragraph or her essay?

7

Revising

Improving Your Paragraph or Essay

YOU KNOW THIS

You often make changes to improve things:

- You dress for an important occasion and then try other clothes you think will be better.
- You go to buy one kind of television set, and then, based on information the salesperson gives you, you rethink your decision.
- You arrange furniture one way and then rearrange it a couple of times until it seems right.

STUDENT VOICES

Chelsea Wilson exchanged messages with her friend Nick Brown about an assignment she had received. Nick had taken the same writing course a semester earlier.

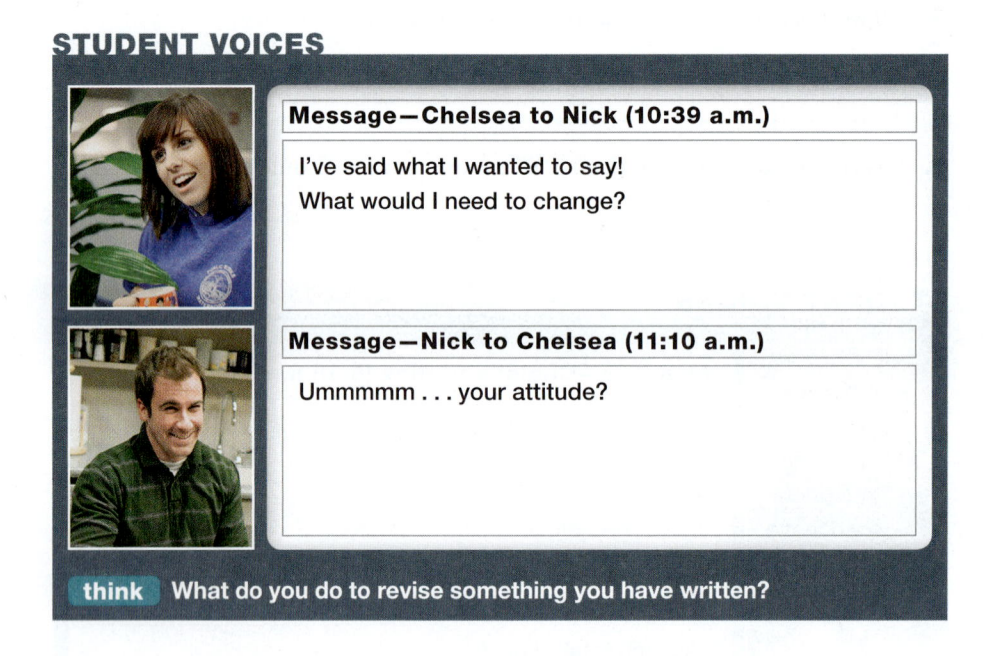

Message—Chelsea to Nick (10:39 a.m.)

I've said what I wanted to say!
What would I need to change?

Message—Nick to Chelsea (11:10 a.m.)

Ummmmm . . . your attitude?

think What do you do to revise something you have written?

Understand What Revision Is

When you finish a draft, you probably wish that you were at the end: You don't want to have to look at it again. But a draft is just the first whole version, a rough cut; it is not the best you can do to represent yourself and your ideas. After taking a break, you need to look at the draft with fresh eyes to revise and edit it.

Revising is making your ideas clearer, stronger, and more convincing. When revising, you are evaluating how well you have made your point.

Editing is finding and correcting problems with grammar, word usage, punctuation, and capitalization. When editing, you are evaluating the words, phrases, and sentences you have used.

Most writers find it difficult to revise and edit well if they try to do both at once. It is easier to solve idea-level problems first (by revising) and then to correct smaller, word-level ones (by editing). This chapter focuses on revising. For editing help, use Chapters 19 through 38.

TIPS FOR REVISING YOUR WRITING

- Wait a few hours or, if possible, a couple of days before starting to revise.
- Read your draft aloud, and listen for places where the writing seems weak or unclear.
- Read critically and ask yourself questions, as if you were reading through someone else's eyes.
- Write notes about changes to make. For small things, like adding a transition (p. 103), you can make the change on the draft. For other things, like adding or getting rid of an idea or reordering your support points, make a note in the margin.
- Get help from a tutor at the writing center, or get feedback from a friend (see the following section for information on peer review).

TIP For more on reading critically, see Chapter 1.

Even the best writers do not get everything right the first time. So, if you finish reading your draft and have not found anything that could be better, you are not reading carefully enough or are not asking the right questions. Use the following checklist to help you make your writing better.

CHECKLIST

Revising Your Writing

- ☐ If someone else just read my topic sentence or thesis statement, what would he or she think the paper is about? Would the main point make a lasting impression? What would I need to do to make it more interesting?
- ☐ Does each support point really relate to my main point? What more could I say about the topic so that someone else will see it my way? Is any of what I have written weak? If so, should I delete it?
- ☐ What about the way the ideas are arranged? Should I change the order so that the writing makes more sense or has more effect on a reader?
- ☐ What about the ending? Does it just droop and fade away? How could I make it better?
- ☐ If, before reading my paragraph or essay, someone knew nothing about the topic or disagreed with my position, would what I have written be enough for him or her to understand the material or be convinced by my argument?

TIP Add transitions as you read to help move from one idea to the next.

Understand What Peer Review Is

Peer review—when students exchange drafts and comment on one another's work—is one of the best ways to get help with revising. Other students can often see things that you might not—parts that are good and parts that need to be strengthened or clarified.

If you are working with one other student, read each other's papers and write down a few comments. If you are working in a small group, you may want to have writers take turns reading their papers aloud. Group members can make notes while listening and then offer comments to the writer that will help improve the paper.

BASICS OF USEFUL FEEDBACK

- It is given in a positive way.
- It offers specific suggestions.
- It may be given in writing or orally.

Often, it is useful for the writer to give the person or people providing feedback a few questions to focus on as they read or listen.

> **CHECKLIST**
> **Questions for Peer Reviewers**
> - What is the main point?
> - Can I do anything to make my opening more interesting?
> - Do I have enough support for my main point? Where could I use more?
> - Where could I use more details?
> - Are there places where you have to stop and reread something to understand it? If so, where?
> - Do I give my reader clues as to where a new point starts? Does one point "flow" smoothly to the next?
> - What about my conclusion? Does it just fade out? How could I make my point more forcefully?
> - Where else could the paper be better? What would you do if it were your paper?
> - If you were going to be graded on this paper, would you turn it in as is? If not, why not?
> - What other comments or suggestions do you have?

Whenever you are reviewing another student's work, remember **2PR**, the critical reading process you learned about in Chapter 1. This process provides another way to question the work and make thoughtful comments about it. In addition, you might refer to the questions in the Reading and Writing Critically chart from that chapter (see pp. 16–17).

Practice Revising for Unity, Detail, and Coherence

You may need to read what you have written several times before deciding what changes would improve it. Remember to consider your audience and your purpose and to focus on three areas: unity, detail, and coherence.

Revise for Unity

Unity in writing means that all the points you make are related to your main point; they are *unified* in support of it. As you draft a paragraph or an essay, you may detour from your main point without even being aware of it, as the writer of the following paragraph did with the underlined sentences. The diagram after the paragraph shows what happens when readers read the paragraph.

First, double-underline the main point in the paragraph that follows to help you see where the writer got off-track.

> If you want to drive like an elderly person, use a cell phone while driving. A group of researchers from the University of Utah tested the reaction times of two groups of people—those between the ages of sixty-five to seventy-four and those who were eighteen to twenty-five—in a variety of driving tasks. All tasks were done with hands-free cell phones. <u>That part of the study surprised me because I thought the main problem was using only one hand to drive. I hardly ever drive with two hands, even when I'm not talking to anyone.</u> Among other results, braking time for both groups slowed by 18 percent. A related result is that the number of rear-end collisions doubled. The study determined that the younger drivers were paying as much—or more—attention to their phone conversations as they were to what was going on around them on the road. The elderly drivers also experienced longer reaction times and more accidents, pushing most of them into the category of dangerous driver. This study makes a good case for turning off the phone when you buckle up.

IDEA JOURNAL Write about your reactions to this study, including your own experiences with cell phones and driving.

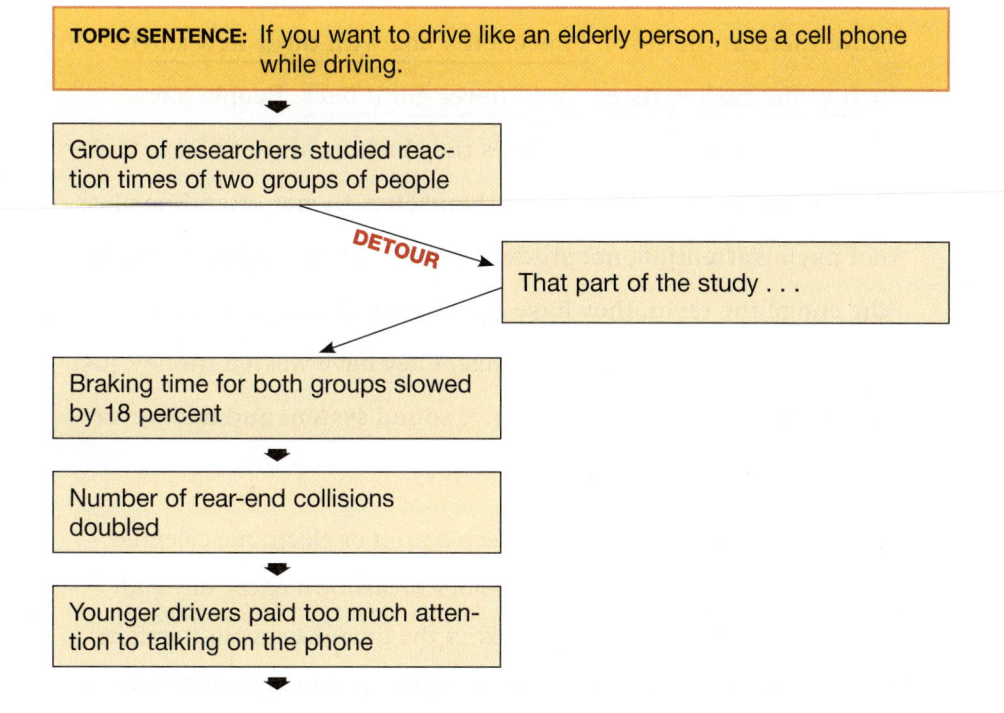

TOPIC SENTENCE: If you want to drive like an elderly person, use a cell phone while driving.

↓

Group of researchers studied reaction times of two groups of people

→ **DETOUR** → That part of the study . . .

↓

Braking time for both groups slowed by 18 percent

↓

Number of rear-end collisions doubled

↓

Younger drivers paid too much attention to talking on the phone

↓

> Elderly drivers also got worse

CONCLUDING SENTENCE: This study makes a good case for turning off the phone when you buckle up.

Detours weaken your writing because readers' focus is shifted from your main point. As you revise, check to make sure your paragraph or essay has unity.

PRACTICE 1   Revising for Unity

Each of the following paragraphs contains a sentence that detours from the main point. First, double-underline the main point. Then, underline the detour in each paragraph.

EXAMPLE:

"Education is one of the few things people are willing to pay for and not get." When we buy something expensive, we make sure we take it home and use it. For example, we wouldn't think of spending a couple of hundred dollars on a new coat and shoes only to hide them away in a closet never to be worn. And we certainly wouldn't pay for those items and then decide to leave them at the store. I once left a bag with three new shirts in it at the cash register, and I never got it back. People pay a lot for education, but sometimes they look for ways to leave the "purchase" behind. They cheat themselves by not attending class, not paying attention, not studying, or not doing assignments. At the end of the term, they have a grade but didn't get what they paid for: education and knowledge. They have wasted money, just as if they had bought an expensive sound system and had never taken it out of the box.

1. One way to manage time is to keep a print or electronic calendar or schedule. It should have an hour-by-hour breakdown of the day and evening, with space for you to write next to the time. As appointments or responsibilities come up, add them on the right day and time. Before the

IDEA JOURNAL Write about the statement "Education is one of the few things people are willing to pay for and not get." Do you agree? How does this statement apply to you?

end of the day, consult your calendar to see what's going on the next day. For example, tomorrow I have to meet Kara at noon, and if I forget, she will be furious with me. Once you are in the habit of using a calendar, you will see that it frees your mind because you are not always trying to think about what you're supposed to do, where you're supposed to be, or what you might have forgotten.

2. As you use a calendar to manage your time, think about how long certain activities will take. A common mistake is to underestimate the time needed to do something, even something simple. For example, when you are planning the time needed to get money from the cash machine, remember that a line of people may be ahead of you. Last week in the line I met a woman I went to high school with. When you are estimating time for a more complex activity, such as reading a chapter in a textbook, block out more time than you think you will need. If you finish in less time than you have allotted, so much the better.

3. Effective time management means allowing time for various "life" activities. For example, it is important to budget time for paying bills, buying food, picking up a child, or going to the doctor. My doctor is always an hour behind schedule. A daily schedule should also account for communication with other people, such as family members and friends. Also, allow yourself a little unscheduled relaxation time when possible. Finally, leave time for unexpected events that are a huge part of life, like last-minute phone calls, a car that won't start, or a bus that is late.

Revise for Detail and Support

When you revise a paper, look carefully at the support you have developed. Will readers have enough information to understand and be convinced by the main point?

In the margin or between the lines of your draft (which should be double-spaced), note ideas that seem weak or unclear. As you revise, build up your support by adding more details.

PRACTICE 2 **Revising for Detail and Support**

Read the following paragraphs, double-underline the main point, and add at least three additional support points or supporting details. Write them in the spaces provided under each paragraph, and indicate where they should go in the paragraph by writing in a caret (∧) and the number.

EXAMPLE:

Sojourner Truth was a brave woman who helped educate people about the evils of slavery. She was a slave herself in New York.¹ ²After she had a religious vision, she traveled from place to place giving speeches about how terrible it was to be a slave. ³But even after the Emancipation Proclamation was signed in 1863, slave owners did not follow the laws. Sojourner Truth was active in the Civil War, nursing soldiers and continuing to give speeches. She was active in the fight for racial equality until her death in 1883.

1. and was not allowed to learn to read or write.
2. Sojourner Truth ran away from her owner because of his cruelty.
3. Although she was beaten for her beliefs, she continued her work and was part of the force that caused Abraham Lincoln to sign the Emancipation Proclamation freeing the slaves.

1. Sports fans can turn from normal people into destructive maniacs. After big wins, a team's fans sometimes riot. Police have to be brought in. Even in school sports, parents of the players can become violent. People get so involved watching the game that they lose control of themselves and are dangerous.

1. _____
2. _____
3. _____

2. If a friend is going through a hard time, try to be as supportive as you can. For one thing, ask if you can help out with any errands or chores. Also, find a time when you can get together in a quiet, nonstressful place. Here, the two of you can talk about the friend's difficulties or just spend time visiting. Let the friend decide how the time is spent. Just knowing that you are there for him or her will mean a lot.

1. _____
2. _____
3. _____

HOW TO WRITE PARAGRAPHS AND ESSAYS
Practice Revising for Unity, Detail, and Coherence

Revise for Coherence

Coherence in writing means that all your support connects to form a whole. In other words, you have provided enough "glue" for readers to see how one point leads to another.

A good way to improve coherence is to use **transitions**—words, phrases, and sentences that connect your ideas so that your writing moves smoothly from one point to the next. The table that starts at the bottom of this page shows some common transitions and what they are used for.

Here are two paragraphs, one that does not use transitions and one that does. Read them and notice how much easier the second paragraph is to follow because of the underlined transitions.

NO TRANSITIONS

It is not difficult to get organized—it takes discipline to stay organized. All you need to do is follow a few simple ideas. You must decide what your priorities are and do these tasks first. You should ask yourself every day: What is the most important task I have to accomplish? Make the time to do it. To be organized, you need a personal system for keeping track of things. Making lists, keeping records, and using a schedule help you remember what tasks you need to do. It is a good idea not to let belongings and obligations stack up. Get rid of possessions you do not need, put items away every time you are done using them, and do not take on more responsibilities than you can handle. Getting organized is not a mystery; it is just good sense.

TRANSITIONS ADDED

It is not difficult to get organized—<u>even though</u> it takes discipline to stay organized. All you need to do is follow a few simple ideas. You must decide what your priorities are and do these tasks first. <u>For example</u>, you should ask yourself every day: What is the most important task I have to accomplish? <u>Then</u>, make the time to do it. To be organized, you <u>also</u> need a personal system for keeping track of things. Making lists, keeping records, and using a schedule help you remember what tasks you need to do. <u>Finally</u>, it is a good idea not to let belongings and obligations stack up. Get rid of possessions you do not need, put items away every time you are done using them, and do not take on more responsibilities than you can handle. Getting organized is not a mystery; it is just good sense.

Common Transitional Words and Phrases

INDICATING SPACE

above	below	near	to the right
across	beside	next to	to the side
at the bottom	beyond	opposite	under
at the top	farther/further	over	where
behind	inside	to the left	→

INDICATING TIME			
after	eventually	meanwhile	soon
as	finally	next	then
at last	first	now	when
before	last	second	while
during	later	since	

INDICATING IMPORTANCE			
above all	in fact	more important	most important
best	in particular	most	worst
especially			

SIGNALING EXAMPLES			
for example	for instance	for one thing	one reason

SIGNALING ADDITIONS			
additionally	and	as well as	in addition
also	another	furthermore	moreover

SIGNALING CONTRAST			
although	however	nevertheless	still
but	in contrast	on the other hand	yet
even though	instead		

SIGNALING CAUSES OR RESULTS			
as a result	finally	so	therefore
because			

PRACTICE 3 Adding Transitions

Read the following paragraphs. In each blank, add a transition that would smoothly connect the ideas. In each case, there is more than one correct answer.

EXAMPLE:

LifeGem, a Chicago company, has announced that it can turn cremated human ashes into high-quality diamonds. ___After___ cremation, the ashes are heated to convert their carbon to graphite. ___Then___, a lab wraps the graphite around a tiny diamond piece and again heats it and pressurizes it. __After__ about a week of crystallizing, the result is a diamond. __Because of__ the time and labor involved, this process can cost as much as $20,000. __Although__ the idea is very creative, many people will think it is also very weird.

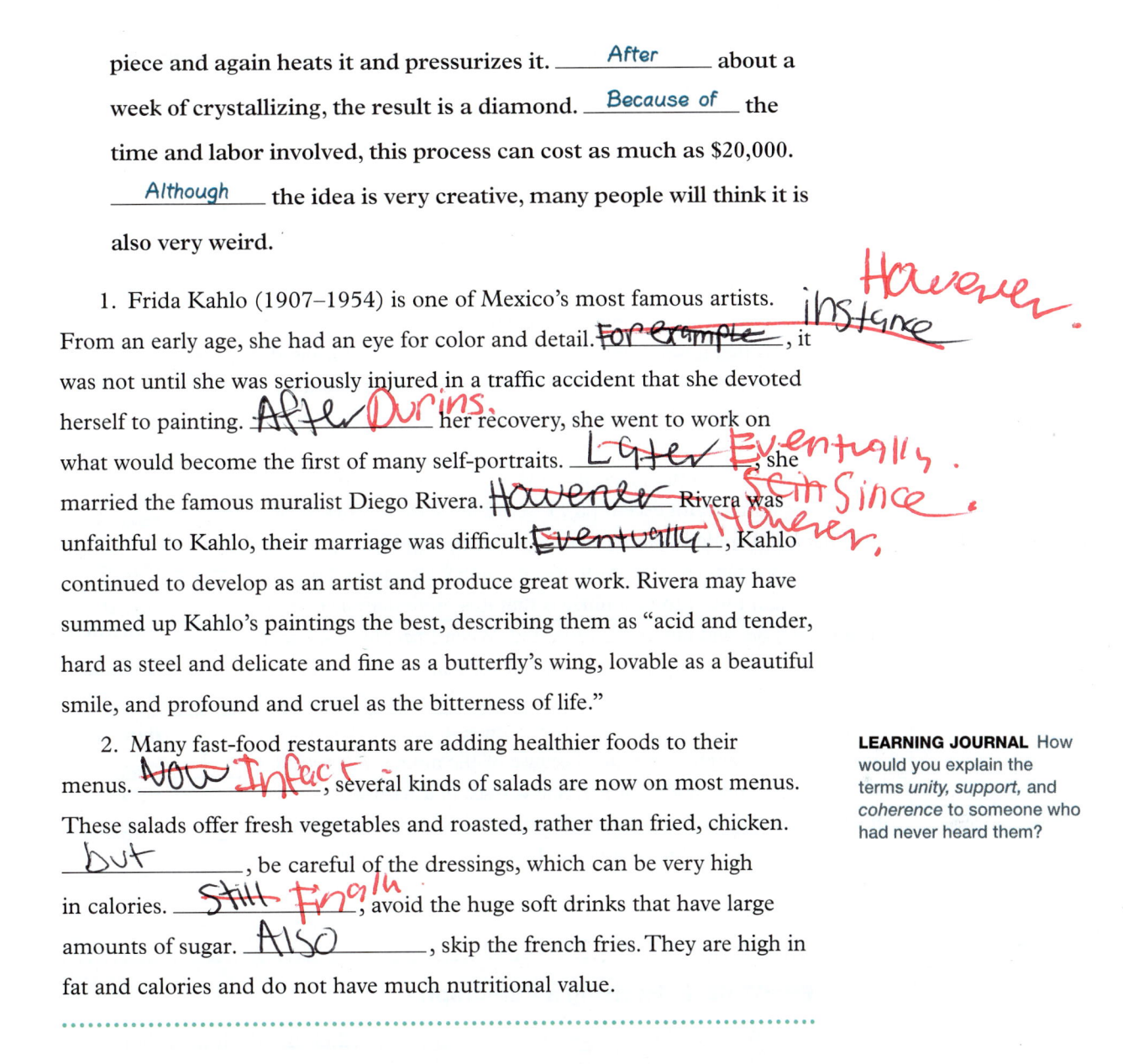

1. Frida Kahlo (1907–1954) is one of Mexico's most famous artists. From an early age, she had an eye for color and detail. ~~For example~~ *However / instance*, it was not until she was seriously injured in a traffic accident that she devoted herself to painting. ~~After~~ *During*, her recovery, she went to work on what would become the first of many self-portraits. ~~Later~~ *Eventually*, she married the famous muralist Diego Rivera. ~~However~~ *Since*, Rivera was unfaithful to Kahlo, their marriage was difficult. ~~Eventually~~ *However*, Kahlo continued to develop as an artist and produce great work. Rivera may have summed up Kahlo's paintings the best, describing them as "acid and tender, hard as steel and delicate and fine as a butterfly's wing, lovable as a beautiful smile, and profound and cruel as the bitterness of life."

2. Many fast-food restaurants are adding healthier foods to their menus. ~~Now~~ *In fact*, several kinds of salads are now on most menus. These salads offer fresh vegetables and roasted, rather than fried, chicken. __But__, be careful of the dressings, which can be very high in calories. ~~Still~~ *Finally*, avoid the huge soft drinks that have large amounts of sugar. __Also__, skip the french fries. They are high in fat and calories and do not have much nutritional value.

LEARNING JOURNAL How would you explain the terms *unity, support,* and *coherence* to someone who had never heard them?

Another way to give your writing coherence is to repeat a **key word—a word that is directly related to your main point.** For example, in the paragraphs on page 103, the writer repeats the word *organized* several times. Repetition of a key word is a good way to keep your readers focused on your main point, but make sure you don't overdo it.

Revise Your Own Paragraph

In Chapter 6, you read Chelsea's draft paragraph (pp. 91–92). Reread that now as if it were your own, asking yourself the questions in the Checklist for Revising Your Writing on page 97. Work either by yourself or with a partner or a small group to answer the questions about Chelsea's draft. Then, read Chelsea's revised paragraph that follows, and compare the changes you suggested with those she made. Make notes on the similarities and differences to discuss with the rest of the class.

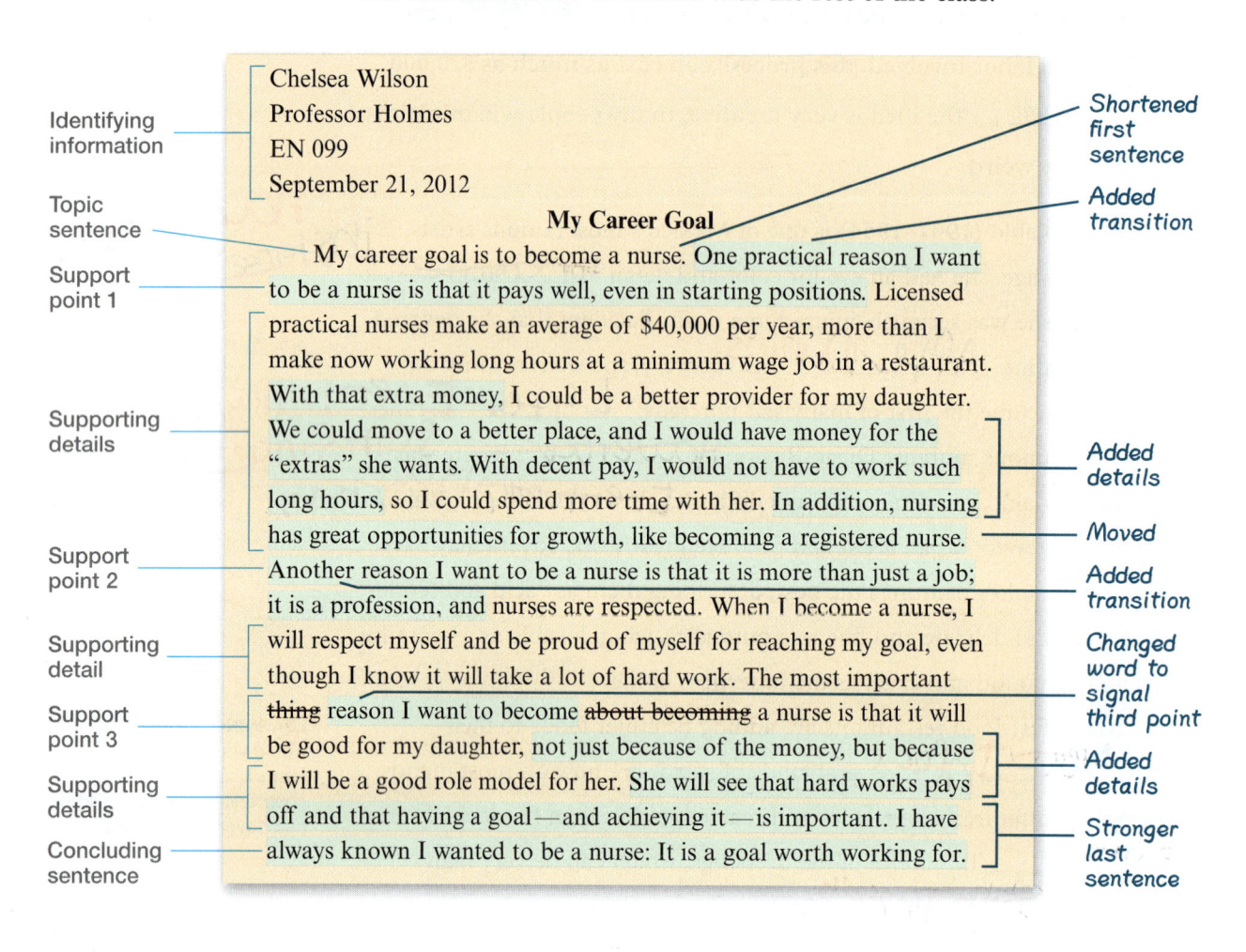

Chelsea Wilson
Professor Holmes
EN 099
September 21, 2012

My Career Goal

My career goal is to become a nurse. One practical reason I want to be a nurse is that it pays well, even in starting positions. Licensed practical nurses make an average of $40,000 per year, more than I make now working long hours at a minimum wage job in a restaurant. With that extra money, I could be a better provider for my daughter. We could move to a better place, and I would have money for the "extras" she wants. With decent pay, I would not have to work such long hours, so I could spend more time with her. In addition, nursing has great opportunities for growth, like becoming a registered nurse. Another reason I want to be a nurse is that it is more than just a job; it is a profession, and nurses are respected. When I become a nurse, I will respect myself and be proud of myself for reaching my goal, even though I know it will take a lot of hard work. The most important ~~thing~~ reason I want to become ~~about becoming~~ a nurse is that it will be good for my daughter, not just because of the money, but because I will be a good role model for her. She will see that hard works pays off and that having a goal—and achieving it—is important. I have always known I wanted to be a nurse: It is a goal worth working for.

Labels (left): Identifying information; Topic sentence; Support point 1; Supporting details; Support point 2; Supporting detail; Support point 3; Supporting details; Concluding sentence

Labels (right): Shortened first sentence; Added transition; Added details; Moved; Added transition; Changed word to signal third point; Added details; Stronger last sentence

---

PRACTICE 4 Revising a Paragraph

1. What major changes did you suggest for Chelsea's draft in response to the Checklist for Revising Your Writing?

2. Did Chelsea make any of the suggested changes? Which ones?

3. Did Chelsea make any changes that were not suggested? Which ones? Were they good changes?

WRITING ASSIGNMENT Paragraph

Revise the draft paragraph you wrote in Chapter 6. After revising your draft, complete the following checklist.

> **CHECKLIST**
> **Evaluating Your Revised Paragraph**
> ☐ My topic sentence is confident, and my main point is clear.
> ☐ My ideas are detailed, specific, and organized logically.
> ☐ My ideas flow smoothly from one to the next.
> ☐ This paragraph fulfills the original assignment.
> ☐ I am ready to turn in this paragraph for a grade.
> ☐ This paragraph is the best I can do.

After you have finished revising your paragraph, you are ready to edit it. See the Important Note about editing on page 109.

Revise Your Own Essay

In Chapter 6, you read Chelsea's draft essay (p. 93). Reread that now as if it were your own, asking yourself the questions in the Checklist for Revising Your Writing on page 97. Work either by yourself or with a partner or a small group to answer the questions about Chelsea's draft. Then, read Chelsea's revised essay that follows, and compare the changes you suggested with those that she made. Make notes on the similarities and differences to discuss with the rest of the class.

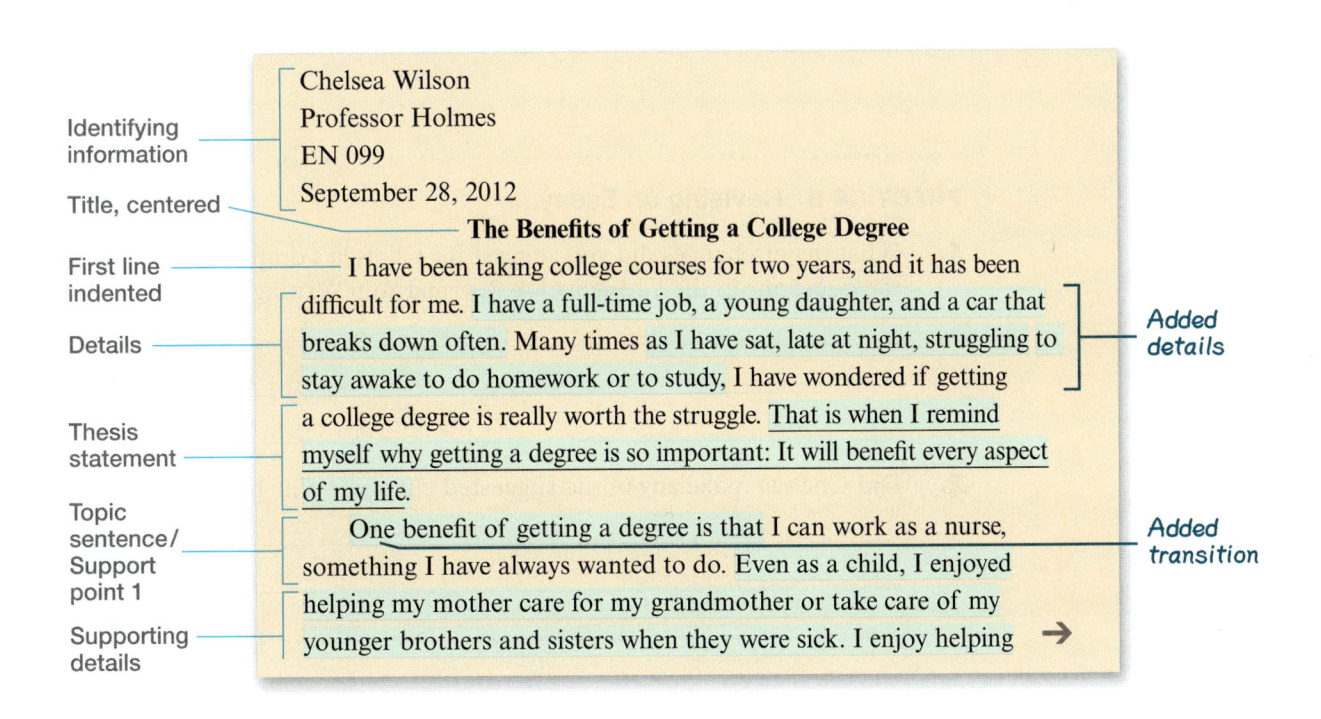

Identifying information — Chelsea Wilson
Professor Holmes
EN 099
September 28, 2012

Title, centered — **The Benefits of Getting a College Degree**

First line indented — I have been taking college courses for two years, and it has been difficult for me. I have a full-time job, a young daughter, and a car that breaks down often. Many times as I have sat, late at night, struggling to stay awake to do homework or to study, I have wondered if getting a college degree is really worth the struggle. That is when I remind myself why getting a degree is so important: It will benefit every aspect of my life.

Details —

Thesis statement —

Topic sentence / Support point 1 — One benefit of getting a degree is that I can work as a nurse, something I have always wanted to do. Even as a child, I enjoyed helping my mother care for my grandmother or take care of my younger brothers and sisters when they were sick. I enjoy helping →

Supporting details

Added details

Added transition

others, and nursing will allow me to do so while making good money. The average salary for a licensed practical nurse is $40,000 per year, substantially more than I make now working at a restaurant. Without a degree, I don't see how that situation will change. Meanwhile, I have almost no time to spend with my daughter.

Another benefit of getting a college degree is that it will allow me to be a better mother. In fact, I didn't get serious about getting a degree until I became a mother. Then, I realized I wanted more for my daughter than I had had: a safer place to live, a bigger apartment, some nice clothes, and birthday presents. I also wanted to have time to raise her properly and keep her safe. She is a good girl, but she sees crime and violence around her. I want to get her away from danger, and I want to show her that there are better ways to live. The job opportunities I will have with a college degree will enable me to do those things.

The most important benefit of getting a college degree is that it will show me that I can achieve something hard. In the past, I have often given up and taken the easy way, which has led to nothing good. The easy way has led to a hard life. Now, however, working toward a goal has moved my life in a good direction. I have confidence and self-respect. I can honestly say that I am proud of myself, and my daughter will be proud of me, too. I will be a good role model as she grows up, not only for her but also for her friends. She will go to college, just like her mother.

So why am I working so hard to get a degree? I am doing it because I see in that degree the kind of life I want to live on this earth and the kind of human being I want to be. Achieving that vision is worth all the struggles.

PRACTICE 5 Revising an Essay

1. What major changes did you suggest for Chelsea's draft in response to the questions in the Checklist for Revising Your Writing?

   _____
   _____
   _____

2. Did Chelsea make any of the suggested changes? Which ones?

   _____
   _____
   _____

3. Did Chelsea make any changes that were not suggested? Which ones? Were they good changes?

_____
_____
_____

WRITING ASSIGNMENT Essay

Revise the draft essay you wrote in Chapter 6. After revising your draft, complete the following checklist.

> **CHECKLIST**
> **Evaluating Your Revised Essay**
> ☐ My thesis statement is confident, and my main point is clear.
> ☐ My ideas are detailed, specific, and organized logically.
> ☐ My ideas flow smoothly from one to the next.
> ☐ This essay fulfills the original assignment.
> ☐ I am ready to turn in this essay for a grade.
> ☐ This essay is the best I can do.

IMPORTANT NOTE: After you have revised your writing to make the ideas clear and strong, you need to edit it to eliminate any distracting or confusing errors in grammar, word use, punctuation, and capitalization. When you are ready to edit your writing, turn to Part 4, the beginning of the editing chapters.

LEARNING JOURNAL In your own words, summarize what you have learned about the writing process.

Chapter Review

1. Highlight the important terms from this chapter (for example, *revising* and *editing*), and list them with their page numbers.

2. Revising is _____
_____

3. Three basic features of useful feedback are
_____
_____

4. As you revise, make sure your paragraph or essay has these three things: _____, _____, and _____.

5. _____ means that all the points you make are related to your main point.

6. Coherence means _____

7. An important way to ensure coherence in your writing is to _____
_____

8. Transitions are _____
_____

9. Write for one minute about "What questions I should ask my instructor."

STUDENT VOICES

Message—Chelsea to Nick (1:56 p.m.)

Do you think there are more changes that would make my paper better, before I turn it in?

Message—Nick to Chelsea (3:15 p.m.)

Well, double-check your grammar and spelling, and make sure all your thoughts are organized.
And then let's all go out to celebrate!

reflect Can you think of other changes that would make Chelsea's paper better?

"I write school essays, performance reviews, and letters to my daughter."
—Sam M., student

Part 2
Writing Different Kinds of Paragraphs and Essays

8	Narration	113
9	Illustration	132
10	Description	152
11	Process Analysis	170
12	Classification	188
13	Definition	207
14	Comparison and Contrast	225
15	Cause and Effect	246
16	Argument	265

8

YOU KNOW THIS

You often use narration:
- You explain a TV episode to a friend who missed it.
- You say, "You won't believe what happened." Then, you tell the story.

write for 2 minutes about what makes a good story or a good telling of events.

Narration

Writing That Tells Important Stories

Understand What Narration Is

Narration is writing that tells the story of an event or an experience.

Four Basics of Good Narration

1. It reveals something of importance to the writer (the main point).
2. It includes all the major events of the story (primary support).
3. It brings the story to life with details about the major events (secondary support).
4. It presents the events in a clear order, usually according to when they happened.

In the following paragraph, the numbers and colors correspond to the Four Basics of Good Narration.

1 Last year, a writing assignment that I hated produced the best writing I have done. **2** When my English teacher told us that our assignment would be to do a few hours of community service and write about it, I was furious. **3** I am a single mother, I work full-time, and I am going to school: Isn't that enough? **2** The next day, I spoke to my teacher during her office hours and told her that I was already so busy that I could hardly make time for homework, never mind housework. My own life was too full to help with anyone else's life. **3** She said that she understood perfectly and that the majority of her students had lives as full as mine. Then, she explained that the service assignment was just for four hours and that other students had enjoyed both doing the assignment

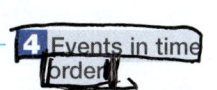

113

[4] Events in time order

and writing about their experiences. She said they were all surprised and that I would be, too. [2] After talking with her, I decided to accept my fate. The next week, I went to the Community Service Club, and was set up to spend a few hours at an adult day-care center near where I live. A few weeks later, I went to the Creative Care Center in Cocoa Beach, not knowing what to expect. [3] I found friendly, approachable people who had so many stories to tell about their long, full lives. [2] The next thing I knew, I was taking notes because I was interested in these people: [3] their marriages, life during the Depression, the wars they fought in, their children, their joys and sorrows. I felt as if I was experiencing everything they lived while they shared their history with me. [2] When it came time to write about my experience, I had more than enough to write about: [3] I wrote the stories of the many wonderful elderly people I had talked with. [2] I got an A on the paper, and beyond that accomplishment, I made friends whom I will visit on my own, not because of an assignment, but because I value them.

Seeing Narration

write What is the story here?

You can use narration in many practical situations.

COLLEGE — In a lab course, you are asked to tell what happened in an experiment.

WORK — Something goes wrong at work, and you are asked to explain to your boss — in writing — what happened.

EVERYDAY LIFE — In a letter of complaint about service you received, you need to tell what happened that upset you.

In college, the word *narration* probably will not appear in writing assignments. Instead, an assignment might ask you to *describe* the events, *report* what happened, or *retell* what happened. Words or phrases that call for an *account of events* are situations that require narration.

Main Point in Narration

In narration, the **main point** is what is important about the story — to you and to your readers. To help you discover the main point for your own narration, complete the following sentence:

MAIN POINT IN NARRATION — What is important to me about the experience is . . .

The topic sentence (paragraph) or thesis statement (essay) usually includes the topic and the main point the writer wants to make about the topic. Let's look at a topic sentence first.

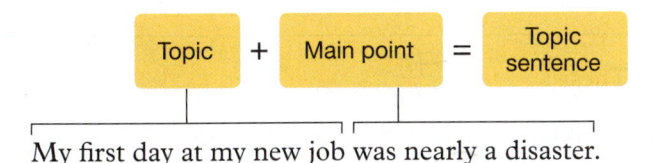

Topic + Main point = Topic sentence

My first day at my new job was nearly a disaster.

Remember that a topic for an essay can be a little broader than one for a paragraph.

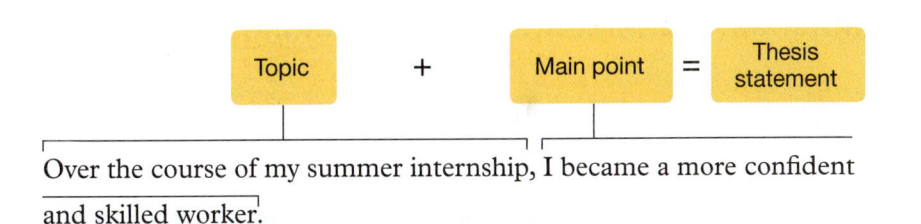

Topic + Main point = Thesis statement

Over the course of my summer internship, I became a more confident and skilled worker.

Whereas the topic sentence is focused on just one work day, the thesis statement considers a season-long internship.

IDEA JOURNAL Write about something that happened to you this week.

WRITER AT WORK

KELLY LAYLAND: I write nursing notes that are narratives about my patients' changing conditions.

(See Kelly Layland's **PROFILE OF SUCCESS** on p. 123)

TIP Sometimes, the same main point can be used for a paragraph and an essay, but the essay must develop this point in more detail. (See pp. 69–70.)

PRACTICE 1   Writing a Main Point

Look at the example narration paragraph on pages 113–14. Fill in the diagram with the paragraph's topic sentence.

[Diagram: Topic — Main point]

PRACTICE 2   Deciding on a Main Point

For each of the following topics, write a main point for a narration. Then, write a sentence that includes your topic and your main point. This sentence would be your topic sentence (paragraph) or thesis statement (essay).

EXAMPLE:

Topic: A fight I had with my sister

Important because: *it taught me something*

Main point: *learned it is better to stay cool*

Topic sentence/Thesis: *After a horrible fight with my sister, I learned the value of staying calm.*

1. Topic: A powerful, funny, or embarrassing experience

   Important because: _____

   Main point: _____

   Topic sentence/Thesis: _____

2. Topic: A strange or interesting incident that you witnessed

   Important because: _____

   Main point: _____

   Topic sentence/Thesis: _____

Support in Narration

In narration, **support** demonstrates the main point—what's important about the story.

The paragraph and essay models on pages 118–19 use the topic sentence (paragraph) and thesis statement (essay) from the Main Point section of this chapter. (The thesis statement has been revised slightly.)

TIP In an essay, the major events may form the topic sentences of paragraphs. The details supporting the major events then make up the body of these paragraphs.

Both models include the support used in all narration writing—major events backed up by details about the events. In the essay model, however, the major support points (events) are topic sentences for individual paragraphs.

CHOOSING MAJOR EVENTS

When you tell a story to a friend, you can include events that are not essential to the story. When you are writing a narration, however, you need to give more careful thought to which events to include, selecting only those that most clearly demonstrate your main point.

PRACTICE 3 Choosing Major Events

Choose two items from Practice 2, and write down the topic sentence or thesis statement you came up with for each. Then, for each topic sentence/thesis statement, write three events that would help you make your main point.

EXAMPLE:

Topic: A fight I had with my sister

Topic sentence/Thesis: *After a horrible fight with my sister, I learned the value of staying calm.*

Events: *We disagreed about who was going to have the family party. She made me so mad that I started yelling at her, and I got nasty. I hung up on her, and now we're not talking.*

1. Topic: A powerful, funny, or embarrassing experience

   Topic sentence/Thesis: _____

   _____

   Events: _____

   _____

   _____

2. Topic: A strange or interesting incident that you witnessed

   Topic sentence/Thesis: _____

   _____

   Events: _____

   _____

   _____

PARAGRAPHS VS. ESSAYS IN NARRATION

For more on the important features of narration, see the Four Basics of Good Narration on page 113.

Paragraph Form

Topic sentence

Support 1 (first major event)

Support 2 (second major event)

Support 3 (third major event)

Support Concluding sentence

My first day at my new job was nearly a disaster. First, a traffic jam from highway construction caused me to be a half hour late. I had left myself plenty of time for the commute, but because of the traffic backup, it took me nearly an hour to travel seven miles. At one point, I tried a detour to avoid traffic, but I ended up getting lost. By the time I finally pulled into the employee parking lot, I was already full of stress. After I arrived in the office, I discovered that I would have to fill in for a sick worker whose job I was not familiar with. I had been trained in accounts payable, while my sick colleague worked in accounts receivable. Although I had some understanding of his job, I was worried about making mistakes and had to ask coworkers a lot of questions, which took a lot of time. For example, I estimate that I spent a half hour on a billing procedure that would take an experienced worker five minutes. Near the end of the day, my computer broke down, erasing two documents that I had been working on. One was a small set of file labels, but the other was a detailed summary of the day's billings. At this point, I wanted to put my head down on my desk and cry. Seeing my distress, my supervisor came by and kindly said, "You have had a long, hard day and done great work. Why don't you go home and make a fresh start tomorrow?" I was grateful for her kindness, and I came around to thinking that if I could handle this type of day on the new job, I could handle just about any day.

Main Point: Often, narrower for a paragraph than for an essay: While the topic sentence (paragraph) is focused on just one workday, the thesis statement (essay) considers a season-long internship.

Major Events Supporting the Main Point

Details about the Events: Usually, 1 to 3 sentences per event for paragraphs and 3 to 8 sentences per event for essays.

Conclusion

Think Critically As You Write Narration

ASK YOURSELF

- Would someone who is unfamiliar with this story be able to follow it and relate to it?
- Have I provided enough detail to bring each event to life?

Essay Form

Thesis statement

Several of my friends question whether summer internships are really worthwhile, especially if the pay is low or nonexistent. However, the right internship definitely pays off professionally in the long run, even if it doesn't financially in the short run. The proof is in my own summer marketing internship, which made me a far more confident and skilled worker.

Topic sentence 1 (first major event)

During the first two weeks of the internship, I received thorough training in every part of my job. For example, my immediate supervisor spent a lot of time going over everything I would need to know about e-mail campaigns, online marketing efforts, and other promotions. She even had me draft a promotional e-mail for a new product and gave me feedback about how to make the message clearer and more appealing. I also spent a lot of time with other staffers, who taught me everything from how to use the photocopier and printers to how to pull together marketing and sales materials for executive meetings. Most impressive, the president of the company took some time out of a busy afternoon to answer my questions about how he got started in his career and what he sees as the keys to success in the marketing field. As I explained to a friend, I got an "insider's view" of the company and its business.

Topic sentence 2 (second major event)

Next, I got hands-on experience with listening to customers and addressing their needs. Specifically, I sat in on meetings with new clients and listened to them describe products and services they would like the company's help in promoting. They also discussed the message they would like to get across about their businesses. After the meetings, I sat in on brainstorming sessions with other staffers in which we came up with as many ideas as we could about campaigns to address the clients' needs. At first, I didn't think anyone would care about my ideas, but others listened to them respectfully and even ended up including some of them in the marketing plans that were sent back to the clients. Later, I learned that some of my ideas would be included in actual promotional campaigns.

Topic sentence 3 (third major event)

By summer's end, I had advanced my skills so much that I was asked to return next summer. My supervisor told me that she was pleased not only with all I had learned about marketing but also with the responsibility I took for every aspect of my job. I did not roll my eyes about having to make photocopies or help at the reception desk, nor did I seem intimidated by bigger, more meaningful tasks. Although I'm not guaranteed a full-time job at the company after graduation, I think my chances are good. Even if I don't end up working there long term, I am very grateful for how the job has helped me grow.

Concluding paragraph

In the end, the greatest benefit of the internship might be the confidence it gave me. I have learned that no matter how challenging the task before me—at work or in real life—I can succeed at it by getting the right information and input on anything unfamiliar, working effectively with others, and truly dedicating myself to doing my best. My time this past summer was definitely well spent.

GIVING DETAILS ABOUT THE EVENTS

When you write a narration, include examples and details that will make each event easier to visualize and understand. You want your readers to share your point of view and see the same message in the story that you do.

PRACTICE 4 Giving Details about the Events

Write down the topic sentence or thesis statement for each item from Practice 3. Then, write the major events in the spaces provided. Give a detail about each event.

EXAMPLE:

Topic sentence/Thesis: *After a horrible fight with my sister, I learned the value of staying calm.*

Event: *We disagreed about who was going to have the family party.*

  Detail: *Even though we both work, she said she was too busy and I would have to do it.*

Event: *She made me so mad I started yelling at her, and I got nasty.*

  Detail: *I brought up times in the past when she had tried to pass responsibilities off on me, and I told her I was sick of being the one who did everything.*

Event: *I hung up on her, and now we are not talking.*

  Detail: *I feel bad, and I know I will have to call her sooner or later because she is my sister. I do love her, even though she is a pain sometimes.*

1. Topic sentence/Thesis: _____

_____

Event: _____

Detail: _____

_____

Event: _____

Detail: _____

_____

Event: _____

Detail: _____

_____

2. Topic sentence/Thesis: _____

_____

Event: _____

Detail: _____

_____

Event: _____

Detail: _____

_____

Event: _____

Detail: _____

_____

Organization in Narration

Narration usually presents events in the order in which they happened, known as **time (chronological) order**. As shown in the paragraph and essay models on pages 117–18, a narration starts at the beginning of the story and describes events as they unfolded.

Transitions move readers from one event to the next.

TIP For more on time order, see page 78.

Common Transitions in Narration

after	eventually	meanwhile	since
as	finally	next	soon
at last	first	now	then
before	last	once	when
during	later	second	while

PRACTICE 5 Using Transitions in Narration

Read the paragraph that follows, and fill in the blanks with time transitions.

 Some historians believe that as many as four hundred women disguised themselves as men so that they could serve in the U.S. Civil War (1861–1865). One of the best known of these women was Sarah Emma Edmonds. _When_____ the war began, Edmonds, an opponent of slavery, felt driven to join the Union Army, which fought for the free states. **When** President Abraham Lincoln asked for army volunteers, she disguised herself as a man, took the name Frank Thompson, and enlisted in the infantry. **During** her military service, Edmonds worked as a male nurse and a messenger. **While** serving as a nurse, she learned that the Union general needed someone to spy on the Confederates. **After** extensive training, Edmonds took on this duty and, disguised as a slave, went behind enemy lines. Here, she learned about the Confederates' military strengths and weaknesses. **Later**, she returned to the Union side and went back to work as a nurse. In 1863, Edmonds left the army after developing malaria. She was worried that hospital workers would discover that she was a woman. As a result of her departure, "Frank Thompson" was listed as a deserter. In later years, Edmonds, under her real name, worked to get a veteran's pension and to get the desertion charge removed from her record. **Finally**, in 1884, a special act of Congress granted her both of these wishes.

Left: Sarah Emma Edmonds; right: Edmonds disguised as Frank Thompson

Read and Analyze Narration

Reading examples of narration will help you write your own. The first example in this section is a Profile of Success from the real world of nursing. In this profile, Kelly Layland shows how she uses narration at work.

The second example is a narration paragraph by a student, and the third example is a narration essay by a professional writer. As you read these selections, pay attention to the vocabulary, and answer the questions in the margin. They will help you read critically.

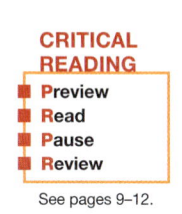

> **CRITICAL READING**
> - Preview
> - Read
> - Pause
> - Review
>
> See pages 9–12.

PROFILE OF SUCCESS

Narration in the Real World

Background   In high school, I was not a good student. I had a lot of other things to do, like having fun. I am a very social person; I loved my friends, and we had a great time. But when I decided I wanted to go to college, I had to pay the price. I had to take lots of noncredit courses to get my skills up to college level because I had fooled around during high school. The noncredit English course I took was very beneficial to me. After I passed it, I took English 101 and felt prepared for it.

Degrees/Colleges   A.S., Monroe Community College; LPN, Isabella Graham Hart School of Nursing; RN, Monroe Community College

Employer   Rochester General Hospital

Writing at work   I write nursing notes that are narratives of patients' changing conditions and the level of care required. When I describe physical conditions, I have to support my descriptions with detailed examples. When I recommend medication for treatment, I have to justify it by explaining the patient's condition and the reasons I am making the recommendation. I also have to write notes that integrate care with Medicare documentation. Basically, I have to write about everything I recommend and all that I do.

How Kelly uses narration   Every day I write brief narratives that recount all that went on with the patient during the day: things that went wrong and things about his or her treatment that need to be changed.

Kelly Layland
Registered Nurse

Kelly's Narration

The following paragraph is an example of the daily reports that Kelly writes on each patient.

Karella Lehmanoff, a two-month-old female infant, is improving steadily. When she was born, her birth weight was 1.3 pounds, but it has increased to 3.1 pounds. Her jaundice has completely disappeared, and her skin has begun to look rosy. Karella's pulse rate is normal for her development, and her resting heart rate has stabilized at about 150 beats per minute. Lung development was a big concern because of Karella's premature birth, but her lungs are now fully developed and largely functional. Dr. Lansing saw Karella at 1 P.M. and pronounced her in good condition. The parents were encouraged, and so am I. The prognosis for little Karella gets better with each day.

1. Double-underline the **main point** of the narration.
2. Underline the **major events**.
3. What order of organization does Kelly use? _____

Student Narration Paragraph

Jelani Lynch

My Turnaround

Vocabulary development
Underline these words as you read Jelani's paragraph.
integrity: honesty; having a sound moral code
mentor: a counselor, a teacher, an adviser

PREDICT What will Jelani's paragraph explain?

Jelani Lynch graduated from Cambridge College/Year Up in 2009 with a degree in information technology. Now, he runs the video production company J/L visual media. As a writer, he says he is interested in exploring "issues that affect the community and the disparities that continue to affect the world." Reflecting on what motivated him to begin this essay, Jelani comments that he viewed his writing as a means of helping those around him: "I wrote this essay after I had just begun to get my life on track. I felt that the struggles that I have encountered needed to be publicized so my mistakes are not repeated by the people who read this essay."

Before my big turnaround, my life was headed in the wrong direction. I grew up in the city and had a typical sad story: broken home, not much money, gangs, and drugs. In this world, few positive male role models are available. I played the game "Street Life": running the streets, stealing bikes, robbing people, carrying a gun, and selling drugs. The men in my neighborhood did not have regular jobs; they got their money outside the system. No one except my mother thought school was worth much. I had a history of poor school performance, a combination of not showing up and not doing any work when I did. My pattern of failure in that area was pretty strong. When I was seventeen, though, things got really bad. I was arrested for possession of crack cocaine. I was kicked out of school for good. During this time, I realized that my life was not going the way I wanted it to be. I was headed nowhere, except a life of crime, violence, and possibly early death. I knew that way of life, because I was surrounded by people who had chosen that direction. I did not want to go there anymore. When I made that decision, my life started to change. First, I met Shawn Brown, a man who had had the same kind of life I did. He got out of that life, though, by graduating from high school and college and getting a good job. He has a house, a wife, and children, along with great clothes. Shawn became my role model, showing me that with honesty, integrity, and hard work I could live a much better life. Since meeting Shawn, I have turned my life around. I started taking school seriously and graduated from high school, something I thought I would never do. Working with Shawn, I have read books and learned I enjoy writing. I have met the mayor of Boston and got a summer job at the State House. I have been part of an educational video and had many opportunities to meet and work with people who are successful. Now, I am a mentor with Diamond Educators, and I work with other young, urban males to give them a role model and help them make good choices. Now, I have a bright future with goals and plans. I have turned my life around and know I will be a success.

REFLECT Have you ever made a decision that changed your life?

SUMMARIZE How did meeting Shawn change Jelani's life?

1. Underline the **topic sentence**.
2. What is important about the story? _____
   _____
   _____

3. Number the **major events**.
4. Circle the **transitions**.
5. Does Jelani's paragraph follow the Four Basics of Good Narration (p. 113)? Be ready to give specific reasons for your answer. _____
   _____
   _____

WRITING DIFFERENT KINDS OF PARAGRAPHS AND ESSAYS

Professional Narration Essay

Vocabulary development
Underline these words as you read the narration essay.
prawns: shrimp or shrimp-like creatures
appalling: horrifying
clamor: noise
murmured: spoke in low tones
belched: burped

Amy Tan
Fish Cheeks

Amy Tan was born in Oakland, California, in 1952, several years after her mother and father emigrated from China. She studied at San Jose City College and later San Jose State University, receiving a B.A. with a double major in English and linguistics. In 1973, she earned an M.A. in linguistics from San Jose State University. In 1989, Tan published her first novel, *The Joy Luck Club*, which was nominated for the National Book Award and the National Book Critics Circle Award. Tan's other books include *The Kitchen God's Wife* (1991), *The Hundred Secret Senses* (1995), and *Saving Fish from Drowning* (2005). Her short stories and essays have been published in the *Atlantic, Grand Street, Harper's,* the *New Yorker,* and other publications.

In the following essay, Tan uses narration to describe an experience that taught her an important lesson.

PREDICT Based on the second paragraph, what do you think will happen?

REFLECT Name an event during which you tried to make a good impression on someone.

1 I fell in love with the minister's son the winter I turned fourteen. He was not Chinese, but as white as Mary in the manger. For Christmas I prayed for this blond-haired boy, Robert, and a slim new American nose.

2 When I found out that my parents had invited the minister's family over for Christmas dinner, I cried. What would Robert think of our shabby Chinese Christmas? What would he think of our noisy Chinese relatives who lacked proper American manners? What terrible disappointment would he feel upon seeing not a roasted turkey and sweet potatoes but Chinese food?

3 On Christmas Eve I saw that my mother had outdone herself in creating a strange menu. She was pulling black veins out of the backs of fleshy prawns. The kitchen was littered with appalling mounds of raw food: A slimy rock cod with bulging eyes that pleaded not to be thrown into a pan of hot oil. Tofu, which looked like stacked wedges of rubbery white sponges. A bowl soaking dried fungus back to life. A plate of squid, their backs crisscrossed with knife markings so they resembled bicycle tires.

4 And then they arrived—the minister's family and all my relatives in a clamor of doorbells and rumpled Christmas packages. Robert grunted hello, and I pretended he was not worthy of existence.

5 Dinner threw me into despair. My relatives licked the ends of their chopsticks and reached across the table, dipping them into the dozen or so plates of food. Robert and his family waited patiently for platters to be passed to them. My relatives murmured with pleasure when my

mother brought out the whole steamed fish. Robert grimaced. Then my father poked his chopsticks just below the fish eye and plucked out the soft meat. "Amy, your favorite," he said, offering me the tender fish cheek. I wanted to disappear.

At the end of the meal my father leaned back and belched loudly, thanking my mother for her fine cooking. "It's a polite Chinese custom to show you are satisfied," explained my father to our astonished guests. Robert was looking down at his plate with a reddened face. The minister managed to muster up a quiet burp. I was stunned into silence for the rest of the night.

After everyone had gone, my mother said to me, "You want to be the same as American girls on the outside." She handed me an early gift. It was a miniskirt in beige tweed. "But inside you must always be Chinese. You must be proud you are different. Your only shame is to have shame."

And even though I didn't agree with her then, I knew that she understood how much I had suffered during the evening's dinner. It wasn't until many years later—long after I had gotten over my crush on Robert—that I was able to fully appreciate her lesson and the true purpose behind our particular menu. For Christmas Eve that year, she had chosen all my favorite foods.

6

7 **REFLECT** Have you ever felt different on the outside than you did on the inside?

8

1. What is Tan's purpose for writing? _____

2. Does she achieve it? _____
3. In your own words, state her **main point**. _____

4. How has Tan organized her essay? _____ Circle the **transitional words and phrases** that indicate this order.

TIP For reading advice, see Chapter 1.

TIP For tools to build your vocabulary, visit the *Student Site for Real Writing* at **bedfordstmartins.com/realwriting**.

Respond to one of the following assignments in a paragraph or essay.

1. Have you ever been embarrassed by your family or by others close to you? Write about the experience, and describe what you learned from it.

2. Write about a time when you felt different from other people. How did you react at the time? Have your feelings about the situation changed since then? If so, how?

3. Write about an experience that was uncomfortable at the time but funny later. Explain how you came to see humor in the situation.

Write Your Own Narration

In this section, you will write your own narration based on one of the following assignments. For help, refer to the "How to Write Narration" checklist on page 130.

ASSIGNMENT OPTIONS Writing about College, Work, and Everyday Life

Write a narration paragraph or essay on one of the following topics or on one of your own choice. If you responded to the idea journal prompt on page 115, you might develop that writing further.

COLLEGE

- Tell the story of how a teacher made a difference in your life.
- Write about a time when you achieved success or experienced a difficulty in school.
- Interview a college graduate about his or her educational experience. Questions might include "Why did you go to college?" "What were your biggest challenges?" and "What were your greatest accomplishments?" Then, write that person's story.

WORK

- Write about a situation or incident that made you decide to leave a job.
- Imagine a successful day at your current or previous job. Then, tell the story of that day, including examples of successes.
- Write your own work history, guided by a statement that you would like to make about this history or your work style. Here is one example: "Being a people person has helped me in every job I have ever had." You might imagine that you are interviewing with a potential employer.

EVERYDAY LIFE

- Write about an experience that triggered a strong emotion: happiness, sadness, fear, anger, regret.
- Find a campus community service club that offers short-term assignments. Take an assignment and write about your experience.
- Tell the story of a community issue that interests you. One example is plans to create a bike lane on a major road. Discuss how the issue arose, and describe key developments. Research details by visiting a local newspaper's Web site.

ASSIGNMENT OPTIONS Reading and Writing Critically

Complete one of the following assignments, which ask you to apply the critical thinking, reading, and writing skills discussed in Chapter 1.

COMMUNITY CONNECTIONS

JENNY HAUN wrote the Four Basics of Good Narration paragraph on page 113. Getting more involved in college and community activities, as Jenny did, can help you feel more connected to others and can even improve the chances that you will stay in school.

For more on this story, ways to make community connections, and writing assignments, visit bedfordstmartins.com/ realwriting.

Writing Critically about Readings

Both Jelani Lynch's "My Turnaround" (p. 124) and Caitlin Prokop's "A Difficult Decision with a Positive Outcome" (p. 257) tell the story of a major life decision with positive results. Review both of these pieces. Then, follow these steps:

1. **Summarize**   Briefly summarize the works, listing major events.

2. **Analyze**   List any types of examples or details you wish had been included in Lynch's or Prokop's story. Also, write down any questions that the pieces raise for you.

3. **Synthesize**   Using examples from both Lynch's and Prokop's stories and from your own experience, write about how a big life decision can have a major effect on one's future.

4. **Evaluate**   Which piece do you think is more effective? Why? To write your evaluation, look back on your responses to step 2.

TIP For a reminder of how to summarize, analyze, synthesize, and evaluate, see the Reading and Writing Critically box on pages 16–17.

Writing about Images

Study the photograph below, and complete the following steps.

1. **Read the image**   Ask yourself: What details does the photographer focus on? What seems to be the photo's message? (For more information on reading images, see Chapter 1.)

2. **Write a narration** Write a narration paragraph or essay about what has happened (or is happening) in the photograph. Be as creative as you like, but be sure to include details and reactions from step 1.

Writing to Solve a Problem

Read or review the discussion of problem solving in Chapter 1 (pp. 24–26). Then, consider the following problem:

> You have learned that a generous scholarship is available for low-income, first-generation college students. You really need the money to cover day-care expenses while you are taking classes (in fact, you had thought you would have to stop going to college for a while). Many people have been applying. Part of the application is to write about yourself and why you deserve the scholarship.

ASSIGNMENT: Write a paragraph or essay that tells your story and why you should be considered for the scholarship. Think about how you can make your story stand out. You might start with the following sentence:

Even though you will be reading applications from many first-generation college students, my story is a little different because _____.

TIP Such scholarships really do exist. Go online or to the college financial aid office to find out about them. If you are pleased with what you have written for this assignment, you could use it as part of your application.

CHECKLIST: HOW TO WRITE NARRATION

STEPS	DETAILS
☐ Narrow and explore your topic. See Chapter 3.	• Make the topic more specific. • Prewrite to get ideas about the narrowed topic.
☐ Write a topic sentence (paragraph) or thesis statement (essay). See Chapter 4.	• State what is most important to you about the topic and what you want your readers to understand.
☐ Support your point. See Chapter 5.	• Come up with examples and details to explain your main point to readers.
☐ Write a draft. See Chapter 6.	• Make a plan that puts events or examples in a logical order. • Include a topic sentence (paragraph) or thesis statement (essay) and all the supporting events, examples, and details.
☐ Revise your draft. See Chapter 7.	• Make sure it has *all* the Four Basics of Good Narration. • Make sure you include transitions to move readers smoothly from one event or example to the next.
☐ Edit your revised draft. See Parts 4 through 7.	• Correct errors in grammar, spelling, word use, and punctuation.

Chapter Review

1. Narration is writing that _____

2. List the Four Basics of Good Narration. _____
   _____
   _____
   _____
   _____

3. The topic sentence in a narration paragraph or the thesis statement in a narration essay usually includes what two things?
   _____

4. What type of organization do writers of narration usually use?
   _____

5. List five common transitions for this type of organization.
   _____

6. Write sentences using the following vocabulary words: *integrity, mentor, appalling, clamor.* _____
   _____
   _____

LEARNING JOURNAL
Reread your idea journal entry about an event that happened to you this week (p. 115). Then, rewrite it using what you now know about narration.

reflect Write for 2 minutes about how to tell a good story. Then, compare what you have written with what you wrote in response to the "write" prompt on page 113.

9

Illustration

Writing That Gives Examples

> **YOU KNOW THIS**
>
> You use examples to illustrate your point in daily communication:
>
> - You answer the question "Like what?"
> - You give a friend some examples of fun things to do this weekend.
>
> **write** for 2 minutes about what you know about writing illustration.

Understand What Illustration Is

Illustration is writing that uses examples to support a point.

Four Basics of Good Illustration

1. It has a point.
2. It gives specific examples that show, explain, or prove the point.
3. It gives details to support the examples.
4. It uses enough examples to get the point across to the reader.

In the following paragraph, the numbers and colors correspond to the Four Basics of Good Illustration.

1 Many people would like to serve their communities or help with causes that they believe in, but they do not have much time and do not know what to do. Now, the Internet provides people with ways to help that do not take much time or money. **2** Web sites now make it convenient to donate online. With a few clicks, an organization of your choice can receive your donation or money from a sponsoring advertiser. For example, if you are interested in helping rescue unwanted and abandoned animals, you can go to www.theanimalrescuesite.com. **3** When you click as instructed, a sponsoring advertiser will make a donation to help provide food and care for the 27 million animals in shelters. Also, a portion of any money you spend in

4 Enough examples to get the point across to the reader

the site's online store will go to providing animal care. **2** If you want to help fight world hunger, go to www.thehungersite.com **3** and click daily to have sponsor fees directed to hungry people in more than seventy countries via the Mercy Corps, Feeding America, and Millennium Promise. Each year, hundreds of millions of cups of food are distributed to one billion hungry people around the world. **2** Other examples of click-to-give sites are www.thechildhealthsite.com, www.theliteracysite.com, and www.breastcancersite.com. **3** Like the animal-rescue and hunger sites, these other sites have click-to-give links, online stores that direct a percentage of sales income to charity, and links to help you learn about causes you are interested in. One hundred percent of the sponsors' donations go to the charities, and you can give with a click every single day. Since I have found out about these sites, I go to at least one of them every day. **1** I have learned a lot about various problems, and every day, I feel as if I have helped a little.

Seeing Illustration

write What do these personal objects illustrate?

WRITING DIFFERENT KINDS OF PARAGRAPHS AND ESSAYS

Chapter 9 • Illustration

WRITER AT WORK

KAREN UPRIGHT: I am a computer scientist, but my writing has to be good.

(See Karen Upright's **PROFILE OF SUCCESS** on p. 140.)

IDEA JOURNAL Give some examples of things that annoy you.

TIP Sometimes, the same main point can be used for a paragraph and an essay, but the essay must develop this point in more detail. (See pp. 69–70.)

It is hard to explain anything without using examples, so you use illustration in almost every communication situation.

COLLEGE	An exam question asks you to explain and give examples of a concept.
WORK	Your boss asks you to tell her what office equipment needs to be replaced and why.
EVERYDAY LIFE	You complain to your landlord that the building superintendent is not doing his job. The landlord asks for examples.

In college, the words *illustration* and *illustrate* may not appear in writing assignments. Instead, you might be asked to *give examples of* _____ or to *be specific about* _____. Regardless of an assignment's wording, to be clear and effective, most types of writing require specific examples. Include them whenever they help you make your point.

Main Point in Illustration

In illustration, the **main point** is the message you want your readers to receive and understand. To help you discover your main point, complete the following sentence:

MAIN POINT IN ILLUSTRATION What I want readers to know about this topic is . . .

The topic sentence (in a paragraph) or thesis statement (in an essay) usually includes the topic and the main point the writer wants to make about the topic. Let's look at a topic sentence first.

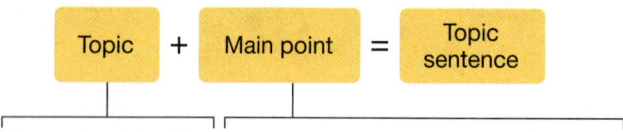

Topic + Main point = Topic sentence

Home health aides provide vital services to the elderly.

Remember that a thesis statement for an essay can be a little broader than a paragraph topic.

Topic + Main point = Thesis statement

Demand for elder-care health workers is increasing rapidly.

Whereas the topic sentence is focused on just home health aides, the thesis statement considers elder-care careers in general.

WRITING DIFFERENT KINDS OF PARAGRAPHS AND ESSAYS
Understand What Illustration Is

PRACTICE 1 Making a Main Point

Each of the items in this practice is a narrowed topic. Think about each of them, and in the space provided, write a main point about each topic.

EXAMPLE: The words to songs I like *relate closely to experiences I have had.*

1. A few moments alone _____
2. A course I am taking _____
3. The busiest time at work _____
4. Being a parent of a newborn baby _____
5. Working with other people _____

Support in Illustration

The paragraph and essay models on pages 136–37 use the topic sentence (paragraph) and thesis statement (essay) from the Main Point section of this chapter. Both models include the **support** used in all illustration writing: examples backed up by details about the examples. In the essay model, however, the major support points (examples) are topic sentences for individual paragraphs.

To generate good detailed examples, use one or more of the prewriting techniques discussed in Chapter 3. First, write down all the examples that come into your mind. Then, review your examples, and choose the ones that will best communicate your point to your readers.

PRACTICE 2 Supporting Your Main Point with Examples

Read the following main points, and give three examples you might use to support each one.

EXAMPLE: My boss's cheapness is unprofessional.

makes us bring in our own calculators

makes us use old, rusted paper clips

will not replace burned-out lightbulbs

1. My (friend, sister, brother, husband, wife — choose one) has some admirable traits.

    _____

    _____

    _____

PARAGRAPHS VS. ESSAYS IN ILLUSTRATION

For more on the important features of narration, see the Four Basics of Good Illustration on page 132.

Paragraph Form

Topic sentence

Support 1 (first example)

Support 2 (second example)

Support 3 (third example)

Concluding sentence

Home health aides provide vital services to the elderly. First, they see to their clients' nutritional and personal-care needs. For instance, they often shop for and prepare meals, following any dietary restrictions clients may have. In addition, they may help clients get in and out of bed, bathe, dress, and accomplish other grooming tasks. Second, home health aides may assist with medical care. For example, they may check clients' vital signs and report any problems to the hospital or to a case manager. Specially trained aides may oversee the operation of medical equipment, such as ventilators; provide therapeutic massage; or assist with physical therapy. Most important, they provide companionship and emotional support. The simple presence of a home health aide is a comfort to clients, but aides who take the time to read to or have conversations with clients are especially valued. Additionally, health aides provide an important link between patients and their families, keeping relatives up to date about the patients' status and about any special needs that may arise. Aside from supplying key information, these updates let family members know that their loved one is in good hands. The bottom line is that for those who are interested in both the personal and the technical sides of health care, a job as a home health aide can be a good start.

Main Point: Often, narrower for a paragraph than for an essay: While the topic sentence (paragraph) is focused on just home health aides, the thesis statement (essay) considers elder-care careers in general.

Examples Supporting the Main Point

Details about the Examples: Usually, 1 to 3 sentences per example for paragraphs and 3 to 8 sentences per example for essays.

Conclusion

Think Critically As You Write Illustration

ASK YOURSELF

- Is each of my current examples clearly related to the main point?
- If my paragraph or essay feels "thin," might I find relevant new examples to enrich it? (For more on generating ideas, see pp. 46–49.)

136

Essay Form

During these difficult economic times, many students are looking to pursue careers in expanding fields with good long-term prospects. One [career they] should seriously consider is elder care. **Because the U.S. population is aging, demand for workers who specialize in the health of the elderly is increasing rapidly.**

One set of workers in great demand consists of physical therapists, who help elderly patients improve their mobility and retain their independence. Some of these therapists are based at hospitals [or rehabilitation] facilities, others at clinics or private offices. [Regardless] of where they work, they provide a variety of services to elderly patients, from helping stroke sufferers relearn how to walk and perform other daily activities to showing others how to live a more active life. Physical therapists can also help patients injured in falls reduce their reliance on painkillers, which can become less effective over time and in certain cases even addictive. According to the U.S. Department of Labor, employment of physical therapists will grow by 30 percent over the next ten years, largely because of the increasing number of elderly Americans.

Also in demand are nutritionists who specialize in older people's dietary needs. These professionals may plan meals and provide nutrition [counseling at] hospitals, nursing homes, and other institutions, or they may counsel individual patients on how to eat more healthfully or on how to prepare meals that meet certain dietary restrictions. For instance, elderly patients suffering from heart disease may need to eat foods that are low in salt and saturated fat. Other patients might have to avoid foods that interfere with the absorption of certain medications. Although the market for nutritionists is not expected to grow as quickly as that for physical therapists, it is projected to increase [steadily as] the population continues to age.

The highest-demand workers are those who provide at-home health care to the elderly. One subset of these workers consists of home nurses, who often provide follow-up care after patients are released from a hospital or other medical facility. These nurses help patients transition from an institutional setting while making sure they continue to receive high-quality care. For instance, they track patients' vital signs, administer and monitor medications, and carry out specific tasks required to manage particular diseases. Another subset of home health workers is made up of home health aides, who assist nurses and other professionals with medical care, see to clients' nutritional and personal-care needs, and provide companionship and emotional support. Both home health aides and nurses provide an important link between patients and their families, keeping relatives up to date about the patients' status and about any special needs that may arise. In addition to supplying key information, these updates let family members know that their loved one is in good hands. Because of home health care workers' vital role in serving the expanding elderly population, their employment is expected to grow significantly: on average, 30 to 40 percent over [the next] ten years.

Given the growing demand for elder-care workers, people pursuing these professions stand an excellent chance of getting jobs with good long-term outlooks. Based on what I have learned about these professions, the best candidates are those who have a strong interest in health or medicine, a willingness to work hard to get the necessary qualifications, and, perhaps most important, an ability to connect with and truly care for others.

137

WRITING DIFFERENT KINDS OF PARAGRAPHS AND ESSAYS
Chapter 9 • Illustration

2. This weekend is particularly busy.

PRACTICE 3   Giving Details about the Examples

In the spaces provided, copy your main points and examples from Practice 2. Then, for each example, write a detail that further shows, explains, or proves what you mean.

EXAMPLE:

Main point: My boss's cheapness is unprofessional.

Example: *makes us bring in our own calculators*

   Detail: *Some people do not have a calculator.*

Example: *makes us use old, rusted paper clips*

   Detail: *They leave rust marks on important documents.*

Example: *will not replace burned-out lightbulbs*

   Detail: *The dim light leads to more errors.*

1. Main point: _Graduate from college_
Example: _Will help get better job_
   Detail: _Job will help get more money._
Example: _____
   Detail: _____
Example: _____
   Detail: _____

2. Main point: _____
Example: _____
   Detail: _____
Example: _____
   Detail: _____
Example: _____
   Detail: _____

Organization in Illustration

Illustration often uses **order of importance**, saving the most powerful example for last. This strategy is used in the paragraph and essay models on pages 135–37. Or, if the examples are given according to when they happened, it might be organized by **time order**.

Transitions in illustration let readers know that you are introducing an example or moving from one example to another.

TIP For more on order of importance and time order, see pages 78 and 79.

Common Transitions in Illustration

also	first, second, and so on	for instance	in addition
another		for one thing/ for another	the most/the least
finally	for example		one example/ another example

PRACTICE 4   Using Transitions in Illustration

Read the paragraph that follows, and fill in the blanks with transitions.

Greek myths include many heroes, such as the great warriors Achilles and Herakles. _____, the myths describe several monsters that tested the heroes' strength. _____ of these frightening creatures was the Hydra, a water serpent with many heads. When a warrior cut off one of these heads, two or more would sprout up in its place. _____ of these mythical monsters was the Gorgons, three sisters who had snakes for hair. Any person who looked into the Gorgons' eyes would turn to stone. _____ terrifying monster was Cerberus, a three-headed dog with snapping jaws. He guarded the gates to the underworld, keeping the living from entering and the dead from leaving. Fortunately, some heroes' cleverness equaled the monsters' hideousness. _____, Herakles discovered that by applying a torch to the wounds of the Hydra, he could prevent the creature from growing more heads. _____, Orpheus, a famous mythical musician, soothed Cerberus by plucking the strings of a lyre. In this way, Orpheus got past the beast and entered the underworld, from which he hoped to rescue his wife.

WRITING DIFFERENT KINDS OF PARAGRAPHS AND ESSAYS

Chapter 9 • Illustration

Painting of Cerberus, by William Blake (1757–1827)

CRITICAL READING
- Preview
- Read
- Pause
- Review

See pages 9–12.

Read and Analyze Illustration

Reading examples of illustration will help you write your own. The first example in this section is a Profile of Success from the real world of business. In this profile, Karen Upright shows how she uses illustration to communicate with her colleagues at Procter & Gamble.

The second example is an illustration paragraph by a student, and the third example is an illustration essay by a professional writer. As you read these pieces, pay attention to the vocabulary, and answer the questions in the margin. They will help you read critically.

PROFILE OF SUCCESS

Illustration in the Real World

Karen Upright
Systems Manager

Background I started college a couple of times but failed most of my courses, mainly because I did not go to class and was not motivated. I was not involved and did not have a particular reason to go to college. I enrolled at FCCJ and took classes irregularly—sometimes full-time, sometimes part-time. I did well in some of the classes and poorly in others.

During this time, I got a job at CityStreet, a global benefits provider, and I realized that I really liked business. I also realized that I would not go far without a college degree. So I decided to try college one more time. My first course then was English, and my teacher, Marian Beaman, was great. I did well in that course and from then on. From FCCJ, I went to Florida State and Purdue University, where I have recently completed an M.B.A. Later, I wrote Professor Beaman to thank her for setting me on a good course; it changed my life.

I now have a great job with lots of potential for advancement.

Degrees/Colleges   A.A., Florida Community College, Jacksonville; B.S., Florida State University; M.B.A., Purdue University

Employer   Procter & Gamble

Writing at work   I write many kinds of documents, like memos, work and development plans, and speeches for presentations. We have structured meetings at P&G, so before meetings we prepare and distribute talk sheets, which provide the necessary background for what will be discussed at the meeting. I write technical design documents with precision analyses of systems. I also write e-mail that is read by senior management. I always make sure that those e-mails are correct because I do not want the executives to be distracted by errors. If I make careless mistakes in writing, I will not get far in the company. I also write about human resources issues. Whenever you manage people, you have to be aware of issues and situations that might offend employees.

I was surprised by how much writing I do as an essential part of the job. I am a computer scientist, but my writing has to be good.

Karen's Illustration

The following memo is an example of the illustration that Karen writes as part of her job. It details the objectives of a workplace initiative to help women already employed by Procter & Gamble plan careers within the company.

From: Upright, Karen
Subject: Women's Network: Assignment Planning Matrix

As you know, we have an enrollment goal for 30 percent of our employees to be women, but we are currently at 20 percent. We need to grow our enrollment, but we also need to retain the women currently in the organization. Greg and I met a few weeks ago to determine how to improve assignment planning for the women in our organization. We agreed to use the Assignment Planning Matrix as a starting point. The matrix is a good career-planning tool, with a section on career interests, rated from "highly desirable" to "undesirable." It also contains a section on specific P&G career interests, with sections to describe aspects that make a particular choice desirable or undesirable and a place to give weight to the various career choices. Completing the matrix requires thought as to what course an individual wants to pursue and why. I have reviewed a sample with and provided training to the women in our organization. Each of them has been asked to complete the matrix, meet with her manager to align on content, and submit a final version to her manager. This information can be shared at the next Leadership Team meeting. →

Vocabulary development
Underline the following words as you read Karen's memo.
retain: to keep
matrix: a grid or table
aspects: parts of
align: to be in line or parallel (in this case, to agree)
objectives: goals

> This initiative has several objectives:
>
> - Have each member of the network start a long-term plan for her career.
> - Use the long-term plan to develop a short-term plan for assignments and competency development.
> - Share this information in written form with the immediate manager and section manager of each member of the network, enabling the manager to speak for each woman's career interests and providing a reference point for each member's career goals.
> - Enable the Leadership Team to plan assignments within the organization for each member of the network, matching individual goals and interests to organizational goals and needs.
>
> I encourage you to support the women on your teams as they work through the Assignment Planning Matrix over the next few weeks. Please let me know if you have any questions.

1. Double-underline the **main point** of the memo.

2. Karen gives examples about two topics. What are the two topics? _____

3. What is the purpose of the memo? _____

Student Illustration Paragraph

Casandra Palmer
Gifts from the Heart

PREDICT After reading the title, what do you think the paragraph will be about?

Casandra Palmer graduated from the University of Akron/Wayne College in 2009. After completing her essay "Gifts from the Heart," Casandra went on to seek publication in her campus paper at the encouragement of her instructor. She spent a few days revising the essay and looked to feedback from others to help strengthen the clarity of her points. With plans to continue writing for publication when time allows, Casandra enjoys reading inspirational novels and offers this advice to other student writers: "Learn all you can and never give up. Follow your dreams!"

REFLECT Have you ever received a gift that made you laugh or cry?

In our home, gift exchanges have always been meaningful items to us. We do not just give things so that everyone has lots of presents. Each item has a purpose, such as a need or something that someone has desired for a long time. Some things have been given that may have made the other person laugh or cry. I remember one Christmas, our daughter Hannah had her boyfriend, who looked a lot like Harry Potter, join us. We wanted to include him, but we did not know him well, so it was hard to know what to give him. We decided to get Hannah a Harry Potter poster and crossed out the name Harry Potter. In place of Harry Potter, we put her boyfriend's name. Everyone thought it was funny, and we were all laughing, including Hannah's boyfriend. It was a personal gift that he knew we had thought about. For some reason, Hannah did not think it was so funny, but she will still remember it. Another meaningful gift came from watching the movie *Titanic* with my other daughter, Tabitha. We both cried hard and hugged each other. She surprised me by getting a necklace that resembled the gem known as "Heart of the Ocean." I was so touched that she gave me something to remind me of the experience we shared. These special moments have left lasting impressions on my heart.

1. Double-underline the **topic sentence**.
2. Underline the **examples** that support the main point.
3. Circle the **transitions**.
4. Does the paragraph have the Four Basics of Good Illustration (p. 132)? Why or why not? _____
   _____
   _____

5. Does the paragraph use a particular kind of organization, like time, space, or importance? Does that choice help the paragraph's effectiveness or not? _____
   _____
   _____

Professional Illustration Essay

Susan Adams
The Weirdest Job Interview Questions and How to Handle Them

Vocabulary development
Underline these words as you read the illustration essay.
- **dovetailed:** matched
- **swimmingly:** smoothly; well
- **perfunctory:** quick
- **studiously:** thoroughly; carefully
- **woefully:** seriously; regrettably
- **tracheotomy:** a cut made into the throat to open a blocked airway
- **grueling:** difficult; tiring
- **Maserati:** a fast Italian sports car
- **Bentley:** a British luxury car known more for elegance than speed

Susan Adams is a senior editor at Forbes, a major publisher of business news. Since joining Forbes in 1995, Adams has written about a wide variety of subjects, including the art and auction market. Previously, she was a reporter for the *MacNeil/Lehrer NewsHour*. Adams holds a B.A. from Brown University and a J.D. from Yale University Law School.

Every week, Adams writes an advice column for Forbes .com, and the following is one of those columns. In it, she gives examples of some of the stranger questions that come up in job interviews.

PREDICT Think of one weird question that might be asked in a job interview.

1 I once interviewed for a job with a documentary producer who made boring if well-meaning films for public TV. By way of preparation, I studied up on the producer's projects and gave a lot of thought to how my interests and experience dovetailed with his. Our chat went swimmingly until he asked me a question that caught me completely off guard: "Who is your favorite comedian?"

2 Wait a second, I thought. Comedy is the opposite of what this guy does. My mind did back flips while I desperately searched for a comedian who might be a favorite of a tweedy, bearded liberal Democrat. After maybe 30 seconds too long, I blurted out my personal favorite: David Alan Grier, an African-American funnyman on the weekly Fox TV show *In Living Color*. My potential boss looked at me blankly as I babbled about how much I liked Grier's characters, especially Antoine Merriweather, one of the two gay reviewers in the brilliantly hilarious sketch "Men on Film."

3 Wrong answer. I had derailed the interview. My potential employer asked me a few more perfunctory questions and then saw me to the door.

4 We all prepare studiously for job interviews, doing our homework about our potential employers and compiling short but detailed stories to illustrate our accomplishments, but how in the world do we prep for an off-the-wall interview question?

5 Glassdoor.com, a three-year-old Sausalito, California, Web site that bills itself as "the TripAdvisor for careers," has compiled a list of "top oddball interview questions" for two years running. Glassdoor gets its information directly from employees who work at 120,000 companies.

Crazy as it sounds, an interviewer at Schlumberger, the giant Houston oilfield services provider, once asked some poor job applicant, "What was your best MacGyver moment?," referring to a 1980s action-adventure TV show. At Goldman Sachs, the question was, "If you were shrunk to the size of a pencil and put in a blender, how would you get out?" At Deloitte, "How many ridges [are there] around a quarter?" At AT&T, "If you were a superhero, which superhero would you be?" And at Boston Consulting: "How many hair salons are there in Japan?"

6 **REFLECT** Pick one of the questions in this paragraph. How would you answer it?

No matter where you apply for work, there is a chance you could get a question from left field. According to Rusty Rueff—a consultant at Glassdoor who is the author of *Talent Force: A New Manifesto for the Human Side of Business* and former head of human resources at PepsiCo and Electronic Arts—most job applicants are woefully unprepared for off-the-wall questions. "Ninety percent of people don't know how to deal with them," he says. Like me, they freeze and their minds go blank.

To deal with that, Rueff advises, first you have to realize that the interviewer isn't trying to make you look stupid, as stupid as the question may seem. For instance, the MacGyver question is meant as an invitation to talk about how you got out of a tough jam. "They're not looking for you to tell about the time you took out your ballpoint and did a tracheotomy," Rueff notes. Rather, you can probably extract an answer from one of the achievement stories you prepared in advance.

With a question like "How many hair salons are there in Japan," the interviewer is giving you an opportunity to demonstrate your thought processes. Rueff says you should think out loud, like the contestants on *Who Wants to Be a Millionaire?* You might start by saying, We'd have to know the population of Japan, and then we'd have to figure out what percentage of them get their hair done and how often. Rueff says it's fine to pull out a pen and paper and start doing some calculations right there in the interview.

Connie Thanasoulis-Cerrachio, a career services consultant at Vault.com, agrees with Rueff. "These are called case interview questions," she says. Another example, which may seem equally impossible to answer: Why are manhole covers round?

In fact the manhole cover question, and "How would you move Mt. Fuji?," were brought to light in a 2003 book, *How Would You Move Mount Fuji? Microsoft's Cult of the Puzzle: How the World's Smartest Company Selects the Most Creative Thinkers*. Microsoft's grueling interview process often includes such problem-solving and logic questions. Just start thinking through the question, out loud, Thanasoulis-Cerrachio advises. "I would say, a round manhole cover could keep the framework of the tunnel stronger, because a round frame is much stronger than a square frame," she suggests. In fact, there are several reasons, including the fact that a round lid can't fall into the hole the way a square one can and the fact that it can be rolled.

12 Business schools teach students how to deal with case interview questions, and Vault has even put out a book on the subject, *Vault Guide to the Case Interview*.

13 Other weird-seeming questions, like "If you were a brick in a wall, which brick would you be and why," or "If you could be any animal, what would you be and why," are really just invitations to show a side of your personality. Thanasoulis-Cerrachio says a friend who is chief executive of a market research company used to ask applicants what kind of car they would be. "She wanted someone fast, who thought quickly," Thanasoulis-Cerrachio says. "She wanted someone who wanted to be a Maserati, not a Bentley." For the brick question, Thanasoulis-Cerrachio advises saying something like, "I would want to be a foundational brick because I'm a solid person. You can build on my experience and I will never let you down."

14 According to Rueff and Thanasoulis-Cerrachio, my comedian question was also a behavioral question, a test of my personality. "You gave a fine answer," says Rueff. Maybe. But I didn't get the job.

EVALUATE Based on Adams's observations, do you think weird interview questions are a good idea or a bad idea?

TIP For reading advice, see Chapter 1.

1. In your own words, state Adams's **main point**. _____
   _____
   _____
   _____

2. Underline the examples of weird interview questions.

3. Circle the **transitional words** in paragraph 8. Can you find more places to add transitions? _____

4. What do you think of this essay? Do you have a better understanding of how to answer strange questions in job interviews? _____
   _____

Respond to one of the following assignments in a paragraph or essay.

1. Write about your own experiences with job interviews, giving examples of anything you found challenging—the stress of preparing for the interview, questions or awkward moments during the interview, and so on. If you were able to address these challenges in any way, explain how. (If you have not had many job interviews, write about the experiences of a friend or relative.)

2. Adams discusses how unusual interview questions can provide useful information. Come up with at least three odd interview questions, and explain how each one would provide an employer with helpful information.

3. In your opinion, what professions would have the strangest interview questions? Write about the questions that employers in these professions might ask, and give examples of answers that would help interviewees get the job. (To get some ideas, you might investigate different professions on the Internet.)

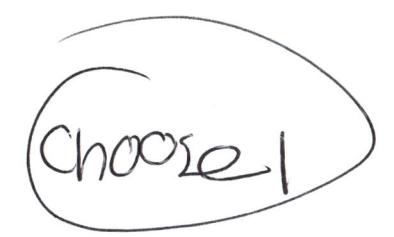

Choose 1

Write Your Own Illustration

In this section, you will write your own illustration based on one of the following assignments. For help, refer to the How to Write Illustration checklist on page 150.

ASSIGNMENT OPTIONS Writing about College, Work, and Everyday Life

Write an illustration paragraph, essay, or other document (as described below) on one of the following topics or on one of your own choice. If you responded to the idea journal prompt on page 134, you might develop that writing further.

COLLEGE

- Describe your goals for this course, making sure to explain the benefits of achieving each goal.

- If you are still deciding on a degree program or major, identify at least two areas of study that interest you. To get some ideas, you might refer to a course catalog. Also, consider visiting a counselor at your college's guidance office or career center. The counselor might be able to recommend some study programs to you based on your goals and interests. Next, write about the areas of study that appeal to you the most, giving examples of what you would learn and explaining how each of your choices matches your goals and interests.

- Produce a one- or two-page newsletter for other students in your class on one of the following topics. Make sure to describe each club, opportunity, and event in enough detail for readers. Also, include contact information, as well as hours and locations for events and club meetings.

    - Student clubs
    - Volunteer opportunities
    - Upcoming campus events (such as lectures, movies, and sports events)
    - Upcoming events in the larger community

COMMUNITY CONNECTIONS

EVELKA RANKINS edits a weekly newsletter that lists events of interest to fellow students at her college. Getting more involved in college and community activities, as Evelka did, can help you feel more connected to others and can even improve the chances that you will stay in school.

For more on this story, ways to make community connections, and writing assignments, visit bedfordstmartins.com/realwriting.

WORK

- What is the best or worst job you have ever had? Give examples of what made it the best or worst job.

- Thinking like a television producer, find a category of jobs—such as "dirty jobs," the name of a popular cable show—that a TV audience would find strange and interesting. Then, give examples of jobs in the category. (Examples of professions covered in the show *Dirty Jobs* include maggot farming, camel ranching, and bologna making.) Give enough details about each job to make it clear why that job is unusual. To get some ideas, you might type "strange jobs" into a search engine.

- Think of the job you would most like to have after graduation. Then, write a list of your skills—both current ones and ones you will be building in college—that are relevant to the job. To identify skills you will be building through your degree program, you might refer to a course catalog. To identify relevant work skills, consider your past or present jobs as well as internships or other work experiences you would like to have before graduation. Finally, write a cover letter explaining why you are the best candidate for your ideal job. Be sure to provide several examples of your skills, referring to the list that you prepared.

TIP For sample cover letters and advice on writing these letters, visit bedfordstmartins.com/realwriting.

EVERYDAY LIFE

- Write about stresses in your life or things that you like about your life. Give plenty of details for each example.

- Give examples of memories that have stayed with you for a long time. For each memory, provide enough details so that readers will be able to share your experience.

- Identify at least three public improvements you think would benefit a significant number of people in your community, such as the addition of sidewalks in residential areas to encourage exercise. These improvements should not include changes, such as the creation of a boat dock on a local lake, that would benefit only a small portion of the community. Then, in a letter to the editor of your local paper, describe each suggested improvement in detail, and explain why it would be an asset to the community.

ASSIGNMENT OPTIONS Reading and Writing Critically

Complete one of the following assignments, which ask you to apply the critical thinking, reading, and writing skills discussed in Chapter 1.

Writing Critically about Readings

Both Susan Adams's "The Weirdest Job Interview Questions and How to Handle Them" (p. 144) and Frances Cole Jones's "Don't Work in a Goat's Stomach" (p. 199) give advice in a humorous way. Read or review both of these pieces, and then follow these steps:

1. **Summarize**   Briefly summarize the works, listing major examples.

2. **Analyze**   What questions do the essays raise for you? Are there any other issues you wish they had covered?

3. **Synthesize**   Using examples from both Adams's and Jones's essays and from your own experience, discuss how the right kind of advice can help people achieve success.

4. **Evaluate**   Which essay, Adams's or Jones's, do you think is more effective? Why? Does the writers' humor help get their points across? Why or why not? In writing your evaluation, you might look back on your responses to step 2.

TIP For a reminder of how to summarize, analyze, synthesize, and evaluate, see the Reading and Writing Critically box on pages 16–17.

Writing about Images

Study the photograph below, and complete the following steps.

1. **Read the image**   Ask yourself: What details does the photographer focus on? How do the colors and lights affect you as a viewer? What main impression does the picture make? (For more information on reading images, see Chapter 1.)

2. **Write an illustration**   The photograph shows a luxury liner whose bright, colorful lights attract onlookers and potential customers. Write an illustration paragraph or essay about businesses that draw customers with colorful displays, loud music, or some other appeal to the senses. Include the types of details you examined in step 1.

Writing to Solve a Problem

Read or review the discussion of problem solving in Chapter 1 (pp. 24–26). Then, consider the following problem.

> Your college is increasing its tuition by $500 next year, and you do not think that you can continue. You have done well so far, and you really want to get a college degree.

ASSIGNMENT: Rather than just giving up and dropping out next year, as many students do, working in a small group or on your own, make a list of resources you could consult to help you, and explain how they might help. You might want to start with the following sentence:

> Before dropping out of school for financial reasons, students should consult _____ because _____.

For a paragraph: Name your best resource, and give examples of how this person or office might help you.

For an essay: Name your three best resources, and give examples of how they might help you.

CHECKLIST: HOW TO WRITE ILLUSTRATION

STEPS	DETAILS
☐ **Narrow and explore your topic.** See Chapter 3.	• Make the topic more specific. • Prewrite to get ideas about the narrowed topic.
☐ **Write a topic sentence (paragraph) or thesis statement (essay).** See Chapter 4.	• State what you want your readers to understand about your topic.
☐ **Support your point.** See Chapter 5.	• Come up with examples and details to show, explain, or prove your main point to readers.
☐ **Write a draft.** See Chapter 6.	• Make a plan that puts examples in a logical order. • Include a topic sentence (paragraph) or thesis statement (essay) and all the supporting examples and details.
☐ **Revise your draft.** See Chapter 7.	• Make sure it has *all* the Four Basics of Good Illustration. • Make sure you include transitions to move readers smoothly from one example to the next.
☐ **Edit your revised draft.** See Parts 4 through 7.	• Correct errors in grammar, spelling, word use, and punctuation.

Chapter Review

1. Illustration is writing that _____
   _____

2. What are the Four Basics of Good Illustration? _____
   _____
   _____
   _____

3. Write sentences using the following vocabulary words: *retain, align, objectives, studiously, woefully, grueling.* _____
   _____
   _____

reflect Write for 2 minutes about what you have learned about writing illustration.

LEARNING JOURNAL
Reread your idea journal entry from page 134. Write another entry about the same topic, using what you have learned about illustration.

10

Description

Writing That Creates Pictures in Words

> **YOU KNOW THIS**
>
> You use description every day:
> - You describe what someone looks like.
> - You describe an item you want to buy.
>
> **write** for 2 minutes about what you know about writing description.

Understand What Description Is

Description is writing that creates a clear and vivid impression of a person, place, or thing, often by appealing to the physical senses.

Four Basics of Good Description

1. It creates a main impression—an overall effect, feeling, or image—about the topic.
2. It uses specific examples to support the main impression.
3. It supports those examples with details that appeal to the five senses: sight, hearing, smell, taste, and touch.
4. It brings a person, place, or physical object to life for the reader.

In the following student paragraph, the numbers and colors correspond to the Four Basics of Good Description.

Scars are stories written on a person's skin and sometimes on his heart. **1** My scar is not very big or very visible. **2** It is only about three inches long and an inch wide. It is on my knee, so it is usually covered, unseen. **3** It puckers the skin around it, and the texture of the scar itself is smoother than my real skin. It is flesh-colored, almost like a raggedy bandage. The story on my skin is a small one. **1** The story on my heart, though, is much deeper. **2** It was night, very cold, **3** my breath pluming into the frigid air. I took deep breaths that smelled like winter, piercing through my nasal passages and into my lungs as I walked to my car. I saw a couple making out against the wall of a building I was nearing. **2** I smiled and thought about them making their own heat. **3** I thought I saw steam coming from them, but maybe I imagined that. As I got near, I heard a familiar giggle: my girlfriend's. Then I saw her scarlet scarf, one I had given her, along with soft red leather gloves. I turned and ran, before they could see me. There was loud pounding in my ears, from the inside, sounding and feeling as if my brain had just become the loudest bass I had ever heard. My head throbbed, and slipping on some ice, I crashed to the ground, landing on my hands and knees, ripping my pants. I knew my knee was bleeding, even in the dark. I didn't care: **4** That scar would heal. The other one would take a lot longer.

Seeing Description

write Describe this photograph in detail. First, look at the image carefully. Then write ten words you want to use in your description.

Being able to describe something or someone accurately and in detail is important in many situations.

gives mental picture to person.

COLLEGE On a physical therapy test, you describe the symptoms you observed in a patient.

example

WRITING DIFFERENT KINDS OF PARAGRAPHS AND ESSAYS

Chapter 10 • Description

WRITER AT WORK

CELIA HYDE: Writing descriptions helps solve crimes.

(See Celia Hyde's **PROFILE OF SUCCESS** on p. 161.)

IDEA JOURNAL Describe what you are wearing.

| WORK | You write a memo to your boss describing how the office could be arranged for increased efficiency. |
| EVERYDAY LIFE | You describe something you lost to the lost-and-found clerk at a store. |

In college assignments, the word *describe* may mean *tell about* or *report*. When an assignment asks you to actually describe a person, place, or thing, however, you will need to use the kinds of specific descriptive details discussed later in this chapter.

Main Point in Description

In description, the **main point** is the main impression you want to create for your readers. To help you discover your main point, complete the following sentence:

| MAIN POINT IN DESCRIPTION | What is most interesting, vivid, and important to me about this topic is . . . |

If you do not have a main impression about your topic, think about how it smells, sounds, looks, tastes, or feels.

PRACTICE 1 Finding a Main Impression

For the following general topics, jot down four impressions that appeal to you, and circle the one you would use as a main impression. Base your choice on what is most interesting, vivid, and important to you.

   EXAMPLE:

   Topic: A vandalized car

   Impressions: *wrecked, smashed, damaged, battered*

1. Topic: A movie-theater lobby

   Impressions: _____

2. Topic: A fireworks display

   Impressions: _____

3. Topic: An elderly person

   Impressions: _____

4. Topic: The room you are in

   Impressions: _____

The topic sentence (paragraph) or thesis statement (essay) in description usually contains both your narrowed topic and your main impression. Here is a topic sentence for a description paragraph:

Topic + Main impression = Topic sentence

The view from the shore of Fisher Lake calms me every time I see it.

Remember that a topic for an essay can be a little broader than one for a paragraph.

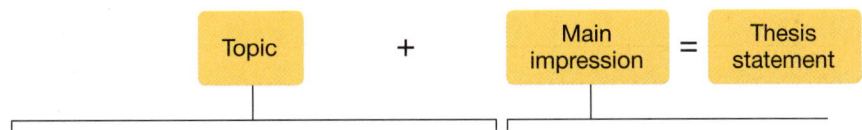

Topic + Main impression = Thesis statement

The views from my sky-high welding jobs are more stunning than any seen through an office window.

Whereas the topic sentence is focused on just one location and view, the thesis statement sets up descriptions of different views from different sites.

To be effective, your topic sentence or thesis statement should be specific. You can make it specific by adding details that appeal to the senses.

TIP Sometimes, the same main point can be used for a paragraph and an essay, but the essay must develop this point in more detail. (See pp. 69–70.)

PRACTICE 2 Writing a Statement of Your Main Impression

For three of the items from Practice 1, write the topic and your main impression. Then, write a statement of your main impression. Finally, revise the statement to make the main impression sharper and more specific.

EXAMPLE:

Topic/Main impression: *A vandalized car/battered*

Statement: *The vandalized car on the side of the highway was battered.*

More specific: *The shell of a car on the side of the road was dented all over, apparently from a bat or club, and surrounded by broken glass.*

1. Topic/Main impression: _____

   Statement: _____

   More specific: _____
   _____

2. Topic/Main impression: _____

   Statement: _____

   More specific: _____
   _____

3. Topic/Main impression: _____

   Statement: _____

   More specific: _____
   _____

Support in Description

In description, **support** consists of the specific examples and details that help readers experience the sights, sounds, smells, tastes, and textures of your topic. Your description should get your main impression across to readers. Here are some qualities to consider.

TIP For tools to build your vocabulary, visit the *Student Site for Real Writing* at bedfordstmartins.com/realwriting.

TIP When writing descriptions, consider this advice from writer Rhys Alexander: "Detail makes the difference between boring and terrific writing. It's the difference between a pencil sketch and a lush oil painting. As a writer, words are your paint. Use all the colors."

SIGHT	SOUND	SMELL
Colors?	Loud/soft?	Sweet/sour?
Shapes?	Piercing/soothing?	Sharp/mild?
Sizes?	Continuous/off and on?	Good? (Like what?)
Patterns?	Pleasant/unpleasant? (How?)	Bad? (Rotten?)
Shiny/dull?	Does it sound like anything else?	New? (New what? Leather? Plastic?)
Does it look like anything else?		Old?
		Does it smell like anything else?

TASTE	TOUCH
Good? (What does "good" taste like?)	Hard/soft?
Bad? (What does "bad" taste like?)	Liquid/solid?
Bitter/sugary? Metallic?	Rough/smooth?
Burning? Spicy?	Hot/cold?
Does it taste like anything else?	Dry/oily?
	Textures?
	Does it feel like anything else?

WRITING DIFFERENT KINDS OF PARAGRAPHS AND ESSAYS
Understand What Description Is

The paragraph and essay models on pages 158–59 use the topic sentence (paragraph) and thesis statement (essay) from the Main Point section of this chapter. Both models include the support used in all descriptive writing—examples that communicate the writer's main impression, backed up by specific sensory details. In the essay model, however, the major support points (examples) are topic sentences for individual paragraphs.

PRACTICE 3 Finding Details to Support a Main Impression

Read the statements below, and write four sensory details you might use to support the main impression.

EXAMPLE:

The physical sensations of a day at the beach are as vivid as the visual ones.

   a. *softness of the sand*

   b. *push and splash of waves*

   c. *chill of the water*

   d. *smoothness of worn stones and beach glass*, feel of sun.

1. My favorite meal smells as good as it tastes.

   a. _____
   b. _____
   c. _____
   d. _____

2. The new office building has a contemporary look.

   a. _____
   b. _____
   c. _____
   d. _____

3. A classroom during an exam echoes with the "sounds of silence."

   a. _____
   b. _____
   c. _____
   d. _____

PARAGRAPHS VS. ESSAYS IN DESCRIPTION

For more on the important features of description, see the Four Basics of Good Description on page 152.

Paragraph Form

Topic sentence

Support 1 (first example)

The view from the shore of Fisher Lake calms me every time I see it. Closest to the shore is the lake's smooth surface, blue by day and sparkling black at night. My favorite time to stand on the shore is midsummer at twilight, when I watch the water's blue darken and become more general, blotting out the day and all its troubles. I listen to waves lapping the dock and think my thoughts, or just let my mind clear. On nights with a bright moon, I stare out at the path of light across the water, losing track of time and sometimes even of myself. Farther out, on the opposite shore, a forest of pine trees reminds me of the cool shade I have enjoyed while hiking there. The pine smell is the first thing to trigger the memories. Evenings when there is still enough light, I look for the break in the trees where the main trail starts, thinking of the many times I have walked it. During the hottest, most trying summer of my life, the cool beauty of the trailside trees, ferns, and moss soothed my nerves and brought me back down to earth. Beyond the forest are rolling hills, soft gray in the morning and near dusk. The expression "old as the hills" comes to mind, and it feels like a just description, not an insult. The soft gray hulk of them makes me think of an ancient, huge, and eternally sleeping creature—something that predated me by millions of years and will outlive me for millions more. For some reason, I always find these thoughts comforting. And they are just one reason that standing on the shore of Fisher Lake is better for me than any medicine.

Support 2 (second example)

Support 3 (third example)

Concluding sentence

Main Point: Often, narrower for a paragraph than for an essay: While the topic sentence (paragraph) is focused on just one location and view, the thesis statement (essay) sets up descriptions of different views from different sites.

Examples Supporting the Main Point (the Writer's Main Impression)

Details about the Examples: Usually, 1 to 3 sentences per example for paragraphs and 3 to 8 sentences per example for essays.

Conclusion

Think Critically As You Write Description

ASK YOURSELF

- Have I included enough examples and details to get across my main impression and to bring my subject to life?
- Do the examples and details appeal to more than one of the senses (sight, hearing, smell, taste, and touch)?

Essay Form

1

I have worked in many places, from a basement-level machine shop to a cubicle in a tenth-floor insurance office. Now that I am in the construction industry, I want to sing the praises of one employment b[**Thesis statement**] not get enough attention: The views from my sky-high welding jobs have been more stunning than any seen through an office window.

From a platform at my latest job, on a high-rise, the streets below look like scenes from a miniature village. The cars and trucks—even the rushing p[**Topic sentence 1 (first example)**] me of my nephews' motorized toys. S breeze carries up to me one of the few reminders that what I see is real: the smell of sausage or roasting chestnuts from street vendors, the honking of taxis or the scream of sirens, the dizzying clouds of diesel smoke. Once, the streets below me were taken over for a fair, and during my lunch break, I sat on a beam and watched the scene below. I spotted the usual things—packs of people strolling by concession stands or game tents, and bands playing to crowds at different ends of the fair. As I finished my lunch, I saw two small flames near the edge

2

of one band stage, nothing burning, nothing to fear. It was, I soon realized, an acrobat carrying two torches. I watched her climb high and walk a rope, juggling the torches as the crowd looked up and I lo[**Topic sentence 2 (second example)**] fascinated.

Even more impressive are the sights from an oil rig. Two years ago, I worked on a rig in Prudhoe Bay, Alaska, right at the water's edge. In the long days of summer, I loved to watch the changing light in the sky and on the water: bright to darker blue as the hours passed, and at day's end, a dying gold. At the greatest heights I could see white dots of ships far out at sea, and looking inland, I might spot musk ox or bears roaming in the distance. In the long winter dark, we worked by spotlights, which blotted the views below. But I still remember one time near nightfall when the spotlights suddenly flashed off. As my eyes adjusted, a crowd of caribou emerged below like ghosts. They snuffled the snow for foo[**Topic sentence 3 (third example)**] to us.

To me, the most amazing views are those from bridges high over rivers. In 2006, I had the privilege of

3

briefly working on one of the tallest bridge-observatories in the world, over the Penobscot River in Maine. As many tourists now do, I reached the height of the observatory's top deck, 437 feet. Unlike them, however, my visits were routine and labor-intensive, giving me little time to appreciate the beauty all around me. But on clear days, during breaks and at the end of our shift, my coworkers and I would admire the wide, sapphire-colored river as it flowed to Penobscot Bay. Looking south, we would track the Maine coast's winding to the Camden Hills. Looking east, we would spot Acadia National Park, the famous Mount Desert Island offshore in the mist. Each sight made up a panoramic view that I will never forget.

[**Concluding paragraph**] My line of work roots me in no one place, and it has a generous share of discomforts and dangers. But there are many reasons I would never trade it for another, and one of the biggest is the height from which it lets me see the world. For stretches of time, I feel nearly superhuman.

Organization in Description

TIP For more on these orders of organization, see pages 78–79.

Description can use any of the orders of organization—**time**, **space**, or **importance**—depending on your purpose. If you are writing to create a main impression of an event (for example, a description of fireworks), you might use time order. If you are describing what someone or something looks like, you might use space order, the strategy used in the paragraph model on page 158. If one detail about your topic is stronger than the others, you could use order of importance and leave that detail for last. This approach is taken in the essay model on page 159.

ORDER	SEQUENCE
Time	first to last/last to first, most recent to least recent/least recent to most recent
Space	top to bottom/bottom to top, right to left/left to right, near to far/far to near
Importance	end with detail that will make the strongest impression

Use **transitions** to move your readers from one sensory detail to the next. Usually, transitions should match your order of organization.

Common Transitions in Description

TIME

as	finally	next	then
at last	first	now	when
before/after	last	second	while
during	later	since	
eventually	meanwhile	soon	

SPACE

above	beneath	inside	over
across	beside	near	to the left/right
at the bottom/top	beyond	next to	to the side
behind	farther/further	on top of	under/underneath
below	in front of	opposite	where

IMPORTANCE

especially	more/even more	most vivid
in particular	most	strongest

WRITING DIFFERENT KINDS OF PARAGRAPHS AND ESSAYS
Read and Analyze Description

PRACTICE 4 Using Transitions in Description

Read the paragraph that follows, and fill in the blanks with transitions.

   I saw the kitchen at Morley's Place on my first day assisting the town restaurant inspector. _____, Morley's was empty of customers, which made sense for 3 p.m. on a Tuesday. _____ my boss and I saw the kitchen, we hoped the restaurant would stay empty. _____ from the kitchen entrance was the food-prep counter, which was covered with a faint layer of grime. _____ the counter were three food bins. _____ I aimed my flashlight into one bin, numerous roaches scuttled away from the light. _____ the counter, a fan whirred loudly in an open window. _____ the stove, we discovered a mouse trap holding a shriveled, long-dead mouse. Because of the violations, the Health Department closed Morley's Place.

Read and Analyze Description

Reading examples of description will help you write your own. In the first example below, police chief Celia Hyde shows how she uses description in a crime scene report. The second example is a description paragraph by a student, and the third is a description essay by a professional writer. As you read, pay attention to the vocabulary, and answer the questions in the margin. They will help you read critically.

CRITICAL READING
- Preview
- Read
- Pause
- Review

See pages 9–12.

PROFILE OF SUCCESS

Description in the Real World

Background When I graduated from high school, I was not interested in academics. I took some courses at a community college but then dropped out to travel. After traveling and trying several different colleges, I returned home. The police chief in town was a family friend and encouraged me to think about law enforcement. I entered that field and have been there since.

Colleges Greenfield Community College, Mt. Wachusett Community College, Fort Lauderdale Community College

Employer Town of Bolton, Massachusetts

Celia Hyde
Chief of Police

Writing at work As chief of police, I do many kinds of writing: policies and procedures for the officers to follow; responses to attorneys' requests for information; letters, reports, and budgets; interviews with witnesses; statements from victims and criminals; accident reports. In all of the writing I do, detail, clarity, and precision are essential. I have to choose my words carefully to avoid any confusion or misunderstanding.

How Celia uses description When I am called to a crime scene, I have to write a report that describes the scene precisely and in detail.

Celia's Description

The following report is one example of the descriptive reports Celia writes.

Report, breaking and entering scene
Response to burglar alarm, 17:00 hours

The house at 123 Main Street is situated off the road with a long, narrow driveway and no visible neighbors. The dense fir trees along the drive block natural light, though it was almost dusk and getting dark. There was snow on the driveway from a recent storm. I observed one set of fresh tire marks entering the driveway and a set of footprints exiting it.

The homeowner, Mr. Smith, had been awakened by the sounds of smashing glass and the squeaking of the door as it opened. He felt a cold draft from the stairway and heard a soft shuffle of feet crossing the dining room. Smith descended the stairs to investigate and was met at the bottom by the intruder, who shoved him against the wall and ran out the front door.

While awaiting backup, I obtained a description of the intruder from Mr. Smith. The subject was a white male, approximately 25–30 years of age and 5′9″–5′11″ in height. He had jet-black hair of medium length, and it was worn slicked back from his forehead. He wore a salt-and-pepper, closely shaved beard and had a birthmark on his neck the size of a dime. The subject was wearing a black nylon jacket with some logo on it in large white letters, a blue plaid shirt, and blue jeans.

---

1. What is your **main impression** of the scene and of the intruder? _____
   _____

2. Underline the **details** that support the main impression.

3. What senses do the details appeal to? _____

4. How is the description organized? _____

Student Description Paragraph

Alessandra Cepeda
Bird Rescue

Alessandra Cepeda became deeply involved in animal welfare during her time at Bunker Hill Community College (BHCC), from which she received associate's degrees in education and early childhood education. While at BHCC, Cepeda assisted the Humane Society with animal-rescue efforts, and she also helped the Phi Beta Kappa organization become more involved in animal welfare.

In the following paragraph, Cepeda describes the scene at a storage unit containing abandoned birds. One of those birds was Samantha, shown in the photo with Cepeda.

When the owner opened the empty storage unit, we could not believe that any living creature could have survived under such horrible conditions. The inside was complete darkness, with no windows and no ventilation. The air hit us with the smell of rot and decay. A flashlight revealed three birds, quiet and huddled in the back corner. They were quivering and looked sickly. Two of the birds had injured wings, hanging from them uselessly at odd angles, obviously broken. They were exotic birds who should have had bright and colorful feathers, but the floor of the unit was covered in the feathers they had molted. We entered slowly and retrieved the abused birds. I cried at how such beautiful and helpless creatures had been mistreated. We adopted two of them, and our Samantha is now eight years old, with beautiful green feathers topped off with a brilliant blue and red head. She talks, flies, and is a wonderful pet who is dearly loved and, I admit, very spoiled. She deserves it after such a rough start to her life.

1. Double-underline the **topic sentence**.
2. What main impression does the writer create? _Depressing in begin, sad in end._
3. Underline the **sensory details** (sight, sound, smell, taste, texture) that create the main impression.
4. Does the paragraph have the Four Basics of Good Description (p. 152)? Why or why not? _____

Professional Description Essay

Oscar Hijuelos

Memories of New York City Snow

Vocabulary development

Underline these words as you read the description essay.

circa: [taken] around
aloft: high
trestles: support structures
tenement houses: apartment buildings, often crowded and in poor shape
girded: reinforced
burlesque houses: theaters that offer live, often humorous performances and/or striptease acts
palatial: palace-like
perilous: dangerous
nary: not even
stint: brief job
toque: hat
to the hilt: [dressed] in the fanciest clothing
nostalgia: a longing for something from the past
connotation: meaning or association
inaccessible divinity: unreachable god

Oscar Hijuelos, the son of Cuban immigrants, was born in New York City in 1951. After receiving undergraduate and master's degrees from the City University of New York, he took a job at an advertising firm and wrote fiction at night. Since then, he has published numerous novels. His first, *The Mambo Kings Play Songs of Love* (1989), was awarded the Pulitzer Prize for fiction, making Hijuelos the first Hispanic writer to receive this honor. His most recent novels include *A Simple Habana Melody* (2002), *Dark Dude* (2008), and *Beautiful Maria of My Soul* (2010). Hijuelos has also published a memoir, *Thoughts Without Cigarettes* (2011).

The following essay was taken from the anthology *Metropolis Found* (2003). In it, Hijuelos describes a New York City winter from the perspective of new immigrants, noting the emotions that the season inspired in them.

PREDICT Why might snow be significant to the author's father and godfather?

1   For immigrants of my parents' generation, who had first come to New York City from the much warmer climate of Cuba in the mid-1940s, the very existence of snow was a source of fascination. A black-and-white photograph that I have always loved, circa 1948, its surface cracked like that of a thawing ice-covered pond, features my father, Pascual, and my godfather, Horacio, fresh up from **Oriente Province**,[1] posing in a snow-covered meadow in Central Park. Decked out in long coats, scarves, and black-rimmed hats, they are holding, in their be-gloved hands, a huge chunk of hardened snow. Trees and their straggly witch's hair branches, glimmering with ice and frost, recede into the distance behind them. They stand on a field of whiteness, the two men seemingly afloat in midair, as if they were being held aloft by the magical substance itself.

2   That they bothered to have this photograph taken—I suppose to send back to family in Cuba—has always been a source of enchantment for me. That something so common to winters in New York would strike them as an object of exotic admiration has always spoken volumes about the newness—and innocence—of their immigrants' experience. How thrilling it all must have seemed to them, for their New York was so very different from the small town surrounded by farms in eastern Cuba that they hailed from. Their New York was a fanciful and bustling city of endless sidewalks and unimaginably high buildings; of great bridges and twisting outdoor elevated train trestles; of walkup tenement houses

---

1. **Oriente Province:** a former province of Cuba, in the eastern part of the country

with mysteriously dark basements, and subways that burrowed through an underworld of girded tunnels; of dancehalls, burlesque houses, and palatial department stores with their complement of Christmas Salvation Army Santa Clauses on every street corner. Delightful and perilous, their New York was a city of incredibly loud noises, of police and air raid sirens and factory whistles and subway rumble; a city where people sometimes shushed you for speaking Spanish in a public place, or could be unforgiving if you did not speak English well or seemed to be of a different ethnic background. (My father was once nearly hit by a garbage can that had been thrown off the rooftop of a building as he was walking along La Salle Street in upper Manhattan.)

Even so, New York represented the future. The city meant jobs and money. Newly arrived, an aunt of mine went to work for Pan Am; another aunt, as a Macy's saleslady. My own mother, speaking nary a word of English, did a stint in the garment district as a seamstress. During the war some family friends, like my godfather, were eventually drafted, while others ended up as factory laborers. Landing a job at the Biltmore Men's Bar, my father joined the hotel and restaurant workers' union, paid his first weekly dues, and came home one day with a brand new white chef's toque in hand. Just about everybody found work, often for low pay and ridiculously long hours. And while the men of that generation worked a lot of overtime, or a second job, they always had their day or two off. Dressed to the hilt, they'd leave their uptown neighborhoods and make an excursion to another part of the city—perhaps to one of the grand movie palaces of Times Square or to beautiful Central Park, as my father and godfather, and their ladies, had once done, in the aftermath of a snowfall.

Snow, such as it can only fall in New York City, was not just about the cold and wintry differences that mark the weather of the north. It was about a purity that would descend upon the grayness of its streets like a heaven of silence, the city's complexity and bustle abruptly subdued. But as beautiful as it could be, it was also something that provoked nostalgia; I am certain that my father would miss Cuba on some bitterly cold days. I remember that whenever we were out on a walk and it began to snow, my father would stop and look up at the sky, with wonderment—what he was seeing I don't know. Perhaps that's why to this day my own associations with a New York City snowfall have a mystical connotation, as if the presence of snow really meant that some kind of inaccessible divinity had settled his breath upon us.

REFLECT What main impression do these descriptions of the city create?

REFLECT What types of weather do you associate with particular feelings or moods?

1. Double-underline the **thesis statement**. ☆ blue
2. Underline the **sensory details** (sight, sound, smell, taste, texture).
   ☆ red

TIP For reading advice, see Chapter 1.

3. Circle the **transitions**.
4. Does the essay create a clear picture of New York City in the winter? Why or why not? _____

Respond to one of the following assignments in a paragraph or essay.

1. Describe a place that is important to you or associated with significant memories. It might be a city, a favorite park, a friend's or relative's home, or a vacation spot.
2. Describe an outdoor scene from your favorite season. You might work from a personal photograph taken during that season.
3. Describe a person who has played a major role in your life. Try to include sensory details that go beyond the person's appearance. For instance, you might describe the sight of his or her usual surroundings, the sound of his or her voice, or the texture of a favorite piece of clothing.

Write Your Own Description

In this section, you will write your own description based on one of the following assignments. For help, refer to the How to Write Description checklist on page 169.

ASSIGNMENT OPTIONS Writing about College, Work, and Everyday Life

Write a description paragraph or essay on one of the following topics or on one of your own choice. If you responded to the idea journal prompt on page 154, you might develop that writing further.

COLLEGE

- Describe the sights, sounds, smells, and tastes in the cafeteria or another dining spot on campus.
- Find a place where you can get a good view of your campus (for instance, a window on an upper floor of one of the buildings). Then, describe the scene using space order (p. 160).
- Think back on a place or scene on campus that has made a strong sensory impression on you. Then, describe the place or scene with specific examples and details, and explain why it made such an impression on you.

WORK

- Describe your workplace, including as many sensory details as you can.
- Describe your boss or a colleague you work with closely. First, think of the main impression you get from this person. Then, choose details that would make your impression clear to readers.

- Take a quick look at Frances Cole Jones's "Don't Work in a Goat's Stomach" (p. 199). Have you ever worked with anyone who creates the kind of messes she discusses? If so, describe the person's work space and/or messes in detail.

EVERYDAY LIFE

- Describe a favorite photograph, using as many details as possible. For a good example of a photograph description, see the first paragraph of Oscar Hijuelos's essay (p. 164).

- Describe a holiday celebration from your past, including as many sensory details as possible. Think back on the people who attended, the food served, the decorations, and so on.

- Visit an organization that serves your community, such as an animal shelter or a food pantry. During your visit, take notes about what you see. Later, write a detailed description of the scene.

ASSIGNMENT OPTIONS Reading and Writing Critically

Complete one of the following assignments, which ask you to apply the critical thinking, reading, and writing skills discussed in Chapter 1.

Writing Critically about Readings

Both Oscar Hijuelos's "Memories of New York City Snow" (p. 164) and Amy Tan's "Fish Cheeks" (p. 126) describe scenes from the past. Read or review both of these pieces, and then follow these steps:

1. **Summarize** Briefly summarize the works, listing major examples and details.

2. **Analyze** Tan uses humor to make her point, whereas Hijuelos's essay is more serious. Why do you think the authors might have chosen these different approaches?

3. **Synthesize** Using examples from both Tan's and Hijuelos's essays and from your own experience, discuss the types of details that make certain things in our lives (such as an event or a photograph) so memorable.

4. **Evaluate** Which essay, Tan's or Hijuelos's, do you think is more effective? Why? In writing your evaluation, you might look back on your responses to step 2.

Writing about Images

Study the photograph on page 168, and complete the following steps.

1. **Read the image** Ask yourself: What part of the photograph draws your attention the most, and why? What main impression does the picture create, and what details contribute to this impression? (For more information on reading images, see Chapter 1.)

COMMUNITY CONNECTIONS

ALESSANDRA CEPEDA (see the paragraph on p. 163) assisted with animal-rescue efforts while she was in college. Getting more involved in college and community activities, as Alessandra did, can help you feel more connected to others and can even improve the chances that you will stay in school.

For more on this story, ways to make community connections, and writing assignments, visit bedfordstmartins.com/realwriting.

TIP For a reminder of how to summarize, analyze, synthesize, and evaluate, see the Reading and Writing Critically box on pages 16–17.

2. **Write a description** Write a paragraph or essay that describes the photograph and explains the main impression it gives. Include the details and reactions from step 1.

Writing to Solve a Problem

Read or review the discussion of problem solving in Chapter 1 (pp. 24–26). Then, consider the following problem.

> An abandoned house on your street is a safety hazard for the children in the neighborhood. Although you and some of your neighbors have called the local Board of Health, nothing has been done. Finally, you and your neighbors decide to write to the mayor.

ASSIGNMENT: Working in a small group or on your own, write to the mayor describing why this house is a safety hazard. Thoroughly describe the house (outside and inside). Imagine a place that is not just ugly; it must also pose safety problems to children. You might start with the following sentence:

> Not only is the abandoned house at 45 Main Street an eyesore, but it is also _____.

For a paragraph: Describe in detail one room on the first floor of the house or just the exterior you can see from the street.

For an essay: Describe in detail at least three rooms in the house or the exterior you can see if you walk entirely around the house.

WRITING DIFFERENT KINDS OF PARAGRAPHS AND ESSAYS
Chapter Review

CHECKLIST: HOW TO WRITE DESCRIPTION

STEPS	DETAILS
☐ Narrow and explore your topic. See Chapter 3.	• Make the topic more specific. • Prewrite to get ideas about the narrowed topic.
☐ Write a topic sentence (paragraph) or thesis statement (essay). See Chapter 4.	• State what is most interesting, vivid, and important about your topic.
☐ Support your point. See Chapter 5.	• Come up with examples and details that create a main impression about your topic.
☐ Write a draft. See Chapter 6.	• Make a plan that puts examples in a logical order. • Include a topic sentence (paragraph) or thesis statement (essay) and all the supporting examples and details.
☐ Revise your draft. See Chapter 7.	• Make sure it has *all* the Four Basics of Good Description. • Make sure you include transitions to move readers smoothly from one detail to the next.
☐ Edit your revised draft. See Parts 4 through 7.	• Correct errors in grammar, spelling, word use, and punctuation.

Chapter Review

1. Description is writing that _____

2. What are the Four Basics of Good Description?
   _____
   _____
   _____

3. The topic sentence in a description paragraph or the thesis statement in a description essay includes what two elements? _____
   _____

4. Write sentences using the following vocabulary words: *aloft, palatial, perilous, stint, nostalgia.* _____
   _____

LEARNING JOURNAL
Reread your idea journal entry from page 154. Write another entry about the same topic, using what you have learned about good description.

> **reflect** Write for 2 minutes about what you have learned about writing description.

11

Process Analysis

Writing That Explains How Things Happen

> **YOU KNOW THIS**
>
> You often use process analysis:
>
> - You teach a friend or a family member how to do something.
> - You learn how to make or do something.
>
> **write** for 2 minutes about how to do something you know about.

Understand What Process Analysis Is

Process analysis either explains how to do something (so that your readers can do it) or explains how something works (so that your readers can understand it).

Four Basics of Good Process Analysis

1. It tells readers what process the writer wants them to know about and makes a point about it.
2. It presents the essential steps in the process.
3. It explains the steps in detail.
4. It presents the steps in a logical order (usually time order).

In the following paragraph, the numbers and colors correspond to the Four Basics of Good Process Analysis.

4 Time order is used

The poet Dana Gioia once said, "Art delights, instructs, consoles. It educates our emotions." **1** Closely observing paintings, sculpture, and other forms of visual art is a great way to have the type of experience that Gioia describes, and following a few basic steps will help you get the most from the experience. **2** First, choose an art exhibit that interests you. **3** You can find listings for exhibits on local museums' Web sites or in the arts section of a newspaper. Links on the Web sites or articles in a newspaper may give you more information about the exhibits, the artists featured in them, and the types of work to be displayed. **2** Second, go to the museum with an open mind and, ideally, with a friend. **3** While moving through the exhibit, take time to examine each work carefully. As you do so, ask yourself questions: What is my eye most drawn to, and why? What questions does this work raise for me, and how does it make me feel? How would I describe it to someone over the phone? Ask your friend the same questions, and consider the responses. You might also consult an exhibit brochure for information about the featured artists and their works. **2** Finally, keep your exploration going after you have left the museum. **3** Go out for coffee or a meal with your friend. Trade more of your thoughts and ideas about the artwork, and discuss your overall impressions. If you are especially interested in any of the artists or their works, you might look for additional information or images on the Internet, or you might consult books at the library. Throughout the whole experience, put aside the common belief that only artists or cultural experts "get" art. The artist Eugène Delacroix described paintings as "a bridge between the soul of the artist and that of the spectator." Trust your ability to cross that bridge and come to new understandings.

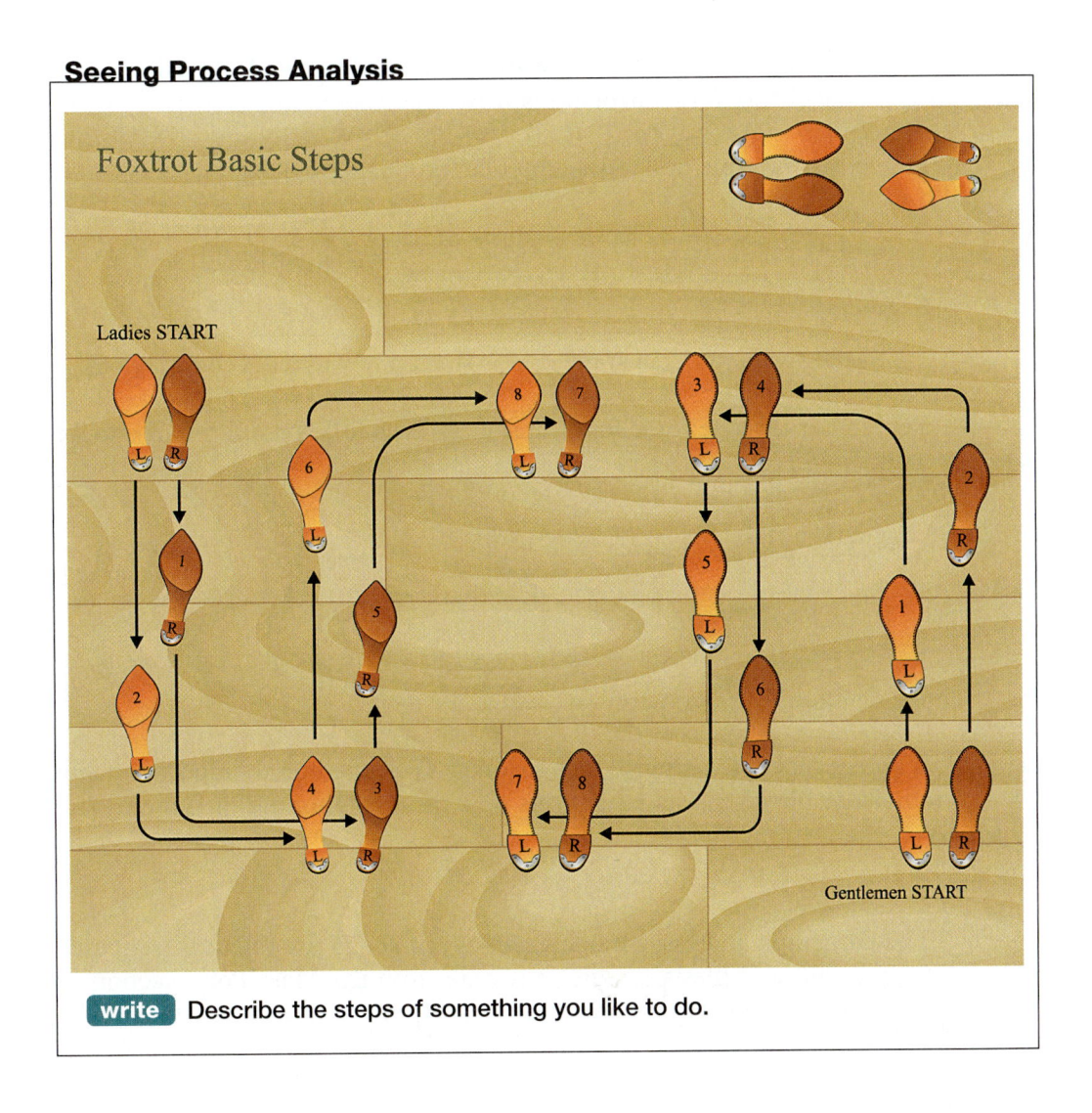

Seeing Process Analysis

Foxtrot Basic Steps

write Describe the steps of something you like to do.

WRITER AT WORK

JEREMY GRAHAM: As a youth pastor, I give youth-group members step-by-step guidance in how to be leaders.

(See Jeremy Graham's **PROFILE OF SUCCESS** on p. 177.)

IDEA JOURNAL Write about something you recently learned how to do—and how you do it.

TIP Sometimes, the same main point can be used for a paragraph and an essay, but the essay must develop this point in more detail. (See pp. 69–70.)

You use process analysis in many situations:

- **COLLEGE** — In a science course, you explain photosynthesis.
- **WORK** — You write instructions to explain how to operate something (the copier, the fax machine).
- **EVERYDAY LIFE** — You write out a recipe for an aunt.

In college, a writing assignment may ask you to *describe the process of*, but you might be asked to *describe the stages of* _____ or *explain how* _____ *works*. Whenever you need to identify and explain the steps or stages of anything, you will use process analysis.

Main Point in Process Analysis

In process analysis, your **purpose** is to explain how to do something or how something works. Your **main point** should tell readers what process you are describing and what you want readers to know about it.

To help you discover the main point for your process analysis, complete the following sentence:

MAIN POINT IN PROCESS ANALYSIS   What I want readers to know about this process is that . . .

Here is an example of a topic sentence for a paragraph:

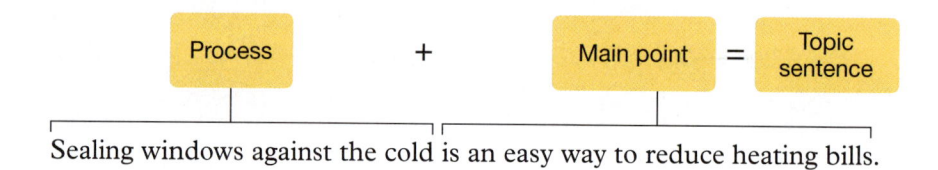

Process + Main point = Topic sentence

Sealing windows against the cold is an easy way to reduce heating bills.

Remember that the topic for an essay can be a little broader than one for a paragraph.

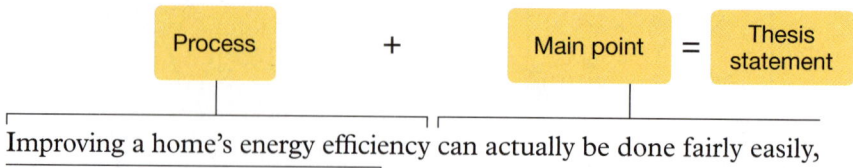

Process + Main point = Thesis statement

Improving a home's energy efficiency can actually be done fairly easily, significantly lowering utility bills.

Whereas the topic sentence focuses on just one method to improve energy efficiency, the thesis statement sets up a discussion of multiple methods.

Support in Process Analysis

The paragraph and essay models on pages 173–74 use the topic sentence (paragraph) and thesis statement (essay) from the Main Point section of this chapter. Both models include the **support** used in all writing about processes: the steps in the process backed up by details about these steps. In the essay model, however, the major support points (steps) are topic sentences for individual paragraphs.

PRACTICE 1 Finding and Choosing the Essential Steps

For each of the following topics, write the essential steps in the order you would perform them.

1. Making (your favorite food) is simple.

   _____

   _____

2. I think I could teach anyone how to _____.

   _____

3. Operating a _____ is _____.

   _____

   _____

PRACTICE 2 Adding Details to Essential Steps

Choose one of the topics from Practice 1. In the spaces that follow, first copy down that topic and the steps you wrote for it in Practice 1. Then, add a detail to each of the steps. If the process has more than three steps, you might want to use a separate sheet of paper.

Topic: _____

Step 1: _____

   Detail: _____

Step 2: _____

   Detail: _____

Step 3: _____

   Detail: _____

Step 4: _____

   Detail: _____

TIP If you have written a narration paragraph already, you will notice that narration and process analysis are alike in that they both usually present events or steps in time order—the order in which they occur. The difference is that narration reports what happened, whereas process analysis describes how to do something or how something works.

PARAGRAPHS VS. ESSAYS IN PROCESS ANALYSIS

For more on the important features of process analysis, see the Four Basics of Good Process Analysis on page 170.

Paragraph Form

Topic sentence

Support 1 (first step)

Support 2 (second step)

Support 3 (third step)

Concluding sentence

Sealing windows against the cold is an easy way to reduce heating bills. First, make sure the inside window frames are clean and clear of dust. Often, it is enough to wipe the frames with a soft, dry cloth. However, if the frames are especially dirty, clean them thoroughly with a damp cloth, and then dry them with paper towels or a blow dryer. Next, apply two-sided adhesive tape on all four sides of the window frame. Begin by peeling the cover from one side of the adhesive. Then, affix this side of the tape to the frame. After you have taped all four sides of the frame, remove the front side of the adhesive cover. Finally, attach the plastic sheeting to the tape. Start by measuring your window and cutting the plastic so that it fits. Next, apply the plastic to the tape, starting at the top of the window and working your way down. When the plastic is fully attached, seal it over the window by running a blow dryer over the plastic from top to bottom. By spending one morning or afternoon covering your windows, you can save $300 on your heating bills and enjoy a much more comfortable home.

Main Point: Often, narrower for a paragraph than for an essay: While the topic sentence (paragraph) focuses on just one method to improve energy efficiency, the thesis statement (essay) sets up a discussion of multiple methods.

Support for the Main Point (the Steps of a Process)

Details about the Steps: Usually, 1 to 3 sentences per step for paragraphs and 3 to 8 sentences per step for essays.

Conclusion

Think Critically As You Write Process Analysis

ASK YOURSELF

- Have I included all the steps necessary for others to complete or understand the process?
- Would any information from experts make my description of the process clearer? (For more on finding and evaluating outside sources, see pp. 304–09.)

Essay Form

Many people are intimidated by the work necessary to make their homes more energy efficient and do not see it as a do-it-yourself job. However, improving a home's energy efficiency can actually be done fairly easily, significantly lowering utility bills.

First, seal air leaks around windows and doors. To seal air leaks around windows, apply caulk between window frames and walls. Also, if you have windows that are not weather-proof, cover them with plastic before the cold temperatures set in. This process involves affixing two-sided adhesive tape to the window frames and then attaching plastic sheeting, which is sealed with the use of a blow dryer. Next, look for drafty spots around doors. Many air leaks at the top or sides of doors can be sealed with adhesive-backed foam strips. Leaks under doors can be stopped with foam draft guards. Alternatively, a rolled-up blanket, rug, or towel can keep the cold from coming in. All of these steps can save up to $600 per season on heating costs.

Second, install water-saving shower heads and faucet aerators. These fixtures are inexpensive and are available in most hardware stores. Also, they are easy to install. First, unscrew the old shower or faucet head. Then, follow the package instructions for affixing the new shower head or aerator. In some cases, you might have to use pipe tape or a rubber washer to ensure a good seal. After this step, run the water to make sure there are no leaks. If you find any leaks, use pliers to tighten the seal. In time, you will discover that the new shower heads and aerators will cut your water usage and water heating by up to 50 percent.

Finally, look for other places where energy efficiency could be increased. One simple improvement is to replace traditional light bulbs with compact fluorescent bulbs, which use up to 80 percent less energy. Also, make sure your insulation is as good as it can be. Many utilities now offer free assessments of home insulation, identifying places where it is missing or inadequate. In some cases, any necessary insulation improvements may be subsidized by the utilities or by government agencies. It is well worth considering such improvements, which, in the case of poorly insulated homes, can save thousands of dollars a year, quickly covering any costs. Although some people prefer to have professionals blow insulating foam into their walls, it is not difficult to add insulation to attics, where a large amount of heat can be lost during cold months.

Taking even one of these steps can make a significant financial difference in your life and also reduce your impact on the environment. My advice, though, is to improve your home's energy efficiency as much as possible, even if it means doing just a little at a time. The long-term payoff is too big to pass up.

175

Organization in Process Analysis

TIP For more on time order, see page 78.

Process analysis is usually organized by **time order** because it explains the steps of the process in the order in which they occur. This is the strategy used in the paragraph and essay models on pages 173–74.

Transitions move readers smoothly from one step to the next.

Common Transitions in Process Analysis

after	eventually	meanwhile	since
as	finally	next	soon
at last	first	now	then
before	last	once	when
during	later	second	while

PRACTICE 3 Using Transitions in Process Analysis

Read the paragraph that follows, and fill in the blanks with transitions.

Scientists have discovered that, like something from a zombie movie, a mind-controlling fungus attacks certain carpenter ants. _____, as if following the fungus's orders, the ants help their invader reproduce. The process begins when an ant is infected. _____, the ant begins to act strangely. For instance, instead of staying in its home high in the trees, it drops to the forest floor. _____ wandering, it searches for a cool, moist place. _____ the zombie-ant finds the right place, it clamps its jaws to a leaf and dies. _____, the fungus within the ant grows until it bursts from the insect's head, and more ants are infected. By studying this process, researchers may find better ways to control the spread of carpenter ants.

Read and Analyze Process Analysis

CRITICAL READING
- Preview
- Read
- Pause
- Review

See pages 9–12.

Reading examples of process analysis will help you write your own. In the first example, Jeremy Graham shows how he uses process analysis in his job as a youth pastor. The second example is a paragraph by a student, and the third example is an essay by a professional writer. As you read, pay attention to the vocabulary, and answer the questions in the margin. They will help you read critically.

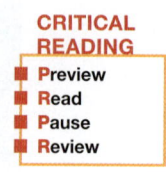

PROFILE OF SUCCESS

Process Analysis in the Real World

Background When I was growing up in New Orleans, my family was well off, and we lived in a nice home. But when I was thirteen, my dad moved out, leaving my mother with the mortgage and the responsibility of raising me and my younger brother. Eventually, we lost our home and were forced to move into a trailer. These changes put a lot of stress on all of us. I ended up dropping out of school and started selling drugs.

In August of 2005, when I was seventeen, Hurricane Katrina hit, and we fled the city for Mississippi, returning to New Orleans later that year. In December, my younger brother got into an altercation with a man in Lacombe, Louisiana, and ended up shooting and killing him, a crime for which he's now serving a life sentence. After his arrest, I moved back to Mississippi and started working menial jobs to get by. Because I had my GED by that time, my mom encouraged me to enroll in college. I entered Hinds Community College but was eventually suspended due to poor academic performance. Fortunately, a pastor in the community, Lionel Joseph Traylor, saw potential in me. He put me to work at his church, where I helped with things like cleaning and raking leaves. Pastor Traylor also gave me suits and other nice clothes to replace the T-shirts and jeans I usually wore, and he pushed me to go back to school.

With his encouragement, I got back into Hinds, and this time I was determined to succeed. I ended up graduating with a 3.0 GPA and a degree in business administration and accounting. Now, I am working on a bachelor's degree in business administration at Mississippi College, where I'm on scholarship. I expect to graduate in December of 2012.

I have also become an ordained minister, and I'm doing full-time ministry work with Pastor Traylor's church, where I am the youth pastor. I have also started sharing my story through public-speaking engagements. Although many people fear public speaking, I find that I get energy and motivation from the crowd.

Jeremy Graham
Youth Pastor and Motivational Speaker

Degree/College A.A., Hinds Community College

Employer Epicenter Church

Writing at work It is important for young people to learn leadership skills. At Epicenter Church, I write instructional materials for members of youth groups to help teach them these skills.

How Jeremy uses process analysis My instructional materials give members of youth groups step-by-step guidance for leadership within the youth group and beyond it. Having the materials in writing helps ensure that the guidance is followed consistently.

Jeremy's Process Analysis

The following paragraph is an example of the instructional materials that Jeremy writes.

PREDICT What do you think one of the steps will be?

> As a member of a youth group, you can become an active leader in the group and in your larger community. Following a few key steps can help you along the way. The first step is to lead by example. Older group members must set the path for younger members by showing them how to conduct themselves, work hard, and keep a positive attitude in any situation. By doing so, the younger members will build healthy relationships, and the skills they learn from older mentors will help them in school and future jobs. Second, youth leaders must encourage their peers to get involved with the community to make positive changes. Gathering together young people to visit homeless shelters, feed the homeless, and clean up the community are just a few things that can be done. These activities teach youth to be grateful for their living conditions and to extend a helping hand to others. The third step is to build good character and moral integrity. This happens naturally as youth leaders become more involved in their communities and serve as role models for other youth. Having good character and integrity improves young leaders' lives and helps them continue to have a positive impact on others. To sum up, all these steps greatly benefit youth leaders and the communities they serve.

1. What **process** is being analyzed? _____
2. How many steps does Jeremy give? _____
3. In your own words, what are the steps to becoming an effective leader?
   _____
   _____

Student Process Analysis Paragraph

Charlton Brown

Buying a Car at an Auction

PREDICT What do you think Charlton will say buyers need to be prepared about?

    Buying a car at an auction is a good way to get a cheap car, but buyers need to be prepared. First, decide what kind of vehicle you want to buy. Then, find a local auction. Scams are common, though, so be careful. Three top sites that are legitimate are www.gov-auctions.org, www.carauctioninc.com, and www.seizecars.com. When you have found an auction and a vehicle you are interested in, become a savvy buyer. Make sure you know the car's actual market value. You can find this out

WRITING DIFFERENT KINDS OF PARAGRAPHS AND ESSAYS
Read and Analyze Process Analysis

from Edmunds.com, Kellybluebook.com, or NADA (the National Automobile Dealers Association). Because bidding can become like a competition, decide on the highest bid you will make, and stick to that. Do not get drawn into the competition. On the day of the auction, get to the auction early so that you can look at the actual cars. If you do not know about cars yourself, bring someone who does with you to the auction so that he or she can examine the car. Next, begin your thorough examination. Check the exterior; especially look for any signs that the car has been in an accident. Also, check the windshield because many states will not give an inspection sticker to cars with any damage to the windshield. Check the interior and try the brakes. Start the engine and listen to how it sounds. Check the heat and air conditioning, the CD player, and all other functions. As a final check before the bidding, look at the car's engine and transmission. Finally, get ready to place your bid, and remember, do not go beyond the amount you settled on earlier. Good luck!

> **Vocabulary development**
> Underline the following words as you read the process analysis paragraph.
> **legitimate:** lawful; genuine; real
> **savvy:** knowledgeable; well informed
> **bid:** an offer, in this case, of a price
> **thorough:** complete; detailed

SUMMARIZE What steps are necessary to buy a car at auction?

1. Double-underline the **topic sentence**.
2. What is Charlton's **main point**? _____
   _____
3. Underline the **major steps**.
4. Circle the words that signal when Charlton moves from one step to the next.
5. Does Charlton's paragraph follow the Four Basics of Good Process Analysis (p. 170)? Why or why not? _____
   _____

Professional Process Analysis Essay

Ian Frazier
How to Operate the Shower Curtain

Born in 1951 in Cleveland, Ohio, writer Ian Frazier is known both for his humorous essays and for his more serious explorations of subjects ranging from American history to fishing. A staff writer for the *New Yorker,* Frazier has contributed pieces to the magazine since 1974, shortly after his graduation from Harvard University. He has also published several books, most recently *Gone to New York: Adventures in the City* (2005), *Lamentations of the Father* (2008), and *Travels in Siberia* (2010).

In the following process analysis essay, Frazier finds humor in one source of annoyance for many people.

> **Vocabulary development**
> Underline these words as you read the process analysis essay.
> **reputable:** having a good reputation
> **owing to:** as a result of
> **disengaged:** removed
> **convection:** a form of air circulation
> **microclimate:** a small climate (set of weather conditions) within a larger one
> **riser:** vertical pipe
> **intervals:** regular distances
> **tamper:** to disturb
> **detaching:** removing
> **inadvertent:** unintentional; accidental
> **scenario:** situation
> **subsequently:** afterward
> **receptacle:** container
> **john:** slang for *toilet*
> **inconsolably:** so dramatically it appears that one is beyond comforting

Dear Guest: The shower curtain in this bathroom has been purchased with care at a reputable "big box" store in order to provide maximum convenience in showering. After you have read these instructions, you will find with a little practice that our shower curtain is as easy to use as the one you have at home.

You'll note that the shower curtain consists of several parts. The top hem, closest to the ceiling, contains a series of regularly spaced holes designed for the insertion of shower-curtain rings. As this part receives much of the everyday strain of usage, it must be handled correctly. Grasp the shower curtain by its leading edge and gently pull until it is flush with the wall. Step into the tub, if you have not already done so. Then take the other edge of shower curtain and cautiously pull it in opposite direction until it, too, adjoins the wall. A little moisture between shower curtain and wall tiles will help curtain to stick.

Keep in mind that normal bathing will cause you unavoidably to bump against shower curtain, which may cling to you for a moment owing to the natural adhesiveness of water. Some guests find the sensation of wet plastic on their naked flesh upsetting, and overreact to it. Instead, pinch the shower curtain between your thumb and forefinger near where it is adhering to you and simply move away from it until it is disengaged. Then, with the ends of your fingers, push it back to where it is supposed to be.

If shower curtain reattaches itself to you, repeat process above. Under certain atmospheric conditions, a convection effect creates air currents outside shower curtain which will press it against you on all sides no matter what you do. If this happens, stand directly under showerhead until bathroom microclimate stabilizes.

Many guests are surprised to learn that all water pipes in our system run off a single riser. This means that the opening of any hot or cold tap, or the flushing of a toilet, interrupts flow to shower. If you find water becoming extremely hot (or cold), exit tub promptly while using a sweeping motion with one arm to push shower curtain aside.

REMEMBER TO KEEP SHOWER CURTAIN *INSIDE* TUB AT ALL TIMES! Failure to do this may result in baseboard rot, wallpaper mildew, destruction of living-room ceiling below, and possible dripping onto catered refreshments at social event in your honor that you are about to attend. So be careful!

This shower curtain comes equipped with small magnets in shape of disks which have been sewn into the bottom hem at intervals. These serve no purpose whatsoever and may be ignored. Please do not tamper with them. The vertical lines, or pleats, which you may have wondered about, are there for a simple reason: user safety. If you have to move from the tub fast, as outlined above, the easy accordion-type folding motion of the pleats makes that possible. The gray substance in some of the inner pleat folds is a kind of insignificant mildew, less toxic than what is found on some foreign cheeses.

When detaching shower curtain from clinging to you or when exiting tub during a change in water temperature, bear in mind that there are seventeen mostly empty plastic bottles of shampoo on tub edge next to wall. These bottles have accumulated in this area over time. Many have been set upside down in order to concentrate the last amounts of fluid in their cap mechanisms, and are balanced lightly. Inadvertent contact with a thigh or knee can cause all the bottles to be knocked over and to tumble into the tub or behind it. If this should somehow happen, we ask that you kindly pick the bottles up and put them back in the same order in which you found them. Thank you.

While picking up the bottles, a guest occasionally will lose his or her balance temporarily, and, in even rarer cases, fall. If you find this occurring, remember that panic is the enemy here. Let your body go limp, while reminding yourself that the shower curtain is not designed to bear your weight. Grabbing onto it will only complicate the situation.

If, in a "worst case" scenario, you do take hold of the shower curtain, and the curtain rings tear through the holes in the upper hem as you were warned they might, remain motionless and relaxed in the position in which you come to rest. If subsequently you hear a knock on the bathroom door, respond to any questions by saying either "Fine" or "No, I'm fine." When the questioner goes away, stand up, turn off shower, and lay shower curtain flat on floor and up against tub so you can see the extent of the damage. With a sharp object — a nail file, a pen, or your teeth — make new holes in top hem next to the ones that tore through.

10 SUMMARIZE What process should a person follow after a fall?

Now lift shower curtain with both hands and reattach it to shower-curtain rings by unclipping, inserting, and reclipping them. If during this process the shower curtain slides down and again goes onto you, reach behind you to shelf under medicine cabinet, take nail file or curved fingernail scissors, and perform short, brisk slashing jabs on shower curtain to cut it back. It can always be repaired later with safety pins or adhesive tape from your toiletries kit.

At this point, you may prefer to get the shower curtain out of your way entirely by gathering it up with both arms and ripping it down with a sharp yank. Now place it in the waste receptacle next to the john. In order that anyone who might be overhearing you will know that you are still all right, sing "Fat Bottomed Girls," by Queen,[1] as loudly as necessary. While waiting for tub to fill, wedge shower curtain into waste receptacle more firmly by treading it underfoot with a regular high-knee action as if marching in place.

We are happy to have you as our guest. There are many choices you could have made, but you are here, and we appreciate that. Operating the shower curtain is kind of tricky. Nobody is denying that. If you do not wish to deal with it, or if you would rather skip the whole subject for reasons you do not care to reveal, we accept your decision. You did not ask to be born. There is no need ever to touch the shower curtain again. If you would like to receive assistance, pound on the door, weep inconsolably, and someone will be along.

REFLECT Have you ever followed any of the steps described in this essay?

TIP For reading advice, see Chapter 1.

1. The first paragraph contains what seems to be the **thesis statement**. Double-underline it.

2. Now, look at this sentence from the last paragraph: "Operating the shower curtain is kind of tricky." Notice how this sentence opposes the thesis statement. What does this opposition say about the process?

   _____
   _____
   _____

3. Circle the **transitions** that introduce steps in the process.

4. Does this essay follow the Four Basics of Good Process Analysis (p. 170)? Why or why not? _____

Respond to one of the following assignments in a paragraph or essay.

1. Identify another process that could be analyzed humorously. Then, write a comical description of this process.

2. Frazier describes, in detail, a process for addressing a frustrating situation. Identify another process that you find frustrating, and write a detailed but serious description of it.

3. Describe to a beginner how to do something that you do well.

---

1. **Queen:** British rock band popular in the 1970s and 1980s

Write Your Own Process Analysis

In this section, you will write your own process analysis based on one of the following assignments. For help, refer to the How to Write Process Analysis checklist on page 186.

ASSIGNMENT OPTIONS   **Writing about College, Work, and Everyday Life**

Write a process analysis paragraph or essay on one of the following topics or on one of your own choice. If you responded to the idea journal prompt on page 172, you might develop that writing further.

COLLEGE

- Describe the process of preparing for an exam.
- Attend a tutoring session at your college's writing center. Afterward, describe the process: What specific things did the tutor do to help you? Also, explain what you learned from the process.
- Interview a college graduate about how he or she achieved success in school. During the interview, ask about the steps of specific processes. For example, one question might be, "What steps did you follow to take good notes?" After the interview, describe the processes in writing.

WORK

- Describe how to make a positive impression at a job interview.
- Think of a challenging task you had to accomplish at work. What steps did you go through to complete it?
- Identify a job that you would like to have after graduation. Then, investigate the process of getting this job, from the search stage to the interview. To gather information, visit the Web site of your college's career center. Better yet, make an appointment to speak with a career counselor. After you have completed your research, describe the process in writing.

EVERYDAY LIFE

- Describe the process of making something, such as a favorite meal, a set of shelves, or a sweater.
- Think of a challenging process that you have completed successfully, such as fixing a leak under the sink, applying for a loan, or finding a good deal on a car or an apartment. Describe the steps specifically enough so that someone else could complete the process just as successfully.
- Take part in a community activity, such as a fund-raising event for a charity, a neighborhood cleanup, or food preparation at a homeless shelter. Then, describe the process you went through.

COMMUNITY CONNECTIONS

While attending college, **ROBIN WYANT** volunteered at a community crisis center in her city. Getting more involved in college and community activities, as Robin did, can help you feel more connected to others and can even improve the chances that you'll stay in school.

For more on this story, ways to make community connections, and writing assignments, visit bedfordstmartins.com/realwriting.

ASSIGNMENT OPTIONS Reading and Writing Critically

Complete one of the following assignments, which ask you to apply the critical thinking, reading, and writing skills discussed in Chapter 1.

Writing Critically about Readings

Although both Charlton Brown's "Buying a Car at an Auction" (p. 178) and Ian Frazier's "How to Operate the Shower Curtain" (p. 179) describe processes, Frazier's process analysis is intended to be entertaining instead of truly useful. Read or review both of these pieces, and then follow these steps:

TIP For a reminder of how to summarize, analyze, synthesize, and evaluate, see the Reading and Writing Critically box on pages 16–17.

1. **Summarize**   Briefly summarize the works, listing steps in the processes described.

2. **Analyze**   Are there any other steps or details that the authors might have included?

3. **Synthesize**   Using examples from both Brown's and Frazier's writings and from your own experience, discuss (1) processes that would be fun to describe humorously and (2) processes that need to be described seriously.

4. **Evaluate**   Which piece, Brown's or Frazier's, do you think is more effective? Why? In writing your evaluation, you might look back on your responses to step 2.

Writing about Images

The following series of photographs, taken by Bill Brummel, accompanied an article about Bryon Widner, a former leader of the white power movement who sought to put his racist past behind him. One part of this effort was the removal of the many tattoos on his face and neck, which featured symbols of racial intolerance and violence. With the help of the Southern Poverty Law Center, Widner received funding for the expensive removal of his tattoos. After undergoing sixteen months of laser surgeries, Widner no longer has any tattoos on his face or neck.

Study the photographs of Widner's transformation, and complete the following steps.

1. **Read the images**   Ask yourself: What changes do you notice from photo to photo? What is the purpose of showing this process? (For more information on reading images, see Chapter 1.)

2. **Write a process analysis**   Write a paragraph or essay that describes the process shown in these photographs. (For more information about Widner's transformation, search for articles about it on the Internet.) In your description, include the changes you observed in step 1.

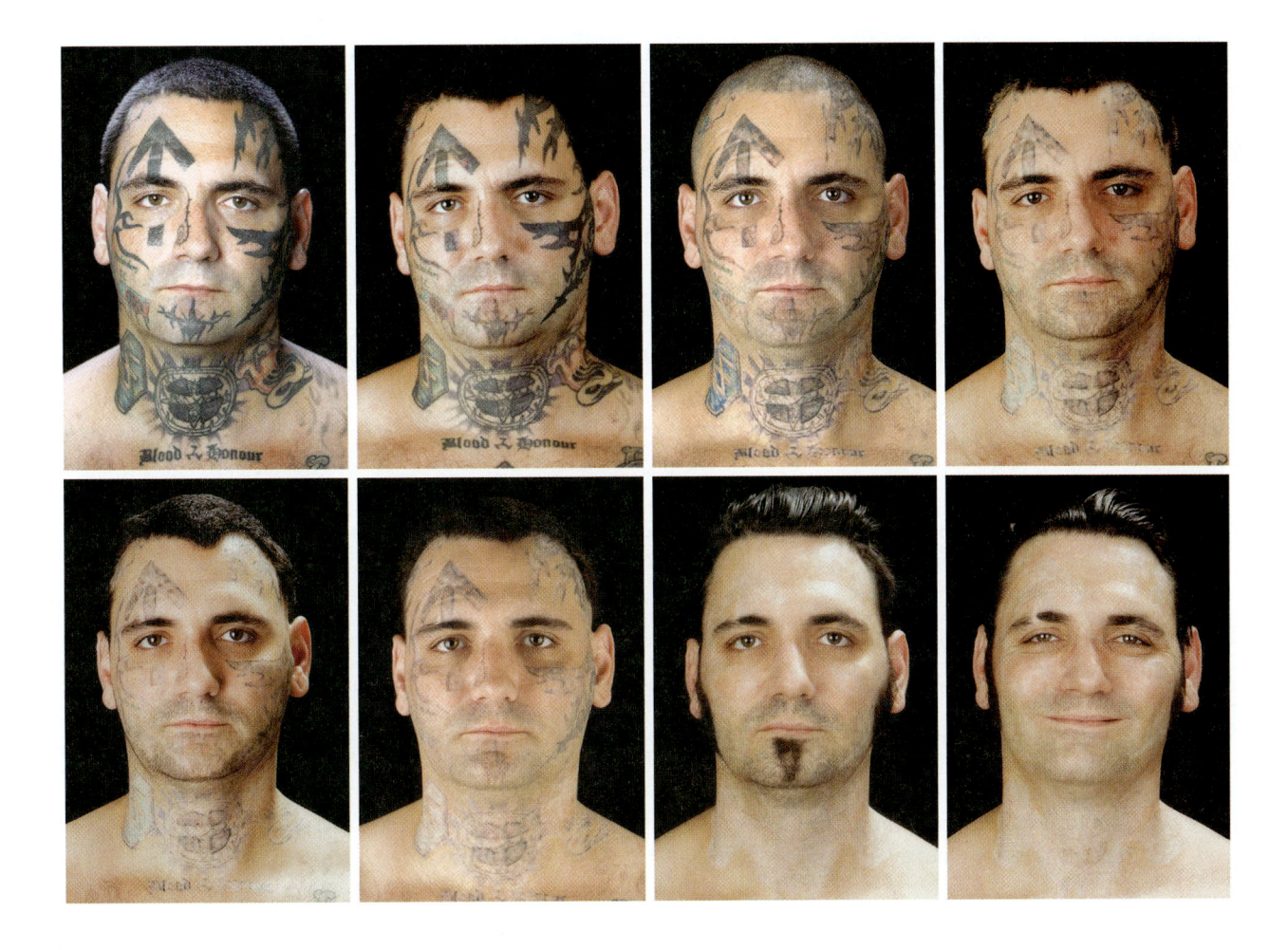

Writing to Solve a Problem

Read or review the discussion of problem solving in Chapter 1 (pp. 24–26). Then, consider the following problem.

> Midway through a course you are taking, your instructor asks the class to tell her how she could improve the course. You have not been happy with the class because the instructor is always late and comes in seeming rushed and tense. She then lectures for most of the class before giving you an assignment that you start on while she sits at her desk, busily grading papers. You are afraid to ask questions about the lecture or assignment. You want to tell the instructor how the course could be better, but you do not want to offend her.

ASSIGNMENT: Working in a small group or on your own, write to your instructor about how she could improve the course. Think of how the class could be structured differently so that you could learn more. Begin with how the class could start. Then, describe how the rest of the class period could go, suggesting specific activities if you can. State your suggestions in positive terms. For example, instead of telling the instructor what *not* to do, make suggestions using phrases like *you could, we could,* or *the class could.* Be sure to use formal English.

You might start in this way:

> Several simple changes might improve our learning. At the start of each class, _____.

At the end, remember to thank your instructor for asking for students' suggestions.

CHECKLIST: HOW TO WRITE PROCESS ANALYSIS

STEPS	DETAILS
☐ **Narrow and explore your topic.** See Chapter 3.	• Make the topic more specific. • Prewrite to get ideas about the narrowed topic, and how you will explain the steps to your audience. • Make sure your topic can be covered in the space given.
☐ **Write a topic sentence (paragraph) or thesis statement (essay).** See Chapter 4.	• Decide what you want readers to know about the process you are describing.
☐ **Support your point.** See Chapter 5.	• Include the steps in the process, and explain the steps in detail.
☐ **Write a draft.** See Chapter 6.	• Make a plan that puts the steps in a logical order (often chronological). • Include a topic sentence (paragraph) or thesis statement (essay) and all the supporting details about each step.
☐ **Revise your draft.** See Chapter 7.	• Make sure it has *all* the Four Basics of Good Process Analysis. • Read to make sure all the steps are present. • Make sure you include transitions to move readers smoothly from one step to the next.
☐ **Edit your revised draft.** See Parts 4 through 7.	• Correct errors in grammar, spelling, word use, and punctuation.

Chapter Review

1. Process analysis is writing that _____

2. What are the Four Basics of Good Process Analysis?

3. Write sentences using the following vocabulary words: *legitimate, savvy, reputable, owing to, intervals.* _____

> **reflect** Write for 2 minutes about what you have learned about writing process analysis.

LEARNING JOURNAL
Reread your idea journal entry about how to do something you recently learned (p. 172). Make another entry about the same process, using what you have learned about process analysis. Assume you are teaching someone else this process.

12

Classification

Writing That Sorts Things into Groups

> **YOU KNOW THIS**
>
> You have had experience classifying various items:
> - You see how movies in a video store are arranged.
> - You sort items for recycling.
>
> **write** for 2 minutes about the kinds of responsibilities you have.

Understand What Classification Is

Classification is writing that organizes, or sorts, people or items into categories. It uses an **organizing principle**: *how* the people or items are sorted. The organizing principle is directly related to the purpose for classifying. For example, you might sort clean laundry (your purpose) using one of the following organizing principles: by ownership (yours, your roommate's) or by where it goes (the bedroom, the bathroom).

Four Basics of Good Classification

1. It makes sense of a group of people or items by organizing them into categories.
2. It has a purpose for sorting the people or items.
3. It categorizes using a single organizing principle.
4. It gives detailed explanations or examples of what fits into each category.

In the following paragraph, the numbers and colors correspond to the Four Basics of Good Classification.

TIP For tools to use in getting a job, visit the *Student Site for Real Writing* at **bedfordstmartins .com/realwriting**.

1 In researching careers I might pursue, I have learned that there are three major types of workers, 2 each having different strengths and preferences. 3 The first type of worker is a big-picture person, who likes to look toward the future and think of new businesses, products, and services. 4 Big-picture people might also identify ways to make their workplaces more successful and productive. Often, they hold leadership positions, achieving their goals by assigning specific projects and tasks

to others. Big-picture people may be drawn to starting their own businesses. Or they might manage or become a consultant for an existing business. **3** The second type of worker is a detail person, who focuses on the smaller picture, whether it be a floor plan in a construction project, a spreadsheet showing a business's revenue and expenses, or data from a scientific experiment. **4** Detail people take pride in understanding all the ins and outs of a task and doing everything carefully and well. Some detail people prefer to work with their hands, doing such things as carpentry or electrical wiring. Others prefer office jobs, such as accounting or clerical work. Detail people may also be drawn to technical careers, such as scientific research or engineering. **3** The third type of worker is a people person, who gets a lot of satisfaction from reaching out to others and helping meet their needs. **4** A people person has good social skills and likes to get out in the world to use them. Therefore, this type of worker is unlikely to be happy sitting behind a desk. A successful people person often shares qualities of the other types of workers; for example, he or she may show leadership potential. In addition, his or her job may require careful attention to detail. Good jobs for a people person include teaching, sales, nursing, and other health-care positions. Having evaluated my own strengths and preferences, I believe that I am equal parts big-picture person and people person. I am happy to see that I have many career options.

Seeing Classification

write What do shoes tell you about their wearer? What types of shoes do you own?

WRITER AT WORK

LEIGH KING: In my fashion blog, I write about many types of clothing, styles, and accessories.

(See Leigh King's **PROFILE OF SUCCESS** on p. 197.)

IDEA JOURNAL Write about the different kinds of students in this class or the different kinds of friends you have.

You use classification anytime you want to organize people or items.

COLLEGE	In a criminal justice course, you are asked to discuss the most common types of chronic offenders.
WORK	For a sales presentation, you classify the kinds of products your company produces.
EVERYDAY LIFE	You classify your typical monthly expenses to make a budget.

In college, writing assignments probably will not use the word *classification*. Instead, you might be asked to *describe the types of* _____ or *explain the types or kinds of* _____. You might also be asked, *How is* _____ *organized?* or *What are the parts of* _____? These are the words and phrases that signal that you need to sort things into categories require classification.

Main Point in Classification

The **main point** in classification uses a single **organizing principle** to sort items in a way that serves your purpose. The categories should help you achieve your purpose.

To help you discover the organizing principle for your classification, complete the following sentences:

MAIN POINT IN CLASSIFICATION

My purpose for classifying my topic is to explain _____ to readers.

It would make most sense to my readers if I sorted this topic by . . .

PRACTICE 1 Using a Single Organizing Principle

For each topic that follows, one of the categories does not fit the same organizing principle as the rest. Circle the letter of the category that does not fit, and, in the space provided, write the organizing principle that the rest follow.

EXAMPLE:

Topic: Shoes

Categories:

a. Running   c. Golf
(b.) Leather   d. Bowling

Organizing principle: *by type of activity*

1. Topic: Relatives

   Categories:
   - a. Aunts
   - b. Uncles
   - c. Sisters
   - d. Nieces

   Organizing principle: _____

2. Topic: Jobs

   Categories:
   - a. Weekly
   - b. Hourly
   - c. Monthly
   - d. Summer

   Organizing principle: _____

3. Topic: Animals

   Categories:
   - a. Dogs
   - b. Cats
   - c. Rabbits
   - d. Whales

   Organizing principle: _____

Sometimes, it helps to think of classification in diagram form. Here is a diagram of the paragraph on pages 188–89.

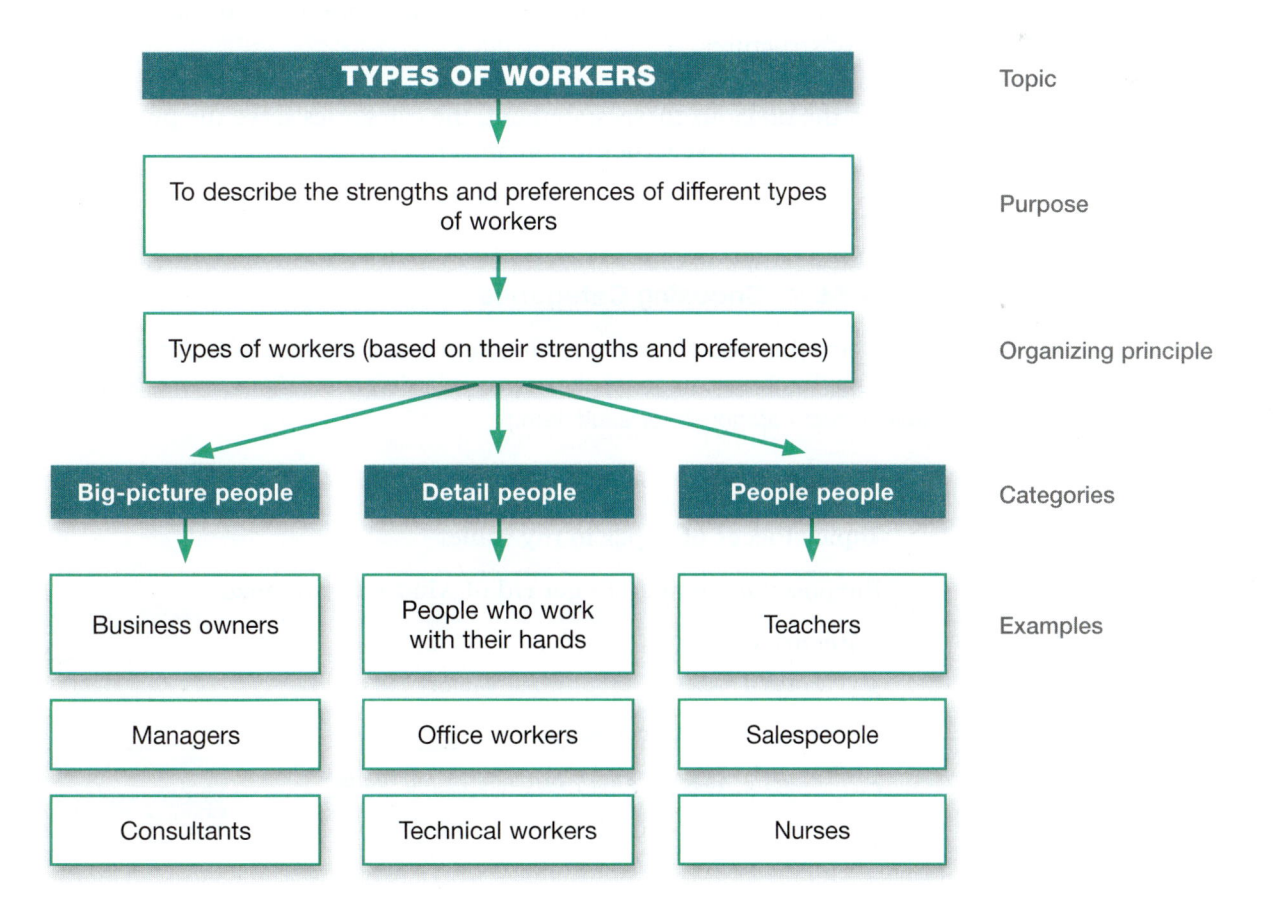

TYPES OF WORKERS — Topic

To describe the strengths and preferences of different types of workers — Purpose

Types of workers (based on their strengths and preferences) — Organizing principle

Categories:
- Big-picture people
- Detail people
- People people

Examples:
- Big-picture people: Business owners, Managers, Consultants
- Detail people: People who work with their hands, Office workers, Technical workers
- People people: Teachers, Salespeople, Nurses

In classification, the main point may or may not state the organizing principle directly. Look at the following examples:

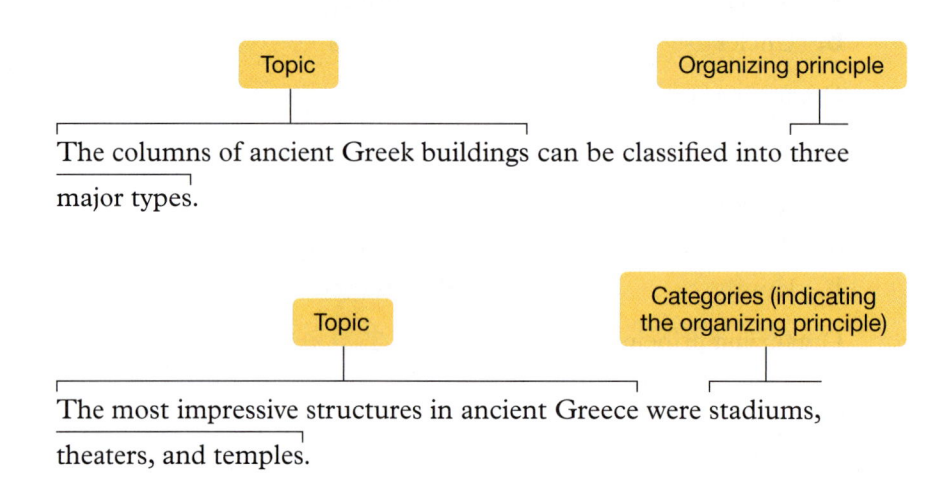

[Topic] [Organizing principle]

The columns of ancient Greek buildings can be classified into three major types.

[Topic] [Categories (indicating the organizing principle)]

The most impressive structures in ancient Greece were stadiums, theaters, and temples.

In both main points, the organizing principle is *types* of things—columns in the case of the paragraph and buildings in the case of the essay. The thesis statement does not state this principle directly, however. Instead, the categories—stadiums, theaters, and temples—make the principle clear.

Also, notice that the topic for the essay is broader than the one for the paragraph. Whereas the topic sentence focuses on just one part of ancient Greek buildings—the columns—the thesis statement considers entire groups of structures.

Make sure that the categories in your classification serve your purpose. In the previous thesis statement, the categories serve the purpose of presenting impressive structures in ancient Greece.

TIP Sometimes, the same main point can be used for a paragraph and an essay, but the essay must develop this point in more detail. (See pp. 69–70.)

PRACTICE 2 Choosing Categories

In the items that follow, you are given a topic and a purpose for sorting. For each item, list three categories that serve your purpose. (There are more than three correct categories for each item.)

EXAMPLE:

Topic: Pieces of paper in my wallet

Purpose for sorting: To get rid of what I do not need

Categories:

a. *Things I need to keep in my wallet*

b. *Things I can throw away*

c. *Things I need to keep, but not in my wallet*

1. Topic: College courses

   Purpose for sorting: To decide what I will register for

   Categories: _____

   a. _____

   b. _____

   c. _____

2. Topic: Stuff in my notebook

   Purpose for sorting: To organize my schoolwork

   Categories: _____

   a. _____

   b. _____

   c. _____

3. Topic: Wedding guests

   Purpose for sorting: To arrange seating at tables

   Categories: _____

   a. _____

   b. _____

   c. _____

4. Topic: Tools for home repair

   Purpose for sorting: To make them easy to find when needed

   Categories: _____

   a. _____

   b. _____

   c. _____

Support in Classification

The paragraph and essay models on pages 194–95 use the topic sentence (paragraph) and thesis statement (essay) from the Main Point section of this chapter. Both models include the **support** used in all classification writing: categories backed up by explanations or examples of each category. In the essay model, however, the major support points (categories) are topic sentences for individual paragraphs.

PARAGRAPHS VS. ESSAYS IN CLASSIFICATION

For more on the important features of classification, see the Four Basics of Good Classification on page 188.

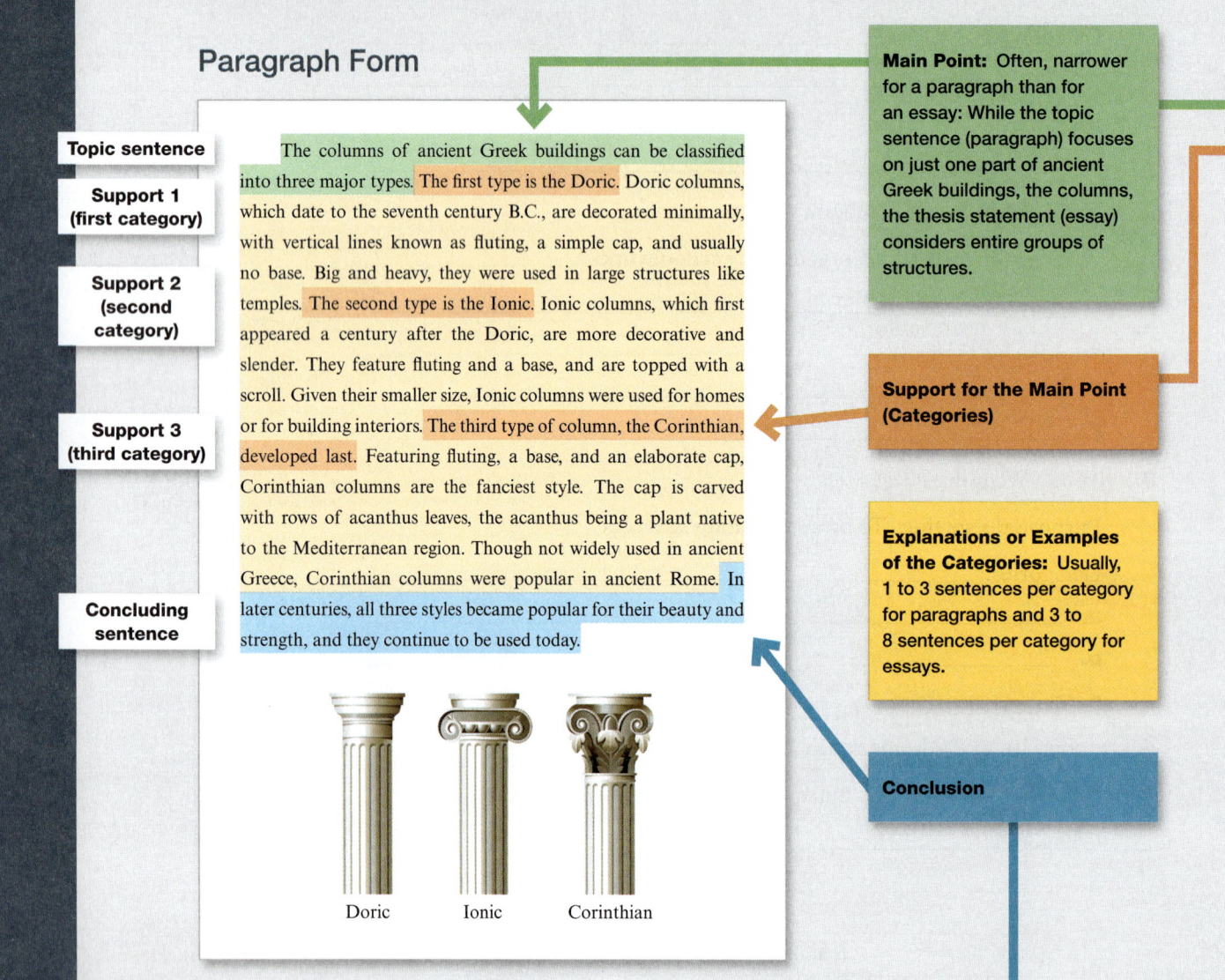

Paragraph Form

Topic sentence

Support 1 (first category)

Support 2 (second category)

Support 3 (third category)

Concluding sentence

The columns of ancient Greek buildings can be classified into three major types. The first type is the Doric. Doric columns, which date to the seventh century B.C., are decorated minimally, with vertical lines known as fluting, a simple cap, and usually no base. Big and heavy, they were used in large structures like temples. The second type is the Ionic. Ionic columns, which first appeared a century after the Doric, are more decorative and slender. They feature fluting and a base, and are topped with a scroll. Given their smaller size, Ionic columns were used for homes or for building interiors. The third type of column, the Corinthian, developed last. Featuring fluting, a base, and an elaborate cap, Corinthian columns are the fanciest style. The cap is carved with rows of acanthus leaves, the acanthus being a plant native to the Mediterranean region. Though not widely used in ancient Greece, Corinthian columns were popular in ancient Rome. In later centuries, all three styles became popular for their beauty and strength, and they continue to be used today.

Doric   Ionic   Corinthian

Main Point: Often, narrower for a paragraph than for an essay: While the topic sentence (paragraph) focuses on just one part of ancient Greek buildings, the columns, the thesis statement (essay) considers entire groups of structures.

Support for the Main Point (Categories)

Explanations or Examples of the Categories: Usually, 1 to 3 sentences per category for paragraphs and 3 to 8 sentences per category for essays.

Conclusion

Think Critically As You Write Classification

ASK YOURSELF

- Will readers be clear about my organizing principle even if my main point doesn't state it directly?
- Do the categories that make up the support for my main point go with my organizing principle? If not, does it make sense to rethink the categories, the organizing principle, or both?
- Are all the explanations or examples for each category relevant?

Essay Form

1

Ancient Greek civilization produced a wealth of architectural wonders that were both **[Thesis statement]** lasting. The most impressive structures were stadiums, theaters, and temples.

The stadiums were designed to hold thousands of spectators. These open-air spaces were s **[Topic sentence 1 (first category)]** so that the seating, often stone benches, from the central space, giving all spectators a decent view. One of the most famous stadiums, built in Delphi in the fifth century B.C., seated audiences of about 7,000 people. Many stadiums featured ornamental details such as dramatic arches, and some of the more sophisticated examples included heated bathhouses with heated floors. Most often, the stadiums hosted sporting events, such as foot races. A common racing distance **[Topic sentence 2 (second category)]** equaling one length of the stadium.

Another type of structure, the theater, was also a popular public gathering place. Like stadiums, the theaters were open-air sites that were set into hillsides. But instead of sports, they featured plays, musical performances, poetry readings, and other cultural events.

2

In the typical Greek theater, a central performance area was surrounded by semicircular seating, which was often broken into different sections. Wooden, and later stone, stages were set up in the central area, and in front of the stage was a space used for singing and dancing. This space was known as the "orchestra." Among the most famous ancient Greek theaters is the one at Epidaurus, built in the fourth century B.C. and seating u people. Performances still take place there. **[Topic sentence 3 (third category)]**

The most beautiful structures were the temples, with their grand entrances and large open spaces. Temples were rectangular in shape, and their outer walls as well as some interior spaces were supported by columns. Their main structures were typically made of limestone or marble, while their roofs might be constructed of terra-cotta or marble tiles. Temples were created to serve as "homes" for particular gods or goddesses, who were represented by statues. People left food or other offerings to these gods or goddesses to stay in their good graces, and communities often held festivals and other celebrations in their honor. Temples tended to be built in either the

3

Doric or Ionic style, with Doric temples featuring simple, heavy columns and Ionic temples featuring slightly more ornate columns. The most famous temple, in the Doric style, is the Parthenon in Athens.

[Concluding paragraph] Turning to the present day, many modern stadiums, theaters, and columned civic buildings show the influence of ancient Greek buildings. Recognizing the lasting strength and beauty of these old structures, architects and designers continue to return to them for inspiration. I predict that this inspiration will last at least a thousand more years.

195

Organization in Classification

Classification can be organized in different ways (**time order**, **space order**, or **order of importance**) depending on its purpose.

PURPOSE	LIKELY ORGANIZATION
to explain changes or events over time	time
to describe the arrangement of people/items in physical space	space
to discuss parts of an issue or problem, or types of people or things	importance

Order of importance is used in the essay model on page 195.

As you write your classification, use **transitions** to move your readers smoothly from one category to another.

TIP For more on the orders of organization, see pages 78–79.

Common Transitions in Classification

another	for example
another kind	for instance
first, second, third, and so on	last
	one example/another example

PRACTICE 3 Using Transitions in Classification

Read the paragraph that follows, and fill in the blanks with transitions. You are not limited to the ones listed in the preceding box.

Every day, I get three kinds of e-mail: work, personal, and junk. The _____ of e-mail, work, I have to read carefully and promptly. Sometimes, the messages are important ones directed to me, but mostly they are group messages about meetings, policies, or procedures. _____, it seems as if the procedure for leaving the building during a fire alarm is always changing. _____ _____ of e-mail, personal, is from friends or my mother. These I read when I get a chance, but I read them quickly and delete any that are jokes or messages that have to be sent to ten friends for good luck. _____ of e-mail is the most common and most annoying: junk. I get at least thirty junk e-mails a day, advertising all kinds of things that I do not want, such as life insurance or baby products. Even when I reply asking that the company stop sending me these messages, they keep coming. Sometimes, I wish e-mail did not exist.

Read and Analyze Classification

Reading examples of classification will help you write your own. In the first example, Leigh King shows how she uses classification in her job as a fashion writer.

The second example is a classification paragraph by a student, and the third example is a classification essay by a professional writer. As you read these pieces, pay attention to the vocabulary, and answer the questions in the margin. They will help you read critically.

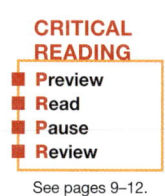

> **CRITICAL READING**
> - Preview
> - Read
> - Pause
> - Review
>
> See pages 9–12.

PROFILE OF SUCCESS

Classification in the Real World

Background I always knew that I wanted to work in the fashion industry, so I entered the Fashion Institute of Design & Merchandising (FIDM), where I studied merchandise marketing. I had to take a noncredit introduction-to-writing course, but it made a big difference for me, and the teacher inspired me to improve my writing.

Later on, while I was still at FIDM, I started a fashion blog, where I write about stylish pieces from up-and-coming designers. Through the blog, I overcame one of the biggest challenges facing people new to the fashion industry: making yourself stand out from the crowd, especially in a place like New York City. People in the industry took note of my blog, and it helped me get an internship in the Web Department at *Teen Vogue*. In that job, I wrote articles for the magazine and blogged about fashion news, celebrities, and many other topics.

My advice to other students is to put yourself out there with your writing, whether through blogging or some other online presence. If you make a good impression with your writing, you can get great results.

Degrees/Colleges A.A., Fashion Institute of Design & Merchandising; pursuing a bachelor of professional studies degree in fashion merchandising at LIM College

Employer Self. Previously interned at *Teen Vogue* and Tory Burch.

Writing at work Blogs, articles, e-mails, and more.

Leigh King
Fashion Writer/Blogger

Leigh's Classification

The following piece is part of an e-mail that Leigh sent to colleagues about upcoming blog posts.

> Now that we're on the eve of prom season, I am going to be writing about some of the most eye-catching prom fashions:
>
> - **Dresses:** The newest looks range from classic and romantic, to glittery and modern, to vintage. And the new styles come in a variety of colors, from understated cream, to striking black and white, to candy colors or pastels.
> - **Clutch purses:** There are plenty of new looks to choose from, including purses made of bold-patterned fabrics or accented with stylish beading.
> - **Shoes:** No matter what style of dress a prom-goer chooses, there are beautiful shoes to go with it: ballet flats, chunky wooden heels, heels with jewels or bows, and more.

1. Double-underline the **main point** of the e-mail.
2. What categories does Leigh break the fashions into? _____
3. Does the e-mail have the Four Basics of Good Classification (p. 188)?

Student Classification Paragraph

Lorenza Mattazi
All My Music

TIP For advice on building your vocabulary, visit the *Student Site for Real Writing* at **bedfordstmartins.com/realwriting**.

From the time I was young, I have always loved music, all kinds of music. My first experience of music was the opera that both of my parents always had playing in our house. I learned to understand the drama and emotion of operas. My parents both spoke Italian, and they told me the stories of the operas and translated the words sung in Italian to English so that I could understand. Because hearing opera made my parents happy, and they taught me about it, I loved it, too. Many of my friends think I am weird when I say I love opera, but to me it is very emotional and beautiful. When I was in my early teens, I found rock music and listened to it no matter what I was doing. I like the music with words that tell a story that I can relate to. In that way, rock can be like opera, with stories that everyone can relate to, about love, heartbreak, happiness, and pain. The best rock has powerful guitars and bass, and a good, strong drumbeat. I love it when I can feel the bass in my chest. Rock has good energy and power. Now, I love rap music, too, not the rap with words that are violent or disrespectful of women, but the rest. The words are poetry, and the energy is so high that I feel as if I just have to move my body to the beat. That rhythm is so steady. I have even written some good rap, which my friends say is really good. Maybe I will try to get it published, even on something like Helium, or I could start a blog. I will always love music because it is a good way to communicate feelings and stories, and it makes people feel good.

1. Double-underline the **topic sentence**.
2. What **categories** of music does Lorenza write about? _____
3. Circle the **transitions**.
4. Does the paragraph have the Four Basics of Good Classification (p. 188)? Why or why not? _____
5. What kind of organization does Lorenza use? _____

Professional Classification Essay

Frances Cole Jones
Don't Work in a Goat's Stomach

Frances Cole Jones, who holds a B.A. in English/creative writing from Connecticut College and an M.A. in liberal studies from New York University, is founder and president of Cole Media Management. This firm focuses on improving clients' communication skills, helping them prepare for media interviews and presentations, among other things. Previously, Jones worked as a book editor, specializing in commercial nonfiction. More recently, she has published her own books: *How to Wow: Proven Strategies for Presenting Your Ideas, Persuading Your Audience, and Perfecting Your Image* (2008) and *The Wow Factor: The 33 Things You Must (and Must Not) Do to Guarantee Your Edge in Today's Business World* (2010). Jones has said of these books, "My goal is to have every person who picks these up . . . feel more confident in their ability to present their best self—in any situation."

In the following excerpt from *The Wow Factor,* Jones discusses the types of workplace clutter that can get in the way of success on the job.

Vocabulary development

Underline these words as you read the classification essay.

inevitably: always; regularly
hazmat: short for *hazardous materials*
hither and yon: from here to there
petri dish: a container used to grow bacteria
disproportionate: unusually large
cull: to reduce (in this case, cluttering items)
self-evident: clear; not needing an explanation
prone to: likely to do; inclined toward
communal: shared
ficus: fig
whimsical: cute
aforementioned: previously mentioned
undermine: weaken
paraphernalia: personal belongings
stowed: stored
pristine: clean
intermittent: regular

When I was working in the nine-to-five world, there was a gentleman down the hall whose office inevitably looked like it had been stirred up with a stick: a desk loaded with piles of paper, dirty cups, takeout containers, a Magic 8 Ball,[1] and a keyboard that looked like you'd be better off wearing a hazmat suit when you touched it, more piles of papers on the desk, on the floor, on the chairs; shelving that was loaded with books, photos, and (bizarrely) pieces of sporting equipment, various items of clothing tossed hither and yon: jackets, sweaters, socks, shoes, hats. . . . One day, our boss walked by and said, "That office looks like the inside of a goat's stomach."

Not surprisingly, the occupant of the messy office wasn't with the company much longer.

IDENTIFY Underline the categories presented in this paragraph.

What I've learned since then is that my colleague had created a petri dish of the three kinds of recognized office clutter. As identified by psychologist Sam Gosling, they are "identity clutter": photos of family, friends, pets, etc. that are designed to remind us we have a life outside the office; "thought and feeling regulators," which are chosen to change our mood: squeezable stress balls, miniature Zen gardens,[2] daily affirmation calendars;[3] and "behavior residues"—old coffee cups, food wrappers, Post-its stuck to the keyboard, etc.

The trouble with having a disproportionate number of these items in and around your office is that it sends a message to those around you that you are out of control. As one of my CEO clients said to me after we'd walked past his junior report's disastrously messy office on the way to his company's conference room, "Doesn't she realize I notice—and care?"

Now I'm not saying you can't have a few personal items. And I am certainly not going to mandate, as one of my clients has done, what kinds of flowers you are allowed to receive. In that office, your loved ones can send you a white orchid. That's it. But I am saying it's important to choose carefully, cull frequently, and clean daily.

In an effort to help you decide what stays and what goes, I have put together two lists: Remove Immediately and Keep Selectively. Given its urgency, let's first look at those items I'd prefer you remove immediately.

Remove Immediately:

- Leftover food: food wrappers; dirty cups, plates, or silverware. While this may seem self-evident, I imagine that more than a few of you have found yourself at five o'clock speaking to your coworkers from

1. **Magic 8 Ball:** a fortune-telling toy that when shaken provides answers to questions
2. **Zen gardens:** miniature (in this case) gardens meant to create a peaceful setting
3. **affirmation calendars:** calendars that include encouraging sayings

amid a small forest of half-empty coffee cups. (And I am hoping there are at least one or two of you who—like me—are still drinking absentmindedly from your 8 a.m. coffee at 5 p.m., a practice I'm prone to if not carefully supervised, which always makes my assistant exclaim with disgust.) All of these must go—again, if you're like me, for your own sake if no one else's. When you do remove them, please don't simply dump them in the sink of the shared kitchen down the hall. I know of one office that based its recent decision as to which of two equally qualified and experienced people was laid off on who was more prone to leaving their dirty dishes in the communal kitchen; deciding factors these days are, indeed, this small.

- Dead flowers/plants. The roses your ex gave you last Valentine's Day shouldn't become a dried flower arrangement on the shelf. That shedding ficus tree will be much happier if given to a friend with a green thumb.
- Stuffed animals/"whimsical" toys (such as the aforementioned Magic 8 Ball). While these can be helpful should your—or your boss's—kids come to the office, day to day they have the potential to undermine others' perceptions of the professionalism you bring to your work.

Keep Selectively:

- Grooming products. Hairbrushes, toothbrushes/paste, shaving and nail paraphernalia can all be handy to have on hand. Please don't, however, leave them in plain sight—or perform any personal maintenance in front of others.
- Extra pairs of shoes/a shirt. Again, both are useful on days when you have an unexpectedly important meeting, or uncooperative weather. They should, however, be stowed out of others' sight lines.
- Photos of family/friends. While these are lovely reminders of your life outside the office and can be great conversation starters, please do make sure everyone in each photo is fully clothed and behaving appropriately. . . .

REFLECT Are there any other items you would put in the "Remove Immediately" or "Keep Selectively" categories?

All this said, I do know that an office has to be worked in—and that worrying about keeping it pristine can, ultimately, detract from focusing on what you need to accomplish. For this reason, it can help to set aside fifteen minutes at the middle and end of each day to clear your desk/chairs/floor of any accumulated clutter. A principle applied by airlines and luxury bus lines, these intermittent sweeps help keep things from piling up.

7 **REFLECT** Would you be willing to devote this much time each day to clearing your work space?

TIP For reading advice, see Chapter 1.

1. Double-underline the **thesis statement**.

2. Within the categories "Remove Immediately" and "Keep Selectively," Jones presents six subcategories of things. Underline them.

3. Do you agree with Jones's categorizations? For instance, do you see value in keeping any of the things Jones thinks should be removed immediately? Why or why not? _____

4. Circle the **transitions**.

Respond to one of the following assignments in a paragraph or essay.

1. Write about whether you are more of a keeper or a thrower-outer of things. Make sure to include examples of items you tend to keep or discard, and explain how you make your decisions.

2. Write about classes of things you think should be kept or thrown out at home (as opposed to work). Explain the reasons for your decisions.

3. Jones recommends avoiding a particular type of behavior: filling work spaces with needless clutter. Can you think of other behaviors that might keep people from reaching their potential at work or school? Give examples of these behaviors, and explain why they are problematic.

Write Your Own Classification

In this section, you will write your own classification based on one of the following assignments. For help, refer to the How to Write Classification checklist on page 205.

ASSIGNMENT OPTIONS Writing about College, Work, and Everyday Life

Write a classification paragraph or essay on one of the following topics or on one of your own choice. If you responded to the idea journal prompt on page 190, you might develop that writing further.

COLLEGE

- Classify the types of resources available in your college's library, giving examples of things in each category. If you don't have time to visit the library, spend time looking at its Web site. (Some library Web sites include virtual tours.)

- Classify the course requirements for your program into different categories, such as easy, challenging, and very challenging. Your purpose could be to help a future student in the program understand what to expect.

- Classify the types of students at your college, giving explanations and examples for each category. You might classify students by such things as their interests, their level of dedication to school, and their backgrounds (for example, *older students returning to college* and *young students*).

WORK

- Classify the different types of bosses, giving explanations and examples for each category.
- Classify the types of skills you need in your current job or a job you held in the past. Give explanations and examples for each category of skill.
- Look back at the paragraph on page 188 that illustrates the Four Basics of Good Classification. Based on your own experiences, think of at least two other ways in which workers might be classified. In writing about your classification, give examples of the types of jobs these workers would like and dislike.

EVERYDAY LIFE

- Using Lorenza Mattazi's paragraph as a guide (see p. 198), classify the types of music you enjoy.
- Write about the types of challenges you face in your everyday life, giving explanations and examples for each category.
- Find out about social-service volunteer opportunities in your community. Write about the types of opportunities that are available. Or research an organization that interests you, and write about the kinds of things it does.

COMMUNITY CONNECTIONS

While attending college, **CAROLINE POWERS** volunteered for Girls, Inc., an organization that inspires girls to be "strong, smart, and bold." Getting more involved in college and community activities, as Caroline did, can help you feel more connected to others and can even improve the chances that you'll stay in school.

For more on this story, ways to make community connections, and writing assignments, visit bedfordstmartins.com/realwriting.

ASSIGNMENT OPTIONS Reading and Writing Critically

Complete one of the following assignments, which ask you to apply the critical thinking, reading, and writing skills discussed in Chapter 1.

Writing Critically about Readings

Both Frances Cole Jones's "Don't Work in a Goat's Stomach" (p. 199) and Shari Beck's "A Classroom Distraction—and Worse" (p. 282) describe annoying behaviors (cluttering one's office in Jones's essay and texting instead of paying attention to others in Beck's). Read or review both of these essays, and then follow these steps:

1. **Summarize** Briefly summarize the works, listing examples they include.
2. **Analyze** Are there any other examples or details that the authors might have provided?
3. **Synthesize** Using examples from both Jones's and Beck's essays and from your own experience, discuss various types of annoying behaviors, and explain why they are bothersome.

TIP For a reminder of how to summarize, analyze, synthesize, and evaluate, see the Reading and Writing Critically box on pages 16–17.

4. **Evaluate** Which piece, Jones's or Beck's, do you think is more effective? Why? In writing your evaluation, you might look back on your responses to step 2.

Writing about Images

Study the visual below, and complete the following steps.

1. **Read the image** Ask yourself: What purpose does the visual serve? How do the drawings in it help viewers understand the different types of barking? (For more information on reading images, see Chapter 1.)

2. **Write a classification** Write a paragraph or essay classifying the types of behaviors that send signals to others. The signals can be from a pet or from a person. You might include or expand on the types of behaviors described in the visual.

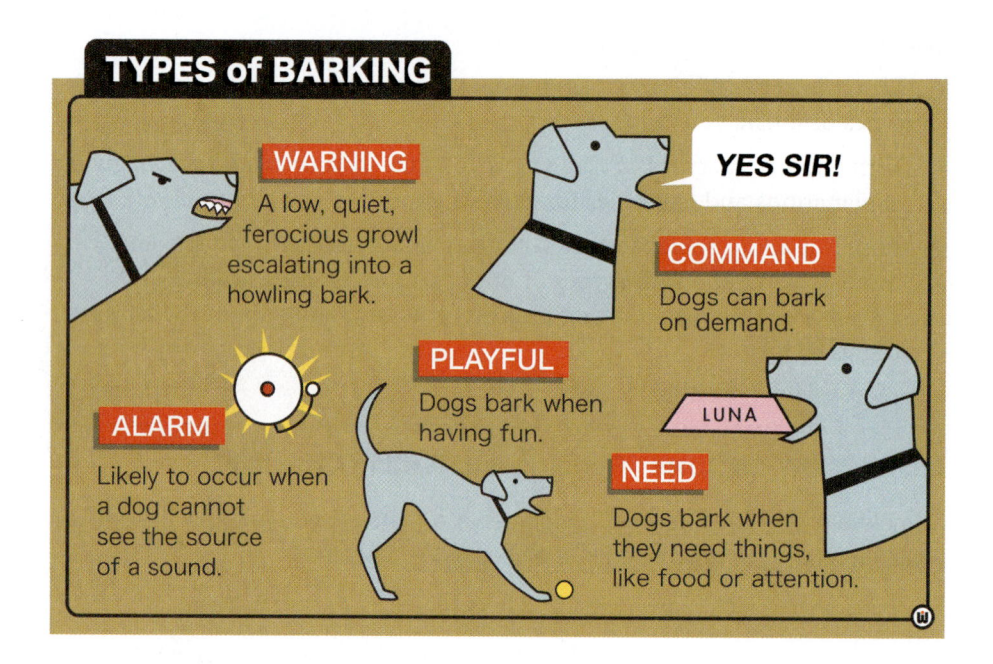

TYPES of BARKING

WARNING A low, quiet, ferocious growl escalating into a howling bark.

COMMAND Dogs can bark on demand. YES SIR!

ALARM Likely to occur when a dog cannot see the source of a sound.

PLAYFUL Dogs bark when having fun.

NEED Dogs bark when they need things, like food or attention.

LUNA

Writing to Solve a Problem

Read or review the discussion of problem solving in Chapter 1 (pp. 24–26). Then, consider the following problem.

> You need a car loan. The loan officer gives you an application that asks for your monthly income and expenses. Because you find yourself short on money every month, you realize that you need to see how you spend your money. You decide to make a monthly budget that categorizes the kinds of expenses you have.

ASSIGNMENT: Working with a group or on your own, break your monthly expenses into categories, thinking of everything that you spend money on. Then, review the expenses carefully to see which ones might be reduced. Next, write a classification paragraph or essay for the loan officer that classifies your monthly expenses, with examples, and ends with one or two suggestions about how you might reduce your monthly spending. You might start with this sentence:

My monthly expenses fall into _____ basic categories: _____, _____, and _____.

CHECKLIST: HOW TO WRITE CLASSIFICATION

STEPS	DETAILS
☐ Narrow and explore your topic. See Chapter 3.	• Make the topic more specific. • Prewrite to get ideas about the narrowed topic.
☐ Write a topic sentence (paragraph) or thesis statement (essay). See Chapter 4.	• State your topic and your organizing principle or categories.
☐ Support your point. See Chapter 5.	• Come up with explanations/examples to support each category.
☐ Write a draft. See Chapter 6.	• Make a plan that puts the categories in a logical order. • Include a topic sentence (paragraph) or thesis statement (essay) and all the supporting categories with explanations and examples.
☐ Revise your draft. See Chapter 7.	• Make sure it has *all* the Four Basics of Good Classification. • Make sure you include transitions to move readers smoothly from one category to the next.
☐ Edit your revised draft. See Parts 4 through 7.	• Correct errors in grammar, spelling, word use, and punctuation.

Chapter Review

1. Classification is writing that _____

2. The organizing principle is _____

WRITING DIFFERENT KINDS OF PARAGRAPHS AND ESSAYS

Chapter 12 • Classification

3. What are the Four Basics of Good Classification?

LEARNING JOURNAL
Reread your idea journal entry (p. 190) about the kinds of students in this class or the kinds of friends you have. Make another entry about the same topic, using what you have learned about classification.

4. Write sentences using the following vocabulary words: *inevitably, disproportionate, prone to, whimsical, undermine.*

> **reflect** Write for 2 minutes about the kinds of responsibilities you have. Then, compare what you have written with what you wrote in response to the "write" prompt on page 188.

13

Definition

Writing That Tells What Something Means

> **YOU KNOW THIS**
>
> You often ask, or are asked, for the meaning of something:
>
> - When a friend tells you a relationship is *serious,* you ask what he means by *serious.*
> - Another student calls a class you are considering *terrible,* and you ask what she means.
>
> **write** for 2 minutes about how you would define a term to someone who had never heard it before.

Understand What Definition Is

Definition is writing that explains what a term or concept means.

> **Four Basics** of Good Definition
>
> 1. It tells readers what is being defined.
> 2. It presents a clear definition.
> 3. It uses examples to show what the writer means.
> 4. It gives details to support the examples.

In the following paragraph, the numbers and colors correspond to the Four Basics of Good Definition.

A **1** stereotype **2** is a conventional idea or image that is simplistic—and often wrong, particularly when it is applied to people or groups of people. Stereotypes can prevent us from seeing people as they really are because stereotypes blind us with preconceived notions about what a certain type of person is like. **3** For example, I had a stereotyped notion of Native Americans until I met my friend Daniel, a Chippewa Indian. **4** I thought all Indians wore feathers and beads, had long black hair, and avoided all contact with non–Native Americans because they resented their land being taken away. Daniel, however, wears jeans and T-shirts, and we talk about everything—even our different ancestries. After meeting him, I understood that my stereotype of Native Americans was completely wrong. **3** Not only was it wrong, but it set up an us-them concept in my mind that made me feel that I, as a non–Native American, would never have anything in common with Native Americans. My stereotype would not have allowed me to see any Native American as an individual: I would have seen him or her as part of a group that I thought was all alike, and all different from me. From now on, I won't assume that any individual fits my stereotype; I will try to see that person as I would like them to see me: as myself, not a stereotyped image.

Seeing Definition

write How do you define "the 99%"?

You can use definition in many practical situations.

COLLEGE On a math exam, you are asked to define *exponential notation*.

WORK On a job application, you are asked to choose one word that describes you and explain why.

EVERYDAY LIFE In a relationship, you define for your partner what you mean by *commitment* or *communication*.

TIP Once you have a basic statement of your definition, try revising it to make it stronger, clearer, or more interesting.

In college, writing assignments may include the word *define*, but they might also use phrases such as *explain the meaning of* _____ and *discuss the meaning of* _____. In these cases, use the strategies discussed in this chapter to complete the assignment.

Main Point in Definition

In definition, the **main point** usually defines a term or concept. The main point is related to your purpose: to help your readers understand the term or concept as you are using it.

When you write your definition, do not just copy the dictionary definition; write it in your own words as you want your readers to understand it. To help you, you might first complete the following sentence:

MAIN POINT IN DEFINITION I want readers to understand that this term means . . .

Then, based on your response, write a topic sentence (paragraph) or thesis statement (essay). These main-point statements can take the following forms.

Term + Class + Detail = Topic sentence

Phototherapy is a treatment for depression caused by inadequate exposure to sunlight.

In this example, "Class" is the larger group the term belongs to. Main-point statements do not have to include a class, however. For example:

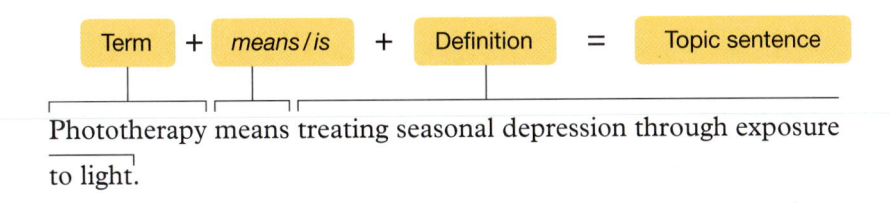

Term + *means/is* + Definition = Topic sentence

Phototherapy means treating seasonal depression through exposure to light.

Now, look at this thesis statement about a related topic.

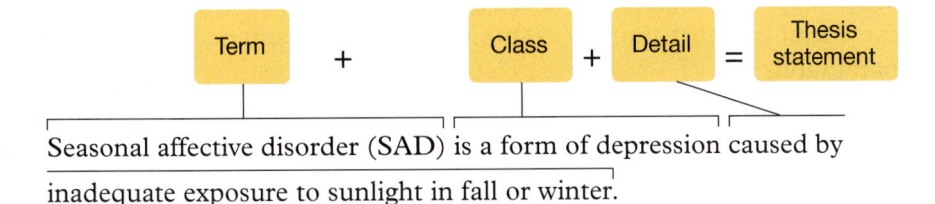

Term + Class + Detail = Thesis statement

Seasonal affective disorder (SAD) is a form of depression caused by inadequate exposure to sunlight in fall or winter.

The thesis statement is broader in scope than the topic sentences, because it sets up a discussion of the larger subject of seasonal affective

---

WRITER AT WORK

WALTER SCANLON: I take my writing seriously because I know that is how people will judge me.

(See Walter Scanlon's **PROFILE OF SUCCESS** on p. 215.)

TIP Sometimes, the same main point can be used for a paragraph and an essay, but the essay must develop this point in more detail. (See pp. 69–70.)

disorder. In contrast, the topic sentences consider one particular treatment for this disorder (phototherapy).

IDEA JOURNAL Write about what success means.

PRACTICE 1 Writing a Statement of Your Definition

For each of the following terms, write a definition statement using the pattern indicated in brackets. You may need to use a dictionary.

EXAMPLE:

Cirrhosis [term + class + detail]:
Cirrhosis is a liver disease often caused by alcohol abuse.

1. Stress [term + class + detail]: _____

2. Vacation [term + *means/is* + definition]: _____

3. Confidence [term + class + detail]: _____

4. Conservation [term + *means/is* + definition]: _____

5. Marriage [term + *means/is* + definition]: _____

Support in Definition

The paragraph and essay models on pages 211–12 use one topic sentence (paragraph) and the thesis statement (essay) from the Main Point section in this chapter. Both models include the **support** used in all definition writing: examples that explain what a term or concept means backed up by details about these examples. In the essay model, however, the major support points (examples) are topic sentences for individual paragraphs.

PRACTICE 2 Selecting Examples and Details to Explain the Definition

List three examples or pieces of information you could use to explain each of the following definitions.

EXAMPLE:

Insomnia means sleeplessness.

a. *hard to fall asleep*

b. *wake up in the middle of the night*

c. *wake up without feeling rested in the morning*

1. Confidence is feeling that you can conquer any obstacle.

   a. _____
   b. _____
   c. _____

2. A real friend is not just someone for the fun times.

   a. _____
   b. _____
   c. _____

3. A family is a group you always belong to, no matter what.

   a. _____
   b. _____
   c. _____

4. Beauty is an important element in life that a viewer needs to be always looking for, even in unlikely places.

   a. _____
   b. _____
   c. _____

PARAGRAPHS VS. ESSAYS IN DEFINITION

For more on the important features of definition, see the Four Basics of Good Definition on page 207.

Paragraph

Topic sentence — Phototherapy means treating seasonal depression through exposure to light.

Support 1 (first example) — One form of phototherapy is spending time outdoors during the brightest time of day. Noon until 2 p.m. is ideal, but going outside earlier or later is better than not getting out at all. Because the sun sets earlier in the winter, it might be necessary to step outdoors before the end of a workday, perhaps during a lunch break. Alternatively, face a bright window for twenty to thirty minutes and absorb the rays.

Support 2 (second example) — Another form of phototherapy is the use of a lamp that mimics outdoor light. Typically, people sit by these lamps as they read, work, or watch television. It is best to use them for at least twenty minutes a day.

Support 3 (third example) — Apart from sunlight, the most effective form of phototherapy is the use of a light-therapy box. Some experts believe that light boxes allow users to absorb more light than is possible with the lamps, which tend to be smaller. However, both phototherapy lamps and light boxes are good ways to counter winter darkness and cloudy days in any season.

Concluding sentence — Whether the solution is a lamp, a light box, or good old-fashioned sunlight, there is no reason to suffer from seasonal depression.

Main Point: Often, narrower for a paragraph than for an essay: While the topic sentence (paragraph) focuses on just one treatment for seasonal affective disorder, the thesis statement (essay) considers the disorder as a whole.

Examples Supporting the Main Point

Details about the Examples: Usually, 1 to 3 sentences per example for paragraphs and 3 to 8 sentences per example for essays.

Conclusion

Think Critically As You Write Definition

ASK YOURSELF

- Have I examined different definitions of this term or concept? (If not, research them and consider broadening or narrowing your definition based on what you learn. For more on finding and evaluating outside sources, see pp. 304–09.)
- Would someone who is unfamiliar with this term or concept understand it based on my definition and my supporting details and examples?

Essay

Thesis statement

Seasonal affective disorder (SAD) is a form of depression caused by inadequate exposure to sunlight in fall or winter. It can seriously affect the daily lives of those who suffer from it.

Topic sentence 1 (first example)

One consequence of SAD is sleepiness and a lack of energy. SAD sufferers may find that they are sleeping longer yet are still drowsy during the day, especially during the afternoon. Connected to the drowsiness may be moodiness and an inability to concentrate. The latter effect can result in poorer performance at work and at other tasks. Those affected by SAD may also find that they move more slowly than usual and that all types of physical activity are more challenging than they used to be. All these difficulties can be a source of stress, sometimes worsening the depression.

Topic sentence 2 (second example)

Another consequence of SAD is loss of interest in work, hobbies, and other activities. To some extent, these symptoms may be connected to a lack of energy. Often, however, the feelings run deeper than that. Activities that once lifted one's spirits may have the opposite effect. For instance, a mother who at one time never missed her child's soccer games might now see attending them as a burden. Someone who was once a top performer at work may find that it is all he or she can do to show up in the morning. Such changes in one's outlook can lead to a feeling of hopelessness.

Topic sentence 3 (third example)

The most serious consequence of SAD is withdrawal from interactions with others. SAD sufferers may find that they are no longer interested in going out with friends, and they may turn down requests to get together for movies, meals, or social events. They may even withdraw from family members, engaging less frequently in conversation or even spending time alone in their room. Furthermore, they may postpone or cancel activities, such as vacation trips, that might require them to interact with family for hours at a time. Withdrawal symptoms may also extend to the workplace, with SAD sufferers becoming less vocal at meetings or avoiding lunches or conversations with colleagues. Concern that family members or coworkers may be noticing such personality changes can cause or worsen anxiety in those with SAD.

Concluding paragraph

Because the effects of SAD can be so significant, it is important to address them as soon as possible. Fortunately, there are many good therapies for the condition, from drug treatment to greater exposure to sunlight, whether real or simulated through special lamps or light boxes. Often, such treatments have SAD sufferers feeling better quickly.

Organization in Definition

TIP For more on order of importance, see page 79.

The examples in definition are often organized by **order of importance**, meaning that the example that will have the most effect on readers is saved for last. This strategy is used in the paragraph and essay models on pages 211–12.

Transitions in definition move readers from one example to the next. Here are some transitions you might use in definition, although many others are possible, too.

Common Transitions in Definition

alternately	first, second, third, and so on
another; one / another	for example
another kind	for instance

PRACTICE 3 Using Transitions in Definition

Read the paragraph that follows, and fill in the blanks with transitions. You are not limited to the ones listed in the preceding box on page 211.

Each year, *Business Week* publishes a list of the most family-friendly companies to work for. The magazine uses several factors to define the organizations as family-friendly. _____ factor is whether the company has flextime, allowing employees to schedule work hours that better fit family needs. _____, a parent might choose to work from 6:30 a.m. to 2:30 p.m. to be able to spend time with children. _____, a parent might split his or her job with a colleague, so each person thus has more time for child care. _____ factor is whether family leave programs are encouraged. In addition to maternity leaves, _____, does the company encourage paternity leaves and leaves for care of elderly parents? Increasingly, companies are trying to become more family-friendly to attract and keep good employees.

Read and Analyze Definition

CRITICAL READING
- Preview
- Read
- Pause
- Review

See pages 9–12.

Reading examples of definition will help you write your own. In the first example, Walter Scanlon shows how he uses definition in his work as a program and workplace consultant.

The second example is a definition paragraph by a student, and the third example is a definition essay by a professional writer. As you read these pieces, pay attention to the vocabulary, and answer the questions in the margin. They will help you read critically.

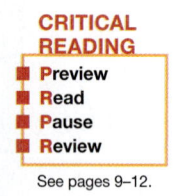

PROFILE OF SUCCESS

Definition in the Real World

Background I grew up in a working-class neighborhood in New York City, in a family with a long history of alcohol problems. From my earliest days in grammar school, I assumed the role of class clown, somehow managing to just get by academically. By the time I reached high school, I was using drugs and alcohol, and I soon dropped out of school. For the next ten years, I was in and out of hospitals and prisons. When I was not in an institution, I lived on the streets—in abandoned buildings and deserted cars.

At one point after being released from yet another prison, I knew I had to do something different if I were to survive. Instead of looking for a drink or a drug this time out of jail, I joined Alcoholics Anonymous. That was the beginning of a new life for me.

I earned a GED, and took a pre-college reading course to improve my reading skills. Then, I took one college-level course, never intending to earn a degree but just to say I went to college. I did not do all that well in the first course, but I kept taking courses and got a bachelor's degree. I then went on for a master's and, finally, a Ph.D. Now, I run my own successful consulting business in which I work with companies' employee assistance programs, private individual clients, and families with a wide range of complex problems. I have also published two books and professional articles.

Walter Scanlon
Program and Workplace Consultant

Degrees/Colleges B.A., Pace University; M.B.A., New York Institute of Technology; Ph.D., Columbus University

Employer Self

Writing at work I do all kinds of writing in my job: letters, proposals, presentations, articles, books, training programs, e-mails, memos, and more. I take my writing seriously because I know that is how people will judge me. Often, I have only a few minutes to present myself, so I work hard to make my point early on and very clearly. I believe that if you write clearly, you think clearly. In most situations, there are many factors that I cannot control, but I can always control my writing and the message it gives people.

I sometimes get e-mails that have all kinds of grammar mistakes in them, and believe me, I notice them and form opinions about the sender. (For an example of an e-mail that Walter received and his reaction to it, see Chapter 22, p. 378.)

How Walter uses definition As I work with clients, I often have to define a term so that they can understand it before I explain its relevance to the situation within which we are working.

Walter's Definition

In the following paragraph, Walter defines *employee assistance program* for a client.

Employee Assistance Program

The "employee assistance program" (EAP) is a confidential, early-intervention workplace counseling service designed to help employees who are experiencing personal problems. It is a social service within a work environment that can be found in most major corporations, associations, and government organizations. EAP services are always free to the employee and benefit the organization as much as the employee. Employees who are free of emotional problems are far more productive than those who are not. An employee whose productivity is negatively affected by a drinking problem, for example, might seek help through the EAP. He/she would be assessed by a counselor and then referred to an appropriate community resource for additional services. The *employee* is helped through the EAP while the *employer* is rewarded with improved productivity. An EAP is a win-win program for all involved.

1. Double-underline the **topic sentence**.
2. Fill in the blanks with the term defined in the paragraph and the definition.

   Term: _____

   Definition: _____

   _____
3. Underline an **example** of what an EAP might do.
4. Double-underline the sentence that makes a final observation about the topic.

Student Definition Paragraph

Corin Costas

What Community Involvement Means to Me

While at Bunker Hill Community College (BHCC), Corin Costas helped start a business club on campus. Later, he took on the leadership of SHOCWAVES (Students Helping Our Community with Activities), an organization focused on community-service projects. Costas initiated several projects, including Light One Little Candle, which asked BHCC students to give $1 to have their names put on a paper candle. The money raised was donated to the Dana-Farber Cancer Institute to buy books for children with cancer. After graduating from BHCC, Costas transferred to the University of Massachusetts Boston with a $14,000 scholarship.

In the following paragraph, Costas defines SHOCWAVES and what it does.

SHOCWAVES is a student organization at Bunker Hill Community College. SHOCWAVES stands for Students Helping Our Community with Activities, and its mission is to get students involved with the community—to become part of it by actively working in it in positive ways. Each year, SHOCWAVES is assigned a budget by the Student Activities Office, and it spends that budget in activities that help the community in a variety of ways. Some of the money is spent, for example, in fund-raising events for community causes. We have money to plan and launch a fund-raiser, which raises far more than we spend. In the process, other students and members of the community also become involved in the helping effort. We get to know lots of people, and we usually have a lot of fun—all while helping others. Recently, we have worked as part of the Charles River Cleanup, the Walk for Hunger, collecting toys for sick and needy children, and Light One Little Candle. While SHOCWAVES's mission is to help the community, it also benefits its members. Working in the community, I have learned so many valuable skills, and I always have something I care about to write about for my classes. I have learned about budgeting, advertising, organizing, and managing. I have also developed my creativity by coming up with new ways to do things. I have networked with many people, including people who are important in the business world. SHOCWAVES has greatly improved my life, and my chances for future success.

1. Double-underline the **topic sentence**.

2. Underline the **examples** of what SHOCWAVES does for the community.

3. Double-underline the sentence that makes a final observation about the topic.

4. Does this paragraph follow the Four Basics of Good Definition (p. 207)? Why or why not? _____

_____

Professional Definition Essay

Janice E. Castro with Dan Cook and Cristina Garcia
Spanglish

Vocabulary development
Underline these words as you read the definition essay.

bemused: surprised and a bit confused
linguistic currency: typical speech
fractured syntax: language that breaks grammatical rules
patter: quick speech
melting pot: a blending of people from different cultures
Anglo: a white, English-speaking person
contemporaries: peers
phenomena: strange experiences or things
implicit: understood but not expressed directly
languorous: long and relaxing
hybrid: a combination of two things
wielded: held
gaffes: mistakes
inadvertently: by mistake; not intentionally
blunders: mistakes

IDEA JOURNAL How important do you think it is for non-Hispanics in the United States to understand at least some Spanish?

SUMMARIZE In your own words, describe how Spanglish differs from the broken English of earlier immigrants to the United States.

PREDICT Based on the first part of the first sentence of paragraph 4, how do you suppose the authors will develop this paragraph?

Janice E. Castro is an assistant professor in the Medill New Media Program at Northwestern University. She worked as a reporter for *Time* for more than twenty years and started the magazine's health policy beat. After the publication of her book, *The American Way of Health: How Medicine Is Changing, and What It Means to You* (1994), she became the managing editor of *Time*'s online division.

Castro wrote "Spanglish" while at *Time* with the help of Dan Cook and Cristina Garcia. In the essay, she defines the language created when Spanish and English speakers come together in our blended culture.

1   In Manhattan a first-grader greets her visiting grandparents, happily exclaiming, "Come here, *siéntate*!" Her bemused grandfather, who does not speak Spanish, nevertheless knows she is asking him to sit down. A Miami personnel officer understands what a job applicant means when he says, "*Quiero un* part time." Nor do drivers miss a beat reading a billboard alongside a Los Angeles street advertising CERVEZA—SIX-PACK!

2   This free-form blend of Spanish and English, known as Spanglish, is common linguistic currency wherever concentrations of Hispanic Americans are found in the U.S. In Los Angeles, where 55 percent of the city's 3 million inhabitants speak Spanish, Spanglish is as much a part of daily life as sunglasses. Unlike the broken-English efforts of earlier immigrants from Europe, Asia, and other regions, Spanglish has become a widely accepted conversational mode used casually—even playfully—by Spanish-speaking immigrants and native-born Americans alike.

3   Consisting of one part Hispanicized English, one part Americanized Spanish, and more than a little fractured syntax, Spanglish is a bit like a Robin Williams comedy routine: a crackling line of cross-cultural patter straight from the melting pot. Often it enters Anglo homes and families through the children, who pick it up at school or at play with their young Hispanic contemporaries. In other cases, it comes from watching TV; many an Anglo child watching *Sesame Street* has learned *uno dos tres* almost as quickly as one two three.

4   Spanglish takes a variety of forms, from the Southern California Anglos who bid farewell with the utterly silly "*hasta la* bye-bye" to the Cuban American drivers in Miami who *parquean* their *carros*. Some

Spanglish sentences are mostly Spanish, with a quick detour for an English word or two. A Latino friend may cut short a conversation by glancing at his watch and excusing himself with the explanation that he must "*ir al* supermarket."

Many of the English words transplanted in this way are simply hardier than their Spanish counterparts. No matter how distasteful the subject, for example, it is still easier to say "income tax" than *impuesto sobre la renta*. At the same time, many Spanish-speaking immigrants have adopted such terms as *VCR*, *microwave*, and *dishwasher* for what they view as largely American phenomena. Still other English words convey a cultural context that is not implicit in the Spanish. A friend who invites you to *lonche* most likely has in mind the brisk American custom of "doing lunch" rather than the languorous afternoon break traditionally implied by *almuerzo*.

Mainstream Americans exposed to similar hybrids of German, Chinese, or Hindi might be mystified. But even Anglos who speak little or no Spanish are somewhat familiar with Spanglish. Living among them, for one thing, are 19 million Hispanics. In addition, more American high school and university students sign up for Spanish than for any other foreign language.

Only in the past ten years [in 1978–1988], though, has Spanglish begun to turn into a national slang. Its popularity has grown with the explosive increases in U.S. immigration from Latin American countries. English has increasingly collided with Spanish in retail stores, offices and classrooms, in pop music, and on street corners. Anglos whose ancestors picked up such Spanish words as *rancho*, *bronco*, *tornado*, and *incomunicado*, for instance, now freely use such Spanish words as *gracias*, *bueno*, *amigo*, and *por favor*.

REFLECT Have you encountered Spanglish? If so, what Spanglish slang are you familiar with?

Among Latinos, Spanglish conversations often flow easily from Spanish into several sentences of English and back.

Spanglish is a sort of code for Latinos: the speakers know Spanish, but their hybrid language reflects the American culture in which they live. Many lean to shorter, clipped phrases in place of the longer, more graceful expressions their parents used. Says Leonel de la Cuesta, an assistant professor of modern languages at Florida International University in Miami: "In the U.S., time is money, and that is showing up in Spanglish as an economy of language." Conversational examples: *taipiar* (type) and *winshiwiper* (windshield wiper) replace *escribir a màquina* and *limpiaparabrisas*.

Major advertisers, eager to tap the estimated $134 billion in spending power wielded by Spanish-speaking Americans, have ventured into Spanglish to promote their products. In some cases, attempts to sprinkle

Spanish through commercials have produced embarrassing gaffes. A Braniff Airlines ad that sought to tell Spanish-speaking audiences they could settle back *en* (in) luxuriant *cuero* (leather) seats, for example, inadvertently said they could fly without clothes (*encuero*). A fractured translation of the Miller Lite slogan told readers the beer was "Filling, and less delicious." Similar blunders are often made by Anglos trying to impress Spanish-speaking pals. But if Latinos are amused by mangled Spanglish, they also recognize these goofs as a sort of friendly acceptance. As they might put it, *no problema*.

1. Double-underline the **thesis statement**.
2. Circle the **transitions** used to introduce examples.
3. Do the writers provide enough examples of what they mean by *Spanglish*? If not, where could more examples be added? _____
   _____
4. Look back at the final paragraph. Why do you suppose the authors chose to conclude in that way? _____
   _____
   _____

Respond to one of the following assignments in a paragraph or essay.

1. Do you have any personal experiences with the use of Spanglish? If so, give examples of the types of words you are familiar with and how they have been used. Also, discuss what using Spanglish means to you. For instance, if you are a native speaker of Spanish, does using Spanglish make you feel more connected to people from different cultures? Or is it just a fun way to communicate?
2. Define an expression common to your group of friends, your workplace, your region, or some other group to which you belong. Make sure to give several examples of how the expression is used.
3. Define a concept that is important to a culture to which you belong. You might, for example, choose to define *success, diversity,* or some other concept in terms of U.S. culture. Explain why the concept is important, and give examples.

Write Your Own Definition

In this section, you will write your own definition based on one of the following assignments. For help, refer to the How to Write Definition checklist on page 223.

WRITING DIFFERENT KINDS OF PARAGRAPHS AND ESSAYS
Write Your Own Definition

ASSIGNMENT OPTIONS Writing about College, Work, and Everyday Life

Write a definition paragraph or essay on one of the following topics or on one of your own choice. If you responded to the idea journal prompt on page 210, you might develop that writing further.

COLLEGE

- How would you define a good student or a bad student? Give examples to explain your definition.
- Identify a difficult or technical term from a class you are taking. Then, define the term, and give examples of different ways in which it might be used.
- Define *learning*, not only in terms of school, but in terms of all the ways in which it can occur. You might start by writing down the different types of learning that go on both in school and in other settings. Then, (1) write a main point that defines learning in a broader way, and (2) support your definition with the examples you came up with.

WORK

- Define a satisfying job, giving explanations and examples.
- If you have ever held a job that used unusual or interesting terminology, write about some of the terms used, what they meant, and their function on the job.
- In many businesses, it's common for workers to use jargon, which can be defined either as insider language or as vague, empty, or overused expressions. Some examples are "going the extra mile," "being on the same page," and "thinking outside the box." Give examples of work jargon that you've heard of, provide definitions, and explain why the jargon is vague or ineffective. Then, for each expression, suggest more specific words.

EVERYDAY LIFE

- What does it mean to be a good friend? Provide a definition, giving explanations and examples.
- What does it mean to be a good parent? Provide a definition, giving explanations and examples.
- Ask three (or more) people to tell you what they think *community service* means. Take notes on their responses, and then write a paragraph or an essay combining their definitions with your own.

ASSIGNMENT OPTIONS Reading and Writing Critically

Complete one of the following assignments, which ask you to apply the critical thinking, reading, and writing skills discussed in Chapter 1.

COMMUNITY CONNECTIONS

CORIN COSTAS (see the paragraph on p. 217) led a community-service organization while attending college. Getting more involved in college and community activities, as Corin did, can help you feel more connected to others and can even improve the chances that you will stay in school.

For more on this story, ways to make community connections, and writing assignments, visit **bedfordstmartins.com/ realwriting**.

Writing Critically about Readings

Both Janice E. Castro's "Spanglish" (p. 218) and Amy Tan's "Fish Cheeks" (p. 126) describe the effects of bringing two different cultures together. Read or review both of these essays, and then follow these steps:

TIP For a reminder of how to summarize, analyze, synthesize, and evaluate, see the Reading and Writing Critically box on pages 16–17.

1. **Summarize** Briefly summarize the works, listing examples they include.

2. **Analyze** What questions do the essays raise for you?

3. **Synthesize** Using examples from both essays and from your own experience, describe ways in which different cultures blend (as in "Spanglish") or maintain distance from each other (as in "Fish Cheeks"). What factors seem to be behind this blending or distancing?

4. **Evaluate** Which essay do you think is more effective? Why? In writing your evaluation, look back on your responses to step 2.

Writing about Images

Study the photograph below, and complete the following steps.

1. **Read the image** You could explain to a friend what a sinkhole is, or you could show your friend the picture below. What makes this photograph such a striking visual definition? (For more on reading images, see Chapter 1.)

WRITING DIFFERENT KINDS OF PARAGRAPHS AND ESSAYS
Write Your Own Definition

2. **Write a definition** Write a paragraph or essay that explains what a visual definition is. To support your definition, use examples of any types of images you are familiar with — signs, advertisements, photographs, and so on.

Writing to Solve a Problem

Read or review the discussion of problem solving in Chapter 1 (pp. 24–26). Then, consider the following problem.

> A recent survey asked business managers what skills or traits they value most in employees. The top five responses were (1) motivation, (2) interpersonal skills, (3) initiative, (4) communication skills, and (5) maturity.
>
> You have a job interview next week, and you want to be able to present yourself well. Before you can do that, though, you need to have a better understanding of the five skills and traits noted above and what examples you might be able to give to demonstrate that you have them.

TIP For tools to use in getting a job, visit the *Student Site for Real Writing* at **bedfordstmartins.com/realwriting**.

ASSIGNMENT: Working in a group or on your own, come up with definitions of three of the five terms, and think of some examples of how the skills or traits could be used at work. Then, do one of the following assignments. You might begin with the following sentence:

I am a person who is (or has) _____.

For a paragraph: Choose one of the terms, and give examples of how you have demonstrated the trait.

For an essay: Write about how you have demonstrated the three traits.

CHECKLIST: HOW TO WRITE DEFINITION	
STEPS	**DETAILS**
☐ Narrow and explore your topic. See Chapter 3.	• Make the topic more specific. • Prewrite to get ideas about the narrowed topic.
☐ Write a topic sentence (paragraph) or thesis statement (essay). See Chapter 4.	• State the term that you are focusing on, and provide a definition for it.
☐ Support your point. See Chapter 5.	• Come up with examples and details to explain your definition.
☐ Write a draft. See Chapter 6.	• Make a plan that puts the examples in a logical order. • Include a topic sentence (paragraph) or thesis statement (essay) and all the supporting examples and details.

WRITING DIFFERENT KINDS OF PARAGRAPHS AND ESSAYS

Chapter 13 • Definition

CHECKLIST: HOW TO WRITE DEFINITION	
STEPS	**DETAILS**
☐ **Revise your draft.** See Chapter 7.	• Make sure it has *all* the Four Basics of Good Definition. • Make sure you include transitions to move readers smoothly from one example to the next.
☐ **Edit your revised draft.** See Parts 4 through 7.	• Correct errors in grammar, spelling, word use, and punctuation.

Chapter Review

1. Definition is writing that _____

2. What are the Four Basics of Good Definition?

   _____
   _____
   _____
   _____

LEARNING JOURNAL
Reread your idea journal entry from page 210. Write another entry on the same topic, using what you have learned about definition.

3. Write sentences using the following vocabulary words: *bemused, contemporaries, phenomena, hybrid, blunders.* _____

   _____
   _____
   _____

> **reflect** Think of a term whose meaning you know. Write for 2 minutes about how you would define the term for someone who isn't familiar with it. Compare your response to what you wrote for the "write" prompt on page 207.

YOU KNOW THIS

You frequently compare and contrast different items or places:

- You compare different pairs of jeans before deciding which pair to buy.
- You compare two Web sites for the best price before buying a new computer.

write for 2 minutes about what you know about making comparisons and when you make them.

14

Comparison and Contrast

Writing That Shows Similarities and Differences

Understand What Comparison and Contrast Are

Comparison is writing that shows the similarities among subjects—people, ideas, situations, or items; **contrast** shows the differences. In conversation, people often use the word *compare* to mean either compare or contrast, but as you work through this chapter, the terms will be separated.

| Compare | = | Similarities |
| Contrast | = | Differences |

Four Basics of Good Comparison and Contrast

1. It uses subjects that have enough in common to be compared/contrasted in a useful way.
2. It serves a purpose—to help readers make a decision, to help them understand the subjects, or to show your understanding of the subjects.
3. It presents several important, parallel points of comparison/contrast.
4. It arranges points in a logical order.

In the following paragraph, written for a biology course, the numbers and colors correspond to the Four Basics of Good Comparison and Contrast.

225

4 Points arranged in a logical order

TIP This paragraph uses point-by-point organization. For more information, see page 232.

1 Although frogs and toads are closely related, **2** they differ in appearance, in habitat, and in behavior. **3** The first major difference is in the creatures' physical characteristics. Whereas most frogs have smooth, slimy skin that helps them move through water, toads tend to have rough, bumpy skin suited to drier surroundings. Also, whereas frogs have long, muscular hind legs that help them leap away from predators or toward food, most toads have shorter legs and, therefore, less ability to move quickly. Another physical characteristic of frogs and toads is their bulging eyes, which help them see in different directions. This ability is important, because neither creature can turn its head to look for food or spot a predator. However, frogs' eyes may protrude more than toads'. The second major difference between frogs and toads is their choice of habitat. Frogs tend to live in or near ponds, lakes, or other sources of water. In contrast, toads live mostly in drier areas, such as gardens, forests, and fields. But, like frogs, they lay their eggs in water. The third major difference between frogs and toads concerns their behavior. Whereas frogs may be active during the day or at night, most toads keep a low profile until nighttime. Some biologists believe that it is nature's way of making up for toads' inability to escape from danger as quickly as frogs can. At night, toads are less likely to be spotted by predators. Finally, although both frogs and toads tend to live by themselves, toads, unlike frogs, may form groups while they are hibernating. Both creatures can teach us a lot about how animals adapt to their environments, and studying them is a lot of fun.

A frog

A toad

WRITING DIFFERENT KINDS OF PARAGRAPHS AND ESSAYS
Understand What Comparison and Contrast Are   **227**

Seeing Comparison and Contrast

write

- What similarities and differences do you see among these three photographs by Asia Kepka?
- Looking at each photo individually, what comparisons and contrasts do you see being set up within each one?
- Choose two photos of the series, and compare and contrast the mood or atmosphere in each photo.
- What do you see as the differences between a real friend and an imaginary one?

WRITER AT WORK

BRAD LEIBOV: Without good written proposals, I don't get jobs.

(See Brad Leibov's **PROFILE OF SUCCESS** on p. 236.)

IDEA JOURNAL Write about some of the differences between dogs and cats as pets.

Many situations require you to understand similarities and differences.

COLLEGE	In a pharmacy course, you compare and contrast the side effects of two drugs prescribed for the same illness.
WORK	You are asked to contrast this year's sales with last year's.
EVERYDAY LIFE	At the supermarket, you contrast brands of the same food to decide which to buy.

In college, writing assignments may include the words *compare and contrast*, but they might also use phrases such as *discuss similarities and differences*, *how is X like (or unlike) Y?*, or *what do X and Y have in common?* Also, assignments may use only the word *compare*.

Main Point in Comparison and Contrast

The **main point** should state the subjects you want to compare or contrast and help you achieve your purpose. (See the second of the Four Basics of Good Comparison and Contrast, p. 225.)

To help you discover your main point, complete the following sentence:

MAIN POINT IN COMPARISON AND CONTRAST

I want my readers to _____ after reading my comparison or contrast.

Then, write a topic sentence (paragraph) or thesis statement (essay) that identifies the subjects and states the main point you want to make about them. Here is an example of a topic sentence for a paragraph:

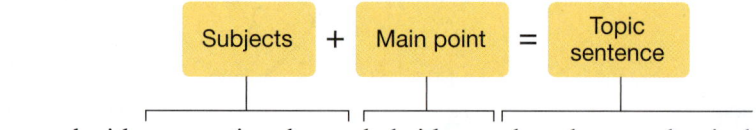

Subjects + Main point = Topic sentence

Compared with conventional cars, hybrid cars show less mechanical wear over time.

[Purpose: to help readers understand mechanical differences between conventional cars and hybrids.]

Remember that the topic for an essay can be a little broader than one for a paragraph.

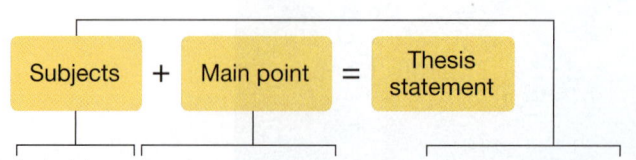

Subjects + Main point = Thesis statement

A hybrid car is a better choice than a conventional car, even one with low gas mileage.

[Purpose: to help readers decide which type of car to buy.]

Whereas the topic sentence focuses on the mechanical advantages of hybrid cars, the thesis statement sets up a broader discussion of these cars' benefits.

TIP Sometimes, the same main point can be used for a paragraph and an essay, but the essay must develop this point in more detail. (See p. 69–70.)

Support in Comparison and Contrast

The paragraph and essay models on pages 230–31 use the topic sentence (paragraph) and thesis statement (essay) from the Main Point section in this chapter. Both models include the **support** used in all comparison and contrast writing: points of comparison/contrast backed up by details. In the essay model, however, the points of comparison/contrast are topic sentences for individual paragraphs.

The support in comparison/contrast should show how your subjects are the same or different. To find support, many people make a list with two columns, one for each subject, with parallel points of comparison or contrast.

TOPIC SENTENCE / THESIS STATEMENT: The two credit cards I am considering offer different financial terms.

BIG CARD	MEGA CARD
no annual fee	$35 annual fee
$1 fee per cash advance	$1.50 fee per cash advance
30 days before interest charges begin	25 days before interest charges begin
15.5% finance charge	17.9% finance charge

Choose points that will be convincing and understandable to your readers. Explain your points with facts, details, or examples.

PRACTICE 1 Finding Points of Contrast

Each of the following items lists some points of contrast. Fill in the blanks with more points.

EXAMPLE:

Contrast hair lengths

Long hair	**Short hair**
takes a long time to dry	dries quickly
can be worn a lot of ways	_only one way to wear it_
does not need to be cut often	needs to be cut every five weeks
gets tangled, needs brushing	_low maintenance_

PARAGRAPHS VS. ESSAYS IN COMPARISON AND CONTRAST

For more on the important features of comparison and contrast, see the Four Basics of Good Comparison and Contrast on page 225.

Paragraph Form

Topic sentence

Support 1 (first point of comparison/contrast)

Support 2 (second point of comparison/contrast)

Concluding sentence

Compared with conventional cars, hybrid cars show less mechanical wear over time. In conventional vehicles, braking and idling place continual stress on the engine and brakes. When braking, drivers of such vehicles rely completely on the friction of the brake pads to come to a stop. As a result, brakes wear down over time, sometimes rather quickly. Additionally, these vehicles burn gas even while idling, making the engine use unnecessary energy and fuel. In contrast, hybrid cars are designed to reduce brake and engine wear. Say that a hybrid driver is moving from a sixty-mile-per-hour stretch of highway to a twenty-five-mile-per-hour off-ramp. When he or she brakes, the hybrid's motor goes into reverse, slowing the car and allowing the driver to place less strain on the brakes. Then, as the driver enters stop-and-start traffic in town, the electric motor takes over from the gas engine, improving energy efficiency during idling and reducing engine wear. These mechanical benefits of hybrids can lead to lower maintenance costs, a significant improvement over conventional cars.

Main Point: Often, narrower for a paragraph than for an essay: While the topic sentence (paragraph) focuses on the mechanical advantages of hybrid cars, the thesis statement (essay) sets up a broader discussion of these cars' benefits.

Support for the Main Point (Points of Comparison/Contrast)

Details about Each Point of Comparison/Contrast: Usually, 1 to 3 sentences per point for paragraphs and 3 to 8 sentences per point for essays.

Conclusion

Think Critically As You Write Comparison and Contrast

ASK YOURSELF

- Have I provided all the information needed to fulfill my purpose: to help readers make a decision or to understand the subjects being compared or contrasted? (This information includes all the important similarities or differences between the subjects, as well as details about these similarities or differences.)
- If my information about similarities or differences feels "thin," might consulting outside sources help me find new details? (For more on finding and evaluating sources, see pp. 304–09.)

Essay Form

They are too expensive. For the last two years, while trying to keep my dying 1999 Chevy on the road, these words have popped into my head every time I have thought about purchasing a hybrid car. **[Thesis statement]** I have done some research, I am finally convinced: A hybrid car is a better choice than a conventional car, even one with low gas mileage.

[Topic sentence 1 (first point of comparison/contrast)] The first advantage of hybrid cars over conventional cars is that buyers can get tax breaks and other hybrid-specific benefits. Although federal tax credits for hybrid purchasers expired in 2010, several states, including Colorado, Louisiana, Maryland, and Oregon, continue to offer such credits. Also, in Arizona, Florida, and several other states, hybrid drivers are allowed to use the less congested high-occupancy vehicle (HOV) lanes even if the driver is the only person on board. Additional benefits for hybrid drivers include longer warranties than those offered for conventional cars and, in some states and cities, rebates, reduced licensing fees, and free parking. None of these benefits are offered to drivers of conventional cars.

[Topic sentence 2 (second point of comparison/contrast)] The second advantage of hybrid cars over conventional cars is that they save money over the long term. In addition to using less fuel, hybrids have less mechanical wear over time, reducing maintenance costs. When braking, drivers of conventional cars rely completely on the friction of the brake pads to come to a stop. As a result, brakes wear down over time, sometimes rather quickly. Additionally, these vehicles burn gas even while idling, making the engine use unnecessary energy and fuel. In contrast, when hybrid drivers hit the brakes, the car's motor goes into reverse, slowing the car and allowing the driver to place less strain on the brakes. Then, as the driver enters stop-and-start traffic in town, the electric motor takes over from the gas engine, improving energy efficiency during idling and reducing engine wear.

[Topic sentence 3 (third point of comparison/contrast)] The most important benefit of hybrid cars over conventional cars is that they have a lower impact on the environment. Experts estimate that each gallon of gas burned by conventional motor vehicles produces 28 pounds of carbon dioxide (CO_2), a greenhouse gas that is a major contributor to global warming. Because hybrid cars use about half as much gas as conventional vehicles, they reduce pollution and greenhouse gases by at least 50 percent. Some experts estimate that they reduce such emissions by as much as 80 percent. The National Resources Defense Council says that if hybrid vehicles are widely adopted, annual reductions in emissions could reach 450 million metric tons by the year 2050. This reduction would be equal to taking 82.5 million cars off the road.

[Concluding paragraph] Although hybrid cars are more expensive than conventional cars, they are well worth it. From an economic standpoint, they save on fuel and maintenance costs. But, to me, the best reasons for buying a hybrid are ethical: By switching to such a vehicle, I will help reduce my toll on the environment. So goodbye, 1999 Chevy, and hello, Toyota Prius!

1. Contrast sports

   Basketball   **Soccer**

   baskets = points   goals = points

   _____   ball is kicked

   _____   _____

2. Contrast pets

   Dogs   **Cats**

   bark   _____

   _____   independent

   _____   _____

PRACTICE 2 Finding Points of Comparison

Each of the following items lists some points of comparison. Fill in the blanks with more.

1. Compare sports

   Basketball   **Soccer**

   team sport   team sport

   _____   _____

   _____   _____

2. Compare pets

   Dogs   **Cats**

   shed fur   _____

   common household pet   _____

   _____   _____

Organization in Comparison and Contrast

Comparison/contrast can be organized in one of two ways: A **point-by-point** organization presents one point of comparison or contrast between the subjects and then moves to the next point. (See the essay model on page 231.) A **whole-to-whole** organization presents all the points of comparison or contrast for one subject and then all the points for the next subject. (See the paragraph model on page 230.) Consider which organization will best explain the similarities or differences to your readers. Whichever organization you choose, stay with it throughout your writing.

WRITING DIFFERENT KINDS OF PARAGRAPHS AND ESSAYS
Understand What Comparison and Contrast Are

PRACTICE 3 Organizing a Comparison/Contrast

The first outline that follows is for a comparison paper using a whole-to-whole organization. Reorganize the ideas and create a new outline (outline 2) using a point-by-point organization. The first blank has been filled in for you.

The third outline is for a contrast paper using a point-by-point organization. Reorganize the ideas, and create a new outline (outline 4) using a whole-to-whole organization. The first blank in outline 4 has been filled in for you.

1. Comparison paper using whole-to-whole organization

    Main point: My daughter is a lot like I was at her age.

    a. Me

    Not interested in school

    Good at sports

    Hard on myself

    b. My daughter

    Does well in school but doesn't study much or do more than the minimum

    Plays in a different sport each season

    When she thinks she has made a mistake, she gets upset with herself

2. Comparison paper using point-by-point organization

    Main point: My daughter is a lot like I was at her age.

    a. Interest in school

    Me: *Not interested in school*

    My daughter: _____

    b. _____

    Me: _____

    My daughter: _____

    c. _____

    Me: _____

    My daughter: _____

3. Contrast paper using point-by-point organization

    Main point: My new computer is a great improvement over my old one.

    a. Weight and portability

    New computer: *small and light*

    Old computer: *heavy, not portable*

    b. *Speed*

    New computer: *fast*

    Old computer: *slow*

c. Cost

New computer: *inexpensive*

Old computer: *expensive*

4. Contrast paper using whole-to-whole organization

Main point: My new computer is a great improvement over my old one.

a. New computer

small and light

b. Old computer

TIP For more on order of importance, see page 79.

Comparison/contrast is often organized by **order of importance**, meaning that the most important point is saved for last. This strategy is used in the essay model on page 231.

Transitions in comparison/contrast move readers from one subject to another and from one point of comparison or contrast to the next.

Common Transitions in Comparison and Contrast

COMPARISON	CONTRAST
both	in contrast
like/unlike	most important difference
most important similarity	now/then
one similarity/another similarity	one difference/another difference
similarly	unlike
	while

PRACTICE 4 Using Transitions in Comparison and Contrast

Read the paragraph that follows, and fill in the blanks with transitions. You are not limited to the ones listed in the preceding box.

Modern coffee shops share many similarities with the coffeehouses that opened hundreds of years ago in the Middle East and Europe. _____ is that the coffeehouses of history, like modern cafés, were popular places to socialize. In sixteenth-century Constantinople (now Istanbul, Turkey) and in seventeenth- and eighteenth-century London, customers shared stories, information, and opinions about current events, politics, and personal matters. The knowledge shared at London coffeehouses led customers to call these places "Penny Universities," a penny being the price of admission. _____ is that the old coffeehouses, like today's coffee shops, were often places of business. However, although most of today's coffee-shop customers work quietly on their laptops, customers of the old shops openly, and sometimes loudly, discussed business and sealed deals. In fact, for more than seventy years, traders for the London Stock Exchange operated out of coffeehouses. _____ similarity between the old coffeehouses and modern coffee shops is that they both increased the demand for coffee and places to drink it. In 1652, a former servant from western Turkey opened the first coffeehouse in London. As a result of its popularity, many more coffeehouses soon sprouted up all over the city, and within a hundred years there were more than 500 coffeehouses in London. _____, in recent years the popularity of Starbucks, and its shops, spread rapidly throughout the United States.

Read and Analyze Comparison and Contrast

Reading examples of comparison and contrast will help you write your own. In the first example, Brad Leibov, president of an urban planning and development firm, shows how he uses comparison and contrast on the job.

The second example is a comparison/contrast paragraph by a student, and the third example is a comparison/contrast essay by a professional writer.

As you read these pieces, pay attention to the vocabulary, and answer the questions in the margin. They will help you read critically.

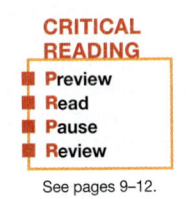

CRITICAL READING
- Preview
- Read
- Pause
- Review

See pages 9–12.

PROFILE OF SUCCESS

Comparison and Contrast in the Real World

Background In high school, I put very little effort into completing my coursework. When I first enrolled at Oakton Community College, I was not motivated and soon dropped all my courses. An instructor from Project Succeed contacted me after my first year, and this program helped me recognize that I really wanted to put in the effort necessary to succeed.

A few years later, I earned a B.A. degree from a four-year university. After working for a few years in community development, I was accepted into a top-tier graduate program in urban planning and policy, from which I graduated with a perfect grade-point average. Later, I started my own urban planning and development company to help revitalize inner-city commercial areas.

Degrees/Colleges B.A., DePaul University; M.A., University of Illinois, Chicago

Writing at work I write contracts, proposals, marketing materials, etc.

How Brad uses comparison and contrast I often give examples of how my company can improve a community—kind of before-and-after contrasts.

Brad Leibov
President, New Chicago Fund, Inc.

Brad's Comparison and Contrast

The following paragraph describes how Brad's company restored a special service area (SSA), a declining community targeted for improvements.

Vocabulary development
Underline these words as you read.
liaison: someone who acts as a communication link
hazardous: dangerous
amenities: attractive features
receptacles: containers
poised: in this sense, ready; also means natural and balanced, relaxed

New Chicago Fund, Inc., is an expert at advising and leading organizations through all the steps necessary to establish an SSA with strong local support. Our experience acting as liaison among various neighborhood groups and individuals affected by an SSA helps us plan for and address the concerns of residents and property owners. In 2005, New Chicago Fund assisted the Uptown Community Development Corporation with establishing an SSA in Uptown, Chicago. Uptown's commercial area was estimated to lose approximately $506 million annually in consumer expenditures to neighboring commercial districts and suburban shopping centers. Community leaders recognized that Uptown's sidewalks were uninviting with litter, hazardous with unshoveled snow, and unappealing in the lack of pedestrian-friendly amenities found in neighboring commercial districts. The Uptown SSA programs funded the transformation of the commercial area. The sidewalks are regularly cleaned and are litter-free. People no longer have to walk around uncleared snow mounds and risk slipping on the ice because maintenance programs provide full-service clearing. Additionally, SSA funds provided new pedestrian-friendly amenities such as benches, trash receptacles, flower planters, and street-pole banners. The Uptown area is now poised for commercial success.

1. Double-underline the **topic sentence**.
2. What subjects are being contrasted? _____
3. What is the purpose of the paragraph? _____
4. What are the points of contrast? _____

Student Comparison/Contrast Paragraph

Said Ibrahim

Eyeglasses vs. Laser Surgery: Benefits and Drawbacks

Although both eyeglasses and laser surgery can address vision problems successfully, each approach has particular benefits and drawbacks. Whereas one pair of eyeglasses is reasonably priced in comparison with laser surgery, eyeglass prescriptions often change over time, requiring regular lens replacements. As a result, over the wearer's lifetime, costs of eyeglasses can exceed $15,000. On the positive side, an accurate lens prescription results in clear vision with few or no side effects. Furthermore, glasses of just the right shape or color can be a great fashion accent. In contrast to eyeglasses, laser vision correction often has to be done only once. Consequently, although the costs average $2,500 per eye, the patient can save thousands of dollars over the following years. On the downside, some recipients of laser surgery report difficulties seeing at night, dry eyes, or infections. Fortunately, these problems are fairly rare. The final advantage of laser surgery applies to those who are happy to forgo the fashion benefits of eyeglasses. Most laser-surgery patients no longer have to wear any glasses other than sunglasses until later in life. At that point, they may need reading glasses. All in all, we are fortunate to live in a time when there are many good options for vision correction. Choosing the right one is a matter of carefully weighing the pros and cons of each approach.

Vocabulary development
Underline these words as you read.
laser: a concentrated beam of light; in this case it is used to reshape part of the eye
reasonably: not excessively
forgo: go without

TIP For tools to build your vocabulary, visit the *Student Site for Real Writing* at bedfordstmartins.com/realwriting.

1. Double-underline the **topic sentence**.
2. Is the **purpose** of the paragraph to help readers make a decision, to help them understand the subjects better, or both? _____
3. Underline **each point of contrast** in the sample paragraph. Give each parallel, or matched, point the same number.
4. Which organization (point by point or whole to whole) does Ibrahim use? _____
5. Circle the **transitions** in the paragraph.

Professional Comparison/Contrast Essay

Mark Twain

Two Ways of Seeing a River

Born Samuel Langhorne Clemens, Mark Twain (1835–1910) is one of America's most admired writers, praised as much for his storytelling as for his humor and wit. He was also a sharp observer of society and politics, and he was known to criticize racial inequality, political corruption, and other injustices.

Twain, a native of Missouri, discovered his love for writing while working as a typesetter and editorial assistant at a local newspaper. Later, he took a job as a river pilot's apprentice. Among the many books Twain was to publish in the following years were *Tom Sawyer* (1876), *Huckleberry Finn* (1884), and *Life on the Mississippi* (1883), from which the following excerpt was taken.

In this essay, Twain paints a vivid picture of the Mississippi River. He also describes an upsetting change to this picture, which occurred during his time as a pilot's apprentice.

Vocabulary development

Underline these words as you read the comparison/contrast essay.

mastered: had become skilled in
trifling: small; of little importance
majestic: great; dignified
hue: color; tint
solitary: single
conspicuous: clearly visible
opal: a gemstone that, typically, is made up of many colors
ruddy: rosy
radiating: extending outward
somber: sad
bough: limb
unobstructed splendor: unblocked (view of) beauty
marvels: wonderful things
bewitched: under a spell; fascinated
rapture: joy; ecstasy
wrought: caused to appear
bluff reef: a type of sandbar that is difficult to see and, therefore, dangerous to boats
yonder: in the distance
shoaling up: becoming shallow
snag: a tree or tree part in the water; it can damage boats
compassing: enabling; providing direction for
break: a wave (in this case)
unwholesome: unhealthy

Now when I had mastered the language of this water and had come to know every trifling feature that bordered the great river as familiarly as I knew the letters of the alphabet, I had made a valuable acquisition. But I had lost something, too. I had lost something which could never be restored to me while I lived. All the grace, the beauty, the poetry, had gone out of the majestic river! I still kept in mind a certain wonderful sunset which I witnessed when steamboating was new to me. A broad expanse of the river was turned to blood; in the middle distance the red hue brightened into gold, through which a solitary log came floating, black and conspicuous; in one place a long, slanting mark lay sparkling upon the water; in another the surface was broken by boiling, tumbling rings that were as many-tinted as an opal; where the ruddy flush was faintest was a smooth spot that was covered with graceful circles and radiating lines, ever so delicately traced; the shore on our left was densely wooded, and the somber shadow that fell from this forest was broken in one place by a long, ruffled trail that shone like silver; and high above the forest wall a clean-stemmed dead tree waved a single leafy bough that glowed like a flame in the unobstructed splendor that was flowing from the sun. There were graceful curves, reflected images, woody heights, soft distances, and over the whole scene, far and near, the dissolving lights drifted steadily, enriching it every passing moment with new marvels of coloring.

REFLECT What do these descriptions say about Twain's early feelings in relation to the river?

I stood like one bewitched. I drank it in, in a speechless rapture. The world was new to me and I had never seen anything like this at home. But as I have said, a day came when I began to cease from noting the glories and the charms which the moon and the sun and the twilight wrought upon the river's face; another day came when I ceased altogether to note them. Then, if that sunset scene had been repeated, I should have looked upon it without rapture and should have commented upon it inwardly after this fashion: "This sun means that we are going to have wind tomorrow; that floating log means that the river is rising, small thanks to it; that slanting mark on the water refers to a bluff reef which is going to kill somebody's steamboat one of these nights, if it keeps on stretching out like that; those tumbling 'boils' show a dissolving bar and a changing channel there; the lines and circles in the slick water over yonder are a warning that that troublesome place is shoaling up dangerously; that silver streak in the shadow of the forest is the 'break' from a new snag and he has located himself in the very best place he could have found to fish for steamboats; that tall dead tree, with a single living branch, is not going to last long, and then how is a body ever going to get through this blind place at night without the friendly old landmark?"

2 **IDENTIFY** Underline the sentence in this paragraph that marks the change in Twain.

No, the romance and beauty were all gone from the river. All the value any feature of it had for me now was the amount of usefulness it could furnish toward compassing the safe piloting of a steamboat. Since those days, I have pitied doctors from my heart. What does the lovely flush in a beauty's cheek mean to a doctor but a "break" that ripples above some deadly disease? Are not all her visible charms sown thick with what are to him the signs and symbols of hidden decay? Does he ever see her beauty at all, or doesn't he simply view her professionally and comment upon her unwholesome condition all to himself? And doesn't he sometimes wonder whether he has gained most or lost most by learning his trade?

3

REFLECT What have you gained or lost by becoming very knowledgeable about something?

1. Double-underline the **thesis statement**.
2. What type of organization does this essay use (point by point or whole to whole)? _____

TIP For reading advice, see Chapter 1.

3. Why do you suppose Twain's perceptions of the river changed?

_____
_____
_____

4. How is the writing in the "before" and "after" sections of the essay similar? How is it different? _____
_____
_____
_____

Respond to one of the following assignments in a paragraph or essay.

1. In the final paragraph of the essay, Twain describes how doctors have lost the ability to see beauty in their patients; instead, they look only for signs of illness. Write about something beautiful (a person, place, or thing) from two different perspectives — one of an expert (such as a doctor, scientist, or architect) and one of an untrained but observant person.

2. Twain argues that knowing too much about something can destroy its appeal. Write a paper that opposes this position, bringing in examples from college, work, or your everyday life.

3. Are there any people, places, or objects that we will always see beauty in, no matter how much knowledge we gain or how much time passes? If you believe that there are, describe these things, and explain why they have a more lasting appeal than some other things. If not, explain your reasons.

Write Your Own Comparison and Contrast

In this section, you will write your own comparison and contrast based on one of the following assignments. For help, refer to the How to Write Comparison and Contrast checklist on page 244.

ASSIGNMENT OPTIONS Writing about College, Work, and Everyday Life

Write a comparison/contrast paragraph or essay on one of the following topics or on one of your own choice. If you responded to the idea journal prompt on page 228, you might develop that writing further.

WRITING DIFFERENT KINDS OF PARAGRAPHS AND ESSAYS
Write Your Own Comparison and Contrast   241

COLLEGE

- Describe similarities and differences between high school and college, and give examples.
- Compare two different approaches you have used to study, such as studying in a group and studying on your own using notes or other aids. Explain whether you prefer one approach over the other or like to use both methods.
- If you are still deciding on a major area of study, see if you can sit in on a class or two from programs that interest you. Then, compare and contrast the classes. If this process helped you decide on a program, explain the reasons for your choice.

WORK

- Compare a job you liked with one you did not like, and give reasons for your views.
- Have you had experience working for both a bad supervisor and a good one? If so, compare and contrast their behaviors, and explain why you preferred one supervisor to another.
- Work styles tend to differ from employee to employee. For instance, some like to work in teams, whereas others prefer to complete tasks on their own. Some like specific directions on how to do things, while others want more freedom. Contrast your own work style with someone else's, someone whose approach and preferences are quite different from yours.

EVERYDAY LIFE

- Compare your life now with the way you would like it to be in five years.
- Mark Twain writes about how his experience working on the river has changed how he sees the river (see p. 238). Have your experiences changed how you see your surroundings? If so, discuss your experiences, and give examples.
- Participate in a cleanup effort in your community, and then compare and contrast how the area looked before the cleanup with how it looked afterward.

COMMUNITY CONNECTIONS

LYNZE SCHILLER helped clean up and paint a storage room in a church, converting it into an Empowerment Room for community members who needed help and support. Getting more involved in college and community activities, as Lynze did, can help you feel more connected to others and can even improve the chances that you will stay in school.

For more on this story, ways to make community connections, and writing assignments, visit bedfordstmartins.com/realwriting.

ASSIGNMENT OPTIONS   Reading and Writing Critically

Complete one of the following assignments, which ask you to apply the critical thinking, reading, and writing skills discussed in Chapter 1.

Writing Critically about Readings

Both Mark Twain's "Two Ways of Seeing a River" (p. 238) and Jelani Lynch's "My Turnaround" (p. 124) describe changes in the writers' lives. Read or review both of these pieces, and then follow these steps:

1. **Summarize**   Briefly summarize the works, listing major events.
2. **Analyze**   What questions do the pieces raise for you?

TIP For a reminder of how to summarize, analyze, synthesize, and evaluate, see the Reading and Writing Critically box on pages 16–17.

3. **Synthesize** Sometimes we are thankful for changes in our lives, as in Lynch's paragraph, but other times we regret them, as in Twain's essay. Using examples from these writings and from your own experience, discuss which types of changes are positive, which types are negative, and why.

4. **Evaluate** Which piece did you connect with more, and why? In writing your evaluation, you might look back on your responses to step 2.

Writing about Images

Study the photographs below, and complete the following steps.

1. **Read the images** Ask yourself: What details are you drawn to in each photograph? What differences do you notice as you move from the 1973 model to the 1985 model and from these cell-phone ancestors to the 1991–2011 phones? (For more on reading images, see Chapter 1.)

2. **Write a comparison and contrast** Choose two or more of the photographs to compare and contrast, and write a paragraph or essay about the changing looks of mobile phones. You might want to address

ANCESTORS OF MODERN CELL PHONES, 1973 AND 1985

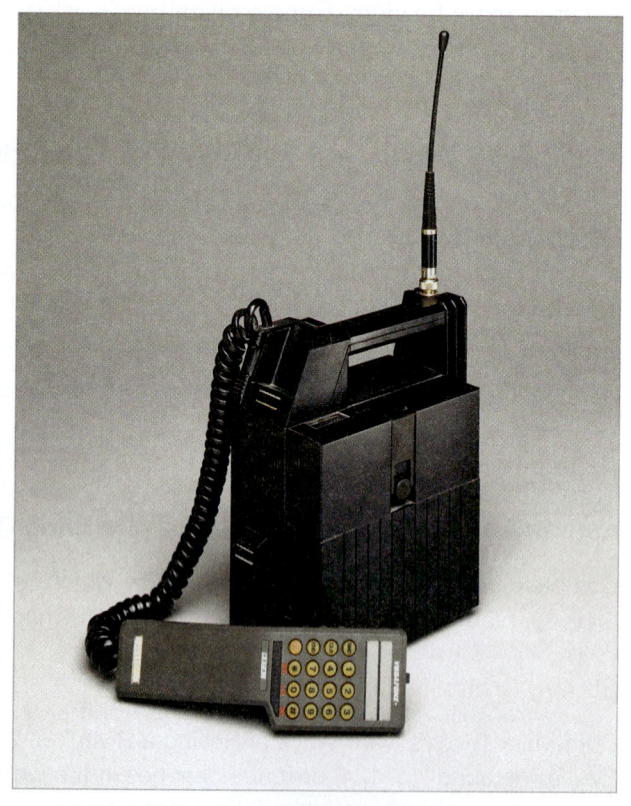

Above left: Martin Cooper, chairman and CEO of ArrayComm, holds a Motorola DynaTAC, a 1973 prototype of the first handheld cellular telephone. Thirty years before this photograph was taken, on April 2, 2003, the first call was made from a cellular phone.
Above right: The Vodafone mobile phone, introduced in 1985. Marketed by Racal-Vodac Limited, this phone was aimed at busy professionals and regular travelers, for portable use or for use in their cars. This phone came with a battery charger and an antenna, for use in areas with poor reception.

WRITING DIFFERENT KINDS OF PARAGRAPHS AND ESSAYS
Write Your Own Comparison and Contrast

CELL PHONES FROM 1991 TO 2011

Brands from left to right: Motorola (1991), Nokia (1999), LG (2005/2006), and Motorola Droid 2 Global (2011).

The Apple iPhone 4 (2011).

how changes in mobile phones represent larger changes in society and culture. Also, answer this question: What do you think phones will look like in another ten years? In writing your comparison/contrast, include the details and differences you identified in step 1.

Writing to Solve a Problem

Read or review the discussion of problem solving in Chapter 1 (pp. 24–26). Then, consider the following problem:

You need a new smartphone, and you want the best one for your money. Before ordering, you do some research.

ASSIGNMENT: Consult a Web site that rates smartphones, such as www.pcworld.com. Identify three features covered by the ratings, and make notes about why each feature is important to you. Then, choose a model based on these features. Finally, write a contrast paragraph or essay that explains your decision and contrasts your choice versus another model. Make sure to support your choice based on the three features you considered.

CHECKLIST: HOW TO WRITE COMPARISON AND CONTRAST

STEPS	DETAILS
☐ **Narrow and explore your topic.** See Chapter 3.	• Make the topic more specific. • Prewrite to get ideas about the narrowed topic.
☐ **Write a topic sentence (paragraph) or thesis statement (essay).** See Chapter 4.	• State the main point you want to make in your comparison/contrast.
☐ **Support your point.** See Chapter 5.	• Come up with points of comparison/contrast and with details about each one.
☐ **Write a draft.** See Chapter 6.	• Make a plan that sets up a point-by-point or whole-to-whole comparison/contrast. • Include a topic sentence (paragraph) or thesis statement (essay) and all the support points.
☐ **Revise your draft.** See Chapter 7.	• Make sure it has *all* the Four Basics of Good Comparison and Contrast. • Make sure you include transitions to move readers smoothly from one subject or comparison/contrast point to the next.
☐ **Edit your revised draft.** See Parts 4 through 7.	• Correct errors in grammar, spelling, word use, and punctuation.

Chapter Review

1. What are the Four Basics of Good Comparison and Contrast?

   _____
   _____
   _____
   _____
   _____

2. The topic sentence (paragraph) or thesis statement (essay) in comparison/contrast should include what two parts? _____

3. What are the two ways to organize comparison/contrast? _____

4. In your own words, explain the two ways of organizing comparison/contrast. _____

5. Write sentences using the following vocabulary words: *liaison, amenities, poised, majestic, somber.* _____

reflect Write for 2 minutes about the elements of a good comparison/contrast.

LEARNING JOURNAL
Reread your idea journal entry (p. 228) about the differences between dogs and cats as pets. Make another entry about the same topic, using what you have learned about comparison and contrast.

15

Cause and Effect

Writing That Explains Reasons or Results

> **YOU KNOW THIS**
>
> You consider causes and effects every day:
>
> - You explain to your boss what caused you to be late.
> - You consider the possible effects of calling in sick.
>
> **write** for 2 minutes about what a cause is and what an effect is.

Understand What Cause and Effect Are

A **cause** is what made an event happen. An **effect** is what happens as a result of the event.

Four Basics of Good Cause and Effect

1. The main point reflects the writer's purpose: to explain causes, effects, or both.
2. If the purpose is to explain causes, the writing presents real causes.
3. If the purpose is to explain effects, it presents real effects.
4. It gives readers detailed examples or explanations of the causes or effects.

In the following paragraph, the numbers and colors correspond to the Four Basics of Good Cause and Effect.

1 Although the thought of writing may be a source of stress for college students, researchers have recently found that it can also be a potent stress reliever. In the winter of 2008, during a time when many people catch colds or the flu or experience other symptoms of ill health, two psychologists conducted an experiment with college students to find out if writing could have positive effects on their minds and/or their bodies. After gathering a large group of college students, a mix of ages, genders, and backgrounds, the psychologists explained the task. The students were asked to write for only 2 minutes, on two consecutive days,

about their choice of three different kinds of experiences: a traumatic experience, a positive experience, or a neutral experience (something routine that happened). The psychologists did not give more detailed directions about the kinds of experiences, rather just a bad one, a good one, or one neither good nor bad. A month after collecting the students' writing, the psychologists interviewed each of the students and asked them to report any symptoms of ill health, such as colds, flu, headaches, or lack of sleep. 3 What the psychologists found was quite surprising. 4 Those students who had written about emotionally charged topics, either traumatic or positive, all reported that they had been in excellent health, avoiding the various illnesses that had been circulating in the college and the larger community. The students who had chosen to write about routine, day-to-day things that didn't matter to them reported the ill health effects that were typical of the season, such as colds, flu, poor sleep, and coughing. From these findings, the two psychologists reported that writing about things that are important to people actually has a positive effect on their health. Their experiment suggests the value to people of regularly recording their reactions to experiences, in a journal of some sort. If writing can keep you well, it is worth a good try. The mind-body connection continues to be studied because clearly each affects the other.

When you are writing about causes and effects, make sure that you do not confuse something that happened before an event with a real cause or something that happened after an event with a real effect. For example, if you have pizza on Monday and get the flu on Tuesday, eating the pizza is not the cause of the flu just because it happened before you got the flu, nor is the flu the effect of eating pizza. You just happened to get the flu the next day.

You use cause and effect in many situations.

COLLEGE	In a nutrition course, you are asked to identify the consequences (effects) of poor nutrition.
WORK	Sales are down in your group, and you have to explain the cause.
EVERYDAY LIFE	You explain to your child why a certain behavior is not acceptable by warning him or her about the negative effects of that behavior.

In college, writing assignments might include the words *discuss the causes (or effects) of*, but they might also use phrases such as *explain the results of, discuss the impact of,* and *how did X affect Y?* In all these cases, use the strategies discussed in this chapter.

WRITER AT WORK

MARY LACUE BOOKER: I started writing rap to teach my students.

(See Mary LaCue Booker's **PROFILE OF SUCCESS** on p. 256.)

WRITING DIFFERENT KINDS OF PARAGRAPHS AND ESSAYS

Chapter 15 • Cause and Effect

Seeing Cause and Effect

WRITING DIFFERENT KINDS OF PARAGRAPHS AND ESSAYS
Understand What Cause and Effect Are

write

- Using these photos as starting points, what are some effects of natural disasters?
- What reactions and responses does a natural disaster cause?

Main Point in Cause and Effect

IDEA JOURNAL Write about a time when something you did caused someone to be happy or unhappy.

The **main point** introduces causes, effects, or both. To help you discover your main point, complete the following sentence:

MAIN POINT IN CAUSE AND EFFECT
(Your topic) causes (or caused) . . .
(Your topic) resulted in (or results in) . . .

Here is an example of a topic sentence for a paragraph:

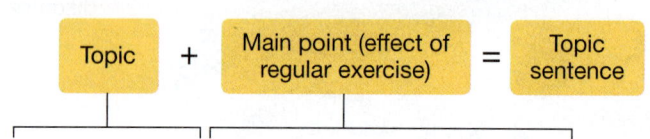

Topic + Main point (effect of regular exercise) = Topic sentence

Regular exercise improves cardiovascular health.

TIP If the writer wanted to explore causes, he or she might look into the factors that motivate people to exercise.

Remember that the main point for an essay can be a little broader than one for a paragraph.

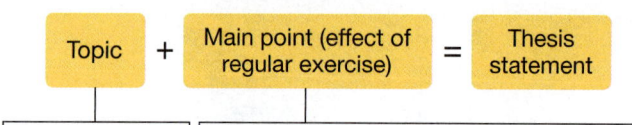

Topic + Main point (effect of regular exercise) = Thesis statement

Regular exercise provides more physical and mental benefits than any medication could offer.

TIP Sometimes, the same main point can be used for a paragraph and an essay, but the essay must develop this point in more detail. (See pp. 69–70.)

Whereas the topic sentence focuses on just one major benefit of regular exercise, the thesis statement considers multiple benefits.

PRACTICE 1 Stating Your Main Point

For each of the following topics, make notes about possible causes and effects on a separate sheet of paper. Then, in each of the spaces below, write a sentence that states a main point. First, look at the following example.

EXAMPLE:

Topic: Bankruptcy

Main point: *Although many different kinds of people declare bankruptcy each year, the causes of bankruptcy are often the same.*

1. Topic: A fire in someone's home

   Main point: _____

2. Topic: An "A" in this course

   Main point: _____

3. Topic: A car accident

   Main point: _____

Support in Cause and Effect

The paragraph and essay models on pages 252–53 use the topic sentence (paragraph) and thesis statement (essay) from the Main Point section of this chapter. Both models include the **support** used in all cause-effect writing: statements of cause or effect backed up by detailed explanations or examples. In the essay plan, however, the major support points (statements of cause/effect) are topic sentences for individual paragraphs.

PRACTICE 2   Giving Examples and Details

Write down two causes or two effects for two of the three topics from Practice 1. Then, give an example or detail that explains each cause or effect.

EXAMPLE:

Topic: Bankruptcy

Cause 1: *Overspending*

   Example/Detail: *bought a leather jacket I liked and charged it*

Cause 2: *Poor budgeting*

   Example/Detail: *not tracking monthly expenses versus income*

1. Topic: A fire in someone's home

   Cause/Effect 1: _____

   Example/Detail: _____

   Cause/Effect 2: _____

   Example/Detail: _____

2. Topic: An "A" in this course

   Cause/Effect 1: _____

   Example/Detail: _____

   Cause/Effect 2: _____

   Example/Detail: _____

3. Topic: A car accident

   Cause/Effect 1: _____

   Example/Detail: _____

PARAGRAPHS VS. ESSAYS IN CAUSE AND EFFECT

For more on the important features of cause and effect, see the Four Basics of Good Cause and Effect on page 246.

Paragraph Form

Topic sentence

Support 1 (cause 1 or effect 1)

Support 2 (cause 2 or effect 2)

Support 3 (cause 3 or effect 3)

Concluding sentence

Regular exercise improves cardiovascular health. One benefit of exercise is that it strengthens the heart. Like any other muscle, the heart becomes stronger with use, and is able to pump blood through the body more efficiently. The result can be lower blood pressure, reducing the risk of heart disease. Another benefit of exercise is that it lessens the toll that excessive weight can take on the heart. In seriously overweight individuals, the strain of carrying extra pounds can cause the heart to enlarge, interfering with its ability to pump blood. By losing weight through exercise and dietary changes, people can reduce the burden on their hearts and also their cardiovascular risk. The most important cardiovascular benefit of exercise is that it lowers the risk of heart disease. As previously noted, exercise can reduce blood pressure and strain on the heart, both risk factors for heart attack, stroke, and heart failure. In addition, it can lower levels of "bad" cholesterol while raising levels of "good" cholesterol. Controlling bad cholesterol is important because when there is too much of this substance in the blood, it can build up on artery walls, causing reduced blood flow. Regular and vigorous aerobic exercise is the best way to reap these cardiovascular benefits, but even a brisk walk a few times a week is better than no activity at all.

Main Point: Often, narrower for a paragraph than for an essay: While the topic sentence (paragraph) focuses on just one major benefit of exercise, the thesis statement (essay) considers multiple benefits.

Support for the Main Point (Statements of Cause or Effect)

Detailed Explanations or Examples of Cause/Effect Statements: Usually, 1 to 3 sentences per statement for paragraphs and 3 to 8 sentences per statement for essays.

Conclusion

Think Critically As You Write Cause and Effect

ASK YOURSELF

- Have I examined a variety of possible causes and/or effects related to my topic? (If not, research them, and consider revising your main point and support based on what you learn. For more on finding and evaluating outside sources, see Chapter 18.)
- Am I certain that my causes are real causes and my effects real effects? (For help with answering this question, see p. 247.)

Essay Form

Thesis statement

Most people know how hard it is to start and stick with an exercise program. However, there is a good reason to build a significant amount of physical activity into every week: Regular exercise provides more physical and mental benefits than any medication could offer.

Topic sentence 1 (cause 1 or effect 1)

First, exercise helps people achieve and maintain a healthy weight. A nutritious diet that is low in calories has a greater effect on weight loss than exercise does. However, regular exercise—ideally, interspersed throughout the day—can make an important contribution. For instance, people trying to lose weight might walk to work or to other destinations instead of driving. Or, they might take the stairs to their office instead of the elevator. If they go the gym at the end of the day, so much the better. Added up, these activities can make a difference.

Topic sentence 2 (cause 2 or effect 2)

Second, exercise boosts mood and energy levels. For example, exercise causes the body to release endorphins, chemicals that give us a sense of well-being, even happiness. Accordingly, exercise can help reduce stress and combat depression. In addition, because exercise can make people look and feel more fit, it can improve their self-esteem. Finally, by improving strength and endurance, exercise gives individuals more energy about their lives.

Topic sentence 3 (cause 3 or effect 3)

The most important benefit of exercise is that it can help prevent disease. For example, exercise can improve the body's use of insulin and, as noted earlier, help people maintain a healthy weight. Therefore, it can help prevent or control diabetes. Additionally, exercise can lower the risk of heart attacks, strokes, and heart failure. For instance, exercise strengthens the heart muscle, helping it pump blood more efficiently and reducing high blood pressure, a heart disease risk factor. Also, exercise can lower levels of "bad" cholesterol while raising levels of "good" cholesterol. Controlling levels of bad cholesterol is important because when there is too much of this substance in the blood, it can build up in the walls of arteries, possibly blocking blood flow. Finally, some research suggests that regular exercise can reduce the risk of certain cancers, including breast, colon, and lung cancer.

Concluding paragraph

In my own life, exercise has made a huge difference. Before starting a regular exercise program, I was close to needing prescription medications to lower my blood pressure and cholesterol. Thanks to regular physical activity, however, both my blood pressure and cholesterol levels are now in the normal range, and I have never felt better. Every bit of time spent at the gym or exchanging a ride in an elevator for a walk up the stairs has been well worth it.

253

Organization in Cause and Effect

TIP For more on the different orders of organization, see pages 78–79.

Cause and effect can be organized in a variety of ways, depending on your purpose.

MAIN POINT	PURPOSE	ORGANIZATION
The "Occupy" protests of 2011 brought attention to the economic difficulties faced by low- and middle-income citizens.	to explain the effects of the protests	order of importance, saving the most important effect for last
A desire to remain at a protest site for an extended period led "Occupy" protesters to create miniature towns, with food service, libraries, and more.	to describe the places where protesters camped out	space order
The "Occupy" protests in New York City inspired other protests throughout the country.	to describe the spread of the protest movement over time	time order

NOTE: If you are explaining both causes and effects, you would present the causes first and the effects later.

Use **transitions** to move readers smoothly from one cause to another, or from one effect to another, or from causes to effects. Because cause and effect can use any method of organization depending on your purpose, the following list shows just a few of the transitions you might use.

Common Transitions in Cause and Effect

also	more important/serious cause or effect
as a result	most important/serious cause or effect
because	one cause/effect; another cause or effect
the final cause or effect	a primary cause; a secondary cause
the first, second, third cause or effect	a short-term effect; a long-term effect

PRACTICE 3   Using Transitions in Cause and Effect

Read the paragraph that follows, and fill in the blanks with transitions.

Recently, neuroscientists, who have long been skeptical about meditation, confirm that it has numerous positive outcomes. _____ is that people who meditate can maintain their focus and attention longer than people who do not. This ability to stay "on task" was demonstrated among students who had been practicing meditation for several weeks. They reported more effective studying and learning because they were able to pay attention. _____ positive outcome was the ability to relax on command. Many people lead busy, stressful lives with multiple pressures on them—family responsibilities, work duties, financial worries, and uncertainties about the future. While meditating, people learned how to reduce their heart rates and blood pressure so that they could relax more easily in all kinds of situations. _____ outcome was a thickening of the brain's cortex. Meditators' cortexes were uniformly thicker than nonmeditators'. Because the cortex enables memorization and the production of new ideas, this last outcome is especially exciting, particularly in fighting Alzheimer's disease and other dementias.

Read and Analyze Cause and Effect

Reading examples of cause and effect will help you write your own. In the first example, a singer shows how she uses cause and effect to write rap lyrics that do more than entertain.

The second example is a cause/effect paragraph by a student, and the third example is a cause/effect essay by a professional writer. As you read these pieces, pay attention to the vocabulary, and answer the questions in the margin. They will help you read critically.

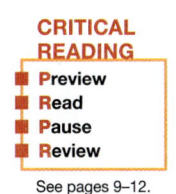

CRITICAL READING
- Preview
- Read
- Pause
- Review

See pages 9–12.

PROFILE OF SUCCESS

Cause and Effect in the Real World

Mary LaCue Booker
Singer, Actor
(stage name: La Q)

Background I grew up in a small town in Georgia but always had big dreams that I followed. Those dreams included becoming a nurse, a teacher, and then a singer and an actor. Before becoming a nurse and teacher, I went to college, studying both nursing and psychology. Later, I followed my dream of performing and left Georgia to attend the competitive American Academy of Dramatic Arts in Los Angeles.

I returned to Georgia and combined teaching and performance as chair of the Fine Arts Department at Columbia Middle School. I wrote rap songs for my students, and my first one, "School Rules," was an immediate hit in Atlanta. I now have three CDs and acted in the movie *We Must Go Forward*, about African American history. In addition to performing, I also am busy giving motivational speeches.

Degrees/Colleges A.A., DeKalb College; B.S., Brenau Women's College; M.Ed., Cambridge College

Writing at work When I taught, I wrote lesson plans, reports for students, and communications with parents. Now, I write song lyrics, speeches, and screenplays. I believe that writing is critical. I write from the heart, and it is a good outlet for my emotions. Sometimes, I freewrite around one word, like *mischievous*, which is the name of one of my CDs.

How La Q uses cause and effect Many of my songs and speeches are about causes and effects, like the effects of how we act or love or what causes pain or happiness. I wrote "School Rules" for my students, who did not listen to regular rules but would listen to a rap song about them.

La Q's Cause and Effect

Following are some lyrics from "School Rules."

> *Now get this, now get this, now get this.*
> If ya wanna be cool, obey the rules
> Cause if ya don't, it's your future you lose.
> I'm a school teacher from a rough school.
> I see students every day breakin' the rules.
> Here comes a new boy with a platinum grill
> Makin' trouble, ringin' the fire drill.
>
> There goes anotha' fool wanna run the school,
> Breakin' all the damn school rules.
> Runnin' in the halls, writin' graffiti on the walls,
> Tellin' a lie without blinkin' an eye,
> Usin' profanity, pleadin' insanity,
> Callin' names, causin' pain,

> Joinin' gangs like it's fame,
> Dissin' the teacha and each otha.
> Regardless of color, they're all sistas and brothas.
>
> *Now get this, now get this, now get this, now get this.*
> Boys and girls are skippin' class,
> Cause they late with no hall pass.
> They wanna have their say, and that's okay,
> But they're outta their minds if they wanna have their way.
>
> *Now get this, now get this, now get this.*
> If ya wanna be free, school's not the place ta be.
> But if ya wanna degree, you gotta feel me.
> So if you wanna be cool, obey the rules
> Cause if ya don't, it's your future you lose.

1. What is La Q's **purpose**? _____

2. What are the **effects** of breaking the rules? _____

3. Underline the **causes** that lead to these effects.

4. With a partner, or as a class, translate this rap into formal English.

TIP For more on using formal English, see Chapter 2.

Student Cause/Effect Paragraph

Caitlin Prokop

A Difficult Decision with a Positive Outcome

Caitlin Prokop wrote the following essay as she was preparing to begin her studies at Brevard Community College in Florida. Later, she went on to pursue a degree in elementary education at the University of Hawaii. She was inspired to write this essay by her parents and their life choices. Caitlin often produces several drafts of her work and understands the balance between inspiration and revision in writing. Of writing, she says, "Follow what the brain is telling the hand. Let it flow. If you cannot write about the topic that is given, put yourself in someone else's shoes and then write. Let your thoughts flow; then, revise and edit to get the finished copy."

> **Vocabulary development**
> Underline these words as you read Caitlin's paragraph.
> **accompany:** to be with; to go with
> **cherish:** to value highly

TIP For advice on building your vocabulary, visit the *Student Site for Real Writing* at **bedfordstmartins.com/realwriting**.

When my mother made the decision to move back to New York, I made the choice to move in with my dad so that I could finish high school. This decision affected me in a positive way because I graduated with my friends, built a better relationship with my father, and had the chance to go to college without leaving home. Graduating with my friends was very important to me because I have known most of them since we were in kindergarten. It was a journey through childhood that we had shared, and I wanted to finish it with them. Accomplishing the goal of graduating from high school with my close friends, those who accompanied me through school, made me a stronger and more confident person. Another good outcome of my difficult decision was the relationship I built with my dad. We never saw eye to eye when I lived with both of my parents. For example, we stopped talking for five months because I always sided against him with my mom. Living together for the past five years has made us closer, and I cherish that closeness we have developed. Every Thursday is our day, a day when we talk to each other about what is going on in our lives, so that we will never again have a distant relationship. A third good outcome of my decision is that I can go to Brevard Community College, which is right down the street. In high school, I had thought that I would want to go away to college, but then I realized that I would miss my home. By staying here, I have the opportunity to attend a wonderful college that is preparing me for transferring to a four-year college and finding a good career. I have done some research and believe I would like to become a police officer, a nurse, or a teacher. Through the school, I can do volunteer work in each of these areas. Right now, I am leaning toward becoming a teacher, based on my volunteer work in a kindergarten class. There, I can explore what grades I want to teach. In every way, I believe that my difficult decision was the right one, giving me many opportunities that I would not have had if I had moved to a new and unfamiliar place.

1. Double-underline the **topic sentence**.

2. Does Caitlin write about causes or effects? _____

3. Circle the **transitions** Caitlin uses to move readers from one point to the next.

4. Does Caitlin's paragraph include the Four Basics of Good Cause and Effect? Why or why not? _____
_____

5. Have you made a difficult decision that turned out to be a good one? Why and how? _____

Professional Cause/Effect Essay

Kristen Ziman
Bad Attitudes and Glowworms

Kristen Ziman is a commander with the Aurora Police Department in Aurora, Illinois, and a columnist for the *Beacon News,* a *Chicago Sun-Times* publication. She holds a B.A. in criminal justice management from Aurora University and an M.A. in criminal justice/organizational leadership from Boston University. She is also a graduate of the Senior Executives in State and Local Government Program at Harvard University's Kennedy School of Government. In addition to writing for the *Beacon News,* Ziman regularly posts to her blog, *Think Different.*

In the following essay, Ziman discusses how keeping a positive attitude helps people maintain control over their lives, even under the most challenging circumstances.

> **Vocabulary development**
> Underline these words as you read the cause/effect essay.
> **epiphany:** a sudden understanding or insight
> **contention:** conflict; displeasure
> **bashful:** shy
> **disdain:** contempt; hatred
> **relatively:** in comparison with (in this case) other times
> **exclusively:** only
> **conceptually:** in abstract or emotional terms, as opposed to factual terms
> **overwhelming:** bordering on unbearable
> **metamorphosis:** transformation
> **motives:** reasons for people's actions
> **hover:** to float in the air above something
> **analytical:** given to studying things carefully
> **gravitated towards:** were drawn to
> **validated:** confirmed; supported
> **proverbial:** related to a proverb or common saying. ("Look at yourself in the mirror" is a common saying.)
> **endure:** to survive; to make it through a difficult situation
> **thrive:** to be successful
> **attitudinally:** in terms of attitude
> **self-imposed:** put upon oneself

1   In my third-grade classroom there was a poster on the wall that read:

I wish I were a glowworm,
A glowworm's never glum.
'Cuz how can you be grumpy
When the sun shines out your bum!

2   I didn't understand what that poem meant until I was in my twenties, and I had an epiphany about attitude. I was partnered with a veteran officer, and two hours into our eight-hour shift, I began to realize that there was not a single thing he enjoyed about his job or his life. Being assigned to ride with me was also a source of contention for him, and he wasn't bashful about telling me so.

3   I found his disdain for life odd—especially given the fact that it was a beautiful summer day and the few calls we answered were relatively uneventful. As we patrolled the streets, I visualized a dark cloud exclusively over his head in contrast to the sunshine surrounding the rest of us, and I laughed out loud as the glowworm poem popped into my head. It was at that moment that I started to understand the effect our attitude has on our entire existence.

4   Throughout my life, I have been bombarded with lessons about attitude. It's not what happens to us in life, but the way we respond that makes a difference. If you can't change a situation, you must change the way you see the situation. I understand these lessons on an intellectual

level, but conceptually, there are times I find it difficult to find the light when darkness seems to be so overwhelming.

IDENTIFY Underline the causes of negative attitudes in this paragraph.

As I gained more experience as a police officer, I began to understand how the metamorphosis from an optimist to a pessimist occurs. I became distrusting of other human beings, though not without reason. I had been lied to, spit on, and physically attacked while doing my job. I saw the evil human beings did to one another and started to become suspicious of motives all around me. There was a moment when I quietly challenged my decision to make this my career, and I felt my own dark cloud begin to hover.

Because I've always been very analytical and self-aware [by my own estimation], I started to pay attention to the negativity of my coworkers, and it suddenly became clear that the miserable ones seemed to feed off each other like vultures. They gravitated towards one another because they validated each other's thoughts and beliefs. They were always victims, and they effortlessly found someone else to blame for all that was wrong. Never did they stop to look in the proverbial mirror and ask themselves if they might be part of the problem.

My favorite book is *Man's Search for Meaning* by Viktor Frankl. In his book, Frankl writes about his experiences in the concentration camps of Nazi Germany. He took particular interest in how some of his fellow prisoners seemed to endure and even thrive, while others gave up and laid down to die. From this, he concluded that "everything can be taken from a man but one thing: the last of human freedom is to choose one's attitude in any given set of circumstances—to choose one's own way."

SUMMARIZE What is the author's main point in this paragraph?

We all struggle in some way with things that are completely out of our control. But the way we gain control over these things—even if only attitudinally—is where our freedom lies. We don't have to experience torture in a concentration camp to apply Frankl's teachings to our own lives. We each have the freedom to make choices that liberate us from our self-imposed prisons.

If Frankl's story doesn't motivate you to choose the way you look at things, maybe you need to surround yourselves with more glowworms.

1. Double-underline the **thesis statement**.

TIP For reading advice, see Chapter 1.

2. Does this essay present causes, effects, or both? Explain how you came to your conclusion. _____
_____
_____
_____

3. Does this essay follow the Four Basics of Good Cause and Effect (p. 246)? Why or why not? _____

Respond to one of the following assignments in a paragraph or essay.

1. At the beginning of her essay, Ziman writes about a time when the words of an old poem popped into her head, helping her see a situation in a new light. Write about a time when something from your past (such as advice from a friend, song lyrics, or a scene from a favorite movie) came into your mind during a challenging time and helped you get through it.

2. We have all met people who, like the police officer in paragraph 3 of Ziman's essay, constantly have a "dark cloud" over their heads. Is it ever a good idea to confront others about their negative attitudes? Or is it better to focus just on our own attitude toward the situation? Explain your position, supporting it with examples.

3. Look back on the Viktor Frankl quotation in paragraph 7 of the essay. Then, write about a time when you had to decide what kind of attitude you were going to take in a difficult situation. How did your attitude affect your view of the situation and of yourself?

Write Your Own Cause and Effect

In this section, you will write your own cause and effect based on one of the following assignments. For help, refer to the How to Write Cause and Effect checklist on page 264.

ASSIGNMENT OPTIONS Writing about College, Work, and Everyday Life

Write a cause/effect paragraph or essay on one of the following topics or on one of your own choice. If you responded to the idea journal prompt on page 250, you might develop that writing further.

COLLEGE

- Write about the causes, effects, or both of not studying for an exam.
- If you have chosen a major or program of study, explain the factors behind your decision. How do you think this choice will shape your future?
- Why do some people stay in college while others drop out? Interview one or two college graduates about the factors behind their decision to stay in school. Also, ask them how staying in school and graduating has affected their lives. Then, write about the causes and effects they describe.

COMMUNITY CONNECTIONS

*While she was in college, **SHAWN ELSWICK** helped found an organization that provides support for victims of domestic abuse. Getting more involved in college and community activities, as Shawn did, can help you feel more connected to others and can even improve the chances that you will stay in school.*

For more on this story, ways to make community connections, and writing assignments, visit bedfordstmartins.com/realwriting.

TIP For a reminder of how to summarize, analyze, synthesize, and evaluate, see the Reading and Writing Critically box on pages 16–17.

WORK

- Write about the causes, effects, or both of stress at work.
- Identify a friend or acquaintance who has been successful at work. Write about the factors behind this person's success.
- Write about the causes, effects, or both of having a good or bad attitude at work. For a description of how our attitudes can affect our lives, see Kristen Ziman's essay on page 259.

EVERYDAY LIFE

- Think of a possession that has great personal meaning for you. Then, write about why you value the possession, and give examples of its importance in your life.
- Try to fill in this blank: "_____ changed my life." Your response can be an event, an interaction with a particular person, or anything significant to you. It can be something positive or negative. After you fill in the blank, explain how and why this event, interaction, or time had so much significance.
- Arrange to spend a few hours at a local soup kitchen or food pantry, or on another volunteer opportunity that interests you. (You can use a search engine to find volunteer opportunities in your area.) Write about how the experience affected you.

ASSIGNMENT OPTIONS Reading and Writing Critically

Complete one of the following assignments, which ask you to apply the critical thinking, reading, and writing skills discussed in Chapter 1.

Writing Critically about Readings

Kristen Ziman's "Bad Attitudes and Glowworms" (p. 259), Caitlin Prokop's "A Difficult Decision with a Positive Outcome" (p. 257), and Jelani Lynch's "My Turnaround" (p. 124) talk about taking control of one's life. Read or review these pieces, and then follow these steps:

1. **Summarize** Briefly summarize the works, listing major examples.

2. **Analyze** What questions do these pieces raise for you? Are there any other issues you wish they had covered?

3. **Synthesize** Using examples from Ziman's, Prokop's, and Lynch's writings and from your own experience, discuss different ways—big and small—in which people can take control of their lives.

4. **Evaluate** Which of the pieces had the deepest effect on you? Why? In writing your evaluation, you might look back on your responses to step 2.

Writing about Images

Researchers have discovered that laughter really is contagious. When we hear someone else laughing, our brain picks up the signal and puts our facial muscles into laughter mode. With that in mind, study the photographs on this page, and complete the following steps.

1. **Read the images** Ask yourself: Why is it a good idea to use a series of photos, instead of a single photo, to show the effects of laughter? (For more information on reading images, see Chapter 1.)

2. **Write a cause/effect paragraph or essay** Write about a time when someone else's laughter caused you to join in—even in a serious situation. What caused you to laugh, and what were the effects on you and everyone else?

Writing to Solve a Problem

Read or review the discussion of problem solving in Chapter 1 (pp. 24–26). Then, consider the following problem.

> You have learned of a cheating ring at school that uses cell phones to give test answers to students taking the test. A few students in your math class, who are also friends of yours, think that this scheme is a great idea and are planning to cheat on a test you will be taking next week. You decide not to participate, partly because you fear getting caught, but also because you think that cheating is wrong. Now you want to convince your friends not to cheat, because you don't want them to get caught and possibly kicked out of school. How do you make your case?

ASSIGNMENT: Working in a group or on your own, list the various effects of cheating—both immediate and long term—you could use to convince your friends. Then, write a cause/effect paragraph or essay that identifies and explains some possible effects of cheating. You might start with this sentence:

> Cheating on tests or papers is not worth the risks.

WRITING DIFFERENT KINDS OF PARAGRAPHS AND ESSAYS
Chapter 15 • Cause and Effect

CHECKLIST: HOW TO WRITE CAUSE AND EFFECT

STEPS	DETAILS
☐ **Narrow and explore your topic.** See Chapter 3.	• Make the topic more specific. • Prewrite to get ideas about the narrowed topic.
☐ **Write a topic sentence (paragraph) or thesis statement (essay).** See Chapter 4.	• State your subject and the causes, effects, or both that your paper will explore.
☐ **Support your point.** See Chapter 5.	• Come up with explanations/examples of the causes, effects, or both.
☐ **Write a draft.** See Chapter 6.	• Make a plan that puts the support points in a logical order. • Include a topic sentence (paragraph) or thesis statement (essay) and all the supporting explanations/examples.
☐ **Revise your draft.** See Chapter 7.	• Make sure it has *all* the Four Basics of Good Cause and Effect. • Make sure you include transitions to move readers smoothly from one cause/effect to the next.
☐ **Edit your revised draft.** See Parts 4 through 7.	• Correct errors in grammar, spelling, word use, and punctuation.

Chapter Review

1. A cause is _____

2. An effect is _____

3. What are the Four Basics of Good Cause and Effect?
   _____
   _____
   _____
   _____

4. Write sentences using the following vocabulary words: *cherish, motives, endure, thrive.* _____
   _____
   _____

LEARNING JOURNAL
Reread your idea journal entry (p. 250) about a time you caused someone to be happy or unhappy. Make another entry about this topic, using what you have learned about cause and effect.

reflect Write for 2 minutes about what you have learned about writing cause and effect.

16

Argument

Writing That Persuades

> **YOU KNOW THIS**
>
> You often try to persuade others or make your opinion known:
>
> - You convince your partner that it's better to save some money than to buy a new television set.
> - You persuade someone to loan you money or let you borrow a car.
>
> **write** for 2 minutes about how you convince others to see something your way.

Understand What Argument Is

Argument is writing that takes a position on an issue and gives supporting evidence to persuade someone else to accept, or at least consider, the position. Argument is also used to convince someone to take (or not take) an action.

Four Basics of Good Argument

1. It takes a strong and definite position.
2. It gives good reasons and supporting evidence to defend the position.
3. It considers opposing views.
4. It has enthusiasm and energy from start to finish.

In the following paragraph, the numbers and colors correspond to the Four Basics of Good Argument.

> **1** Even though I write this blog post on an 88-degree day, I am truly glad that I stopped using my air conditioner, and I urge you to follow my lead. **2** For one thing, going without air conditioning can save a significant amount of money. Last summer, this strategy cut my electricity costs by nearly $2,000, and I am on my way to achieving even higher savings this summer. For another thing, living without air conditioning reduces humans' effect on the environment. Agricultural researcher Stan Cox estimates that air conditioning creates 300 million tons of carbon dioxide (CO_2) emissions each year. This amount, he says, is the equivalent of every U.S. household buying an additional car and driving

4 Argument is enthusiastic and energetic.

266 Chapter 16 • Argument

4 Argument is enthusiastic and energetic.

it 7,000 miles annually. Because CO_2 is one of the greenhouse gases responsible for trapping heat in our atmosphere, reducing CO_2 emissions is essential to curbing climate change. The final reason for going without air conditioning is that it is actually pretty comfortable. The key to staying cool is keeping the blinds down on south-facing windows during the day. It is also a good idea to open windows throughout the home for cross ventilation while turning on ceiling fans to improve air circulation. **3** Although some people argue that using fans is just as bad as switching on the air conditioner, fans use far less electricity. In closing, let me make you a promise: The sooner you give up air conditioning, the sooner you will get comfortable with the change—and the sooner you and the planet will reap the rewards.

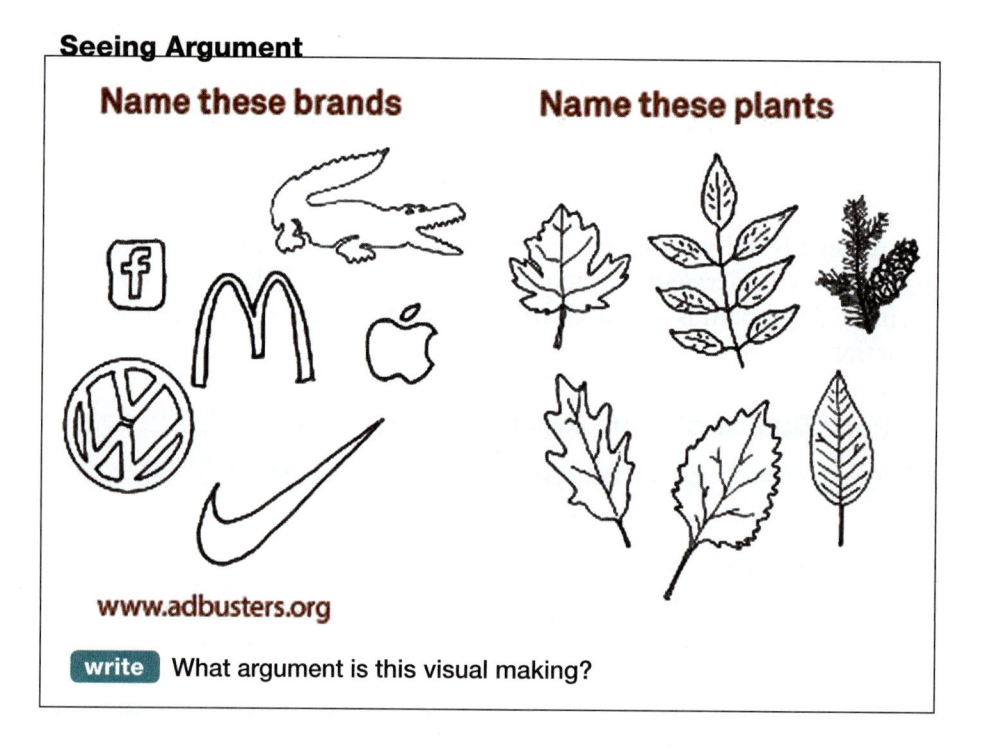

Seeing Argument

Name these brands **Name these plants**

www.adbusters.org

write What argument is this visual making?

Knowing how to make a good argument is one of the most useful skills you can develop.

COLLEGE	You argue for or against makeup exams for students who do not do well the first time.
WORK	You need to leave work an hour early one day a week for twelve weeks to take a course. You persuade your boss to allow you to do so.
EVERYDAY LIFE	You try to negotiate a better price on an item you want to buy.

In college, writing assignments might include questions or statements such as the following: *Do you agree or disagree with _____? Defend or refute _____. Is _____ fair and just?* In all these cases, use the strategies discussed in this chapter.

Main Point in Argument

Your **main point** in argument is the position you take on the issue (or topic) about which you are writing. When you are free to choose an issue, choose something that matters to you. When you are assigned an issue, try to find some part of it that matters to you. You might try starting with a "should" or "should not" sentence:

| MAIN POINT IN ARGUMENT | College football players should/should not be paid. |

If you have trouble seeing how an issue matters, talk about it with a partner or write down ideas about it using the following tips.

TIPS FOR BUILDING ENTHUSIASM AND ENERGY

- Imagine yourself arguing your position with someone who disagrees.
- Imagine that your whole grade rests on persuading your instructor to agree with your position.
- Imagine how this issue could affect you or your family personally.
- Imagine that you are representing a large group of people who care about the issue very much and whose lives will be forever changed by it. It is up to you to win their case.

In argument, the topic sentence (in a paragraph) or thesis statement (in an essay) usually includes the issue/topic and your position about it. Here is an example of a topic sentence for a paragraph:

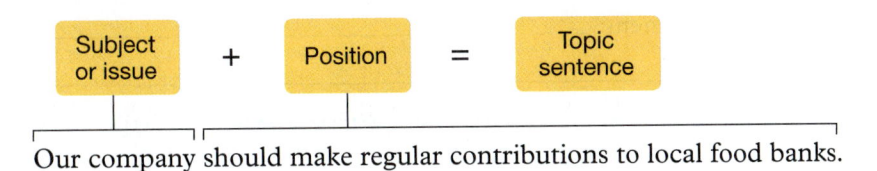

Subject or issue + Position = Topic sentence

Our company should make regular contributions to local food banks.

Remember that the main point for an essay can be a little broader than one for a paragraph.

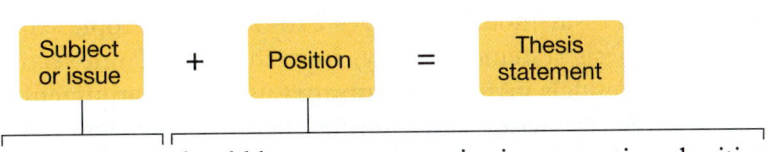

Subject or issue + Position = Thesis statement

Our company should become more active in supporting charities.

WRITER AT WORK

DIANE MELANCON: As a doctor, I make cases for diagnoses and treatments.

(See Diane Melancon's **PROFILE OF SUCCESS** on p. 279.)

IDEA JOURNAL Persuade a friend who has lost his job to take a course at your college.

WRITING DIFFERENT KINDS OF PARAGRAPHS AND ESSAYS

Chapter 16 • Argument

TIP Sometimes, the same main point can be used for a paragraph and an essay, but the essay must develop this point in more detail. (See pp. 69–70.)

Whereas the topic sentence focuses on just one type of charitable organization, the thesis statement sets up a discussion of different ways to help different charities.

PRACTICE 1   Writing a Statement of Your Position

Write a statement of your position for each item.

EXAMPLE:

Issue: Prisoners' rights

Position statement: *Prisoners should not have more rights and privileges than law-abiding citizens.*

1. Issue: Lab testing on animals

   Position statement: _____

2. Issue: Use of cell phones while driving

   Position statement: _____

3. Issue: Athletes' salaries

   Position statement: _____

4. Issue: Treadmill desks

   Position statement: _____

5. Issue: Organic farming

   Position statement: _____

Support in Argument

TIP For more on evidence, see page 271.

The paragraph and essay models on pages 270–71 use the topic sentence (paragraph) and thesis statement (essay) from the Main Point section of this chapter. Both models include the **support** used in all argument writing: the **reasons** for the writer's position backed up by **evidence**. In the essay model, however, the major support points (reasons) are topic sentences for individual paragraphs.

A good way to find strong support for an argument is to return to some of the critical-thinking strategies you learned about in Chapter 1. Let's take another look at the basics.

Four Basics of Critical Thinking

1. Be alert to assumptions made by you and others.
2. Question those assumptions.
3. Consider and connect various points of view, even those different from your own.
4. Do not rush to conclusions; instead, remain patient with yourself and others, and keep an open mind.

Jess, a student you might remember from Chapter 1, applied some of these basics while working on an argument paper for her English class. She got an idea for the paper while waiting to start her shift at a local restaurant. On the TV over the restaurant's bar, a political commentator and a doctor were debating whether a tax on soda would help reduce obesity.

Jess was in favor of just about any reasonable approach to fighting obesity, although she wasn't sure that a tax on soda (and other sugary beverages) would work. Even the doctor seemed a little unsure.

After finishing her shift, Jess thought about the issue some more, and she began to see how the pros of such a tax might outweigh the cons, but she decided to sleep on the issue before coming to any final conclusions. Here is the working main point she wrote down in her notebook before going to bed.

MAIN POINT   Taxing sugary drinks might be a good way to reduce obesity.

QUESTIONING ASSUMPTIONS TO BUILD EVIDENCE

The next morning, Jess used a key critical-thinking strategy to explore her main point in more depth. Specifically, she tried to identify some of the **assumptions** (unquestioned ideas or opinions) behind her main point. She wrote them down on one half of a sheet of notebook paper. Next, she questioned each of her assumptions, trying to put herself in the shoes of someone opposed to beverage taxes. She wrote these questions on the other half of the notebook paper.

TIP Consider this advice from actor Alan Alda: "Begin challenging your own assumptions. Your assumptions are your windows on the world. Scrub them off every once in a while, or the light won't come in."

ASSUMPTIONS BEHIND MAIN POINT	QUESTIONS ABOUT ASSUMPTIONS
Sugary drinks, like soda, energy drinks, and sweetened tea, can make people fat.	But why target sugary drinks instead of other junk food? Aren't french fries just as bad for the waistline as soda is? →

PARAGRAPHS VS. ESSAYS IN ARGUMENT

For more on the important features of argument, see the Four Basics of Good Argument on page 265.

Paragraph Form

Topic sentence

Support 1 (reason 1)

Support 2 (reason 2)

Support 3 (reason 3)

Concluding sentence

Our company should make regular contributions to local food banks. The first reason for making these contributions is that, as a food wholesaler, we have the resources to do so. Often, we find that we have a surplus of certain items, such as canned goods and pasta, and it would be a waste not to donate this food to organizations that need it so desperately. We could also donate food that is safe to consume but that we cannot sell to stores or institutions. These items include market-testing products from manufacturers and goods with torn labels. Second, these contributions will improve our image among clients. All other things being equal, grocers, schools, hospitals, and other institutions will be more likely to purchase food from a wholesaler that gives something back to the community than one focused on its financial interests alone. The most important reason for making these contributions is to help our company become a better corporate citizen. Especially in challenging economic times, many people see corporations as heartless, and motivated by profits alone. It is important to show not only clients but also the wider community that we are one of the "good guys." That is, we are willing to do what is right, not only within our organization but also in society. Although some question the need for a donation program, arguing that it would take too much time to organize, the good that will come from the program will far exceed the effort devoted to it.

Main Point: Often, narrower for a paragraph than for an essay: While the topic sentence (paragraph) focuses on just one type of charitable organization, the thesis statement (essay) sets up a discussion of different ways to help different charities.

Support for the Main Point (Reasons for the Writer's Position)

Evidence to Back Up Each Reason: Usually, 1 to 3 sentences per reason for paragraphs and 3 to 8 sentences per reason for essays.

Conclusion

Think Critically As You Write Argument

ASK YOURSELF

- Have I questioned the assumptions behind my main point?
- Have I looked for evidence to respond to these questions and to develop support for my argument? (For more on finding and evaluating outside sources, see pp. 304–09.)
- Have I tested this evidence before including it in my paper? (For more on testing evidence, see p. 274.)

Essay Form

At the last executive meeting, we discussed several possible ways to improve our company's marketing and advertising and to increase employee morale. Since attending the meeting, I have become con[vinced that one] effort would help in those areas and more: **Our company should become more active in supporting charities.**

First, giving time and money to community organizations is a good way to promote our organization. This approach has worked well for [some of our] competitors. For example, Lanse Industrie[s is known] for sponsoring Little League teams throughout the city. Its name is on the back of each uniform, and banners promoting Lanse's new products appear on the ball fields. Lanse gets free promotion of these efforts through articles in the local papers, and according to one company source quoted in the *Hillsburg Gazette,* Lanse's good works in the community have boosted its sales by 5 to 10 percent. Another competitor, Great Deals, has employees serve meals at soup kitchens over the holidays and at least once during the spring or summer. It, too, has gotten great publicity from these efforts, including a spot on a local TV news show. It is time for our company to s[tart getting] these kinds of benefits.

Second, activities like group volunteering will help employees feel more connected to one another and to their community. Kay Rodriguez, a manager at Great Deals and a good friend of mine, organized the company's group volunteering efforts at the soup kitchens, and she cannot say enough good things about the results. Aside from providing meals to the needy, the volunteering has boosted the morale of Great Deals employees because they understand that they are supporting an important cause in their community. Kay has also noticed that as employees work together at the soup kitchens, they form closer bonds. She says, "Some of these people work on different floors and rarely get to see each other during the work week. Or they just do not have time to talk. But while they work together on the volunteering, I see real connections forming." I know that some members of our executive committee might think it would be too time-consuming to organize companywide volunteering efforts. Kay assures me, however, that this is not the case and that the rewards of such efforts far exceed the costs in time.

The most important reason for supporting charities is that it is the right thing to do. As a successful business that depends on the local community for a large share of revenue and employees, I believe we owe that community something in return. If our home city does not thrive, how can we? By giving time and money to local organizations, we provide a real service to people, and we present our company as a good and caring neighbor instead of a faceless corporation that could not care less if local citizens went hungry, had trash and graffiti in their parks, or couldn't afford sports teams for their kids. We could make our community proud to have us around.

I realize that our main goal is to run a profitable and growing business. I do not believe, however, that this aim must exclude doing good in the community. In fact, I see these two goals moving side-by-side, and hand-in-hand. When companies give back to local citizens, their businesses benefit, the community benefits, and everyone is pleased by the results.

271

ASSUMPTIONS BEHIND MAIN POINT	QUESTIONS ABOUT ASSUMPTIONS
Taxes on sugary drinks would make people less likely to buy these beverages.	Really? It's easy for me to say that this tax would work because I'm not a big fan of these drinks. But if they taxed coffee, the taxes would have to be pretty big to break my four-cups-a-day habit.
The tax revenues would benefit the public.	How much difference would they really make?

To answer these questions, Jess turned to some sources recommended by a college librarian later that day. She also drew on information she found through a Google search, and on a few of her own experiences and observations. In doing so, she gathered the following four types of evidence used most often in support of arguments.

- **FACTS:** Statements or observations that can be proved. Statistics—real numbers from actual studies—can be persuasive factual evidence.

- **EXAMPLES:** Specific information or experiences that support your position.

- **EXPERT OPINIONS:** The opinions of people considered knowledgeable about your topic because of their educational or work background, their research into the topic, or other qualifications. It is important to choose these sources carefully. For example, an economics professor might be very knowledgeable about the possible benefits and drawbacks of beverage taxes. He or she probably wouldn't be the best source of information on the health effects of soda, however.

- **PREDICTIONS:** Forecasts of the possible outcomes of events or actions. These forecasts are the informed views of experts, not the best guesses of nonexperts.

TIP When looking for evidence about assumptions, always seek the most reliable sources of information. For more details on finding reliable sources, see Chapter 18.

The following chart shows the evidence Jess pulled together to address her assumptions and her questions about them. (She revised and expanded her original questions as she explored her topic further.)

ASSUMPTIONS / QUESTIONS TO INVESTIGATE	EVIDENCE IN RESPONSE
To what degree do sugary drinks contribute to obesity?	**Fact:** According to the Centers for Disease Control and Prevention, about half of all Americans get a major portion of their daily calories from sweetened beverages. **Fact:** In the *Journal of Pediatrics,* Robert Murray reported that one-fourth of U.S. teenagers drink as many as four cans of soda or fruit drinks a day, each one containing about 150 calories. That translates to a total of 600 calories a day, the equivalent of an additional meal. **Expert opinion:** Dr. Richard Adamson, senior scientific consultant for the American Beverage Association, says, "Blaming one specific product or ingredient as the root cause of obesity defies common sense. Instead, there are many contributing factors, including regular physical activity."

WRITING DIFFERENT KINDS OF PARAGRAPHS AND ESSAYS
Understand What Argument Is

ASSUMPTIONS / QUESTIONS TO INVESTIGATE	EVIDENCE IN RESPONSE
Do sugary drinks deserve to be targeted more than other dietary factors that can contribute to obesity?	**Example (from Jess's personal experience):** My brother, his wife, and their three kids are all big soda drinkers, and they are all overweight. They also eat lots of junk food, however, so it is hard to tell how much the soda is to blame for their weight. **Fact:** The Center for Science in the Public Interest says that sugary beverages are more likely to cause weight gain than solid foods are. After eating solid food, people tend to reduce their consumption of other calorie sources. Unlike solid foods, however, sugary beverages do not make people feel full. Therefore, they may add on calories to satisfy their hunger.
To what degree would taxes on sugary drinks discourage people from buying these beverages and also reduce obesity?	**Expert opinion/fact:** Several researchers say that the taxes would have to be pretty significant to affect consumer behavior. The average national tax on a 12-ounce bottle of soda is 5 cents, and that has not provided enough discouragement. **Prediction:** In the *New England Journal of Medicine,* Kelly D. Brownell says that a penny-per-ounce tax on sugary beverages could reduce consumption of these beverages by more than 10 percent.
Would the taxes have any other benefits?	**Prediction:** Kelly D. Brownell says that by reducing the consumption of sugary beverages, the taxes could help cut public expenditures on obesity. Each year, about $79 billion goes toward the health-care costs of overweight and obese individuals. Approximately half of these costs are paid by taxpayers. **Expert opinion:** Brownell also believes that the tax revenues could/should be used for programs to prevent childhood obesity.

PRACTICE 2 Deepening the Search for Evidence

Come up with at least one other question that could be raised about Jess's topic. Then, list the type(s) of evidence (such as personal examples, an expert opinion from a scientific study, or a prediction from a business leader) that could help answer the question.

QUESTION(S): _____

_____

TYPE(S) OF EVIDENCE: _____

In the process of investigating her assumptions, Jess not only gathered good support; she also encountered some opposing views (one of the Four Basics of Good Argument). One of the opposing views, from Dr. Richard Adamson of the American Beverage Association, gave her a little pause. Because he represents the interests of the beverage industry, he might not offer a completely balanced opinion on the health effects of sweetened drinks, but Jess decided that as long as she mentioned his affiliation with the beverage industry, his point might be worth including in her paper.

In reviewing her evidence, Jess also referred to the following tips from her instructor.

TESTING EVIDENCE

- Consider your audience's view of the issue. Are audience members likely to agree with you, to be uncommitted, or to be hostile? Then, make sure your evidence would be convincing to a typical member of your audience.

- Reread your evidence from an opponent's perspective, looking for ways to knock it down. Anticipate your opponent's objections, and include evidence to answer them.

- Do not overgeneralize. Statements about what everyone else does or what always happens are easy to disprove. It is better to use facts (including statistics), specific examples, expert opinions, and informed predictions.

- Make sure you have considered every important angle of the issue.

- Reread the evidence to make sure it provides good support for your position. Also, the evidence must be relevant to your argument.

PRACTICE 3 Reviewing the Evidence

For each of the following positions, one piece of evidence is weak: It does not support the position. Circle the letter of the weak evidence, and, in the space provided, state why it is weak.

EXAMPLE:

Position: Advertisements should not use skinny models.

Reason: Skinny should not be promoted as ideal.
 a. Three friends of mine became anorexic trying to get skinny.
 (b.) Everyone knows that most people are not that thin.
 c. A survey of girls shows that they think that they should be as thin as models.
 d. People can endanger their health trying to fit the skinny "ideal" promoted in advertisements.

Not strong evidence because *"everyone knows" is not strong evidence; everyone obviously doesn't know that.*

1. Position: People who own guns should not be allowed to keep them at home.

   Reason: It is dangerous to keep a gun in the house.
    a. Guns can go off by accident.
    b. Keeping guns at home has been found to increase the risk of home suicides and adolescent suicides.
    c. Just last week, a story in the newspaper told about a man who, in a fit of rage, took his gun out of the drawer and shot his wife.
    d. Guns can be purchased easily.

Not strong evidence because _____

2. Position: Schoolchildren in the United States should go to school all year.

   Reason: Year-round schooling promotes better learning.

   a. All my friends have agreed that we would like to end the long summer break.
   b. A survey of teachers across the country showed that children's learning improved when they had multiple shorter vacations rather than entire summers off.
   c. Many children are bored and restless after three weeks of vacation and would be better off returning to school.
   d. Test scores improved when a school system in Colorado went to year-round school sessions.

   Not strong evidence because _____

3. Position: The "three strikes and you're out" law that forces judges to send people to jail after three convictions should be revised.

   Reason: Basing decisions about sentencing on numbers alone is neither reasonable nor fair.

   a. A week ago, a man who stole a slice of pizza was sentenced to eight to ten years in prison because it was his third conviction.
   b. The law makes prison overcrowding even worse.
   c. Judges always give the longest sentence possible anyway.
   d. The law too often results in people getting major prison sentences for minor crimes.

   Not strong evidence because _____

After Jess reviewed her evidence, she decided to refine her initial position.

REVISED MAIN POINT   To help address the obesity crisis, states should place significant taxes on sugary beverages.

Notice that Jess got rid of the "might" wording that had been part of her original main point. Having done some research, she now believes strongly that the taxes are a good idea—as long as they are high enough to make a significant dent in consumption.

Before writing her paper, Jess created a rough outline stating her main point and her major support points—the reasons for the position expressed in her main point. The reasons are based on the evidence Jess gathered.

ROUGH OUTLINE

Main point: To help address the obesity crisis, states should place significant taxes on sugary beverages.

Support/reasons:

Sugary drinks are a major contributor to obesity.

As long as they are significant, taxes on these drinks could reduce consumption.

The taxes could fund programs targeting childhood obesity.

WRITING THE CONCLUSION

Your conclusion is your last opportunity to convince readers of your position. Make it memorable and forceful. Remind readers of the stand you are taking and the rightness of this stand, even in the face of opposing views.

Before writing your conclusion, imagine that you are an attorney making a final, impassioned appeal to the judge in an important case. Then, put this energy into words with a conclusion that drives your point home. (See Jess's conclusion on p. 277.)

Organization in Argument

TIP For more on order of importance, see page 79.

Most arguments are organized by **order of importance**, starting with the least important evidence and saving the most convincing reason and evidence for last.

Use **transitions** to move your readers smoothly from one supporting reason to another. Here are some of the transitions you might use in your argument.

Common Transitions in Argument

above all	more important
also	most important
best of all	one fact / another fact
especially	one reason / another reason
for example	one thing / another thing
in addition	remember
in fact	the first (second, third) point
in particular	worst of all
in the first (second, third) place	

Jess used order of importance to organize her argument in favor of taxes on sugary drinks, which follows. The transitions have been highlighted in bold.

You will notice that Jess didn't incorporate all the evidence from the chart on pages 272–73; instead, she chose the evidence she believed offered the strongest support for her main point. She also included an opposing view.

> To help address the obesity crisis, states should place significant taxes on sugary beverages, such as soda, sweetened tea and fruit juices, and energy drinks. These drinks are a good target for taxation because they are a major contributor to obesity. According to the Centers for Disease Control and Prevention, about half of all Americans get a major portion of their daily calories from sweetened beverages. **In addition**, the *Journal of Pediatrics* reports that one-fourth of U.S. teenagers get as many as 600 calories a day from soda or fruit drinks. This consumption is the equivalent of an additional meal. **Another reason to tax sugary drinks is that** such taxation could reduce consumption. However, it is important that these taxes be significant, because taxes of just a few additional pennies per can or bottle probably wouldn't deter consumers. According to Kelly D. Brownell, director of the Rudd Center for Food Policy and Obesity, a penny-per-ounce tax on sugary beverages could cut consumption of these beverages by more than 10 percent. It could also reduce the estimated $79 billion of taxpayer money spent each year on health care for overweight and obese individuals. **The most important reason to tax sugary drinks is that** the money from such taxes could be used to prevent future cases of obesity. As Brownell notes, the taxes could fund antiobesity programs aimed at educating children about healthy diets and encouraging them to exercise. Some people who are opposed to taxing sugary beverages, such as Dr. Richard Adamson of the American Beverage Association, argue that it is unfair to blame one product for our expanding waistlines. It is true that overconsumption of soda and other sweetened beverages is just one cause of obesity. Nevertheless, targeting this one cause could play a vital, lasting role in a larger campaign to bring this major health crisis under control.

PRACTICE 4 Using Transitions in Argument

The following argument essay encourages students to get involved in service work during college. It was written by Jorge Roque, an Iraq War veteran and Miami-Dade College student who is vice president of a service fraternity.

After reading Jorge's essay, fill in the blanks with transitions. You are not limited to the ones listed in the box on page 276.

Even for the busiest student, getting involved in service organizations is worth the time and effort it takes. At one point, after I had returned from Iraq, was homeless, and was experiencing post-traumatic stress disorder, I was referred to Veteran Love, a nonprofit organization that helps disabled ex-soldiers, and they helped when I needed it most. When I was back on track, I knew that I wanted to help others. I was working and going to school with very little extra time, but getting involved has been important in ways I had not expected.

_____

_____ you meet many new people and form a new and larger network of friends and colleagues. You also learn new skills, like organization, project management, communication, teamwork, and public speaking. The practical experience I have now is more than I could have gotten from a class, and I have met people who want to help me in my career.

_____

_____ you help other people and learn about them. You feel as if you have something valuable to give. You also feel part of something larger than yourself. So often, students are not connected to meaningful communities and work, and service helps you while you help others.

_____

service work makes you feel better about yourself and your abilities. What I am doing is important and real, and I feel better than I ever have because of my service involvement. If you get involved with community service of any kind, you will become addicted to it. You get more than you could ever give.

Read and Analyze Argument

Reading examples of argument will help you write your own. In the first example, Diane Melancon, an oncologist (cancer doctor), shows how she uses persuasive writing at work. The second examples are opposing argument essays by two students.

As you read these pieces, pay attention to the vocabulary, and answer the questions in the margin. They will help you read critically.

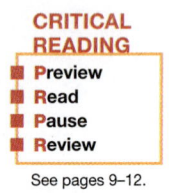

CRITICAL READING
- Preview
- Read
- Pause
- Review

See pages 9–12.

PROFILE OF SUCCESS

Argument in the Real World

Background Although I graduated second in my high school class in Fall River, Massachusetts, my family did not encourage me to go to college. Instead, it was expected that I would marry and get some kind of job that did not require a college degree. Nevertheless, after finishing high school I entered Southeastern Massachusetts University (now part of the University of Massachusetts) as a biology major. I had no idea what I really wanted to do, however, and I ended up leaving college after the first year and going to a vocational school to be a medical assistant. When I finished that training, I got a job as an EKG technician. After doing that for a year and a half, I applied to X-ray school at Northeastern University, where I eventually received my associate's degree. For two years after graduation, I worked at Boston University Medical Center. During this time I started to have doubts about whether I wanted to be an X-ray tech for the rest of my life. Some of my friends started saying, "You really should try to go to medical school." But to go to med school, I first needed to get a bachelor's degree, so I applied to and was accepted at Wellesley College. Wellesley was tough for me at the beginning because I started there when I was twenty-five, and to seventeen- and eighteen-year-olds, I was kind of an old lady. But I got through, and after graduating with a biology degree, I was accepted into Dartmouth Medical School.

After graduating from medical school I practiced internal medicine in Massachusetts, New Hampshire, and Texas. In 2005, I happened to see an advertisement for a job in the hematology/oncology group of St. Mary's Hospital in Grand Junction, Colorado. I got the job, and after a year of training, I became a member of the hematology/oncology group, where I focus mostly on breast and gynecological cancers.

Although I followed kind of a curvy path to get to where I am now, I think I found what I was meant to do, and I love my work. As my experience shows, people can do much more than they ever think they can if they believe in themselves and persevere.

Degrees/Colleges Medical assistant certificate, Diman Regional Vocational Technical High School; A.S., Northeastern University; B.A., Wellesley College; M.D., Dartmouth Medical School

Employer St. Mary's Hospital

Writing at work The major types of writing that I do are (1) patient assessments, in which I pull together information about a patient's condition to specify a diagnosis, and (2) treatment plans.

Diane Melancon
Oncologist

Diane's Argument

In the following piece of writing, Diane argues for advance directives. In these legal documents, individuals spell out how they wish their medical treatment to be handled in a life-threatening situation. If you have studied definition, notice as you read that Diane uses elements of definition to make her argument.

Vocabulary development

Underline these words as you read.

chemotherapy: drug therapy aimed at killing cancer cells
strains: difficulties
sustaining: preserving
ventilators: machines that help with or perform the breathing process
aggressive: powerful
cardiopulmonary resuscitation: a method of restoring someone's heart and lung function in an emergency situation
incapable: unable
contradicted: opposed
scenario: situation

Consider these difficult situations: (1) A car accident seriously damages a young man's brain, leaving his family to decide whether or not he should be kept on life support. (2) A patient's cancer is not responding well to chemotherapy. She must decide whether to continue with the therapy, despite its physical and emotional strains, or to receive only care that reduces pain and provides comfort. Nothing will make such decisions any easier for these patients or their families. However, people who are able to provide guidance for their treatment in advance of a medical crisis can help ensure that their wishes are followed, even under the most difficult circumstances. Therefore, everyone should seriously consider preparing advance directives for medical care.

One major reason for preparing advance directives is that they make it clear to care providers, family, and other loved ones which medical measures patients do or do not want to be taken during a health crisis. Directives specify these wishes even after patients are no longer able to do so themselves — because, for example, they have lost consciousness. Advance directives include living wills, legal documents that indicate which life-sustaining measures are acceptable to patients and under what circumstances. These measures include the use of breathing aids, such as ventilators, and of feeding aids, such as tube-delivered nutrition. Living wills may also indicate a point at which a patient wishes to receive only comfort care, as opposed to aggressive treatment. Furthermore, living wills may specify whether patients wish to receive cardiopulmonary resuscitation if their heart and breathing stop. Finally, through a legal document known as a medical power of attorney, patients may select another person to make medical decisions on their behalf if they become incapable of doing so themselves. All of these parts of advance directives help reduce the risk that patients' wishes will be overlooked or contradicted during any point of the treatment process.

Another important reason for preparing advanced directives is that they can reduce stress and confusion in the delivery of care. Ideally, patients should complete these directives while they are still relatively healthy in mind and body and capable of giving thoughtful and informed instructions for their own medical care. In contrast, waiting until a health problem is far advanced can increase the difficulty and stress of making medical decisions; at this point, patients and their loved ones may be feeling too overwhelmed to think carefully through the various options. In the worst-case scenario, patients may have moved beyond the ability to contribute to medical decisions at all. In such cases, family members and others close to patients may be forced to make their own judgments about which treatments should or should not be given, possibly resulting in disagreements and confusion. However, when patients have made their preferences clear in advance, care delivery moves more smoothly for them and everyone else.

> Some people may believe that advance directives are too depressing to think about or that they are even unnecessary. They may take the attitude "Let's cross that bridge when we come to it." However, as has been noted, by the time the bridge is in sight it might already be too late. Although making advance plans for life-threatening medical situations can be difficult and emotional, avoiding such planning can create more stress for patients and their loved ones. Worse, it may mean that the patients' true wishes are never known or acted upon.

1. Double-underline the **thesis statement**.
2. Circle the **transitions** that introduce the different reasons supporting the argument.
3. Underline the part of the essay that presents an opposing view.
4. Does this essay follow the Four Basics of Good Argument (p. 265)? Why or why not? _____

The next two student essays argue about the wisdom of using social media, like Facebook and Twitter, as educational aids in college. Read both essays, and answer the questions after the second one.

Student Argument Essay 1: "Yes" to Social Media in Education

Jason Yilmaz

A Learning Tool Whose Time Has Come

Efforts to incorporate social media into courses at our college have drawn several complaints. A major objection is that Facebook and Twitter are distractions that have no place in the classroom. Based on my own experiences, I must completely disagree. Social media, when used intelligently, will get students more involved with their courses and help them be more successful in college.

In the first place, social media can help students engage deeply with academic subjects. For example, in a sociology class that I took in high school, the instructor encouraged students to use Twitter in a research

Vocabulary development
Underline the following words as you read.
incorporate: to add; to bring into
objection: an argument against something
distractions: things that draw attention away from something else
engage: to become involved in

2 **REFLECT** Do you think using social media in your classes would help you get more out of your education?

281

assignment. This assignment called for us to record, over one week, the number of times we observed students of different races and ethnic groups interacting outside of the classroom. Each of us made observations in the lunch room, in the courtyard where students liked to hang out between classes, and in other public areas. We tweeted our findings as we did our research, and in the end, we brought them together to write a group report. The Twitter exchanges gave each of us new ideas and insights. Also, the whole process helped us understand what a research team does in the real world.

In the second place, social media are a good way for students to get help and support outside of class. As a commuter student with a job, it is hard for me to get to my instructors' office hours, let alone meet with other students. Therefore, I would value Facebook groups that would let me post questions about assignments and other homework and get responses from instructors and other students. Also, I would be able to form online study groups with classmates.

Finally, social networking can make students feel more confident and connected. In the sociology course where I used Twitter, I found that other students valued and respected the information that I shared, just as I valued their contributions. Also, all of us felt like we were "in this together"—an uncommon experience in most classrooms. I have heard that feeling connected to other students and to the larger college community can make people less likely to drop out, and I believe it.

PREDICT What points do you think will be raised in the opposing argument?

New things often scare people, and the use of social media in education is no exception. However, I would hate to see fears about social media get in the way of efforts to make students more engaged with and successful in college. We owe it to students to overcome such fears.

Vocabulary development
Underline these words as you read.
spell: a state of being enchanted or fascinated by something
initiative: a program or process
compromise: to interfere with
savvy: knowledgeable or sophisticated
plagiarism: using other people's words as your own

Student Argument Essay 2: "No" to Social Media in Education

Shari Beck

A Classroom Distraction—and Worse

Last week, I saw the campus newspaper's story about new efforts to incorporate Twitter, Facebook, and other social media into courses. What did I think about these efforts? To get my answer, I only had to lower the newspaper. Across the table from me was my fourteen-year-old son, whom I'd just told, for the third time, to go upstairs and do his homework.

Instead, he was still under the spell of his phone, thumbs flying as he continued to text a friend about who knows what.

As you might have guessed already, my answer to my own question is this: Making social media part of a college education is a terrible idea, for a whole lot of reasons.

One reason is the distraction factor, illustrated by my phone-addicted son. I am confident that he is not the only person incapable of turning his full attention to any subject when the competition is an incoming or outgoing text message, or anything happening on a computer screen. Supporters of the college's social-media initiative say that students will benefit from discussing course material on Facebook or Twitter. I am concerned, however, that such discussions—when and if they ever take place—would quickly go off-topic, turning into social exchanges. Also, participants' attention could easily wander to other links and news flashes.

Another reason I am opposed to social media in education is that students' postings on Facebook or Twitter might compromise their privacy. I am not confident that all teachers will educate students about the importance of limiting the personal information that they make available in public forums. Tech-savvy students probably know how to maximize their privacy settings, but I doubt that all students do.

My biggest concern is that students will use social media to cheat. According to proponents of the social-media initiative, one of the biggest educational advantages of Facebook and Twitter is that students can exchange information and form study groups. But it is also possible that they will share answers to homework or test questions or take credit for information posted or tweeted by others. They may not realize that such information theft is plagiarism—something that could cause them to fail a course, or worse. In responding to a 2011 survey by the Pew Research Center, 55 percent of college presidents said that student plagiarism had increased over the previous ten years. Of those who reported this increase, 89 percent said computers and the Internet played "a major role." It would be a shame to make this growing problem even worse through programs like the college's social-media initiative.

From where I sit—once again, across the table from my phone-distracted son—the disadvantages of this initiative far outweigh the benefits. I plan to send an e-mail opposing it to the Student Affairs Office. First, though, I'm taking my son's phone away for the night.

1. Double-underline the **thesis statement** in both essays.
2. Underline the **reasons** for the position taken in each essay.

3. Does each essay follow the Four Basics of Good Argument (p. 265)? Give examples to support your answer. _____

4. Write down at least one additional support point/reason that one of the authors might have included. Then, describe the types of evidence that could be used to back up this support point. _____

Respond to one of the following assignments in a paragraph or essay.

1. Write a letter to Jason or Shari, either in support of or against his or her argument. Make sure to back up the reasons for your position with evidence.

2. The previous essays focus on the educational applications of social media. Now, think about the possible uses of social media in the workplace. Do you see any benefits to this usage, or do you think that social media would be just another distraction at work? Support your argument with evidence.

3. Think of (1) a new policy or program you would like to see adopted at your school or (2) an existing or proposed policy or program you would like to see discontinued or dropped from consideration. Provide at least two reasons for your position, and make sure to back up your argument with evidence.

Write Your Own Argument

In this section, you will write your own argument based on one of the following assignments. For help, refer to the How to Write Argument checklist on page 287.

ASSIGNMENT OPTIONS Writing about College, Work, and Everyday Life

Write an argument paragraph or essay on one of the following topics or on one of your own choice. If you responded to the idea journal prompt on page 267, you might develop that writing further.

COLLEGE

- Take a position on a controversial issue on your campus. If you need help coming up with topics, you might consult the campus newspaper.
- Argue for or against the use of standardized tests or placement tests. Make sure to research different positions on the tests to support your argument and address opposing views. One Web site you might consult is standardizedtests.procon.org.

- In 2011, "Occupy" protests swept college campuses. In them, students argued for a fairer economic system nationally, lower tuition, and other measures to reduce financial burdens on them and other citizens. If you support their arguments, explain why, providing specific reasons and examples. If you oppose their arguments, give reasons and examples for your position.

WORK

- Argue for a change in a company policy.
- Argue for something that you would like to get at work, such as a promotion, a raise, or a flexible schedule. Explain why you deserve what you are asking for, and give specific examples.
- Argue for an improvement in your workplace, such as the addition of a bike rack, new chairs in the break room, or a place to swap books or magazines. Make sure your request is reasonable in cost and will be beneficial to a significant number of employees.

EVERYDAY LIFE

- Take a position on a controversial issue in your community.
- Choose a community organization that you belong to, and write about why it is important. Try to persuade your readers to join.
- Oscar Wilde (1854–1900), a famous Irish writer, once commented, "Most people are other people. Their thoughts are someone else's opinions, their lives a mimicry,[1] their passions a quotation." Write an argument that supports or opposes Wilde's views, giving reasons and examples for your position.

COMMUNITY CONNECTIONS

JORGE ROQUE (see the essay on p. 278) is vice president of a service fraternity at his college. Getting more involved in college and community activities, as Jorge did, can help you feel more connected to others and can even improve the chances that you will stay in school.

For more on this story, ways to make community connections, and writing assignments, visit bedfordstmartins.com/realwriting.

ASSIGNMENT OPTIONS Reading and Writing Critically

Complete one of the following assignments, which ask you to apply the critical thinking, reading, and writing skills discussed in Chapter 1.

Writing Critically about Readings

The pro/con essays by Jason Yilmaz and Shari Beck (see pp. 281–83) are strongly focused on arguing a position. Sometimes, however, arguments can take a more subtle form. See, for instance, Frances Cole Jones's "Don't Work in a Goat's Stomach" (p. 199) and Kristen Ziman's "Bad Attitudes and Glow-worms" (p. 259). Read or review these pieces, and then follow these steps:

1. **Summarize**   Briefly summarize at least two of the works, listing major examples and details.

2. **Analyze**   What features of argument do you see in the essays by Jones and Ziman?

---

1. **mimicry:** an imitation of something else

TIP For a reminder of how to summarize, analyze, synthesize, and evaluate, see the Reading and Writing Critically box on pages 16–17.

3. **Synthesize** Using examples from at least two of the previously mentioned essays and from your own experience, describe the features that make an argument successful and convincing. Think of features beyond those in the Four Basics of Good Argument.

4. **Evaluate** In your opinion, are strongly focused arguments or subtler arguments more effective? Or do both types of writing have a place? Explain your answer.

Writing about Images

The following photograph is of an installation by Brazilian sculptor Nele Azevedo, who travels around the world and sets up ice sculptures of people on the steps of government buildings. Throughout the day, the sculptures melt, helping to illustrate the effect of climate change.

Study the photograph, and complete the following steps.

1. **Read the image** Ask yourself: What details are you drawn to, and why? What emotions or reactions do the melting sculptures bring about in you? (For more information on reading images, see Chapter 1.)

2. **Write an argument** Write a paragraph or essay in which you respond to Azevedo's work and discuss the argument you think that she's making with it. How effective do you find her visual argument? Is it a good way to convey the effects of climate change? Why or why not? Include the details and reactions from step 1.

Writing to Solve a Problem

Read or review the discussion of problem solving in Chapter 1 (pp. 24–26). Then, consider the following problem.

> Your friend/child/relative has just turned sixteen and is planning to drop out of high school. He has always done poorly, and if he drops out, he can increase his hours at the restaurant where he works. You think that this idea is terrible for many reasons.

ASSIGNMENT: In a group or on your own, come up with various reasons in support of your decision. Consider, too, your friend's/child's/relative's possible objections to your argument, and account for them. Then, write an argument paragraph or essay to persuade him to complete high school. Give at least three solid reasons, and support your reasons with good evidence or examples. You might start with the following sentence:

> There are so many important reasons to stay in school and get your high school diploma.

CHECKLIST: HOW TO WRITE ARGUMENT

STEPS	DETAILS
☐ Narrow and explore your topic. See Chapter 3.	• Make the topic more specific. • Prewrite to get ideas about the narrowed topic.
☐ Write a topic sentence (paragraph) or thesis statement (essay). See Chapter 4.	• State your position on your topic.
☐ Support your point. See Chapter 5.	• Come up with reasons and evidence to back up your position.
☐ Write a draft. See Chapter 6.	• Make a plan that puts the reasons in a logical order. • Include a topic sentence (paragraph) or thesis statement (essay) and all the reasons and supporting evidence.
☐ Revise your draft. See Chapter 7.	• Make sure it has *all* the Four Basics of Good Argument. • Make sure you include transitions to move readers smoothly from one reason to the next.
☐ Edit your revised draft. See Parts 4 through 7.	• Correct errors in grammar, spelling, word use, and punctuation.

Chapter Review

1. Argument is writing _____

2. What are the Four Basics of Good Argument?

3. The topic sentence (paragraph) or thesis statement (essay) in an argument should include what two elements? _____

4. What three types of information make good evidence? _____

5. Why do you need to be aware of opposing views? _____

6. Write sentences using the following vocabulary words: *aggressive, contradicted, distractions, compromise, plagiarism.* _____

LEARNING JOURNAL
Reread your idea journal entry (p. 267) about why your friend should take a college course. Make another entry about this topic, using what you have learned about argument.

reflect Write for 2 minutes about what you have learned about writing a good argument.

"I write presentations and speeches for work and school."
—Katie F., student

Part 3

Special College Writing Projects

17 Writing Summaries, Reports, and Essay Exams 291

18 Writing the Research Essay 302

17

YOU KNOW THIS

You often share what you have learned with others:

- You summarize events or TV shows for friends.
- You tell a classmate who missed class what happened.
- You report on a meeting at work for your boss.

Writing Summaries, Reports, and Essay Exams

Showing What You Have Learned

Write a Summary

A **summary** is a condensed, or shortened, version of something—often, a longer piece of writing, a movie or TV show, a situation, or an event. It presents the main ideas and major support, stripping the information to its essential elements.

Four Basics of a Good Summary

1. It has a topic sentence (in a paragraph) or a thesis statement (in an essay) that states what is being summarized and its main idea.
2. It identifies the major support points.
3. It includes any final observations or recommendations made in the original piece.
4. It is written in your own words and presents information without your opinions.

1 The essay "A Classroom Distraction—and Worse" argues against using social media as an educational tool in college. **2** The first reason the author gives for her position is that social media might draw students' attention away from course content instead of encouraging them to focus on it. For example, online discussions of course material might turn into chit-chat sessions. **2** Second, the author argues that students

TIP Shari Beck's essay, "A Classroom Distraction—and Worse," appears on pages 282–83.

SPECIAL COLLEGE WRITING PROJECTS

292   Chapter 17 • Writing Summaries, Reports, and Essay Exams

> might post too much information about themselves, harming their privacy. Finally, she says that students might use social media to give one another answers to test questions or homework assignments or to plagiarize—a growing problem, according to college presidents. **3** The author concludes by saying that any benefits provided by using social media in education are small in comparison to the drawbacks.

4 Summary is in the writer's own words.

There are many uses for summarizing.

COLLEGE	To answer a test question for a history course, you summarize the causes of the Great Depression.
WORK	You write a summary of a telephone conversation to send to a client and your boss.
EVERYDAY LIFE	You summarize a car accident for your insurance company.

The Reading Process for Summaries

To write a summary, you must first understand what you are reading. To note what is important as you read, you might follow this process:

READING TO SUMMARIZE

1. Double-underline the main point, and write "main point" in the margin next to it.
2. Underline the major support points, and write "major support" in the margin.
3. Underline the final observations, recommendations, or conclusions, and write "conclusion" in the margin.
4. After you finish reading, write a sentence or two, in your own words, about what is important about the piece.

TIP Instead of underlining, you could use two different-colored highlighters for steps 1 and 2.

Here is the paragraph from the Four Basics of a Good Summary, underlined and annotated using the steps of the reading process.

Main point ——— The essay "A Classroom Distraction—and Worse" argues against using social media as an educational tool in college. The first reason the author gives for her position is that social media might draw students' attention away from course content instead of encouraging them to focus on it. For example, online discussions of course material might turn into chit-chat sessions. Second, the author argues that students might post too much information about themselves, harming their privacy. Finally, she says that students might use social media to give one another answers to test questions or homework assignments or to plagiarize—a growing problem, according to college presidents.

Major support

Major support

Major support

The author concludes by saying that any benefits provided by using social media in education are small in comparison to the drawbacks. ⎯⎯ Conclusion

WHAT'S IMPORTANT: The writer argues that using social media in college does more harm than good.

PRACTICE 1 Reading to Summarize

Read the following essay, and mark it according to the four steps of Reading to Summarize.

In 2010, Congress passed a law to bring tighter regulations to Wall Street and prevent another major economic crisis. Despite this law's passage, the threat of another financial meltdown remains.

One reason the threat remains is that financial institutions have little incentive to change the practices that got them into trouble in the first place. In 2009, billions of dollars of taxpayer money went to rescuing banks and other financial interests perceived as "too big to fail." Even though the Wall Street Reform and Consumer Protection Act, also known as the Dodd-Frank law, seeks to reduce the need for future bailouts of this kind, it may have little effect in the long run. As business reporter Shahien Nasiripour writes, large financial institutions have come to believe that if they get into more trouble, the government will always come to their rescue; therefore, it is likely that they will continue to take risks, such as making careless loans.

Furthermore, continuing resistance to the Dodd-Frank law is reducing its effectiveness. Nasiripour reports that one year after passage of the legislation, only 38 of its 400 new rules had been finalized. One reason for this slow progress is financial institutions' reservations about various parts of the law, expressed in ongoing meetings with federal regulators. According to an article by *New York Times* reporter Edward Wyatt, financial lobbyists spent more than $50 million in 2011 to try to change Dodd-Frank. They are getting help from Senate and House members who are taking steps to repeal the law, to further reduce its power, or to cut the budgets of regulatory bodies, such as the Securities and Exchange Commission, charged with enforcing the new rules (Nasiripour). Although the Dodd-Frank law is far from ideal, any successes in weakening or overturning it will place the U.S. economic system at greater risk.

TIP Summaries and reports often use specific passages or quotations from a piece. For more information on citing and documenting source material, see Chapter 18.

Most big banks and other large financial institutions have come out of the economic crisis thriving and relieved that, for the most part, it is business as usual for them. But business as usual in financial regulation could have devastating consequences for the economy as a whole.

Works Cited

Nasiripour, Shahien. "A Year after Dodd-Frank, Too Big to Fail Remains Bigger Problem Than Ever." *Huffingtonpost.com*. Huffington Post, 20 July 2011. Web. 5 Dec. 2011.

Wyatt, Edward. "Dodd-Frank Under Fire a Year Later." *Nytimes.com*. New York Times, 18 July 2011. Web. 5 Dec. 2011.

WHAT'S IMPORTANT: _____

_____

PRACTICE 2   Reading to Summarize

Read Janice E. Castro's essay on pages 218–220, and mark it according to the four steps of Reading to Summarize.

The Writing Process for Summaries

Use the following checklist to help you write summaries.

CHECKLIST: HOW TO WRITE A SUMMARY	
STEPS	**DETAILS**
☐ Focus.	• Think about why you are writing the summary and for whom. How much information will your audience need?
☐ Read the selection carefully.	• Underline the main idea, the major support, and the conclusion(s), noting each in the margin.
☐ Write a short statement about what you have read.	• In your own words, write what is important about the piece.
☐ Reread the sections you underlined and annotated, along with your written statement.	• Make additional notes or annotations.
☐ Draft the summary.	• For an essay-length summary, make an outline. • While drafting your summary, refer to the original piece, but use your own words. • Work in the points you have annotated, using your outline if you wrote one.

CHECKLIST: HOW TO WRITE A SUMMARY

STEPS	DETAILS
☐ Revise the summary.	• Make sure it has *all* the Four Basics of a Good Summary (p. 291). • Add transitions to move readers smoothly from one point to another. • Have you clearly told your reader what article, essay, or other source you are summarizing?
☐ Edit your work. (See Parts 4 through 7.)	• Check for errors in grammar, spelling, and punctuation.

Summary Assignments

Choose one of the following assignments, and complete it using the previous checklist.

- Using your notes from Practice 1, write a summary of the piece in Practice 1.
- Summarize a section of a textbook from one of your other courses.
- Summarize an editorial from a print or online magazine or newspaper.
- Summarize an entry from a blog that you have read.
- Summarize the plot of a movie or television program.
- Summarize one of the essays in Chapters 8 through 16.

Write a Report

A **report** usually begins with a short summary of a piece of writing, a conversation, or a situation. Then, it analyzes the information, providing reactions, opinions, or recommendations. Unlike a summary, a report often includes the writer's opinions.

The following apply to reports on pieces of writing.

Four Basics of a Good Report

1. In the first sentence or paragraph, it states the title and author of the piece and gives a brief overview.
2. It summarizes the piece, including the main idea and major support points.
3. It then moves to the writer's reactions and reasons for those reactions.
4. It concludes with an opinion (such as whether the piece is good or bad) or a general observation from the writer.

TIP Notice that the present tense is used to describe the action in essays and literary works.

"A Brother's Murder": A Painful Story That Is as True as Ever

Title, author, and brief overview

1 In the essay "A Brother's Murder," Brent Staples writes about his younger brother, Blake, who took a different path in life than Staples did.

2 The essay starts with a phone call in which Staples learns that Blake has been murdered, shot six times by a former friend (554). The essay goes on to tell about the conditions in which Blake grew up. The neighborhood in which the brothers lived was violent, and young men grew into dangerous adults. Staples recalls a conversation he overheard there between two Vietnam veterans, in which one of them said how much he preferred to fight with young men from the inner city, who wear "their manhood on their sleeves." They weren't afraid to fight, believing that violence proved they were *real* men (554–55).

Direct reference

Summary with major events/support

The author leaves the neighborhood to go to college, and he never returns. Blake, however, stays, and the author recalls a visit home when he sees that his brother has been transformed and now hangs out with drug dealers and gangs (555). When Staples notices a wound on his brother's hand, Blake shrugs it off as "kickback from a shotgun" (555). The author wants to help his brother and makes a date to see him the next night (556). Blake does not show up, and the author returns to Chicago, where he lives. Sometime later, he gets the phone call that announces Blake's death, and he regrets that he had not done something to help his brother.

Direct reference

3 "A Brother's Murder" is a moving and sad story about how men growing up in the inner city are destroyed. Although the essay was written in 1986, its message is at least as true today as it was then. Staples shows how his brother is sucked into the routine violence of the streets, shooting and being shot because that is what he knows and that is how a man shows that he is a man.

Writer's reactions

4 Today, thousands of young men live this life and die before they are thirty. This essay makes me wonder why this situation continues, but it also makes me wonder how two brothers could go such different ways. What happened to save Brent Staples? Could he have saved Blake? What can we do to stop the violence? "A Brother's Murder" is an excellent and thought-provoking essay about a dangerous and growing societal problem.

Conclusion with writer's observations and opinion

Work Cited

Staples, Brent. "A Brother's Murder." *Real Skills with Readings: Sentences and Paragraphs for College, Work, and Everyday Life.* Ed. Susan Anker. 2nd ed. Bedford/St. Martin's: 2010. 554–56. Print.

SPECIAL COLLEGE WRITING PROJECTS
Write a Report

You may need to write a report in a number of situations.

COLLEGE	You are assigned to write a book report.
WORK	You are asked to report on a product or service your company is considering.
EVERYDAY LIFE	You write an e-mail to a friend reporting on how your first months of college are going.

The Reading Process for Reports

Reading to write a report is like reading to write a summary except that, in the last step, you write your response to the piece instead of just noting what is important about it.

READING TO REPORT

1. Double-underline the main point, and write "main point" in the margin next to it.
2. Underline the major support points, and write "major support" in the margin.
3. Underline the final observations, recommendations, or conclusions, and write "conclusion" in the margin.
4. After you finish reading, write a sentence or two, in your own words, about how you responded to the piece and why.

PRACTICE 3   Reading to Report

Read Frances Cole Jones's essay on pages 199–201. Then, mark it according to the four steps of Reading to Report.

The Writing Process for Reports

Use the following checklist to help you write reports.

CHECKLIST: HOW TO WRITE A REPORT	
STEPS	**DETAILS**
☐ Focus.	• Think about why you are writing the report and for whom. What do you think of the piece, and how can you get that view across to readers?
☐ Read the selection carefully.	• Underline the main idea, the major support, and the conclusion(s), noting each in the margin. →

CHECKLIST: HOW TO WRITE A REPORT	
STEPS	**DETAILS**
☐ Write a short statement about what you have read.	• In your own words, write your reactions to the piece and reasons for those reactions.
☐ Reread your underlinings, marginal notes, and reactions.	• Make additional notes, and look for specific statements from the piece you might use in your report.
☐ Draft the report.	• For an essay-length report, make an outline. • While drafting your report, refer to the original piece, but use your own words. • Start with a summary, including the major support points. • Work from your outline if you wrote one, including your reactions.
☐ Revise the report.	• Make sure it has *all* the Four Basics of a Good Report (p. 295). • Add transitions to move readers smoothly from one point to another. • Make sure the report (aside from quotations) is all in your own words.
☐ Edit your work. (See Parts 4 through 7.)	• Check for errors in grammar, spelling, and punctuation.

Report Assignments

Complete one of the following assignments, using the checklist above.

- Using your notes from Practice 3, write a report on Frances Cole Jones's essay (pp. 199–201).
- Report on a movie or a concert you have seen recently.
- Report on an event in your community.
- Report on an article in a print or online magazine or news source.
- Report on one of the essays in Chapters 8 through 16.

Write a Response to an Essay Exam Question

In this course and others, you may be asked to complete an **essay exam**. In these exams, you must write an essay in response to questions like the following one from a sociology course:

> Define *groupthink* and identify three of its major characteristics, giving explanations and examples.

> **Four Basics** of a Good Response to an Essay Question
>
> 1. It includes a thesis statement that directly responds to the essay question.
> 2. It supports the thesis statement—again, by directly responding to the essay question.
> 3. It provides enough explanations, examples, and details for each support point.
> 4. It ends with a conclusion that refers back to the thesis statement and makes an observation.

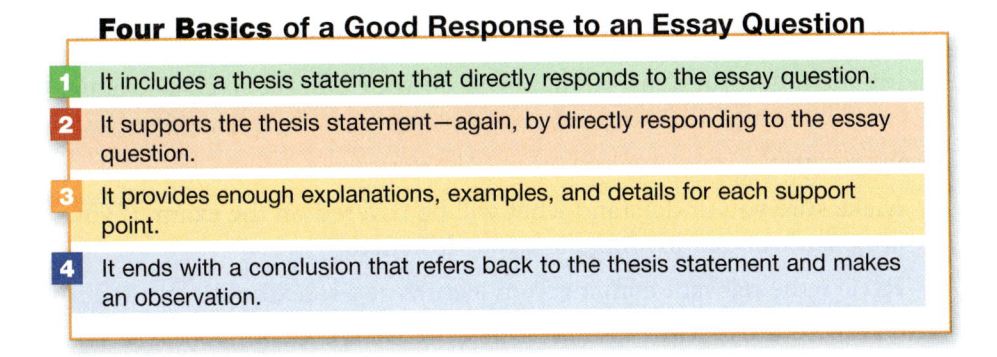

The following essay responds to the exam question from the sociology course.

In *groupthink*, the members of a group value complete agreement among themselves over individuals' thoughts and ideas. **1** It has the following major characteristics.

2 One characteristic of groupthink is that group members are pressured to conform with the beliefs and practices of the group. **3** If they have any doubts or concerns about these beliefs or practices, they usually do not express them and continue to go along with the group. According to psychologist Irving Janis, group members known as *mindguards* contribute to conformity by trying to block or counter any outside information that goes against the group's beliefs. Also, if a mindguard notices that any members of the group are starting to disagree with the group's ideas, he or she will put pressure on them to end their opposition.

2 Another characteristic of groupthink is that anyone who does not belong to the group is portrayed in a negative way. **3** This viewpoint helps group members feel superior to outsiders. It also helps dehumanize outsiders, making it easier for group members to mistreat them or, in the worst cases, kill them. One of the most horrifying examples of dehumanization under groupthink was Nazi Germany's oppression and murder of millions of Jews during World War II.

2 A third characteristic of groupthink is that group members believe that they are morally just, even if they have committed crimes against humanity. **3** Group conformity contributes to this perception. For example, group members tend to think, "How can this action be wrong if all of us think it is the right thing to do?" Terrorist organizations, such as al-Qaeda, provide just one example of this type of groupthink.

4 In any group, even those with the best intentions, it is a good idea for members to look for these signs of groupthink and work against them—or, if this approach fails, to leave the group. The best groups welcome the ideas and views of members and respect non-members. In the long run, such openness can help them achieve better outcomes.

The Process of Succeeding on Essay Exams

Taking the following steps will help you do your best on an essay exam.

BEFORE THE TEST

1. Make sure you understand what will be covered on the exam. If you are unsure about anything, ask your instructor.
2. Review the relevant content from lecture notes, textbooks, or other materials. Begin this review as early as possible.
3. Come up with a sample essay question, and write a response to it. Give yourself only as much time as you will have for the actual test.

DURING THE TEST

1. Underline key words in the essay question—the words that tell you what you need to do or provide. (In the essay exam question on p. 298, the key words are *define, identify, three . . . major characteristics,* and *explanations and examples*.)
2. Divide your time carefully. For example, for a 50-minute exam, you might devote 10 minutes to planning, 30 minutes to drafting, and 10 minutes to revising and editing.
3. Try to write a scratch outline for your essay. Your outline should include your thesis statement and at least three support points.
4. Stay focused on your topic by keeping the key words in mind as you write.
5. Make sure you have followed all the steps in the checklist on page 301.

PRACTICE 4 Identifying Key Words

Underline the key words in the following essay exam questions.

EXAMPLE: <u>Discuss</u> the <u>effects</u> of radiation on humans.

1. Describe the process of cell division in prokaryotes and eukaryotes.
2. Summarize the controversy surrounding the use of graphic antismoking images on cigarette packages.
3. Discuss the causes and effects of delayed adoption of children.
4. Identify and explain the major differences between the brains of teenagers and adults.
5. Evaluate Joe Klein's argument in favor of legalizing marijuana, giving reasons for your responses.

The Writing Process for Essay Exams

Use the following checklist to help you write an effective response to an essay exam question.

| CHECKLIST: HOW TO WRITE A RESPONSE TO AN ESSAY EXAM QUESTION ||
STEPS	DETAILS
☐ Focus.	• Underline the key words in the essay question, and think about what they are asking you to do.
☐ Draft the essay.	• Make an outline, and refer to it as you write. • Conclude with an observation about your topic.
☐ Revise the essay.	• Make sure it has *all* the Four Basics of a Good Response to an Essay Question (p. 299). • Add transitions to move readers smoothly from one point to another.
☐ Edit your work. (See Parts 4 through 7.)	• Check for errors in grammar, spelling, word use, and punctuation.

Chapter Review

1. What are the Four Basics of a Good Summary?

   _____
   _____
   _____
   _____

2. How is a summary different from a report? _____
   _____

3. What is the first thing you should do when you get an essay exam question? _____

18
Writing the Research Essay

Using Sources in Your Writing

> **YOU KNOW THIS**
>
> You have done research and reported on it:
>
> - You go online to find information about something you want to do or buy.
> - You ask a coworker about how to do a certain job, and you take notes.

In all areas of your life, doing research makes you better informed and strengthens any point you want to make. Here are some situations in which you might use research skills.

COLLEGE	In a criminal justice course, you are asked to write about whether the death penalty deters crime.
WORK	You are asked to do some research about a major office product (such as a phone or computer system) that your company wants to purchase.
EVERYDAY LIFE	Your child's doctor has prescribed a certain medication, and you want information about it.

This chapter explains the major steps of writing a college research essay: how to make a schedule; how to choose a topic and guiding research question; and how to find, evaluate, and document sources. A checklist guides you through the process of writing a research essay.

Make a Schedule

Writing a college research essay takes time: It cannot be started and finished in a day or two. To make sure you allow enough time, make a schedule, and stick to it.

You can use the following schedule as a model for making your own.

SAMPLE RESEARCH ESSAY SCHEDULE

Assignment: (Write out what your instructor has assigned.) _____
_____

Number of outside sources required: _____

Length (if specified): _____

Draft due date: _____

Final due date: _____

My general topic: _____

DO BY	STEP
_____	Choose a topic.
_____	Find and evaluate sources; decide which ones to use.
_____	Take notes, keeping publication information for each source.
_____	Write a working thesis statement by answering a research question.
_____	Review all notes; choose the best support for your working thesis.
_____	Make an outline that includes your thesis statement and support.
_____	Write a draft, including a title.
_____	Revise the draft.
_____	Prepare a list of Works Cited using the correct form of documentation.
_____	Edit the revised draft.
_____	Submit the final copy.

TIP For detailed information about writing a research essay, visit **bedfordstmartins .com/researchroom**.

Choose a Topic

Your instructor may assign a research paper topic or may want you to think of your own topic. If you are free to choose your own topic, find a subject that interests you and that you would like to explore. Ask yourself some questions such as the following:

1. What is going on in my own life that I want to know more about?
2. What do I daydream about? What frightens me? What inspires or encourages me?
3. What am I interested in doing in the future, either personally or professionally?
4. What famous person or people interest me?
5. What current issue do I care about?

Here are some current topics you might want to research:

Alternative energy sources	Jobs of the future
Behavior disorders	Music/musical groups
A career you are interested in	Obesity in the United States
Education issues	Online dating services
Environmental issues	Privacy and the Internet
Gay/lesbian marriage	Travel
Health/medical issues	Violence in the media
Immigration trends/policies	Volunteer opportunities

Before writing a working thesis statement, you need to learn more about your topic. It helps to come up with a **guiding research question**, which is often a variation of "What do I want to find out about my topic?" This question will help direct and focus your research.

The following is a guiding research question used by Dara Riesler, who chose the topic of dogs trained to help war veterans suffering from post-traumatic stress disorder (PTSD). (To learn how Dara answered this question, see her research paper on p. 319.)

GUIDING RESEARCH QUESTION	What benefits do service dogs provide to veterans suffering from PTSD?

Find Sources

With both libraries and the Internet available to you, finding information is not a problem. Knowing how to find good, reliable sources of information, however, can be a challenge. The following strategies will help you.

Consult a Reference Librarian

Reference librarians are essential resources in helping you find appropriate information in both print and electronic forms. They will save you time and possible frustration in your search for relevant material.

If your library allows, schedule an appointment with a librarian. Before your appointment, write down some questions to ask, such as the following. Begin your conversation by telling the librarian your research topic.

QUESTIONS FOR THE LIBRARIAN

- How do I use an online catalog? What information will the library's catalog give me?
- Can I access the library catalog and article databases from home or other locations?

TIP A catalog is a searchable register of all a library's holdings.

- What other reference tools would you recommend as a good starting place for research on my topic?
- Once I identify a source that might be useful, how do I find it?
- Can you recommend an Internet search engine that will help me find information on my topic? Can you also recommend some useful keywords?
- Does the college have access to a research database, such as *EBSCO*, *InfoTrac*, or *LexisNexis*?
- How can I tell whether a Web site is reliable?
- I have already found some articles related to my topic. Can you suggest some other places to look for sources?
- I have found good online sources, but how can I find some good print sources on my topic?

Use the Online Catalog

Most libraries now list their holdings online rather than in a card catalog. You can search by keyword, title, author, subject, publication data, and call number. Online catalog help is usually easy to find (generally on the screen or in a Help menu) and easy to follow. If you are just beginning your research, use the keyword search.

Dara Riesler, who wrote the research essay that appears later in this chapter, searched the library's online catalog using the keywords "service dogs and veterans." Here is one source she found:

TIP For more on conducting keyword searches, see page 306.

Author:	Montalván, Luis Carlos
Additional contributors:	Witter, Bret
Title:	Until Tuesday: A Wounded Warrior and the Golden Retriever Who Saved Him
Published:	New York - Hyperion
Location:	Main Library
Call #:	HV1569.6.M56 2011
Status:	Available
Physical description:	xi, 252 p. : ill. ; 22 cm.
Contents:	The story of how a trained service dog has helped a traumatized Iraq War veteran live a better life.

A call number is an identification number that helps you locate a book in the library. Once you find the book you are looking for, browse the nearby shelves, where you may find other sources related to your topic.

If the book is available only at another library, ask a librarian to have the book sent to your library, or request it at your library's Web site.

Look at Your Library's Web Site

Most libraries have a Web site that can help researchers find useful information. The home page may have links to electronic research sources that the library subscribes to and that are free to library users. These databases are usually reliable and legitimate sources of information. The library home page may also list the library's hours, provide search tools, and offer research tips and other valuable information.

Use Your Library's Online Databases and Other Reference Materials

Magazines, journals, and newspapers are called *periodicals*. Periodical indexes help you locate information published in these sources. Online periodical indexes are called *periodical databases* and often include the full text of magazine, journal, or newspaper articles. Libraries often subscribe to these online services. Here are some of the most popular periodical indexes and databases:

EBSCO   *LexisNexis*
InfoTrac   *NewsBank*
JSTOR   *ProQuest*

Use the Internet

TIP Visit www.census.gov, the official Web site of the U.S. Census Bureau, for current state and national statistical data related to population, economics, and geography.

This section will offer some basics on finding what you need on the Internet. To start, visit sites that categorize information on the Web, such as the Internet Public Library at www.ipl.org.

Some Internet sites charge fees for information (such as archived newspaper or magazine articles). Before using any of these sources, check to see whether they are available free through your library's databases.

SEARCH ENGINES AND KEYWORD SEARCHES

Google (www.google.com) is the most commonly used search engine. Others include Yahoo! at www.yahoo.com, www.duckduckgo.com, and www.bing.com.

To use a search engine, type in keywords related to your subject. Adding more specific keywords or phrases and using an Advanced Search option may narrow the number of entries (called *hits*) you have to sift through to find relevant information. Adding additional search terms can narrow a search even more. (With many search engines, you get the best results by enclosing phrases in quotation marks.)

When you discover a Web site to which you might want to return, save the Web address so that you do not have to remember it each time you want to go to the site. Different browsers have different ways of saving Web addresses; use the Bookmarks menu in Netscape or Firefox, or the Favorites menu in Microsoft Internet Explorer.

OTHER HELPFUL ONLINE RESEARCH SITES

Go to the following sites for tutorials on research processes and for other research advice. To access these sites, type their names and sponsors into a search engine.

- **The Bedford Research Room** (from Bedford/St. Martin's). This site provides advice on finding and evaluating sources and on writing research papers.
- **Citing Electronic Information** (from the Internet Public Library). This site contains links to various sources that explain how to document information found online.
- **Evaluating Web Sites** (from Cornell University). This site lists ways to evaluate Internet sources. Your own college library may have a similar Web site.

TIP Many instructors do not consider Wikipedia a good reference source. You might ask your instructor whether you may use Wikipedia for your research paper.

Interview People

Personal interviews can be excellent sources of information. Before interviewing anyone, however, plan carefully. First, consider what kind of person to interview. Do you want information from an expert on the subject or from someone directly affected by the issue? The person should be knowledgeable about the subject and have firsthand experience. When you have decided whom to interview, schedule an appointment.

Next, prepare a list of five to ten open-ended questions, such as *What do you think of the proposal to build a new library?* Closed questions, such as *Are you in favor of building a new library?*, will only lead to simple yes-or-no responses.

At the time of the interview, record the person's full name and qualifications and the date. Listen carefully to the responses to your questions and ask follow-up questions. Write down important ideas. If you plan to use any of the person's exact words, put them in quotation marks in your notes so that you can identify direct quotations later. For more on using direct quotations, see page 313 and Chapter 36.

Using a small recorder during the interview can be helpful. If you want to do so, make sure you ask the person for permission.

Evaluate Sources

Whether you are doing research for a college course, a work assignment, or personal reasons, make sure the sources you use are reliable. Reliable sources present accurate, up-to-date information written by authors with appropriate credentials for the subject matter. Research materials found in a college library (books, journals, and newspapers, for example) are generally considered reliable sources.

Materials found on the Internet must be approached with more caution. When you are doing research on the Internet, try to determine each source's purpose. A Web site set up solely to provide information might be

Quik-LEAN™ NUTRITIONAL SUPPLEMENT

Members Login / Not a member yet? Register NOW!

About Quik-Lean™ | Guarantee | Links | Ordering

Shed 20 pounds in 20 days!

...and build *muscle mass* without changing your diet or heading to the gym!

With its unique, patented combination of safe, natural ingredients Quik-Lean™
- increases lean muscle mass
- reduces body fat
- boosts metabolism

Satisfied customers say...
"I lost more weight, more quickly than ever before!" —A Quik-Lean fan from MA
"I was thrilled by the results I got." —A Quik-Lean fan from KY
"Quik-Lean is safe and effective!" —A certified health trainer, CA

Annotations:
- Site sponsored by a business to sell a product
- Unrealistic and unsupported claims
- No names supplied
- Is this person in a position to say what is safe and effective?

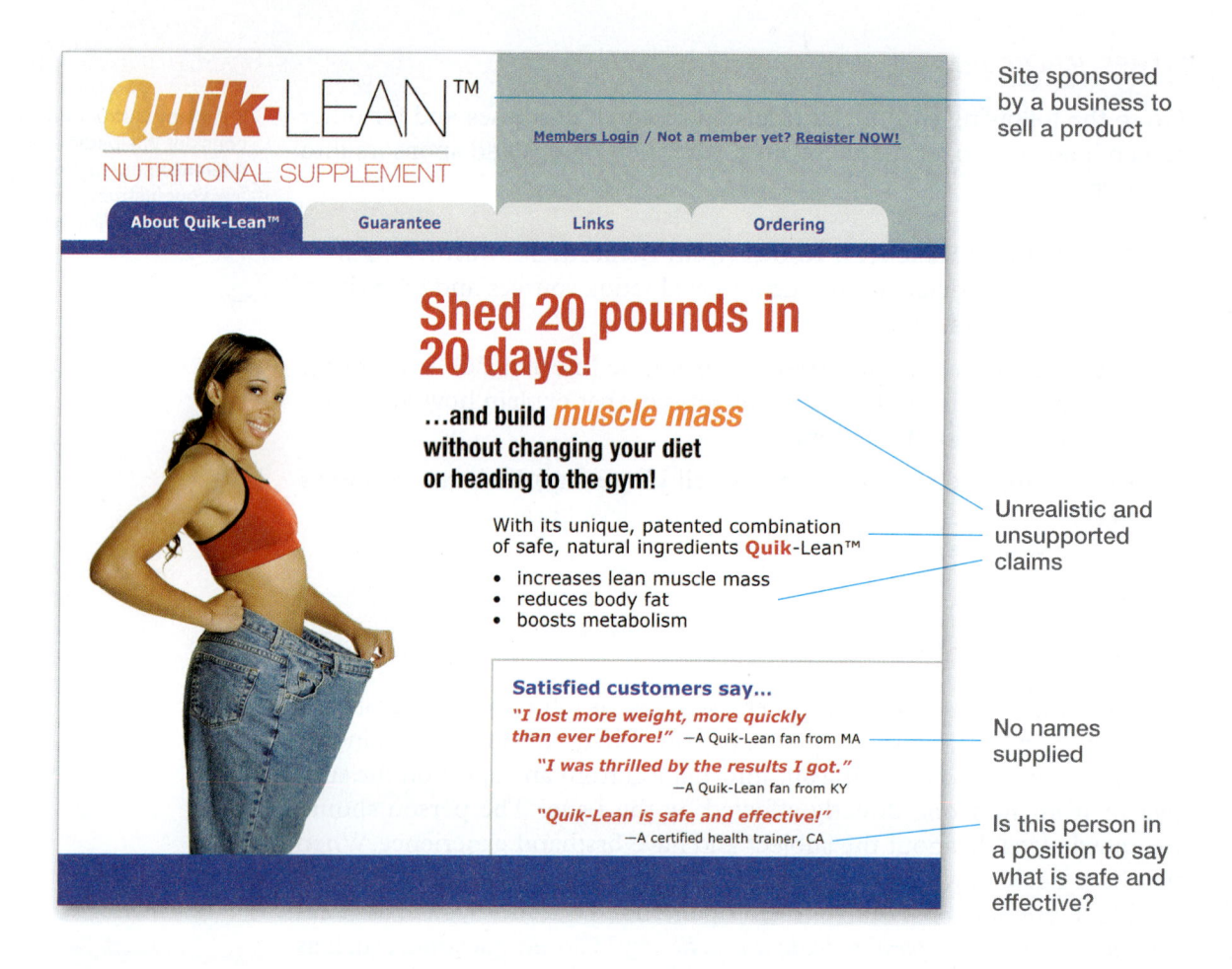

more reliable than an online product advertisement. A keyword search on "how to lose weight," for example, would point a researcher to thousands of sites; the two shown above and on the facing page are just samples. Which site do you think contains more reliable information?

Here are some questions you can ask to evaluate a source. If you answer "no" to any of these questions, do not use the source.

QUESTIONS FOR EVALUATING A PRINT OR ELECTRONIC SOURCE

- Is the source reliable? It should be a well-known magazine or publisher or from a reputable Web site. (For Web sites, also consider the Internet address extension; see the box on page 309 for guidance.)

- Is the author qualified to write reliably about the subject? If there is no biographical information, do an online search using the author's name, to learn more about the author's qualifications.

- Do you know who sponsored the publication or Web site? Be aware of the sponsor's motives (for example, to market a product).

- Does the author provide adequate support for key points, and does he or she cite the sources of this support?

SPECIAL COLLEGE WRITING PROJECTS
Evaluate Sources

Site sponsored by a nonprofit medical organization to educate the public

Access to expert viewpoints

Realistic information

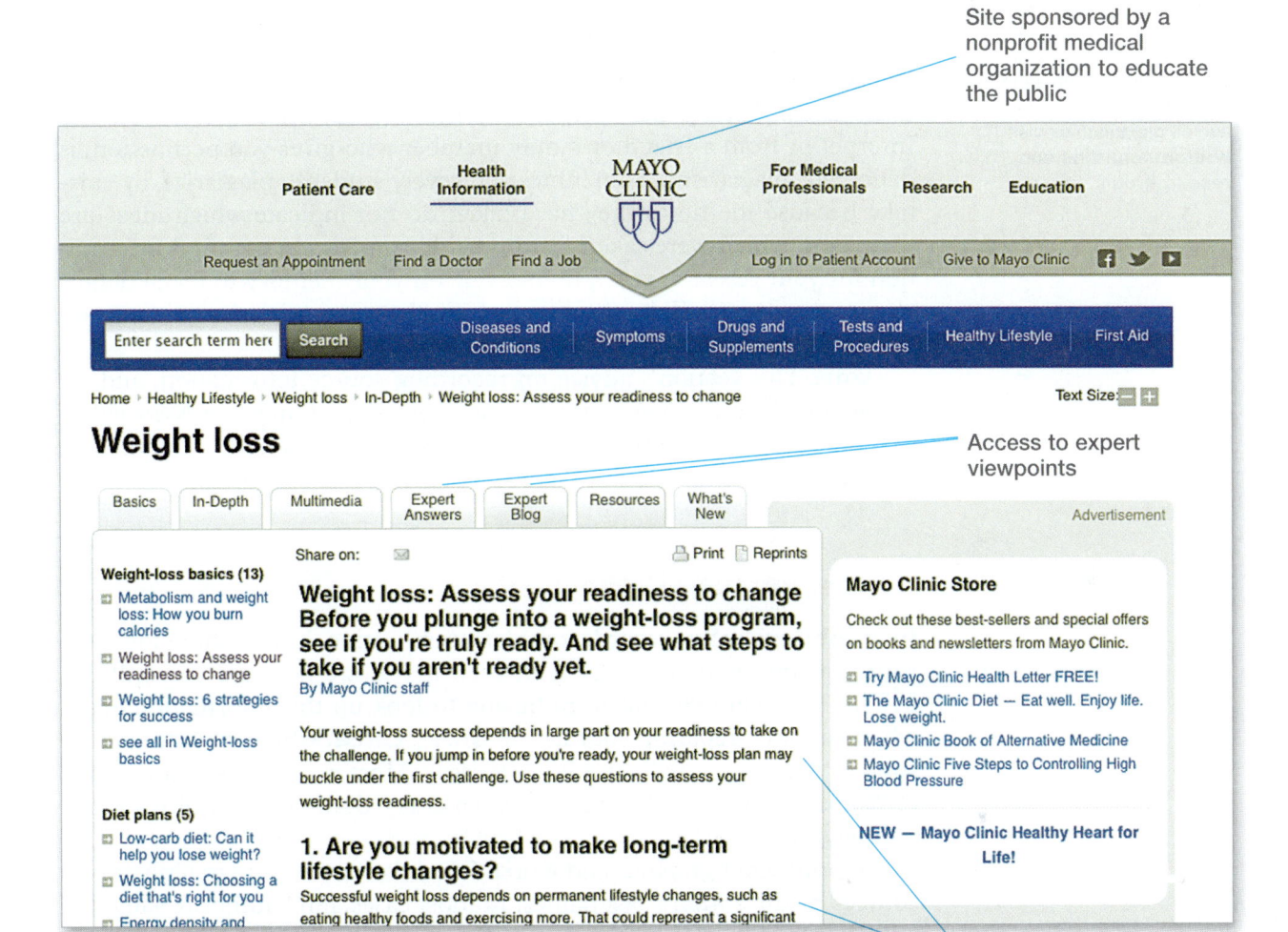

Guide to Internet Address Extensions

EXTENSION	SPONSOR OF SITE	HOW RELIABLE?
.com	A commercial or business organization	Varies. Consider whether you have heard of the organization, and be sure to read its home page or "About us" link carefully.
.edu	An educational institution	Reliable, but may include materials of varying quality.
.gov	A government agency	Reliable.
.net	A commercial organization	Varies. See the advice for ".com" extensions.
.org	A nonprofit organization	Generally reliable, although each volunteer or professional group promotes its own interests.

Avoid Plagiarism

TIP For more information on evaluating sources and avoiding plagiarism, visit **bedfordstmartins.com/ researchroom**.

Plagiarism is passing off someone else's ideas and information as your own. Turning in a paper written by someone else, whether it is from the Internet or from a friend or family member who gives you permission, is deliberate plagiarism. Sometimes, however, students plagiarize by mistake because the notes they have taken do not indicate which ideas are theirs and which were taken from outside sources. As you find information for your research essay, do not rely on your memory to recall details about your sources. Take good notes from the start, using the guidance on the following pages.

NOTE: This section's advice on recording source information, and on citing and documenting sources, reflects Modern Language Association (MLA) style, the preferred style for English classes and other humanities courses.

Keep a Running Bibliography

In a **bibliography**, record complete publication information for each source at the time you consult it, even if you are not sure you will use it. This step will save you from having to look up this information again when you are preparing your list of **Works Cited**, which includes all the sources that you actually use in your essay. Most instructors require a list of Works Cited at the end of a research essay. Some may require a bibliography as well.

In both bibliographies and Works Cited lists, make sure to alphabetize sources by the authors' last names. In most cases, if no author is named, a source should be alphabetized by its title. (For Dara Riesler's Works Cited list, see p. 323.)

TIP Go to **bedfordstmartins .com/researchroom**, and click on "The Bedford Bibliographer" for help with your bibliography.

Here is a list of information to record for each source while you are taking notes.

BOOKS	ARTICLES	WEB SITES
Author name(s)	Author name(s)	Author name(s) (if any)
Title and subtitle	Title of article	Title of page or site
Publisher and location of publisher	Page number(s) (for print sources)	Date of publication or latest update (if available)
Year of publication	Title of magazine, journal, or newspaper	Name of sponsoring organization
	Year, month, day of publication (2012 Jan. 4)	Date on which you accessed the source
	Main address for Web-based articles (for example, Nytimes.com)	Optional: Web address in angle brackets (</>)

When keeping a bibliography, think ahead to how you will use the good sources you find. You will probably integrate source material into your paper by summary, paraphrase, and direct quotation. In both summaries and paraphrases, you will put information from sources in your own words. Often, summaries condense whole works, and they include the source's main idea and support. Usually, they are significantly shorter than the original work. In contrast, paraphrases may condense only part of a larger work. Usually, they are slightly shorter than the source material. In all cases, give credit where credit is due. Let your readers know the source of words and ideas not your own.

As you take notes, record which method you are using so that you do not accidentally plagiarize. Tips for summarizing, paraphrasing, and using direct quotations follow.

Indirect Quotation: Summary

Be careful if you choose to summarize (or paraphrase). It is easy to think that you are using your own words when you are actually using only some of your own and some of the author's or speaker's words. When you summarize, follow these guidelines:

- Check your summary against the source to make sure you have not used the author's words or copied the author's sentence structure.

- Make sure to introduce the outside source when it is first mentioned—for example,

    > In an article from the military publication *Stars and Stripes* ("PTSD Treatment Goes to the Dogs: DOD Research Pairs Soldiers with K-9s"), Alan Bavley describes a study. . . .

- Include in parentheses the page number(s), if available, of the entire section you have summarized. (You will need to provide full publication information later, in the Works Cited list.)

SUMMARY OF AN ARTICLE

In an article from the military publication *Stars and Stripes* ("PTSD Treatment Goes to the Dogs: DOD Research Pairs Soldiers with K-9s"), Alan Bavley describes a study aimed at determining whether specially trained dogs can help soldiers who are suffering from post-traumatic stress disorder (PTSD) (5). The study, funded by $300,000 from the Department of Defense, will examine the benefits that the dogs may provide to soldiers returning from Iraq and Afghanistan. These benefits might include calming a soldier who is about to have a panic attack or helping a hallucinating owner distinguish between real and imagined events. Craig Love and Joan Esnayra will be conducting the study. In previous research, Love and Esnayra found that among 39 PTSD sufferers paired with service dogs, 82% reported fewer PTSD symptoms. In addition, 40% reported that they were able to reduce their use of medications. The DOD was not put off by some scientists' view that Love and Esnayra's investigations are too "touchy-feely" (Esnayra's words). If a new approach shows real potential, the department is willing to sponsor research into it.

Identifying information

Page reference

TIP For more on writing summaries, see Chapter 17.

Indirect Quotation: Paraphrase

To paraphrase responsibly, use the following guidelines:

- Check your paraphrase against the original source to make sure you have not used too many of the author's words or copied the author's sentence structure.

- Make sure to introduce the outside source—for example, "According to Alicia Miller, an Army veteran who. . . ."

- Include in parentheses the page number(s), if available, of the section you have paraphrased.

The following are examples of unacceptable and acceptable paraphrases.

ORIGINAL SOURCE

The first documented use of animal-assisted therapy in the United States occurred from 1944 through 1945. The Pawling Army Air Force Convalescent Hospital (located in Dutchess County, approximately 60 miles north of New York City) treated soldiers suffering from either battle injuries or psychological trauma. In this rural setting, the patients interacted with farm animals including horses, chickens and cows. But there was no scientific data collected to assess the impact these animals had on the recuperating veterans when the program ceased at the end of World War II.

—From page 4 of *Animal-Assisted Therapy* by Donald Altschiller

UNACCEPTABLE PARAPHRASE: TOO CLOSE TO ORIGINAL

The first recorded use of animal therapy in the United States was in 1944–1945. This occurred at the Pawling Army Air Force Convalescent Hospital in Dutchess County, north of New York City. The soldiers there were being treated either for combat injuries or mental trauma. At the hospital, the patients interacted with such animals as horses, chickens, and cows. However, because no scientific information was gathered, it was not possible to assess the effectiveness of the animal therapy on the veterans.

This paraphrase is unacceptable for several reasons:

- The paraphrase too closely follows the original source in wording and sentence structure.

- The writer has not included identifying information or page numbers for the source.

- The writer has not expressed the ideas in his or her own words.

Identifying phrase — **ACCEPTABLE PARAPHRASE**

Donald Altschiller reports that as far back as the final years of World War II (1944–1945), animal companionship was attempted as a treatment for both the mental and physical consequences of combat (4). This approach was used by the Pawling Army Air Force Convalescent Hospital in Dutchess County, New York. However, the effectiveness of the animal therapy was never determined because no one kept information on this treatment program.

— Page reference

The acceptable paraphrase presents the basic ideas, but in the writer's own words and structures. It also includes a parenthetical reference.

Direct Quotation

Use these guidelines when you write direct quotations:

- Record the exact words of the source.
- Include the name of the writer or speaker. If there is more than one author or speaker, record all names.
- Enclose the writer's or speaker's words in quotation marks.
- For print sources, include the page number on which the quotation appeared in the original source. The page number should go in parentheses after the end quotation mark but before the period. If the person quoted is not the author of the book or the article, include "qtd. in," the author's name, and the page number in parentheses. If there are two or three authors, give all names.
- If a direct quotation is more than five typed lines, indent the whole quotation, and do not use quotation marks.

DIRECT QUOTATION

According to Alicia Miller, an Army veteran who cofounded an organization that donates and trains service dogs for PTSD sufferers, "Medication works 50 percent of the time. Talk therapy, alone, works 30 percent of the time, and dogs work 84.5 percent of the time" (qtd. in Caprioli).

— Identifying phrase

— Quotation in quotation marks

Cite and Document Your Sources

You need to not only document your sources at the end of your research essay in a Works Cited list, but also to include in-text citations of sources as you use them in the essay. No one can remember the specifics of correct citation and documentation, so be sure to refer to this section or a reference that your instructor directs you to. Include all the correct information, and pay attention to where punctuation marks such as commas, periods, and quotation marks should go.

There are several different systems of documentation. Most English instructors prefer the Modern Language Association (MLA) system, which is used in this chapter. When you are writing a research paper in another course, you may be required to use another system.

TIP For more information on documenting sources, visit **bedfordstmartins.com/researchroom**.

Use In-Text Citations within Your Essay

In-text citations such as the ones shown below are used for books and periodicals. For Web sites and other electronic sources, you typically will not be able to include page numbers, although you can note any paragraph, section, chapter, or part numbers used in place of page numbers.

When you refer to the author (or authors) in an introductory phrase, write just the relevant page number(s), if available, in parentheses at the end of the quotation.

> **DIRECT QUOTATION:** In an article by Alan Bavley, veteran and PTSD sufferer Chris Kornkven was quoted as saying the following about service dogs he had observed: "They seemed like they would be really helpful, particularly for individuals living alone" (5).
>
> **INDIRECT QUOTATION:** In an article by Alan Bavley, veteran and PTSD sufferer Chris Kornkven expressed the belief that service dogs would be especially beneficial to vets who live by themselves (5).

When you do not refer to the author(s) in an introductory phrase, write the author's name followed by the page number(s), if available, at the end of the quotation. If an author is not named, use the title of the source.

> **DIRECT QUOTATION:** "Today's all-volunteer military is far smaller than past draftee-fed forces, requiring troops to be repeatedly recycled through combat zones" (*Issues in Peace and Conflict Studies* 395).
>
> **INDIRECT QUOTATION:** Because the current wars are not supported by a draft, military forces are smaller than in past wars, and troops are being deployed multiple times (*Issues in Peace and Conflict Studies* 395).

The following section shows you how to include an in-text citation for various kinds of sources, inserting the citation after the material you have used. For a direct quotation, insert the citation after the end quote and before the period ending the sentence.

DIRECTORY OF MLA IN-TEXT CITATIONS

One author 315	Author not named 315
Two or three authors 315	Encyclopedia or other reference work 315
Four or more authors 315	
Group, corporation, or government agency 315	Work in an anthology 316
	Interview, e-mail, speech 316

NOTE: The formats given below are for print sources. To cite a Web source, use page numbers if available; if not, use a paragraph number instead. If there are no paragraphs, cite the author, title of the part of the Web site, or the site sponsor.

The series of dots (called ellipses) in the following examples indicate that words have been left out. Two examples are provided for each citation: (1) The author is named in an introductory phrase, with the page or paragraph number in parentheses. (2) The author's name and page or paragraph number appear in parentheses.

One author

As David Shipler states, ". . ." (16).

The number of people who work and fall below the poverty line has increased dramatically (Shipler 16).

Two or three authors   Use all authors' last names.

Quigley and Morrison found that . . . (243).

Banks and credit card companies are charging many more fees . . . (Quigley and Morrison 243).

Four or more authors   Use the first author's last name and the words *et al.* (*et al.* means "and others").

According to Sen et al., . . . (659).

The overuse of antibiotics can result in . . . (Sen et al. 659).

Group, corporation, or government agency   Use the name of the group, corporation, or government agency. The source can be abbreviated in the parentheses, as shown in the second example.

The Texas Parks and Wildlife Department offers guidelines for landscaping . . . (26).

Texas has more native plants than any other . . . (Texas Parks and Wildlife Dept. 26).

Author not named   Use article title in quotations, shortened if it is a long title.

In the article "Texas Wildscapes," . . . (7).

Many areas of Texas are filled with drought-tolerant native . . . ("Texas Wildscapes" 7).

Encyclopedia or other reference work   Use the name of the entry you are using as a source.

In its entry on xeriscaping, the *Landscape Encyclopedia* claims that . . . ("Xeriscaping").

Xeriscaping is often used in . . . ("Xeriscaping").

Work in an anthology Use the name of the author(s) of the piece you are using as a source.

> As Rich Chiappone believes, . . . (200).
>
> Fly-fishing is as much a spiritual . . . (Chiappone 200).

Interview, e-mail, speech Use the name of the person interviewed or speaker, or the author of an e-mail.

> As University of Texas Vice President of Student Affairs Juan Gonzalez said in an interview. . . .
>
> Students have many resources available to . . . (Gonzalez).

Use a Works Cited List at the End of Your Essay

Following are model Works Cited entries for major types of sources. At the end of your paper, you will need to include such entries for each source you cite in the body of the paper.

TIP If you have additional questions about MLA style, visit *Research and Documentation Online* by entering the title of this site and "Bedford/St. Martin's" into a search engine. Then, click on the "Humanities" link.

DIRECTORY OF MLA WORKS CITED

Books
One author 316
Two or three authors 317
Four or more authors 317
Editor 317
Work in an anthology 317
Encyclopedia article 317

Periodicals
Magazine article 317
Newspaper article 317
Editorial in a magazine or newspaper 317

Electronic Sources
An entire Web site 318
Part of a larger Web site 318

Article from a database 318
Article in an online magazine or newspaper 318
Government publication 318
Weblog (blog) 318
Digital file 319
E-mail 319

Multimedia
Film 319
Film on DVD 319
Television and radio 319
Podcast online 319
Recording 319
Personal interview 319

Books

Book with one author

Author, last name first — Full title

Anker, Susan. *Real Writing: Paragraphs and Essays for College, Work, and Everyday Life.* 6th ed. Boston: Bedford/St. Martin's, 2013. Print.

— Edition number — Place of publication — Publisher — Publication date

All lines after first line of entry are indented.

Book with two or three authors

Baumeister, Roy F., and John Tierney. *Willpower: Rediscovering the Greatest Human Strength*. New York: Penguin, 2011. Print.

Hudson, Valerie M., Bonnie Ballif-Spanvill, Mary Caprioli, and Chad F. Emmett. *Sex and World Peace*. New York: Columbia UP, 2012. Print.

Book with four or more authors *Et al.* means "and others."

McKay, John P., et al. *A History of World Societies*. 9th ed. Boston: Bedford/St. Martin's, 2012. Print.

TIP For help creating source citations, try using the "Autocite" tool at **www.easybib.com**.

Book with an editor

Price, Steven D., ed. *The Best Advice Ever Given: Life Lessons for Success in the Real World*. Guilford: Lyons Press, 2006. Print.

Work in an anthology

Vowell, Sarah. "Shooting Dad." *50 Essays: A Portable Anthology*. 3rd ed. Ed. Samuel Cohen. Boston: Bedford/St. Martin's, 2011. 412–19. Print.

Encyclopedia article

"Metaphor." *The Columbia Encyclopedia*. 6th ed. 2000. Print.

Periodicals

Magazine article

Author | Title | Name of periodical | Publication date | Inclusive page numbers

Kapur, Akash. "The Shandy." *New Yorker* 10 Oct. 2011: 72–79. Print.

Newspaper article

Oliveira, Rebeca. "The Art of Storytelling Is Alive and Well." *Jamaica Plain Gazette* 7 Oct. 2011: 10–11. Print.

Editorial in a magazine or newspaper

Escobar, Veronica. "All Quiet on the Southern Front." Opinion. *New York Times* 6 Oct. 2011: A27. Print.

Electronic Sources

Electronic sources include Web sites; databases or subscription services such as *ERIC*, *InfoTrac*, *LexisNexis*, and *ProQuest*; and electronic communications such as e-mail. Because electronic sources change often, always note the date you accessed or read the source as well as the date on which the source was posted or updated online, if this information is available. If no date is available, write "n.d."

An entire Web site

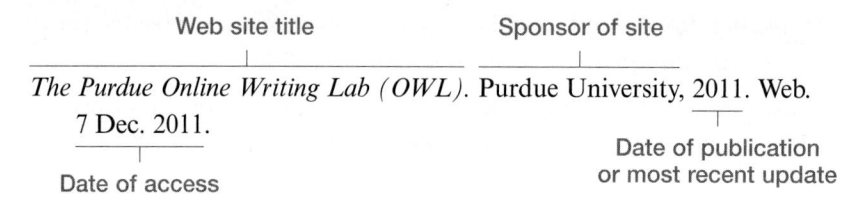

The Purdue Online Writing Lab (OWL). Purdue University, 2011. Web. 7 Dec. 2011.

- Web site title: *The Purdue Online Writing Lab (OWL)*
- Sponsor of site: Purdue University
- Date of publication or most recent update: 2011
- Date of access: 7 Dec. 2011

Part of a larger Web site

"How to Evaluate Sources: Introduction." *The Bedford Research Room*. Bedford/St. Martin's, n.d. Web. 7 Jan. 2012.

Article from a database

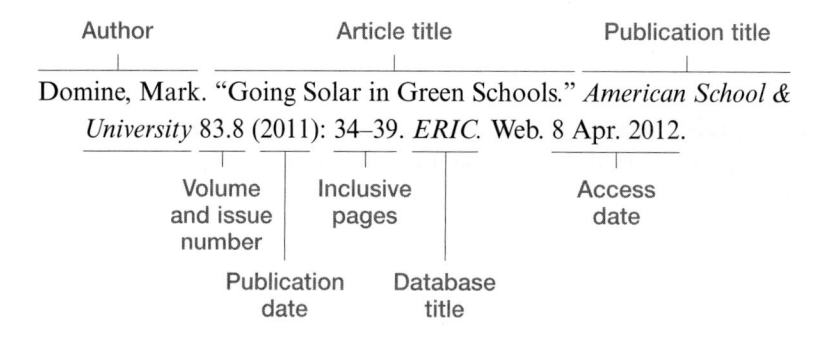

Domine, Mark. "Going Solar in Green Schools." *American School & University* 83.8 (2011): 34–39. *ERIC*. Web. 8 Apr. 2012.

- Author: Domine, Mark
- Article title: "Going Solar in Green Schools."
- Publication title: *American School & University*
- Volume and issue number: 83.8
- Publication date: (2011)
- Inclusive pages: 34–39
- Database title: *ERIC*
- Access date: 8 Apr. 2012

Article in an online magazine or newspaper

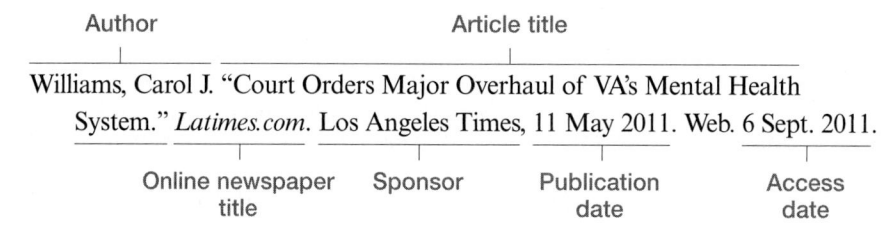

Williams, Carol J. "Court Orders Major Overhaul of VA's Mental Health System." *Latimes.com*. Los Angeles Times, 11 May 2011. Web. 6 Sept. 2011.

- Author: Williams, Carol J.
- Article title: "Court Orders Major Overhaul of VA's Mental Health System."
- Online newspaper title: *Latimes.com*
- Sponsor: Los Angeles Times
- Publication date: 11 May 2011
- Access date: 6 Sept. 2011

Government publication

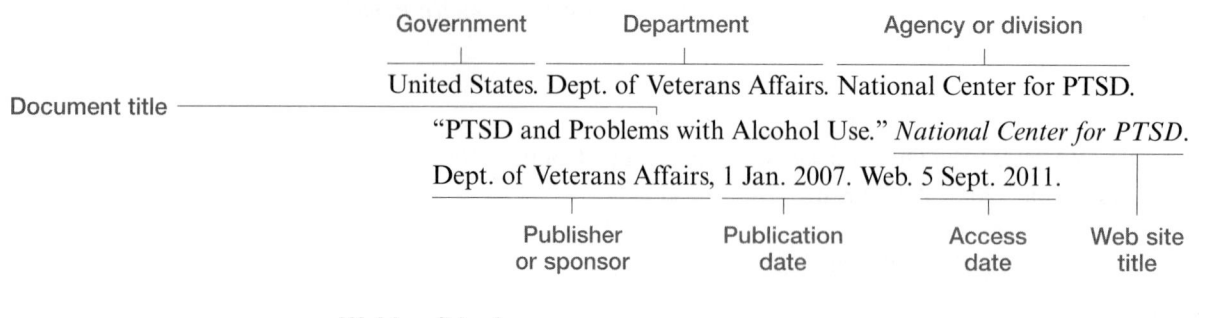

United States. Dept. of Veterans Affairs. National Center for PTSD. "PTSD and Problems with Alcohol Use." *National Center for PTSD*. Dept. of Veterans Affairs, 1 Jan. 2007. Web. 5 Sept. 2011.

- Government: United States
- Department: Dept. of Veterans Affairs
- Agency or division: National Center for PTSD
- Document title: "PTSD and Problems with Alcohol Use."
- Web site title: *National Center for PTSD*
- Publisher or sponsor: Dept. of Veterans Affairs
- Publication date: 1 Jan. 2007
- Access date: 5 Sept. 2011

Weblog (blog)

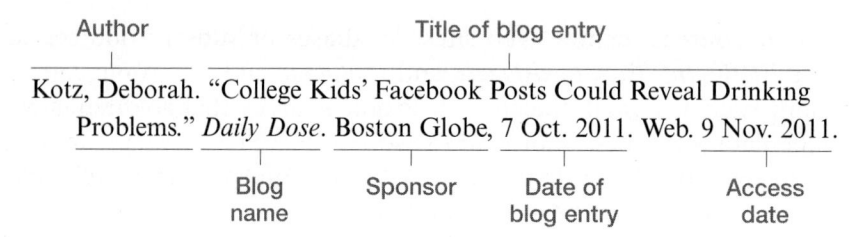

Kotz, Deborah. "College Kids' Facebook Posts Could Reveal Drinking Problems." *Daily Dose*. Boston Globe, 7 Oct. 2011. Web. 9 Nov. 2011.

- Author: Kotz, Deborah
- Title of blog entry: "College Kids' Facebook Posts Could Reveal Drinking Problems."
- Blog name: *Daily Dose*
- Sponsor: Boston Globe
- Date of blog entry: 7 Oct. 2011
- Access date: 9 Nov. 2011

Digital file

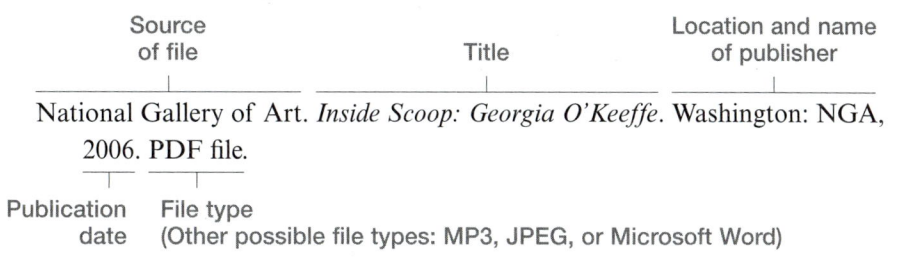

Source of file — Title — Location and name of publisher

National Gallery of Art. *Inside Scoop: Georgia O'Keeffe*. Washington: NGA, 2006. PDF file.

Publication date — File type (Other possible file types: MP3, JPEG, or Microsoft Word)

E-mail

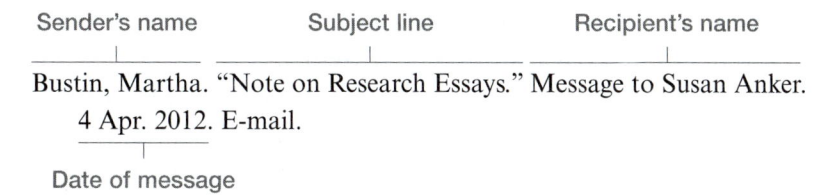

Sender's name — Subject line — Recipient's name

Bustin, Martha. "Note on Research Essays." Message to Susan Anker. 4 Apr. 2012. E-mail.

Date of message

Multimedia

Film

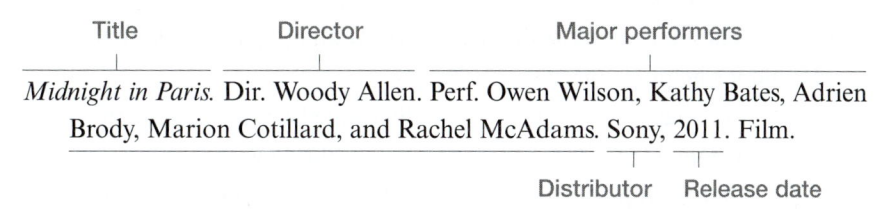

Title — Director — Major performers

Midnight in Paris. Dir. Woody Allen. Perf. Owen Wilson, Kathy Bates, Adrien Brody, Marion Cotillard, and Rachel McAdams. Sony, 2011. Film.

Distributor — Release date

Film on DVD

Campion, Jane, dir. *Bright Star*. Perf. Abbie Cornish, Ben Whishaw, and Paul Schneider. Apparition, 2009. DVD.

Television and radio

"Dogs Decoded." *Nova*. PBS. 12 Oct. 2011. Television.

Podcast online

"Hidden Costs of Energy." Narr. Ann Merchant. *Sounds of Science*. National Academies, 29 Jan. 2010. Web. 13 Dec. 2011.

Recording

Jay-Z and Kanye West. "Made in America." *Watch the Throne*. Roc-A-Fella, 2011. CD.

Personal interview

Hain, Carla. Personal interview. 5 Sept. 2011.

Student Research Essay

Here is Dara Riesler's research essay, with annotations pointing out standard characteristics of content, documentation, and formatting.

Dara Riesler
Professor Gomes
English 99
4 October 2011

Service Dogs Help Heal the Mental Wounds of War

Whenever Ken Costich, a former army colonel, is on the edge of a panic attack, his dog, Bandit, senses it immediately, nuzzling Costich until he feels calm again (Caprioli). Across the country, another dog, Maya, is also looking out for her owner, veteran Jacob Hyde. When Hyde, feeling nervous in a crowd, gives the command "block," Maya stands between him and other people, easing Hyde's fears (Lorber). Elsewhere, Mush, a Siberian husky, is helping her owner, Margaux Vair, get out and meet people—something Vair had avoided since returning from her service in Iraq (Albrecht). "Because [Mush] is a Husky and very pretty, everybody wants to pet her," Vair says. "What's happening is that people are coming up and talking to me, and it's helping with my confidence."

Bandit, Maya, and Mush—specially trained service dogs—are making a significant difference in the lives of their owners, all of whom suffer from post-traumatic stress disorder (PTSD) as a result of military service. As the benefits of service dogs become clearer, and as more PTSD sufferers return from the wars in Iraq and Afghanistan, demand for these helpful and caring pets is growing; in fact, at the present time, demand far exceeds supply.

PTSD, as defined by the United States Department of Veterans Affairs (VA), is an anxiety disorder that can result from a traumatic experience, such as personal injury in combat or witnessing the deaths or injuries of others. According to the VA, symptoms of the condition include flashbacks of the trauma or nightmares about it. PTSD sufferers may also have difficulty forming or maintaining relationships with others. Additionally, some of them are constantly "keyed up" and "on the lookout for danger," as if they are still in a war zone ("What Are the Symptoms of PTSD?"). According to the RAND Corporation, a nonprofit research group, an estimated 300,000 of veterans from the wars in Afghanistan and Iraq suffer from PTSD or major depression. In attempts to escape or to numb the effects of PTSD, sufferers may turn to alcohol or drugs, possibly leading to addiction ("PTSD and Problems with Alcohol Use").

Riesler 2

Worse, they may decide to end their lives, as an estimated 6,500 veterans do each year (Williams).

A variety of treatments are available to veterans with PTSD. They include one-on-one discussions with a therapist, group therapy, and medicines—usually antidepressants—that address the symptoms of the condition ("Treatment of PTSD"). The use of service dogs as an additional therapy for PTSD is a relatively new practice. According to researchers Joan Esnayra and Craig Love, a key benefit of these dogs is that they are constant companions to PTSD sufferers, helping them go about their daily lives and directly addressing their symptoms. For example, service dogs may be trained to alert easily startled veterans that someone is approaching, to scan surroundings for possible threats, or to turn on the lights and wake up veterans suffering from nightmares (Esnayra and Love). These pets can also soothe veterans experiencing panic attacks and remind their owners when it is time to take medications (Caprioli).

Some veterans, however, find that their dog companions outshine medication as a PTSD treatment. "This dog [did] more for me in three weeks than any medication," says Ken Costich (qtd. in Caprioli; see fig. 1). Alicia Miller, an Army veteran who cofounded an organization that donates and trains service dogs for vets, agrees. "Medication works 50 percent of the time," says Miller, who also experiences symptoms of PTSD. "Talk therapy, alone, works 30 percent of the time, and dogs work 84.5 percent of the time" (qtd. in Caprioli).

In a recent study, Esnayra and Love found that among 39 PTSD sufferers paired with service dogs, 82% reported fewer PTSD symptoms (Bavley 5). In addition, 40% reported that they were able to reduce their use of medications. Recognizing that more research into the effectiveness of service-dog therapy is needed, the United States Department of Defense is funding a $300,000 study on this topic (Bavley 5). Esnayra and Love are conducting the research.

Fig. 1. Ken Costich and his service dog, Bandit (Caprioli).

Riesler 3

Topic sentence — Although service-dog therapy has many benefits, organizations that train these dogs have trouble keeping up with the demand created by the thousands of veterans who have returned from Iraq or Afghanistan with PTSD (Dreazen). Training is time-consuming and demanding; the dogs are taught to respond to as many as 150 commands and to notice subtle changes in vets—such as a quickening pulse—that signal emotional distress (Montalván and Witter 4). During a two-year period that ended in the spring of 2010, Puppies Behind Bars, a program in which prisoners train service dogs, placed 23 dogs with veterans suffering from PTSD (Lorber). Other nonprofit training organizations report similar, or lower, numbers of vet-ready dogs (Caprioli). Given the labor-intensive training, these numbers are understandable; however, the need remains.

Topic sentence — Another challenge is the expense of the training, which in the case of many nonprofit organizations, like Puppies Behind Bars, is paid for by donations, not by the veterans (Caprioli; Dreazen). At Puppies Behind Bars, $26,000 is needed to train each dog. Other training organizations report similar expenses.

Topic sentence — Some lawmakers are taking steps to meet vets' growing need for helper dogs. In 2009, President Obama signed into law the Service Dogs for Veterans Act, which was sponsored by Senator Al Franken and Senator Johnny Isakson. According to Franken's office, this legislation matches at least 200 veterans with VA–funded service dogs, and it requires that at least 50% of these vets suffer mainly from mental-health problems, as opposed to physical disabilities. It also calls for a study of the participating veterans to learn more about the therapeutic and economic benefits of service dogs. Additionally, in January 2011, the Veterans Dog Training Therapy Act was introduced in the U.S. House of Representatives. Under this legislation, vets with PTSD would be taught how to train service dogs which, in turn, would be used by other vets (Peters).

Conclusion — With luck, and with the continuing efforts of legislators and concerned citizens, more helper dogs will find homes with veterans, providing not only valued service but also lasting friendship. As Army veteran Luis Carlos Montalván says of his service dog, Tuesday: "We are bonded, dog and man, in a way able-bodied people can never understand, because they will never experience anything like it. As long as Tuesday is alive, he will be with me. Neither of us will ever be alone. We will never be without companionship" (Montalván and Witter 6).

Riesler 4

Works Cited

Albrecht, Brian. "Psychiatric Service Dogs Aid Northeast Ohio Veterans." *Cleveland.com*. Cleveland.com, 13 July 2011. Web. 8 Sept. 2011.

Bavley, Alan. "PTSD Treatment Goes to the Dogs: DOD Research Pairs Soldiers with K-9s." *Stars and Stripes* 10 Sept. 2009, Mideast ed.: 5. Print.

Caprioli, Jennifer M. "Dogs Go the Distance: Program Provides Service to Veterans with PTSD." *www.army.mil: The Official Homepage of the United States Army*. United States Army, 4 Mar. 2010. Web. 8 Sept. 2011.

Dreazen, Yochi J. "'Sit! Stay! Snuggle!': An Iraq Vet Finds His Dog Tuesday." *Wsj.com*. Wall Street Journal, 11 July 2009. Web. 9 Sept. 2011.

Esnayra, Joan, and Craig Love. "A Survey of Mental Health Patients Utilizing Psychiatric Service Dogs." *PSD Lifestyle*. Psychiatric Service Dog Society, 2008. Web. 8 Sept. 2011.

"Franken-Isakson Service Dogs for Veterans Act Passes Senate." *Al Franken: U.S. Senator for Minnesota*. Al Franken: U.S. Senator for Minnesota, 24 July 2009. Web. 7 Sept. 2011.

"Invisible Wounds: Mental Health and Cognitive Care Needs of America's Returning Veterans." *RAND Corporation*. RAND Corporation, 2008. Web. 7 Sept. 2011.

Lorber, Janie. "For the Battle-Scarred, Comfort at Leash's End." *Nytimes.com*. New York Times, 3 Apr. 2010. Web. 8 Sept. 2011.

Montalván, Luis Carlos, and Bret Witter. *Until Tuesday: A Wounded Warrior and the Golden Retriever Who Saved Him*. New York: Hyperion, 2011. Print.

Peters, Sharon L. "Man's Best Friend Could Soon Be Veteran's Best Medicine." *Usatoday.com*. USA Today, 19 Jan. 2011. Web. 7 Sept. 2011.

United States. Dept. of Veterans Affairs. National Center for PTSD. "PTSD and Problems with Alcohol Use." *National Center for PTSD*. Dept. of Veterans Affairs, 1 Jan. 2007. Web. 5 Sept. 2011.

---. ---. National Center for PTSD. "Treatment of PTSD." *National Center for PTSD*. Dept. of Veterans Affairs, 1 Jan. 2007. Web. 5 Sept. 2011.

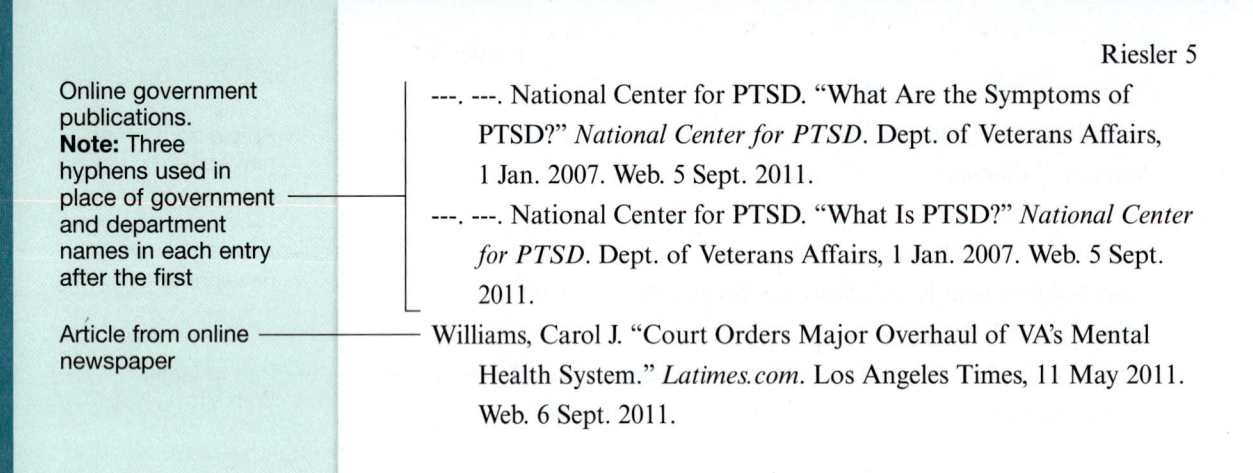

---. ---. National Center for PTSD. "What Are the Symptoms of
   PTSD?" *National Center for PTSD*. Dept. of Veterans Affairs,
   1 Jan. 2007. Web. 5 Sept. 2011.

---. ---. National Center for PTSD. "What Is PTSD?" *National Center
   for PTSD*. Dept. of Veterans Affairs, 1 Jan. 2007. Web. 5 Sept.
   2011.

Williams, Carol J. "Court Orders Major Overhaul of VA's Mental
   Health System." *Latimes.com*. Los Angeles Times, 11 May 2011.
   Web. 6 Sept. 2011.

Online government publications.
Note: Three hyphens used in place of government and department names in each entry after the first

Article from online newspaper

To write a research essay, use the checklist below.

CHECKLIST: HOW TO WRITE A RESEARCH ESSAY	
STEPS	**DETAILS**
☐ **Make a schedule.** (See the model on p. 303.)	• Include the due date and dates for doing the research, finishing a draft, and revising.
☐ **Choose a topic.** (See pp. 303–04.)	• Ask yourself the five questions on page 303. • Choose a topic that interests you.
☐ **Ask a guiding research question.** (See p. 304.)	• Ask a question about your topic that you will begin to answer as you do your initial research.
☐ **Find sources.** (See pp. 304–07.)	• Go to the library and find out what resources are available to you, both in print and online.
☐ **Evaluate your sources.** (See pp. 307–09.)	• Particularly for Web sites, look for the sponsor, and judge whether the site is reliable and accurate.
☐ **Avoid plagiarism.** (See pp. 310–13.)	• As you make notes from your sources, write down the publication information you will need. • Think ahead to how you will integrate your sources into your paper, giving source information as you summarize, paraphrase, and use direct quotation.
☐ **Write a thesis statement.** (For more on writing a thesis statement, see Chapter 4.)	• Try turning your guiding research question (see p. 304) into a statement.
☐ **Support your thesis statement.** (For more on supporting your point, see Chapter 5.)	• Review all your notes, and choose the points that best support your thesis statement. • If you do not have enough support to make your point, do a little more reading.
☐ **Write a draft essay.** (For more on writing a draft, see Chapter 6.)	• Make an outline that includes your thesis statement and major support, arranged logically. • Write an introduction that includes your thesis statement. • Write topic sentences for each major support, and include supporting evidence. • Cite sources in the body of your essay, and provide full publication information at the end, in the list of Works Cited. • Write a conclusion that reminds readers of your thesis statement and makes a final observation.

CHECKLIST: HOW TO WRITE A RESEARCH ESSAY

STEPS	DETAILS
☐ **Revise your draft.** (For more on revising, see Chapter 7.) Consider getting comments from a peer first. For more information, see pages 97–98.	Ask yourself: • Do I have enough support that my readers are likely to understand my position on my topic? • Have I included transitions that will help readers move smoothly from one point to the next? • Have I integrated source material smoothly into the essay? • Are all sources cited and documented correctly?
☐ **Edit your essay.** (See Parts 4 through 7.)	• Reread your essay, looking for errors in grammar, spelling, and punctuation.

"I write directions, instructions, captions for photographs, and descriptions of my art."
—Ali K., student

Part 4

The Four Most Serious Errors

19	The Basic Sentence 329
20	Fragments 341
21	Run-Ons 359
22	Problems with Subject-Verb Agreement 377
23	Verb Tense 397

19

The Basic Sentence

An Overview

> **EVER THOUGHT THIS?**
>
> "Grammar. I never get it. There's too much to remember."
> —Tony Mancuso, Student
>
> *This chapter*
> - tells you which four errors are the most important to find and fix.
> - gives you practice working with the basic elements of a sentence.
> - keeps grammar terms to a minimum.
> - simplifies grammar so that you can get it.
>
> **write** for 2 minutes on what you know about a sentence.

The Four Most Serious Errors

This part of the book focuses first on four grammar errors that people most often notice.

THE FOUR MOST SERIOUS ERRORS

1. Fragments (Chapter 20)
2. Run-ons (Chapter 21)
3. Problems with subject-verb agreement (Chapter 22)
4. Problems with verb form and tense (Chapter 23)

If you can edit your writing to correct these four errors, your grades will improve.

This chapter reviews the basic sentence elements that you will need to understand to find and fix the four most serious errors.

✓ **LearningCurve**
Parts of Speech:
Nouns and Pronouns;
Verbs, Adjectives, and
Adverbs; Prepositions
and Conjunctions
**bedfordstmartins
.com/realwriting/LC**

The Parts of Speech

There are seven basic parts of speech:

1. **Noun:** names a person, place, thing, or idea (for information on making nouns plural, see p. 561). A **noun phrase** is a group of words that includes a noun, or a word that functions as a noun, and any surrounding article and modifiers.

    <u>Jaime</u> <u>dances</u>.

THE FOUR MOST SERIOUS ERRORS

330 Chapter 19 • The Basic Sentence

TIP In the examples in this chapter, subjects are underlined once, and verbs are underlined twice.

TIP For a definition of *subject*, see page 331.

2. **Pronoun:** replaces a noun in a sentence. *He, she, it, we,* and *they* are pronouns.

   <u>She</u> <u>dances</u>.

3. **Verb:** tells what action the subject does or links a subject to another word that describes it.

   <u>Jaime</u> **<u>dances</u>**. [The verb *dances* is what the subject, Jaime, does.]

   <u>She</u> **<u>is</u>** a dancer. [The verb *is* links the subject, Jaime, to a word that describes her, *dancer*.]

4. **Adjective:** describes a noun or a pronoun (can also be a participle, a verb that functions as a noun).

   <u>Jaime</u> <u>is</u> **thin**. [The adjective *thin* describes the noun *Jaime*.]

   <u>She</u> <u>is</u> **graceful**. [The adjective *graceful* describes the pronoun *She*.]

TIP Some grammar experts consider **interjections** to be a part of speech. Interjections are words or phrases that are often used to convey emotion—for example, "Ouch!", "Oh no!", and "Good grief!"

5. **Adverb:** describes an adjective, a verb, or another adverb. Adverbs often end in *-ly*.

   <u>Jaime</u> <u>is</u> **extremely** graceful. [The adverb *extremely* describes the adjective *graceful*.]

   <u>She</u> <u>practices</u> **often**. [The adverb *often* describes the verb *practices*.]

   <u>Jaime</u> <u>dances</u> **quite** beautifully. [The adverb *quite* describes another adverb, *beautifully*.]

6. **Preposition:** connects a noun, pronoun, or verb with information about it. *Across, around, at, in, of, on,* and *out* are prepositions (there are many others).

   <u>Jaime</u> <u>practices</u> **at** the studio. [The preposition *at* connects the verb *practices* with the noun *studio*.]

TIP For more on coordinating conjunctions, see pages 465–66. For more on subordinating conjunctions (dependent words), see pages 344–46.

7. **Conjunction:** connects words to each other. An easy way to remember the seven common conjunctions is to connect them in your mind to **FANBOYS**: *for, and, nor, but, or, yet, so.*

   The <u>studio</u> <u>is</u> expensive **but** good.

TIP For more practice with the parts of speech, visit *Exercise Central* at bedfordstmartins.com/realwriting.

PRACTICE 1 Using the Parts of Speech

Fill in the blanks with the part of speech indicated.

EXAMPLE: More and more wild animals are coming into towns and cities, making life ___challenging___ (adjective) for them and humans.

1. Two _____ (adjective) hawks built a _____ (noun) on the roof _____ (preposition) a city apartment building.

2. The female laid _____ (noun) there, and _____ (pronoun) hatched a few days later, releasing four _____ (adverb) noisy chicks.

3. Some of the building's residents _____ (verb) about the hawks, _____ (conjunction) others loved to stand _____ (preposition) the street from the birds and watch _____ (pronoun).

4. Because of the complaints, the _____ (noun) was removed, _____ (conjunction) the people who liked the hawks got _____ (adverb) upset.

5. The supporters _____ (preposition) the birds eventually won, and the hawks were allowed to _____ (verb) to rebuild their _____ (noun).

The Basic Sentence

A **sentence** is the basic unit of written communication. A complete sentence in written standard English must have these three elements:

- A **subject**
- A **verb**
- A **complete thought**

Subjects

The **subject** of a sentence is the person, place, thing, or idea that a sentence is about. The subject of a sentence can be a noun or a pronoun. For a list of common pronouns, see page 426.

To find the subject, ask yourself, **Whom or what is the sentence about?**

PERSON AS SUBJECT   Isaac arrived last night.
[**Whom** is the sentence about? *Isaac*]

THING AS SUBJECT   The restaurant has closed.
[**What** is the sentence about? The *restaurant*]

A **compound subject** consists of two or more subjects joined by *and*, *or*, or *nor*.

TWO SUBJECTS Kelli and Kate love animals of all kinds.

SEVERAL SUBJECTS The baby, the cats, and the dog play well together.

The subject of a sentence is *never* in a **prepositional phrase**, a word group that begins with a preposition and ends with a noun or pronoun, called the **object of a preposition**.

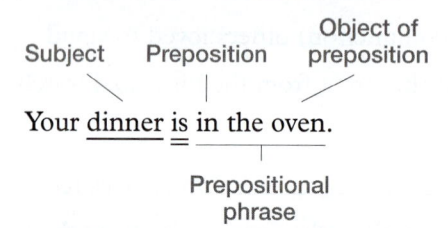

```
                        Object of
Subject   Preposition   preposition
   \          |             |
  Your dinner is in the oven.
       ===    =      |
                Prepositional
                   phrase
```

PREPOSITION	OBJECT	PREPOSITIONAL PHRASE
from	the bakery	from the bakery
to	the next corner	to the next corner
under	the table	under the table

LANGUAGE NOTE: *In* and *on* can be tricky prepositions for people whose native language is not English. Keep these definitions and examples in mind:

in = inside of (in the box, in the office) or at a certain time (in January, in the fall, in three weeks)

on = on top of (on the table, on my foot), located in a certain place (on the page, on Main Street), or at a certain time (on January 31)

If you have trouble deciding what prepositions to use, see Chapter 30.

Common Prepositions

about	before	for	on	until
above	behind	from	out	up
across	below	in	outside	upon
after	beneath	inside	over	with
against	beside	into	past	within
along	between	like	since	without
among	by	near	through	
around	down	next to	to	
at	during	of	toward	
because of	except	off	under	

TIP For common prepositional phrases, see Chapter 30.

See if you can identify the subject of the following sentence.

One of my best friends races cars.

Although you might think that the word *friends* is the subject, it isn't. *One* is the subject. The word *friends* cannot be the subject because it is in the prepositional phrase *of my best friends*. When you are looking for the subject of a sentence, cross out the prepositional phrase.

PREPOSITIONAL PHRASE CROSSED OUT

One ~~of the students~~ won the science prize.

The rules ~~about the dress code~~ are very specific.

> **LANGUAGE NOTE:** The example sentences use the word *the* before the noun (*the rules, the dress code*). *The, a,* and *an* are called *articles*. If you have trouble deciding which article to use with which nouns, see Chapter 30.

PRACTICE 2 Identifying Subjects and Prepositional Phrases

In each of the following sentences, cross out any prepositional phrases, and underline the subject of the sentence.

EXAMPLE: Coupons ~~from newspapers and Web sites~~ are just one way to save money.

1. A friend ~~from my neighborhood~~ packs her lunch every day.
2. Sandwiches ~~in her~~ workplace cafeteria cost five dollars.
3. Restaurants ~~near her job~~ charge even more.
4. Therefore, sandwiches from ~~her own kitchen~~ are saving my friend twenty-five dollars or more each week.
5. Savings in gasoline expenses ~~are also possible~~.
6. ~~Everything in~~ the trunk of a car increases the car's weight and gasoline usage.
7. Recently, a hiker ~~down the street~~ cleaned out his trunk.
8. The amount of old hiking gear ~~in the trunk~~ was surprisingly large.
9. The result of his cleanup was greatly reduced gasoline expenses.
10. Savings during just one week reached thirty dollars.

TIP For more practices on sentence basics, visit *Exercise Central* at bedfordstmartins.com/realwriting.

Verbs

TIP Verbs do not always immediately follow the subject: Other words may come between the subject and the verb. **Example:** The boy who came in first won a prize.

Every sentence has a **main verb**, the word or words that tell what the subject does or that link the subject to another word that describes it. There are three kinds of verbs: action verbs, linking verbs, and helping verbs.

ACTION VERBS

An **action verb** tells what action the subject performs.

To find the main action verb in a sentence, ask yourself: **What action does the subject perform?**

ACTION VERBS	The band played all night.
	The alarm rings loudly.

LINKING VERBS

A **linking verb** connects (links) the subject to another word or group of words that describes the subject. Linking verbs show no action. The most common linking verb is *be* (*am, is, are,* and so on). Other linking verbs, such as *seem* and *become,* can usually be replaced by a form of the verb *be,* and the sentence will still make sense.

To find linking verbs, ask yourself: **What word joins the subject and the words that describe the subject?**

LINKING VERBS	The bus is late.
	My new shoes look shiny. (My new shoes are shiny.)
	The milk tastes sour. (The milk is sour.)

Some words can be used as either action verbs or linking verbs, depending on how the verb is used in a particular sentence.

ACTION VERB	Justine smelled the flowers.
LINKING VERB	The flowers smelled wonderful.

Common Linking Verbs

FORMS OF BE	FORMS OF SEEM AND BECOME	FORMS OF SENSE VERBS
am	seem, seems, seemed	look, looks, looked
are		appear, appears, appeared
is	become, becomes, became	
was		smell, smells, smelled
were		taste, tastes, tasted
		feel, feels, felt

THE FOUR MOST SERIOUS ERRORS
The Basic Sentence

> **LANGUAGE NOTE:** The verb *be* cannot be left out of sentences in English.
>
> **INCORRECT**   Tonya well now.
>
> **CORRECT**   Tonya **is** well now.

HELPING VERBS

A **helping verb** joins the main verb in a sentence to form the **complete verb** (also known as a verb phrase—the main verb and all of its helping verbs). The helping verb is often a form of the verb *be*, *have*, or *do*. A sentence may have more than one helping verb along with the main verb.

Helping verb + Main verb = Complete verb

Sharon was listening to the radio as she was studying for the test.
[The helping verb is *was*; the complete verbs are *was listening* and *was studying*.]

I am saving my money for a car.

Colleen might have borrowed my sweater.

You must pass this course before taking the next one.

You should stop smoking.

Common Helping Verbs

FORMS OF *BE*	FORMS OF *HAVE*	FORMS OF *DO*	OTHER
am	have	do	can
are	has	does	could
been	had	did	may
being			might
is			must
was			should
were			will
			would

Before you begin Practice 3, look at these examples to see how action, linking, and helping verbs are different.

ACTION VERB   Kara graduated last year.
[The verb *graduated* is an action that Kara performed.]

LINKING VERB   Kara is a graduate.
[The verb *is* links Kara to the word that describes her: *graduate*. No action is performed.]

THE FOUR MOST SERIOUS ERRORS

Chapter 19 • The Basic Sentence

HELPING VERB Kara is graduating next spring.

[The helping verb *is* joins the main verb *graduating* to make the complete verb *is graduating*, which tells what action the subject is taking.]

PRACTICE 3 Identifying the Verb (Action, Linking, or Helping Verb + Main Verb)

In the following sentences, underline each subject and double-underline each verb. Then, identify each verb as an action verb, a linking verb, or a helping verb + a main verb.

Helping verb + main verb
EXAMPLE: Bowling was created a long time ago.

1. The ancient Egyptians invented bowling.
2. Dutch settlers were responsible for bowling's introduction to North America.
3. They bowled outdoors on fields of grass.
4. One area in New York City is called Bowling Green because the Dutch bowled there in the 1600s.
5. The first indoor bowling alley in the United States opened in 1840 in New York.
6. Indoor bowling soon became popular across the country.
7. The largest bowling alley in the United States offers more than a hundred lanes.
8. Visitors to Las Vegas can bowl there.
9. Most people would not think of bowling as more popular than basketball.
10. However, more Americans participate in bowling than in any other sport.

Complete Thoughts

A **complete thought** is an idea, expressed in a sentence, that makes sense by itself, without additional words. An incomplete thought leaves readers wondering what's going on.

INCOMPLETE THOUGHT because my alarm did not go off

COMPLETE THOUGHT I was late because my alarm did not go off.

THE FOUR MOST SERIOUS ERRORS
The Basic Sentence   337

| INCOMPLETE THOUGHT | the people who won the lottery |
| COMPLETE THOUGHT | The people who won the lottery were old. |

To determine whether a thought is complete, ask yourself: **Do I have to ask a question to understand?**

INCOMPLETE THOUGHT	in my wallet
	[You would have to ask a question to understand, so it is not a complete thought.]
COMPLETE THOUGHT	My ticket is in my wallet.

PRACTICE 4 Identifying Complete Thoughts

Some of the following items contain complete thoughts, and others do not. In the space to the left of each item, write either "C" for complete thought or "I" for incomplete thought. If you write "I," add words to make a sentence.

EXAMPLE: __I__ My love of the outdoors *is well known.*

_____ 1. Therefore, I decided to study golf management.

_____ 2. So far, have learned about plant and soil nutrition as well as irrigation.

_____ 3. These skills will help me maintain landscapes for golfing.

_____ 4. Knowing how to fix golfing equipment.

_____ 5. Thanks to my studies, now comfortable repairing different types of golf clubs.

_____ 6. Next, I will start learning about golf cart maintenance.

_____ 7. One-third of my time outdoors each week.

_____ 8. Being outside is my favorite part of my studies.

_____ 9. However, the classroom work.

_____ 10. In one class, I am learning how to run a profitable pro shop.

Six Basic English Sentence Patterns

In English, there are six basic sentence patterns, some of which you have just worked through in this chapter. Although there are other patterns, they build on these six.

1. **Subject-Verb (S-V).** This pattern is the most basic one, as you have already seen.

   S   V
   Babies cry.

2. **Subject-Linking Verb-Noun (S-LV-N)**

   S   LV   N
   They are children.

3. **Subject-Linking Verb-Adjective (S-LV-ADJ)**

   S   LV ADJ
   Parents are tired.

4. **Subject-Verb-Adverb (S-V-ADV)**

   S   V   ADV
   They sleep poorly.

5. **Subject-Verb-Direct Object (S-V-DO).** A *direct object* directly receives the action of the verb.

   S   V   DO
   Teachers give tests.   [The *tests* are given.]

6. **Subject-Verb-Direct Object-Indirect Object.** An *indirect object* does not directly receive the action of the verb.

   S   V   DO   IO
   Teachers give tests to students.   [The *tests* are given; the *students* are not.]

   This pattern can also have the indirect object before the direct object.

   S   V   IO   DO
   Teachers give students tests.

PRACTICE 5 Identifying Basic Sentence Patterns

Using the sentence pattern indicated, write a sentence for each of the following items.

1. (Subject-verb-direct object) _____

2. (Subject-linking verb-noun) _____

3. (Subject-verb-adverb) _____

THE FOUR MOST SERIOUS ERRORS
Chapter Review 339

4. (Subject-verb-direct object-indirect object) _____

5. (Subject-verb-indirect object-direct object) _____

PRACTICE 6 Identifying Complete Sentences

In this essay, underline the subject of each sentence, and double-underline the verb. Correct five incomplete thoughts.

(1) Space travel fascinates my grandpa Bill. (2) He watches every space movie at least a dozen times. (3) Before 1996, he never even thought about the moon, Mars, or beyond. (4) He was too old to be an astronaut. (5) Now, however, he is on board a satellite. (6) It analyzes particles in the atmosphere. (7) He has the company of millions of other people. (8) And me, too. (9) Truthfully, only our names travel to Mars or beyond. (10) We are happy with that.

(11) In 1996, the Planetary Society flew the names of members into space. (12) Using the Mars *Pathfinder*. (13) At first, individuals signed a paper. (14) Then, Planetary Society members put the signatures into electronic form. (15) Now, people submit names on the Internet. (16) By filling out a form. (17) The names go on a microchip. (18) One spacecraft to the moon had more than a million names on board. (19) Some people have placed their names on a spacecraft going past Pluto and out of our solar system. (20) Their names are on a CD. (21) Which could survive for billions of years.

(22) Grandpa and I feel good about our journey into space. (23) In a way, we will travel to places only dreamed about. (24) After signing up, we received colorful certificates to print out. (25) To tell about our mission. (26) My certificate hangs on my wall. (27) My grandpa and I travel proudly into space.

Chapter Review

1. List the seven parts of speech. _____

LEARNING JOURNAL What is the main thing you learned from this chapter? What is one thing that is unclear to you?

THE FOUR MOST SERIOUS ERRORS

Chapter 19 • The Basic Sentence

2. A sentence must have three things: ___subject, noun verb___

3. A ___noun___ is the person, place, or thing that a sentence is about.

4. A prepositional phrase is ___add details to sentence can be removed___

5. Write an example of a prepositional phrase (not from one of the examples presented earlier): _____

6. An action verb tells _____

7. A linking verb _____

8. A helping verb _____

Chapter Test

Circle the correct choice for each of the following items.

1. Identify the underlined part of speech in this sentence.

    Devon <u>walks</u> so fast that I can never keep up with him.

    a. Noun   **b.** Verb   **c.** Preposition   **d.** Adjective

2. Identify the underlined part of speech in this sentence.

    In spring, the trees around our house are a <u>beautiful</u> shade of green.

    a. Adjective   **b.** Adverb   **c.** Preposition   **d.** Verb

3. Identify the underlined part of speech in this sentence.

    <u>Shopping</u> is Jerimiah's favorite hobby.

    a. Noun   **b.** Verb   **c.** Adjective   **d.** Adverb

4. Identify the type of verb in this sentence.

    The baby always <u>seems</u> tired after lunch.

    a. Action verb   **b.** Linking verb   **c.** Helping verb

5. Choose the item that is a complete sentence.
    a. Driving to the store.
    b. Driving to the store, I saw Rick jogging.
    c. Driving to the grocery store last Wednesday.

20

Fragments

Incomplete Sentences

EVER THOUGHT THIS?

"When my sentence gets too long, I think it probably needs a period, so I put one in, even though I'm not sure it goes there."

—Naomi Roman, Student

This chapter
- explains what fragments are.
- gives you practice finding and correcting five common kinds of fragments.

Understand What Fragments Are

A **fragment** is a group of words that is missing one or more parts of a complete sentence: a subject, a verb, or a complete thought.

SENTENCE	I was hungry, so I ate some cold pizza and drank a soda.
FRAGMENT	I was hungry, so I ate some cold pizza. *And drank a soda.* [*And drank a soda* contains a verb (*drank*) but no subject.]

LANGUAGE NOTE: Remember that any idea that ends with a period needs a subject and verb to be complete. As a quick review, a subject is the person, place, or thing that a sentence is about. A verb tells what the subject does, links the subject to another word that describes it, or "helps" another verb form a complete verb.

LearningCurve
Fragments
bedfordstmartins
.com/realwriting/LC

In the Real World, Why Is It Important to Correct Fragments?

People outside the English classroom notice fragments and consider them major mistakes.

SITUATION: Justina is interested in starting a blog to establish an online presence and attract potential employers, just as Leigh King did (see p. 197). Here is part of an e-mail that Justina sent to Leigh:

> I am getting in touch with you about starting a blog on dress design. Because I have heard about your success with your fashion blog. For a long time, I have designed and sewn many dresses for myself and my

friends, and I have a good sense of style. On my blog, I would like to share sewing tips and patterns based on my dress designs. Which should appeal to many readers. I would like to ask your opinion about many things. Especially about how to write clear, interesting blog posts. I have to admit that my dream would be for my blog to catch the eye of a major fashion house looking for talent. To come up with new looks for its dress line. Could we set up a time to talk in person?

WRITER AT WORK

Here are Leigh's thoughts about Justina's e-mail.

LEIGH KING'S RESPONSE: Justina seems to be a talented designer who has a lot of good information to share with others. However, her e-mail has a lot of mistakes in it, and if the writing in her blog will be as careless as the writing in the e-mail, I am concerned that readers—including potential employers—will not take her seriously. When I meet with Justina, I will recommend that she brush up on her writing skills and carefully edit her blog entries before posting them. If she can do all that, I think she could produce an appealing blog.

(See Leigh's **PROFILE OF SUCCESS** on p. 197.)

Find and Correct Fragments

To find fragments in your own writing, look for the five trouble spots in this chapter. They often signal fragments.

When you find a fragment in your own writing, you can usually correct it in one of two ways.

BASIC WAYS TO CORRECT A FRAGMENT

- Add what is missing (a subject, a verb, or both).
- Attach the fragment to the sentence before or after it.

PRACTICE 1   Finding Fragments

Find and underline the four fragments in Justina's e-mail above.

THE FOUR MOST SERIOUS ERRORS
Find and Correct Fragments

Seeing Fragments

Saw shoe
didn't chew

write What elements are missing from this sentence? Rewrite it to make it complete.

1. Fragments That Start with Prepositions

Whenever a preposition starts what you think is a sentence, check for a subject, a verb, and a complete thought. If the group of words is missing any of these three elements, it is a fragment.

FRAGMENT I pounded as hard as I could. *Against the door.*
[*Against the door* lacks both a subject and a verb.]

Correct a fragment that starts with a preposition by connecting it to the sentence either before or after it. If you connect such a fragment to the sentence after it, put a comma after the fragment to join it to the next sentence.

TIP Remember that the subject of a sentence is *never* in a prepositional phrase (see p. 332).

TIP In the examples in this chapter, subjects are underlined once, and verbs are underlined twice.

FINDING AND FIXING FRAGMENTS:
Fragments That Start with a Preposition

Find

I pounded as hard as I could. (Against) the door.

1. **Circle** any preposition that starts a word group.
2. **Ask:** Does the word group have a subject? *No.* A verb? *No.* **Underline** any subject, and **double-underline** any verb.
3. **Ask:** Does the word group express a complete thought? *No.*
4. If the word group is missing a subject or verb or does not express a complete thought, it is a fragment. *This word group is a fragment.*

Fix

I pounded as hard as I could / ᵃAgainst the door.

5. **Correct the fragment** by joining it to the sentence before or after it.

Common Prepositions

about	before	for	on	until
above	behind	from	out	up
across	below	in	outside	upon
after	beneath	inside	over	with
against	beside	into	past	within
along	between	like	since	without
among	by	near	through	
around	down	next to	to	
at	during	of	toward	
because of	except	off	under	

TIP For more practice correcting fragments, visit *Exercise Central* at bedfordstmartins.com/realwriting.

2. Fragments That Start with Dependent Words

A **dependent word** (also called a **subordinating conjunction**) is the first word in a dependent clause (a clause is a group of words that has a subject and a verb).

SENTENCE WITH A DEPENDENT WORD
We arrived early *because* we left early.
[*Because* is a dependent word introducing the dependent clause *because we left early.*]

A dependent clause cannot be a sentence because it does not express a complete thought, even though it has a subject and a verb. Whenever a dependent word starts what you think is a sentence, stop to check for a subject, a verb, and a complete thought.

FRAGMENT	*Since I moved.* I have eaten out every day.
	[*Since I moved* has a subject (*I*) and a verb (*moved*), but it does not express a complete thought.]
CORRECTED	Since I moved, I have eaten out every day.

Common Dependent Words

after	if/if only	until
although	now that	what (whatever)
as/as if/as though	once	when (whenever)
as long as/as soon as	since	where (wherever)
because	so that	whether
before	that	which
even if/even though	though	while
how	unless	who/whose

When a word group starts with *who*, *whose*, or *which*, it is not a complete sentence unless it is a question.

FRAGMENT	That woman is the police officer. *Who gave me a ticket last week.*
QUESTION	*Who* gave you a ticket last week?
FRAGMENT	He is the goalie. *Whose team is so bad.*
QUESTION	*Whose* team are you on?
FRAGMENT	Sherlene went to the HiHo Club. *Which does not serve alcohol.*
QUESTION	*Which* club serves alcohol?

Correct a fragment that starts with a dependent word by connecting it to the sentence before or after it. If the dependent clause is joined to the sentence after it, put a comma after the dependent clause.

THE FOUR MOST SERIOUS ERRORS

Chapter 20 • Fragments

FINDING AND FIXING FRAGMENTS:
Fragments That Start with a Dependent Word

Find

(Because) a job search is important. People should take the time to do it correctly.

1. **Circle** any dependent word that starts either word group.
2. **Ask:** Does the word group beginning with a dependent word have a subject? *Yes.* A verb? *Yes.* **Underline** any subject, and **double-underline** any verb.
3. **Ask:** Does this word group express a complete thought? *No.*
4. If the word group is missing a subject or verb or does not express a complete thought, it is a fragment. *This word group is a fragment.*

Fix

Because a job search is important, people should take the time to do it correctly.

5. **Correct the fragment** by joining it to the sentence before or after it. Add a comma if the dependent word group comes first.

TIP For more on commas with dependent clauses, see Chapters 27 and 34.

PRACTICE 2 Correcting Fragments That Start with Prepositions or Dependent Words

In the following items, circle any prepositions or dependent words that start a word group. Then, correct each fragment by connecting it to the sentence before or after it.

EXAMPLE: The fire at the Triangle Waist Company in New York City marked a turning point, (in) U.S. labor history.

1. Before the fire occurred, on March 25, 1911. Labor activists had raised complaints against the company, a maker of women's blouses.

2. The activists demanded shorter hours and better wages. For the company's overworked and underpaid sewing-machine operators.

3. The owners refused these requests, however. Because they placed profits over their employees' welfare.

4. When activists demanded better safety measures, such as sprinkler systems. The owners again refused to do anything.

5. On the day of the fire. A scrap bin on the eighth floor of the blouse factory ignited by accident.

6. Although workers threw buckets of water on the flames. Their efforts could not keep the fire from spreading to other floors.

7. Without access to safe or unlocked exits. Many workers died in the smoke and flames or jumped to their deaths.

8. One hundred and forty-six workers had lost their lives. By the end of this tragic day.

9. After news of the tragedy spread. The public reacted with outrage and greater demands for better working conditions.

10. Within a few years of the fire. Legislatures in New York and in other states passed laws to improve workplace safety and worker rights.

PRACTICE 3 Correcting Fragments That Start with Prepositions or Dependent Words

Read the following paragraph, and circle the ten fragments that start with prepositions or dependent words. Then, correct the fragments.

Staying focused at an office job can be difficult. Because of these jobs' many distractions. After making just a few changes. Workers will find that they are less distracted and more productive. A good first step is to clear away clutter, such as old paperwork. From the desk. Once the workspace is cleared. It is helpful to make a list of the most important tasks for the day. It is best for workers to do brain-demanding tasks when they are at their best. Which is often the start of the day. Workers can take on simpler tasks, like filing. When they are feeling less energetic. While they are doing something especially challenging. Workers might want to disconnect themselves from e-mail and turn off their cell phones. Although it is tempting to answer e-mails and phone calls immediately. They are among the worst workplace distractions. Some people set up a special electronic folder. For personal e-mails. They check this folder only while they are on break or between tasks. Finally, it is important for workers to remember the importance of breaks. Which recharge the mind and improve its focus.

3. Fragments That Start with *-ing* Verb Forms

An ***-ing* verb form** (also called a **gerund**) is the form of a verb that ends in *-ing: walking, writing, running*. Sometimes, an *-ing* verb form is used at the beginning of a complete sentence.

SENTENCE Walking is good exercise.
[The *-ing* verb form *walking* is the subject; *is* is the verb. The sentence expresses a complete thought.]

Sometimes, an *-ing* verb form introduces a fragment. When an *-ing* verb form starts what you think is a sentence, stop and check for a subject, a verb, and a complete thought.

FRAGMENT I ran as fast as I could. *Hoping to get there on time.*
[*Hoping to get there on time* lacks a subject, and it does not express a complete thought.]

Correct a fragment that starts with an *-ing* verb form either by adding whatever sentence elements are missing (usually a subject and a helping verb) or by connecting the fragment to the sentence before or after it. Usually, you will need to put a comma before or after the fragment to join it to the complete sentence.

FINDING AND FIXING FRAGMENTS:
Fragments That Start with *-ing* Verb Forms

Find

I was running as fast as I could. (Hoping) to get there on time.

1. **Circle** any *-ing* verb that starts a word group.
2. **Ask:** Does the word group have a subject? *No.* A verb? *Yes.* **Underline** any subject, and **double-underline** any verb.
3. **Ask:** Does the word group express a complete thought? *No.*
4. If the word group is missing a subject or a verb or does not express a complete thought, it is a fragment. *This word group is a fragment.*

Fix

I was running as fast as I could, hoping to get there on time.

I was running as fast as I could. I was hoping ~~Hoping~~ to get there on time.

5. **Correct the fragment** by joining it to the sentence before or after it. **Alternative:** Add the missing sentence elements.

THE FOUR MOST SERIOUS ERRORS
Find and Correct Fragments

PRACTICE 4 Correcting Fragments That Start with *-ing* Verb Forms

Circle any *-ing* verb that appears at the beginning of a word group in the paragraph. Then, read the word group to see if it has a subject and a verb and expresses a complete thought. Not *all* the word groups that start with an *-ing* verb are fragments, so read carefully. In the space provided, record the numbers of the word groups that are fragments. Then, correct each fragment either by adding the missing sentence elements or by connecting it to the sentence before or after it.

Which word groups are fragments? _____

(1) People sometimes travel long distances in unusual ways trying to set new world records. (2) Walking is one unusual way to set records. (3) In 1931, Plennie Wingo set out on an ambitious journey. (4) Walking backward around the world. (5) Wearing sunglasses with rearview mirrors, he started his trip early one morning. (6) After eight thousand miles, Wingo's journey was interrupted by a war in Pakistan. (7) Ending his ambitious journey. (8) Hans Mullikan spent more than two years in the late 1970s traveling to the White House by crawling from Texas to Washington, D.C. (9) Taking time out to earn money as a logger and a Baptist minister. (10) Alvin Straight, suffering from poor eyesight, traveled across the Midwest on a lawn mower. (11) Looking for his long-lost brother.

4. Fragments That Start with *to* and a Verb

When what you think is a sentence begins with *to* and a verb (called the *infinitive* form of the verb), you need to make sure it is not a fragment.

FRAGMENT	Each day, I check freecycle.org. *To see if it has anything I need.*
CORRECTED	Each day, I check freecycle.org to see if it has anything I need.

If a word group begins with *to* and a verb, it must have another verb; if not, it is not a complete sentence. When you see a word group that begins with *to* and a verb, first check to see if there is another verb. If there is no other verb, the word group is a fragment.

SENTENCE	*To run* a complete marathon *was* my goal. [*To run* is the subject; *was* is the verb.]

FRAGMENT	Cheri got underneath the car. *To change the oil.*
	[No other verb appears in the word group that begins with *to change.*]
LANGUAGE NOTE:	Do not confuse the infinitive (*to* before the verb) with *that*.
INCORRECT	My brother wants *that* his girlfriend cook.
CORRECT	My brother wants his girlfriend *to cook*.

To correct a fragment that starts with *to* and a verb, join it to the sentence before or after it, or add the missing sentence elements.

FINDING AND FIXING FRAGMENTS:
Fragments That Start with *to* and a Verb

Find

Cheri got underneath the car. *To change* the oil.

1. **Circle** any *to*-plus-verb combination that starts a word group.
2. **Ask:** Does the word group have a subject? **No.** A verb? **Yes.** **Underline** any subject, and **double-underline** any verb.
3. **Ask:** Does the word group express a complete thought? **No.**
4. If the word group is missing a subject or a verb or does not express a complete thought, it is a fragment. *This word group is a fragment.*

Fix

Cheri got underneath the car/ *t*o change the oil.

To change the oil,
Cheri got underneath the car. ~~To change the oil.~~

She needed to
Cheri got underneath the car. ~~To~~ change the oil.

5. **Correct the fragment** by joining it to the sentence before or after it. If you put the *to*-plus-verb word group first, put a comma after it. **Alternative:** Add the missing sentence elements.

PRACTICE 5 Correcting Fragments That Start with *to* and a Verb

Circle any *to*-plus-verb combination that appears at the beginning of a sentence in the paragraph. Then, read the word group to see if it has a subject and a verb and expresses a complete thought. Not *all* the word groups that start with *to* and a verb are fragments, so read carefully. In the space provided, record the numbers of the word groups that are fragments. Then, correct each fragment either by adding the missing sentence elements or by connecting it to the sentence before or after it.

Which word groups are fragments? _____

(1) For people older than twenty-five, each hour spent watching TV lowers life expectancy by nearly twenty-two minutes. (2) This finding is the result of Australian researchers' efforts. (3) To investigate the health effects of TV viewing. (4) To put it another way, watching an hour of television is about the same as smoking two cigarettes. (5) The problem is that most people are inactive while watching TV. (6) They are not doing anything, like walking or playing sports. (7) To strengthen their heart and maintain a healthy weight. (8) Fortunately, it is possible. (9) To counteract some of TV's negative health effects. (10) To increase their life expectancy by three years. (11) People need to exercise just fifteen minutes a day. (12) To accomplish this goal, they might exchange a ride in an elevator for a climb up the stairs. (13) Or they might walk around the block during a lunch break at work.

5. Fragments That Are Examples or Explanations

As you edit your writing, pay special attention to groups of words that are examples or explanations of information you presented in the previous sentence. They may be fragments.

FRAGMENT	More and more people are reporting food allergies. *For example, allergies to nuts or milk.*
FRAGMENT	My body reacts to wheat-containing foods. *Such as bread or pasta.*
	[*For example, allergies to nuts or milk* and *Such as bread or pasta* are not complete thoughts.]

This last type of fragment is harder to recognize because there is no single word or kind of word to look for. The following words may signal a fragment, but fragments that are examples or explanations do not always start with these words.

especially   for example   like   such as

When a group of words gives an example or explanation connected to the previous sentence, stop to check it for a subject, a verb, and a complete thought.

TIP *Such as* and *like* do not often begin complete sentences.

FRAGMENT	I have found great things at freecycle.org. *Like a nearly new computer.*
FRAGMENT	Freecycle.org is a good site. *Especially for household items.*
FRAGMENT	It lists many gently used appliances. *Such as DVD players.*

[*Like a nearly new computer, Especially for household items,* and *Such as DVD players* are not complete thoughts.]

Correct a fragment that starts with an example or explanation by connecting it to the sentence before or after it. Sometimes, you can add whatever sentence elements are missing (a subject, a verb, or both) instead. When you connect the fragment to a sentence, you may need to change some punctuation. For example, fragments that are examples are often set off by a comma.

FINDING AND FIXING FRAGMENTS:
Fragments That Are Examples or Explanations

Find

Freecycle.org recycles usable items. (Such as clothing.)

1. **Circle** the word group that is an example or explanation.
2. **Ask:** Does the word group have a subject, a verb, and a complete thought? *No.*
3. If the word group is missing a subject or a verb or does not express a complete thought, it is a fragment. *This word group is a fragment.*

Fix

Freecycle.org recycles usable items, such as clothing.

You may need to add some words to correct fragments:

I should list some things on freecycle.org. The sweaters I never wear *could keep others warm*.

4. **Correct the fragment** by joining it to the sentence before or after it or by adding the missing sentence elements.

PRACTICE 6 Correcting Fragments That Are Examples or Explanations

Circle word groups that are examples or explanations. Then, read the word group to see if it has a subject and verb and expresses a complete thought. In the space provided, record the numbers of the word groups that are fragments.

Then, correct each fragment either by adding the missing sentence elements or by connecting it to the sentence before or after it.

Which word groups are fragments? __2) 6 5__

(1) Being a smart consumer can be difficult. (2) Especially when making a major purchase. (3) At car dealerships, for example, important information is often in small type. (4) Like finance charges or preparation charges. (5) Advertisements also put negative information in small type. (6) Such as a drug's side effects. (7) Credit-card offers often use tiny, hard-to-read print for the terms of the card. (8) Like interest charges and late fees, which can really add up. (9) Phone service charges can also be hidden in small print. (10) Like limits on text messaging and other functions. (11) Especially now, as businesses try to make it seem as if you are getting a good deal, it is important to read any offer carefully.

Edit for Fragments

Use the chart on page 358, Finding and Fixing Fragments, to help you complete the practices in this section and edit your own writing.

PRACTICE 7 Correcting Various Fragments

In the following items, circle each word group that is a fragment. Then, correct fragments by connecting them to the previous or next sentence or by adding the missing sentence elements.

EXAMPLE: (With the high cost of producing video games,) ~~Game~~ game publishers are turning to a new source of revenue.

1. To add to their income. Publishers are placing advertisements in their games.
2. Sometimes, the ads show a character using a product. For example, drinking a specific brand of soda to earn health points.
3. One character, a race-car driver, drove his ad-covered car. Across the finish line.
4. When a warrior character picked up a sword decorated with an athletic-shoe logo. Some players complained.

5. Worrying that ads are distracting. Some publishers are trying to limit the number of ads per game.

6. But most players do not seem to mind seeing ads in video games. If there are not too many of them.

7. These players are used to seeing ads in all kinds of places. Like grocery carts and restroom walls.

8. For video game publishers. The goal is making a profit, but most publishers also care about the product.

9. To strike a balance between profitable advertising and high game quality. That is what publishers want.

10. Doing market research. Will help publishers find that balance.

PRACTICE 8 Editing Paragraphs for Fragments

Find and correct ten fragments in the following paragraphs.

1. Ida Lewis was born on February 25, 1842, in Newport, Rhode Island. Her father, Hosea, had been a coast pilot but was transferred to the Lighthouse Service. Although he was in failing health. In 1853, he was appointed lighthouse keeper at Lime Rock in Newport. Many lighthouse keepers were forced to leave family behind when they assumed their duties. Because the lighthouses were in remote locations and the living situations were poor. At first, Lime Rock had only a shed. For the keeper and a temporary lantern for light. Appropriate housing was constructed in 1857, and Hosea moved his family to Lime Rock.

2. Hosea was completely disabled by a stroke. In only a few months. Ida, who was already caring for an ill sister, took care of her father and the lighthouse as well. Keeping the lighthouse lamp lit. At sunset, the lamp had to be filled with oil and refilled at midnight. The reflectors needed constant polishing, and the light had to be extinguished in the morning. Since schools were on the mainland, Ida rowed her brothers and sisters to school every day. Strengthening her rowing ability, which ultimately saved many lives. In 1872, Hosea died, and Ida's mother was appointed keeper. Even though Ida did all the work. Finally, in 1879, Ida became the keeper and received a salary of $500 a year.

3. She was the best-known lighthouse keeper because of her many rescues. Some called her "The Bravest Woman in America." Saving eighteen

lives during her time of service. In 1867, during a storm, sheepherders had gone into the water after a lost sheep. Ida saved both the sheep and the sheepherders. She became famous, and many important people came to see her. For example, President Ulysses S. Grant. All the ships anchored in the harbor tolled their bells. To honor her after her death. Later, the Rhode Island legislature changed the name of Lime Rock to Ida Lewis Rock, the first and only time this honor was awarded.

PRACTICE 9   Editing Fragments and Using Formal English

Your friend wants to send this thank-you note to an employer who interviewed her for a job. She knows that the note has problems and has asked for your help. Correct the fragments in the note. Then, edit the informal English in it.

TIP For more advice on using formal English, see Chapter 2. For advice on choosing appropriate words, see Chapter 31.

Dear Ms. Hernandez,

(1) Thank you so much for taking the time. (2) To meet with me this past Wednesday. (3) I am more psyched than ever about the administrative assistant position at Fields Corporation. (4) Learning more about the stuff I would need to do. Was very cool. (5) Also, I enjoyed meeting you and the other managers. (6) With my strong organizational skills, professional experience, and friendly personality. (7) I'm sure that I would be awesome for the job. (8) Because I'm totally jazzed about the position. (9) I hope you will keep me in mind. (10) Please let me know if you need any other info.

(11) Like references or a writing sample.

(12) Thank U much,

Sincerely,

Terri Hammons

PRACTICE 10   Editing Justina's E-mail

Look back at Justina's e-mail on page 341. You may have already underlined the fragments in her e-mail; if not, do so now. Next, using what you have learned in this chapter, correct each fragment in the e-mail.

PRACTICE 11   Editing Your Own Writing for Fragments

Edit fragments in a piece of your own writing—a paper for this course or another one, or something you have written for work or your everyday life. Use the chart on page 358 to help you.

Chapter Review

LEARNING JOURNAL What kind of fragments do you find in your writing? What is the main thing you have learned about fragments that will help you? What is unclear to you?

1. A *sentence* is a group of words that has three elements: a _____, a _____, and a _____.

2. A _____ seems to be a complete sentence but is only a piece of one. It lacks a _____, a _____, or a _____.

3. What are the five trouble spots that signal possible fragments?
   _____
   _____
   _____
   _____

4. What are the two basic ways to correct fragments?
   _____
   _____

Chapter Test

Circle the correct choice for each of the following items. For help, refer to the chart on page 358, Finding and Fixing Fragments.

1. If an underlined portion of this sentence is incorrect, select the revision that fixes it. If the sentence is correct as written, choose d.

   Natalie did not go on our bike trip. Because she could not ride a
   ................................A........................B...C
   bike.

   a. go. On
   b. trip because
   c. ride; a
   d. No change is necessary.

2. Choose the item that has no errors.
   a. Since Gary is the most experienced hiker here, he should lead the way.
   b. Since Gary is the most experienced hiker here. He should lead the way.
   c. Since Gary is the most experienced hiker here; he should lead the way.

3. If an underlined portion of this sentence is incorrect, select the revision that fixes it. If the sentence is correct as written, choose d.

   Planting fragrant flowers will attract wildlife. Such as butterflies.
       A   B   C

   a. When planting
   b. flowers; will
   c. wildlife, such
   d. No change is necessary.

4. Choose the item that has no errors.
   a. To get to the concert hall; take exit 5 and drive for 3 miles.
   b. To get to the concert hall. Take exit 5 and drive for 3 miles.
   c. To get to the concert hall, take exit 5 and drive for 3 miles.

5. If an underlined portion of this sentence is incorrect, select the revision that fixes it. If the sentence is correct as written, choose d.

   Buying many unnecessary groceries. Can result in wasted food
                                  A   B

   and wasted money.
        C

   a. groceries can
   b. : in wasted
   c. : wasted money
   d. No change is necessary.

6. If an underlined portion of this sentence is incorrect, select the revision that fixes it. If the sentence is correct as written, choose d.

   Some scientists predict that people will soon take vacation
                         A   B

   cruises. Into space.
      C

   a. predict, that
   b. soon; take
   c. cruises into
   d. No change is necessary.

7. Choose the item that has no errors.
   a. Walking for 10 miles after her car broke down. Pearl became tired and frustrated.
   b. Walking for 10 miles after her car broke down; Pearl became tired and frustrated.
   c. Walking for 10 miles after her car broke down, Pearl became tired and frustrated.

8. Choose the item that has no errors.
   a. Many people find it hard. To concentrate during stressful times.
   b. Many people find it hard to concentrate during stressful times.
   c. Many people find it hard, to concentrate during stressful times.

9. If an underlined portion of this sentence is incorrect, select the revision that fixes it. If the sentence is correct as written, choose d.

Growing suspicious, the secret agent discovered a tiny recording
   A   B
device inside a flower vase.
       C

   a. Growing, suspicious   c. inside, a flower vase
   b. agent. Discovered   d. No change is necessary.

10. If an underlined portion of this sentence is incorrect, select the revision that fixes it. If the sentence is correct as written, choose d.

Early in their training, doctors learn that there is a fine
   A   B
line. Between life and death.
       C

   a. Early, in   c. line between
   b. doctors. Learn   d. No change is necessary.

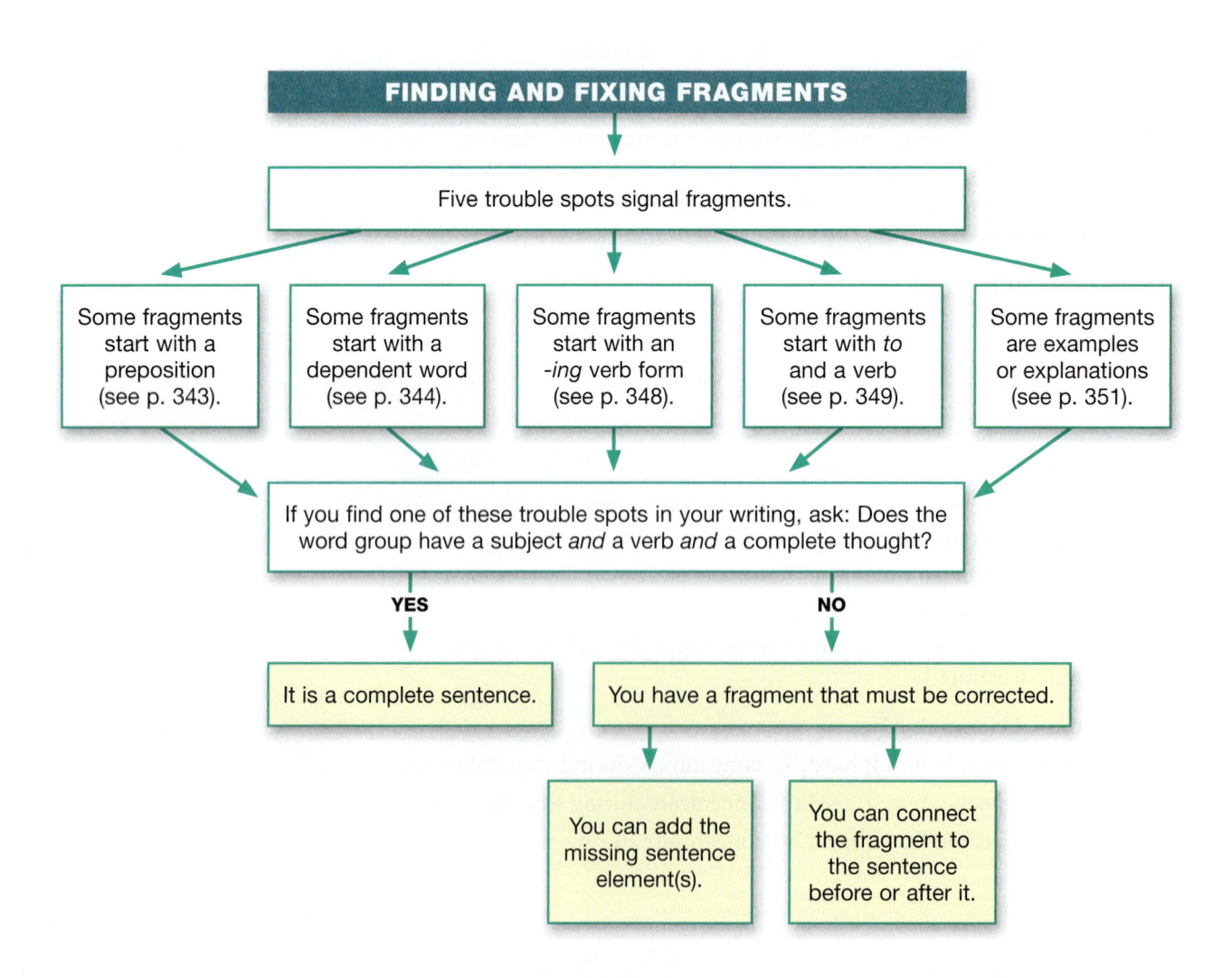

FINDING AND FIXING FRAGMENTS

Five trouble spots signal fragments.

- Some fragments start with a preposition (see p. 343).
- Some fragments start with a dependent word (see p. 344).
- Some fragments start with an *-ing* verb form (see p. 348).
- Some fragments start with *to* and a verb (see p. 349).
- Some fragments are examples or explanations (see p. 351).

If you find one of these trouble spots in your writing, ask: Does the word group have a subject *and* a verb *and* a complete thought?

YES → It is a complete sentence.

NO → You have a fragment that must be corrected.
- You can add the missing sentence element(s).
- You can connect the fragment to the sentence before or after it.

21

Run-Ons

Two Sentences Joined Incorrectly

EVER THOUGHT THIS?

"I tried putting in commas instead of periods so that I wouldn't have fragments. But now my papers get marked for 'comma splices.'"
—Jimmy Lester, Student

This chapter
- explains what run-ons are.
- gives you practice finding run-ons and shows five ways to correct them.

Understand What Run-Ons Are

A sentence is also called an **independent clause**, a group of words with a subject and a verb that expresses a complete thought. Sometimes, two independent clauses can be joined to form one larger sentence.

SENTENCE WITH TWO INDEPENDENT CLAUSES

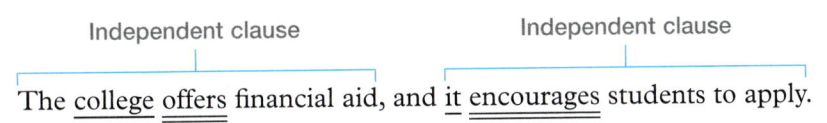

[Independent clause] [Independent clause]
The college offers financial aid, and it encourages students to apply.

A **run-on** is two complete sentences (independent clauses) joined incorrectly as one sentence. There are two kinds of run-ons: **fused sentences** and **comma splices**.

A **fused sentence** is two complete sentences joined without a coordinating conjunction (*for, and, nor, but, or, yet, so*) or any punctuation.

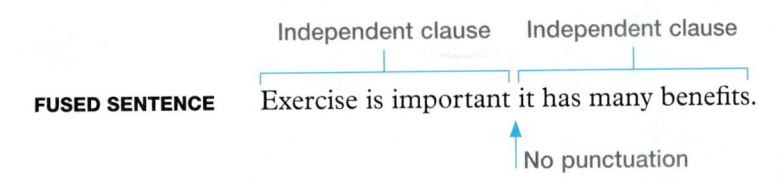

FUSED SENTENCE [Independent clause] [Independent clause]
Exercise is important it has many benefits.
   No punctuation

A **comma splice** is two complete sentences joined by only a comma.

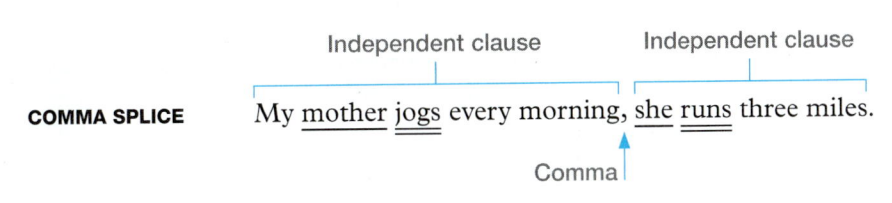

COMMA SPLICE [Independent clause] [Independent clause]
My mother jogs every morning, she runs three miles.
   Comma

✓ **LearningCurve**
Run-On Sentences
bedfordstmartins.com/realwriting/LC

TIP To find and correct run-ons, you need to be able to identify a complete sentence. For a review, see Chapter 19.

TIP In the examples throughout this chapter, subjects are underlined once, and verbs are underlined twice.

When you join two sentences, use the proper punctuation.

CORRECTIONS Exercise is important; it has many benefits.

My mother jogs every morning; she runs 3 miles.

In the Real World, Why Is It Important to Correct Run-Ons?

People outside the English classroom notice run-ons and consider them major mistakes.

SITUATION: Naomi is applying to a special program for returning students at Cambridge College. Here is one of the essay questions on the application, followed by a paragraph from Naomi's answer.

STATEMENT OF PURPOSE: In two hundred words or less, describe your intellectual and professional goals and how a Cambridge College education will assist you in achieving them.

For many years, I did not take control of my life, I just drifted without any goals. I realized one day as I met with my daughter's guidance counselor that I hoped my daughter would not turn out like me. From that moment, I decided to do something to help myself and others. I set a goal of becoming a teacher. To begin on that path, I took a math course at night school, then I took another in science. I passed both courses with hard work, I know I can do well in the Cambridge College program. I am committed to the professional goal I finally found it has given new purpose to my whole life.

WRITER AT WORK

Mary LaCue Booker, a master's degree recipient from Cambridge College, read Naomi's answer and commented.

MARY LACUE BOOKER'S RESPONSE: Cambridge College wants students who are thoughtful, hardworking, and mature. Although Naomi's essay indicates that she has some of these qualities, her writing gives another impression. She makes several noticeable errors; I wonder if she took the time to really think about this essay. If she is careless on a document that represents her for college admission, will she be careless in other areas as well? It is too bad, because her qualifications are quite good otherwise.

(See Mary's **PROFILE OF SUCCESS** on p. 256.)

Find and Correct Run-Ons

To find run-ons, focus on each sentence in your writing, one at a time, looking for fused sentences and comma splices. Pay special attention to sentences longer than two lines. By spending this extra time, your writing will improve.

PRACTICE 1 Finding Run-Ons

Find and underline the four run-ons in Naomi's writing on page 360.

Once you have found a run-on, there are five ways to correct it.

FIVE WAYS TO CORRECT RUN-ONS

1. **Add a period.**

   I saw the man. ~~he~~ *He* did not see me.

2. **Add a semicolon.**

   I saw the man; he did not see me.

3. **Add a semicolon, a conjunctive adverb, and a comma.**

   I saw the man; *however,* he did not see me.

4. **Add a comma and a coordinating conjunction.**

   I saw the man, *but* he did not see me.

5. **Add a dependent word.**

   When I saw the man, he did not see me.

Add a Period

You can correct run-ons by adding a period to make two separate sentences. After adding the period, capitalize the letter that begins the new sentence. Reread your two sentences to make sure they each contain a subject, a verb, and a complete thought.

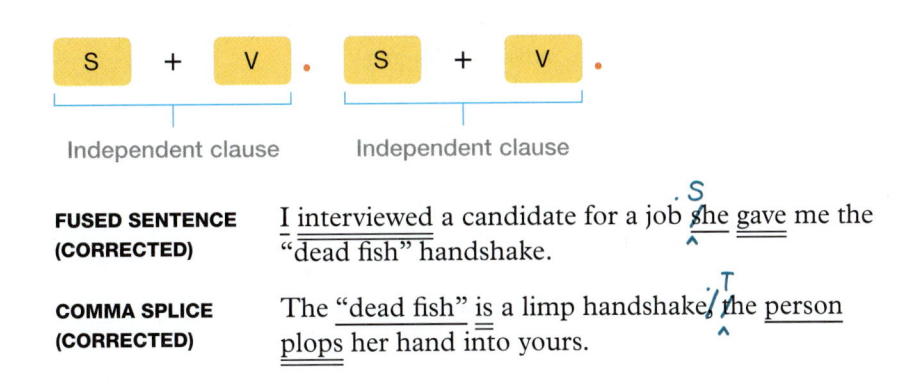

[S + V] . [S + V] .
Independent clause   Independent clause

FUSED SENTENCE (CORRECTED) I interviewed a candidate for a job. *S*he gave me the "dead fish" handshake.

COMMA SPLICE (CORRECTED) The "dead fish" is a limp handshake. *T*he person plops her hand into yours.

Add a Semicolon

A second way to correct run-ons is to use a semicolon (;) to join the two sentences. Use a semicolon only when the two sentences express closely related ideas and the words on each side of the semicolon can stand alone as a complete sentence. Do not capitalize the word that follows a semicolon unless it is the name of a specific person, place, or thing that is usually capitalized—for example, Mary, New York, or the Eiffel Tower.

FUSED SENTENCE (CORRECTED)   Slouching creates a terrible impression; it makes a person seem uninterested, bored, or lacking in self-confidence.

COMMA SPLICE (CORRECTED)   It is important in an interview to hold your head up; it is just as important to sit up straight.

Add a Semicolon, a Conjunctive Adverb, and a Comma

A third way to correct run-ons is to add a semicolon followed by a **conjunctive adverb** and a comma.

Common Conjunctive Adverbs

consequently	indeed	moreover	still
finally	instead	nevertheless	then
furthermore	likewise	otherwise	therefore
however	meanwhile	similarly	

I stopped by the market; however, it was closed.
(Semicolon / Conjunctive adverb / Comma)

Sharon is a neighbor; moreover, she is my friend.
(Semicolon / Conjunctive adverb / Comma)

THE FOUR MOST SERIOUS ERRORS
Find and Correct Run-Ons   363

> **FINDING AND FIXING RUN-ONS:**
> Adding a Period, a Semicolon,
> or a Semicolon, a Conjunctive Adverb, and a Comma

Find

Few people know the history of many popular holidays Valentine's Day is one of these holidays.

1. To see if there are two independent clauses in a sentence, **underline** the subjects, and **double-underline** the verbs.
2. **Ask:** If the sentence has two independent clauses, are they separated by either a period or a semicolon? *No. It is a run-on.*

Fix

Few people know the history of many popular holidays. Valentine's Day is one of these holidays.

Few people know the history of many popular holidays; Valentine's Day is one of these holidays.

Few people know the history of many popular holidays; *indeed,* Valentine's Day is one of these holidays.

3. **Correct** the error by adding a period, a semicolon, or a semicolon, a conjunctive adverb, and a comma.

PRACTICE 2 Correcting Run-Ons by Adding a Period or a Semicolon

For each of the following items, indicate in the space to the left whether it is a fused sentence ("FS") or a comma splice ("CS"). Then, correct the error by adding a period or a semicolon. Capitalize the letters as necessary to make two sentences.

EXAMPLE: _FS_ Being a farmer can mean dealing with all types of challenges ; one of the biggest ones comes from the sky.

____ 1. Farmers have been trying to keep hungry birds out of their crops for centuries, the first scarecrow was invented for this reason.

____ 2. Some farmers have used a variety of chemicals, other farmers have tried noise, such as small cannons.

____ 3. Recently, a group of berry farmers tried something new they brought in bigger birds called falcons.

TIP For more practices on run-ons, visit *Exercise Central* at **bedfordstmartins.com/realwriting**.

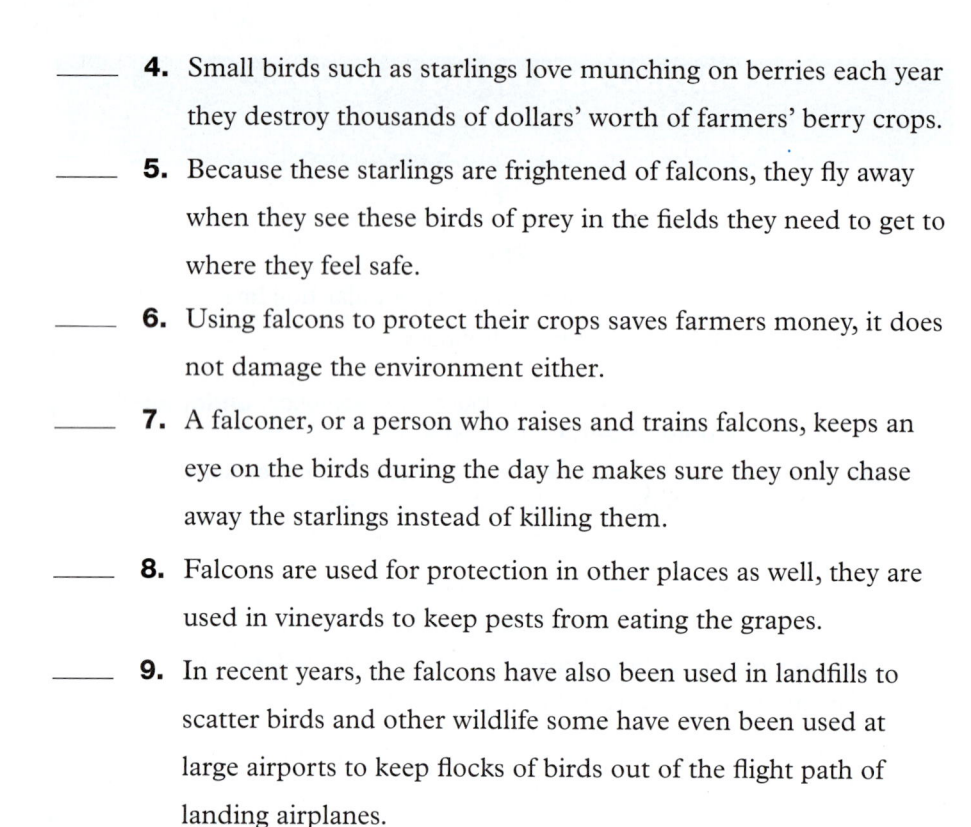

_____ 4. Small birds such as starlings love munching on berries each year they destroy thousands of dollars' worth of farmers' berry crops.

_____ 5. Because these starlings are frightened of falcons, they fly away when they see these birds of prey in the fields they need to get to where they feel safe.

_____ 6. Using falcons to protect their crops saves farmers money, it does not damage the environment either.

_____ 7. A falconer, or a person who raises and trains falcons, keeps an eye on the birds during the day he makes sure they only chase away the starlings instead of killing them.

_____ 8. Falcons are used for protection in other places as well, they are used in vineyards to keep pests from eating the grapes.

_____ 9. In recent years, the falcons have also been used in landfills to scatter birds and other wildlife some have even been used at large airports to keep flocks of birds out of the flight path of landing airplanes.

Seeing Run-Ons

> Please do not run on these stairs
> Its better to miss your train than break your leg
> GER
> GREAT EASTERN RAILWAY
>
> ↑ Platforms 2 & 3 🚆 one

write How would you fix the run-on in this sign? What other errors do you notice? Write two more closely related sentences, and then connect them using a semicolon or a semicolon, a conjunctive adverb, and a comma. Make sure that all your punctuation is correct.

_____ **10.** Although a falconer's services are not cheap, they cost less than some other methods that farmers have tried for example, putting nets over a berry field can often cost more than $200,000.

Add a Comma and a Coordinating Conjunction

A fourth way to correct run-ons is to add a comma and a **coordinating conjunction**: a link that joins independent clauses to form one sentence. The seven coordinating conjunctions are *and, but, for, nor, or, so, yet*. Some people remember these words by thinking of **FANBOYS:** *for, and, nor, but, or, yet, so*.

To correct a fused sentence this way, add a comma and a coordinating conjunction. A comma splice already has a comma, so just add a coordinating conjunction that makes sense in the sentence.

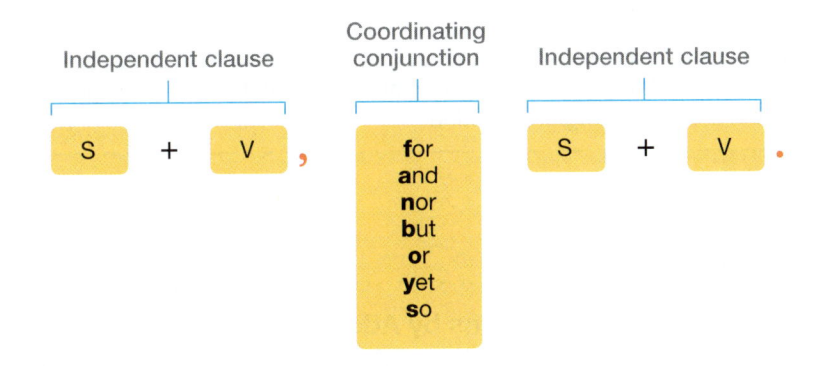

[Diagram: Independent clause (S + V), Coordinating conjunction (for, and, nor, but, or, yet, so), Independent clause (S + V).]

TIP Notice that the comma does not follow the conjunction. The comma follows the word before the conjunction.

FUSED SENTENCE (CORRECTED) Nakeisha was qualified for the job, but she hurt her chances by mumbling.

COMMA SPLICE (CORRECTED) The candidate smiled, and she waved to the crowd.

Coordinating conjunctions need to connect two independent clauses. They are not used to join a dependent and an independent clause.

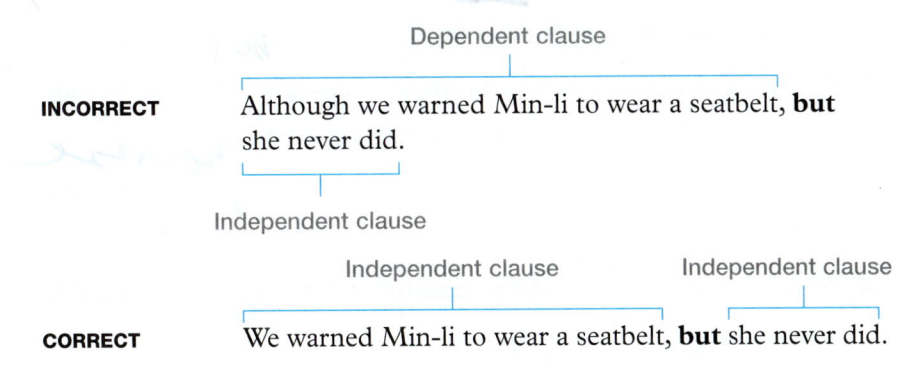

INCORRECT Although we warned Min-li to wear a seatbelt, **but** she never did. [Dependent clause / Independent clause]

CORRECT We warned Min-li to wear a seatbelt, **but** she never did. [Independent clause / Independent clause]

> **FINDING AND FIXING RUN-ONS:**
> Using a Comma and/or a Coordinating Conjunction

Find

Foods <u>differ</u> from place to place your favorite <u>treat</u> <u><u>might disgust</u></u> someone from another culture.

1. To see if there are two independent clauses in a sentence, **underline** the subjects, and **double-underline** the verbs.
2. **Ask:** If the sentence has two independent clauses, are they separated by either a period or a semicolon? *No. It is a run-on.*

Fix

Foods differ from place to place **, and** your favorite treat might disgust someone from another culture.

3. **Correct** a fused sentence by adding a comma and a coordinating conjunction between the two independent clauses. Correct a comma splice by adding just a coordinating conjunction.

PRACTICE 3 Correcting Run-Ons by Adding a Comma and/or a Coordinating Conjunction

Correct each of the following run-ons by adding a comma, if necessary, and an appropriate coordinating conjunction. First, underline the subjects, and double-underline the verbs.

> **EXAMPLE:** Most <u>Americans</u> <u><u>do not like</u></u> the idea of eating certain kinds of food, **and** most of <u>us</u> <u><u>would</u></u> probably <u><u>reject</u></u> horse meat.

1. In most cultures, popular <u>foods</u> depend on availability and tradition, people tend to eat old familiar favorites.

2. Sushi shocked many Americans thirty years ago, *but* today some young people in the United States have grown up eating raw fish. *because*

3. In many societies, certain foods are allowed to age, this process adds flavor.

4. Icelanders bury eggs in the ground to rot for months, these aged eggs are considered a special treat.

THE FOUR MOST SERIOUS ERRORS

Find and Correct Run-Ons 367

5. As an American, you might not like such eggs the thought of eating them might even revolt you.

6. In general, aged foods have a strong taste, the flavor is unpleasant to someone unaccustomed to those foods.

7. Many Koreans love to eat kimchee, a spicy aged cabbage, Americans often find the taste odd and the smell overpowering.

8. Herders in Kyrgyzstan drink kumiss this beverage is made of aged horse's milk.

9. Americans on a visit to Kyrgyzstan consider themselves brave for tasting kumiss, local children drink it regularly.

10. We think of familiar foods as normal, favorite American foods might horrify people in other parts of the world.

Add a Dependent Word

A fifth way to correct run-ons is to make one of the complete sentences a dependent clause by adding a dependent word (a **subordinating conjunction** or a **relative pronoun**), such as *after, because, before, even though, if, that, though, unless, when, who,* and *which.* (For a more complete list of these words, see the graphic on p. 368.) Choose the dependent word that best expresses the relationship between the two clauses.

Turn an independent clause into a dependent one when it is less important than the other clause or explains it, as in the following sentence.

> *When* I get *to the train station,* I will call *Josh.*

The italicized clause is dependent (subordinate) because it just explains when the most important part of the sentence—calling Josh—will happen. It begins with the dependent word *when.*

Because a dependent clause is not a complete sentence (it has a subject and verb but does not express a complete thought), it can be joined to a sentence without creating a run-on. When the dependent clause is the second clause in a sentence, you usually do not need to put a comma before it unless it is showing contrast.

TWO SENTENCES

> Halloween was originally a religious holiday. People worshipped the saints.

DEPENDENT CLAUSE: NO COMMA NEEDED

> Halloween was originally a religious holiday *when* people worshipped the saints.

DEPENDENT CLAUSE SHOWING CONTRAST: COMMA NEEDED

Many holidays have religious origins, *though some celebrations have moved away from their religious roots.*

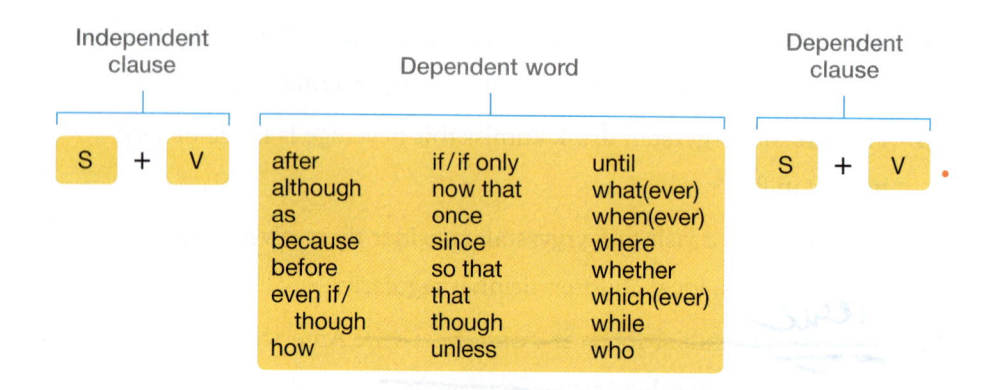

Independent clause | Dependent word | Dependent clause

S + V

after	if/if only	until
although	now that	what(ever)
as	once	when(ever)
because	since	where
before	so that	whether
even if/	that	which(ever)
though	though	while
how	unless	who

S + V.

FUSED SENTENCE (CORRECTED) Your final statement should express your interest in the position, although you do not want to sound desperate.
[The dependent clause *although you do not want to sound des-perate* shows contrast, so a comma comes before it.]

COMMA SPLICE (CORRECTED) It is important to end an interview on a positive note/ because that final impression is what the interviewer will remember.

You can also put the dependent clause first. When the dependent clause comes first, be sure to put a comma after it.

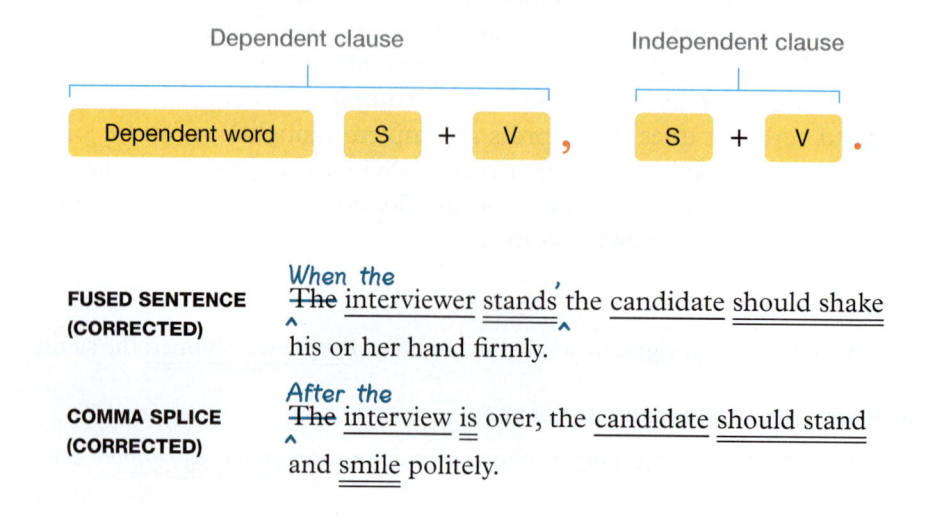

Dependent clause | Independent clause

Dependent word   S + V ,   S + V .

FUSED SENTENCE (CORRECTED) When the ~~The~~ interviewer stands, the candidate should shake his or her hand firmly.

COMMA SPLICE (CORRECTED) After the ~~The~~ interview is over, the candidate should stand and smile politely.

THE FOUR MOST SERIOUS ERRORS
Find and Correct Run-Ons

FINDING AND FIXING RUN-ONS:
Making a Dependent Clause

Find

Alzheimer's disease is a heartbreaking illness, it causes a steady decrease in brain capacity.

1. To see if there are two independent clauses in a sentence, **underline** the subjects, and **double-underline** the verbs.
2. **Ask:** If the sentence has two independent clauses, are they separated by a period, a semicolon, or a comma and a coordinating conjunction? *No. It is a run-on.*

Fix

Alzheimer's disease is a heartbreaking illness, *because* it causes a steady decrease in brain capacity.

3. If one part of the sentence is less important than the other, or if you want to make it so, add a dependent word to the less important part.

PRACTICE 4 Correcting Run-Ons by Adding a Dependent Word

Correct run-ons by adding a dependent word to make a dependent clause. First, underline the subjects, and double-underline the verbs. Although these run-ons can be corrected in different ways, in this exercise correct by adding dependent words. You may want to refer to the graphic on page 368.

> **EXAMPLE:** *When many* ~~Many~~ soldiers returned from Iraq and Afghanistan missing arms or legs, demand for better artificial limbs increased.

1. Computer chips were widely used artificial limbs remained largely unchanged for decades.

2. Computer chips now control many artificial limbs, these limbs have more capabilities than the ones of the past.

3. The i-LIMB artificial hand picks up electrical signals from nearby arm muscles the amputee can move individual fingers of the hand.

4. Lighter-weight materials were introduced artificial limbs were not as easy to move as they are today.

5. Now, the C-Leg artificial leg is popular it is lightweight, flexible, and technically advanced.

6. A C-Leg user wants to jog, bike, or drive instead of walk he or she can program the leg for the necessary speed and motion.

7. Major advances have been made in artificial limbs, researchers believe the technology has not reached its full potential.

8. Many will not be satisfied the human brain directly controls the motion of artificial limbs.

9. A thought-controlled artificial arm is being tested on patients, that time may not be far off.

10. The artificial arm passes those tests it may be introduced to the market within the next few years.

A Word That Can Cause Run-Ons: *Then*

Many run-ons are caused by the word *then*. You can use *then* to join two sentences, but if you add it without the correct punctuation or added words, your sentence will be a run-on. Often, writers use just a comma before *then*, but that makes a comma splice.

COMMA SPLICE   I picked up my laundry, then I went home.

Some of the methods you have just practiced can be used to correct errors caused by *then*. These methods are shown in the following examples.

I picked up my laundry. Then I went home.

I picked up my laundry; then I went home.

I picked up my laundry, and then I went home.

I picked up my laundry before I went home.
[dependent word *before* added to make a dependent clause]

Edit for Run-Ons

Use the chart on page 376, Finding and Fixing Run-Ons, to help you complete the practices in this section and edit your own writing.

PRACTICE 5 Correcting Various Run-Ons

In the following items, correct any run-ons. Use each method of correcting such errors—adding a period, adding a semicolon, adding a semicolon, a conjunctive adverb, and a comma, adding a comma and a coordinating conjunction, or adding a dependent word—at least once.

EXAMPLE: *Although some* ~~Some~~ people doubt the existence of climate change, few can deny that the weather has become more extreme and dangerous.

1. More than sixteen hundred tornadoes tore through the United States in 2011, hundreds of people lost their lives. [edits: "*When* More than..." and strike-throughs]

2. That same year, parts of the Midwest experienced severe flooding *and* droughts in Texas cost farmers more than $7 billion.

3. Some cities are taking steps to adapt to environmental changes, *because* they are focusing on the biggest threats.

4. Global temperatures are rising, sea levels are also rising—a threat to coastal regions.

5. As a result, some coastal cities are planning to build protective walls, *and, while* others are raising road beds.

6. Extreme heat is another major problem, urban planners are studying different ways to address it.

7. New York City is painting some rooftops white, light and heat will be reflected away from the city.

8. In Chicago, landscapers are planting heat-tolerant trees, these trees should help cool the environment and reduce flooding during heavy rains.

9. All these efforts are encouraging most parts of the United States are doing little or nothing to plan for ongoing environmental changes.

10. One study reports that only fourteen states are undertaking such planning the threats of severe weather remain.

PRACTICE 6 Editing Paragraphs for Run-Ons

Find and correct the six run-ons in the following paragraphs.

(1) For the first time, monster-size squids were filmed while still in the wild. (2) The images were caught on camera in the North Pacific Ocean the site is located just off the coast of southeastern Japan. (3) A team of Japanese scientists followed a group of sperm whales to locate the rare squids the whales like to eat the eight-legged creatures. (4) Wherever the whales went, the squids were likely to be found as well.

(5) From aboard their research ship, the team located the squids thousands of feet under the water, the scientists lowered bait over the side to attract them. (6) Next, they sent down cameras alongside the bait to catch images of these bizarre animals as soon as they appeared.

(7) The Dana octopus squid, also known as *Taningia danae,* often grows to the size of a human being or even larger. (8) Its eight arms are covered in suckers, as most squid species are, these particular types of arms end in catlike claws. (9) Two of the arms contain special organs on the ends called photophores. (10) These photophores produce flashing bursts of light they are designed to lure and capture prey. (11) The burst of light stuns other creatures, giving a squid a chance to capture and eat its victim. (12) When the squid isn't hunting, it still glows. (13) Experts believe that squids remain lighted as a way of communicating with other squids about potential dangers or as a way of attracting mates. (14) These lights appear eerie, the scientists were glad for them, as the lights made the giant squids slightly easier to find and finally film.

PRACTICE 7 Editing Run-Ons and Using Formal English

Your brother has been overcharged for an MP3 player he ordered online, and he is about to send this e-mail to the seller's customer-service department. Help him by correcting the run-ons. Then, edit the informal English.

(1) I'm writing 2U cuz I was seriously ripped off for the Star 3 MP3 player I ordered from your Web site last week. (2) U listed the price as $50 $150 was charged to my credit card. (3) Check out any competitors'

TIP For more advice on using formal English, see Chapter 2. For advice on choosing appropriate words, see Chapter 31.

sites, U will see that no one expects people 2 cough up that much cash for the Star model, the prices are never higher than $65. (4) I overpaid big bucks on this, I want my money back as soon as possible.

(5) Seriously bummin',

Chris Langley

PRACTICE 8 Editing Naomi's Application Answer

Look back at Naomi's writing on page 360. You may have already underlined the run-ons; if not, underline them now. Then, correct each error.

PRACTICE 9 Editing Your Own Writing for Run-Ons

Edit run-ons in a piece of your own writing—a paper for this course or another one, or something you have written for work or your everyday life. Use the chart on page 376 to help you.

Chapter Review

1. A sentence can also be called an _____.
2. A _____ is two complete sentences joined without any punctuation.
3. A _____ is two complete sentences joined by only a comma.
4. What are the five ways to correct run-ons?

   _____
   _____
   _____
   _____
   _____

5. What word in the middle of a sentence may signal a run-on?

   _____

6. What are the seven coordinating conjunctions?

   _____

LEARNING JOURNAL If you found run-ons in your writing, how did you correct them? What is the main thing you have learned about run-ons that you will use? What is one thing that remains unclear?

Chapter Test

Circle the correct choice for each of the following items. For help, refer to the Finding and Fixing Run-Ons chart on page 376.

1. Choose the item that has no errors.
   a. Please fill this prescription for me, it is for my allergies.
   b. Please fill this prescription for me. It is for my allergies.
   c. Please fill this prescription for me it is for my allergies.

2. If an underlined portion of this sentence is incorrect, select the revision that fixes it. If the sentence is correct as written, choose d.

   Harlan is busy <u>now ask</u> <u>him if</u> he can do his <u>report next</u> week.
                   A   B   C

   a. now, so
   b. him, if
   c. report; next
   d. No change is necessary.

3. Choose the item that has no errors.
   a. You cut all the onion slices to the same thickness, they will finish cooking at the same time.
   b. You cut all the onion slices to the same thickness they will finish cooking at the same time.
   c. If you cut all the onion slices to the same thickness, they will finish cooking at the same time.

4. Choose the correct answer to fill in the blank.

   I have told Jervis several times not to tease the baby _____ he never listens.

   a. ,
   b. , but
   c. No word or punctuation is necessary.

5. Choose the item that has no errors.
   a. I am in no hurry to get a book I order it online.
   b. I am in no hurry to get a book, I order it online.
   c. When I am in no hurry to get a book, I order it online.

6. If an underlined portion of this sentence is incorrect, select the revision that fixes it. If the sentence is correct as written, choose d.

   <u>Many people</u> think a tomato is a <u>vegetable</u> <u>it is</u> really a fruit.
        A   B   C

    a. Many, people
    b. vegetable; it
    c. really; a
    d. No change is necessary.

 7. Choose the item that has no errors.
    a. Although air conditioning makes hot days more comfortable, it will increase your energy bills.
    b. Air conditioning makes hot days more comfortable it will increase your energy bills.
    c. Air conditioning makes hot days more comfortable, it will increase your energy bills.

 8. If an underlined portion of this sentence is incorrect, select the revision that fixes it. If the sentence is correct as written, choose d.

    In northern Europe, bodies that are thousands of years <u>old have</u>
                                                                              A
    been found in <u>swamps, some</u> bodies are so well preserved that they
                            B
    <u>look like</u> sleeping people.
       C

    a. old, have
    b. swamps. Some
    c. look, like
    d. No change is necessary.

 9. Choose the item that has no errors.
    a. Do not be shy about opening doors for strangers, courtesy is always appreciated.
    b. Do not be shy about opening doors for strangers; courtesy is always appreciated.
    c. Do not be shy about opening doors for strangers courtesy is always appreciated.

10. Choose the correct answer to fill in the blank.

    You can ride with me to work _____ you can take the train.

    a. , or
    b. if
    c. No word or punctuation is necessary.

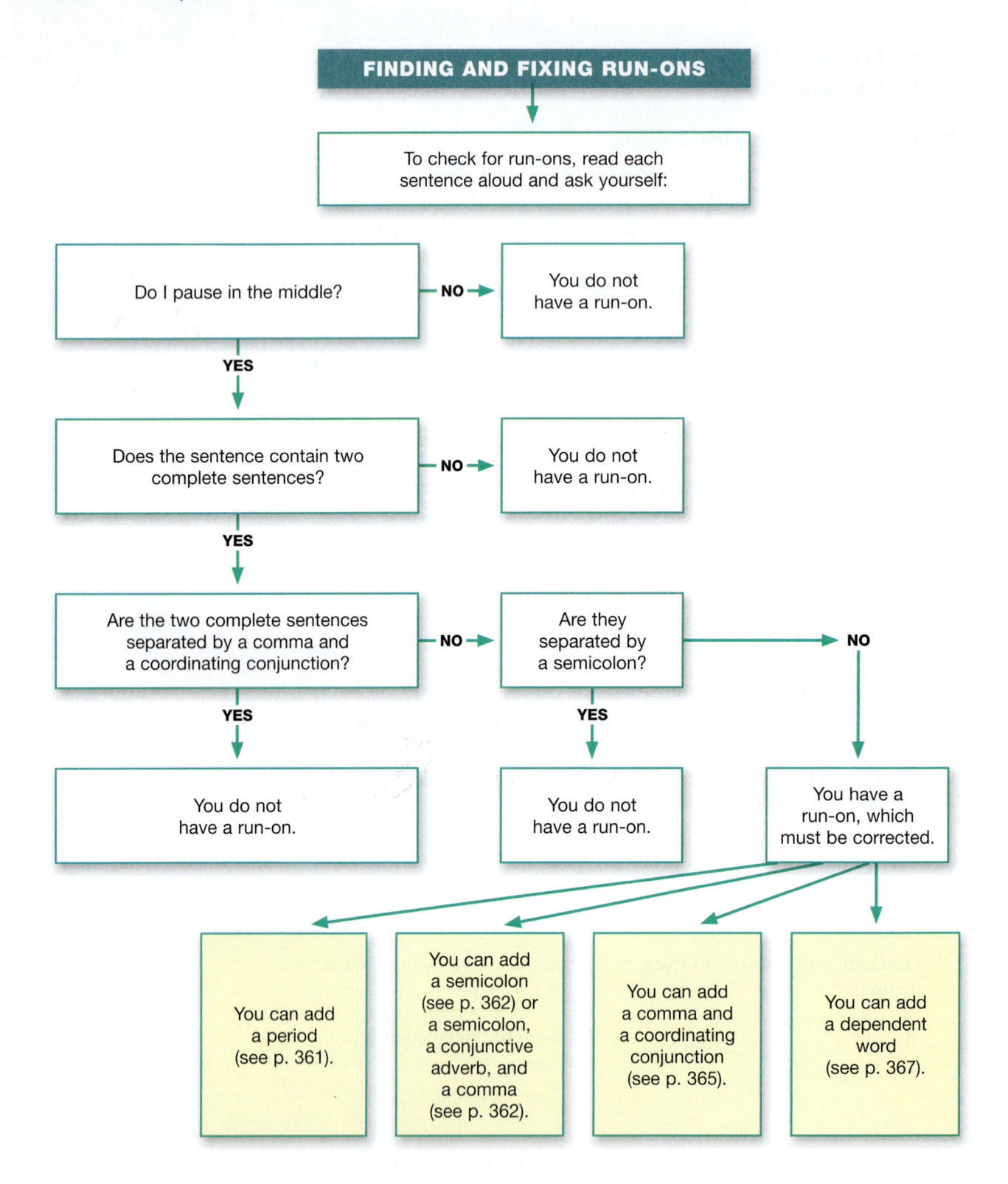

FINDING AND FIXING RUN-ONS

To check for run-ons, read each sentence aloud and ask yourself:

Do I pause in the middle? — NO → You do not have a run-on.

YES ↓

Does the sentence contain two complete sentences? — NO → You do not have a run-on.

YES ↓

Are the two complete sentences separated by a comma and a coordinating conjunction? — NO → **Are they separated by a semicolon?** — NO → **You have a run-on, which must be corrected.**

YES ↓ (left) You do not have a run-on.

YES ↓ (middle) You do not have a run-on.

From "You have a run-on, which must be corrected":

- You can add a period (see p. 361).
- You can add a semicolon (see p. 362) or a semicolon, a conjunctive adverb, and a comma (see p. 362).
- You can add a comma and a coordinating conjunction (see p. 365).
- You can add a dependent word (see p. 367).

22

Problems with Subject-Verb Agreement

EVER THOUGHT THIS?

"I know sometimes the verb is supposed to end with -s and sometimes it isn't, but I always get confused."
—Mayerlin Fana, Student

This chapter
- explains what *agreement* between subjects and verbs is.
- explains the simple rules for *regular verbs*.
- identifies five trouble spots that can cause confusion.
- gives you practice finding and fixing errors in subject-verb agreement.

When Subjects and Verbs Don't Match

Understand What Subject-Verb Agreement Is

In any sentence, the **subject and the verb must match—or agree—**in number. If the subject is singular (one person, place, or thing), the verb must also be singular. If the subject is plural (more than one), the verb must also be plural.

LearningCurve
Subject-Verb Agreement
bedfordstmartins
.com/realwriting/LC

| SINGULAR | The skydiver jumps out of the airplane. |
| PLURAL | The skydivers jump out of the airplane. |

Regular Verbs, Present Tense

	SINGULAR		PLURAL
First person	I walk.	} no -s	We walk.
Second person	You walk.		You walk.
Third person	He (she, it) walks.		They walk.
	Joe walks.	} all end in -s	Joe and Alice walk.
	The student walks.		The students walk.

TIP In the examples throughout this chapter, subjects are underlined, and verbs are double-underlined.

377

Regular verbs (with forms that follow standard English patterns) have two forms in the present tense: one that ends in *-s* and one that has no ending. The third-person subjects—*he, she, it*—and singular nouns always use the form that ends in *-s*. First-person subjects (*I*), second-person subjects (*you*), and plural subjects use the form with no ending.

In the Real World, Why Is It Important to Correct Errors in Subject-Verb Agreement?

People outside the English classroom notice subject-verb agreement errors and consider them major mistakes.

SITUATION: Regina Toms (name changed) wrote the following brief report about a company employee whom she was sending to the employee assistance program. These programs help workers with various problems, such as alcoholism or mental illness, that may affect their job performance.

Mr. XXX, who has been a model employee of the company for five years, have recently behaved in ways that is inappropriate. For example, last week he was rude when a colleague asked him a question. He has been late to work several times and has missed work more often than usual. When I spoke to him about his behavior and asked if he have problems, he admitted that he had been drinking more than usual. I would like him to speak to someone who understand more about this than I do.

WRITER AT WORK

When Walter Scanlon, program and workplace consultant, received Regina's report, he responded in this way:

WALTER SCANLON'S RESPONSE: I immediately formed an opinion of her based on this short piece of correspondence: that she was either not well educated or not considerate of the addressee. Ms. Toms may indeed be intelligent and considerate, but those qualities are not reflected in this report. In this fast-paced world we live in, rapid-fire e-mails and brief telephone conversations are likely to be our first mode of contact. Since one never gets a second chance to make a first impression, make the first one count!

(See Walter's **PROFILE OF SUCCESS** on p. 215.)

Find and Correct Errors in Subject-Verb Agreement

To find problems with subject-verb agreement in your own writing, look for five trouble spots that often signal these problems.

1. The Verb Is a Form of *Be, Have,* or *Do*

The verbs *be, have,* and *do* do not follow the rules for forming singular and plural forms; they are **irregular verbs**.

Forms of the Verb *Be*

PRESENT TENSE	SINGULAR	PLURAL
First person	I am	we are
Second person	you are	you are
Third person	she, he, it is	they are
	the student is	the students are

PAST TENSE		
First person	I was	we were
Second person	you were	you were
Third person	she, he, it was	they were
	the student was	the students were

Forms of the Verb *Have,* Present Tense

	SINGULAR	PLURAL
First person	I have	we have
Second person	you have	you have
Third person	she, he, it has	they have
	the student has	the students have

Forms of the Verb *Do*, Present Tense

	SINGULAR	PLURAL
First person	I do	we do
Second person	you do	you do
Third person	she, he, it does	they do
	the student does	the students do

These verbs cause problems for writers who in conversation use the same form in all cases: *He do the cleaning; they do the cleaning.* People also sometimes use the word *be* instead of the correct form of *be*: *She be on vacation.*

In college and at work, use the correct forms of the verbs *be*, *have*, and *do* as shown in the charts above.

They ~~is~~ *are* sick today.

Joan ~~have~~ *has* the best jewelry.

Carlos ~~do~~ *does* the laundry every Wednesday.

FINDING AND FIXING PROBLEMS WITH SUBJECT-VERB AGREEMENT:
Making Subjects and Verbs Agree When the Verb Is *Be, Have,* or *Do*

Find

<u>I</u> (am / is / are) a true believer in naps.

1. **Underline** the subject.
2. **Ask:** Is the subject in the first (*I*), second (*you*), or third person (*he/she*)? *First person.*
3. **Ask:** Is the subject singular or plural? *Singular.*

Fix

<u>I</u> (**am**)/ is / are) a true believer in naps.

4. **Choose** the verb by matching it to the form of the subject (first person, singular).

THE FOUR MOST SERIOUS ERRORS
Find and Correct Errors in Subject-Verb Agreement 381

PRACTICE 1 Identifying Problems with Subject-Verb Agreement

Find and underline the four problems with subject-verb agreement in Regina Toms's report on page 378.

PRACTICE 2 Using the Correct Form of *Be, Have,* or *Do*

In each sentence, underline the subject of the verb *be, have,* or *do*, and fill in the correct form of the verb indicated in parentheses.

EXAMPLE: She ___has___ (*have*) often looked at the stars on clear, dark nights.

1. Stars ___are___ (*be*) clustered together in constellations.
2. Every constellation ___has___ (*have*) a name.
3. I ___do___ (*do*) not know how they got their names.
4. Most constellations ___do___ (*do*) not look much like the people or creatures they represent.
5. You ___have___ (*have*) to use your imagination to see the pictures in the stars.
6. Twelve constellations ___are___ (*be*) signs of the zodiac.
7. One ___is___ (*be*) supposed to look like a crab.
8. Other star clusters ___have___ (*have*) the names of characters from ancient myths.
9. Orion, the hunter, ___is___ (*be*) the only one I can recognize.
10. He ___does___ (*do*) not look like a hunter to me.

TIP For more practices on subject-verb agreement, visit *Exercise Central* at **bedfordstmartins.com/realwriting**.

2. Words Come between the Subject and the Verb

When the subject and verb are not directly next to each other, it is more difficult to find them to make sure they agree. Most often, either a prepositional phrase or a dependent clause comes between the subject and the verb.

PREPOSITIONAL PHRASE BETWEEN THE SUBJECT AND THE VERB

A **prepositional phrase** starts with a preposition and ends with a noun or pronoun: I took my bag *of books* and threw it *across the room*.

The subject of a sentence is never in a prepositional phrase. When you are looking for the subject of a sentence, you can cross out any prepositional phrases.

TIP For a list of common prepositions, see page 344.

THE FOUR MOST SERIOUS ERRORS

382 Chapter 22 • Problems with Subject-Verb Agreement

A volunteer ~~in the Peace Corps~~ (serve / **serves**) two years.

FINDING AND FIXING PROBLEMS WITH SUBJECT-VERB AGREEMENT:
Making Subjects and Verbs Agree When They Are Separated by a Prepositional Phrase

Find

Learners ~~with dyslexia~~ (face / faces) many challenges.

1. **Underline** the subject.
2. **Cross out** any prepositional phrase that follows the subject.
3. **Ask:** Is the subject singular or plural? *Plural.*

Fix

Learners with dyslexia (**face** / faces) many challenges.

4. **Choose** the form of the verb that matches the subject.

PRACTICE 3 Making Subjects and Verbs Agree When They Are Separated by a Prepositional Phrase

In each of the following sentences, cross out the prepositional phrase between the subject and the verb, and circle the correct form of the verb. Remember that the subject of a sentence is never in a prepositional phrase.

EXAMPLE: Tomatoes ~~from the supermarket~~ (is / **are**) often tasteless.

1. Experts ~~in agriculture and plant science~~ (identifies / **identify**) several reasons ~~for flavorless tomatoes~~.

2. ~~First,~~ many commercial growers ~~in the United States~~ (chooses / **choose**) crop yield over taste.

3. Specially engineered breeds ~~of tomatoes~~ (produces / **produce**) many more bushels per planting ~~than traditional breeds do~~.

4. Unfortunately, the tomatoes ~~inside each bushel~~ (tastes / **taste**) nothing like their sweet, juicy homegrown relatives.

5. Growing conditions ~~at commercial farms~~ also (contributes / **contribute**) to the problem.

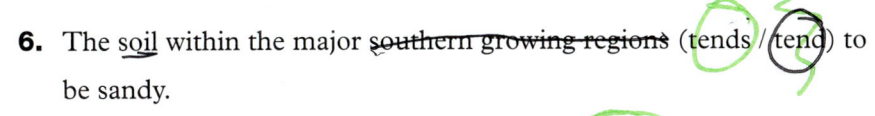

6. The soil within the major ~~southern growing regions~~ (tends / tend) to be sandy.

7. Sandy soil because of ~~its low nutrient levels~~ (results / result) in ~~less-flavorful tomatoes.~~

8. One way around the tasteless supermarket tomato (is / are) to purchase local ~~farm-stand tomatoes.~~

9. Also, many gardeners ~~across the country~~ (grows / grow) delicious tomatoes ~~on their own land.~~

10. Tomatoes from farm stands or home gardens (lasts / last) through the winter when they are canned.

DEPENDENT CLAUSE BETWEEN THE SUBJECT AND THE VERB

A **dependent clause** has a subject and a verb, but it does not express a complete thought. When a dependent clause comes between the subject and the verb, it usually starts with the word *who, whose, whom, that,* or *which*.

The subject of a sentence is never in a dependent clause. When you are looking for the subject of a sentence, you can cross out any dependent clauses.

The coins ~~that I found last week~~ (seem / seems) valuable.

FINDING AND FIXING PROBLEMS WITH SUBJECT-VERB AGREEMENT:
Making Subjects and Verbs Agree When They Are Separated by a Dependent Clause

Find

The security systems ~~that shopping sites on the Internet provide~~ (is / are) surprisingly effective.

1. **Underline** the subject.
2. **Cross out** any dependent clause that follows the subject. (Look for the words *who, whose, whom, that,* and *which* because they can signal such a clause.)
3. **Ask:** Is the subject singular or plural? *Plural.*

Fix

The security systems that shopping sites on the Internet provide (is / are) surprisingly effective.

4. **Choose** the form of the verb that matches the subject.

THE FOUR MOST SERIOUS ERRORS

384   Chapter 22 • Problems with Subject-Verb Agreement

PRACTICE 4   Making Subjects and Verbs Agree When They Are Separated by a Dependent Clause

In each of the following sentences, cross out any dependent clauses. Then, correct any problems with subject-verb agreement. If the subject and the verb agree, write "OK" next to the sentence.

> **EXAMPLE:** My cousins ~~who immigrated to this country from Ecuador~~ **has** jobs in a fast-food restaurant. *(have)*

1. The restaurant that hired my cousins are not treating them fairly.
2. People who work in the kitchen has to report to work at 7:00 a.m.
3. The boss who supervises the morning shift tells the workers not to punch in until 9:00 a.m.
4. The benefits that full-time workers earn have not been offered to my cousins.
5. Ramón, whose hand was injured slicing potatoes, need to have physical therapy.
6. No one who works with him has helped him file for worker's compensation.
7. The doctors who cleaned his wound and put in his stitches at the hospital expects him to pay for the medical treatment.
8. The managers who run the restaurant insists that he is not eligible for medical coverage.
9. My cousins, whose English is not yet perfect, feels unable to leave their jobs.
10. The restaurant that treats them so badly offers the only opportunity for them to earn a living.

3. The Sentence Has a Compound Subject

A **compound subject** is two (or more) subjects joined by *and*, *or*, or *nor*.

And/Or Rule: If two subjects are joined by *and*, use a plural verb. If two subjects are joined by *or* (or *nor*), they are considered separate, and the verb should agree with whatever subject it is closer to.

Plural subject = Plural verb

The <u>teacher</u> *and* her <u>aide</u> <u>grade</u> all the exams.

TIP Whenever you see a compound subject joined by *and*, try replacing it in your mind with *they*.

THE FOUR MOST SERIOUS ERRORS
Find and Correct Errors in Subject-Verb Agreement

Subject *or* Singular subject = Singular verb

Either the teacher *or* her aide grades all the exams.

Subject *or* Plural subject = Plural verb

The teacher *or* her aides grade all the exams.

Subject *nor* Plural subject = Plural verb

Neither the teacher *nor* her aides grade all the exams.

FINDING AND FIXING PROBLEMS WITH SUBJECT-VERB AGREEMENT:
Making Subjects and Verbs Agree in a Sentence with a Compound Subject

Find

Watermelon (or) cantaloupe (makes / make) a delicious and healthy snack.

1. **Underline** the subjects.
2. **Circle** the word between the subjects.
3. **Ask:** Does that word join the subjects to make them plural or keep them separate? *Keeps them separate.*
4. **Ask:** Is the subject that is closer to the verb singular or plural? *Singular.*

Fix

Watermelon or cantaloupe (makes)/ make) a delicious and healthy snack.

5. **Choose** the verb form that agrees with the subject that is closer to the verb.

PRACTICE 5 Choosing the Correct Verb in a Sentence with a Compound Subject

In each of the following sentences, underline the word (*and* or *or*) that joins the parts of the compound subject. Then, circle the correct form of the verb.

EXAMPLE: My mother <u>and</u> my sister (has /(have)) asked a nutritionist for advice on a healthy diet.

Seeing Subject-Verb Agreement Errors

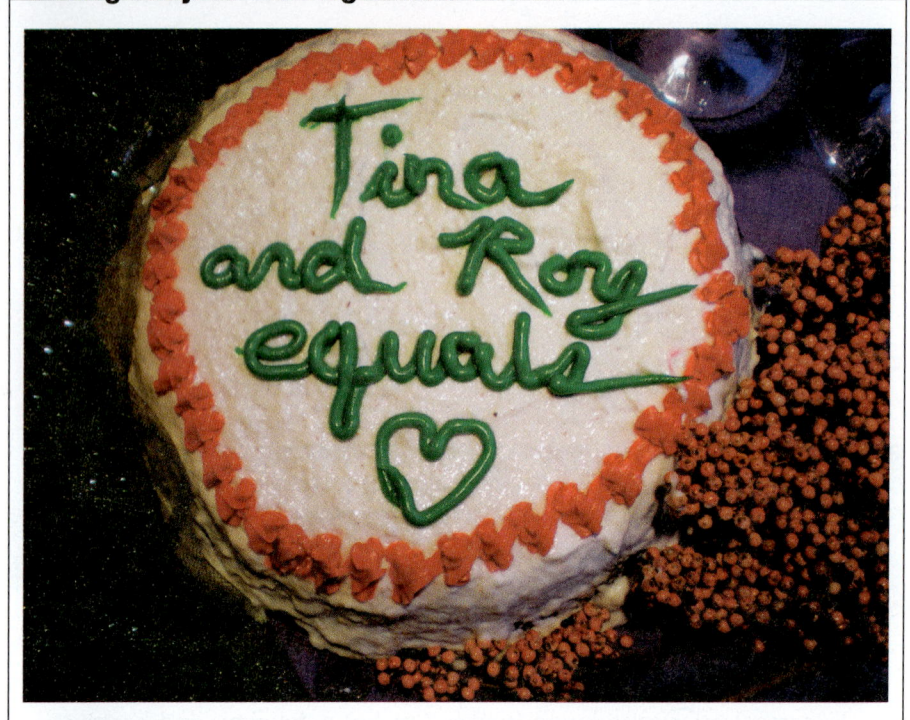

write What is wrong with the verb here? Write two sentences—one with a compound subject joined by *and* and one with a compound subject joined by *or*. Make sure the verbs agree with the subjects.

1. A tomato and a watermelon (shares / share) more than just red-colored flesh.

2. A cooked tomato or a slice of watermelon (contains / contain) a nutrient called lycopene that seems to protect the human body from some diseases.

3. Fruits and vegetables (is / are) an important part of a healthy diet, most experts agree.

4. Nutrition experts and dietitians (believes / believe) that eating a variety of colors of fruits and vegetables is best for human health.

5. Collard greens or spinach (provides / provide) vitamins, iron, and protection from blindness to those who eat them.

6. Carrots and yellow squash (protects / protect) against cancer and some kinds of skin damage.

7. Too often, a busy college student or worker (finds / find) it hard to eat the recommended five to nine servings of fruits and vegetables a day.

8. A fast-food restaurant or vending machine (is / are) unlikely to have many fresh vegetable and fruit selections.

9. A salad or fresh fruit (costs / cost) more than a hamburger in many places where hurried people eat.

10. Nevertheless, a brightly colored vegetable and fruit (adds / add) vitamins and healthy fiber to any meal.

4. The Subject Is an Indefinite Pronoun

An **indefinite pronoun** replaces a general person, place, or thing or a general group of people, places, or things. Indefinite pronouns are often singular, although there are some exceptions, as shown in the chart below.

SINGULAR	Everyone wants the semester to end.
PLURAL	Many want the semester to end.
SINGULAR	Either of the meals is good.

Often, an indefinite pronoun is followed by a prepositional phrase or dependent clause. Remember that the verb of a sentence must agree with the subject of the sentence, and the subject of a sentence is *never in a prepositional phrase or dependent clause*. To choose the correct verb, cross out the prepositional phrase or dependent clause.

Everyone ~~in all the classes~~ (want / wants) the term to end.

Several ~~who have to take the math exam~~ (is / are) studying together.

Indefinite Pronouns

ALWAYS SINGULAR			MAY BE SINGULAR OR PLURAL
another	everybody	no one	all
anybody	everyone	nothing	any
anyone	everything	one (of)	none
anything	much	somebody	some
each (of)*	neither (of)*	someone	
either (of)*	nobody	something	

*When one of these words is the subject, mentally replace it with *one*. *One* is singular and takes a singular verb.

FINDING AND FIXING PROBLEMS WITH SUBJECT-VERB AGREEMENT:
Making Subjects and Verbs Agree When the Subject Is an Indefinite Pronoun

Find

One ~~of my best friends~~ (lives / live) in California.

1. **Underline** the subject.
2. **Cross out** any prepositional phrase or dependent clause that follows the subject.
3. **Ask:** Is the subject singular or plural? *Singular.*

Fix

One of my best friends (**lives**/ live) in California.

4. **Choose** the verb form that agrees with the subject.

PRACTICE 6   Choosing the Correct Verb When the Subject Is an Indefinite Pronoun

In each of the following sentences, cross out any prepositional phrase or dependent clause that comes between the subject and the verb. Then, underline the subject, and circle the correct verb.

EXAMPLE: One ~~of the strangest human experiences~~ (**results**/ result) from the "small-world" phenomenon.

1. Everyone (**remembers**/ remember) ~~an example of a "small-world"~~ phenomenon.   *no*
2. Someone whom you ~~have just met~~ (**tells**/ tell) you a story.
3. During the story, ~~one~~ of you (**realizes**/ realize) that you are connected somehow.
4. One of your friends (**lives**/ live) next door ~~to the person~~.
5. Someone ~~in your family~~ (**knows**/ know) someone ~~in the person's family~~.
6. Each of your families (**owns**/ own) a home ~~in the same place~~.
7. One of your relatives (**plans**/ plan) to ~~marry his cousin~~.

8. Some (believes / **believe**) that if ~~you~~ "you" know one hundred people and talk to someone who knows one hundred people, together you are linked to one million people ~~through friends and acquaintances~~.

9. Someone in this class probably (**connects** / connect) to you ~~in one way or another~~.

10. Each of you probably (**knows** / know) a good "small-world" story ~~of your own~~.

5. The Verb Comes before the Subject

In most sentences, the subject comes before the verb. Two kinds of sentences often reverse the usual subject-verb order: questions and sentences that begin with *here* or *there*. In these two types of sentences, check carefully for errors in subject-verb agreement.

QUESTIONS

In questions, the verb or part of the verb comes before the subject. To find the subject and verb, you can turn the question around as if you were going to answer it.

Where is the bookstore? / The bookstore is . . .

Are you excited? / You are excited.

LANGUAGE NOTE: For reference charts showing how to form questions, see pages 512–14 and pages 515–18, in Chapter 30.

NOTE: Sometimes the verb in a sentence appears before the subject even in sentences that are not questions:

Most inspiring of all were her speeches on freedom.

SENTENCES THAT BEGIN WITH *HERE* OR *THERE*

When a sentence begins with *here* or *there,* the subject often follows the verb. Turn the sentence around to find the subject and verb.

Here is your key to the apartment. / Your key to the apartment is here.

There are four keys on the table. / Four keys are on the table.

FINDING AND FIXING PROBLEMS WITH SUBJECT-VERB AGREEMENT:
Making Subjects and Verbs Agree When the Verb Comes before the Subject

Find

What classes (is / are) the professor teaching?

There (is / are) two good classes in the music department.

1. If the sentence is a question, **turn the question into a statement**: *The professor (is/are) teaching the classes.*
2. If the sentence begins with *here* or *there*, **turn it around**: *Two good classes (is/are) in the music department.*
3. **Identify** the subject in each of the two new sentences. *It is "professor" in the first sentence and "classes" in the second.*
4. **Ask:** Is the subject singular or plural? *"Professor" is singular; "classes" is plural.*

Fix

What classes (**is**/ are) the professor teaching?

There (is / **are**) two good classes in the music department.

5. **Choose** the form of the verb in each sentence that matches the subject.

PRACTICE 7 Correcting a Sentence When the Verb Comes before the Subject

Correct any problem with subject-verb agreement in the following sentences. If a sentence is already correct, write "OK" next to it.

EXAMPLE: What electives ~~do~~ *does* the school offer?

1. What are the best reason to study music?
2. There is several good reasons.
3. There is evidence that music helps students with math.
4. What is your favorite musical instrument?
5. Here is a guitar, a saxophone, and a piano.
6. There is very few people with natural musical ability.
7. What time of day does you usually practice?

8. There is no particular time.

9. What musician does you admire most?

10. Here are some information about the importance of regular practice.

Edit for Subject-Verb Agreement

Use the chart on page 396, Finding and Fixing Problems with Subject-Verb Agreement, to help you complete the practices in this section and edit your own writing.

PRACTICE 8 Correcting Various Subject-Verb Agreement Problems

In the following sentences, identify any verb that does not agree with its subject. Then, correct the sentence using the correct form of the verb.

EXAMPLE: Some twenty-somethings in Washington, D.C., ~~wakes~~ *wake* before dawn to read the news.

1. They does so, not out of interest in current events.
2. Instead, their jobs in government and business requires them to read and summarize the latest information related to these jobs.
3. Each of their bosses need this information early in the morning to be prepared for the day.
4. For example, a politician who introduces new legislation want to know the public's reaction as soon as possible.
5. Learning of new complaints about such legislation by 8 a.m. give the politician time to shape a thoughtful response for a 10 a.m. news conference.
6. What is the benefits of the reading-and-summarizing job?
7. There is several, according to the young people who do such work.
8. Information and power goes together, some of them say.
9. A reputation for being in-the-know help them rise through the ranks at their workplaces.
10. Also, they has a chance to build skills and connections that can lead to other jobs.

PRACTICE 9 Editing Paragraphs for Subject-Verb Agreement

Find and correct six problems with subject-verb agreement in the following paragraphs.

(1) You probably does not have a mirror at your computer desk, but if you did, you might notice something about yourself you had not been aware of before. (2) As you sit there, hour after hour, your shoulders are rounded, your back is slumped, and your posture are awful.

(3) Do not worry; you are not alone. (4) Most students spend hours in front of a computer monitor with terrible posture. (5) Then, they make things worse by getting up and heading off to school with painfully heavy backpacks on their backs. (6) Young people who carry a heavy burden is forced to hunch forward even more to balance the weight, adding strain to already seriously fatigued muscles. (7) Everyone who studies these trends are concerned.

(8) The study of people and their surroundings is known as ergonomics. (9) Improperly slouching at the computer and toting around a heavy backpack are both examples of poor ergonomics. (10) These bad habits is two causes of chronic back pain that can interfere with school, work, and sports. (11) Everyone, according to experts, need to sit up straight while at the computer, take frequent breaks to get up and walk around, and carry less in his or her backpack.

PRACTICE 10 Editing Subject-Verb Agreement Errors and Using Formal English

A friend of yours has been turned down for a course because of high enrollment, even though she registered early. She knows that her e-mail to the instructor teaching the course has a few problems in it. Help her by correcting any subject-verb agreement errors. Then, edit the informal English in the e-mail.

TIP For more advice on using formal English, see Chapter 2. For advice on choosing appropriate words, see Chapter 31.

(1) Hey Prof Connors,

(2) I am e-mailing you to make sure you gets the e-mail I sent before about registering for your Business Writing course this semester. (3) IMHO, it is one of the best classes this college offers. (4) I does not miss the deadline; I signed up on the first day, in fact. (5) I plans to graduate with a degree in business and economics, so your class is important to me.

(6) Could you please check yur class roster to see if I was somehow skipped or missed? (7) I would sure appreciate it a ton, LOL. (8) Plz let me know what you finds out. (9) If I cannot get into your class this semester, I will have to rearrange my schedule so that I can takes it next semester instead. (10) I look forward to taking your class and learning all about business writing. (11) You rocks, prof.

(12) Sincerely,

Cameron Taylor

PRACTICE 11 Editing Regina's Report

Look back at Regina Toms's report on page 378. You may have already underlined the subject-verb agreement errors; if not, do so now. Next, using what you have learned in this chapter, correct each error.

PRACTICE 12 Editing Your Own Writing for Subject-Verb Agreement

Edit for subject-verb agreement problems in a piece of your own writing—a paper for this course or another one, or something you have written for work or your everyday life. Use the chart on page 396 to help you.

Chapter Review

1. The _____ and the _____ in a sentence must agree (match) in terms of number. They must both be _____, or they must both be plural.

2. Five trouble spots can cause errors in subject-verb agreement:

   When the verb is a form of _____, _____, or _____.

   When a _____ or a _____ comes between the subject and the verb.

   When the sentence has a _____ subject joined by *and*, *or*, or *nor*.

   When the subject is an _____ pronoun.

   When the _____ comes _____ the subject.

LEARNING JOURNAL If you found errors in subject-verb agreement in your writing, were they one of the trouble spots (pp. 379–90)? What is the main thing you have learned about subject-verb agreement that you will use? What is one thing that remains unclear?

THE FOUR MOST SERIOUS ERRORS

Chapter 22 • Problems with Subject-Verb Agreement

Chapter Test

Circle the correct choice for each of the following items. For help, refer to the Finding and Fixing Problems with Subject-Verb Agreement chart on page 396.

1. If an underlined portion of this sentence is incorrect, select the revision that fixes it. If the sentence is correct as written, choose d.

    There <u>is</u> only certain times when <u>you can</u> call to get technical
        A   B   C
    support for this computer.

    a. There are   c. getting
    b. you could   d. No change is necessary.

2. Choose the correct word to fill in the blank.

    Dana's dog Bernard _____ just a puppy, but he moves so slowly that he seems old.

    a. be   c. being
    b. am   d. is

3. If an underlined portion of this sentence is incorrect, select the revision that fixes it. If the sentence is correct as written, choose d.

    The <u>umpire was</u> not happy to see that <u>everyone were</u> watching
           A   B
    him <u>argue with</u> the baseball player.
            C

    a. umpire were   c. argues with
    b. everyone was   d. No change is necessary.

4. Choose the correct word to fill in the blank.

    The woman who rented us our kayaks _____ now paddling her own kayak down the river.

    a. are   b. be   c. is

5. Choose the item that has no errors.

    a. Alex and Dane likes to travel now that they have retired from their jobs.
    b. Alex and Dane liking to travel now that they have retired from their jobs.
    c. Alex and Dane like to travel now that they have retired from their jobs.

6. Choose the correct word to fill in the blank.

   The builders of this house _____ used the best materials they could find.

   a. have   b. having   c. has

7. Choose the correct word to fill in the blank.

   The calm before hurricanes _____ most people with anxiety.

   a. fill   b. filling   c. fills

8. Choose the item that has no errors.
   a. Sheryl and her sons go to the beach whenever they can find the time.
   b. Sheryl and her sons goes to the beach whenever they can find the time.
   c. Sheryl and her sons is going to the beach whenever they can find the time.

9. Choose the correct word to fill in the blank.

   Where _____ the children's wet swimsuits?

   a. are   b. is   c. be

10. If an underlined portion of this sentence is incorrect, select the revision that fixes it. If the sentence is correct as written, choose d.

    Anybody who can speak several languages are in great demand to
                    A   B
    work for the government, especially in foreign embassies.
    C

    a. could   c. working
    b. is   d. No change is necessary.

THE FOUR MOST SERIOUS ERRORS

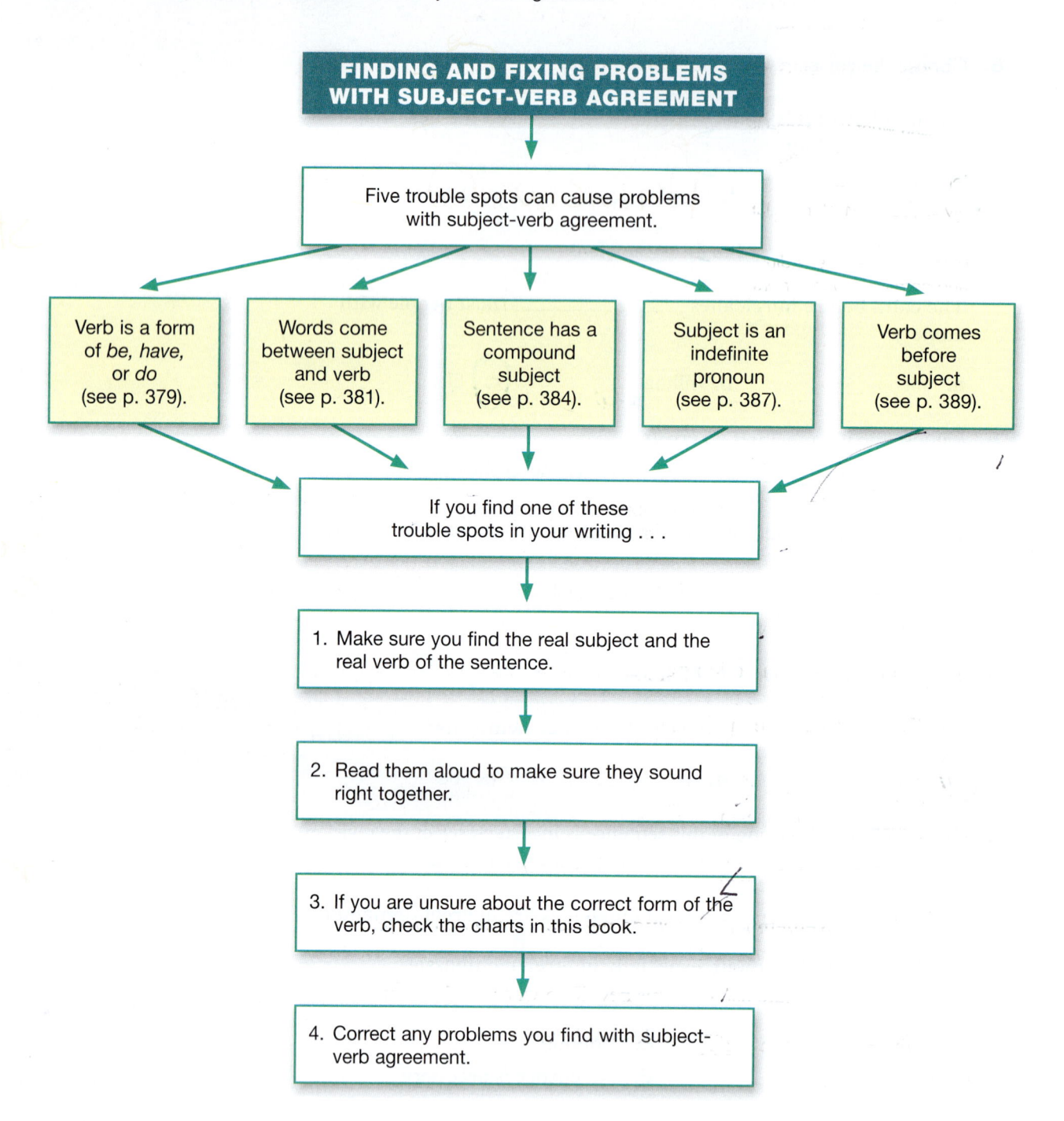

Chapter 22 • Problems with Subject-Verb Agreement

FINDING AND FIXING PROBLEMS WITH SUBJECT-VERB AGREEMENT

Five trouble spots can cause problems with subject-verb agreement.

- Verb is a form of *be*, *have*, or *do* (see p. 379).
- Words come between subject and verb (see p. 381).
- Sentence has a compound subject (see p. 384).
- Subject is an indefinite pronoun (see p. 387).
- Verb comes before subject (see p. 389).

If you find one of these trouble spots in your writing . . .

1. Make sure you find the real subject and the real verb of the sentence.

2. Read them aloud to make sure they sound right together.

3. If you are unsure about the correct form of the verb, check the charts in this book.

4. Correct any problems you find with subject-verb agreement.

23

Verb Tense

EVER THOUGHT THIS?

"I hear the word *tense* and I get all tense. I don't understand all the terms."
—Ken Hargreaves, Student

This chapter
- explains what *verb tense* is.
- explains the present and past tenses of verbs.
- gives you a list of irregular verbs.
- gives you practice finding and correcting verb errors.

Using Verbs to Express Different Times

Understand What Verb Tense Is

Verb tense tells *when* an action happened: in the past, in the present, or in the future. Verbs change their **base form** or use the helping verbs *have, be,* or *will* to indicate different tenses.

PRESENT TENSE	Rick hikes every weekend.
PAST TENSE	He hiked 10 miles last weekend.
FUTURE TENSE	He will hike again on Saturday.

✓ **LearningCurve**
Verbs; Active and Passive Voice
bedfordstmartins
.com/realwriting/LC

LANGUAGE NOTE: Remember to include needed endings on present-tense and past-tense verbs, even if they are not noticed in speech.

| PRESENT TENSE | Nate listens to his new iPod wherever he goes. |
| PAST TENSE | Nate listened to his iPod while he walked the dog. |

In the Real World, Why Is It Important to Use the Correct Verb Tense?

People outside the English classroom notice errors in verb tense and consider them major mistakes.

SITUATION: Cal is a summer intern in the systems division of a large company. He would like to get a part-time job there during the school year because he is studying computer science and knows that the experience would help him get a job after graduation. He sends this e-mail to his supervisor.

397

THE FOUR MOST SERIOUS ERRORS

Chapter 23 • Verb Tense

I have work hard since coming to Technotron and learn many new things. Mr. Joseph tell me that he likes my work and that I shown good motivation and teamwork. As he knows I spended many hours working on a special project for him. I would like to continue my work here beyond the summer. Therefore, I hope that you will consider me for future employment.

Sincerely,

Cal Troppo

WRITER AT WORK

Karen Upright, systems manager, read Cal's e-mail and made the following comments:

KAREN UPRIGHT'S RESPONSE: I would probably not hire him because of the many errors in his writing. While he is in school, he should take a writing course and learn more about using correct verbs and verb tenses. Otherwise, his writing will be a barrier to his employment, not just at Procter & Gamble, but anywhere.

(See Karen's **PROFILE OF SUCCESS** on p. 140.)

Practice Using Correct Verbs

TIP To find and correct problems with verbs, you need to be able to identify subjects and verbs. For a review, see Chapter 19.

This section will teach you about verb tenses and give you practice with using them. The best way to learn how to use the various verb tenses correctly, however, is to read, write, and speak them as often as possible.

PRACTICE 1 Identifying Verb Errors

Find and underline the seven verb errors in Cal's e-mail above.

Regular Verbs

Most verbs in English are **regular verbs** that follow standard rules about what endings to use to express time.

PRESENT-TENSE ENDINGS: -S AND NO ENDING

TIP A complete verb, also known as a verb phrase, is made up of the main verb and all of its helping verbs.

The **present tense** is used for actions that are happening at the same time that they are being written about (the present) and for things that happen all the time. Present-tense, regular verbs either end in -s or have no ending added.

THE FOUR MOST SERIOUS ERRORS
Practice Using Correct Verbs

-S ENDING	NO ENDING
jumps	jump
walks	walk
lives	live

Use the *-s* ending when the subject is *he*, *she*, *it*, or the name of one person or thing. Use no ending for all other subjects.

Regular Verbs in the Present Tense

	SINGULAR	PLURAL
First person	I jump.	We jump.
Second person	You jump.	You jump.
Third person	She (he, it) jumps.	They jump.
	The child jumps.	The children jump.

TIP For more about making verbs match subjects, see Chapter 22. For more about using present-tense and past-tense verbs, see Chapter 30.

Do not confuse the simple present tense with the **present progressive**, which is used with a form of the helping verb *be* to describe actions that are in progress right now.

SIMPLE PRESENT	I eat a banana every day.
PRESENT PROGRESSIVE	I am eating a banana.

TIP In the examples throughout this chapter, subjects are underlined, and verbs are double-underlined.

LANGUAGE NOTE: Some languages do not use progressive tenses. If you have trouble using progressive tenses, see Chapter 30.

PRACTICE 2 Using Present-Tense Regular Verbs Correctly

In each of the following sentences, first underline the subject, and then circle the correct verb form.

TIP For more practices on verb problems, visit *Exercise Central* at bedfordstmartins.com/realwriting.

EXAMPLE: I (tries /(try)) to keep to my budget.

1. My classes (requires /(require)) much of my time these days.
2. In addition to attending school, I (works /(work)) 20 hours a week in the college library.
3. The other employees (agrees /(agree)) that the work atmosphere is pleasant.
4. Sometimes, we even (manages /(manage)) to do homework at the library.

400 Chapter 23 • Verb Tense

5. The job (**pays** / pay) a fairly low wage, however.
6. My roommate (**helps** / help) with the rent on the apartment.
7. Because he is not in school, he often (**wonders** / wonder) how I get by.
8. I (uses / **use**) my bicycle to get everywhere I need to go.
9. The bicycle (**allows** / allow) me to stay in shape both physically and financially.
10. I know that I will not be in school forever, so for now, life on a budget (**satisfies** / satisfy) me.

ONE REGULAR PAST-TENSE ENDING: -ED

The **past tense** is used for actions that have already happened. An *-ed* ending is needed on all regular verbs in the past tense.

	PRESENT TENSE	PAST TENSE
First person	I avoid her.	I avoid**ed** her.
Second person	You help me.	You help**ed** me.
Third person	He walks quickly.	He walk**ed** quickly.

TIP If a verb already ends in *-e*, just add *-d*: dance / danced. If a verb ends in *-y*, usually the *-y* changes to *-i* when *-ed* is added: spy / spied; try / tried.

PRACTICE 3 Using the Past Tense of Regular Verbs Correctly

In each of the following sentences, fill in the correct past-tense forms of the verbs in parentheses.

(1) Last winter, I **displayed** (display) the clear signs of a cold. (2) I **sneezed** (sneeze) often, and I **developed** (develop) a sore throat. (3) The congestion in my nose and throat **annoyed** (annoy) me, and it **seemed** (seem) that blowing my nose was useless. (4) However, I **visited** (visit) with my friends and **attended** (attend) classes at college. (5) I **assumed** (assume) that I could not give anyone else my cold once I showed the symptoms. (6) Unfortunately, many people **joined** (join) me in my misery because of my ignorance. (7) Later, I **learned** (learn) that I **remained** (remain) contagious for several days after I first showed symptoms. (8) My doctor **explained** (explain) to me that I **started** (start) spreading my cold about one day after I became infected with it. (9) However, after my symptoms **disappeared** (disappear), I **passed** (pass) on my cold to others for up to three days more. (10) I **wanted** (want) to apologize to everyone I had

infected, but I also __realized__ (realize) that others had given me their colds as well.

ONE REGULAR PAST-PARTICIPLE ENDING: -ED

The **past participle** is a verb that is used with a helping verb (also called a modal auxiliary), such as *have* or *be*. For all regular verbs, the past-participle form is the same as the past-tense form: It uses an *-ed* ending. (To learn about when past participles are used, see pp. 410–14.)

TIP The modal auxiliary verbs are *can, could, may, might, must, shall, should, will,* and *would*.

PAST TENSE	PAST PARTICIPLE
My kids watched cartoons.	They have watched cartoons before.
George visited his cousins.	He has visited them every year.

PRACTICE 4 Using the Past Participle of Regular Verbs Correctly

In each of the following sentences, underline the helping verb (a form of *have*), and fill in the correct form of the verb in parentheses.

EXAMPLE: Because of pressure to keep up with others, families have ___started___ (*start*) to give fancier and fancier birthday parties.

1. We have all __received__ (*receive*) invitations to simple birthday parties where children played games and had cake, but those days are gone.
2. Kids' birthday parties have __turned__ (*turn*) into complicated and expensive events.
3. Price tags for some of these parties have __climbed__ (*climb*) to $1,000 or more.
4. By the time she had finished planning her daughter's birthday, one mother had __devoted__ (*devote*) hundreds of dollars to the event.
5. She discovered that she had __handed__ (*hand*) out $50 for a clubhouse rental, $200 for a cotton-candy maker, and $300 for an actor dressed as Woody from *Toy Story*.
6. The money spent on gifts has __increased__ (*increase*) as well.
7. At the end of each year, many parents find that they have __purchased__ (*purchase*) an average of twenty gifts costing $20 each — $400 total.

8. However, some families have _decided_ (decide) to go against the trend.
9. My best friend has _saved_ (save) money and effort by having small birthday parties for her son.
10. The savings have _reached_ (reach) $500, and she is putting the money toward his college education.

Irregular Verbs

Irregular verbs do not follow the simple rules of regular verbs, which have just two present-tense endings (*-s* or *-es*) and two past-tense endings (*-d* or *-ed*). Irregular verbs show past tense with a change in spelling, although some irregular verbs, such as *cost, hit,* and *put,* do not change their spelling. The most common irregular verbs are *be* and *have* (see p. 405). As you write and edit, use the following chart to make sure you use the correct form of irregular verbs.

NOTE: What is called "Present Tense" in the chart below is sometimes called the "base form of the verb."

Irregular Verbs

PRESENT TENSE (BASE FORM OF VERB)	PAST TENSE	PAST PARTICIPLE (USED WITH HELPING VERB)
be (am/are/is)	was/were	been
become	became	become
begin	began	begun
bite	bit	bitten
blow	blew	blown
break	broke	broken
bring	brought	brought
build	built	built
buy	bought	bought
catch	caught	caught
choose	chose	chosen
come	came	come
cost	cost	cost

PRESENT TENSE (BASE FORM OF VERB)	PAST TENSE	PAST PARTICIPLE (USED WITH HELPING VERB)
dive	dived, dove	dived
do	did	done
draw	drew	drawn
drink	drank	drunk
drive	drove	driven
eat	ate	eaten
fall	fell	fallen
feed	fed	fed
feel	felt	felt
fight	fought	fought
find	found	found
fly	flew	flown
forget	forgot	forgotten
get	got	gotten
give	gave	given
go	went	gone
grow	grew	grown
have/has	had	had
hear	heard	heard
hide	hid	hidden
hit	hit	hit
hold	held	held
hurt	hurt	hurt
keep	kept	kept
know	knew	known
lay	laid	laid
lead	led	led
leave	left	left
let	let	let
lie	lay	lain

PRESENT TENSE (BASE FORM OF VERB)	PAST TENSE	PAST PARTICIPLE (USED WITH HELPING VERB)
light	lit	lit
lose	lost	lost
make	made	made
mean	meant	meant
meet	met	met
pay	paid	paid
put	put	put
quit	quit	quit
read	read	read
ride	rode	ridden
ring	rang	rung
rise	rose	risen
run	ran	run
say	said	said
see	saw	seen
seek	sought	sought
sell	sold	sold
send	sent	sent
shake	shook	shaken
show	showed	shown
shrink	shrank	shrunk
shut	shut	shut
sing	sang	sung
sink	sank	sunk
sit	sat	sat
sleep	slept	slept
speak	spoke	spoken
spend	spent	spent
stand	stood	stood
steal	stole	stolen

PRESENT TENSE (BASE FORM OF VERB)	PAST TENSE	PAST PARTICIPLE (USED WITH HELPING VERB)
stick	stuck	stuck
sting	stung	stung
strike	struck	struck, stricken
swim	swam	swum
take	took	taken
teach	taught	taught
tear	tore	torn
tell	told	told
think	thought	thought
throw	threw	thrown
understand	understood	understood
wake	woke	woken
wear	wore	worn
win	won	won
write	wrote	written

PRESENT TENSE OF *BE* AND *HAVE*

The present tense of the verbs *be* and *have* is very irregular, as shown in the following chart.

Present Tense of *Be* and *Have*

BE		HAVE	
I am	we are	I have	we have
you are	you are	you have	you have
he, she, it is	they are	he, she, it has	they have
the editor is	the editors are		
Beth is	Beth and Christina are		

PRACTICE 5 Using *Be* and *Have* in the Present Tense

In each of the following sentences, fill in the correct form of the verb indicated in parentheses.

> **EXAMPLE:** Because of my university's internship program, I ____*am*____ (*be*) able to receive academic credit for my summer job.

1. I ____have____ (*have*) a job lined up with a company that provides private security to many local businesses and residential developments.
2. The company ____has____ (*have*) a good record of keeping its clients safe from crime.
3. The company ____is____ (*be*) part of a fast-growing industry.
4. Many people no longer ____have____ (*have*) faith in the ability of the police to protect them.
5. People with lots of money ____are____ (*be*) willing to pay for their own protection.
6. Concern about crime ____is____ (*be*) especially noticeable in so-called gated communities.
7. In these private residential areas, no one ____has____ (*have*) the right to enter without permission.
8. If you ____are____ (*be*) a visitor, you must obtain a special pass.
9. Once you ____have____ (*have*) the pass, you show it to the security guard when you reach the gate.
10. In a gated community, the residents ____are____ (*be*) likely to appreciate the security.

PAST TENSE OF *BE*

The past tense of the verb *be* is tricky because it has two different forms: *was* and *were*.

THE FOUR MOST SERIOUS ERRORS
Practice Using Correct Verbs

Past Tense of *Be*

	SINGULAR	PLURAL
First person	I was	we were
Second person	you were	you were
Third person	she, he, it was	they were
	the student was	the students were

PRACTICE 6 Using *Be* in the Past Tense

In the paragraph that follows, fill in each blank with the correct past tense of the verb *be*.

EXAMPLE: During college, my sister ____was____ excited about a big decision she had made.

(1) My sister ____was____ always afraid of visits to the doctor. (2) Therefore, my parents and I ____were____ surprised when she announced that she wanted to become a doctor herself. (3) We thought that medicine ____was____ a strange choice for her. (4) "Since you ____were____ a little girl, you have disliked doctors," I reminded her. (5) I ____was____ sure she would quickly change her mind. (6) She admitted that she ____was____ still afraid, but she hoped that understanding medicine would help her overcome her fears. (7) Her premedical courses in college ____were____ difficult, but finally she was accepted into medical school. (8) We ____were____ very proud of her that day, and we knew that she would be a great doctor.

PRACTICE 7 Using Irregular Verbs in the Past Tense

In the following paragraph, replace any incorrect present-tense verbs with the correct past tense of the verb. If you are unsure of the past-tense forms of irregular verbs, refer to the chart on pages 402–05.

(1) For years, Homer and Langley Collyer ~~are~~ *were* known for their strange living conditions. (2) Neighbors who passed by the brothers' New York City townhouse ~~see~~ *saw* huge piles of trash through the windows. (3) At night,

Langley roamed the streets in search of more junk. (4) In March 1947, an anonymous caller tells the police that someone had died in the Collyers' home. (5) In response, officers break through a second-floor window and tunneled through mounds of newspapers, old umbrellas, and other junk. (6) Eventually, they find the body of Homer Collyer, who seemed to have died of starvation. (7) But where was Langley? (8) In efforts to locate him, workers spend days removing trash from the house—more than one hundred tons' worth in total. (9) They bring a strange variety of items to the curb, including medical equipment, bowling balls, fourteen pianos, and the frame of a Model T car. (10) In early April, a worker finally discovered Langley's body. (11) It lies just 10 feet from where Homer had been found. (12) Apparently, Langley died while bringing food to his disabled brother. (13) As he tunneled ahead, a pile of trash falls on him and crushed him. (14) This trash was part of a booby trap that Langley had created to stop intruders. (15) Not long after the brothers' deaths, the city demolished their former home. (16) In 1965, community leaders do something that might have surprised Homer and Langley: Where the trash-filled home once stands, workers created a neat and peaceful park. (17) In the 1990s, this green space becomes the Collyer Brothers Park.

A police inspector in the Collyer brothers' home, 1947

The Collyer Brothers Park today

For irregular verbs, the past participle is often different from the past tense.

	PAST TENSE	PAST PARTICIPLE
REGULAR VERB	I walked home.	I have walked home before.
IRREGULAR VERB	I drove home.	I have driven home before.

It is difficult to predict how irregular verbs form the past participle. Until you are familiar with them, find them in the chart on pages 402–05.

PRACTICE 8 Using the Past Participle of Irregular Verbs

In each of the following sentences, fill in the correct helping verb (a form of *have*) and the correct past-participle form of the verb in parentheses. If you do not know the correct form, find the word in the chart on pages 402–05.

EXAMPLE: Even though she has passed her seventy-fourth birthday, Ernestine Shepherd ____has become____ (become) a star in the fitness world.

1. In 2010, recognizing the work Shepherd _____ (do) to build her muscles, the *Guinness Book of World Records* named her the oldest female bodybuilder.

2. Since then, Shepherd _____ (tell) many fans the story of her success.

3. She and her sister started working out in their fifties because they _____ (grow) tired of carrying extra pounds.

4. Tragically, Shepherd's sister died soon afterward; nevertheless, by the end of a long mourning period, Shepherd _____ (make) an even stronger commitment to staying in shape.

5. From that time on, she _____ (keep) a busy workout schedule.

6. For years, she _____ (run) up to 80 miles a week.

7. In addition, she _____ (get) a lot of attention for her ability to bench-press 150 pounds.

8. Since becoming a personal trainer, Shepherd _____ (teach) many other senior citizens how to stay in shape.

9. Also, she _____ (give) hope to many elderly people who want to live more active lives.

10. Throughout her busy days, Shepherd _____ (stick) to her belief that growing older does not necessarily mean growing weaker; sometimes, it can mean the exact opposite.

Past Participles

TIP For more about using perfect-tense verbs, see Chapter 30.

A **past participle**, by itself, cannot be the main verb of a sentence. When a past participle is combined with another verb, called a **helping verb**, however, it can be used to make the present perfect tense and the past perfect tense.

Have/Has + Past participle = Present perfect tense

The **present perfect** tense is used for an action that began in the past and either continues into the present or was completed at some unknown time in the past.

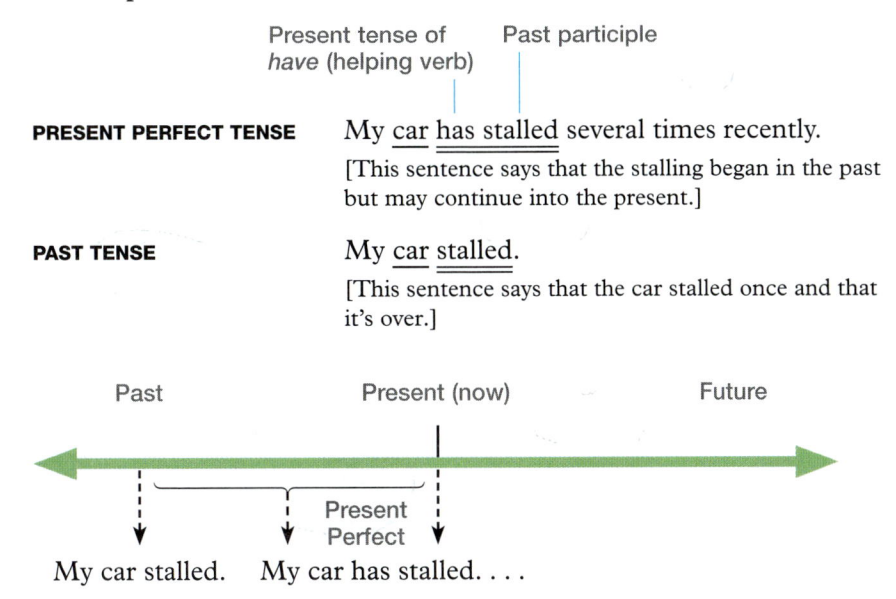

	Present tense of *have* (helping verb)	Past participle

PRESENT PERFECT TENSE   My car has stalled several times recently.
[This sentence says that the stalling began in the past but may continue into the present.]

PAST TENSE   My car stalled.
[This sentence says that the car stalled once and that it's over.]

Past — Present (now) — Future

My car stalled.   Present Perfect   My car has stalled. . . .

Present Perfect Tense

	SINGULAR	PLURAL
First person	I have laughed.	We have laughed.
Second person	You have laughed.	You have laughed.
Third person	She/he/it has laughed.	They have laughed.
	The baby has laughed.	The babies have laughed.

LANGUAGE NOTE: Be careful not to leave out *have* when it is needed for the present perfect. Time-signal words like *since* and *for* may mean that the present perfect is required.

| INCORRECT | I drive since 1985. | We wait for 2 hours. |
| CORRECT | I **have** driven since 1985. | We **have** waited for 2 hours. |

PRACTICE 9 Using the Present Perfect Tense

In each of the following sentences, circle the correct verb tense.

EXAMPLE: For many years now, the laws of most states (allowed / (have allowed)) only doctors to write prescriptions for patients.

1. In the past few years, a number of states (began / **have begun**) to allow physician assistants and nurse practitioners to write prescriptions.

2. Before the changes in the laws, physician assistants and nurse practitioners (**saw** / have seen) patients with common illnesses.

3. However, if the patients (**needed** / have needed) a prescription, a doctor had to write it.

4. Many doctors (said / **have said**) that the changes are a good idea.

5. Physician assistants and nurse practitioners (spent / **have spent**) years in training by the time they get their licenses.

6. Since the new laws took effect, physician assistants and nurse practitioners (wrote / **have written**) many common prescriptions.

7. Recently, some people (expressed / **have expressed**) concern that physician assistants and nurse practitioners might make mistakes in writing prescriptions.

8. However, the possibility of a mistake in a prescription (always existed / **has always existed**).

9. For the past several years, pharmacists (kept / **have kept**) track of prescription errors.

10. Doctors made all but one of the mistakes that they (found / **have found**) so far.

| Had | + | Past participle | = | Past perfect tense |

Use *had* plus the past participle to make the **past perfect tense**. The past perfect tense is used for an action that began in the past and ended before some other past action.

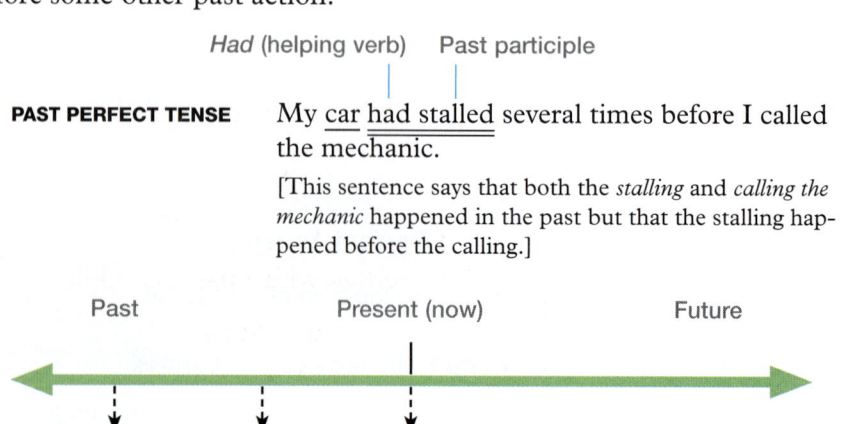

Had (helping verb)   Past participle

PAST PERFECT TENSE   My car had stalled several times before I called the mechanic.

[This sentence says that both the *stalling* and *calling the mechanic* happened in the past but that the stalling happened before the calling.]

Past — car stalled
Present (now) — mechanic called
Future

THE FOUR MOST SERIOUS ERRORS
Practice Using Correct Verbs

PRACTICE 10 Using the Past Perfect Tense

In each of the following sentences, circle the correct verb tense.

EXAMPLE: When musician Ray Charles was born in September 1930, the Great Depression already (caused / **had caused**) many Americans to lose hope.

1. His family (was / **had been**) poor even before the Great Depression started.
2. Until he was four years old, Ray (**enjoyed** / had enjoyed) normal vision.
3. However, by the time he was seven, he (became / **had become**) totally blind.
4. When he (**tripped** / had tripped) over furniture and asked for his mother's help, often she just watched him and remained silent.
5. In this way, she (**encouraged** / had encouraged) him to learn how to help himself get back up.
6. She (**came** / had come) to recognize how important it was for Ray to find his way on his own.
7. Ray later (spent / **had spent**) several years in Florida's state school for the deaf and blind.
8. By the time he left the school, he (developed / **had developed**) his unusual gift for playing, composing, and arranging music.
9. By the time he became a star, Ray Charles (refined / **had refined**) his unique musical style.
10. By the time of his death in 2004, Charles understood that he (inspired / **had inspired**) many people.

| Be | + | Past participle | = | Passive voice |

A sentence that is written in the **passive voice** has a subject that does not perform an action. Instead, the subject is acted upon. To create the passive voice, combine a form of the verb *be* with a past participle.

            Form of *be*   Past participle
            (helping verb)

PASSIVE   The newspaper was thrown onto the porch.
[The subject, *newspaper*, did not throw itself onto the porch. Some unidentified person threw the newspaper.]

Most sentences should be written in the **active voice**, which means that the subject performs the action.

ACTIVE	The delivery person threw the newspaper onto the porch.
	[The subject, *delivery person*, performed the action: He or she threw the newspaper.]

Use the passive voice when no one person performed the action, when you do not know who performed the action, or when you want to emphasize the receiver of the action. When you know who performed the action, it is usually preferable to identify the actor.

ACTIVE	The bandleader chose Kelly to do a solo.
PASSIVE	Kelly was chosen to do a solo.
	[If you wanted to emphasize Kelly's being chosen rather than the bandleader's choice, you might decide to use the passive voice.]

FINDING AND FIXING VERB-TENSE ERRORS:
Changing from Passive to Active Voice

Find

The game was turned around by (Jo Cortez's touchdown pass).

1. **Underline** the subject, and **double-underline** the verb (in this case, a form of *be* with a past participle).
2. **Circle** any word or words that describe who or what performed the action in the sentence.

Fix

Jo Cortez's touchdown pass
The game was turned around. ~~by Jo Cortez's touchdown pass.~~

3. Make the circled words the subject of the sentence, and delete the word *by*.

Jo Cortez's touchdown pass
The game ~~was~~ turned around. ~~by Jo Cortez's touchdown pass.~~

4. Change the verb from a past-participle form, using the correct tense.

Jo Cortez's touchdown pass turned the game
~~The game was turned~~ around. ~~by Jo Cortez's touchdown pass.~~

5. Move the former subject so that it receives the action.

NOTE: If you do not have specific information on who or what performed the action, you might use a general word like *someone* or *people*.

Someone left flowers
~~Flowers were left~~ on my desk.

PRACTICE 11 Changing the Passive Voice to the Active Voice

Rewrite the following sentences, changing them from the passive voice to the active voice.

EXAMPLE: ~~Funding~~ for animal shelters ~~was cut by the legislature.~~
The legislature cut funding

1. Some shelters were going to be closed by the owners.
2. What would become of the animals was unknown.
3. A campaign was started by animal lovers.
4. Interviews were given by the owners and volunteers at shelters.
5. The animals were filmed by news teams.
6. The stories were aired on all the local television stations.
7. A protest was staged by animal lovers across the state.
8. Fund-raisers of all sorts were held.
9. Some funds were restored by the legislature.
10. Enough money was raised to keep the shelters open.

Consistency of Verb Tense

Consistency of verb tense means that all actions in a sentence that happen (or happened) at the same time are in the same tense. If all the actions happen in the present or happen all the time, use the present for all verbs in the sentence. If all the actions happened in the past, use the past tense for all verbs.

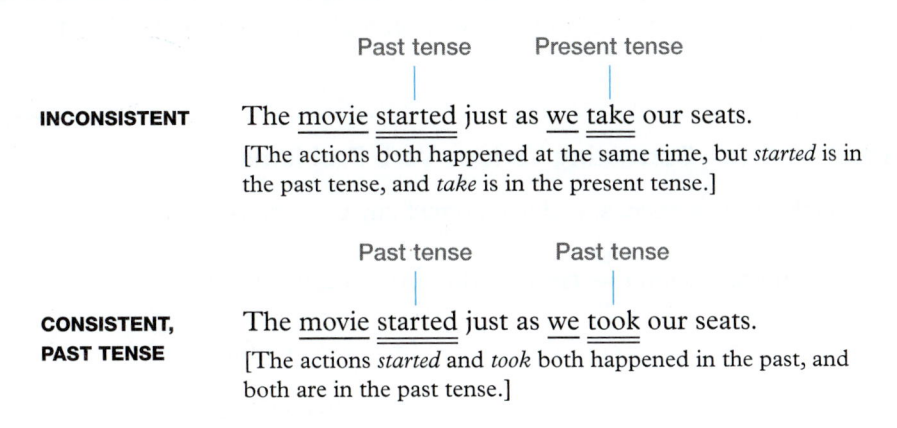

INCONSISTENT   The movie started [Past tense] just as we take [Present tense] our seats.
[The actions both happened at the same time, but *started* is in the past tense, and *take* is in the present tense.]

CONSISTENT, PAST TENSE   The movie started [Past tense] just as we took [Past tense] our seats.
[The actions *started* and *took* both happened in the past, and both are in the past tense.]

Use different tenses only when you are referring to different times.

My daughter hated math as a child, but now she loves it.
[The sentence uses two different tenses because the first verb (*hated*) refers to a past condition, whereas the second verb (*loves*) refers to a present one.]

THE FOUR MOST SERIOUS ERRORS

416 Chapter 23 • Verb Tense

PRACTICE 12 Using Consistent Verb Tense

In each of the following sentences, double-underline the verbs, and correct any unnecessary shifts in verb tense. Write the correct form of the verb in the blank space provided.

EXAMPLE: ____have____ Although some people dream of having their picture taken by a famous photographer, not many had the chance.

1. _____ Now, special stores in malls take magazine-quality photographs of anyone who wanted one.

2. _____ The founder of one business got the idea when she hear friends complaining about how bad they looked in family photographs.

3. _____ She decide to open a business to take studio-style photographs that did not cost a lot of money.

4. _____ Her first store included special lighting and offers different sets, such as colored backgrounds and outdoor scenes.

5. _____ Now, her stores even have makeup studios for people who wanted a special look for their pictures.

Edit for Verb Problems

Use the chart on page 421, Finding and Fixing Verb-Tense Errors, to help you complete the practices in this section and edit your own writing.

PRACTICE 13 Correcting Various Verb Problems

In the following sentences, find and correct any verb problems.

EXAMPLE: Sheena ~~be~~ *is* tired of the tattoo on her left shoulder.

1. Sheena had never consider a tattoo until several of her friends got them.

2. Sheena was twenty-two when she goes to the tattoo parlor.

3. After looking at many designs, she choose a purple rose design, which she gave to the tattoo artist.

4. Her sister liked the tattoo, but her mother faints.

5. Like Sheena, many people who now reached their thirties want to get rid of their old tattoos.

6. A few years ago, when a person decides to have a tattoo removed, doctors had to cut out the design.

7. That technique leaved scars.

8. Today, doctors using laser light to break up the ink molecules in the skin.

9. Six months ago, Sheena start to have treatments to remove her tattoo.

10. The procedure hurted every time she saw the doctor, but she hoped it would be worth the pain.

PRACTICE 14 Editing Paragraphs for Verb Problems

Find and correct seven problems with verb tense in the following paragraphs.

(1) When you thought about a farm, you probably imagine acres of cornfields and stalls full of noisy animals. (2) Although that is an understandable vision, it may not be a particularly accurate one in the near future. (3) Some experts believes that farms of the future will be found inside the top floors of a city's tallest skyscrapers. (4) This concept have been referred to as "vertical gardening."

(5) Indoor city gardening not only would help make places become more self-sufficient but also could provide new uses for the variety of abandoned buildings that are finded scattered throughout large cities. (6) Experts has suggested that the water used for these small farms and gardens could be recycled from indoor fishponds. (7) False sunlight could be created through the use of artificial lights. (8) Thermostats could control the indoor temperatures.

(9) Although this technology is not currently available, architects has been toying with possible designs. (10) In the future, farms will most likely include everything from solar panels and windmills to generators that run on biofuels. (11) It is about five to ten years before all these ideas will be commonplace.

PRACTICE 15 Editing Verb Problems and Using Formal English

Your sister has a bad case of laryngitis and wants to bring a note about her condition to her doctor. Help her by correcting the verb problems in the note. Then, edit the informal English.

THE FOUR MOST SERIOUS ERRORS

418 Chapter 23 • Verb Tense

(1) What's up, Doc Kerrigan?

(2) Your assistant ask me to tell you about my symptoms, so I will describe them as well as I can. (3) I becomed sick about a day ago. (4) Now, my throat hurt every time I swallowed, and I cannot speak. (5) Also, I has a high fever, and I be wicked tired. (6) I do not think I has ever feeled so crappy before. (7) I looked forward to seeing you during my appointment.

(8) Thanks mucho,

Corrine Evans

PRACTICE 16 Editing Cal's E-mail

Look back at Cal's e-mail on page 398. You may have already underlined the seven verb errors; if not, do so now. Next, using what you have learned in this chapter, correct each error.

PRACTICE 17 Editing Your Own Writing for Verb Problems

Edit verb-tense problems in a piece of your own writing — a paper for this course or another one, or something you have written for work or your everyday life. Use the chart on page 421 to help you.

Chapter Review

LEARNING JOURNAL If you found verb errors in your writing, what kind were they? What is the main thing you have learned about verb tense that you will use? What is one thing that remains unclear?

1. Verb _____ indicates when the action in a sentence happens (past, present, or future).

2. What are the two present-tense endings for regular verbs? _____

3. How do regular verbs in the past tense end? _____

4. The past participle is used with a _____ verb.

5. Verbs that do not follow the regular pattern for verbs are called _____.

6. An action that started in the past but might continue into the present uses the _____.

7. An action that happened in the past before something else that happened in the past uses the _____.

8. You should usually avoid using the _____ voice, which has a subject that performs no action but is acted upon.

9. Verb tenses are consistent when actions that happen at the same _____ are in the same _____.

Chapter Test

Circle the correct choice for each of the following items. For help, refer to the Finding and Fixing Verb-Tense Errors chart on page 421.

1. If an underlined portion of this sentence is incorrect, select the revision that fixes it. If the sentence is correct as written, choose d.

   It has became difficult to tell whether Trisha is tired of her work or
         A   B
   tired of her boss.
      C

   a. become
   b. be
   c. tiring
   d. No change is necessary.

2. Choose the item that has no errors.
   a. By the time we arrived, Michelle already gave her recital.
   b. By the time we arrived, Michelle had already given her recital.
   c. By the time we arrived, Michelle has already given her recital.

3. If an underlined portion of this sentence is incorrect, select the revision that fixes it. If the sentence is correct as written, choose d.

   I likes Manuel's new car, but I wish he wouldn't park it in my
     A   B
   space when he comes home from work.
                 C

   a. like
   b. wishing
   c. came
   d. No change is necessary.

4. Choose the item that has no errors.
   a. Patrick has such a bad memory that he has to write down everything he is supposed to do.
   b. Patrick had such a bad memory that he has to write down everything he is supposed to do.
   c. Patrick had such a bad memory that he having to write down everything he is supposed to do.

5. Choose the correct word(s) to fill in the blank.

   For many years, Steven _____ the manual typewriter his grandfather had given to him.

   a. keeped
   b. kept
   c. was keeping

6. Choose the item that has no errors.
   a. I have be cutting back on the amount of coffee I drink.
   b. I has been cutting back on the amount of coffee I drink.
   c. I have been cutting back on the amount of coffee I drink.

7. Choose the correct word(s) to fill in the blank.

   We had intended to visit Marina's parents while we _____ in town, but we did not have time.

   a. was
   b. had were
   c. were

8. Choose the correct word(s) to fill in the blank.

   Each family _____ a dish and brought it to our knitting club's annual dinner.

   a. prepares
   b. prepared
   c. have prepared

9. If an underlined portion of this sentence is incorrect, select the revision that fixes it. If the sentence is correct as written, choose d.

   The boy jumped out of the way just before the car is about to hit him.
              A   B   C

   a. jumping
   b. was
   c. hitted
   d. No change is necessary.

10. Choose the correct word to fill in the blank.

    Who has _____ the train to New York before?

    a. taken
    b. take
    c. taked

THE FOUR MOST SERIOUS ERRORS

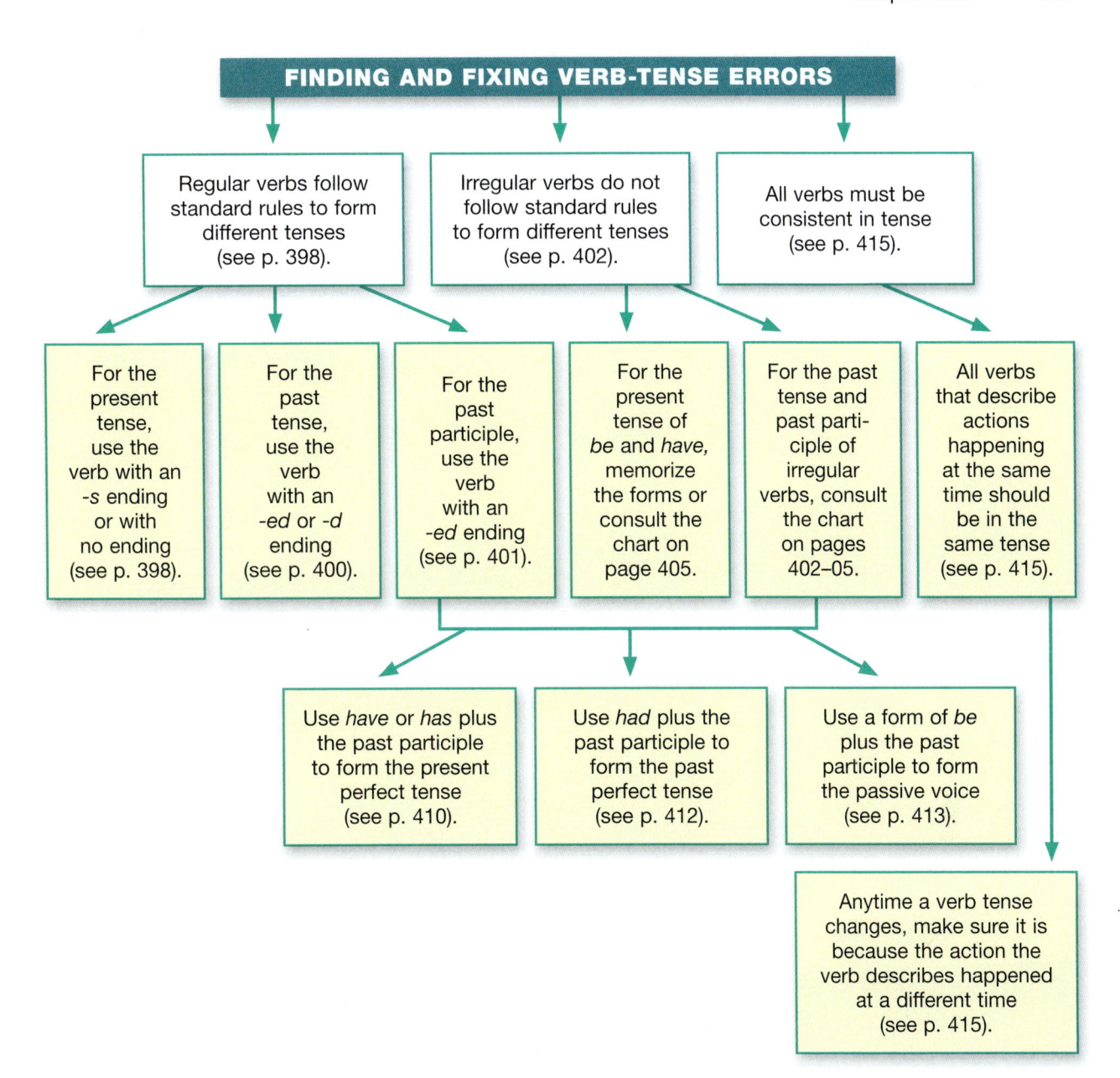

FINDING AND FIXING VERB-TENSE ERRORS

- Regular verbs follow standard rules to form different tenses (see p. 398).
- Irregular verbs do not follow standard rules to form different tenses (see p. 402).
- All verbs must be consistent in tense (see p. 415).

From "Regular verbs":
- For the present tense, use the verb with an -s ending or with no ending (see p. 398).
- For the past tense, use the verb with an -ed or -d ending (see p. 400).
- For the past participle, use the verb with an -ed ending (see p. 401).

From "Irregular verbs":
- For the present tense of *be* and *have*, memorize the forms or consult the chart on page 405.
- For the past tense and past participle of irregular verbs, consult the chart on pages 402–05.

From "All verbs must be consistent in tense":
- All verbs that describe actions happening at the same time should be in the same tense (see p. 415).

From past participle:
- Use *have* or *has* plus the past participle to form the present perfect tense (see p. 410).
- Use *had* plus the past participle to form the past perfect tense (see p. 412).
- Use a form of *be* plus the past participle to form the passive voice (see p. 413).

- Anytime a verb tense changes, make sure it is because the action the verb describes happened at a different time (see p. 415).

"I write proposals for my Web clients, and I write texts and e-mails to friends."

—Chris E., student

Part 5

Other Grammar Concerns

24	Pronouns	425
25	Adjectives and Adverbs	448
26	Misplaced and Dangling Modifiers	458
27	Coordination and Subordination	465
28	Parallelism	478
29	Sentence Variety	486
30	Formal English and ESL Concerns	499

24

Pronouns

Using Substitutes for Nouns

THIS CHAPTER
- explains what the different kinds of pronouns are.
- explains how to make your pronouns agree with your nouns.
- shows how to avoid pronoun problems.
- gives you practice using the different kinds of pronouns correctly.

Understand What Pronouns Are

A **pronoun** is used in place of a noun or other pronoun mentioned earlier. Pronouns enable you to avoid repeating those nouns or other pronouns mentioned earlier.

> Sheryl got into ~~Sheryl's~~ *her* car.
>
> I like Mario. ~~Mario~~ *He* is a good dancer.

The noun or pronoun that a pronoun replaces is called the **antecedent**. In most cases, a pronoun refers to a specific antecedent nearby.

> Antecedent
> I picked up my new **glasses**. **They** are cool.
> Pronoun replacing antecedent

✓ **LearningCurve**
Pronoun Agreement and Reference
bedfordstmartins.com/realwriting/LC

Practice Using Pronouns Correctly

Identify Pronouns

Before you practice finding and correcting common pronoun errors, it is helpful to practice identifying pronouns.

425

Common Pronouns

PERSONAL PRONOUNS	POSSESSIVE PRONOUNS	INDEFINITE PRONOUNS	
I	my	all	much
me	mine	any	neither (of)
you	your/yours	anybody	nobody
she/he	hers/his	anyone	none (of)
her/him	hers/his	anything	no one
it	its	both	nothing
we	our/ours	each (of)	one (of)
us	our/ours	either (of)	some
they	their/theirs	everybody	somebody
them	their/theirs	everyone	someone
		everything	something
		few (of)	

PRACTICE 1 Identifying Pronouns

In each of the following sentences, circle the pronoun, underline the noun it refers to, and draw an arrow from the pronoun to the noun.

TIP For more practice with pronoun usage, visit *Exercise Central* at bedfordstmartins.com/ realwriting.

EXAMPLE: People can have a hard time seeing stars at night if they live in or near a big city.

1. Each night, the stars fill the skies, but in many large cities, they are impossible to see.

2. The huge amount of light coming from homes, businesses, and streets creates a type of pollution, and it makes seeing the stars difficult.

3. The average night sky has approximately 2,500 stars in it, and they can be seen with the human eye.

4. In many neighborhoods, however, only two hundred or three hundred stars can be spotted, whereas in a big city, only about a dozen of them can be seen.

5. The International Dark Sky Association focuses on reducing light pollution as its main goal and has several recommendations.

6. Pointing lights down toward the ground instead of allowing them to shine up toward the sky is one suggestion.

7. To help battle light pollution, some cities and towns have passed laws limiting what lights they will allow.

8. Experts have been studying light pollution, and they have reported that it can affect many things, including wildlife and even human health.

9. Migrating birds sometimes fly over brightly lit cities and, confused by the unnatural light, fly in circles until they become exhausted.

10. Too much light has also been shown to be harmful to humans, and studies are being done to determine just how this overexposure affects them.

Check for Pronoun Agreement

A pronoun must agree with (match) the noun or pronoun it refers to in number. It must be either singular (one) or plural (more than one).

If a pronoun is singular, it must also match the noun or pronoun it refers to in gender (*he, she,* or *it*).

CONSISTENT	Magda sold *her* old television set.
	[*Her* agrees with *Magda* because both are singular and feminine.]
CONSISTENT	The Wilsons sold *their* old television set.
	[*Their* agrees with *the Wilsons* because both are plural.]

Watch out for singular, general nouns. If a noun is singular, the pronoun that refers to it must be singular as well.

INCONSISTENT	Any student can tell you what *their* least favorite course is.
	[*Student* is singular, but the pronoun *their* is plural.]
CONSISTENT	Any student can tell you what *his* or *her* least favorite course is.
	[*Student* is singular, and so are the pronouns *his* and *her*.]

To avoid using the awkward phrase *his or her*, make the subject plural when you can.

CONSISTENT	Most students can tell you what *their* least favorite course is.

Two types of words often cause errors in pronoun agreement: indefinite pronouns and collective nouns.

INDEFINITE PRONOUNS

An **indefinite pronoun** does not refer to a specific person, place, or thing: It is general. Indefinite pronouns often take singular verbs. Whenever a pronoun refers to an indefinite pronoun, check for agreement.

The monks got up at dawn. Everybody had ~~their~~ *his* chores for the day.

Indefinite Pronouns

ALWAYS SINGULAR			MAY BE PLURAL OR SINGULAR
another	everyone	nothing	all
anybody/anyone	everything	one (of)	any
anything	much	somebody	none
each (of)	neither (of)	someone	some
either (of)	nobody	something	
everybody	no one		

NOTE: Many people object to the use of only the masculine pronoun *he* when referring to a singular indefinite pronoun, such as *everyone*. Although grammatically correct, using the masculine form alone to refer to an indefinite pronoun is considered sexist. Here are two ways to avoid this problem:

1. Use *his or her*.

    Someone posted *his or her* e-mail address to the Web site.

2. Change the sentence so that the pronoun refers to a plural noun or pronoun.

    Some students posted *their* e-mail addresses to the Web site.

PRACTICE 2 Using Indefinite Pronouns

Circle the correct pronoun or group of words in parentheses.

(1) Anyone who wants to start (their / his or her) own business had better be prepared to work hard. (2) One may find, for example, that (his or her / their) work is never done. (3) Something is always waiting, with

(its / their) own peculiar demands. (4) Nothing gets done on (their / its) own. (5) Anybody who expects to have more freedom now that (he or she no longer works / they no longer work) for a boss may be disappointed. (6) After all, when you work as an employee for a company, someone above you makes decisions as (they see / he or she sees) fit. (7) When you are your own boss, no one else places (themselves / himself or herself) in the position of final responsibility.

(8) Somebody starting a business may also be surprised by how much tax (they / he or she) must pay. (9) Each employee at a company pays only about half as much toward social security as what (they / he or she) would pay if self-employed. (10) Neither medical nor dental coverage can be obtained as inexpensively as (it / they) can when a person is an employee at a corporation.

COLLECTIVE NOUNS

A **collective noun** names a group that acts as a single unit.

Common Collective Nouns

audience	company	group
class	crowd	jury
college	family	society
committee	government	team

Collective nouns are usually singular, so when you use a pronoun to refer to a collective noun, it is also usually singular.

The team had ~~their~~ *its* sixth consecutive win of the season.

If the people in a group are acting as individuals, however, the noun is plural and should be used with a plural pronoun.

The class brought *their* papers to read.

FINDING AND FIXING PRONOUN PROBLEMS: Using Collective Nouns and Pronouns

Find

The committee changed (its / their) meeting time.

1. **Underline** any collective nouns.
2. **Ask:** Is the collective noun singular (a group acting as a single unit) or plural (people in a group acting as individuals)? *Singular.*

Fix

The committee changed (**its**/ their) meeting time.

3. **Choose** the pronoun that agrees with the subject.

PRACTICE 3   Using Collective Nouns and Pronouns

Fill in the correct pronoun (*it, its,* or *their*) in each of the following sentences.

EXAMPLE: The Vidocq Society is known for _____its_____ unusual approach to investigating unsolved murders, or "cold cases."

1. The Philadelphia-based club got _____ name from Eugène François Vidocq, a French detective who also worked on unsolved crimes.

2. A police department with a cold case may find that _____ can benefit from the Vidocq Society's services.

3. During the society's monthly meetings, a team of crime investigators, psychologists, scientists, and others bring _____ varied skills to such cases.

4. When guests with knowledge about a case speak to the society, the audience gives _____ full attention to the information.

5. A group of police officers who worked a particular murder case might describe _____ original findings in detailed presentations.

6. Next, as a group, the society considers the evidence before _____; with their combined skills and fresh eyes, members sometimes see things that earlier investigators missed.

7. The 2000 murder of an Oregon teen was unsolved for years until the club used _____ expertise to help authorities find the victim's killer: her former boyfriend.

8. In 2011, the jury assigned to the case returned _____ verdict: The ex-boyfriend was found guilty of manslaughter.

9. The slain teen's family could not hide _____ emotions, which ranged from joy over the conviction to tears of relief.

10. The Vidocq Society has an excellent reputation because of successes like this case and because a committee carefully evaluates potential new members before _____ decides to admit them.

Make Pronoun Reference Clear

In an **ambiguous pronoun reference**, the pronoun could refer to more than one noun.

AMBIGUOUS	Enrico told Jim that *he* needed a better résumé.
	[Did Enrico tell Jim that Enrico himself needed a better résumé? Or did Enrico tell Jim that Jim needed a better résumé?]
EDITED	Enrico advised Jim to revise his résumé.
AMBIGUOUS	I put the glass on the shelf, even though *it* was dirty.
	[Was the glass dirty? Or was the shelf dirty?]
EDITED	I put the dirty glass on the shelf.

In a **vague pronoun reference**, the pronoun does not refer clearly to any particular person, place, or thing. To correct a vague pronoun reference, use a more specific noun instead of the pronoun.

VAGUE	When Tom got to the clinic, *they* told him it was closed.
	[Who told Tom the clinic was closed?]
EDITED	When Tom got to the clinic, the nurse told him it was closed.

VAGUE	Before I finished printing my report, *it* ran out of paper. [What ran out of paper?]
EDITED	Before I finished printing my report, the printer ran out of paper.

> ### FINDING AND FIXING PRONOUN PROBLEMS:
> Avoiding Ambiguous or Vague Pronoun References
>
> **Find**
>
> The <u>cashier</u> said that (they) were out of milk.
>
> 1. **Underline** the subject.
> 2. **Circle** the pronoun.
> 3. **Ask:** Who or what does the pronoun refer to? *No one. "They" does not refer to "cashier."*
>
> **Fix**
>
>   *the store was*
> The cashier said that ~~they were~~ out of milk.
>
> 4. **Correct the pronoun reference** by revising the sentence to make the pronoun more specific.

PRACTICE 4 Avoiding Ambiguous or Vague Pronoun References

Edit each sentence to eliminate ambiguous or vague pronoun references. Some sentences may be revised in more than one way.

EXAMPLE: I am always looking for good advice on controlling my weight, but ~~they~~ *experts* have provided little help.

1. My doctor referred me to a physical therapist, and she said that I needed to exercise more.

2. I joined a workout group and did exercises with the members, but it did not solve my problem.

3. I tried a lower-fat diet along with the exercising, but it did not really work either.

4. They used to say that eliminating carbohydrates is the easiest way to lose weight.

5. Therefore, I started eating fats again and stopped consuming carbs, but this was not a permanent solution.

6. Although I lost weight and loved eating fatty foods, it did not keep me from eventually gaining the weight back.

7. Last week, I overheard my Uncle Kevin talking to my brother, and he explained how he stayed slender even while traveling a lot.

8. Uncle Kevin eats fruit and vegetables instead of junk food while traveling, and it has kept off the pounds.

9. He says that it is not hard to pack carrots or apples for a trip, so anyone can do this.

10. I now try to plan better, eat less at each meal, and ignore all diet books, and I hope it works.

In a **repetitious pronoun reference**, the pronoun repeats a reference to a noun rather than replacing the noun.

The nurse at the clinic ~~he~~ told Tom that it was closed.

The newspaper/~~it~~ says that the new diet therapy is promising.

FINDING AND FIXING PRONOUN PROBLEMS:
Avoiding Repetitious Pronoun References

Find

Television advertising (it) sometimes has a negative influence on young viewers.

1. **Underline** the subject, and **double-underline** the verb.
2. **Circle** any pronouns in the sentence.
3. **Ask:** What noun does the pronoun refer to? *Advertising.*
4. **Ask:** Do the noun and the pronoun that refers to it share the same verb? *Yes.* Does the pronoun just repeat the noun rather than replace it? *Yes.* If the answer to one or both questions is yes, the pronoun is repetitious.

OTHER GRAMMAR CONCERNS
Chapter 24 • Pronouns

> **Fix**
>
> Television advertising ~~it~~ sometimes has a negative influence on young viewers.
>
> 5. **Correct the sentence** by crossing out the repetitious pronoun.

PRACTICE 5 Avoiding Repetitious Pronoun References

Correct any repetitious pronoun references in the following sentences.

> EXAMPLE: Car commercials ~~they~~ want viewers to believe that buying a certain brand of car will bring happiness.

1. Young people they sometimes take advertisements too literally.
2. In a beer advertisement, it might suggest that drinking alcohol makes people more attractive and popular.
3. People who see or hear an advertisement they have to think about the message.
4. Parents should help their children understand why advertisements they do not show the real world.
5. A recent study, it said that parents can help kids overcome the influence of advertising.

Use the Right Type of Pronoun

Three important types of pronouns are **subject pronouns**, **object pronouns**, and **possessive pronouns**. Notice their uses in the following sentences.

Object pronoun / Subject pronoun
The dog barked at *him,* and *he* laughed.

Possessive pronoun
As Josh walked out, *his* phone started ringing.

OTHER GRAMMAR CONCERNS
Practice Using Pronouns Correctly

TIP Never put an apostrophe in a possessive pronoun.

Pronoun Types

	SUBJECT	OBJECT	POSSESSIVE
First-person singular/plural	I/we	me/us	my, mine/ our, ours
Second-person singular/plural	you/you	you/you	your, yours/ your, yours
Third-person singular	he, she, it	him, her, it	his, her, hers, its
	who	whom	whose
Third-person plural	they	them	their, theirs
	who	whom	whose

LANGUAGE NOTE: Notice that pronouns have gender (*he/she*, *him/her*, *his/her/hers*). The pronoun must agree with the gender of the noun it refers to.

INCORRECT Carolyn went to see *his* boyfriend.

CORRECT Carolyn went to see *her* boyfriend.

Also, notice that English has different forms for subject and object pronouns, as shown in the previous chart.

Read the following sentence, and replace the underlined nouns with pronouns. Notice that the pronouns are all different.

When Andreas made an A on <u>Andreas's</u> final exam, <u>Andreas</u> was proud of himself, and the teacher congratulated <u>Andreas</u>.

SUBJECT PRONOUNS

Subject pronouns serve as the subject of a verb.

You live next door to a coffee shop.

I opened the door too quickly.

OBJECT PRONOUNS

Object pronouns either receive the action of a verb or are part of a prepositional phrase.

TIP For a list of common prepositions, see page 332.

| **OBJECT OF THE VERB** | Jay gave *me* his watch. |
| **OBJECT OF THE PREPOSITION** | Jay gave his watch to *me*. |

POSSESSIVE PRONOUNS

Possessive pronouns show ownership.

> Dave is *my* uncle.

Three trouble spots make it difficult to know what type of pronoun to use; compound subjects and objects; comparisons; and sentences that need *who* or *whom*.

OTHER TYPES OF PRONOUNS

Intensive pronouns emphasize a noun or other pronoun. **Reflexive pronouns** are used when the performer of an action is also the receiver of the action. Both types of pronouns end in *-self* or *-selves*.

> **REFLEXIVE**　　He taught *himself* how to play the guitar.
>
> **INTENSIVE**　　The club members *themselves* have offered to support the initiative.

Relative pronouns refer to a noun already mentioned, and introduce a group of words that describe this noun (*who, whom, whose, which, that*).

> Tomatoes, *which* are popular worldwide, were first grown in South America.

Interrogative pronouns are used to begin questions (*who, whom, whose, which, what*).

> *What* did the senator say at the meeting?

Demonstrative pronouns specify which noun is being referred to (*this, these, that, those*).

> Use *this* simple budgeting app, not *that* complicated one.

Reciprocal pronouns refer to individuals when the antecedent is plural (*each other, one another*).

> My friend and I could not see *one another* in the crowd.

PRONOUNS USED WITH COMPOUND SUBJECTS AND OBJECTS

A **compound subject** has more than one subject joined by *and* or *or*. A **compound object** has more than one object joined by *and* or *or*.

> **COMPOUND SUBJECT**　　Chandler and *I* worked on the project.
>
> **COMPOUND OBJECT**　　My boss gave the assignment to Chandler and *me*.

TIP When you are writing about yourself and someone else, always put yourself after everyone else. *My friends and I went to a club*, not *I and my friends went to a club*.

> **FINDING AND FIXING PRONOUN PROBLEMS:**
> Using Pronouns in Compound Constructions
>
> **Find**
>
> ~~My friend and~~ me talk at least once a week.
>
> 1. **Underline** the subject, **double-underline** the verb, and **circle** any object or objects.
> 2. **Ask:** Does the sentence have a compound subject or object? *Yes—"friend and me" is a compound subject.*
> 3. **Ask:** Do the nouns in the compound construction share a verb? *Yes—"talk."*
> 4. **Cross out** one of the subjects so that only the pronoun remains.
> 5. **Ask:** Does the sentence sound correct with just the pronoun as the subject? *No.*

> **Fix**
>
> My friend and ~~me~~ I talk at least once a week.
>
> 6. **Correct the sentence** by replacing the incorrect pronoun with the correct one.

To decide what type of pronoun to use in a compound construction, try leaving out the other part of the compound and the *and* or *or*. Then, say the sentence aloud to yourself.

Compound subject

~~Joan and~~ (me / **I**) went to the movies last night.
[Think: *I* went to the movies last night.]

Compound object

The car was headed right for ~~Tom and~~ (she / **her**).
[Think: The car was headed right for *her*.]

If a pronoun is part of a compound object in a prepositional phrase, use an object pronoun.

Compound object

I will keep that information just between you and (I / **me**).
[*Between you and me* is a prepositional phrase, so an object pronoun, *me*, is required.]

TIP Many people make the mistake of using *I* in the phrase *between you and I*. The correct pronoun with *between* is the object *me*.

OTHER GRAMMAR CONCERNS

438   Chapter 24 • Pronouns

PRACTICE 6   Editing Pronouns in Compound Constructions

Correct any pronoun errors in the following sentences. If a sentence is already correct, write a "C" next to it.

EXAMPLE: Marie Curie made several major contributions to science, but in 1898, ~~her~~ *she* and her husband, Pierre Curie, announced their greatest achievement: the discovery of radium.

1. Before this discovery, Marie and Pierre understood that certain substances gave off rays of energy, but them and other scientists were just beginning to learn why and how.

2. Eventually, the Curies made a discovery that intrigued they and, soon afterward, hundreds of other researchers.

3. Two previously unknown elements, radium and polonium, were responsible for the extra radioactivity; fascinated by this finding, Marie began thinking about the consequences of the work that she and her husband had done.

4. As them and other researchers were to discover, radium was especially valuable because it could be used in X-rays and for other medical purposes.

5. Marie was deeply moved when, in 1903, the scientific community honored she and Pierre with the Nobel Prize in physics.

PRONOUNS USED IN COMPARISONS

Using the right type of pronoun in comparisons is particularly important because using the wrong type changes the meaning of the sentence. Editing comparisons can be tricky because they often imply (suggest the presence of) words that are not actually included in the sentence.

> Bob trusts Donna more than *I*.
> [This sentence means that Bob trusts Donna more than I trust her. The implied words are *trust her*.]

TIP To find comparisons, look for the word *than* or *as*.

> Bob trusts Donna more than *me*.
> [This sentence means that Bob trusts Donna more than he trusts me. The implied words are *he trusts*.]

To decide whether to use a subject or object pronoun in a comparison, try adding the implied words and saying the sentence aloud.

The registrar is much more efficient than (us /(we)).
[Think: The registrar is much more efficient than *we are*.]

Susan rides her bicycle more than ((he)/ him).
[Think: Susan rides her bicycle more than *he does*.]

TIP Add the additional words to the comparison when you speak and write. Then, others will not think you are incorrect.

FINDING AND FIXING PRONOUN PROBLEMS: Using Pronouns in Comparisons

Find

The other band attracts a bigger audience (than) us on Friday nights.

1. **Circle** the word that indicates a comparison.
2. **Ask:** What word or words that would come after the comparison word are implied but missing from the sentence? *"Do."*
3. **Ask:** If you add the missing word or words, does the pronoun make sense? *No.*

Fix

The other band attracts a bigger audience than ~~us~~ *we (do)* on Friday nights.

4. **Correct the sentence** by replacing the incorrect pronoun with the correct one.

PRACTICE 7 Editing Pronouns in Comparisons

Correct any pronoun errors in the following sentences. If a sentence is correct, put a "C" next to it.

EXAMPLE: The camping trip we planned did not seem dangerous to Hannah, so she was not as nervous about it as ~~me~~ *I*.

1. In addition, I was nowhere near as well equipped for camping as her.
2. In the store, Hannah rather than me did all the talking.
3. At the campground, I could see that some of the other camping groups were not as prepared as we.
4. The park ranger chatted with the other campers more than we.
5. He seemed to believe that we were more experienced than them.

6. On the hiking trail, the other campers walked faster than we.

7. They all hurried past us, but Hannah kept hiking just as slowly as me.

8. Our boots had been crunching on the trail for hours when we suddenly heard that a group ahead was being much louder than us.

9. When Hannah and I saw the group running back toward us, I was more alarmed than her.

10. When we spotted the bear that was chasing the other hikers, Hannah ran to hide a lot faster than I.

CHOOSING BETWEEN *WHO* AND *WHOM*

Who is always a subject; *whom* is always an object. If a pronoun performs an action, use the subject form *who*. If a pronoun does not perform an action, use the object form *whom*.

TIP In the examples here, subjects are underlined, and verbs are double-underlined.

| **WHO = SUBJECT** | I would like to know *who* delivered this package. |
| **WHOM = OBJECT** | He told me to *whom* I should report. |

TIP *Whoever* is a subject pronoun; *whomever* is an object pronoun.

In sentences other than questions, when the pronoun (*who* or *whom*) is followed by a verb, use *who*. When the pronoun (*who* or *whom*) is followed by a noun or pronoun, use *whom*.

The pianist (who / whom) played was excellent.
[The pronoun is followed by the verb *played*. Use *who*.]

The pianist (who / whom) I saw was excellent.
[The pronoun is followed by another pronoun: *I*. Use *whom*.]

PRACTICE 8 Choosing between *Who* and *Whom*

In each sentence, circle the correct word, *who* or *whom*.

EXAMPLE: Police officers (who / whom) want to solve a crime—or prevent one—are now relying more than ever on technology.

1. Face-recognition software is supposed to identify possible criminals (who / whom) cameras have photographed in public places.

2. Use of such software, which compares security-camera images with photos from a criminal database, can help law enforcement officials determine (who / whom) they want to question about a crime.

3. Police will try to detain any person (who / whom) is identified by the software as a criminal.

4. Police know that the software will single out some innocent people (who / whom) resemble criminals.

5. However, police and nervous Americans are hopeful that this method can help identify terrorists (who / whom) appear in airports or other locations.

Make Pronouns Consistent in Person

Person is the point of view a writer uses — the perspective from which he or she writes. Pronouns may be in first person (*I* or *we*), second person (*you*), or third person (*he, she,* or *it*). (See the chart on p. 435.)

INCONSISTENT	As soon as *a shopper* walks into the store, *you* can tell it is a weird place.
	[The sentence starts with the third person (*a shopper*) but shifts to the second person (*you*).]
CONSISTENT, SINGULAR	As soon as *a shopper* walks into the store, *he* or *she* can tell it is a weird place.
CONSISTENT, PLURAL	As soon as *shoppers* walk into the store, *they* can tell it is a weird place.

FINDING AND FIXING PRONOUN PROBLEMS:
Making Pronouns Consistent in Person

Find

I had the correct answer, but to win the tickets (you) had to be the ninth caller.

1. **Underline** all the subject nouns and pronouns in the sentence.
2. **Circle** any pronouns that refer to another subject noun or pronoun in the sentence.
3. **Ask:** Is the subject noun or pronoun that the circled pronoun refers to in the first (*I* or *we*), second (*you*), or third person (*he, she,* or *it*)? *First person.*
4. **Ask:** What person is the pronoun in? *Second.*

> **Fix**
>
> I had the correct answer, but to win the tickets ~~you~~ *I* had to be the ninth caller.

5. **Correct the sentence** by changing the pronoun to be consistent with the noun or pronoun it refers to.

PRACTICE 9 Making Pronouns Consistent in Person

In the following sentences, correct the shifts in person. There may be more than one way to correct some sentences.

EXAMPLE: Many college students have access to a writing center where ~~you~~ *they* can get tutoring.

1. A writing tutor must know your way around college writing assignments.
2. I have gone to the writing center at my school because sometimes you need a second pair of eyes to look over a paper.
3. Students signing up for tutoring at the writing center may not be in your first semester of college.
4. Even a graduate student may need help with your writing at times.
5. The writing-center tutor is careful not to correct their students' papers.
6. My tutor told me that you had to learn to edit a paper.
7. Every student has to learn to catch your own mistakes.
8. A student's tutor is not like your English professor.
9. No student gets their grade on a paper from a writing tutor.
10. Tutors do not judge but simply help students with your papers.

Edit for Pronoun Problems

PRACTICE 10 Correcting Various Pronoun Problems

In the following sentences, find and correct problems with pronoun use. You may be able to revise some sentences in more than one way, and you may need to rewrite some sentences to correct errors.

EXAMPLE: ~~Everyone with a busy schedule has~~ *Students with busy schedules have* probably been tempted to take shortcuts on their coursework.

1. My class received its term paper grades yesterday.
2. My friend Gene and me were shocked to see that he had gotten an F on his paper.
3. I usually get better grades than him, but he does not usually fail.
4. Mr. Padilla, the instructor, who most students consider strict but fair, scheduled an appointment with Gene.
5. When Gene went to the department office, they told him where to find Mr. Padilla.
6. Mr. Padilla told Gene that he did not think he had written the paper.
7. The paper it contained language that was unusual for Gene.
8. The instructor said that you could compare Gene's in-class writing with this paper and see differences.
9. Mr. Padilla, whom had typed some passages from Gene's paper into a search engine, found two online papers containing sentences that were also in Gene's paper.
10. Gene told Mr. Padilla that he had made a terrible mistake.
11. Gene told my girlfriend and I later that he did not realize that borrowing sentences from online sources was plagiarism.
12. We looked at the paper, and you could tell that parts of it did not sound like Gene's writing.
13. Anyone doing Internet research must be especially careful to document their sources, as Gene now knows.
14. The department decided that they would not suspend Gene from school.
15. Mr. Padilla will let Gene take the class again and will help him avoid accidental plagiarism, and Gene said that no one had ever been more relieved than him to hear that news.

OTHER GRAMMAR CONCERNS

444 Chapter 24 • Pronouns

PRACTICE 11 Editing Paragraphs for Pronoun Problems

Find and correct seven errors in pronoun use in the following paragraphs.

(1) Ask anyone who has moved to a city, and they will tell you: At first, life can feel pretty lonely. (2) Fortunately, it is possible to make friends just about anywhere. (3) One good strategy is to get involved in a group that interests you, such as a sports team or arts club. (4) In many cases, a local baseball team or theater group will open their arms to new talent. (5) Joining in on practices, games, or performances is a great way to build friendships with others whom have interests like yours. (6) Also, most community organizations are always in need of volunteers. (7) It is a great way to form new friendships while doing something positive for society.

(8) Getting a pet or gardening, it is another great way to meet new people. (9) In many cities, you can walk down the street for a long time and never be greeted by another person. (10) If you are walking a dog, though, it is likely that others will say hello. (11) Some may even stop to talk with you and pet your dog. (12) Also, gardeners tend to draw other gardeners. (13) If you are planting flowers and other flower growers stop by to chat, them and you will have plenty to talk about.

(14) To sum up, newcomers to any city do not have to spend all their nights alone in front of the TV. (15) You have plenty of opportunities to get out and feel more connected.

PRACTICE 12 Editing Your Own Writing for Pronoun Problems

Edit pronoun errors in a piece of your own writing—a paper for this course or another one, or something you have written for work or your everyday life. Use the chart on page 447 to help you.

Chapter Review

1. Pronouns replace _____ or other _____ in a sentence.

2. A pronoun must agree with (match) the noun or pronoun it replaces in _____ and _____ .

3. In an _____ pronoun reference, the pronoun could refer to more than one noun.

4. Subject pronouns serve as the subject of a verb. Write a sentence using a subject pronoun. _____

5. What are two other types of pronouns? _____

6. What are three trouble spots in pronoun use?

LEARNING JOURNAL Did you find pronoun errors in your writing? What is the main thing you have learned about pronouns that will help you? What is unclear to you?

Chapter Test

Circle the correct choice for each of the following items.

1. Choose the item that has no errors.
   a. When he skis, Jim never falls down as much as me.
   b. When he skis, Jim never falls down as much as I.
   c. When he skis, Jim never falls down as much as mine.

2. Choose the correct word(s) to fill in the blank.

   Everyone hopes that the jury will deliver _____ verdict by the end of this week.

   a. his or her   b. their   c. its

3. If an underlined portion of this sentence is incorrect, select the revision that fixes it. If the sentence is correct as written, choose d.

   She is the one <u>who</u> Jake always calls whenever <u>he</u> wants a favor.
      A   B   C

   a. Her
   b. whom
   c. him
   d. No change is necessary.

4. If an underlined portion of this sentence is incorrect, select the revision that fixes it. If the sentence is correct as written, choose d.

   Somebody has left <u>their</u> camera here, and <u>we</u> do not know to <u>whom</u>
                         A   B   C

   it belongs.

a. his or her
b. us
c. who
d. No change is necessary.

5. Choose the item that has no errors.
   a. Becky told Lydia that she needed to help clean up after the party.
   b. Becky told Lydia to help clean up after the party.
   c. Becky told Lydia that she needed to help clean up after it.

6. Choose the item that has no errors.
   a. When I applied for the tour operator job, I was told that you needed a special certificate.
   b. When I applied for the tour operator job, you were told that you needed a special certificate.
   c. When I applied for the tour operator job, I was told that I needed a special certificate.

7. Choose the correct word(s) to fill in the blank.

   Nicole's _____ must be lonely because he barks all the time.

   a. dog he
   b. dog him
   c. dog

8. Choose the correct words to fill in the blank.

   The other players in my soccer club like me because _____ agree on the importance of teamwork.

   a. they and I
   b. them and me
   c. them and I

9. If an underlined portion of this sentence is incorrect, select the revision that fixes it. If the sentence is correct as written, choose d.

   I think that <u>my next-door</u> neighbor has mice in <u>him house</u> because
              A   B
   he keeps asking me to <u>lend him</u> my cat.
                          C

   a. me next-door
   b. his house
   c. lend he
   d. No change is necessary.

10. Choose the item that has no errors.
    a. Any lifeguard can tell you about a scary experience they have had on the job.
    b. Any lifeguard can tell you about a scary experience her have had on the job.
    c. Most lifeguards can tell you about a scary experience they have had on the job.

FINDING AND FIXING PRONOUN PROBLEMS

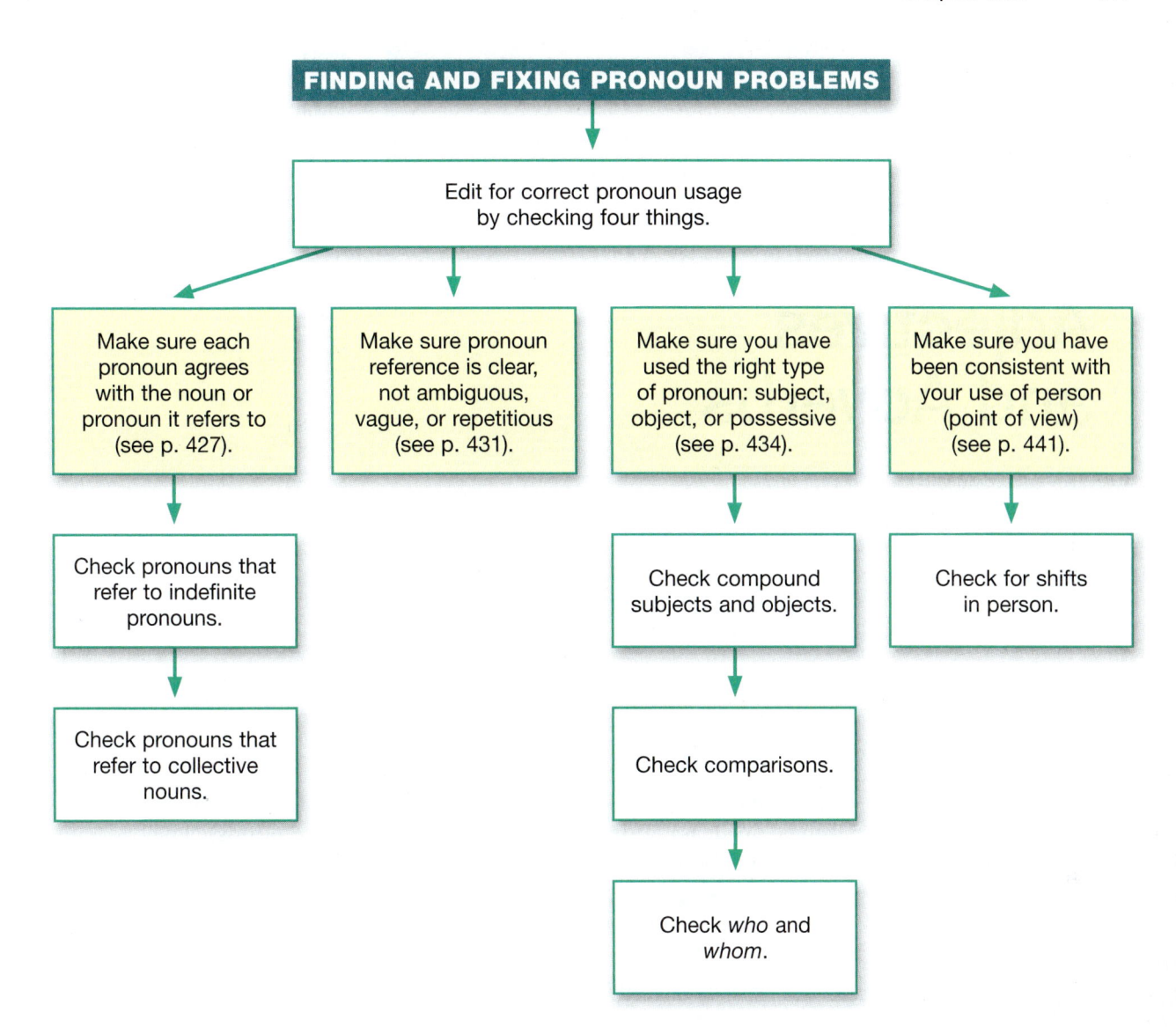

Edit for correct pronoun usage by checking four things.

- **Make sure each pronoun agrees with the noun or pronoun it refers to (see p. 427).**
  - Check pronouns that refer to indefinite pronouns.
  - Check pronouns that refer to collective nouns.

- **Make sure pronoun reference is clear, not ambiguous, vague, or repetitious (see p. 431).**

- **Make sure you have used the right type of pronoun: subject, object, or possessive (see p. 434).**
  - Check compound subjects and objects.
  - Check comparisons.
  - Check *who* and *whom*.

- **Make sure you have been consistent with your use of person (point of view) (see p. 441).**
  - Check for shifts in person.

25

Adjectives and Adverbs

Using Descriptive Words

THIS CHAPTER
- explains what adjectives and adverbs are and do.
- explains when to use an adjective and when to use an adverb.
- gives you practice using adjectives and adverbs correctly.

Understand What Adjectives and Adverbs Are

Adjectives describe or modify nouns (words that name people, places, things, or ideas) and pronouns (words that replace nouns). They add information about *what kind*, *which one*, or *how many*.

The *final* exam was today.

It was *long* and *difficult*.

The *three shiny new* coins were on the dresser.

LANGUAGE NOTE: In English, adjectives do not indicate whether the words they describe are singular or plural.

INCORRECT The three babies are *adorables*.
[The adjective *adorables* should not end in *-s*.]

CORRECT The three babies are *adorable*.

Adverbs describe or modify verbs (words that tell what happens in a sentence), adjectives, or other adverbs. They add information about *how*, *how much*, *when*, *where*, *why*, or *to what extent*.

MODIFYING VERB Sharon *enthusiastically* accepted the job.

MODIFYING ADJECTIVE The *very* young lawyer handled the case.

MODIFYING ANOTHER ADVERB The team played *surprisingly* well.

TIP To understand this chapter on adjectives and adverbs, you need to know what nouns and verbs are. For a review, see Chapter 19.

448

Adjectives usually come before the words they modify; adverbs come before or after. You can use more than one adjective or adverb to modify a word.

LANGUAGE NOTE: The *-ed* and *-ing* forms of adjectives are sometimes confused. Common examples include *bored/boring*, *confused/confusing*, *excited/exciting*, and *interested/interesting*.

Often, the *-ed* form describes a person's reaction, whereas the *-ing* form describes the thing to which a person is reacting.

INCORRECT	Janelle is interesting in ghosts and ghost stories.
CORRECT	Janelle is interested in ghosts and ghost stories.
CORRECT	Janelle finds ghosts and ghost stories interesting.

Practice Using Adjectives and Adverbs Correctly

Choosing between Adjectives and Adverbs

Many adverbs are formed by adding *-ly* to the end of an adjective.

ADJECTIVE	ADVERB
She received a *quick* answer.	Her sister answered *quickly*.
Our *new* neighbors just got married.	The couple is *newly* married.
That is an *honest* answer.	Please answer *honestly*.

To decide whether to use an adjective or an adverb, find the word being described. If that word is a noun or pronoun, use an adjective. If it is a verb, adjective, or another adverb, use an adverb.

PRACTICE 1 Choosing between Adjectives and Adverbs

In each sentence, underline the word in the sentence that is being described or modified. Then, circle the correct word in parentheses.

EXAMPLE: People are (common / (commonly)) aware that smoking causes health risks.

1. Many smokers are (stubborn / stubbornly) about refusing to quit.
2. Others who are thinking about quitting may decide (sudden / suddenly) that the damage from smoking has already been done.

TIP For more practice with adjective and adverb usage, visit *Exercise Central* at bedfordstmartins.com/realwriting.

OTHER GRAMMAR CONCERNS

Chapter 25 • Adjectives and Adverbs

3. In such cases, the (typical / typically) smoker sees no reason to stop.

4. The news about secondhand smoke may have made some smokers stop (quick / quickly) to save the health of their families.

5. Research now shows that pet lovers who smoke can have a (terrible / terribly) effect on their cats.

6. Cats who live with smokers (frequent / frequently) develop cancer.

7. Veterinarians point out that the cats of smokers may smell (strong / strongly) of smoke.

8. Cats like to have their fur (clean / cleanly), and they lick the fur to groom themselves.

9. When they are grooming, cats may inhale a (large / largely) dose of tobacco smoke.

10. Perhaps some smokers who believe that it is too late for their own health will (serious / seriously) consider quitting for the sake of their pets.

Using Adjectives and Adverbs in Comparisons

To compare two people, places, or things, use the **comparative** form of adjectives or adverbs. Comparisons often use the word *than*.

Carol ran *faster* than I did.
Johan is *more intelligent* than his sister.

To compare three or more people, places, or things, use the **superlative** form of adjectives or adverbs.

Carol ran the *fastest* of all the women runners.
Johan is the *most intelligent* of the five children.

If an adjective or adverb is short (one syllable), add the endings *-er* to form the comparative and *-est* to form the superlative. Also use this pattern for adjectives that end in *-y* (but change the *-y* to *-i* before adding *-er* or *-est*).

For all other adjectives and adverbs, add the word *more* to make the comparative and the word *most* to make the superlative.

Forming Comparatives and Superlatives

ADJECTIVE OR ADVERB	COMPARATIVE	SUPERLATIVE
ADJECTIVES AND ADVERBS OF ONE SYLLABLE		
tall	taller	tallest
fast	faster	fastest
ADJECTIVES ENDING IN -Y		
happy	happier	happiest
silly	sillier	silliest
OTHER ADJECTIVES AND ADVERBS		
graceful	more graceful	most graceful
gracefully	more gracefully	most gracefully
intelligent	more intelligent	most intelligent
intelligently	more intelligently	most intelligently

Use either an ending (*-er* or *-est*) or an extra word (*more* or *most*) to form a comparative or superlative—not both at once.

Lance Armstrong is the ~~most~~ greatest cyclist in the world.

TIP Some people refer to the correct use of comparatives and superlatives as *appropriate degree forms*.

PRACTICE 2 Using Adjectives and Adverbs in Comparisons

In the space provided in each sentence, write the correct form of the adjective or adverb in parentheses. You may need to add *more* or *most* to some adjectives and adverbs.

EXAMPLE: It was one of the ____scariest____ (scary) experiences of my life.

1. I was driving along Route 17 and was _____ (relaxed) than I ought to have been.

2. Knowing it was a busy highway, I was _____ (careful) than usual to make sure my cell phone was ready in case of an accident.

3. I had run the cord for the phone's earbud over my armrest, where it would be in the _____ (easy) place to reach if the phone rang.

4. I was in the _____ (heavy) traffic of my drive when the cell phone rang.

5. I saw that the earbud was _____ (hard) to reach than before because the cord had fallen between the front seats of the car.

6. When I reached down to get the earbud, a pickup truck to my right suddenly started going _____ (fast).

7. The truck swerved toward my lane, coming _____ (close) than I wanted it to be.

8. I took the _____ (quick) action I could think of, shifting to the left lane and just barely avoiding the pickup.

9. _____ (Calm) now, I decided to give up trying to find the earbud.

10. I wanted the cell phone ready for safety's sake, but I now think that concentrating on my driving is the _____ (intelligent) thing to do.

Using *Good, Well, Bad,* and *Badly*

Four common adjectives and adverbs have irregular forms: *good, well, bad,* and *badly.*

TIP *Irregular* means not following a standard rule.

Forming Irregular Comparatives and Superlatives

	COMPARATIVE	SUPERLATIVE
ADJECTIVE		
good	better	best
bad	worse	worst
ADVERB		
well	better	best
badly	worse	worst

People often get confused about whether to use *good* or *well. Good* is an adjective, so use it to describe a noun or pronoun. *Well* is an adverb, so use it to describe a verb or an adjective.

ADJECTIVE   She has a *good* job.

ADVERB   He works *well* with his colleagues.

Well can also be an adjective to describe someone's health: I am not *well* today.

PRACTICE 3 Using *Good* and *Well*

Complete each sentence by circling the correct word in parentheses. Underline the word that *good* or *well* modifies.

EXAMPLE: A (**good**/ well) <u>pediatrician</u> spends as much time talking with parents as he or she does examining patients.

1. The ability to communicate (good / well) is something that many parents look for in a pediatrician.
2. With a firstborn child, parents see a doctor's visit as a (good / well) chance to ask questions.
3. Parents can become worried when their infant does not feel (good / well) because the child cannot say what the problem is.
4. Doctors today have (good / well) diagnostic tools, however.
5. An otoscope helps a doctor see (good / well) when he or she looks into a patient's ear.
6. A fever and an inflamed eardrum are (good / well) signs of a middle-ear infection.
7. Children who have many ear infections may not hear as (good / well) as children who have fewer infections.
8. If the pediatrician presents clear options for treatment, parents can make a (good / well)-informed decision about treating their child's illness.
9. Some parents decide that ear-tube surgery is a (good / well) solution to the problem of frequent ear infections.
10. Within an hour after ear-tube surgery, most children are (good / well) enough to go home.

PRACTICE 4 Using Comparative and Superlative Forms of *Good* and *Bad*

Complete each sentence by circling the correct comparative or superlative form of *good* or *bad* in parentheses.

EXAMPLE: One of the (worse /**worst**) outcomes of heavy drinking is severe impairment of mental and physical functioning.

1. Research has shown that if a man and a woman drink the same amount of alcohol, the woman may experience (worse / worst) effects.

2. The (better / best) explanation for this difference concerns the physical differences between women and men.

3. Men are (better / best) at processing alcohol because they have a higher proportion of water in their bodies than women do, and this higher water content helps lower the concentration of alcohol in men's blood.

4. Also, because of additional physical differences between women and men, the same amount of alcohol may have a (worse / worst) effect on women's livers.

5. The (worse / worst) effect of heavy drinking on the liver is cirrhosis, in which normal liver cells are replaced with scar tissue.

6. Hearing about what alcohol can do to their bodies, some women may think that it is (better / best) not to drink at all.

7. Not all women who drink have (worse / worst) health outcomes than women who do not, however.

8. In fact, recent studies have shown that women who drink one alcoholic beverage a day have a (better / best) chance of aging healthfully than those who drink more heavily or not at all.

9. Women who drink more heavily, though, may do (worse / worst) than nondrinkers and minimal drinkers because they can increase their risk of breast cancer.

10. The (better / best) approach for those who enjoy wine, beer, or cocktails is to drink these beverages in moderation—advice that both women and men should follow.

Edit for Adjective and Adverb Problems

PRACTICE 5 Editing Paragraphs for Correct Adjectives and Adverbs

Find and correct seven adjective and adverb errors in the following paragraphs.

(1) Every day, many people log on to play one of the popularest computer games of all time, *World of Warcraft*. (2) This multiplayer game was first introduced by Blizzard Entertainment in 1994 and has grown quick

ever since. (3) More than 11 million players participate in the game every month, according to the recentest figures.

(4) Computer game experts call *World of Warcraft* a "massively multi-player online role-playing game," or MMORPG for short. (5) Players of this game select a realm in which to play. (6) They choose from among four differently realms. (7) Each realm has its own set of rules and even its own language. (8) Players also choose if they want to be members of the Alliance or the Horde, which are groups that oppose each other. (9) Each side tends to think that it is gooder than the other one.

(10) In *World of Warcraft,* questing is one of the funnest activities. (11) Questing players undertake special missions or tasks to earn experience and gold. (12) The goal is to trade these earnings for better skills and equipment. (13) Players must proceed careful to stay in the game and increase their overall power and abilities.

PRACTICE 6 Editing Your Own Writing for Correct Adjectives and Adverbs

Edit a piece of your own writing for correct use of adjectives and adverbs. It can be a paper for this course or another one, or something you have written for work or your everyday life. Use the chart on page 457 to help you.

Chapter Review

1. Adjectives modify _____ and _____.
2. Adverbs modify _____, _____, or _____.
3. Many adverbs are formed by adding an _____ ending to an adjective.
4. The comparative form of an adjective or adverb is used to compare how many people, places, things, or ideas? _____
5. The superlative form of an adjective or adverb is used to compare how many people, places, things, or ideas? _____
6. What four words have irregular comparative and superlative forms? _____

LEARNING JOURNAL Did you find adjective or adverb errors in your writing? What is the main thing you have learned about adjectives and adverbs that will help you? What is unclear to you?

Chapter Test

Circle the correct choice for each of the following items.

1. Choose the correct word to fill in the blank.

   We performed _____ in the debate, so we will have to be better prepared next time.

   a. bad   **b.** worse   **c.** badly

2. If an underlined portion of this sentence is incorrect, select the revision that fixes it. If the sentence is correct as written, choose d.

   After the <u>beautiful</u> wedding, the groom danced <u>happy</u> down the
                A   B
   church's <u>stone</u> steps.
           C

   a. beautifully   **c.** stonily
   b. happily   **d.** No change is necessary.

3. Choose the item that has no errors.
   a. Sarah's foot is healing well, and she is making a good recovery.
   b. Sarah's foot is healing good, and she is making a good recovery.
   c. Sarah's foot is healing good, and she is making a well recovery.

4. Choose the correct word(s) to fill in the blank.

   With Kenneth's wild imagination, he is a _____ choice than Conor for writing the play's script.

   a. gooder   **b.** better   **c.** more good

5. If an underlined portion of this sentence is incorrect, select the revision that fixes it. If the sentence is correct as written, choose d.

   When asked about the <u>thoughtfulest</u> person I know, I immediately
                                      A
   gave the name of my <u>best</u> friend, who is <u>kind</u> to everyone.
                       B   C

   a. most thoughtful   **c.** kindest
   b. bestest   **d.** No change is necessary.

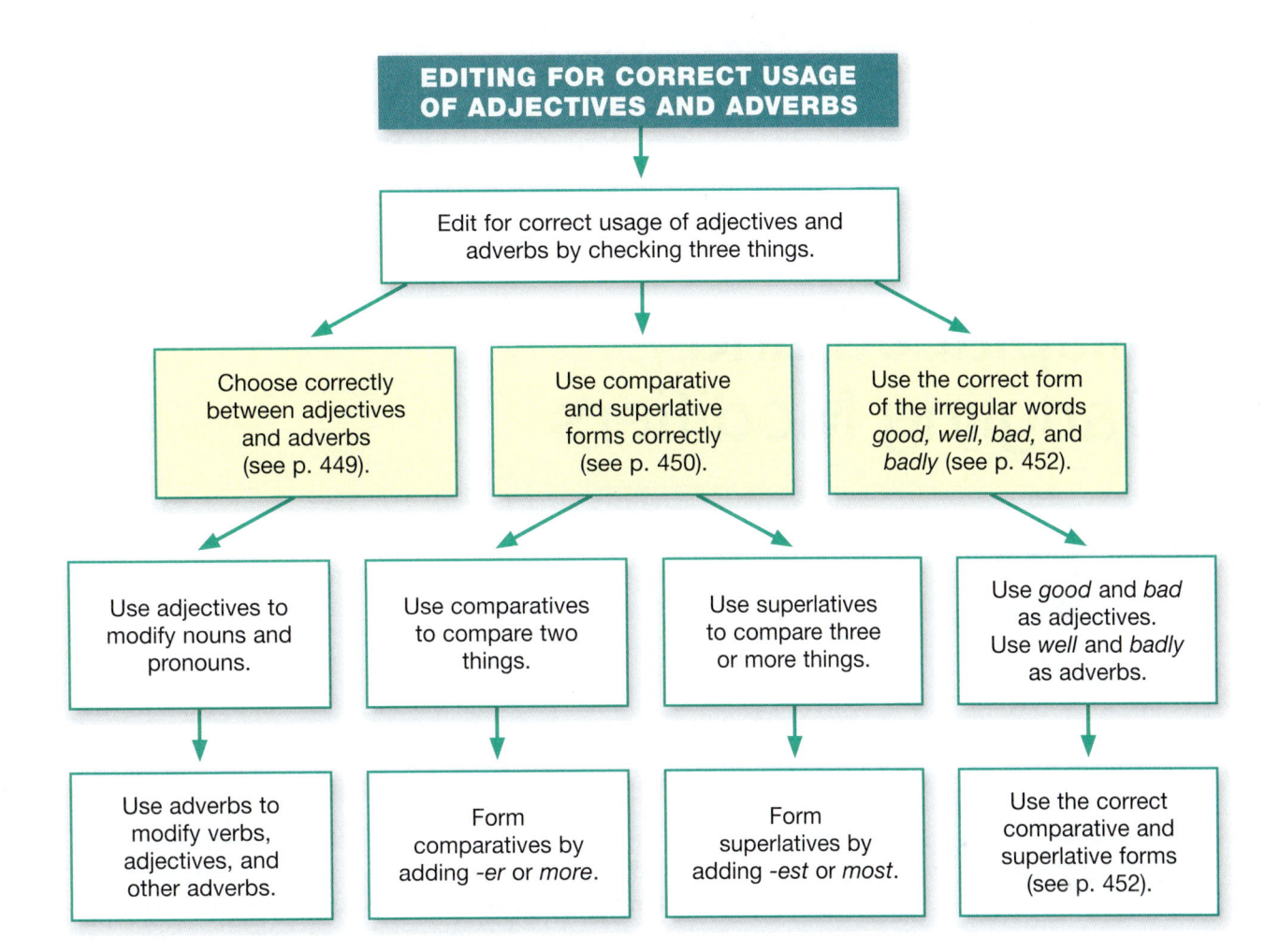

EDITING FOR CORRECT USAGE OF ADJECTIVES AND ADVERBS

Edit for correct usage of adjectives and adverbs by checking three things.

- Choose correctly between adjectives and adverbs (see p. 449).
  - Use adjectives to modify nouns and pronouns.
    - Use adverbs to modify verbs, adjectives, and other adverbs.

- Use comparative and superlative forms correctly (see p. 450).
  - Use comparatives to compare two things.
    - Form comparatives by adding *-er* or *more*.
  - Use superlatives to compare three or more things.
    - Form superlatives by adding *-est* or *most*.

- Use the correct form of the irregular words *good*, *well*, *bad*, and *badly* (see p. 452).
  - Use *good* and *bad* as adjectives. Use *well* and *badly* as adverbs.
    - Use the correct comparative and superlative forms (see p. 452).

26

Misplaced and Dangling Modifiers

Avoiding Confusing Descriptions

> **THIS CHAPTER**
> - explains what misplaced and dangling modifiers are.
> - gives examples of the kinds of modifiers that are often misplaced.
> - gives you practice correcting misplaced and dangling modifiers.

Understand What Misplaced Modifiers Are

TIP For a review of basic sentence elements, see Chapter 19.

Modifiers are words or word groups that describe other words in a sentence. Modifiers should be near the words they modify; otherwise, the sentence can be unintentionally funny. A **misplaced modifier**, because it is in the wrong place, describes the wrong word or words.

MISPLACED Linda saw the White House *flying over Washington, D.C.*
[Was the White House flying over Washington?]

CLEAR *Flying over Washington, D.C.,* Linda saw the White House.

To correct a misplaced modifier, place the modifier as close as possible to the word or words it modifies, often directly before it.

Wearing my bathrobe, I went outside to get the paper. ~~wearing my bathrobe.~~

Four constructions often lead to misplaced modifiers.

1. **Modifiers such as *only, almost, hardly, nearly,* and *just*.** These words need to be immediately before—not just close to—the words or phrases they modify.

   I ~~only~~ *only* found two old photos in the drawer.
   [The intended meaning is that just two photos were in the drawer.]

   Joanne ~~almost~~ *almost* ate the whole cake.
   [Joanne actually ate; she did not "almost" eat.]

458

Thomas ~~nearly~~ *nearly* spent 2 hours waiting for the bus.

[Thomas spent close to 2 hours waiting; he did not "nearly" spend them.]

2. **Modifiers that are prepositional phrases.**

   The cashier found money *from the cash register* on the floor. ~~from the cash register.~~

   Jen served punch *in plastic cups* to the seniors. ~~in plastic cups.~~

3. **Modifiers that start with *-ing* verbs.**

   Using jumper cables, Darlene started the car. ~~using jumper cables.~~

   [The car was not using jumper cables; Darlene was.]

   Wearing flip-flops, Javier climbed the mountain. ~~wearing flip-flops.~~

   [The mountain was not wearing flip-flops; Javier was.]

4. **Modifier clauses that start with *who, whose, that,* or *which*.**

   Joel found the computer virus *that was infecting my hard drive* attached to an e-mail message. ~~that was infecting my hard drive.~~

   [The e-mail did not infect the hard drive; the virus did.]

   The baby *who was crying* on the bus ~~who was crying~~ had curly hair.

   [The bus was not crying; the baby was.]

Practice Correcting Misplaced Modifiers

PRACTICE 1 Correcting Misplaced Modifiers

Find and correct misplaced modifiers in the following sentences.

EXAMPLE: I write things in my blog that I used to ~~only~~ *only* tell my best friends.

1. I used to write about all kinds of personal things and private observations in a diary.

2. Now, I nearly write the same things in my blog.

3. Any story might show up in my blog that is entertaining.

4. The video I was making was definitely something I wanted to write about in my blog of my cousin Tim's birthday.

5. I had invited to the birthday party my loudest, wildest friends wanting the video to be funny.

TIP For more practice correcting misplaced and dangling modifiers, visit *Exercise Central* at bedfordstmartins.com/realwriting.

OTHER GRAMMAR CONCERNS

Chapter 26 • Misplaced and Dangling Modifiers

6. We jumped off tables, had mock swordfights, and almost used ten cans of whipped cream in a food fight.

7. Unfortunately, the battery in the smartphone died that I was using to make the video.

8. I told my friends that I would write a blog post about the party anyway apologizing to them.

9. I explained how I would include the funny story about the failed video session in the blog post.

10. My friends hardly said that they could wait until we tried again to make the video.

Understand What Dangling Modifiers Are

A **dangling modifier** "dangles" because the word or word group it modifies is not in the sentence. Dangling modifiers usually appear at the beginning of a sentence and seem to modify the noun or pronoun that immediately follows them, but they are really modifying another word or group of words.

> **DANGLING**   *Rushing to class,* the books fell out of my bag.
> [The books were not rushing to class.]
>
> **CLEAR**   *Rushing to class,* I dropped my books.

There are two basic ways to correct dangling modifiers. Use the one that makes more sense. One way is to add the word being modified immediately after the opening modifier so that the connection between the two is clear.

Trying to eat a hot dog, ~~my bike~~ I swerved on my bike.

Another way is to add the word being modified in the opening modifier itself.

While I was trying ~~Trying~~ to eat a hot dog, my bike swerved.

Practice Correcting Dangling Modifiers

PRACTICE 2   Correcting Dangling Modifiers

Find and correct any dangling modifiers in the following sentences. If a sentence is correct, write a "C" next to it. It may be necessary to add new words or ideas to some sentences.

EXAMPLE: ~~Inviting~~ *Because I had invited* my whole family to dinner, the kitchen was filled with all kinds of food.

1. Preparing a big family dinner, the oven suddenly stopped working.
2. In a panic, we searched for Carmen, who can solve any problem.
3. Trying to help, the kitchen was crowded.
4. Looking into the oven, the turkey was not done.
5. Discouraged, the dinner was about to be canceled.
6. Staring out the window, a pizza truck went by.
7. Using a credit card, Carmen ordered six pizzas.
8. With one quick phone call, six large pizzas solved our problem.
9. Returning to the crowd in the kitchen, family members still surrounded the oven.
10. Delighted with Carmen's decision, cheers filled the room.

Edit for Misplaced and Dangling Modifiers

PRACTICE 3 Editing Paragraphs for Misplaced and Dangling Modifiers

Find and correct any misplaced or dangling modifiers in the following paragraphs.

(1) Carrying overfilled backpacks is a common habit, but not necessarily a good one. (2) Bulging with books, water bottles, and sports equipment and weighing an average of 14 to 18 pounds, students' backs can gradually become damaged. (3) Because they have to plan ahead for the whole day and often need books, extra clothes, and on-the-go meals, backpacks get heavier and heavier. (4) An increasing number of doctors, primarily physical therapists, are seeing young people with chronic back problems.

(5) Researchers have recently invented a new type of backpack from the University of Pennsylvania and the Marine Biological Laboratory. (6) Designed with springs, the backpack moves up and down as a person walks. (7) This new backpack creates energy, which is then collected and transferred to an electrical generator. (8) Experiencing relief from the wear and tear on muscles, the springs make the pack more comfortable.

(9) What is the purpose of the electricity generated by these new backpacks? (10) Needing electricity for their night-vision goggles, the backpacks could solve a problem for soldiers. (11) Soldiers could benefit from such an efficient energy source to power their global positioning systems and other electronic gear. (12) Instead of being battery operated, the soldiers could use the special backpacks and would not have to carry additional batteries. (13) For the average student, these backpacks might one day provide convenient energy for video games, television, and music players, all at the same time. (14) Designed with this technology, kids would just have to look both ways before crossing the street.

> **PRACTICE 4** **Editing Your Own Writing for Misplaced and Dangling Modifiers**
>
> Edit a piece of your own writing for misplaced and dangling modifiers. It can be a paper for this course or another one, or something you have written for work or your everyday life. You may want to use the chart on page 464.

Chapter Review

LEARNING JOURNAL Do you sometimes write sentences with misplaced or dangling modifiers? What is the main thing you have learned about correcting them? What remains unclear to you?

1. _____ are words or word groups that describe other words in a sentence.

2. A _____ describes the incorrect word or word group because it is in the wrong place in a sentence.

3. When an opening modifier does not modify any word in the sentence, it is a _____ .

4. Which four constructions often lead to misplaced modifiers?

   _____

   _____

   _____

   _____

Chapter Test

Circle the correct choice for each of the following items.

1. If an underlined portion of this sentence is incorrect, select the revision that fixes it. If the sentence is correct as written, choose d.

   Annoyed by the flashing cameras, the limousine drove the celebrity
         A   B
   away from the crowd in front of the restaurant.
                           C

   a. Annoying
   b. the celebrity got into the limousine, which drove
   c. the restaurant in front of
   d. No change is necessary.

2. Choose the item that has no errors.
   a. The thief found the code in the bank clerk's desk for the alarm system.
   b. The thief found the code for the alarm system in the bank clerk's desk.
   c. For the alarm system, the thief found the code in the bank clerk's desk.

3. If an underlined portion of this sentence is incorrect, select the revision that fixes it. If the sentence is correct as written, choose d.

   Talking on his cell phone, his shopping cart rolled over my foot.
     A   B   C

   a. Talking and concentrating too much
   b. his cell phones
   c. he rolled his shopping cart
   d. No change is necessary.

4. If an underlined portion of this sentence is incorrect, select the revision that fixes it. If the sentence is correct as written, choose d.

   I only bought two tickets to the game, so one of the three of us
        A   B   C
   cannot go.

   a. bought only
   b. to go to the game
   c. of the us three of
   d. No change is necessary.

EDITING FOR MISPLACED AND DANGLING MODIFIERS

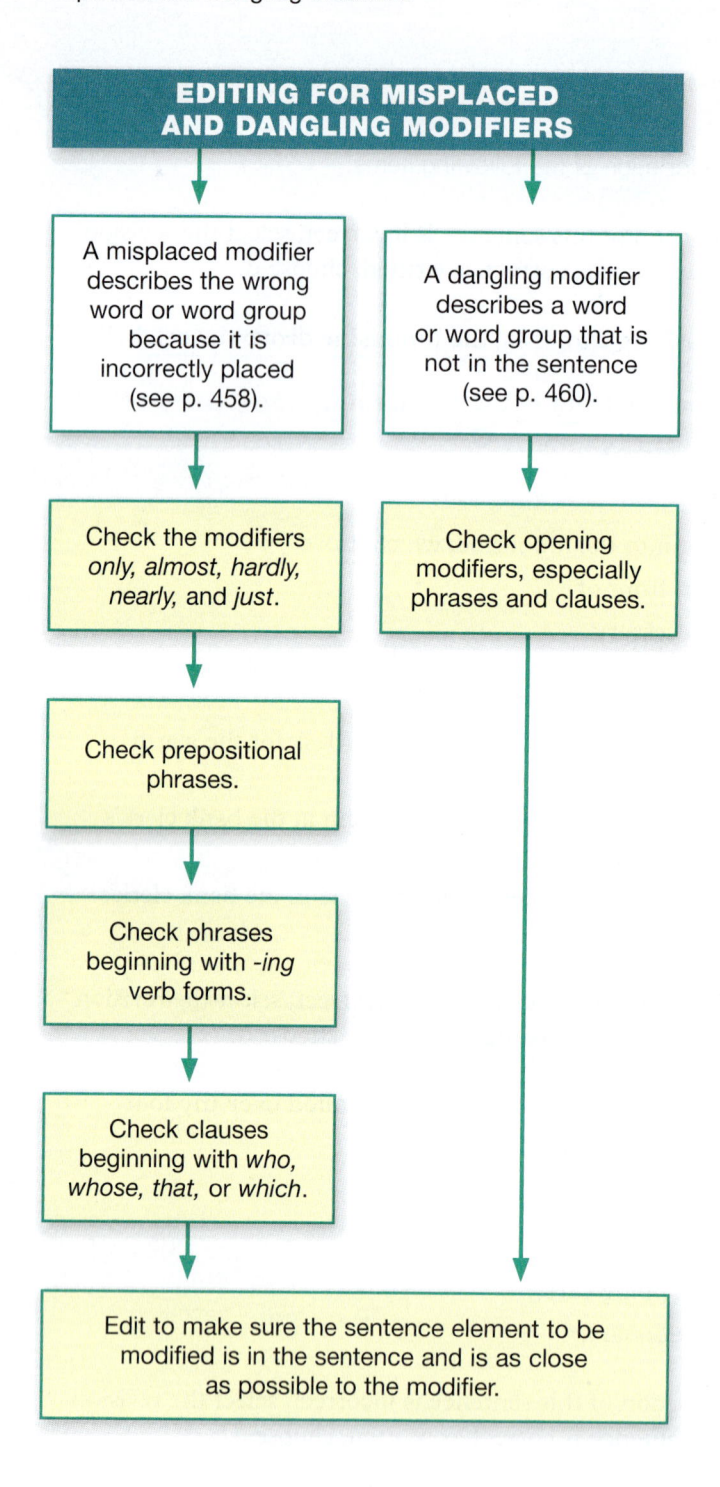

- A misplaced modifier describes the wrong word or word group because it is incorrectly placed (see p. 458).
  - Check the modifiers *only, almost, hardly, nearly,* and *just*.
  - Check prepositional phrases.
  - Check phrases beginning with *-ing* verb forms.
  - Check clauses beginning with *who, whose, that,* or *which*.

- A dangling modifier describes a word or word group that is not in the sentence (see p. 460).
  - Check opening modifiers, especially phrases and clauses.

Edit to make sure the sentence element to be modified is in the sentence and is as close as possible to the modifier.

27

THIS CHAPTER

- explains what coordination and subordination are.
- explains how to use coordination and subordination to combine sentences.
- gives you practice joining sentences with coordination and subordination.

Coordination and Subordination

Joining Sentences with Related Ideas

Understand What Coordination Is

Coordination is used to join two sentences with related ideas, and it can make your writing less choppy. The sentences remain complete and independent, but they are joined with a comma and a coordinating conjunction.

TIP To understand this chapter, you need to be familiar with basic sentence elements. For a review, see Chapter 19.

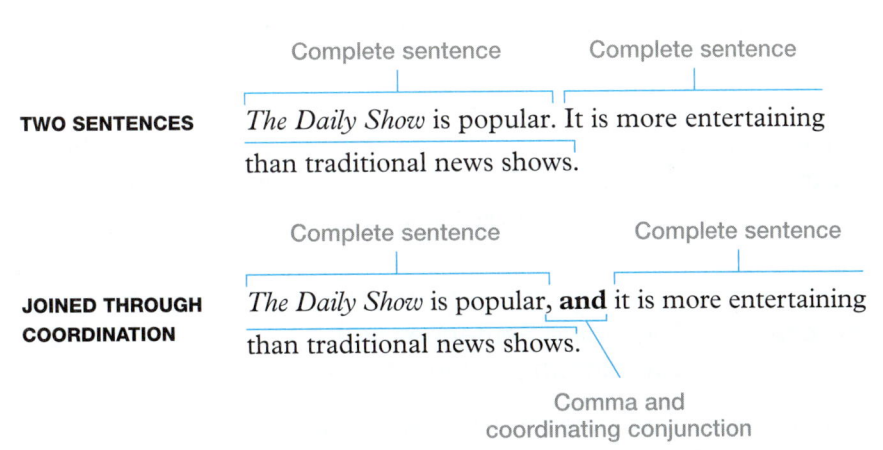

TWO SENTENCES — *The Daily Show* is popular. [Complete sentence] It is more entertaining than traditional news shows. [Complete sentence]

JOINED THROUGH COORDINATION — *The Daily Show* is popular, **and** it is more entertaining than traditional news shows.
(Comma and coordinating conjunction)

Practice Using Coordination

Using Coordinating Conjunctions

Conjunctions join words, phrases, or clauses. **Coordinating conjunctions** join ideas of equal importance. (You can remember them by thinking of **FANBOYS**—*for, and, nor, but, or, yet, so*.) To join two sentences through coordination, put a comma and one of these conjunctions

465

between the sentences. Choose the conjunction that makes the most sense for the meaning of the two sentences.

Complete sentence	, for , and , nor , but , or , yet , so	Complete sentence

TIP For more on the use of commas, see Chapter 34.

| Wikipedia is a popular encyclopedia | , for | it is easily available online. |

[*For* indicates a reason or cause.]

| The encyclopedia is open to all | , and | anyone can add information to it. |

[*And* simply joins two ideas.]

| Often, inaccurate entries cannot be stopped | , nor | is there any penalty for them. |

[*Nor* indicates a negative.]

| People have complained about errors | , but | the mistakes may or may not be fixed. |

[*But* indicates a contrast.]

| Some people delete information | , or | they add their own interpretations. |

[*Or* indicates alternatives.]

| Many people know that Wikipedia is flawed | , yet | they continue to use it. |

[*Yet* indicates a contrast or possibility.]

| Wikipedia now has trustees | , so | perhaps it will be monitored more closely. |

[*So* indicates a result.]

PRACTICE 1 Combining Sentences with Coordinating Conjunctions

Combine each pair of sentences into a single sentence by using a comma and a coordinating conjunction. In some cases, there may be more than one correct answer.

TIP For more practice with coordination and subordination, visit *Exercise Central* at bedfordstmartins.com/realwriting.

EXAMPLE: In business, e-mails can make a good or bad impression,/
~~People~~ so people should mind their e-mail manners.

1. Many professionals use e-mail to keep in touch with clients and contacts, and ~~They~~ they must be especially careful not to offend anyone with their e-mail messages.

OTHER GRAMMAR CONCERNS
Practice Using Coordination

2. However, anyone who uses e-mail should be cautious. It is dangerously easy to send messages to the wrong person.

3. Employees may have time to send personal messages from work. They should remember that employers often have the ability to read their workers' messages.

4. R-rated language and jokes may be deleted automatically by a company's server. They may be read by managers and cause problems for the employee sending or receiving them.

5. No message should be forwarded to everyone in a sender's address book. Senders should ask permission before adding someone to a mass-mailing list.

6. People should check the authenticity of mailings about lost children, dreadful diseases, and terrorist threats before passing them on. Most such messages are hoaxes.

7. Typographical errors and misspellings in e-mail make the message appear less professional. Using all capital letters—a practice known as *shouting*—is usually considered even worse.

8. People who use e-mail for business want to be taken seriously. They should make their e-mails as professional as possible.

Using Semicolons

A **semicolon** is a punctuation mark that can join two sentences through coordination. Use semicolons *only* when the ideas in the two sentences are closely related. Do not overuse semicolons.

Complete sentence	;	Complete sentence
Antarctica is a mystery	;	few people know much about it.
Its climate is extreme	;	few people want to endure it.
My cousin went there	;	he loves to explore the unknown.

TIP When you connect two sentences with a conjunctive adverb, the statement following the semicolon remains a complete thought. If you use a subordinating word such as *because*, however, the second statement becomes a dependent clause, and a semicolon is not needed: *The desert is cold at night because sand does not store heat well.*

A semicolon alone does not tell readers much about the relationship between the two ideas. To give more information about the relationship, use a **conjunctive adverb** after the semicolon. Put a comma after the conjunctive adverb.

OTHER GRAMMAR CONCERNS
Chapter 27 • Coordination and Subordination

Complete sentence	; also, ; as a result, ; besides, ; furthermore, ; however, ; in addition, ; in fact, ; instead, ; moreover, ; still, ; then, ; therefore,	Complete sentence
Antarctica is largely unexplored	; as a result,	it is unpopulated.
It receives little rain	; also,	it is incredibly cold.
It is a huge area	; therefore,	scientists are becoming more interested in it.

EDITING FOR COORDINATION:
Joining Sentences with Related Ideas

Find

I go to bed late at night. I get up early in the morning.

1. **Ask:** Should the sentences be joined by a coordinating conjunction (FANBOYS) or by a semicolon and a conjunctive adverb? *These sentences could be joined in either way.*
2. **Ask:** What coordinating conjunction(s) or conjunctive adverb(s) best expresses the relationship between the two sentences? *"And" could join the two ideas; "but," "yet," or "however" could show a contrast.*

Edit

I go to bed late at night, and I get up early in the morning.
I go to bed late at night, but I get up early in the morning.
I go to bed late at night, yet I get up early in the morning.
I go to bed late at night; however, I get up early in the morning.

3. **Join the two sentences** with a coordinating conjunction or a semicolon and a conjunctive adverb.

PRACTICE 2 Combining Sentences with Semicolons and Conjunctive Adverbs

Combine each pair of sentences by using a semicolon and a conjunctive adverb. In some cases, there may be more than one correct answer.

EXAMPLE: More and more people are researching their family history, or genealogy; in fact, this type of research is now considered one of the fastest-growing hobbies in North America.

1. Before the Internet, genealogy researchers had to contact public offices to get records of ancestors' births, marriages, occupations, and deaths. Some visited libraries to search for old newspaper articles mentioning the ancestors.

2. There was no quick and easy way to search records or article databases. With the rise of the Internet and new digital tools, genealogy research became much simpler.

3. These tools allow people to search a wide range of records with key words. Researchers can gather details about their ancestors' lives much more quickly and efficiently.

4. Recently, people have started using social-networking tools to find out about living and dead relatives. Some of them are getting more information even more quickly.

5. One researcher, Lauren Axelrod, used Ancestry.com to gather some information on the birth mother of her husband, who had been adopted. Using this information, she searched for his birth mother on Facebook.

6. The entire search, which ended successfully, took only 2 hours. In less than a week, Axelrod's husband was talking on the phone with his birth mother.

7. Not everyone thinks that genealogy research has to be a purely serious hobby. Some people see it as a great way to have fun.

8. In the online Family Village Game, players create characters, or avatars, representing their ancestors. Using genealogical records, they add background information on these ancestors.

9. Players have a lot of fun creating the characters and their worlds. They get additional genealogical information by following the research suggestions provided by the game.

10. Some parents play Family Village Game with their children. The children see their connection to the past.

PRACTICE 3 Choosing the Right Coordinating Conjunctions and Conjunctive Adverbs

Fill in the blanks with a coordinating conjunction or conjunctive adverb that makes sense in the sentence. Make sure to add the correct punctuation.

EXAMPLE: Rebates sound like a good deal _____, but_____ they rarely are.

1. Rebate offers are common _____ you have probably seen many of them on packages for appliances and electronics.

2. These offers may promise to return hundreds of dollars to consumers _____ many people apply for them.

3. Applicants hope to get a lot of money back soon _____ they are often disappointed.

4. They might have to wait several months _____ they might not get their rebate at all.

5. Rebate applications are not short _____ are they easy to fill out.

6. One applicant compared completing a rebate form to filling out tax forms _____ he spent more than an hour on the process.

7. Manufacturers sometimes use rebates to move unpopular products off the shelves _____ they can replace these products with newer goods.

8. Only about 10 to 30 percent of people who apply for a rebate eventually get it _____ consumer groups are warning people to be careful.

9. Problems with rebates are getting more attention _____ companies that offer them might have to improve their processes for giving refunds.

10. Manufacturers have received a lot of complaints about rebates _____ they will probably never stop making these offers.

Understand What Subordination Is

Like coordination, **subordination** is a way to join short, choppy sentences with related ideas into a longer sentence. With subordination, you put a dependent word (such as *after*, *although*, *because*, or *when*) in front of one of the sentences, which then becomes a dependent clause and is no longer a complete sentence.

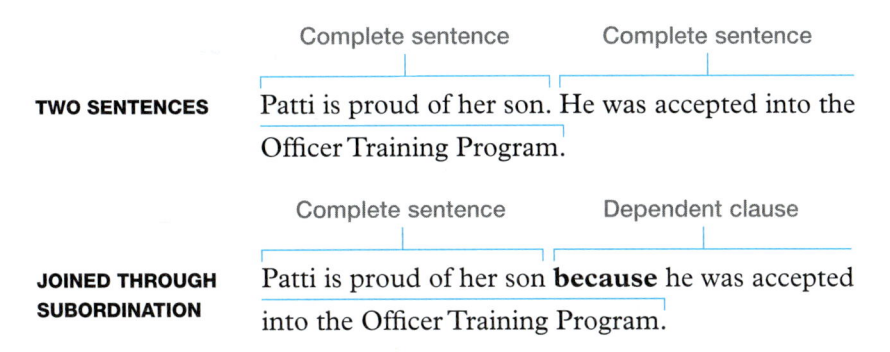

TWO SENTENCES: Patti is proud of her son. [Complete sentence] He was accepted into the Officer Training Program. [Complete sentence]

JOINED THROUGH SUBORDINATION: Patti is proud of her son [Complete sentence] **because** he was accepted into the Officer Training Program. [Dependent clause]

Practice Using Subordination

To join two sentences through subordination, use a **subordinating conjunction**. Choose the conjunction that makes the most sense with the two sentences. Here are some of the most common subordinating conjunctions.

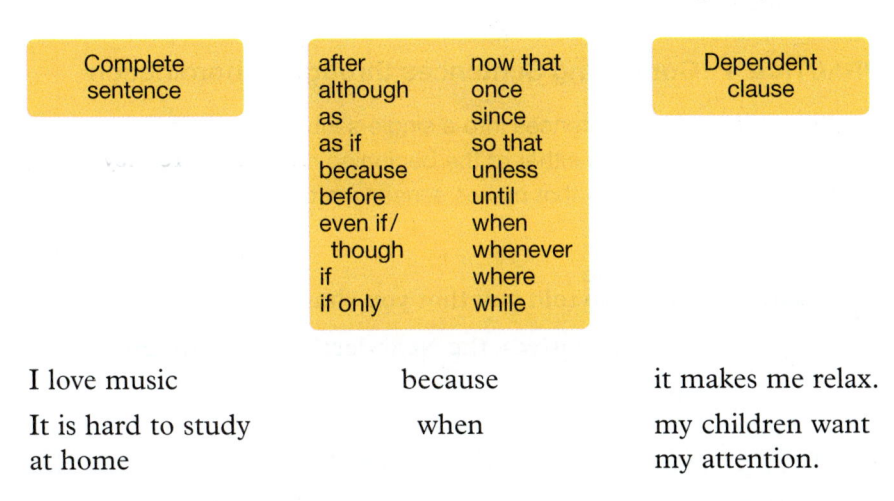

Complete sentence	Subordinating conjunctions	Dependent clause
	after, although, as, as if, because, before, even if/though, if, if only, now that, once, since, so that, unless, until, when, whenever, where, while	

I love music	because	it makes me relax.
It is hard to study at home	when	my children want my attention.

When a dependent clause ends a sentence, it usually does not need to be preceded by a comma unless it is showing a contrast.

When the dependent clause begins a sentence, use a comma to separate it from the rest of the sentence.

Subordinating conjunction	Dependent clause	,	Complete sentence
When	I eat out	,	I usually have steak.
Although	it is harmful	,	young people still smoke.

OTHER GRAMMAR CONCERNS

472 Chapter 27 • Coordination and Subordination

EDITING FOR SUBORDINATION:
Joining Ideas with Related Ideas

↓

Find

It is hard to sleep in the city. It is always very noisy.

1. **Ask:** What is the relationship between the two complete sentences? *The second sentence explains the first.*
2. **Ask:** What subordinating conjunctions express that relationship? *"Because," "as," or "since."*

↓

Edit

It is hard to sleep in the city/ ~~It~~ *because it* is always very noisy.

3. **Join the two sentences** with a subordinating conjunction that makes sense.

PRACTICE 4 Combining Sentences through Subordination

Combine each pair of sentences into a single sentence by using an appropriate subordinating conjunction either at the beginning of or between the two sentences. Use a conjunction that makes sense with the two sentences, and add commas where necessary.

> EXAMPLE: *If someone* ~~Someone~~ told you that you share DNA with humans' extinct relatives, the Neanderthals/ *, you* ~~You~~ might be surprised.

1. In fact, scientists have found that mating between humans and Neanderthals occurred. Groups of humans migrated north and east from Africa.

2. Scientists examined the DNA of modern humans. They made a startling discovery: 1 to 4 percent of all non-Africans' DNA is Neanderthal DNA.

3. Old illustrations present Neanderthals as bent over and primitive looking. It may be hard to believe that humans would want to mate with them.

4. However, a Neanderthal man got a good shave and a nice set of clothes. He might pass for a modern man.

5. Researchers are learning more about Neanderthals. Many mysteries remain.

6. Researchers continue their investigations. They are trying to answer one key question: What are the specific genetic differences between humans and Neanderthals?

7. They have started sequencing the entire Neanderthal genome. They can answer this question.

8. The genome is the entire set of genetic material for an organism. Comparing the Neanderthal genome to the human one might help researchers identify a number of differences between the two species.

9. These differences have yet to be identified. Scientists are growing more and more certain about the answer to one question: Why did Neanderthals become extinct?

10. Humans mated with Neanderthals. They also contributed to Neanderthals' extinction, either by killing them or by outcompeting them for food and other resources.

PRACTICE 5 Combining Sentences through Coordination and Subordination

Join each of the following sentence pairs in two ways, first by coordination and then by subordination.

EXAMPLE: Rick has many talents. He is still deciding what to do with his life.

JOINED BY COORDINATION: *Rick has many talents, but he is still deciding what to do with his life.*

JOINED BY SUBORDINATION: *Although Rick has many talents, he is still deciding what to do with his life.*

1. Rick rides a unicycle. He can juggle four oranges.

   JOINED BY COORDINATION: _____

   JOINED BY SUBORDINATION: _____

OTHER GRAMMAR CONCERNS

474 Chapter 27 • Coordination and Subordination

2. A trapeze school opened in our town. Rick signed up immediately.

JOINED BY COORDINATION: _____

_____

JOINED BY SUBORDINATION: _____

_____

3. Rick is now at the top of his class. He worked hard practicing trapeze routines.

JOINED BY COORDINATION: _____

_____

JOINED BY SUBORDINATION: _____

_____

4. Rick asks me for career advice. I try to be encouraging.

JOINED BY COORDINATION: _____

_____

JOINED BY SUBORDINATION: _____

_____

5. He does not want to join the circus. He could study entertainment management.

JOINED BY COORDINATION: _____

_____

JOINED BY SUBORDINATION: _____

_____

Edit for Coordination and Subordination

PRACTICE 6 Editing Paragraphs for Coordination and Subordination

In the following paragraphs, combine the six pairs of underlined sentences. For three of the sentence pairs, use coordination. For the other three sentence pairs, use subordination. Do not forget to punctuate correctly, and keep in mind that there may be more than one way to combine each sentence pair.

(1) Washington, D.C., was the first city in the United States to offer a public bicycle-sharing program. (2) The idea has been popular in Europe for years. (3) In fact, Paris has more than twenty thousand bikes available

for people to rent and ride around the city. (4) Called Capital Bikeshare, the Washington program costs citizens $7 a day, $25 a month, or $75 a year to join. (5) For that fee, they have access to more than one thousand bikes available at 110 stations set up all over Washington and in Arlington, Virginia. (6) After using the bikes, people must return them to one of the stations. (7) Other riders might be waiting. (8) Regular users have come to depend on Capital Bikeshare for short trips and errands. (9) The popularity of the program is growing.

(10) Throughout the United States, cycling has become much more popular in recent years. (11) Gasoline prices have increased. (12) A number of other cities are now considering bike-sharing programs. (13) Studies show that these programs can reduce city traffic by 4 to 5 percent. (14) Some companies are already creating similar programs to encourage their employees to exercise more and drive less. (15) Company leaders are aware that fit employees and a healthier environment are important goals to achieve. (16) It means that the company spends a little extra time, money, and effort to start and run a bike-sharing program.

PRACTICE 7 Editing Your Own Writing for Coordination and Subordination

Edit a piece of your own writing for coordination and subordination. It can be a paper for this course or another one, or something you have written for work or your everyday life. You may want to use the chart on page 477.

Chapter Review

1. What are the two ways to join sentences through coordination?

    _____

    _____

    _____

2. Use a semicolon *only* when the sentences are _____ .

3. Write two sentences using coordination.

    _____

    _____

LEARNING JOURNAL Did you find coordination or subordination errors in your writing? What is the main thing you have learned about coordination and subordination that will help you? What is unclear to you?

OTHER GRAMMAR CONCERNS

Chapter 27 • Coordination and Subordination

4. With subordination, you put a _____ in front of one of two related sentences.

5. Write two sentences using subordination.
   _____
   _____

Chapter Test

Circle the correct choice to fill in each blank.

1. We were delighted when Eva was transferred to our department, _____ she does not seem pleased with the change.

   a. or   b. and   **c. but** (circled)

2. _____ the candidate stepped up to the podium, a group of protesters began to shout criticisms of her.

   a. So that   b. As if   **c. As** (circled)

3. Daniel is very clever _____ he can convince anyone that he is right.

   a. , but   **b. ;** (circled)   c. ,

4. _____ you are sure that the lightning has stopped, don't let the kids get back into the pool.

   a. Until (circled)   b. Before   c. As if

5. I do not have a smartphone; _____ I cannot access the Internet when I am away from my computer.

   a. besides,   b. however,   **c. therefore,** (circled)

6. Matt speaks out against glorifying college sports _____ he himself is the star of our football team.

   a. until   **b. even though** (circled)   c. unless

7. I did not like the teacher's criticism of my paper; _____ I must admit that everything she said was right.

   a. as a result,   b. in addition,   **c. still,** (circled)

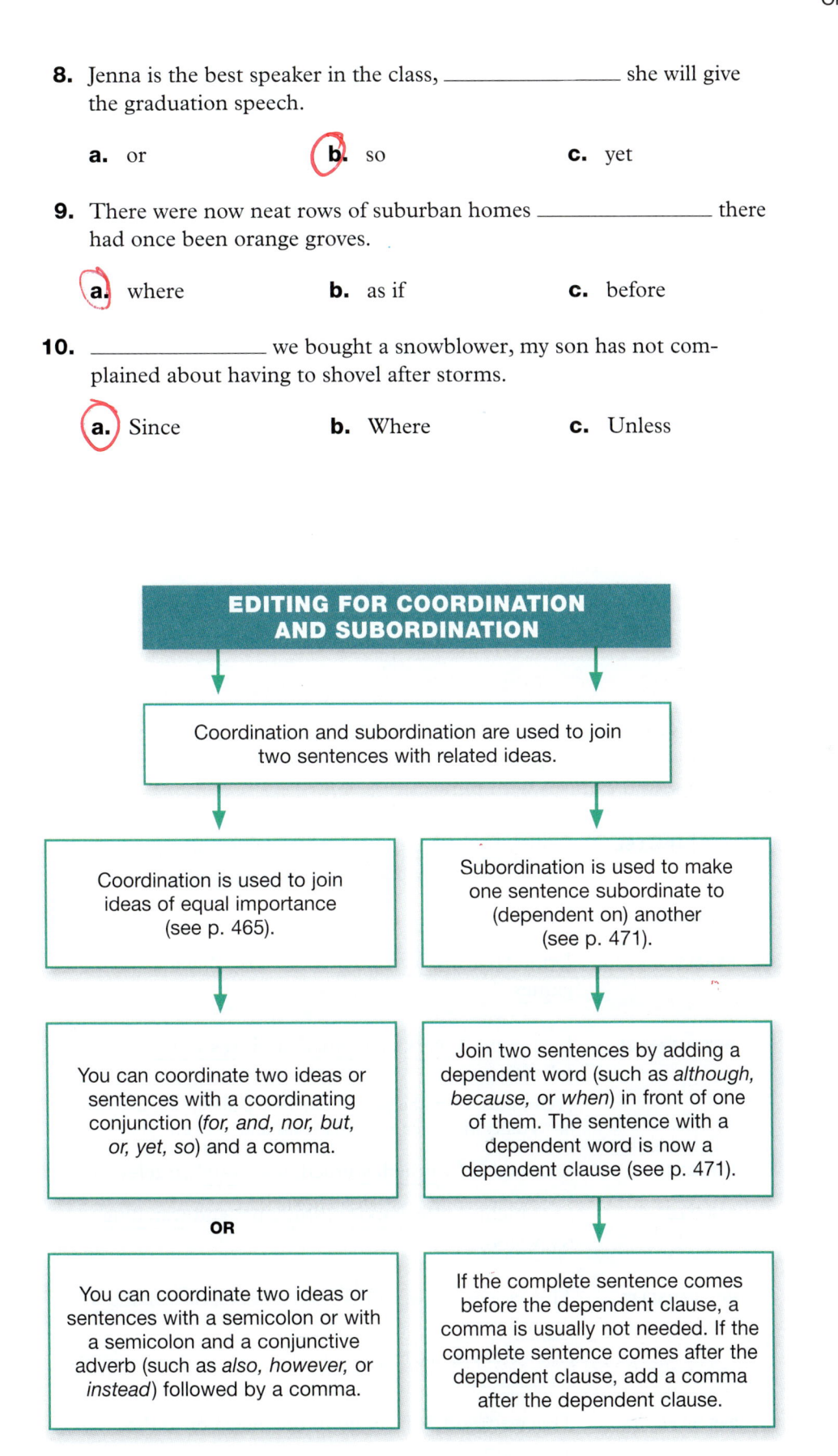

8. Jenna is the best speaker in the class, _____ she will give the graduation speech.

   a. or   **b. so** (circled)   c. yet

9. There were now neat rows of suburban homes _____ there had once been orange groves.

   a. where (circled)   b. as if   c. before

10. _____ we bought a snowblower, my son has not complained about having to shovel after storms.

    a. Since (circled)   b. Where   c. Unless

EDITING FOR COORDINATION AND SUBORDINATION

Coordination and subordination are used to join two sentences with related ideas.

- Coordination is used to join ideas of equal importance (see p. 465).

  - You can coordinate two ideas or sentences with a coordinating conjunction (*for, and, nor, but, or, yet, so*) and a comma.

  OR

  - You can coordinate two ideas or sentences with a semicolon or with a semicolon and a conjunctive adverb (such as *also, however,* or *instead*) followed by a comma.

- Subordination is used to make one sentence subordinate to (dependent on) another (see p. 471).

  - Join two sentences by adding a dependent word (such as *although, because,* or *when*) in front of one of them. The sentence with a dependent word is now a dependent clause (see p. 471).

  - If the complete sentence comes before the dependent clause, a comma is usually not needed. If the complete sentence comes after the dependent clause, add a comma after the dependent clause.

28

Parallelism

Balancing Ideas

THIS CHAPTER
- explains what parallelism is.
- explains how to use parallelism when writing lists and comparisons.
- explains how to write parallel sentences with paired words.
- gives you practice writing parallel sentences.

Understand What Parallelism Is

LearningCurve
Parallelism
bedfordstmartins.com/
realwriting/LC

Parallelism in writing means that similar parts in a sentence have the same structure: Their parts are balanced. Use nouns with nouns, verbs with verbs, and phrases with phrases.

NOT PARALLEL	I enjoy basketball more than playing video games.
	[*Basketball* is a noun, but *playing video games* is a phrase.]
PARALLEL	I enjoy basketball more than video games.
PARALLEL	I enjoy playing basketball more than playing video games.
NOT PARALLEL	Last night, I worked, studied, and was watching television.
	[Verbs must be in the same tense to be parallel. *Was watching* has a different structure from *worked* and *studied*.]
PARALLEL	Last night, I worked, studied, and watched television.
PARALLEL	Last night, I was working, studying, and watching television.
NOT PARALLEL	This weekend, we can go to the beach or walking in the mountains.
	[*To the beach* should be paired with another prepositional phrase: *to the mountains*.]
PARALLEL	This weekend, we can go to the beach or to the mountains.

TIP To understand this chapter, you need to be familiar with basic sentence elements, such as nouns and verbs. For a review, see Chapter 19.

478

OTHER GRAMMAR CONCERNS
Practice Writing Parallel Sentences   479

Practice Writing Parallel Sentences

Parallelism in Pairs and Lists

When two or more items in a series are joined by *and* or *or*, use a similar form for each item.

NOT PARALLEL   The professor assigned readings, practices to do, and a paper.

PARALLEL   The professor assigned readings, practices, and a paper.

NOT PARALLEL   The story was in the newspaper, on the radio, and the television.
[*In the newspaper* and *on the radio* are prepositional phrases. *The television* is not.]

PARALLEL   The story was in the newspaper, on the radio, and on the television.

PRACTICE 1   Using Parallelism in Pairs and Lists

In each sentence, underline the parts of the sentence that should be parallel. Then, edit the sentence to make it parallel.

EXAMPLE: Coyotes roam the western mountains, the central plains, and ~~they are in the suburbs of~~ the East Coast ~~of the United States~~.

1. Wild predators, such as wolves, are vanishing because people hunt them and are taking over their land.
2. Coyotes are surviving and they do well in the modern United States.
3. The success of the coyote is due to its varied diet and adapting easily.
4. Coyotes are sometimes vegetarians, sometimes scavengers, and ~~sometimes they~~ hunt.
5. Today, they are spreading and populate the East Coast for the first time.
6. The coyotes' appearance surprises and is worrying many people.
7. The animals have chosen an area that is more populated and it's not as wild as their traditional home.
8. Coyotes can adapt to rural, suburban, and even living in a city.
9. One coyote was identified, tracked, and they captured him in Central Park in New York City.
10. Suburbanites are getting used to the sight of coyotes and hearing them.

TIP For more practice with making sentences parallel, visit Exercise Central at bedfordstmartins.com/realwriting.

Parallelism in Comparisons

Comparisons often use the word *than* or *as*. When you edit for parallelism, make sure the items on either side of those words have parallel structures.

NOT PARALLEL	Taking the bus downtown is as fast as the drive there.
PARALLEL	Taking the bus downtown is as fast as driving there.
NOT PARALLEL	To admit a mistake is better than denying it.
PARALLEL	To admit a mistake is better than to deny it.
	Admitting a mistake is better than denying it.

Sometimes you need to add or delete a word or two to make the parts of a sentence parallel.

NOT PARALLEL	A tour package is less expensive than arranging every travel detail yourself.
PARALLEL, WORD ADDED	*Buying* a tour package is less expensive than arranging every travel detail yourself.
NOT PARALLEL	The sale price of the shoes is as low as paying half of the regular price.
PARALLEL, WORDS DROPPED	The sale price of the shoes is as low as half of the regular price.

PRACTICE 2 Using Parallelism in Comparisons

In each sentence, underline the parts of the sentence that should be parallel. Then, edit the sentence to make it parallel.

EXAMPLE: Leasing a new car may be less expensive than ~~to buy~~ *buying* one.

1. Car dealers often require less money down for leasing a car than for ~~the purchase of one~~ *for buying one*.
2. The monthly payments for a leased car may be as low as ~~paying for a loan~~ *loan payments*.
3. You should check the terms of leasing to make sure they are as favorable as ~~to buy~~ *terms of buying*.
4. You may find that to lease is a safer bet ~~than buying~~ *than to buy*.
5. You will be making less of a financial commitment by leasing a car than to ~~own~~ *owning* it.

OTHER GRAMMAR CONCERNS
Practice Writing Parallel Sentences   481

6. Buying a car may be better than a ~~lease~~ leasing on one if you plan to keep it for several years.

7. A used car can be more economical than ~~getting~~ a new one.

8. However, maintenance of a new car may be easier than ~~taking care~~ managing of a used car.

9. A used car may not be as impressive as ~~buying a brand-new vehicle~~ to pay for a new car.

10. To get a used car from a reputable source can be a better decision than a new vehicle that loses value the moment you drive it home.

Parallelism with Certain Paired Words

Certain paired words, called **correlative conjunctions**, link two equal elements and show the relationship between them. Here are the paired words:

| both . . . and | neither . . . nor | rather . . . than |
| either . . . or | not only . . . but also | |

Make sure the items joined by these paired words are parallel.

NOT PARALLEL Bruce wants *both* freedom *and* to be wealthy.
[*Both* is used with *and*, but the items joined by them are not parallel.]

PARALLEL Bruce wants *both* freedom *and* wealth.

PARALLEL Bruce wants *both* to have freedom *and* to be wealthy.

NOT PARALLEL He can *neither* fail the course and quitting his job is also impossible.

PARALLEL He can *neither* fail the course *nor* quit his job.

PRACTICE 3   Using Parallelism with Certain Paired Words

In each sentence, circle the paired words, and underline the parts of the sentence that should be parallel. Then, edit the sentence to make it parallel. You may need to change one of the paired elements to make the sentence parallel.

EXAMPLE: A cell phone can be (either) a lifesaver (or) ~~it can be annoying~~ an annoyance.

1. Twenty years ago, most people neither had cell phones nor did they want them.

2. Today, cell phones are not only used by people of all ages but also are carried everywhere.

3. Cell phones are not universally popular: Some commuters would rather ban cell phones on buses and trains than being forced to listen to other people's conversations.

4. No one denies that a cell phone can be both useful and convenience is a factor.

5. A motorist stranded on a deserted road would rather have a cell phone than to walk to the nearest gas station.

6. When cell phones were first introduced, some people feared that they either caused brain tumors or they were a dangerous source of radiation.

7. Most Americans today neither worry about radiation from cell phones nor other injuries.

8. The biggest risk of cell phones is either that drivers are distracted by them or people getting angry at someone talking too loudly in public on a cell phone.

9. Cell phones probably do not cause brain tumors, but some experiments on human cells have shown that energy from the phones may both affect people's reflexes and it might alter the brain's blood vessels.

10. Some scientists think that these experiments show that cell phone use might have not only physical effects on human beings but it also could influence mental processes.

PRACTICE 4 Completing Sentences with Paired Words

For each sentence, complete the correlative conjunction, and add more information. Make sure the structures on both sides of the correlative conjunction are parallel.

EXAMPLE: I am both impressed by your company *and enthusiastic to work for you*.

1. I could bring to this job not only youthful enthusiasm _____ _____.

2. I am willing to work either in your main office _____ _____.

3. My current job neither encourages initiative _____.

4. I would rather work in a challenging job _____.

5. In college, I learned a lot both from my classes _____
_____.

Edit for Parallelism Problems

PRACTICE 5 **Editing Paragraphs for Parallelism Problems**

Find and correct five parallelism errors in the following paragraphs.

(1) On a mountainous island between Norway and the North Pole is a special underground vault. (2) It contains neither gold and other currency. (3) Instead, it is full of a different kind of treasure: seeds. (4) They are being saved for the future in case something happens to the plants that people need to grow for food.

(5) The vault has the capacity to hold 4.5 million types of seed samples. (6) Each sample contains an average of five hundred seeds, which means that up to 2.25 billion seeds can be stored in the vault. (7) To store them is better than planting them. (8) Stored, they are preserved for future generations to plant. (9) On the first day that the vault's storage program began, 268,000 different seeds were deposited, put into sealed packages, and collecting into sealed boxes. (10) Some of the seeds were for maize (corn), while others were for rice, wheat, and barley.

(11) Although some people call it the "Doomsday Vault," many others see it as a type of insurance policy against starvation in the case of a terrible natural disaster. (12) The vault's location keeps it safe from floods, earthquakes, and storming. (13) Carefully storing these seeds not only will help ensure people will have food to eat plus make sure important crops never go extinct.

PRACTICE 6 **Editing Your Own Writing for Parallelism**

Edit a piece of your own writing for parallelism. It can be a paper for this course or another one, or something you have written for work or your everyday life. You may want to use the chart on page 485.

OTHER GRAMMAR CONCERNS

Chapter 28 • Parallelism

Chapter Review

LEARNING JOURNAL Did you find parallelism errors in your writing? What is the main thing you have learned about parallelism that will help you? What is unclear to you?

1. Parallelism in writing means that _____
   _____.

2. In what three situations do problems with parallelism most often occur? _____
   _____

3. What are two pairs of correlative conjunctions? _____
   _____

4. Write two sentences using parallelism.
   _____
   _____

Chapter Test

Circle the correct choice for each of the following items.

1. If an underlined portion of this sentence is incorrect, select the revision that fixes it. If the sentence is correct as written, choose d.

   For our home renovation, we are planning to <u>expand the kitchen</u>,
                                                          A
   <u>retile the bathroom</u>, and <u>we also want to add a bedroom</u>.
           B   **C**

   a. add space to the kitchen   c. add a bedroom
   b. replace the tile in the bathroom   d. No change is necessary.

2. Choose the correct word(s) to fill in the blank.

   In my personal ad, I said that I like taking long walks on the beach, dining over candlelight, and _____ sculptures with a chain saw.

   a. to carve   b. carving   c. carved

3. If an underlined portion of this sentence is incorrect, select the revision that fixes it. If the sentence is correct as written, choose d.

   To get her elbow back into shape, <u>she wants</u> <u>exercising</u> and not
                                         A   **B**
   <u>to take pills</u>.
         C

a. To getting
c. taking pills
b. to do exercises
d. No change is necessary.

4. Choose the correct word(s) to fill in the blank.

I have learned that _____ a pet is better than buying one from a pet store.

a. adopting
b. have adopted
c. to adopt

5. Choose the correct words to fill in the blank.

You can travel by car, by plane, or _____.

a. boating is fine
b. by boat
c. on boat

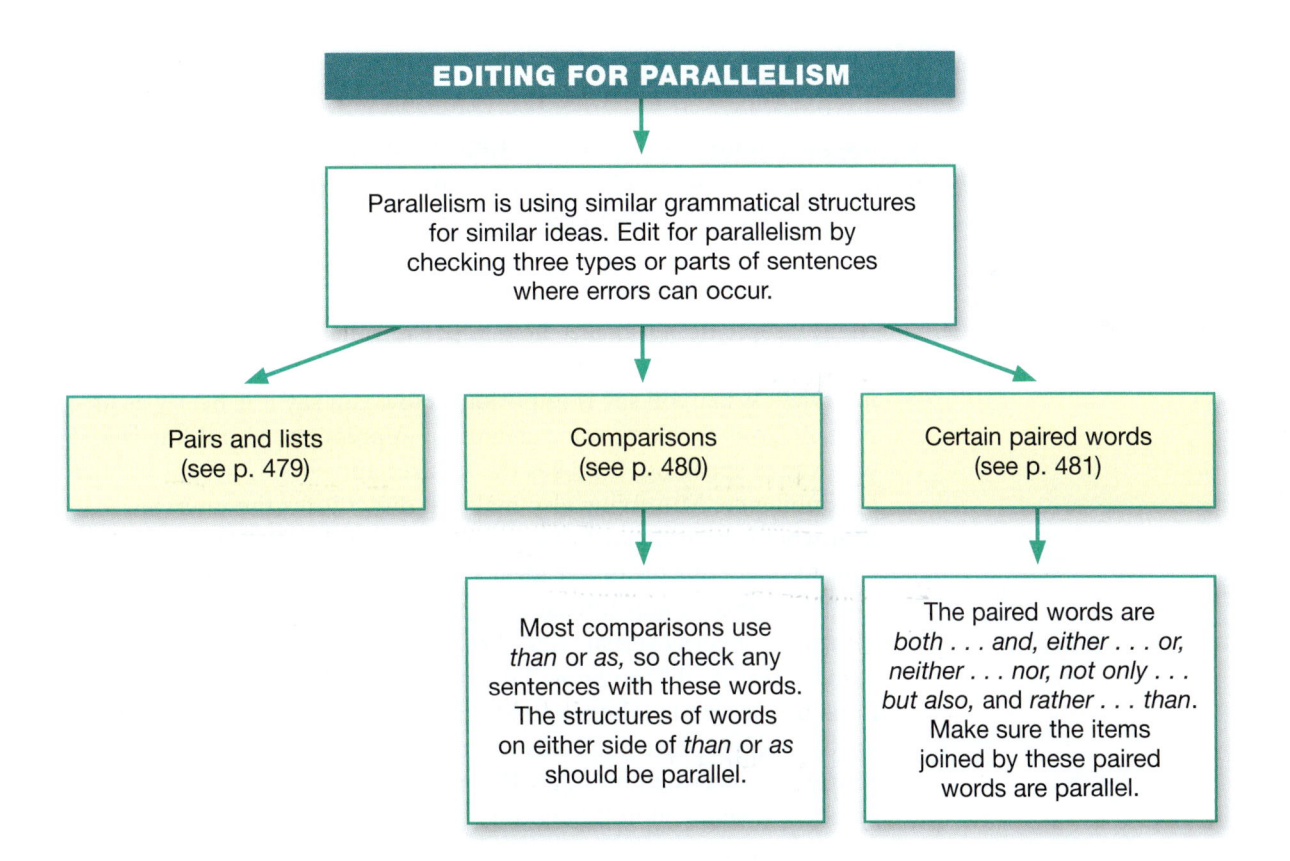

EDITING FOR PARALLELISM

Parallelism is using similar grammatical structures for similar ideas. Edit for parallelism by checking three types or parts of sentences where errors can occur.

- **Pairs and lists** (see p. 479)
- **Comparisons** (see p. 480)
- **Certain paired words** (see p. 481)

Most comparisons use *than* or *as*, so check any sentences with these words. The structures of words on either side of *than* or *as* should be parallel.

The paired words are *both . . . and, either . . . or, neither . . . nor, not only . . . but also,* and *rather . . . than*. Make sure the items joined by these paired words are parallel.

29

Sentence Variety

Putting Rhythm in Your Writing

THIS CHAPTER
- gives you five ways to vary your sentences as you write.
- gives you practice using those ways to achieve variety.

Understand What Sentence Variety Is

Sentence variety means using different sentence patterns and lengths to give your writing good rhythm and flow. Notice how the first example below does not have any rhythm.

WITH SHORT, SIMPLE SENTENCES

Many people do not realize how important their speaking voice and style are. Speaking style can make a difference, particularly in a job interview. What you say is important. How you say it is nearly as important. Your speaking voice creates an impression. Mumbling is a bad way of speaking. It makes the speaker appear sloppy and lacking in confidence. Mumbling also makes it difficult for the interviewer to hear what is being said. Talking too fast is another bad speech behavior. The speaker runs his or her ideas together. The interviewer cannot follow them or distinguish what is important. A third common bad speech behavior concerns verbal "tics." Verbal tics are empty filler phrases like "um," "like," and "you know." Practice for an interview. Sit up straight. Look the person to whom you are speaking directly in the eye. Speak up. Slow down. One good way to find out how you sound is to leave yourself a voice-mail message. If you sound bad to yourself, you need practice speaking aloud. Do not let poor speech behavior interfere with creating a good impression.

WITH SENTENCE VARIETY

Many people do not realize how important their speaking voice and style are, particularly in a job interview. What you say is important, but how you say it is nearly as important in creating a good impression. Mumbling is a bad way of speaking. Not only does it make the speaker appear sloppy and lacking in confidence, but mumbling also makes it difficult for the interviewer to hear what is being said. Talking too fast is another bad speech behavior. The speaker runs his or her ideas together, and the interviewer cannot follow them or distinguish what is important. A third common bad speech behavior is called verbal "tics," empty filler expressions such as "um," "like," and "you know." When you practice for an interview, sit up straight, look the person to whom you are speaking directly in the eye, speak up, and slow down. One good way to find out how you sound is to leave yourself a voice-mail message. If you sound bad to yourself, you need practice speaking aloud. Do not let poor speech behavior interfere with creating a good impression.

Practice Creating Sentence Variety

Most writers tend to write short sentences that start with the subject, so this chapter will focus on techniques for starting with something other than the subject and for writing a variety of longer sentences. Two additional techniques for achieving sentence variety—coordination and subordination—are covered in Chapter 27.

Start Some Sentences with Adverbs

Adverbs are words that describe verbs, adjectives, or other adverbs; they often end with *-ly*. As long as the meaning is clear, adverbs can be placed at the beginning of a sentence instead of in the middle. Adverbs at the beginning of a sentence are usually followed by a comma.

TIP For more about adverbs, see Chapter 25.

ADVERB IN MIDDLE	Stories about haunted houses *frequently* surface at Halloween.
ADVERB AT BEGINNING	*Frequently*, stories about haunted houses surface at Halloween.
ADVERB IN MIDDLE	These stories *often* focus on ship captains lost at sea.
ADVERB AT BEGINNING	*Often*, these stories focus on ship captains lost at sea.

PRACTICE 1 Starting Sentences with an Adverb

Edit each sentence so that it begins with an adverb.

EXAMPLE: *Unfortunately, rabies* ~~Rabies unfortunately~~ remains a problem in the United States.

TIP For more practice with sentence variety, visit *Exercise Central* at bedfordstmartins.com/realwriting.

1. Rabies once was a major threat to domestic pets in this country.
2. The disease is now most deadly to wildlife such as raccoons, skunks, and bats.

3. People frequently fail to have their pets vaccinated against rabies.

4. They believe mistakenly that their dogs and cats are no longer in danger.

5. An oral vaccine that prevents rabies in raccoons and skunks has been developed, thankfully.

PRACTICE 2 Writing Sentences That Start with an Adverb

Write three sentences that start with an adverb. Use commas as necessary. Choose among the following adverbs: *often, sadly, amazingly, luckily, lovingly, aggressively, gently, frequently, stupidly.*

1. _____
2. _____
3. _____

Join Ideas Using an -*ing* Verb

One way to combine sentences is to add -*ing* to the verb in the less important of the two sentences and to delete the subject, creating a phrase.

TWO SENTENCES   A pecan roll from our bakery is not a health food. It contains 800 calories.

JOINED WITH -*ING* VERB FORM   *Containing* 800 calories, a pecan roll from our bakery is not a health food.

You can add the -*ing* phrase to the beginning or the end of the other sentence, depending on what makes more sense.

The fat content is also high/~~It equals~~ *, equaling* the fat in a huge country breakfast.

If you add the -*ing* phrase to the beginning of a sentence, you will usually need to put a comma after it. If you add the phrase to the end of a sentence, you will usually need to put a comma before it. A comma should *not* be used only when the -*ing* phrase is essential to the meaning of the sentence.

TWO SENTENCES   Experts examined the effects of exercise on arthritis patients. The experts found that walking, jogging, or swimming could reduce pain.

OTHER GRAMMAR CONCERNS
Practice Creating Sentence Variety 489

JOINED WITHOUT COMMAS   Experts examining the effects of exercise on arthritis patients found that walking, jogging, or swimming could reduce pain.

[The phrase *examining the effects of exercise on arthritis patients* is essential to the meaning of the sentence.]

If you put a phrase starting with an *-ing* verb at the beginning of a sentence, be sure the word that the phrase modifies follows immediately. Otherwise, you will create a dangling modifier.

TIP For more on finding and correcting dangling modifiers, see Chapter 26, and for more on joining ideas, see Chapter 27.

TWO SENTENCES   I ran through the rain. My raincoat got all wet.

DANGLING MODIFIER   Running through the rain, my raincoat got all wet.

EDITED   Running through the rain, I got my raincoat all wet.

PRACTICE 3   Joining Ideas Using an *-ing* Verb

Combine each pair of sentences into a single sentence by using an *-ing* verb. Add or delete words as necessary.

EXAMPLE: Some people read faces amazingly well**, interpreting** ~~They interpret~~ nonverbal cues that other people miss.

1. A recent study tested children's abilities to interpret facial expressions. The study made headlines.

2. Physically abused children participated in the study. They saw photographs of faces changing from one expression to another.

3. The children told researchers what emotion was most obvious in each face. The children chose among fear, anger, sadness, happiness, and other emotions.

4. The study also included nonabused children. They served as a control group for comparison with the other children.

5. All the children in the study were equally good at identifying most emotions. They all responded similarly to happiness or fear.

6. Battered children were especially sensitive to one emotion on the faces. These children identified anger much more quickly than the other children could.

7. The abused children have learned to look for anger. They protect themselves with this early-warning system.

8. Their sensitivity to anger may not help the abused children later in life. It perhaps hurts them socially.

OTHER GRAMMAR CONCERNS

Chapter 29 • Sentence Variety

9. The abused children tend to run from anger they observe. They have difficulty connecting with people who exhibit anger.

10. The human brain works hard to acquire useful information. It often hangs on to the information after its usefulness has passed.

PRACTICE 4 Joining Ideas Using an -ing Verb

Write two sets of sentences, and join them using an -ing verb form.

EXAMPLE: a. *Carol looked up.*

b. *She saw three falling stars in the sky.*

Combined: *Looking up, Carol saw three falling stars in the sky.*

1. a. _____
   b. _____
   Combined: _____

2. a. _____
   b. _____
   Combined: _____

Join Ideas Using a Past Participle

TIP For more on helping verbs, see Chapters 19 and 23. Chapter 23 also covers past participles.

Another way to combine sentences is to use a past participle (often, a verb ending in *-ed*) to turn the less important of the two sentences into a phrase.

| TWO SENTENCES | Henry VIII was a powerful English king. He is *remembered* for his many wives. |
| JOINED WITH A PAST PARTICIPLE | *Remembered* for his many wives, Henry VIII was a powerful English king. |

Past participles of irregular verbs do not end in *-ed*; they take different forms.

| TWO SENTENCES | Tim Treadwell was *eaten* by a grizzly bear. He showed that wild animals are unpredictable. |
| JOINED WITH A PAST PARTICIPLE | *Eaten* by a grizzly bear, Tim Treadwell showed that wild animals are unpredictable. |

Notice that sentences can be joined this way when one of them has a form of *be* along with a past participle (*is remembered* in the first Henry VIII example and *was eaten* in the first Tim Treadwell example).

To combine sentences this way, delete the subject and the *be* form from the sentence that has the *be* form and the past participle. You now have a phrase that can be added to the beginning or the end of the other sentence, depending on what makes more sense.

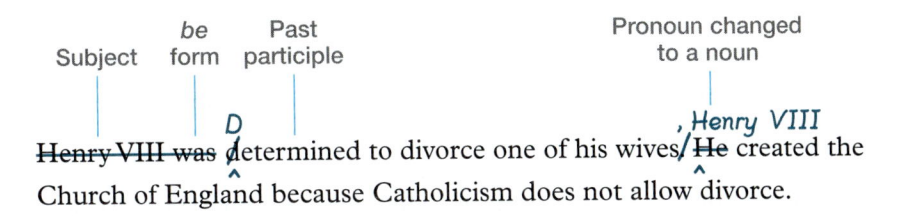

~~Henry VIII was~~ **D**etermined to divorce one of his wives**/** ~~He~~ **, Henry VIII** created the Church of England because Catholicism does not allow divorce.

If you add a phrase that begins with a past participle to the beginning of a sentence, put a comma after it. If you add the phrase to the end of the sentence, put a comma before it.

TIP If you put a phrase starting with a past participle at the beginning of a sentence, be sure the word that the phrase modifies follows immediately. Otherwise, you will create a dangling modifier.

PRACTICE 5 Joining Ideas Using a Past Participle

Combine each pair of sentences into a single sentence by using a past participle.

EXAMPLE: **Forced** ~~The oil company was forced~~ to take the local women's objections seriously**/** ~~The~~ **, the oil** company had to close for ten days during their protest.

1. The women of southern Nigeria were angered by British colonial rule in 1929. They organized a protest.

2. Nigeria is now one of the top ten oil-producing countries. The nation is covered with pipelines and oil wells.

3. The oil is pumped by American and other foreign oil companies. The oil often ends up in wealthy Western economies.

4. The money from the oil seldom reaches Nigeria's local people. The cash is stolen by corrupt rulers in many cases.

5. The Nigerian countryside is polluted by the oil industry. The land then becomes a wasteland.

6. Many Nigerians are insulted by the way the oil industry treats them. They want the oil companies to pay attention to their problems.

OTHER GRAMMAR CONCERNS

492 Chapter 29 • Sentence Variety

7. Local Nigerian women were inspired by the 1929 women's protests. They launched a series of protests against the oil industry in the summer of 2002.

8. The women prevented workers from entering or leaving two oil company offices. The offices were located in the port of Warri.

9. Workers at the oil company were concerned about the women's threat to take their clothes off. Many workers told company officials that such a protest would bring a curse on the company and shame to its employees.

10. The company eventually agreed to hire more local people and to invest in local projects. The projects are intended to supply electricity and provide the villagers with a market for fish and poultry.

PRACTICE 6 Joining Ideas Using a Past Participle

Write two sets of sentences, and join them with a past participle.

EXAMPLE: a. *Chris is taking intermediate accounting.*

b. *It is believed to be the most difficult course in the major.*

Combined: *Chris is taking intermediate accounting, believed to be the most difficult course in the major.*

1. a. _____
   b. _____
   Combined: _____

2. a. _____
   b. _____
   Combined: _____

Join Ideas Using an Appositive

An **appositive** is a noun or noun phrase that renames a noun or pronoun. Appositives can be used to combine two sentences into one.

TWO SENTENCES   Brussels sprouts can be roasted for a delicious flavor. They are a commonly disliked food.

JOINED WITH AN APPOSITIVE	Brussels sprouts, a commonly disliked food, can be roasted for a delicious flavor.

[The phrase *a commonly disliked food* renames the noun *brussels sprouts*.]

TIP Usually, you will want to turn the less important of the two sentences into an appositive.

Notice that the sentence that renames the noun was turned into a noun phrase by dropping the subject and the verb (*They* and *are*). Also, commas set off the appositive.

PRACTICE 7 Joining Ideas Using an Appositive

Combine each pair of sentences into a single sentence by using an appositive. Be sure to use a comma or commas to set off the appositive.

EXAMPLE: Levi's jeans , perhaps the most famous work clothes in the world, have looked the same for well over a century. ~~They are perhaps the most famous work clothes in the world.~~

1. Jacob Davis was a Russian immigrant working in Reno, Nevada. He was the inventor of Levi's jeans.

2. Davis came up with an invention that made work clothes last longer. The invention was the riveted seam.

3. Davis bought denim from a wholesaler. The wholesaler was Levi Strauss.

4. In 1870, he offered to sell the rights to his invention to Levi Strauss for the price of the patent. Patents then cost about $70.

5. Davis joined the firm in 1873 and supervised the final development of its product. The product was the famous Levi's jeans.

6. Davis oversaw a crucial design element. The jeans all had orange stitching.

7. The curved stitching on the back pockets was another choice Davis made. It also survives in today's Levi's.

8. The stitching on the pockets has been a trademark since 1942. It is very recognizable.

9. During World War II, Levi Strauss temporarily stopped adding the pocket stitches because they wasted thread. It was a valuable resource.

10. Until the war ended, the pocket design was added with a less valuable material. The company used paint.

Join Ideas Using an Adjective Clause

TIP For more about adjectives, see Chapter 25.

An **adjective clause** is a group of words with a subject and a verb that describes a noun. An adjective clause often begins with the word *who*, *which*, or *that*, and it can be used to combine two sentences into one.

| TWO SENTENCES | Lauren has won many basketball awards. She is captain of her college team. |
| JOINED WITH AN ADJECTIVE CLAUSE | Lauren, *who is captain of her college team*, has won many basketball awards. |

To join sentences this way, use *who*, *which*, or *that* to replace the subject in a sentence that describes a noun in the other sentence. You now have an adjective clause that you can move so that it follows the noun it describes. The sentence with the more important idea (the one you want to emphasize) should become the main clause. The less important idea should be in the adjective clause.

TIP Use *who* to refer to a person, *which* to refer to places or things (but not to people), and *that* for places or things.

Leigh got an internship because of her blog, which caught the eye of people in the fashion industry.

[The more important idea here is that Leigh got an internship because of her blog. The less important idea is that the blog caught the eye of people in the fashion industry.]

NOTE: If an adjective clause can be taken out of a sentence without completely changing the meaning of the sentence, put commas around it.

Lauren, *who is captain of her college team*, has won many basketball awards.

[The phrase *who is captain of her college team* adds information about Lauren, but it is not essential.]

If an adjective clause is an essential part of a sentence, do not put commas around it.

Lauren is an award-winning basketball player who overcame childhood cancer.

[*Who overcame childhood cancer* is an essential part of this sentence.]

OTHER GRAMMAR CONCERNS
Practice Creating Sentence Variety   495

PRACTICE 8   Joining Ideas Using an Adjective Clause

Combine each pair of sentences into a single sentence by using an adjective clause beginning with *who*, *which*, or *that*.

EXAMPLE: My friend Erin, *who has been going to college for the past three years,* had her first child last June. ~~She has been going to college for the past three years.~~

1. While Erin goes to classes, her baby boy stays at a day-care center. The day-care center costs Erin about $100 a week.
2. Twice when her son was ill, Erin had to miss her geology lab. The lab is an important part of her grade for that course.
3. Occasionally, Erin's parents come up and watch the baby while Erin is studying. They live about 70 miles away.
4. Sometimes Erin feels discouraged by the extra costs. The costs have come from having a child.
5. She believes that some of her professors are not very sympathetic. These professors are the ones who have never been parents themselves.
6. Erin understands that she must take responsibility for both her child and her education. She wants to be a good mother and a good student.
7. Her grades have suffered somewhat since she had her son. They were once straight A's.
8. Erin wants to graduate with honors. She hopes to go to graduate school someday.
9. Her son is more important than an A in geology. He is the most important thing to her.
10. Erin still expects to have a high grade point average. She has simply given up expecting to be perfect.

PRACTICE 9   Joining Ideas Using an Adjective Clause

Fill in the blank in each of the following sentences with an appropriate adjective clause. Add commas, if necessary.

EXAMPLE: The firefighters *who responded to the alarm* entered the burning building.

OTHER GRAMMAR CONCERNS

496 Chapter 29 • Sentence Variety

1. A fire _____ began in our house in the middle of the night.

2. The members of my family _____ were all asleep.

3. My father _____ was the first to smell smoke.

4. He ran to our bedrooms _____ and woke us up with his shouting.

5. The house _____ was damaged, but everyone in my family reached safety.

Edit for Sentence Variety

PRACTICE 10 Editing Paragraphs for Sentence Variety

Create sentence variety in the following paragraphs by joining at least two sentences in each of the paragraphs. Use several of the techniques covered in this chapter. More than one correct answer is possible.

(1) Few people would associate the famous English poet and playwright William Shakespeare with prison. (2) However, Shakespeare has taken on an important role in the lives of certain inmates. (3) They are serving time at the Luther Luckett Correctional Complex in Kentucky. (4) These inmates were brought together by the Shakespeare Behind Bars program. (5) They spend nine months preparing for a performance of one of the great writer's plays.

(6) Recently, prisoners at Luckett performed *The Merchant of Venice*. (7) It is one of Shakespeare's most popular plays. (8) Many of the actors identified with Shylock. (9) He is a moneylender who is discriminated against because he is Jewish. (10) When a rival asks Shylock for a loan to help a friend, Shylock drives a hard bargain. (11) He demands a pound of the rival's flesh if the loan is not repaid. (12) One inmate shared his views of this play with a newspaper reporter. (13) The inmate said, "It deals with race. It deals with discrimination. It deals with gambling, debt, cutting people. It deals with it all. And we were all living that someway, somehow."

(14) Through the Shakespeare performances, the inmates form bonds not only with the characters but also with one another. (15) Additionally, they are able to explore their own histories and their responsibility for the crimes they committed. (16) Many feel changed by their experience on the stage. (17) One actor was affected deeply by his role in *The Merchant of Venice*. (18) He said, "You feel like you're in a theater outside of here. You don't feel the razor wire."

PRACTICE 11 Editing Your Own Writing for Sentence Variety

Add more sentence variety to a piece of your own writing—a paper for this course or another one, or something you have written for work or your everyday life. You may want to use the chart on page 498.

Chapter Review

1. Having sentence variety means _____ .

2. If you tend to write short, similar-sounding sentences, what five techniques should you try? _____

3. An _____ is a noun or noun phrase that renames a noun.

4. An _____ clause often starts with *who*, _____, or _____ . It describes a noun or pronoun.

5. Use commas around an adjective clause when the information in it is (essential / not essential) to the meaning of the sentence.

LEARNING JOURNAL Did you find short, choppy sentences in your writing? What is the main thing you have learned about sentence variety that will help you? How would you explain how to vary sentences to someone else? What is unclear to you?

Chapter Test

For each of the following sentence pairs, choose the answer that joins the sentences logically using one of the strategies in this chapter.

1. Luis straightened his tie. He waited to be called in for his job interview.
    a. Straightened his tie, Luis waited to be called in for his job interview.
    b. Straightening his tie, Luis waited to be called in for his job interview.

2. The auditorium was noisy and chaotic. It was filled with people in Superman outfits.
   a. Filled with people in Superman outfits, the auditorium was noisy and chaotic.
   b. Filled with people in Superman outfits; the auditorium was noisy and chaotic.

3. My niece is a star softball player. She loves to watch baseball on TV.
   a. My niece, a star softball player, loves to watch baseball on TV.
   b. Starring as a softball player, my niece loves to watch baseball on TV.

4. Chocolate is a favorite sweet worldwide. It has compounds that might lower the risk of certain diseases.
   a. Chocolate is a favorite sweet worldwide, for it has compounds that might lower the risk of certain diseases.
   b. Chocolate, a favorite sweet worldwide, has compounds that might lower the risk of certain diseases.

5. The lawyer believed passionately in his client's innocence. He convinced the jury to come to a verdict of not guilty.
   a. The lawyer, who believed passionately in his client's innocence, convinced the jury to come to a verdict of not guilty.
   b. The lawyer believed passionately in his client's innocence, yet he convinced the jury to come to a verdict of not guilty.

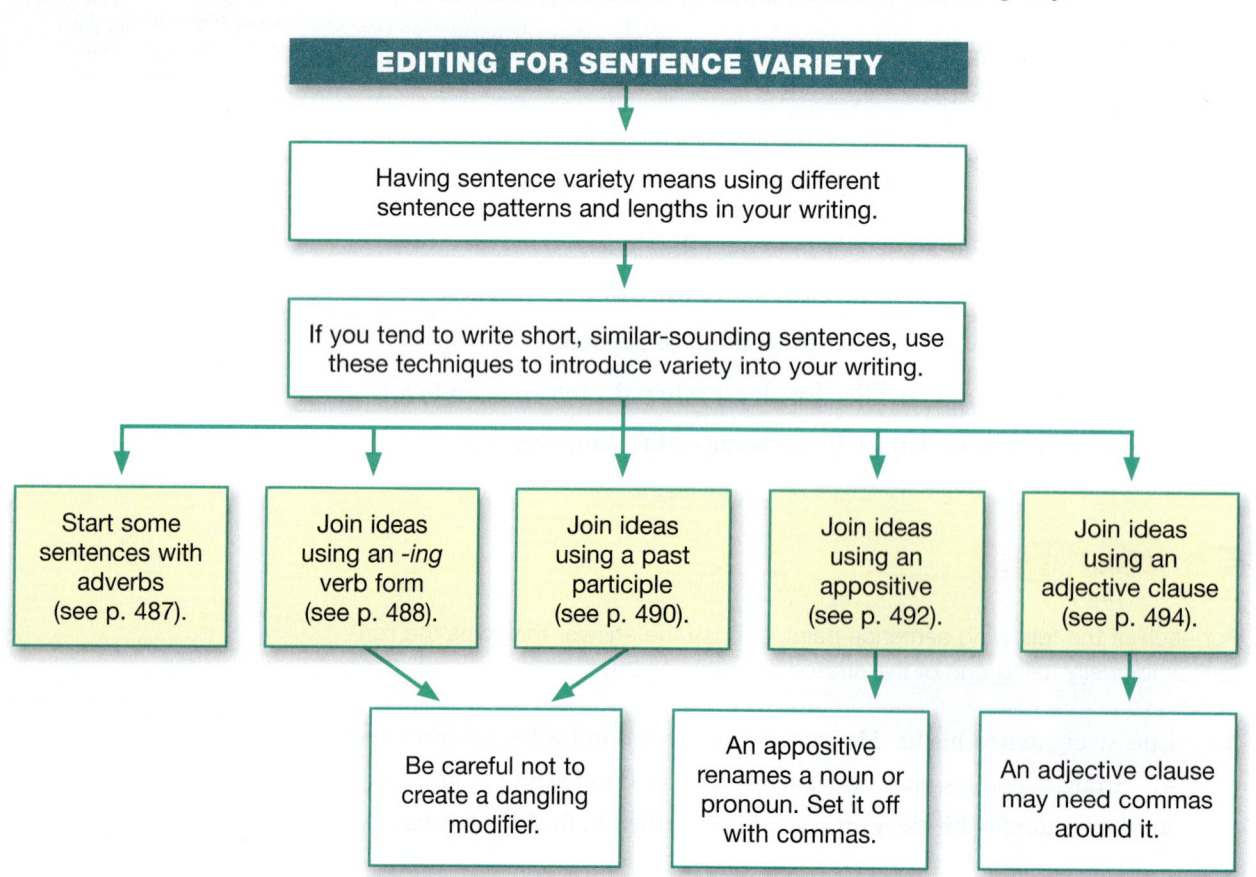

EDITING FOR SENTENCE VARIETY

Having sentence variety means using different sentence patterns and lengths in your writing.

If you tend to write short, similar-sounding sentences, use these techniques to introduce variety into your writing.

- Start some sentences with adverbs (see p. 487).
- Join ideas using an *-ing* verb form (see p. 488).
- Join ideas using a past participle (see p. 490).
- Join ideas using an appositive (see p. 492).
- Join ideas using an adjective clause (see p. 494).

Be careful not to create a dangling modifier.

An appositive renames a noun or pronoun. Set it off with commas.

An adjective clause may need commas around it.

30

Formal English and ESL Concerns

Grammar Trouble Spots for Multilingual Students

THIS CHAPTER
- explains four basic sentence patterns.
- shows how to form negatives and questions.
- explains the different kinds of pronouns and how to use them.
- shows some verb tenses that can be tricky and gives you summary charts to refer to.
- explains how to use articles and prepositions correctly.

Academic, or formal, English is the English you will be expected to use in college and in most work situations, especially in writing. If you are not accustomed to using formal English or if English is not your native language, this chapter will help you avoid the most common problems with key sentence parts.

TIP In this chapter, we use the word *English* to refer to formal English. Throughout the chapter, subjects are underlined, and verbs are double-underlined.

Basic Sentence Patterns

Statements

Every sentence in English must have at least one subject and one verb **(S-V)** that together express a complete idea. The subject performs the action, and the verb names the action, as in the sentence that follows.

    S   V
The pitcher throws.

Other English sentence patterns build on that structure. One of the most common patterns is subject-verb-object **(S-V-O)**.

    S   V   O
The pitcher throws the ball.

499

There are two kinds of objects.

DIRECT OBJECTS receive the action of the verb.

```
S      V     DO
```
The <u>pitcher</u> <u>throws</u> the ball.

[The ball directly receives the action of the verb *throws*.]

INDIRECT OBJECTS do not receive the action of the verb. Instead, the action is performed *for* or *to* the person.

```
S     V    IO    DO
```
The <u>pitcher</u> <u>throws</u> me the ball.

PRACTICE 1 Sentence Patterns

Label the subject (S), verb (V), direct object (DO), and indirect object (IO), if any, in the following two sentences.

1. John sent the letter.

2. John sent Beth the letter.

TIP For more on prepositions, see pages 332–33. For more on the parts of sentences, see Chapter 19.

Another common sentence pattern is subject-verb-prepositional phrase. In standard English, the prepositional phrase typically follows the subject and verb.

```
S    V    Prepositional phrase
```
Lilah went to the movies.

PRACTICE 2 Using Correct Word Order

Read each of the sentences that follow. If the sentence is correct, write "C" in the blank to the left of it. If it is incorrect, write "I"; then, rewrite the sentence using correct word order.

EXAMPLE: __I__ My friend to me gave a present.

Revision: *My friend gave me a present.*

_____ 1. Presents I like very much.

Revision: _____

_____ 2. To parties I go often.

Revision: _____

_____ 3. To parties, I always bring a present.

Revision: _____

_____ 4. At my parties, people bring me presents, too.

Revision: _____

_____ 5. Always write to them a thank-you note.

Revision: _____

Negatives

To form a negative statement, use one of the words listed here, often with a helping verb such as *can/could, does/did, has/have,* or *should/will/would.*

| never | nobody | no one | nowhere |
| no | none | not | |

Notice in these examples that the word *not* comes *after* the helping verb.

SENTENCE   Dina can sing.

NEGATIVE   Dina ~~no can~~ sing. *(cannot)*

SENTENCE   The store sells cigarettes.

NEGATIVE   The store ~~no~~ sells cigarettes. *(does not)*

SENTENCE   Bruce will call.

NEGATIVE   Bruce ~~no~~ will call. *(not)*

SENTENCE   Caroline walked.

NEGATIVE   Caroline ~~no~~ did walk. *(not)*

Common Helping Verbs

FORMS OF *BE*	FORMS OF *HAVE*	FORMS OF *DO*	OTHER VERBS
am	have	do	can
are	has	does	could
is	had	did	may
been			might
being			must
was			should
were			will
			would

TIP For more on helping verbs and their forms, see Chapter 23.

The helping verb cannot be omitted in expressions using *not*.

INCORRECT	The store *not sell* cigarettes.
CORRECT	The store *does not sell* cigarettes.
	[*Does*, a form of the helping verb *do*, must come before *not*.]
CORRECT	The store *is not selling* cigarettes.
	[*Is*, a form of *be*, must come before *not*.]

Double negatives are not standard in English.

INCORRECT	Shane *does not have no* ride.
CORRECT	Shane *does not have a* ride.
CORRECT	Shane *has no* ride.

When forming a negative in the simple past tense, use the past tense of the helping verb *do*.

> did + not + Base verb without an *-ed* = Negative past tense

SENTENCE	I *talked* to Jairo last night.
	[*Talked* is the past tense.]
NEGATIVE	I *did not talk* to Jairo last night.
	[Notice that *talk* in this sentence does not have an *-ed* ending because the helping verb *did* conveys the past tense.]

PRACTICE 3 Forming Negatives

Rewrite the sentences to make them negative.

EXAMPLE: Hassan's son is ^not talking now.

1. He can say several words.
2. Hassan remembers when his daughter started talking.
3. He thinks it was at the same age.
4. His daughter was an early speaker.
5. Hassan expects his son to be a talkative adult.

Questions

To turn a statement into a question, move the helping verb so that it comes before the subject. Add a question mark (**?**) to the end of the question.

STATEMENT	Johan *can go* tonight.
QUESTION	*Can* Johan *go* tonight**?**

If the only verb in the statement is a form of *be,* it should be moved before the subject.

STATEMENT	Jamie *is* at work.
QUESTION	*Is* Jamie at work**?**

If the statement does not contain a helping verb or a form of *be,* add a form of *do* and put it before the subject. Be sure to end the question with a question mark (**?**).

STATEMENT	Norah sings in the choir.	Tyrone goes to college.
QUESTION	*Does* Norah sing in the choir**?**	*Does* Tyrone go to college**?**
STATEMENT	The building burned.	The plate broke.
QUESTION	*Did* the building burn**?**	*Did* the plate break**?**

Notice that the verb changed once the helping verb *did* was added.
Do is used with *I, you, we,* and *they. Does* is used with *he, she,* and *it.*

EXAMPLES	*Do* [I/you/we/they] practice every day?
	Does [he/she/it] sound terrible?

TIP Sometimes the verb appears before the subject in sentences that are not questions: *Behind the supermarket is the sub shop.*

PRACTICE 4 Forming Questions

Rewrite the sentences to make them into questions.

EXAMPLE: *Does* Brad knows how to cook **?**

1. He makes dinner every night for his family.
2. He goes to the grocery store once a week.
3. He uses coupons to save money.
4. Brad saves a lot of money using coupons.

There Is and There Are

English sentences often include *there is* or *there are* to indicate the existence of something.

There is a man at the door.
[You could also say, *A man is at the door.*]

There are many men in the class.
[You could also say, *Many men are in the class.*]

When a sentence includes the words *there is* or *there are*, the verb (*is*, *are*) comes before the noun it goes with (which is actually the subject of the sentence). The verb must agree with the noun in number. For example, the first sentence above uses the singular verb *is* to agree with the singular noun *man*, and the second sentence uses the plural verb *are* to agree with the plural noun *men*.

In questions, *is* or *are* comes before *there*.

STATEMENTS	*There is* plenty to eat.
	There are some things to do.
QUESTIONS	*Is there* plenty to eat?
	Are there some things to do?

PRACTICE 5 Using *There Is* and *There Are*

In each of the following sentences, fill in the blank with *there is* or *there are*, using the correct word order for any questions.

EXAMPLE: Although my parents are busy constantly, they say that ____there is____ always more that can be done.

1. Every morning, _____ flowers to water and weeds to pull.

2. Later in the day, _____ more chores, like mowing the lawn or cleaning out the garage.

3. I always ask, "_____ anything I can do?"

4. They are too polite to say that _____ work that they need help with.

5. If _____ more productive parents in the world, I would be surprised.

Pronouns

Pronouns replace nouns or other pronouns in a sentence so that you do not have to repeat them. There are three types of pronouns: subject pronouns, object pronouns, and possessive pronouns.

SUBJECT PRONOUNS serve as the subject of the verb (and remember that every English sentence *must* have a subject).

>   He
> Rob is my cousin. ~~Rob~~ lives next to me.

OBJECT PRONOUNS receive the action of the verb or are part of a prepositional phrase.

> Rob asked *me* for a favor.
> [The object pronoun *me* receives the action of the verb *asked*.]

> Rob lives next door *to me*.
> [*To me* is the prepositional phrase; *me* is the object pronoun.]

POSSESSIVE PRONOUNS show ownership.

> Rob is *my* cousin.

Use the following chart to check which type of pronoun to use.

TIP For more on pronouns, see Chapter 24.

Pronoun Types

SUBJECT		OBJECT		POSSESSIVE	
SINGULAR	**PLURAL**	**SINGULAR**	**PLURAL**	**SINGULAR**	**PLURAL**
I	we	me	us	my/mine	our/ours
you	you	you	you	your/yours	your/yours
he/she/it	they	him/her/it	them	his/her/hers/its	theirs

RELATIVE PRONOUNS

who, which, that

The singular pronouns *he/she*, *him/her*, and *his/hers* show gender. *He*, *him*, and *his* are masculine pronouns; *she*, *her*, and *hers* are feminine.

Here are some examples of common pronoun errors, with corrections.

Confusing Subject and Object Pronouns

Use a subject pronoun for the word that *performs* the action of the verb, and use an object pronoun for the word that *receives* the action.

Tashia is a good student. ~~Her~~ **She** gets all A's.
[The pronoun performs the action *gets*, so it should be the subject pronoun, *she*.]

Tomas gave the keys to ~~she~~ **her**. Banh gave the coat to ~~he~~ **him**.
[The pronoun receives the action of *gave*, so it should be the object pronoun, *her* or *him*.]

Confusing Gender

Use masculine pronouns to replace masculine nouns, and use feminine pronouns to replace feminine nouns.

Nick is sick. ~~She~~ **He** has the flu.
[*Nick* is a masculine noun, so the pronoun must be masculine.]

The jacket belongs to Jane. Give it to ~~him~~ **her**.
[*Jane* is feminine, so the pronoun must be feminine.]

Leaving Out a Pronoun

Some sentences use the pronoun *it* as the subject or object. Do not leave *it* out of the sentence.

~~Is~~ **It is** a holiday today.

Maria will bring the food. ~~Will~~ **It will** be delicious.

I tried calamari last night and liked **it** very much.

Using a Pronoun to Repeat a Subject

A pronoun *replaces* a noun, so do not use both a subject noun and a pronoun.

My father ~~he~~ is very strict.
[*Father* is the subject noun, so the sentence should not also have the subject pronoun *he*.]

The bus ~~it~~ was late.
[*Bus* is the subject noun, so the sentence should not also have the subject pronoun *it*.]

Using Relative Pronouns

The words *who*, *which*, and *that* are **relative pronouns**. Use relative pronouns in a clause that gives more information about the subject.

- Use *who* to refer to a person or people.

The man *who* lives next door plays piano.

- Use *which* or *that* to refer to nonliving things.

  The plant, *which* was a gift, died.

  The phone *that* I bought last week is broken.

PRACTICE 6 Using Correct Pronouns

Using the chart of pronouns on page 505, fill in the blanks with the correct pronoun.

EXAMPLE: Tennis is popular, for _____*it*_____ is an exciting sport.

1. Since the first time I played tennis, I have liked _____ very much.
2. _____ favorite player is John McEnroe.
3. _____ is famous for his bad temper.
4. Even though he is now middle-aged, _____ serve is perfect.
5. No matter how much I practice, _____ serve will never be as good.
6. McEnroe got a lot of publicity when _____ challenged Venus and Serena Williams to a match.
7. _____ declined.
8. Venus said that she did not know if she could fit him into _____ schedule.
9. Both of the sisters were busy with _____ tournament matches.
10. Who is _____ favorite tennis player?

Verbs

Verbs have different tenses to show when something happened: in the past, present, or future.

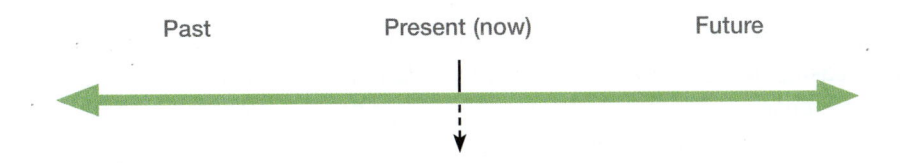

Past   Present (now)   Future

This section contains time lines, examples, and common errors for the simple and perfect tenses; coverage of progressive tenses; and more. See Chapter 23 for full coverage of the simple tenses and the perfect tenses, as well as practice exercises.

The Simple Tenses

SIMPLE PRESENT

Use the simple present to describe situations that exist now.

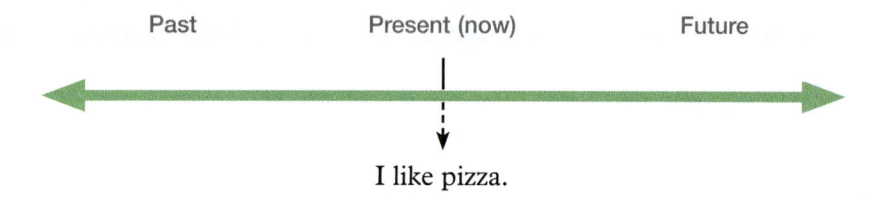

Past — Present (now) — Future

I like pizza.

I/You/We/They like pizza.

She/He likes pizza.

The third-person singular (*she/he*) of regular verbs ends in *-s* or *-es*. For irregular verb endings, see pages 402–05.

SIMPLE PAST

Use the simple past to describe situations that began and ended in the past.

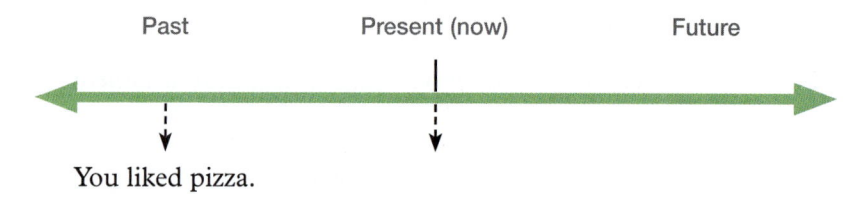

Past — Present (now) — Future

You liked pizza.

I/You/She/He/We/They liked pizza.

For regular verbs, the simple past is formed by adding either *-d* or *-ed* to the verb. For the past forms of irregular verbs, see the chart on pages 402–05.

SIMPLE FUTURE

Use the simple future to describe situations that will happen in the future. It is easier to form than the past tense. Use this formula for forming the future tense.

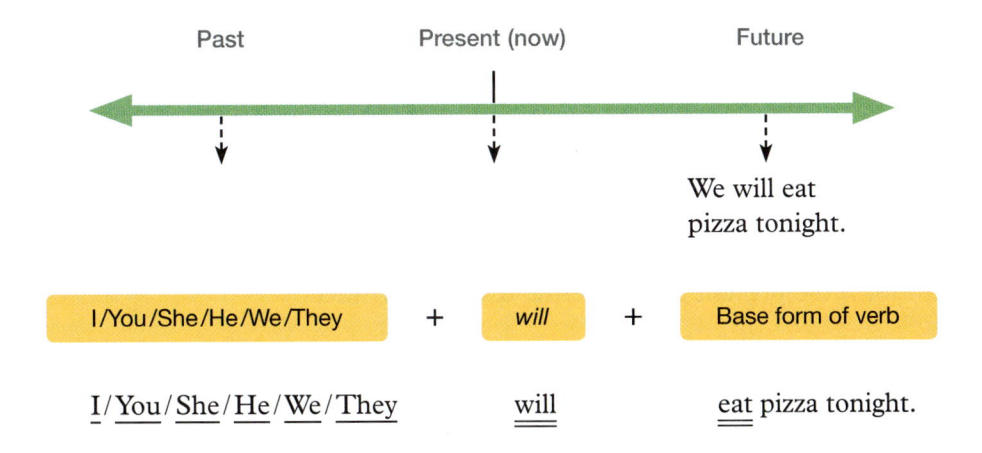

Past — Present (now) — Future

We will eat pizza tonight.

[I/You/She/He/We/They] + [will] + [Base form of verb]

I/You/She/He/We/They   will   eat pizza tonight.

COMMON ERRORS IN USING SIMPLE TENSES

Following are some common errors in using simple tenses.

Simple present. Forgetting to add -s or -es to verbs that go with third-person singular subjects (*she/he/it*)

INCORRECT	She know the manager.
CORRECT	She know**s** the manager.

TIP The subject and the verb must agree in number. For more on subject-verb agreement, see Chapter 22.

Simple past. Forgetting to add -d or -ed to regular verbs

INCORRECT	Gina work late last night.
CORRECT	Gina work**ed** late last night.

Forgetting to use the correct past forms of irregular verbs (see the chart of irregular verb forms on pages 402–05)

INCORRECT	Gerard speaked to her about the problem.
CORRECT	Gerard **spoke** to her about the problem.

Forgetting to use the base verb without an ending for negative sentences

INCORRECT	She does not wants money for helping.
CORRECT	She does not **want** money for helping.

TIP Double negatives (*Johnetta will **not** call **no** one*) are not standard in English. One negative is enough (*Johnetta will **not** call **anybody***).

The Perfect Tenses

PRESENT PERFECT

Use the present perfect to describe situations that started in the past and either continue into the present or were completed at some unknown time in the past.

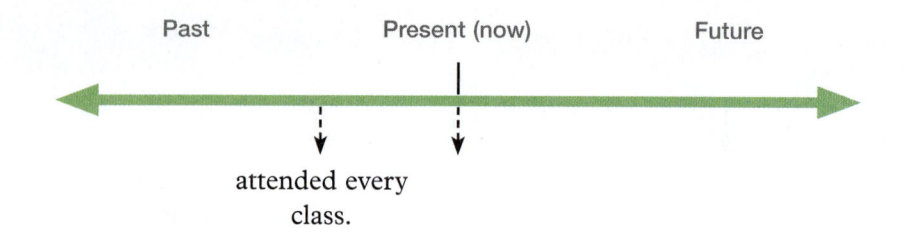

attended every class.

To form the present perfect tense, use this formula:

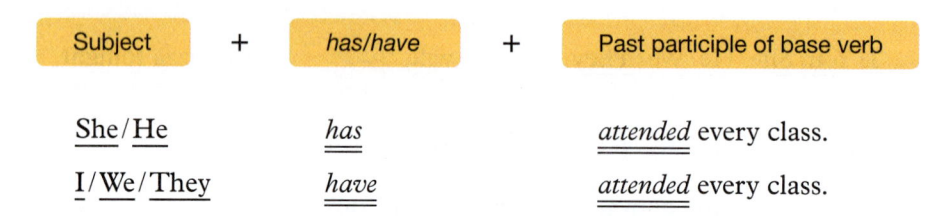

| Subject | + | has/have | + | Past participle of base verb |

She/He   has   *attended* every class.
I/We/They   have   *attended* every class.

Notice that *I/We/They* use *have* and that *She/He* use *has*.

PAST PERFECT

Use the past perfect to describe situations that began and ended before some other situation happened.

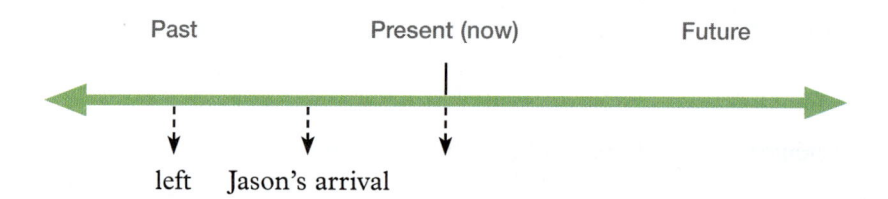

left   Jason's arrival

To form the past perfect tense, use this formula:

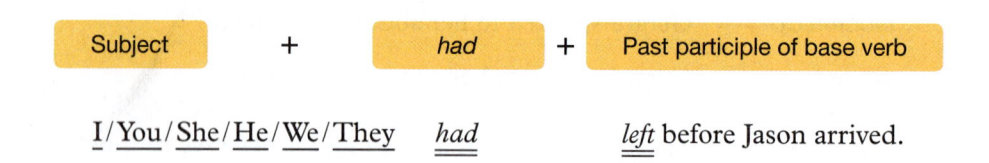

| Subject | + | had | + | Past participle of base verb |

I/You/She/He/We/They   had   *left* before Jason arrived.

FUTURE PERFECT

Use the future perfect to describe situations that begin and end before another situation begins.

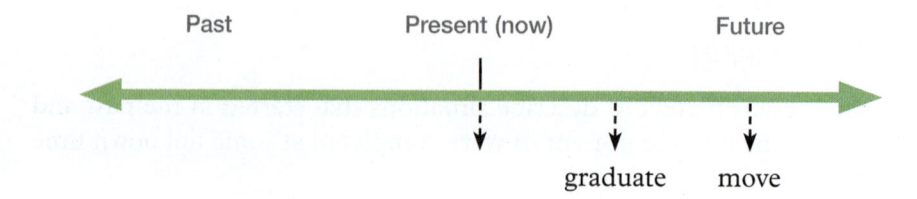

graduate   move

Use this formula to form the future perfect tense:

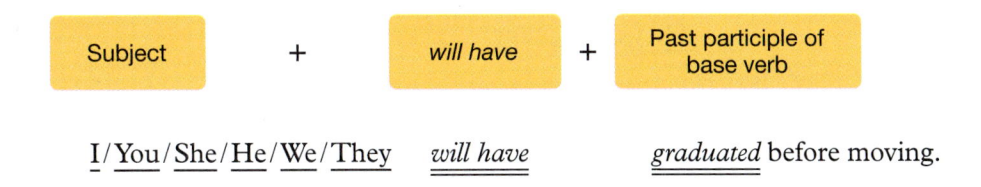

[Subject] + [*will have*] + [Past participle of base verb]

I/You/She/He/We/They   *will have*   *graduated* before moving.

COMMON ERRORS IN FORMING THE PERFECT TENSE

Using *had* instead of *has* or *have* for the present perfect

| INCORRECT | We **had** lived here since 2003. |
| CORRECT | We **have** lived here since 2003. |

Forgetting to use past participles (with *-d* or *-ed* endings for regular verbs)

| INCORRECT | She has attend every class. |
| CORRECT | She has attend**ed** every class. |

Using *been* between *have* or *has* and the past participle of a base verb

INCORRECT	I have **been** attended every class.
CORRECT	I have attended every class.
INCORRECT	I will have **been** graduated before I move.
CORRECT	I will have graduated before I move.

The Present Progressive Tenses

The progressive tense is used to describe ongoing actions in the present, past, or future. Following are some common errors in using the present progressive tense.

Forgetting to add *-ing* to the verb

INCORRECT	I am type now.
	She/he is not type now.
CORRECT	I am typ**ing** now.
	She/he is not typ**ing** now.

OTHER GRAMMAR CONCERNS

Forgetting to include a form of *be* (*am/is/are*)

INCORRECT	He typing now.
	They typing now.
CORRECT	He **is** typing now.
	They **are** typing now.

Forgetting to use a form of *be* (*am/is/are*) to start questions

INCORRECT	They typing now?
CORRECT	**Are** they typing now?

The following charts show how to use the present, past, and future progressive tenses in regular statements, negative statements, and questions.

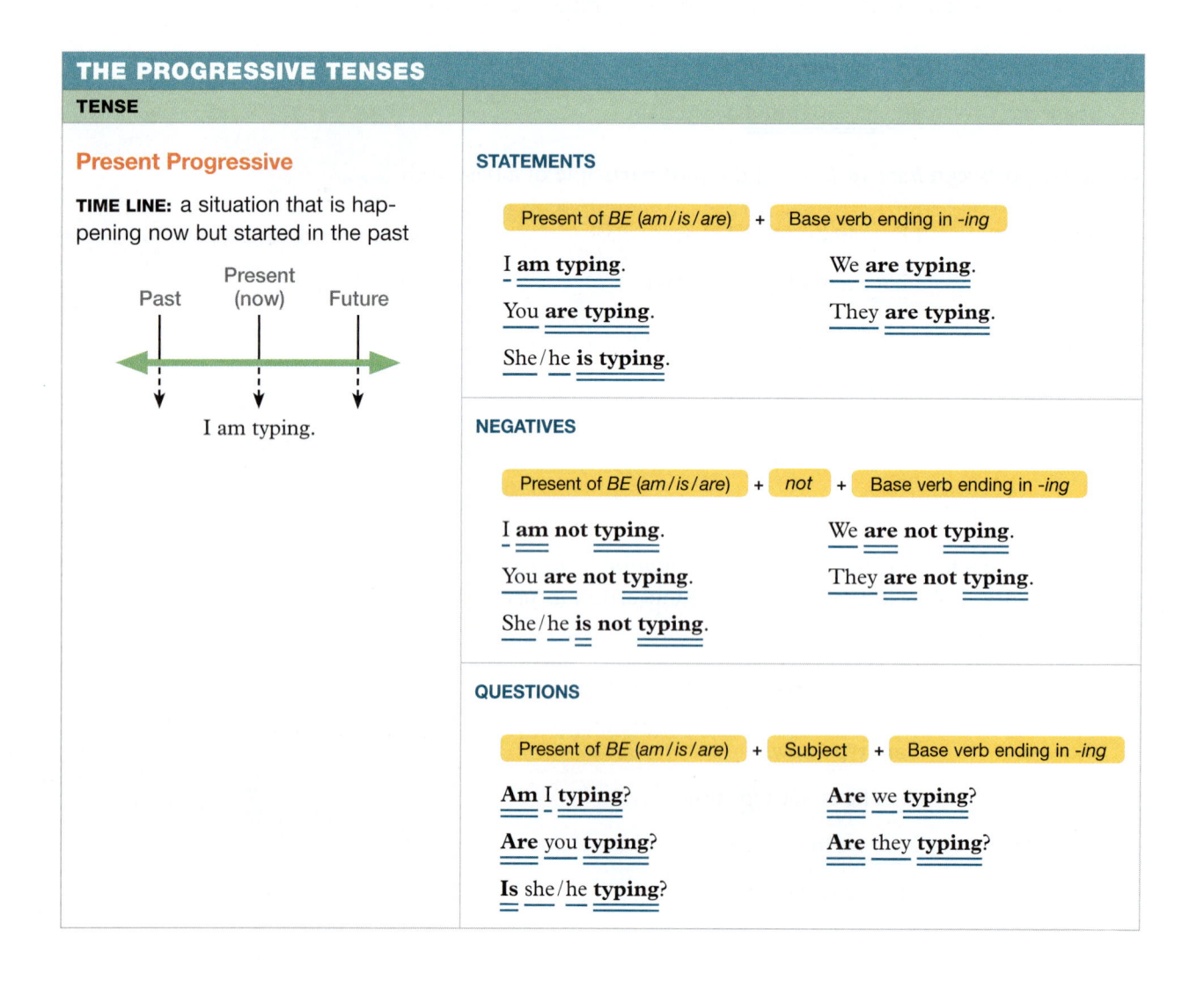

THE PROGRESSIVE TENSES

TENSE

Present Progressive

TIME LINE: a situation that is happening now but started in the past

Past — Present (now) — Future

I am typing.

STATEMENTS

Present of BE (*am/is/are*) + Base verb ending in *-ing*

I **am typing**. We **are typing**.
You **are typing**. They **are typing**.
She/he **is typing**.

NEGATIVES

Present of BE (*am/is/are*) + not + Base verb ending in *-ing*

I **am not typing**. We **are not typing**.
You **are not typing**. They **are not typing**.
She/he **is not typing**.

QUESTIONS

Present of BE (*am/is/are*) + Subject + Base verb ending in *-ing*

Am I **typing**? **Are** we **typing**?
Are you **typing**? **Are** they **typing**?
Is she/he **typing**?

OTHER GRAMMAR CONCERNS
Verbs

TENSE		
Past Progressive **TIME LINE:** a situation that was going on in the past Past — Present (now) — Future raining — arrival at restaurant	**STATEMENTS** `Past of BE (was/were)` + `Base verb ending in -ing` It **was raining** when I got to the restaurant at 7:00. The students **were studying** all night.	
	NEGATIVES `Past of BE (was/were)` + `not` + `Base verb ending in -ing` It **was not raining** when I got to the restaurant at 7:00. The students **were not studying** all night.	
	QUESTIONS `Past of BE (was/were)` + `Subject` + `Base verb ending in -ing` **Was** it **raining** when I got to the restaurant at 7:00? **Were** the students **studying** all night?	
Future Progressive **TIME LINE:** a situation that will be on-going at some point in the future Past — Present (now) — Future working — Jan's arrival	**STATEMENTS** `will be` + `Base verb ending in -ing` I/you **will be working** when Jan gets home. She/he **will be working** when Jan gets home. We **will be working** when Jan gets home. They **will be working** when Jan gets home.	
	NEGATIVES `will` + `not` + `be` + `Base verb ending in -ing` I/you **will not be working** when Jan gets home. She/he **will not be working** when Jan gets home. We **will not be working** when Jan gets home. They **will not be working** when Jan gets home.	

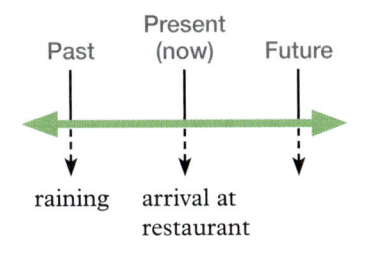

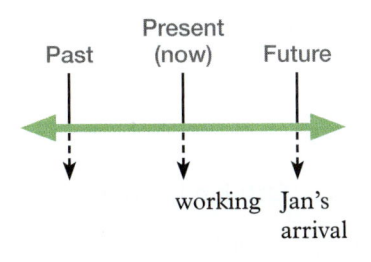

TENSE	
	QUESTIONS *will* + Subject + *be* + Base verb ending in *-ing* **Will** I/you **be working** when Jan gets home? **Will** she/he **be working** when Jan gets home? **Will** we **be working** when Jan gets home? **Will** they **be working** when Jan gets home?

PRACTICE 7 Using the Progressive Tense

Fill in the correct progressive form of the verb in parentheses after each blank.

EXAMPLE: My friend Maria and I are _____*trying*_____ (try) to be healthier.

1. First, we are _____ (start) to walk every day.

2. Why are we _____ (make) this change?

3. Last week, when Maria _____ (visit) me, she said that I didn't seem like myself.

4. I answered, "Yes, I am _____ (feel) kind of sad."

5. "Are you _____ (sleep) well?" she asked.

6. "Oh, yes," I said. "I _____ (get) plenty of sleep."

7. "What about your diet? Are you _____ (eat) right?" she asked.

8. "I eat in the cafeteria," I explained. "The chefs there are always _____ (cook) healthy options."

9. "What about activities? Are you _____ (exercise) at all?"

10. "Not really, unless you count my brain while I am _____ (study)!" I admitted.

PRACTICE 8 Forming Negative Statements and Questions

Rewrite the following sentences as indicated.

1. Betsy is golfing today. *Make the sentence a question:* _____
   _____

2. It was snowing when we got up. *Make the sentence a negative statement:*
   _____

3. You are going to the mall. *Make the sentence a question:* _____
   _____

4. They are losing the game. *Make the sentence a negative statement:*
   _____

5. Meriam was eating when you arrived. *Make the sentence into a question:*
   _____

Modal (Helping) Verbs

Modal verbs (or modal auxiliary verbs) are helping verbs that express the writer's attitude about an action. You do not have to learn too many modal verbs—just the eight in the chart that follows.

TIP For more on helping verbs, see Chapter 19.

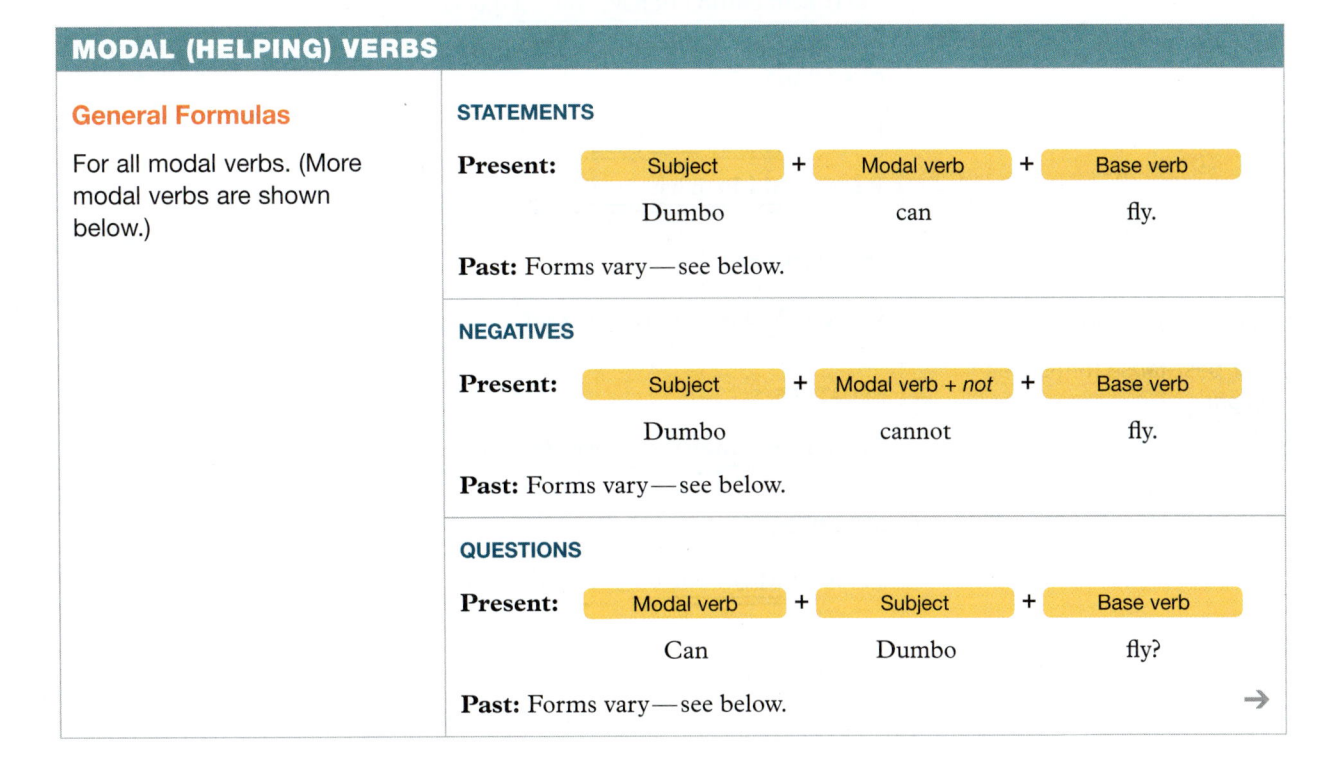

MODAL (HELPING) VERBS

General Formulas

For all modal verbs. (More modal verbs are shown below.)

STATEMENTS

Present: Subject + Modal verb + Base verb

　　　　　Dumbo　　　can　　　fly.

Past: Forms vary—see below.

NEGATIVES

Present: Subject + Modal verb + *not* + Base verb

　　　　　Dumbo　　　cannot　　　fly.

Past: Forms vary—see below.

QUESTIONS

Present: Modal verb + Subject + Base verb

　　　　　Can　　　Dumbo　　　fly?

Past: Forms vary—see below.

MODAL (HELPING) VERBS

Can Means *ability*	**STATEMENTS** **Present:** Beth **can** work fast. **Past:** Beth **could** work fast.
	NEGATIVES **Present:** Beth **can**not work fast. **Past:** Beth **could** not work fast.
	QUESTIONS **Present: Can** Beth work fast? **Past: Could** Beth work fast?
Could Means *possibility*. It can also be the past tense of *can*.	**STATEMENTS** **Present:** Beth **could** work quickly if she had more time. **Past:** Beth **could** have worked quickly if she had had more time.
	NEGATIVES *Can* is used for present negatives. (See above.) **Past:** Beth **could** not have worked quickly.
	QUESTIONS **Present: Could** Beth work quickly? **Past: Could** Beth have worked quickly?
May Means *permission* For past-tense forms, see *might*.	**STATEMENTS** **Present:** You **may** borrow my car.
	NEGATIVES **Present:** You **may** not borrow my car.
	QUESTIONS **Present: May** I borrow your car?

MODAL (HELPING) VERBS

Might
Means *possibility*. It can also be the past tense of *may*.

STATEMENTS

Present (with *be*): Lou **might** be asleep.

Past (with *have* + past participle of *be*): Lou **might** have been asleep.

Future: Lou **might** sleep.

NEGATIVES

Present (with *be*): Lou **might** not be asleep.

Past (with *have* + past participle of *be*): Lou **might** not have been asleep.

Future: Lou **might** not sleep.

QUESTIONS

Might in questions is very formal and not often used.

Must
Means *necessary*

STATEMENTS

Present: We **must** try.

Past (with *have* + past participle of base verb): We **must** have tried.

Past (with *had* + *to* + base verb): We **had to** try.

NEGATIVES

Present: We **must** not try.

Past (with *have* + past participle of base verb): We **must** not have tried.

QUESTIONS

Present: **Must** we try?

Past-tense questions with *must* are unusual.

Should
Means *duty* or *expectation*

STATEMENTS

Present: They **should** call.

Past (with *have* + past participle of base verb): They **should** have called.

NEGATIVES

Present: They **should** not call.

Past (with *have* + past participle of base verb): They **should** not have called.

QUESTIONS

Present: **Should** they call?

Past (with *have* + past participle of base verb): **Should** they have called?

MODAL (HELPING) VERBS

Will Means *intend to* (future) For past-tense forms, see *would*.	**STATEMENTS** **Future:** I **will** succeed. **NEGATIVES** **Future:** I **will** not succeed. **QUESTIONS** **Future: Will** I succeed?
Would Means *prefer* or used to start a future request. It can also be the past tense of *will*.	**STATEMENTS** **Present:** I **would** like to travel. **Past** (with *have* + past participle of base verb): I **would** have traveled if I had had the money. **NEGATIVES** **Present:** I **would** not like to travel. **Past** (with *have* + past participle of base verb): I **would** not have traveled if it had not been for you. **QUESTIONS** **Present: Would** you like to travel? *Or* to start a request: **Would** you help me? **Past** (with *have* + past participle of base verb): **Would** you have traveled with me if I had asked you?

COMMON ERRORS WITH MODAL VERBS

Following are some common errors in using modal verbs.

Using more than one helping verb

    INCORRECT   They **will can** help.

    CORRECT   They **will** help. (future intention)

                     They **can** help. (are able to)

Using *to* between the modal verb and the main (base) verb

    INCORRECT   Emilio **might to** come with us.

    CORRECT   Emilio **might** come with us.

Using *must* instead of *had to* to form the past tense

INCORRECT	She **must** work yesterday.
CORRECT	She **had to** work yesterday.

Forgetting to change *can* to *could* to form the past negative

INCORRECT	Last night, I **can**not sleep.
CORRECT	Last night, I **could** not sleep.

Forgetting to use *have* with *could/should/would* to form the past tense

INCORRECT	Tara **should** called last night.
CORRECT	Tara **should have** called last night.

Using *will* instead of *would* to express a preference in the present tense

INCORRECT	I **will** like to travel.
CORRECT	I **would** like to travel.

PRACTICE 9 Using Modal Verbs

Fill in the appropriate modal verbs in the sentences below.

EXAMPLE: Lilly ____would____ like to help the homeless.

1. What _____ she do?
2. First, she _____ find out what programs exist in her community.
3. For example, there _____ be a chapter of Habitat for Humanity.
4. Religious organizations _____ have started soup kitchens.
5. If she _____ find anything in her community, she should contact a national organization, such as the National Coalition for the Homeless.
6. The organization _____ definitely give her some ideas.
7. Also, she _____ feel as though she must volunteer alone.
8. Surely, there are other people who _____ want to help.
9. How _____ she get them involved?
10. She _____ spread the word, perhaps through e-mail.

OTHER GRAMMAR CONCERNS
Chapter 30 • Formal English and ESL Concerns

PRACTICE 10 Using the Correct Tense

Fill in the blanks with the correct form of the verbs in parentheses, adding helping verbs as needed. Refer to the verb charts if you need help.

EXAMPLE: Many critics ___have argued___ (argue) that *Citizen Kane*, directed by Orson Welles, is the greatest movie ever made.

1. You might not want to watch a movie from 1941, but *Citizen Kane* _____ (convince) you to give older films a chance.
2. The story _____ (begin) with the death of Charles Foster Kane, who was once a powerful man.
3. By the time of his death, Kane _____ (lose) much of his power.
4. Charles's parents were poor, but he _____ (inherit) a lot of money as a child.
5. He also inherited a failing newspaper, *The Inquirer*, and _____ (turn) it into a success.
6. In the beginning, his marriage was also a success, but his wife divorced him when she discovered that he _____ (have) an affair.
7. At the time of the discovery, Kane _____ (run) for governor.
8. Because of the scandal, he _____ (lose) the election.
9. Kane's last word was "Rosebud." What _____ (can) he _____ (mean) by that?
10. You _____ (watch) the movie to find out.

PRACTICE 11 Using the Correct Tense

Fill in the blanks with the correct form of the verbs in parentheses, adding helping verbs as needed. Refer to the verb charts if you need help.

EXAMPLE: ___Have___ you ___heard___ (hear) of volcano boarding?

(1) In a November 5, 2002, article in *National Geographic Today*, Zoltan Istvan _____ (report) on a new sport: volcano boarding. (2) Istvan first _____ (get) the idea in 1995, when he

_____ (sail) past Mt. Yasur, an active volcano on an island off the coast of Australia. (3) For centuries, Mt. Yasur _____ (have) the reputation of being a dangerous volcano. (4) For example, it regularly _____ (spit) out lava bombs. (5) These large molten rocks _____ often _____ (strike) visitors on the head.

(6) There is a village at the base of Mt. Yasur. (7) When Istvan arrived with his snowboard, the villagers _____ not _____ (know) what to think. (8) He _____ (make) his way to the volcano, _____ (hike) up the highest peak, and rode his board all the way down. (9) After he _____ (reach) the bottom, Istvan admitted that volcano boarding is more difficult than snowboarding. (10) Luckily, no lava bombs _____ (fall) from the sky, although the volcano _____ (erupt) seconds before his descent. (11) Istvan hopes that this new sport _____ (become) popular with snowboarders around the world.

Gerunds and Infinitives

A **gerund** is a verb form that ends in *-ing* and acts as a noun. An **infinitive** is a verb form that is preceded by the word *to*. Gerunds and infinitives cannot be the main verbs in sentences; each sentence must have another word that is the main verb.

GERUND Mike loves **swimming**.
[*Loves* is the main verb, and *swimming* is a gerund.]

INFINITIVE Mike loves **to run**.
[*Loves* is the main verb, and *to run* is an infinitive.]

How do you decide whether to use a gerund or an infinitive? The decision often depends on the main verb in a sentence. Some verbs can be followed by either a gerund or an infinitive.

Verbs That Can Be Followed by Either a Gerund or an Infinitive

begin	hate	remember	try
continue	like	start	
forget	love	stop	

TIP To improve your ability to write and speak standard English, read print or online articles, and listen to television and radio news programs. Also, reading articles aloud will help your pronunciation.

Sometimes, using a gerund or an infinitive after one of these verbs results in the same meaning.

| GERUND | Joan likes **playing** the piano. |
| INFINITIVE | Joan likes **to play** the piano. |

Other times, however, the meaning changes depending on whether you use a gerund or an infinitive.

| INFINITIVE | Carla stopped **helping** me. |

[This wording means Carla no longer helps me.]

| GERUND | Carla stopped **to help** me. |

[This wording means Carla stopped what she was doing and helped me.]

Verbs That Are Followed by a Gerund

admit	discuss	keep	risk
avoid	enjoy	miss	suggest
consider	finish	practice	
deny	imagine	quit	

The politician risked **losing** her supporters.
Sophia considered **quitting** her job.

Verbs That Are Followed by an Infinitive

agree	decide	need	refuse
ask	expect	offer	want
beg	fail	plan	
choose	hope	pretend	
claim	manage	promise	

Aunt Sally wants **to help**.
Cal hopes **to become** a millionaire.

Do not use the base form of the verb when you need a gerund or an infinitive.

INCORRECT, BASE VERB	*Swim* is my favorite activity.
	[*Swim* is the base form of the verb, not a noun; it cannot be the subject of the sentence.]
CORRECT, GERUND	*Swimming* is my favorite activity.
	[*Swimming* is a gerund that can be the subject of the sentence.]
INCORRECT, BASE VERB	My goal is *graduate* from college.
CORRECT, GERUND	My goal is *graduating* from college.
CORRECT, INFINITIVE	My goal is *to graduate* from college.
INCORRECT, BASE VERB	I need *stop* at the store.
	[*Need* is the verb, so there cannot be another verb that shows the action of the subject, *I*.]
CORRECT, INFINITIVE	I need *to stop* at the store.

PRACTICE 12 Using Gerunds and Infinitives

Read the paragraphs, and fill in the blanks with either a gerund or an infinitive as appropriate.

EXAMPLE: If you want ____to be____ (be) an actor, be aware that the profession is not all fun and glamour.

(1) When you were a child, did you pretend _____ (be) famous people? (2) Did you imagine _____ (play) roles in movies or on television? (3) Do you like _____ (take) part in plays? (4) If so, you might want _____ (make) a career out of acting.

(5) Be aware of some drawbacks, however. (6) If you hate _____ (work) with others, acting may not be the career for you. (7) Also, if you do not enjoy _____ (repeat) the same lines over and over, you will find acting dull. (8) You must practice _____ (speak) lines to memorize them. (9) Despite these drawbacks, you will gain nothing if you refuse _____ (try). (10) Anyone who hopes _____ (become) an actor has a chance at succeeding through hard work and determination.

Articles

Articles announce a noun. English uses only three articles—*a*, *an*, and *the*—and the same articles are used for both masculine and feminine nouns.

Definite and Indefinite Articles

The is a **definite article** and is used before a specific person, place, or thing. *A* and *an* are **indefinite articles** and are used with a person, place, or thing whose specific identity is not known.

DEFINITE ARTICLE	*The* car crashed into the building.
	[A specific car crashed into the building.]
INDEFINITE ARTICLE	*A* car crashed into the building.
	[Some car, we don't know which one exactly, crashed into the building.]

When the word following the article begins with a vowel (*a, e, i, o, u*), use *an* instead of *a*.

An old car crashed into the building.

To use the correct article, you need to know what count and noncount nouns are.

Count and Noncount Nouns

Count nouns name things that can be counted, and they can be made plural, usually by adding *-s* or *-es*. **Noncount nouns** name things that cannot be counted, and they are usually singular. They cannot be made plural.

COUNT NOUN/SINGULAR	I got a **ticket** for the concert.
COUNT NOUN/PLURAL	I got two **tickets** for the concert.
NONCOUNT NOUN	The Internet has all kinds of **information**.
	[You would not say, *The Internet has all kinds of information**s**.*]

Here is a brief list of several count and noncount nouns. In English, all nouns are either count or noncount.

COUNT	NONCOUNT	
apple / apples	beauty	grass
chair / chairs	flour	grief
dollar / dollars	furniture	happiness

COUNT	NONCOUNT	
letter/letters	health	poverty
smile/smiles	homework	rain
tree/trees	honey	rice
	information	salt
	jewelry	sand
	mail	spaghetti
	milk	sunlight
	money	thunder
	postage	wealth

Use the chart that follows to determine when to use *a, an, the,* or no article.

Articles with Count and Noncount Nouns

COUNT NOUNS	ARTICLE USED

SINGULAR

Specific → ***the***

I want to read **the book** on taxes that you recommended.

[The sentence refers to one particular book: the one that was recommended.]

I cannot stay in **the sun** very long.

[There is only one sun.]

Not specific → ***a*** or ***an***

I want to read **a** book on taxes.

[It could be any book on taxes.]

PLURAL

Specific → ***the***

I enjoyed **the books** that we read.

[The sentence refers to a particular group of books: the ones that we read.]

Not specific → **no article or *some***

I usually enjoy **books**.

[The sentence refers to books in general.]

She found **some books**.

[I do not know which books she found.] →

NONCOUNT NOUNS		ARTICLE USED
SINGULAR		
Specific	→	*the*
		I put away **the food** that we bought.
		[The sentence refers to particular food: the food that we bought.]
Not specific	→	no article or *some*
		There is **food** all over the kitchen.
		[The reader does not know what food the sentence refers to.]
		Give **some food** to the neighbors.
		[The sentence refers to an indefinite quantity of food.]

PRACTICE 13 Using Articles Correctly

Fill in the correct article (*a*, *an*, or *the*) in each of the following sentences. If no article is needed, write "no article."

EXAMPLE: Children who go to ___no article___ preschool have several advantages over those who do not.

1. First, _____ good preschool will help students learn about letters and numbers.

2. These skills can make _____ big difference when preschoolers move on to kindergarten.

3. Research shows that _____ prereading and math skills of children who have attended preschool are stronger than those of kids who have not.

4. Additionally, preschoolers learn everyday information, such as _____ names of the days of the week.

5. But _____ biggest advantage of preschool is that it teaches social skills.

6. Children who have spent most of their time at _____ home might be uncomfortable with other kids.

7. For example, they might cry when they are asked to share _____ toy.

8. Preschool teaches children how to share, take turns, and enjoy _____ others' company.

9. By the time preschooled children enter kindergarten, they are used to being part of _____ classroom.

10. Also, they have learned how to be more independent from their parents or _____ other caretakers.

Prepositions

A **preposition** is a word (such as *of, above, between,* or *about*) that connects a noun, pronoun, or verb with information about it. The correct preposition to use is often determined by common practice rather than by the preposition's actual meaning.

TIP For more on prepositions, see Chapter 19.

Prepositions after Adjectives

Adjectives are often followed by prepositions. Here are some common examples.

afraid of	full of	scared of
ashamed of	happy about	sorry about/sorry for
aware of	interested in	tired of
confused by	proud of	
excited about	responsible for	

Peri is afraid ~~to~~ ^of walking alone.

We are happy ~~of~~ ^about Dino's promotion.

Prepositions after Verbs

Many verbs consist of a verb plus a preposition. The meaning of these combinations is not usually the meaning that the verb and the preposition would each have on its own. Often, the meaning of the verb changes completely depending on which preposition is used with it.

You must **take out** the trash.   [*take out* = bring to a different location]

You must **take in** the exciting sights of New York City.   [*take in* = observe]

Here are a few common verb/preposition combinations.

call in (telephone)	You can *call in* your order.
call off (cancel)	They *called off* the party.
call on (ask for a response)	The teacher always *calls on* me.
drop in (visit)	*Drop in* the next time you are around.
drop off (leave behind)	Juan will *drop off* the car for service.
drop out (quit)	Many students *drop out* of school.
fight against (combat)	He tried to *fight against* the proposal.
fight for (defend)	We will *fight for* our rights.
fill out (complete)	Please *fill out* the form.
fill up (make full)	Do not *fill up* with junk food.
find out (discover)	Did you *find out* the answer?
give up (forfeit)	Do not *give up* your chance to succeed.
go by (visit, pass by)	I may *go by* the store on my way home.
go over (review)	Please *go over* your notes before the test.
grow up (mature)	All children *grow up*.
hand in (submit)	Please *hand in* your homework.

Seeing Preposition Errors

No Eating ~~on~~ *in* This Area

write As the editing of this sign shows, *in* is the correct preposition to use when referring to someone or something *within* a particular place or enclosure (*the clerk **in** the store, the papers **in** the box*). *On* is used to refer to something *on* a surface (*the teapot **on** the table, the picture **on** the wall*). Write two sentences that use *in* correctly and two sentences that use *on* correctly.

lock up (secure)	*Lock up* the apartment before leaving.
look up (check)	*Look up* the meaning in the dictionary.
pick out (choose)	*Pick out* a good apple.
pick up (take or collect)	Please *pick up* some drinks.
put off (postpone)	Do not *put off* starting your paper.
sign in (register)	*Sign in* when you arrive.
sign out (borrow)	You can *sign out* a book from the library.
sign up (register for)	I want to *sign up* for the contest.
think about (consider)	Simon *thinks about* moving.
turn in (submit)	Please *turn in* your homework.

PRACTICE 14 Editing Paragraphs for Preposition Problems

Edit the following paragraphs to make sure the correct prepositions are used.

EXAMPLE: At some point, many people think ~~out~~ *about* having a more flexible work schedule.

(1) If they are responsible in child care, they might want to get home from work earlier than usual. (2) Or they might be interested on having one workday a week free for studying or other activities. (3) Employees shouldn't be afraid to asking a supervisor about the possibility of a flexible schedule. (4) For instance, the supervisor might be very willing to allow the employee to do 40 hours of work in four days instead of five days. (5) Or a worker who wants to leave a little earlier than usual might give out half of a lunch hour to do so.

(6) The wide use of computers also allows for flexibility. (7) For example, busy parents might use their laptops to work from home a day or two a week. (8) They can stay in touch with the office by e-mailing supervisors or coworkers, or they might call on.

(9) Often, employers who allow more flexibility find in that they benefit, too. (10) Workers are happy on having more control over their own time; therefore, they are less stressed out and more productive than they would have been on a fixed schedule.

Chapter Review

LEARNING JOURNAL Did you find errors in your writing? Record the types of errors in your learning journal, and review them before you edit your own writing.

1. What is a pronoun? _____

   What are the three types of pronouns in English? _____

2. Rewrite this sentence in the simple past and the simple future.

   Melinda picks flowers every morning.

   Past: _____

   Future: _____

3. Rewrite this sentence so that it uses the perfect tense correctly.

   They have call an ambulance. _____

4. Using the progressive tenses, first rewrite this sentence as a question. Then, rewrite the question in the past tense and in the future tense.

   Chris is learning Spanish.

   Question: _____

   Past: _____

   Future: _____

5. Rewrite these sentences so that they use the modal verb correctly.

   Jennifer should to help her mother. _____

   Yesterday, I cannot work. _____

6. What is a gerund? _____

   Write a sentence with a gerund in it. _____

7. What is an infinitive? _____

   Write a sentence with an infinitive in it. _____

8. Give an example of a count noun. _____ Give an example of a noncount noun. _____

9. What is a preposition? _____

   Write a sentence using a preposition. _____

Chapter Test

Circle the correct choice for each of the following items.

1. Choose the correct word(s) to fill in the blank.

   You need _____ me if you have a problem.

   a. telling   **b.** to tell   **c.** told

2. Choose the sentence that has no errors.
   a. I have been written to my congressman three times, but I have never heard back from him.
   b. I have been writing to my congressman three times, but I have never heard back from him.
   c. I have written to my congressman three times, but I have never heard back from him.

3. Choose the sentence that has no errors.
   a. I walked 5 miles yesterday.
   b. I walk 5 miles yesterday.
   c. I walking 5 miles yesterday.

4. Choose the correct word to fill in the blank.

   In January, they _____ to vacation in Florida.

   a. going   **b.** is going   **c.** are going

5. If an underlined portion of this sentence is incorrect, select the revision that fixes it. If the sentence is correct as written, choose d.

   Pasquale <u>might to</u> get a job <u>at</u> his father's <u>construction</u> business.
                    A   B   C

   a. might   **c.** constructing
   b. on   **d.** No change is necessary.

6. Choose the correct word to fill in the blank.

   Elena tells the funniest jokes. _____ always makes me laugh.

   a. Her   **b.** Him   **c.** She

7. Choose the sentence that is in the correct order.
   a. One pound of chocolate I ate last week.
   b. I ate one pound of chocolate last week.
   c. Chocolate one pound I ate last week.

8. If an underlined portion of this sentence is incorrect, select the revision that fixes it. If the sentence is correct as written, choose d.

   The healths of our employees is very important.
   ‾‾‾ ‾‾‾‾‾‾‾   ‾‾
    A   B   C

   a. A
   b. health
   c. were
   d. No change is necessary.

9. Choose the sentence that has no errors.
   a. Was it snowing when you got to the mountain?
   b. Snowing it was when you got to the mountain?
   c. When you got to the mountain, snowing it was?

10. Choose the correct word to fill in the blank.

    Because it rained, we called _____ the picnic.

    a. on
    b. in
    c. off

"I write to clear my mind and to get my point across."
—Jade E., student

Part 6

Word Use

31 Word Choice 535

32 Commonly Confused Words 545

33 Spelling 557

31

THIS CHAPTER

- explains two resources for finding words and their meanings.
- explains four common word-choice problems and gives you practice avoiding them.

Word Choice

Using the Right Words

Understand the Importance of Choosing Words Carefully

In conversation, you show much of your meaning through facial expression, tone of voice, and gestures. In writing, you have only the words on the page to make your point, so you must choose them carefully. If you use vague or inappropriate words, your readers may not understand you.

Two resources will help you find the best words for your meaning: a dictionary and a thesaurus.

Dictionary

Dictionaries give you all kinds of useful information about words: spelling, division of words into syllables, pronunciation, parts of speech, other forms of words, definitions, and examples of use. Following is a sample dictionary entry.

TIP A number of good dictionaries are now available free online. An excellent resource is at **www.dictionary.com**.

Spelling and end-of-line division | Pronunciation | Parts of speech | Other forms

con • crete (kon′krēt, kong′-, kon-krēt′), *adj., n., v.* **-cret • ed,
-cret • ing**, *adj.* **1.** constituting an actual thing or instance; real; perceptible; substantial: *concrete proof.* **2.** pertaining to or concerned with realities or actual instances rather than abstractions; particular as opposed to general: *concrete proposals.* **3.** referring to an actual substance or thing, as opposed to an abstract quality: The words *cat, water,* and *teacher* are concrete, whereas the words *truth, excellence,* and *adulthood* are abstract.

— Definition
— Example

—*Random House Webster's College Dictionary*

535

Thesaurus

TIP To look up words online in both a dictionary and a thesaurus, go to the free online resource www.merriam-webster.com.

A thesaurus gives **synonyms** (words that have the same meaning) for the word you look up. Use a thesaurus when you cannot find the right word for what you mean. Be careful, however, to choose a word that has the precise meaning you intend. Following is a sample thesaurus entry.

> **Concrete**, *adj.* 1. Particular, specific, single, certain, special, unique, sole, peculiar, individual, separate, isolated, distinct, exact, precise, direct, strict, minute; definite, plain, evident, obvious; pointed, emphasized; restrictive, limiting, limited, well-defined, clear-cut, fixed, finite; determining, conclusive, decided.
>
> —J. I. Rodale, *The Synonym Finder*

Practice Avoiding Four Common Word-Choice Problems

Four common problems with word choice may make it hard for readers to understand your point.

Vague and Abstract Words

TIP For tools to build your vocabulary, visit the *Student Site for Real Writing* at bedfordstmartins.com/realwriting. Also, try the word games at www.dictionary.com.

Vague and abstract words are too general. They do not give your readers a clear idea of what you mean. Here are some common vague and abstract words.

Vague and Abstract Words			
a lot	cute	nice	stuff
amazing	dumb	OK (okay)	terrible
awesome	good	old	thing
bad	great	pretty	very
beautiful	happy	sad	whatever
big	huge	small	young

When you see one of these words or another general word in your writing, replace it with a concrete or more specific word or description. A **concrete** word names something that can be seen, heard, felt, tasted, or smelled. A **specific** word names a particular person or quality. Compare these two sentences:

VAGUE AND ABSTRACT   An old man crossed the street.

CONCRETE AND SPECIFIC   An eighty-seven-year-old priest stumbled along Main Street.

WORD USE
Practice Avoiding Four Common Word-Choice Problems 537

The first version is too general to be interesting. The second version creates a clear, strong image. Some words are so vague that it is best to avoid them altogether.

VAGUE AND ABSTRACT   It is awesome.
[This sentence is neither concrete nor specific.]

PRACTICE 1   Avoiding Vague and Abstract Words

In the following sentences, underline any words that are vague or abstract. Then, edit each sentence by replacing the vague or abstract words with concrete, specific ones. You may invent details or base them on brief online research into physician assistant careers.

EXAMPLE: It would be <u>cool</u> to be a physician assistant (PA). *It would be rewarding to be a physician assistant (PA).*

1. I am drawn to this career because it would let me do neat things for others. _____

2. I know that becoming a PA would require tons of work. _____

3. Also, each day in the classroom or clinic would be long. _____

4. Furthermore, I would have to be able to tolerate some rough sights. _____

5. However, I would learn a lot. _____

6. And in meetings with patients, I would be able to apply my great listening skills. _____

7. All this stuff would be interesting. _____

8. I am confident that my PA education would have a good outcome. _____

9. Also, my starting salary would be decent. _____

TIP For more practice on choosing words effectively, visit *Exercise Central* at **bedfordstmartins.com/realwriting**.

10. Getting accepted into a PA program would be awesome. _____

Slang

Slang, informal and casual language, should be used only in informal situations. Avoid it when you write, especially for college classes or at work. Use language that is appropriate for your audience and purpose.

SLANG	EDITED
S'all good.	Everything is going well.
Dawg, I don't deserve this grade.	Professor, I don't deserve this grade.

PRACTICE 2 Avoiding Slang

In the following sentences, underline any slang words. Then, edit the sentences by replacing the slang with language appropriate for a formal audience and purpose. Imagine that you are writing to a boss where you work.

EXAMPLE: ~~Yo~~, Randy, I need to talk ~~at~~ you for a minute.
         Hello,   *to*

1. That reference letter you wrote for me was really awesome sweet.
2. I am grateful because the one my English instructor did for me sucked.
3. She said that I thought I was all that, but that is not true.
4. I would be down with doing a favor for you in return if you need it.
5. Maybe you and I could hang sometime one of these weekends?
6. I know that we cannot be best buds, but we could shoot some hoops or something.
7. You could let me know whazzup when I see you at work next week.
8. If you are too stressed, do not go all emo on me.
9. Just chill out, and forget about it.
10. Text me when you get a mo.

Wordy Language

People sometimes use too many words to express their ideas. They may think that using more words will make them sound smart, but too many words can weaken a writer's point.

WORD USE
Practice Avoiding Four Common Word-Choice Problems

WORDY   I am not interested *at this point in time*.

EDITED   I am not interested now.
[The phrase *at this point in time* uses five words to express what could be said in one word: *now*.]

Common Wordy Expressions

WORDY	EDITED
As a result of	Because
Due to the fact that	Because
In spite of the fact that	Although
It is my opinion that	I think (*or just make the point*)
In the event that	If
The fact of the matter is that	(*Just state the point.*)
A great number of	Many
At that time	Then
In this day and age	Now
At this point in time	Now
In this paper I will show that . . .	(*Just make the point; do not announce it.*)
Utilize	Use

PRACTICE 3 Avoiding Wordy Language

In the following sentences, underline the wordy or repetitive language. Then, edit each sentence to make it more concise. Some sentences may contain more than one wordy phrase.

EXAMPLE: Sugar substitutes are a popular diet choice for people ~~of all ages~~ when they are searching for ways to ~~cut down~~ *reduce* ~~on all~~ the calories they ingest ~~on a daily basis~~ *each day*.

1. It is a well-known fact that dieting is difficult for most people.

2. Due to the fact that people are trying to cut calories, sugar substitutes are used in sodas, snacks, and other products.

3. The fact of the matter is that these substitutes provide a sweet taste, but without the calories of sugar or honey.

4. A great number of researchers have stated at this time that such substitutes are not necessarily safe or healthy to use in large quantities.

5. Some of the current experts on the matter are of the opinion that sugar substitutes can cause cancer, allergies, and other serious health problems.

6. At this point in time, other experts on the same subject believe that using these substitutes maintains a person's addiction to sugar and leads people to eat more junk food.

7. Despite these warnings, negative evaluations, and critical opinions from the experts, nearly 200 million people consume sugar-free or low-calorie products each year.

8. In this day and age, people are consuming an average of four of these items each day.

9. In spite of the fact that people know sugar is bad for them, their tastes will probably not change anytime in the near future.

10. It is my opinion that it would be better if people just learned to consume foods that do not contain sweeteners of any kind.

Clichés

Clichés are phrases used so often that people no longer pay attention to them. To get your point across and to get your readers' attention, replace clichés with fresh and specific language.

CLICHÉS	EDITED
I cannot *make ends meet*.	I do not have enough money to live on.
My uncle *worked his way up the corporate ladder*.	My uncle started as a shipping clerk but ended up as a regional vice president.
This roll is *as hard as a rock*.	This roll is so hard I could bounce it.

Common Clichés

as big as a house	few and far between	spoiled brat
as light as a feather	hell on earth	starting from scratch
better late than never	last but not least	sweating blood/bullets
break the ice	no way on earth	too little, too late
crystal clear	110 percent	24/7
a drop in the bucket	playing with fire	work like a dog
easier said than done		

WORD USE
Practice Avoiding Four Common Word-Choice Problems

PRACTICE 4 Avoiding Clichés

In the following sentences, underline the clichés. Then, edit each sentence by replacing the clichés with fresh and specific language.

> **TIP** Hundreds of clichés exist. To check if you have used one, go to www.clichesite.com.

EXAMPLE: Riding a bicycle 100 miles a day can be ~~hell on earth~~ *excruciating* unless you are willing to ~~give 110 percent~~ *work extremely hard*.

1. You have to persuade yourself to sweat blood and work like a dog for up to 10 hours.
2. There's no way on earth you can do it without extensive training.
3. Staying on your bike until the bitter end, of course, is easier said than done.
4. It is important to keep the fire in your belly and keep your goal of finishing the race crystal clear in your mind.
5. No matter how long it takes you to cross the finish line, remind yourself that it's better late than never.
6. Even if you are not a champion racer, training for a bike race will keep you fit as a fiddle.
7. It may take discipline to make yourself train, but you should keep your nose to the grindstone.
8. Bike racers should always play it safe by wearing helmets.
9. When you train for road racing, keep an eye peeled for cars.
10. You do not want to end up flat on your back in the hospital or six feet under!

A FINAL NOTE: Language that favors one gender over another or that assumes that only one gender performs a certain role is called *sexist*. Such language should be avoided.

> **TIP** See Chapter 24 for more advice on using pronouns.

SEXIST	A doctor should politely answer *his* patients' questions. [Not all doctors are male, as suggested by the pronoun *his*.]
REVISED	A doctor should politely answer *his or her* patients' questions. *Doctors* should politely answer *their* patients' questions. [The first revision changes *his* to *his or her* to avoid sexism. The second revision changes the subject to a plural noun (*Doctors*) so that a genderless pronoun (*their*) can be used. Usually, it is preferable to avoid *his or her*.]

Edit for Word Choice

PRACTICE 5 Editing Paragraphs for Word Choice

Find and edit six examples of vague or abstract language, slang, wordy language, or clichés in the following paragraphs.

(1) Imagine spending almost two weeks living in the coolest home in the world. (2) That is what scientist Lloyd Godson did when he lived at the bottom of a lake in Australia for thirteen days. (3) While there is no way on earth I would want to do that, it sure sounds fascinating.

(4) Godson's home was an 8-by-11-foot-long yellow steel box that he dubbed the BioSUB. (5) His air supply came from the algae plants growing inside the BioSUB. (6) Divers brought him food, water, and other junk through a manhole built in the bottom of his underwater home. (7) To keep busy, he rode on an exercise bicycle, which created electricity for him to recharge his laptop and run the lights for his plants. (8) He used his computer to talk to students all over the world and to watch movies.

(9) Godson paid for this experiment with money he had won in the "Live Your Dream" contest. (10) At this point in time, I have to say that for most people, the BioSUB home would be less appealing than a regular, aboveground room, apartment, or house. (11) Indeed, by the time his two weeks were over, Godson was ready to come up, feel the sunshine and wind on his face again, and "smell the roses."

PRACTICE 6 Editing Your Own Writing for Word Choice

Edit a piece of your own writing for word choice. It can be a paper for this course or another one, or something you have written for work or your everyday life. You may want to use the chart on page 544.

Chapter Review

LEARNING JOURNAL Did you find problems with word choice in your writing? What is the main thing you have learned about word choice that will help you? What is unclear to you?

1. What two resources will help you choose the best words to get your ideas across in writing? _____

2. What are four common word-choice problems? _____
_____

3. Replace vague and abstract words with _____ and _____ words.

4. When is it appropriate to use slang in college writing or in writing at work? _____

5. Give two examples of wordy expressions. _____
_____

Chapter Test

For each of the following items, choose words or sentences that are specific and appropriate for a formal (academic or work) audience.

1. Choose the item that uses words most effectively.
   a. My dorm is just an OK place to study.
   b. My dorm is so noisy and full of activity that it is difficult to study there.
   c. My dorm is not where I go when I want to study.

2. Choose the best words to fill in the blank.

   I am afraid that all your hard work did not _____ .

   a. solve our problem   b. do the trick   c. do it for us

3. Choose the best word(s) to fill in the blank.

   Kevin was extremely _____ about his new job.

   a. juiced   b. turned on   c. enthusiastic

4. Choose the item that uses words most effectively.
   a. I like that thing Nikki does whenever she scores a goal.
   b. I like the way Nikki goes nuts whenever she scores a goal.
   c. I like the way Nikki does a backflip whenever she scores a goal.

5. Choose the item that uses words most effectively.
   a. In the event that you are ever in River City, stop by to see me.
   b. If you are ever in River City, stop by to see me.
   c. If by chance you are ever in River City, stop by to see me.

EDITING FOR WORD CHOICE

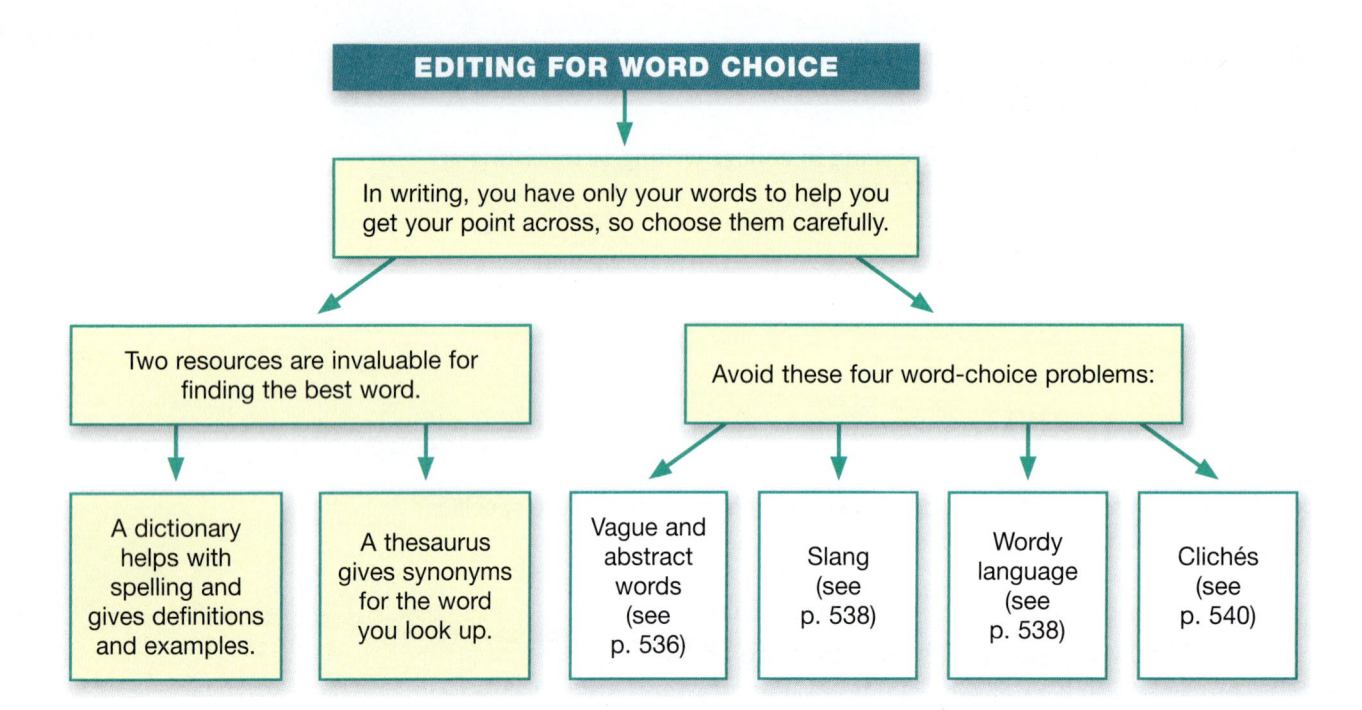

In writing, you have only your words to help you get your point across, so choose them carefully.

Two resources are invaluable for finding the best word.

- A dictionary helps with spelling and gives definitions and examples.
- A thesaurus gives synonyms for the word you look up.

Avoid these four word-choice problems:

- Vague and abstract words (see p. 536)
- Slang (see p. 538)
- Wordy language (see p. 538)
- Clichés (see p. 540)

THIS CHAPTER
- gives you twenty-seven sets of commonly confused words.
- explains what the words mean and how they should be used.
- gives you practice using them correctly.

32

Commonly Confused Words

Avoiding Mistakes with Soundalike Words

Understand Why Certain Words Are Commonly Confused

People often confuse certain words in English because they sound alike and may have similar meanings. In speech, words that sound alike are not a problem. In writing, however, words that sound alike may be spelled differently, and readers rely on the spelling to understand what you mean. Edit your writing carefully to make sure you have used the correct words.

- **Proofread carefully**, using the techniques discussed on page 558.
- **Use a dictionary** to look up any words you are unsure about.
- **Focus on finding and correcting mistakes** you make with the twenty-seven sets of commonly confused words covered in this chapter.
- **Develop a personal list of soundalike words** you confuse often. In your learning journal, record words that you confuse in your writing and their meanings. Before you turn in any piece of writing, consult your personal word list to make sure you have used words correctly.

Practice Using Commonly Confused Words Correctly

Study the different meanings and spellings of these twenty-seven sets of commonly confused words. Complete the sentence after each set of words, filling in each blank with the correct word.

TIP Some commonly confused words sound similar but not exactly alike, such as *conscience* and *conscious*, *loose* and *lose*, and *of* and *have*. To avoid confusing these words, practice pronouncing them correctly.

A / AN / AND

a: used before a word that begins with a consonant sound

A friend of mine just won the lottery.

an: used before a word that begins with a vowel sound

An old friend of mine just won the lottery.

and: used to join two words

My friend *and* I went out to celebrate.

A friend *and* I ate at *an* Italian restaurant.

Other lottery winners were _____ algebra teacher _____ bowling team.

ACCEPT / EXCEPT

accept: to agree to receive or admit (verb)

I will *accept* the job offer.

except: but, other than

All the stores are closed *except* the Quik-Stop.

I *accept* all the job conditions *except* the low pay.

Do not _____ gifts from clients _____ those who are also personal friends.

ADVICE / ADVISE

advice: opinion (noun)

I would like your *advice* before I make a decision.

advise: to give an opinion (verb)

Please *advise* me what to do.

Please *advise* me what to do; you always give me good *advice*.

If you do not like my _____, please _____ me how to proceed.

AFFECT / EFFECT

affect: to make an impact on, to change something (verb)

The whole city was *affected* by the hurricane.

effect: a result (noun)

What *effect* will the hurricane have on the local economy?

Although the storm will have many negative *effects*, it will not *affect* the price of food.

The _____ of the disaster will _____ many people.

ARE / OUR

are: a form of the verb *be*

The workers *are* about to go on strike.

our: a pronoun showing ownership

The children played on *our* porch.

My relatives *are* staying at *our* house.

_____ new neighbors _____ moving in today.

BY / BUY / BYE

by: next to, before, or past

Meet me *by* the entrance.

Make sure the bill is paid *by* the fifteenth of the month.

The motorcycle raced *by* me.

buy: to purchase (verb)

I would like to *buy* a new laptop.

bye: an informal way to say *goodbye*

"Bye, Grandma!"

Seeing Commonly Confused Words

write What error do you see in this sign? Write a sentence that uses *by, buy,* and *bye* correctly.

I said "_____" from the window as we drove _____ our friends, who were standing next to the house I wanted to _____ .

CONSCIENCE / CONSCIOUS

TIP Remember that one of the words is *con-science*; the other is not.

conscience: a personal sense of right and wrong (noun)

Jake's *conscience* would not allow him to cheat.

conscious: awake, aware (adjective)

The coma patient is now *conscious*.

I am *conscious* that it is getting late.

The judge was *conscious* that the accused had acted according to his *conscience* even though he had broken the law.

The man said that he was not _____ that what he had done was illegal, or his _____ would not have let him do it.

FINE / FIND

fine: of high quality (adjective); feeling well (adjective); a penalty for breaking a law (noun)

This jacket is made of *fine* leather.

After a day in bed, Jacob felt *fine*.

The *fine* for exceeding the speed limit is $50.

find: to locate, to discover (verb)

Did Clara *find* her glasses?

I *find* gardening to be a *fine* pastime.

Were you able to _____ a place to store your _____ jewelry?

ITS / IT'S

its: a pronoun showing ownership

The dog chased *its* tail.

it's: a contraction of the words *it is*

It's about time you got here.

It's very hard for a dog to keep *its* teeth clean.

TIP If you are not sure whether to use *its* or *it's* in a sentence, try substituting *it is*. If the sentence does not make sense with *it is*, use *its*.

_____ no surprise that the college raised _____ tuition.

Seeing Commonly Confused Words

> **write** What error do you see in this sign? What other types of errors have you noticed on signs, on television, in newspapers or magazines, or in online content?

KNEW / NEW / KNOW / NO

knew: understood; recognized (past tense of the verb *know*)

I *knew* the answer, but I could not think of it.

new: unused, recent, or just introduced (adjective)

The building has a *new* security code.

know: to understand; to have knowledge of (verb)

I *know* how to bake bread.

no: used to form a negative

I have *no* idea what the answer is.

I never *knew* how much a *new* car costs.

The _____ teacher _____ many of her students already.

There is _____ way Tom could _____ where Celia is hiding.

I _____ that there is _____ cake left.

LOOSE / LOSE

loose: baggy; relaxed; not fixed in place (adjective)

　In hot weather, people tend to wear *loose* clothing.

lose: to misplace; to forfeit possession of (verb)

　Every summer, I *lose* about three pairs of sunglasses.

If the ring is too *loose* on your finger, you might *lose* it.

I _____ my patience with the _____ rules on Wall Street.

MIND / MINE

mind: to object to (verb); the thinking or feeling part of one's brain (noun)

　Toby does not *mind* if I borrow his tool chest.

　Estela has a good *mind*, but often she does not use it.

mine: belonging to me (pronoun); a source of ore and minerals (noun)

　That coat is *mine*.

　My uncle worked in a coal *mine* in West Virginia.

That writing problem of *mine* was on my *mind*.

If you do not _____, the gloves you just took are _____.

OF / HAVE

of: coming from; caused by; part of a group; made from (preposition)

　The leader *of* the band played bass guitar.

have: to possess (verb; also used as a helping verb)

　I *have* one more course to take before I graduate.

　I should *have* started studying earlier.

The president *of* the company should *have* resigned.

Sidney could _____ been one _____ the winners.

NOTE: Do not use *of* after *would*, *should*, *could*, and *might*. Use *have* after those words (*would have*, *should have*).

PASSED / PAST

passed: went by or went ahead (past tense of the verb *pass*)

　We *passed* the hospital on the way to the airport.

past: time that has gone by (noun); gone by, over, just beyond (preposition)

    In the *past*, I was able to stay up all night and not be tired.

    I drove *past* the burning warehouse.

This *past* school year, I *passed* all my exams.

Trish _____ me as we ran _____ the 1-mile marker.

PEACE / PIECE

peace: no disagreement; calm

    Could you quiet down and give me a little *peace*?

piece: a part of something larger

    May I have a *piece* of that pie?

The feuding families found *peace* after they sold the *piece* of land.

To keep the _____, give your sister a _____ of candy.

PRINCIPAL / PRINCIPLE

principal: main (adjective); head of a school or leader of an organization (noun)

    Brush fires are the *principal* risk in the hills of California.

    Ms. Edwards is the *principal* of Memorial Elementary School.

    Corinne is a *principal* in the management consulting firm.

principle: a standard of beliefs or behaviors (noun)

    Although tempted, she held on to her moral *principles*.

The *principal* questioned the delinquent student's *principles*.

The _____ problem is that you want me to act against my _____.

QUIET / QUITE / QUIT

quiet: soft in sound; not noisy (adjective)

    The library was *quiet*.

quite: completely; very (adverb)

    After cleaning all the windows, Alex was *quite* tired.

quit: to stop (verb)

    She *quit* her job.

After the band *quit* playing, the hall was *quite quiet*.

If you would _____ shouting and be _____, you would find that the scenery is _____ pleasant.

RIGHT / WRITE

right: correct; in a direction opposite from left (adjective)

You definitely made the *right* choice.

When you get to the stoplight, make a *right* turn.

write: to put words on paper (verb)

Will you *write* your phone number for me?

Please *write* the *right* answer in the space provided.

You were _____ to _____ to the senator.

SET / SIT

set: a collection of something (noun); to place an object somewhere (verb)

Paul has a complete *set* of Johnny Cash records.

Please *set* the package on the table.

sit: to rest in a chair or other seatlike surface; to be located in a particular place

I need to *sit* on the sofa for a few minutes.

The shed *sits* between the house and the garden.

If I *sit* down now, I will not have time to *set* the plants outside.

Before you _____ on that chair, _____ the magazines on the floor.

SUPPOSE / SUPPOSED

suppose: to imagine or assume to be true

I *suppose* you would like something to eat.

Suppose you won a million dollars.

supposed: past tense of *suppose*; intended

Karen *supposed* Thomas was late because of traffic.

I *suppose* you know that Rita was *supposed* to be home by 6:30.

I _____ you want to leave soon because we are _____ to arrive before the guests.

THAN / THEN

than: a word used to compare two or more people, places, or things

It is colder inside *than* outside.

then: at a certain time; next in time

I got out of the car and *then* realized the keys were still in it.

Clara ran more miles *than* she ever had before, and *then* she collapsed.

Back _____, I smoked more _____ three packs a day.

THEIR / THERE / THEY'RE

their: a pronoun showing ownership

   I borrowed *their* clippers to trim the hedges.

there: a word indicating location or existence

   Just put the keys *there* on the desk.

   There are too many lawyers.

they're: a contraction of the words *they are*

   They're about to leave.

There is a car in *their* driveway, which indicates that *they're* home.

TIP If you are not sure whether to use *their* or *they're*, substitute *they are*. If the sentence does not make sense, use *their*.

_____ beach house is empty except for the one week that _____ vacationing _____.

THOUGH / THROUGH / THREW

though: however; nevertheless; in spite of (conjunction)

   Though he is short, he plays great basketball.

through: finished with (adjective); from one side to the other (preposition)

   I am *through* arguing with you.

   The baseball went right *through* the window.

threw: hurled; tossed (past tense of the verb *throw*)

   She *threw* the basketball.

Even *though* it was illegal, she *threw* the empty cup *through* the window onto the road.

_____ she did not really believe it would bring good luck, Jan _____ a penny _____ the air into the fountain.

TO / TOO / TWO

to: a word indicating a direction or movement (preposition); part of the infinitive form of a verb

   Please give the message *to* Sharon.

   It is easier *to* ask for forgiveness than *to* get permission.

too: also; more than enough; very (adverb)

   I am tired *too*.

   Dan ate *too* much and felt sick.

   That dream was *too* real.

two: the number between one and three (noun)

    The lab had only *two* computers.

They went *to* a restaurant and ordered *too* much food for *two* people.

When Marty went _____ pay for his meal, the cashier charged him _____ times, which was _____ bad.

USE / USED

use: to employ or put into service (verb)

    How do you plan to *use* that blueprint?

used: past tense of the verb *use*. *Used to* can indicate a past fact or state, or it can mean "familiar with."

    He *used* his lunch hour to do errands.

    He *used* to go for a walk during his lunch hour.

She *used* to be a chef, so she knows how to *use* all kinds of kitchen gadgets.

She is also *used* to improvising in the kitchen.

Tom _____ the prize money to buy a boat; his family hoped he would _____ the money for his education, but Tom was _____ to getting his way.

TIP Writing *use to* instead of *used to* is a common error. Train yourself not to make that mistake.

WHO'S / WHOSE

who's: a contraction of the words *who is*

    Who's at the door?

whose: a pronoun showing ownership

    Whose car is parked outside?

Who's the person *whose* car sank in the river?

The student _____ name is first on the list is the one _____ in charge.

TIP If you are not sure whether to use *whose* or *who's*, substitute *who is*. If the sentence does not make sense, use *whose*.

YOUR / YOU'RE

your: a pronoun showing ownership

    Did you bring *your* wallet?

you're: a contraction of the words *you are*

    You're not telling me the whole story.

You're going to have *your* third exam tomorrow.

_____ teacher says that _____ good with numbers.

TIP If you are not sure whether to use *your* or *you're*, substitute *you are*. If the sentence does not make sense, use *your*.

Edit for Commonly Confused Words

PRACTICE 1 Editing Paragraphs for Commonly Confused Words

Edit the following paragraphs to correct eighteen errors in word use.

(1) More and more women are purchasing handguns, against the advise of law enforcement officers. (2) Few of these women are criminals or plan to commit crimes. (3) They no the risks of guns, and they except those risks. (4) They buy weapons primarily because their tired of feeling like victims. (5) They do not want to contribute too the violence in are society, but they also realize that women are the victims of violent attacks far to often. (6) Many women loose they're lives because they cannot fight off there attackers. (7) Some women have made a conscience decision to arm themselves for protection.

(8) But does buying a gun make things worse rather then better? (9) Having a gun in you're house makes it three times more likely that someone will be killed there—and that someone is just as likely to be you or one of your children as a criminal. (10) Most young children cannot tell the difference between a real gun and a toy gun when they fine one. (11) Every year, their are tragic examples of children who accidentally shoot and even kill other youngsters while they are playing with guns. (12) A mother who's children are injured while playing with her gun will never again think that a gun provides piece of mind. (13) Reducing the violence in are society may be a better solution.

PRACTICE 2 Editing Your Own Writing for Commonly Confused Words

Edit a piece of your own writing for commonly confused words. It can be a paper for this course or another one, or something you have written for work or your everyday life.

Chapter Review

LEARNING JOURNAL
Record your personal list of commonly confused words, and look at it when you edit your own writing.

1. What are four strategies you can use to avoid confusing words that sound alike or have similar meanings? _____
   _____
   _____
   _____

2. What are the top five commonly confused words on your personal list?
   _____

Chapter Test

Use the words in parentheses to correctly fill in the blanks in each of the following sentences.

1. The coin machine will _____ any coins _____ foreign ones. (*accept, except*)

2. _____ going to arrive _____ late, but they will be sure to bring all _____ tools. (*their, there, they're*)

3. There is _____ much confusion in our department now that _____ supervisors have been asked _____ perform the same job. (*to, too, two*)

4. Everyone thinks that _____ going to get a perfect score on _____ exam. (*your, you're*)

5. The veterinarian told me _____ not necessary to wash a cat because a cat keeps _____ own fur clean. (*its, it's*)

THIS CHAPTER

- gives you strategies for finding and correcting spelling errors.
- gives you methods to become a better speller.
- gives you a list of one hundred commonly misspelled words to use as a reference.

33

Spelling

Using the Right Letters

Finding and Correcting Spelling Mistakes

Some extremely smart people are poor spellers. Unfortunately, spelling errors are easy for readers to spot, and they make a bad impression. Learn to find and correct spelling mistakes in your writing by using the following strategies.

Use a Dictionary

When proofreading your papers, consult a dictionary whenever you are unsure about the spelling of a word. *Checking a dictionary is the single most important thing you can do to improve your spelling.*

TIP Online dictionaries, such as **www.merriamwebster.com**, can help you spell, as they often allow you to type in an incorrectly spelled word and get the correct spelling.

Use a Spell Checker—with Caution

Use a spell checker after you have completed a piece of writing but before you print it out. This word-processing tool finds and highlights a word that may be misspelled, suggests other spellings, and gives you the opportunity to change the spelling of the word.

However, never rely on a spell checker to do your editing for you. It ignores anything it recognizes as a word, so it will not help you find words that are misused or misspellings that are also words. For example, a spell checker would not highlight any of the problems in these phrases:

Just *to* it. (Correct: Just *do* it.)
pain in the *nick* (Correct: pain in the *neck*)
my writing *coarse* (Correct: my writing *course*)

Use Proofreading Techniques

TIP For more spelling practice, visit *Exercise Central* at **bedfordstmartins.com/realwriting**.

Use some of the following proofreading techniques to focus on the spelling of one word at a time. Try them all. Then, decide which ones work best for you.

- Print out your paper before proofreading. (Many writers find it easier to detect errors on paper than on a computer screen.)
- Put a piece of paper under the line that you are reading.
- Proofread your paper backward, one word at a time.
- Print out a version of your paper that looks noticeably different: Make the words larger, make the margins larger, triple-space the lines, or make all these changes.
- Read your paper aloud. This strategy will help you if you tend to leave words out.
- Exchange papers with a partner, and proofread each other's papers, identifying only possible misspellings.

Make a Personal Spelling List

Set aside a section of your course notebook or learning journal for your spelling list. Every time you edit a paper, write down the words that you misspelled. Every couple of weeks, go back to your spelling list to see if your problem words have changed. Are you misspelling fewer words in each paper?

For each word on your list, create a memory aid or silly phrase to help you remember the correct spelling. For example, if you often misspell *a lot*, you could remember that "*a lot* is a lot of words."

Strategies for Becoming a Better Speller

Here are three good strategies for becoming a better speller.

Master Commonly Confused Words

Chapter 32 covers twenty-seven sets of words that are commonly confused because they sound similar, such as *write* and *right*. If you can master these commonly confused words, you will avoid many spelling mistakes.

Learn Six Spelling Rules

If you can remember the following six rules, you can correct many of the spelling errors in your writing.

First, here is a quick review of vowels and consonants.

VOWELS: *a, e, i, o,* and *u*

CONSONANTS: *b, c, d, f, g, h, j, k, l, m, n, p, q, r, s, t, v, w, x,* and *z*

The letter *y* can be either a vowel or a consonant. It is a vowel when it sounds like the *y* in *fly* or *hungry*. It is a consonant when it sounds like the *y* in *yellow*.

Rule 1.   "*I* before *e*, except after *c*. Or when sounded like *a*, as in *neighbor* or *weigh*."

Many people repeat this rhyme to themselves as they decide whether a word is spelled with an *ie* or an *ei*.

pi**e**ce (*i* before *e*)

rec**ei**ve (except after *c*)

eight (sounds like *a*)

EXCEPTIONS: *either, neither, foreign, height, seize, society, their, weird*

Rule 2.   **Drop the final *e*** when adding an ending that begins with a vowel.

hop**e** + ing = hoping

imagin**e** + ation = imagination

Keep the final *e* when adding an ending that begins with a consonant.

achiev**e** + ment = achievement

definit**e** + ly = definitely

EXCEPTIONS: *argument, awful, judgment, simply, truly,* and others

Rule 3.   When adding an ending to a word that ends in *y*, **change the *y* to *i*** when a consonant comes before the *y*.

lone**ly** + est = loneliest

hap**py** + er = happier

apolo**gy** + ize = apologize

like**ly** + hood = likelihood

Do not change the *y* when a vowel comes before the *y*.

b**oy** + ish = boyish

p**ay** + ment = payment

surv**ey** + or = surveyor

b**uy** + er = buyer

EXCEPTIONS:

1. When adding *-ing* to a word ending in *y*, always keep the *y*, even if a consonant comes before it: stu**dy** + ing = stud**y**ing.

2. Other exceptions include *daily, dryer, said,* and *paid*.

Rule 4. When adding an ending that starts with a vowel to a one-syllable word, follow these rules.

Double the final consonant only if the word ends with a consonant-vowel-consonant.

t**rap** + ed = trapped   k**nit** + ed = knitted

d**rip** + ed = dripped   f**at** + er = fatter

Do not double the final consonant if the word ends with some other combination.

VOWEL-VOWEL-CONSONANT	VOWEL-CONSONANT-CONSONANT
cl**ean** + est = cleanest	sl**ick** + er = slicker
p**oor** + er = poorer	t**each** + er = teacher
cl**ear** + ed = cleared	l**ast** + ed = lasted

Rule 5. When adding an ending that starts with a vowel to a word with two or more syllables, follow these rules.

Double the final consonant only if the word ends with a consonant-vowel-consonant and the stress is on the last syllable.

sub**mit** + ing = submitting

pre**fer** + ed = preferred

Do not double the final consonant in other cases.

understand + ing = understanding

offer + ed = offered

Rule 6. Add *-s* to most nouns to form the plural, including words that end in *o* preceded by a vowel.

MOST WORDS	WORDS THAT END IN VOWEL PLUS *O*
book + **s** = books	video + **s** = videos
college + **s** = colleges	stereo + **s** = stereos

Add *-es* to words that end in *o* preceded by a consonant and words that end in *s, sh, ch,* or *x*.

WORDS THAT END IN CONSONANT PLUS O	WORDS THAT END IN S, SH, CH, OR X
pota**to** + **es** = potato**es**	cla**ss** + **es** = class**es**
he**ro** + **es** = hero**es**	pu**sh** + **es** = push**es**
	ben**ch** + **es** = bench**es**
	fa**x** + **es** = fax**es**

Exceptions When Forming Plurals

A **compound noun** is formed when two nouns are joined, with a hyphen (*in-law*), a space (*life vest*), or no space (*keyboard, stockpile*). Plurals of compound nouns are generally formed by adding an *-s* to the end of the last noun (*in-laws, life vests*) or to the end of the combined word (*keyboards, stockpiles*). Some hyphenated compound words such as *mother-in-law* or *hole-in-one* form plurals by adding an *-s* to the chief word (*mothers-in-law, holes-in-one*).

Some words form plurals in different ways, as in the list below.

Different Types of Plurals

SINGULAR	PLURAL	SINGULAR	PLURAL
analysis	analyses	louse	lice
bacteria	bacterium	loaf	loaves
bison	bison	medium	media
cactus	cacti	man	men
calf	calves	mouse	mice
child	children	phenomenon	phenomena
deer	deer	roof	roofs
die	dice	sheep	sheep
foot	feet	shelf	shelves
focus	foci	tooth	teeth
goose	geese	thief	thieves
half	halves	vertebra	vertebrae
hoof	hooves	wife	wives
knife	knives	wolf	wolves
leaf	leaves	woman	women

Consult a List of Commonly Misspelled Words

Use a list like the one below as an easy reference to check your spelling.

One Hundred Commonly Misspelled Words

absence	cruelty	height	recognize
achieve	daughter	humorous	recommend
across	definite	illegal	restaurant
aisle	describe	immediately	rhythm
a lot	develop	independent	roommate
already	dictionary	interest	schedule
analyze	different	jewelry	scissors
answer	disappoint	judgment	secretary
appetite	dollar	knowledge	separate
argument	eighth	license	sincerely
athlete	embarrass	lightning	sophomore
awful	environment	loneliness	succeed
basically	especially	marriage	successful
beautiful	exaggerate	meant	surprise
beginning	excellent/excellence	muscle	truly
believe	exercise	necessary	until
business	fascinate	ninety	usually
calendar	February	noticeable	vacuum
career	finally	occasion	valuable
category	foreign	perform	vegetable
chief	friend	physically	weight
column	government	prejudice	weird
coming	grief	probably	writing
commitment	guidance	psychology	written
conscious	harass	receive	
convenient			

Seeing Spelling Errors

WE ARE COMMITTED TO EXCELLENSE

write Which word is misspelled? Use the correct form of this word in a sentence.

Chapter Review

1. What are two important tools for finding and correcting spelling mistakes? _____
   _____

2. What three strategies can you use to become a better speller?
   _____
   _____

LEARNING JOURNAL What spelling errors do you make most often? How will you remember to spell them correctly?

Chapter Test

In each sentence, fill in the blank with the correctly spelled word.

1. Your joining us for dinner is a pleasant _____.
   - **a.** suprise
   - **b.** surprize
   - **c.** surprise

2. When can I expect to _____ the package?
   - **a.** recieve
   - **b.** receive
   - **c.** reeceive

3. The solar technology program is _____ many new students.
   a. admiting   b. admitting   c. addmitting

4. Colin's roommate is _____ weird.
   a. definately   b. definitely   c. definitly

5. After my doctor diagnosed my injury, she _____ me to a physical therapist.
   a. refered   b. reffered   c. referred

6. We will have to go in _____ cars.
   a. separate   b. seperate   c. sepurate

7. I have not seen her since _____ grade.
   a. eith   b. eigth   c. eighth

8. The date is circled on the _____.
   a. callender   b. calendar   c. calander

9. Dana got her _____ last week.
   a. lisense   b. liscence   c. license

10. That ring is _____.
    a. valuble   b. valuable   c. valueble

> "I write e-mails to clients, asking them questions to help them figure out what they want."
>
> —Daniel B., student

Part 7
Punctuation and Capitalization

34 Commas 567

35 Apostrophes 582

36 Quotation Marks 590

37 Other Punctuation 598

38 Capitalization 604

EDITING REVIEW TESTS 609

34

THIS CHAPTER
- shows you how and where to use commas (and tells you where *not* to use them).
- gives you practice using commas correctly.

Commas (,)

Understand What Commas Do

Commas (,) are punctuation marks that help readers understand a sentence. Read aloud the following three sentences. How does the use of commas change the meaning?

NO COMMA	When you call Sarah I will start cooking.
ONE COMMA	When you call Sarah**,** I will start cooking.
TWO COMMAS	When you call**,** Sarah**,** I will start cooking.

To get your intended meaning across to your readers, it is important that you understand when and how to use commas.

✓ **LearningCurve**
Commas
bedfordstmartins.com/realwriting/LC

Practice Using Commas Correctly

Commas between Items in a Series

Use commas to separate the items in a series (three or more items), including the last item in the series, which usually has *and* before it.

[Item] **,** [Item] **,** [Item] **,** and [Item]

To get from South Dakota to Texas, we will drive through *Nebraska***,** *Kansas***,** and *Oklahoma*.

We can *sleep in the car***,** *stay in a motel***,** or *camp outside*.

As I drive, I see many beautiful sights, such as *mountains***,** *plains***,** and *prairies*.

567

TIP How does a comma change the way you read a sentence aloud? Many readers pause when they come to a comma.

NOTE: Writers do not always use a comma before the final item in a series. In college writing, however, it is best to include it.

Commas between Coordinate Adjectives

Coordinate adjectives are two or more adjectives that independently modify the same noun and are separated by commas.

> Conor ordered a *big*, *fat*, *greasy* burger.
>
> The diner food was *cheap*, *unhealthy*, and *delicious*.

Do *not* use a comma between the final adjective and the noun it describes.

INCORRECT	Joelle wore a *long*, *clingy*, *red*, dress.
CORRECT	Joelle wore a *long*, *clingy*, *red* dress.

Cumulative adjectives describe the same noun but are not separated by commas because they form a unit that describes the noun. You can identify cumulative adjectives because separating them by *and* does not make any sense.

> The store is having its *last storewide clearance* sale.
>
> [Putting *and* between *last* and *storewide* and between *storewide* and *clearance* would make an odd sentence: The store is having its *last* and *storewide* and *clearance* sale. The adjectives in the sentence are cumulative adjectives and should not be separated by commas.]

In summary:

- **Do** use commas to separate two or more **coordinate adjectives**.
- **Do not** use commas to separate **cumulative adjectives**.

PRACTICE 1   Using Commas in Series and with Adjectives

Edit the following sentences by underlining the items in the series and adding commas where they are needed. If a sentence is already correct, put a "C" next to it.

EXAMPLE: In 1935, the U.S. government hired <u>writers</u>,<u>teachers</u>, <u>historians</u>,<u>and others</u> to work for the Federal Writers' Project (FWP).

1. The FWP was part of an effort to create jobs during the long devastating economic crisis known as the Great Depression.

TIP For more practice using commas correctly, visit *Exercise Central* at bedfordstmartins.com/ realwriting.

2. Many famous writers, such as John Cheever Ralph Ellison and Zora Neale Hurston, joined the FWP.

3. The FWP's Folklore Unit dedicated itself to interviewing ordinary Americans writing down their stories and bringing together this information so that it could be shared with the public.

4. Folklore Unit workers were able to collect not only life stories but also songs folktales and superstitions.

5. The director of the Folklore Unit hoped that by publishing this information, the FWP might make Americans more accepting of fellow citizens whose experiences, beliefs, and interests were different from their own.

6. Through all its efforts, the FWP helped to create a more vivid engaging and personal history of the country.

7. Some of the most striking FWP records are interviews with former slaves who lived in Georgia, South Carolina, Virginia, and other parts of the South.

8. Interviewers asked the former slaves to tell their personal stories and also to describe their working conditions diets and experiences with racism.

9. Eventually, the government published a thorough highly informative collection of these interviews: *Slave Narratives: A Folk History of Slavery in the United States from Interviews with Former Slaves.*

10. This collection is a valued resource for historians social scientists and anyone interested in American history.

Commas in Compound Sentences

A **compound sentence** contains two complete sentences joined by a coordinating conjunction: *and, but, for, nor, or, so, yet*. Use a comma before the joining word to separate the two complete sentences.

TIP Remember the coordinating conjunctions with *FANBOYS: for, and, nor, but, or, yet,* and *so*. For more information, see Chapter 27.

| Sentence | **,** | and, but, for, nor, or, so, yet | Sentence. |

I called my best friend**,** and she agreed to drive me to work.

I asked my best friend to drive me to work**,** but she was busy.

I can take the bus to work**,** or I can call another friend.

LANGUAGE NOTE: A comma alone cannot separate two sentences in English. Doing so creates a run-on (see Chapter 21).

EDITING FOR CORRECT COMMA USAGE:
Using Commas in Compound Sentences

Find

Many college students are the first in their families to go to college (and) these students' relatives are proud of them.

1. To determine if the sentence is compound, **underline** the subjects, and **double-underline** the verbs.
2. **Ask:** Is the sentence compound? Yes.
3. **Circle** the word that joins them.

Edit

Many college students are the first in their families to go to college, and these students' relatives are proud of them.

4. **Put a comma** before the word that joins the two sentences.

PRACTICE 2 Using Commas in Compound Sentences

Edit the following compound sentences by adding commas where they are needed. If a sentence is already correct, put a "C" next to it.

EXAMPLE: Marika wanted to get a college education, but her husband did not like the idea.

1. Marika's hospital volunteer work had convinced her to become a physical therapist, but she needed a college degree to qualify.

2. Deciding to apply to college was difficult for her so she was excited when she was admitted.

3. She had chosen the college carefully for it had an excellent program in physical therapy.

4. Marika knew that the courses would be difficult but she had not expected her husband to oppose her plan.

5. They had been married for twelve years, and he was surprised that she wanted a career.

6. She tried to tell him about the exciting things she was learning but he did not seem interested.

7. It was hard for her to manage the house and keep up with her classes, but he would not help.

8. Maybe he was upset that she wanted more education than he had or perhaps he was afraid that they would grow apart.

9. She did not want to have to choose between her husband and an education and she did not have to.

10. They talked about their problems and now he thinks that her career might even help their marriage.

Commas after Introductory Words

Use a comma after an introductory word, phrase, or clause. The comma lets your readers know when the main part of the sentence is starting.

| Introductory word or word group | , | Main part of sentence. |

INTRODUCTORY WORD: *Yesterday*, I went to the game.

INTRODUCTORY PHRASE: *By the way*, I do not have a babysitter for tomorrow.

INTRODUCTORY CLAUSE: *While I waited outside*, Susan went backstage.

PRACTICE 3 Using Commas after Introductory Word Groups

In each item, underline introductory words or word groups. Then, add commas after introductory word groups where they are needed. If a sentence is already correct, put a "C" next to it.

EXAMPLE: <u>In the 1960s</u>, John Mackey became famous for his speed and strength as a tight end for the Baltimore Colts football team.

1. In his later years the National Football League Hall-of-Famer was in the news for another reason: He suffered from dementia possibly linked to the head blows he received on the football field.

2. According to medical experts, repeated concussions can severely damage the brain over time, and they are especially harmful to young people, whose brains are still developing.

3. Based on these warnings and on stories like John Mackey's athletic associations, coaches, and parents of young athletes are taking new precautions.

4. For example more football coaches are teaching players to tackle and block with their heads up, reducing the chance that they will receive a blow to the top of the head.

5. Also when players show signs of a concussion—such as dizziness, nausea, or confusion—more coaches are taking them out of the game.

6. Ideally coaches then make sure injured players receive immediate medical attention.

7. Once concussion sufferers are back home, they should take a break from sports until the symptoms of their injury are gone.

8. During their recovery they should also avoid any activity that puts too much stress on the brain; these activities can include playing video games, studying, and driving.

9. When concussion sufferers feel ready to get back into the game a doctor should confirm that it is safe for them to do so.

10. As a result of these new precautions young athletes may avoid experiencing anything like the long, difficult decline of John Mackey, who died in 2011.

Commas around Appositives and Interrupters

An **appositive** comes directly before or after a noun or pronoun and renames it.

TIP For more on appositives, see Chapter 29.

Lily, *a senior*, will take her nursing exam this summer.

The prices are outrageous at Beans, *the local coffee shop*.

An **interrupter** is an aside or transition that interrupts the flow of a sentence and does not affect its meaning.

My sister, *incidentally*, has good reasons for being late.

Her child had a fever, *for example*.

PUNCTUATION AND CAPITALIZATION
Practice Using Commas Correctly

Putting commas around appositives and interrupters tells readers that these elements give extra information but are not essential to the meaning of a sentence. If an appositive or interrupter is in the middle of a sentence, set it off with a pair of commas, one before and one after. If an appositive or interrupter comes at the beginning or end of a sentence, separate it from the rest of the sentence with one comma.

By the way, your proposal has been accepted.

Your proposal, *by the way*, has been accepted.

Your proposal has been accepted, *by the way*.

NOTE: Sometimes, an appositive is essential to the meaning of a sentence. When a sentence would not have the same meaning without the appositive, the appositive should not be set off with commas.

The actor *Leonardo DiCaprio* has never won an Oscar.
[The sentence *The actor has never won an Oscar* does not have the same meaning.]

EDITING FOR CORRECT COMMA USAGE:
Using Commas to Set Off Appositives and Interrupters

Find

Tamara my sister-in-law moved in with us last week.

1. **Underline** the subject.
2. **Underline** any appositive (which renames the subject) or interrupter (which interrupts the flow of the sentence).
3. **Ask:** Is the appositive or interrupter essential to the meaning of the sentence? *No.*

Edit

Tamara, my sister-in-law, moved in with us last week.

4. If it is not essential, **set it off with commas**.

PRACTICE 4 Using Commas to Set Off Appositives and Interrupters

Underline all the appositives and interrupters in the following sentences. Then, use commas to set them off.

EXAMPLE: Harry, an attentive student, could not hear his teacher because the radiator in class made a constant rattling.

1. Some rooms in fact are full of echoes, dead zones, and mechanical noises that make it hard for students to hear.
2. The American Speech-Language-Hearing Association experts on how noise levels affect learning abilities has set guidelines for how much noise in a classroom is too much.
3. The association recommends that background noise the constant whirring or whining sounds made by radiators, lights, and other machines be no more than 35 decibels.
4. That level 35 decibels is about as loud as a whispering voice 15 feet away.
5. One study found a level of 65 decibels the volume of a vacuum cleaner in a number of classrooms around the country.
6. Other classroom noises came for example from ancient heating systems, whirring air-conditioning units, rattling windows, humming classroom computers, buzzing clocks, and the honking of traffic on nearby streets.
7. An increasing number of school districts are beginning to pay more attention to acoustics the study of sound when they plan new schools.
8. Some changes such as putting felt pads on the bottoms of chair and desk legs to keep them from scraping against the floor are simple and inexpensive.
9. Other changes however can be costly and controversial; these changes include buying thicker drapes, building thicker walls, or installing specially designed acoustic ceiling tiles.
10. School administrators often parents themselves hope that these improvements will result in a better learning environment for students.

Commas around Adjective Clauses

An **adjective clause** is a group of words that begins with *who, which,* or *that*; has a subject and a verb; and describes a noun right before it in a sentence.

If an adjective clause can be taken out of a sentence without completely changing the meaning of the sentence, put commas around the clause.

Lily, *who is my cousin*, will take her nursing exam this summer.

Beans, *which is the local coffee shop*, charges outrageous prices.

I complained to Mr. Kranz, *who is the shop's manager*.

PUNCTUATION AND CAPITALIZATION
Practice Using Commas Correctly

If an adjective clause is essential to the meaning of a sentence, do not put commas around it. You can tell whether a clause is essential by taking it out and seeing if the meaning of the sentence changes significantly, as it would if you took the clauses out of the following examples.

The only grocery store *that sold good bread* went out of business.

Students *who do internships* often improve their hiring potential.

Salesclerks *who sell liquor to minors* are breaking the law.

| Noun | Adjective clause essential to meaning | Rest of sentence. |

| Noun , | Adjective clause not essential to meaning , | Rest of sentence. |

EDITING FOR CORRECT COMMA USAGE:
Using Commas to Set Off Adjective Clauses

Find

The woman who had octuplets received much publicity.

1. **Underline** any adjective clause (a word group that begins with *who, which,* or *that*).
2. **Read** the sentence without this clause.
3. **Ask:** Does the meaning change significantly without the clause? Yes.

Edit

The woman who had octuplets received much publicity.

4. If the meaning *does* change, as in this case, **do not put in commas**. (Add commas only if the meaning *does not* change.)

PRACTICE 5 Using Commas to Set Off Adjective Clauses

In each item, underline the adjective clauses. Then, put commas around these clauses where they are needed. Remember that if an adjective clause is essential to the meaning of a sentence, commas are not necessary. If a sentence is already correct, put a "C" next to it.

EXAMPLE: Daniel Kish, who has been blind since the age of one, has changed many people's ideas about what blind people can and cannot do.

1. Kish who runs the organization World Access for the Blind regularly rides his bike down busy streets and goes on long hikes.
2. His system for "seeing" his surroundings which is known as echo-location uses sound waves to create mental pictures of buildings, cars, trees, and other objects.
3. As Kish bikes around his neighborhood or hikes to sites that are deep in the wilderness, he clicks his tongue and listens to the echoes.
4. The echoes which differ depending on the distance and physical features of nearby objects allow him to map his surroundings in his mind.
5. This mental map which he constantly revises as he moves ahead helps him avoid running into cars, trees, and other obstacles.
6. Researchers who recently investigated Kish's echolocation made some interesting discoveries.
7. They found that Kish's visual cortex which is the part of the brain that processes visual information was activated during his sessions of mapping with sound.
8. This finding which received a lot of attention in the scientific community suggests that Kish's way of seeing the world is indeed visual.
9. Other blind people who have been trained in echolocation have learned to be as active and independent as Kish is.
10. The successes that they and Kish have achieved offer additional proof that blindness does not equal helplessness.

Other Uses for Commas

COMMAS WITH QUOTATION MARKS

Quotation marks are used to show that you are repeating exactly what someone said. Use commas to set off the words inside quotation marks from the rest of the sentence.

"Let me see your license**,**" demanded the police officer.

"Did you realize**,**" she asked**,** "that you were going 80 miles per hour?"

I exclaimed**,** "No!"

Notice that a comma never comes directly after a quotation mark.

TIP For more on quotation marks, see Chapter 36.

When quotations are not attributed to a particular person, commas may not be necessary.

"Pretty is as pretty does" never made sense to me.

COMMAS IN ADDRESSES

Use commas to separate the elements of an address included in a sentence. However, do not use a comma before a zip code.

My address is 2512 Windermere Street, Jackson, Mississippi 40720.

If a sentence continues after a city-state combination or after a street address, put a comma after the state or the address.

I moved here from Detroit, Michigan, when I was eighteen.

I've lived at 24 Heener Street, Madison, since 1989.

COMMAS IN DATES

Separate the day from the year with a comma. If you give just the month and year, do not separate them with a comma.

My daughter was born on November 8, 2004.

The next conference is in August 2014.

If a sentence continues after the date, put a comma after the date.

On April 21, 2013, the contract will expire.

COMMAS WITH NAMES

Put a comma after (and sometimes before) the name of someone being addressed directly.

Don, I want you to come look at this.

Unfortunately, Marie, you need to finish the report by next week.

COMMAS WITH YES OR NO

Put a comma after the word *yes* or *no* in response to a question.

Yes, I believe that you are right.

PRACTICE 6 Using Commas in Other Ways

Edit the following sentences by adding commas where they are needed. If a sentence is already correct, put a "C" next to it.

EXAMPLE: On August 12,2011,beachfront property was badly damaged by a fast-moving storm.

1. Some homeowners were still waiting to settle their claims with their insurance companies in January 2012.
2. Rob McGregor of 31 Hudson Street Wesleyville is one of those homeowners.
3. Asked if he was losing patience, McGregor replied "Yes I sure am."
4. "I've really had it up to here," McGregor said.
5. His wife said "Rob don't go mouthing off to any reporters."
6. "Betty I'll say what I want to say" Rob replied.
7. An official of Value-Safe Insurance of Wrightsville Ohio said that the company will process claims within the next few months.
8. "No there is no way we can do it any sooner" the official said.
9. Customers unhappy with their service may write to Value-Safe Insurance, P.O. Box 225, Wrightsville, Ohio 62812.
10. The company's home office in Rye New York can be reached by a toll-free number.

Edit for Commas

PRACTICE 7 Editing Paragraphs for Commas

Edit the following paragraphs by adding commas where they are needed.

(1) By the end of 2011, communities in California Texas Washington and several other states had banned the use of plastic bags. (2) One grocery store chain Whole Foods Market was an early leader in restricting the use of these bags. (3) As of April 22 2008 Whole Foods stopped asking customers if they wanted paper bags or plastic bags. (4) The store which cares about environmental issues now offers only paper bags made from recycled paper.

(5) The president of Whole Foods stated "We estimate we will keep 100 million new plastic grocery bags out of our environment between Earth Day and the end of this year." (6) The company also sells cloth bags, hoping to encourage shoppers to bring their own reusable bags with them when they go shopping.

(7) Experts believe that plastic bags do a great deal of damage to the environment. (8) They clog drains harm wildlife and take up an enormous amount of space in the nation's landfills. (9) According to the experts it takes more than a thousand years for a plastic bag to break down, and Americans use 100 billion of them every single year.

PRACTICE 8 **Editing Your Own Writing for Commas**

Edit a piece of your own writing for comma usage. It can be a paper for this course or another one, or something you have written for work or your everyday life.

Chapter Review

1. A comma (,) is a _____ that helps readers understand a sentence.

2. How do you use commas in these three situations?

    In a series of items, _____.

    In a compound sentence, _____
    _____.

    With introductory words, _____
    _____.

3. An appositive comes before or after a noun or pronoun and _____
    _____.

4. An interrupter is an _____ that interrupts the flow of a sentence.

5. Put commas around an adjective clause when it is _____ to the meaning of a sentence.

LEARNING JOURNAL Did you find comma errors in your writing? What is the main thing you have learned about using commas that will help you? What is unclear to you?

Chapter Test

Circle the correct choice for each of the following items.

1. If an underlined portion of this sentence is incorrect, select the revision that fixes it. If the sentence is correct as written, choose d.

   The company <u>owners, for</u> your <u>information are</u> planning to inspect
                           A   **B**
   our <u>department this</u> afternoon.
          C

   a. owners for
   b. information, are
   c. department, this
   d. No change is necessary.

2. Choose the item that has no errors.
   a. I used to hate parties but now I like to socialize with others.
   b. I used to hate parties, but now I like to socialize with others.
   c. I used to hate parties, but, now I like to socialize with others.

3. Choose the item that has no errors.
   a. If you do not file your income tax forms by April 15, 2013 you could face penalties.
   b. If you do not file your income tax forms by April 15, 2013, you could face penalties.
   c. If you do not file your income tax forms by April 15 2013 you could face penalties.

4. If an underlined portion of this sentence is incorrect, select the revision that fixes it. If the sentence is correct as written, choose d.

   Henry's <u>favorite hobbies</u> <u>are watching birds,</u> collecting <u>stamps, and</u>
               A   **B**   **C**
   fixing up old cars.

   a. favorite, hobbies
   b. are watching, birds
   c. stamps and
   d. No change is necessary.

5. Choose the item that has no errors.
   a. Roger, who teaches dance at a local studio, will be my partner for the ballroom competition.
   b. Roger who teaches dance at a local studio will be my partner for the ballroom competition.
   c. Roger who teaches dance at a local studio, will be my partner for the ballroom competition.

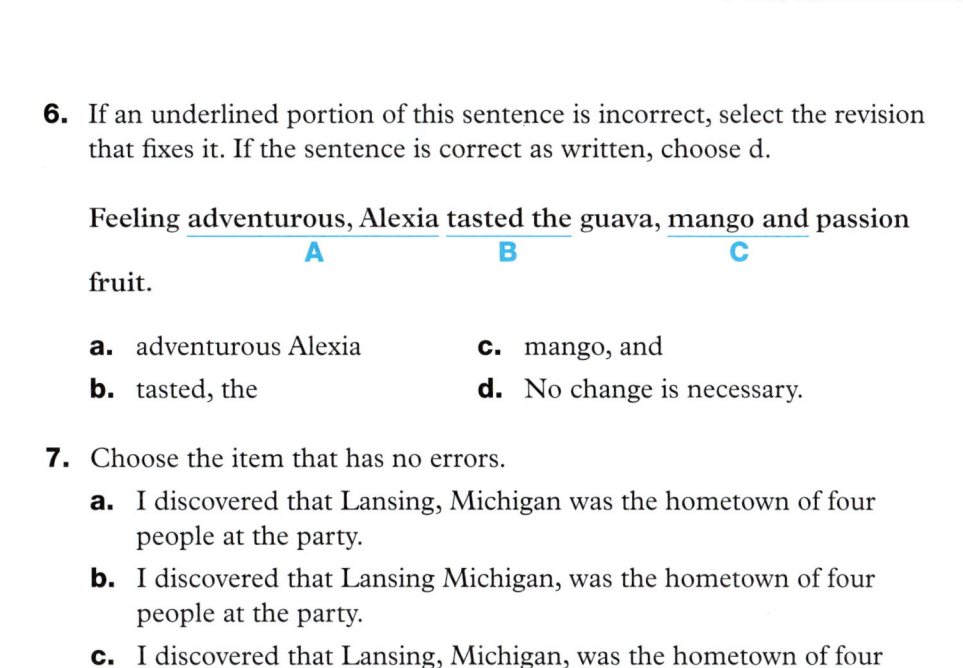

6. If an underlined portion of this sentence is incorrect, select the revision that fixes it. If the sentence is correct as written, choose d.

Feeling adventurous, Alexia tasted the guava, mango and passion fruit.
          A   B   C

- **a.** adventurous Alexia
- **b.** tasted, the
- **c.** mango, and
- **d.** No change is necessary.

7. Choose the item that has no errors.
- **a.** I discovered that Lansing, Michigan was the hometown of four people at the party.
- **b.** I discovered that Lansing Michigan, was the hometown of four people at the party.
- **c.** I discovered that Lansing, Michigan, was the hometown of four people at the party.

8. If an underlined portion of this sentence is incorrect, select the revision that fixes it. If the sentence is correct as written, choose d.

Just to be different I decided to wear a top hat to all my classes today.
         A   B   C

- **a.** different, I
- **b.** decided, to
- **c.** hat, to
- **d.** No change is necessary.

9. Choose the item that has no errors.
- **a.** "If you follow my instructions precisely" said the manager, "I will consider you for a promotion."
- **b.** "If you follow my instructions precisely," said the manager "I will consider you for a promotion."
- **c.** "If you follow my instructions precisely," said the manager, "I will consider you for a promotion."

10. If an underlined portion of this sentence is incorrect, select the revision that fixes it. If the sentence is correct as written, choose d.

No Bob, I cannot swim, paddle a kayak, or steer a sailboat.
  A   B   C

- **a.** No, Bob,
- **b.** swim paddle
- **c.** kayak or
- **d.** No change is necessary.

35

Apostrophes (')

Understand What Apostrophes Do

An **apostrophe (')** is a punctuation mark that either shows ownership (*Susan's*) or indicates that a letter has been intentionally left out to form a contraction (*I'm, that's, they're*).

LearningCurve
Apostrophes
bedfordstmartins.com/
realwriting/LC

Practice Using Apostrophes Correctly

Apostrophes to Show Ownership

Add -'s to a singular noun to show ownership even if the noun already ends in -s.

Karen's apartment is on the South Side.

James's roommate is looking for him.

If a noun is plural and ends in -s, just add an apostrophe. If it is plural but does not end in -s, add -'s.

TIP Use apostrophes to show ownership for abbreviations: *The NBA's playoff system has changed.*

My *books*' covers are falling off.
[more than one book]

The *twins*' father was building them a playhouse.
[more than one twin]

The *children*'s toys were broken.

The *men*'s locker room is being painted.

582

The placement of an apostrophe makes a difference in meaning.

My *sister's* six children are at my house for the weekend.
[one sister who has six children]

My *sisters'* six children are at my house for the weekend.
[two or more sisters who together have six children]

Do not use an apostrophe to form the plural of a noun.

Gina went camping with her *sister~~'~~s* and their children.

All the *highway~~'~~s* to the airport are under construction.

Do not use an apostrophe with a possessive pronoun. These pronouns already show ownership (possession).

Is that bag *your~~'~~s*?   No, it is *our~~'~~s*.

Possessive Pronouns

my	his	its	their
mine	her	our	theirs
your	hers	ours	whose
yours			

The single most common error with apostrophes and pronouns is confusing *its* (a possessive pronoun) with *it's* (a contraction meaning "it is"). Whenever you write *it's*, test correctness by replacing it with *it is* and reading the sentence aloud to hear if it makes sense.

PRACTICE 1 Using Apostrophes to Show Ownership

Edit the following sentences by adding -'s or an apostrophe alone to show ownership and by crossing out any incorrect use of an apostrophe or -'s.

EXAMPLE: Not long ago, my cousin's résumé was looking thin because he was young and had not held many job~~'~~s.

1. Also, his previous jobs as a welders assistant and a line cook did not relate to what he most wanted to do: landscaping.

Seeing Apostrophe Errors

TIP The "Restroom's" photo was taken by Jeff Deck, coauthor of *The Great Typo Hunt: Two Friends Changing the World, One Correction at a Time.* For more typos hunted down by Jeff and others, visit the book's Web site at **greattypohunt.com**.

write How would you correct the apostrophe errors in these signs? Also, in the sign on the left, what is the correct plural form of *hero*?

2. He had some contacts in the landscaping business: Two friends sisters were landscapers, and another friends father managed the grounds at a golf course.

3. But my cousin couldn't get jobs through these contacts because he had no experience working on a landscapers crew or with a professional gardener.

4. To build up the right kind of skills, he spent six month's of last year volunteering at a community garden.

5. Under the guidance of the community gardens most expert member, my cousin learned about soil drainage, composting, and chemical-free pest control.

6. Last month, when my cousin applied for a job as a landscaping assistant, the interviewer told him that there had been many other applicants but that his skills were far more impressive than their's.

7. He was very excited about getting the job, and he is pleased with it's benefits.

8. As my cousins' example shows, many peoples résumés can be improved through volunteering.

9. Volunteering provides a way not only to acquire new skills but also to test different career path's.

10. For instance, volunteers who comfort patients families at a local hospital will get a sense of whether working in a medical setting is a good choice for them.

TIP For more practice using apostrophes correctly, visit *Exercise Central* at **bedfordstmartins.com/ realwriting**.

Apostrophes in Contractions

A **contraction** is formed by joining two words and leaving out one or more of the letters. When writing a contraction, put an apostrophe where the letter or letters have been left out.

*She**'**s* on her way. = *She is* on her way.

*I**'**ll* see you there. = *I will* see you there.

Be sure to put the apostrophe in the correct place.

It *does*/n**'**t really matter.

TIP Ask your instructor if contractions are acceptable in papers.

TIP To shorten the full year to only the final two numbers, replace the first two numbers: The year 2013 becomes '13.

Common Contractions

aren't = are not	I'd = I would, I had
can't = cannot	I'll = I will
couldn't = could not	I'm = I am
didn't = did not	I've = I have
don't = do not	isn't = is not
he'd = he would, he had	it's = it is, it has
he'll = he will	let's = let us
he's = he is, he has	she'd = she would, she had →

she'll = she will	who'll = who will
she's = she is, she has	who's = who is, who has
there's = there is	won't = will not
they'd = they would, they had	wouldn't = would not
they'll = they will	you'd = you would, you had
they're = they are	you'll = you will
they've = they have	you're = you are
who'd = who would, who had	you've = you have

PRACTICE 2 Using Apostrophes in Contractions

Read each sentence carefully, looking for any words that have missing letters. Edit these words by adding apostrophes where needed and crossing out incorrectly used apostrophes.

EXAMPLE: Although we observe personal space boundaries in our daily lives, they're not something we spend much time thinking about.

1. Youll notice right away if a stranger leans over and talks to you so that his face is practically touching yours.
2. Perhaps youd accept this kind of behavior from a family member.
3. There is'nt one single acceptable boundary wed use in all situations.
4. An elevator has its own rules: Dont stand right next to a person if there is open space.
5. With coworkers, were likely to keep a personal space of 4 to 12 feet.
6. Well accept a personal space of 4 feet down to 18 inches with friends.
7. The last 16 inches are reserved for people were most intimate with.
8. When people hug or kiss, theyre willing to surrender their personal space to each other.
9. A supervisor whos not aware of the personal space boundaries of his or her employees might make workers uncomfortable.
10. Even if the supervisor does'nt intend anything by the gestures, its his or her responsibility to act appropriately.

PUNCTUATION AND CAPITALIZATION
Edit for Apostrophes

Apostrophes with Letters, Numbers, and Time

For capital letters, such as letter grades, do not use an apostrophe to form the plural.

He got all As.

For lowercase letters, use -'s to form the plural. The apostrophe prevents confusion or misreading.

In Scrabble games, *a's* are valuable tiles to draw.

Do not use an apostrophe to form the plural of numbers.

In women's shoes, size *8s* are more common than size *10s*.

Use an apostrophe or -'s in certain expressions in which time nouns are treated as if they possess something. The apostrophe takes the place of an implied *of*: four *weeks'* maternity leave, this *year's* graduating class.

PRACTICE 3 Using Apostrophes with Letters, Numbers, and Time

Edit the following sentences by adding apostrophes where needed and crossing out incorrectly used apostrophes.

EXAMPLE: When I returned to work after two weeks' vacation, I had what looked like a decade's worth of work in my inbox.

1. I sorted letters alphabetically, starting with *A*s.
2. There were more letters by names' starting with *M*s than any other.
3. The screen flashed 8s to show that I had eight e-mail messages.
4. In two weeks time I had received twenty-five messages.
5. I needed another weeks time just to return all the e-mails.

Edit for Apostrophes

PRACTICE 4 Editing Paragraphs for Apostrophes

Edit the following paragraphs by adding two apostrophes where needed and crossing out five incorrectly used apostrophes.

(1) Have you noticed many honeybee's when you go outside? (2) If not, it is'nt surprising. (3) For reasons that scientists still don't quite understand, these bees have been disappearing all across the country. (4) This mass

disappearance is a problem because bees are an important part of growing a wide variety of flowers, fruits, vegetables, and nuts as they spread pollen from one place to another.

(5) In the last year, more than one-third, or billions, of the honeybees in the United States' have disappeared. (6) As a consequence, farmers have been forced either to buy or to rent beehives for their crops. (7) Typically, people who are in the bee business ship hives to farmers fields by truck. (8) The hives often have to travel hundreds of miles.

(9) Scientist's have been trying to find out what happened to the once-thriving bee population. (10) They suspect that either a disease or chemicals harmed the honeybee's.

PRACTICE 5 Editing Your Own Writing for Apostrophes

Edit a piece of your own writing for apostrophes. It can be a paper for this course or another one, or something you have written for work or your everyday life.

Chapter Review

LEARNING JOURNAL Did you find apostrophe errors in your writing? What is the main thing you have learned about apostrophes that will help you? What is unclear to you?

1. An apostrophe (') is a punctuation mark that either shows _____ or indicates that a letter or letters have been intentionally left out to form a _____.

2. To show ownership, add _____ to a singular noun, even if the noun already ends in -s. For a plural noun, add an _____ alone if the noun ends in -s; add _____ if the noun does not end in -s.

3. Do not use an apostrophe with a _____ pronoun.

4. Do not confuse *its* and *it's*. *Its* shows _____; *it's* is a _____ meaning "it is."

5. A _____ is formed by joining two words and leaving out one or more of the letters.

Chapter Test

Circle the correct choice for each of the following items.

1. If an underlined portion of this sentence is incorrect, select the revision that fixes it. If the sentence is correct as written, choose d.

    I've always believed that <u>its</u> a crime to use software that you
           A   B
    <u>haven't</u> paid for.
      C

    a. Ive
    b. it's
    c. havent
    d. No change is necessary.

2. Choose the item that has no errors.
    a. The thieves boldness made them a lot of money, but it eventually landed them in jail.
    b. The thieves's boldness made them a lot of money, but it eventually landed them in jail.
    c. The thieves' boldness made them a lot of money, but it eventually landed them in jail.

3. Choose the item that has no errors.
    a. By playing that slot machine, your throwing away money.
    b. By playing that slot machine, you're throwing away money.
    c. By playing that slot machine, youre' throwing away money.

4. If an underlined portion of this sentence is incorrect, select the revision that fixes it. If the sentence is correct as written, choose d.

    The house is now <u>Renee's</u>, but <u>she'll</u> regret having an address with
                            A   B
    five <u>3's</u> in it.
       C

    a. Renees
    b. sh'ell
    c. 3s
    d. No change is necessary.

5. Choose the item that has no errors.
    a. Her eighteen months' service overseas has somehow made her seem older.
    b. Her eighteen month's service overseas has somehow made her seem older.
    c. Her eighteen months service overseas has somehow made her seem older.

36

Quotation Marks (" ")

THIS CHAPTER
- explains how quotation marks are used.
- gives you practice using quotation marks correctly.

Understand What Quotation Marks Do

Quotation marks (" ") always appear in pairs. Quotation marks have two common uses in college writing:

- They are used with **direct quotations**, which exactly repeat, word for word, what someone said or wrote. (*Nick said, "You should take the downtown bus."*)
- They are used to set off **titles**. (*My favorite song is "Sophisticated Lady."*)

Practice Using Quotation Marks Correctly

Quotation Marks for Direct Quotations

When you write a direct quotation, use quotation marks around the quoted words. Quotation marks tell readers that the words used are exactly what was said or written.

1. "I do not know what she means," I said to my friend Lina.
2. Lina asked, "Do you think we should ask a question?"
3. "Excuse me, Professor Soames," I called out, "but could you explain that again?"
4. "Yes," said Professor Soames. "Let me make sure you all understand."
5. After further explanation, Professor Soames asked, "Are there any other questions?"

When you are writing a paper that uses outside sources, use quotation marks to indicate where you quote the exact words of a source.

> We all need to become more conscientious recyclers. A recent editorial in the *Bolton Common* reported, "When recycling volunteers spot-checked bags that were supposed to contain only newspaper, they found a collection of nonrecyclable items such as plastic candy wrappers, aluminum foil, and birthday cards."

When quoting, writers usually use words that identify who is speaking, such as *I said to my friend Lina* in the first example on the previous page. The identifying words can come after the quoted words (example 1), before them (example 2), or in the middle of them (example 3). Here are some guidelines for capitalization and punctuation.

TIP For more on incorporating outside source material through quoting and other methods, see Chapter 18.

GUIDELINES FOR CAPITALIZATION AND PUNCTUATION

- Capitalize the first letter in a complete sentence that is being quoted, even if it comes after some identifying words (example 2 on the previous page).
- Do not capitalize the first letter in a quotation if it is not the first word in a complete sentence (*but* in example 3).
- If it is a complete sentence and it is clear who the speaker is, a quotation can stand on its own (second sentence in example 4).
- Identifying words must be attached to a quotation; they cannot be a sentence on their own.
- Use commas to separate any identifying words from quoted words in the same sentence.
- Always put quotation marks after commas and periods. Put quotation marks after question marks and exclamation points if they are part of the quoted sentence.

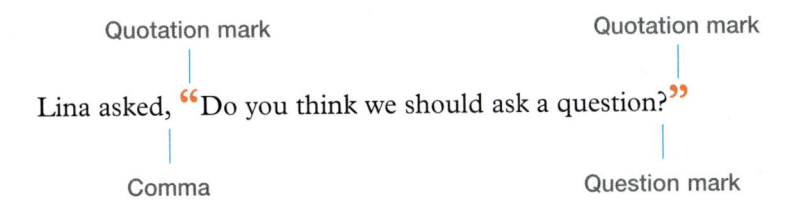

Lina asked, "Do you think we should ask a question?"

(Comma, Quotation mark, Quotation mark, Question mark)

TIP For more on commas with quotation marks, see Chapter 34.

- If a question mark or exclamation point is part of your own sentence, put it after the quotation mark.

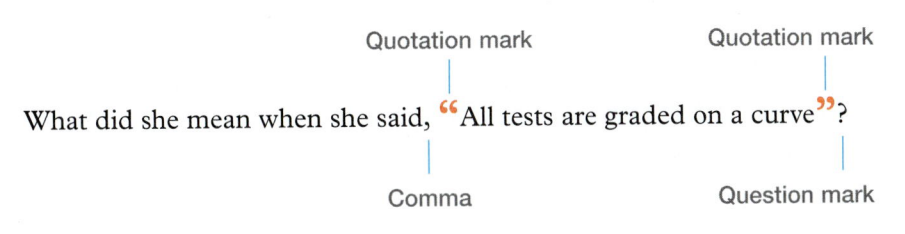

What did she mean when she said, "All tests are graded on a curve"?

(Comma, Quotation mark, Quotation mark, Question mark)

SETTING OFF A QUOTATION WITHIN ANOTHER QUOTATION

Sometimes, when you quote someone directly, part of what that person said quotes words that someone else said or wrote. Put single quotation marks (' ') around the quotation within a quotation so that readers understand who said what.

> The student handbook says, "Students must be given the opportunity to make up work missed for legitimate reasons."

> Terry told his instructor, "I am sorry I missed the exam, but that is not a reason to fail me for the term. Our student handbook says, 'Students must be given the opportunity to make up work missed for legitimate reasons,' and I have a good reason."

PRACTICE 1 Punctuating Direct Quotations

Edit the following sentences by adding quotation marks and commas where needed.

TIP For more practice using quotation marks correctly, visit *Exercise Central* at bedfordstmartins.com/realwriting.

EXAMPLE: A radio journalist asked a nurse at a critical-care facility, "Do you believe that the medical community needlessly prolongs the life of the terminally ill?"

1. If I could answer that question quickly the nurse replied I would deserve an honorary degree in ethics.
2. She added But I see it as the greatest dilemma we face today.
3. How would you describe that dilemma? the reporter asked the nurse.
4. The nurse said It is a choice of when to use our amazing medical technology and when not to.
5. The reporter asked So there are times when you would favor letting patients die on their own?
6. Yes the nurse replied I would.
7. The reporter asked Under what circumstances should a patient be allowed to die?
8. I cannot really answer that question because so many variables are involved the nurse replied.
9. Is this a matter of deciding how to allocate scarce resources? the reporter asked.

10. In a sense, it is the nurse replied. As a colleague of mine says, We should not try to keep everyone alive for as long as possible just because we can.

No Quotation Marks for Indirect Quotations

When you report what someone said or wrote but do not use the person's exact words, you are writing an **indirect quotation**. Do not use quotation marks for indirect quotations. Indirect quotations often begin with the word *that*.

INDIRECT QUOTATION	DIRECT QUOTATION
Sam said that there was a fire downtown.	Sam said, "There was a fire downtown."
The police told us to move along.	"Move along," directed the police.
Tara told me that she is graduating.	Tara said, "I am graduating."

PRACTICE 2 Punctuating Direct and Indirect Quotations

Edit the following sentences by adding quotation marks where needed and crossing out quotation marks that are used incorrectly. If a sentence is already correct, put a "C" next to it.

EXAMPLE: Three days before her apartment was robbed, Jocelyn told a friend, "I worry about the safety of this building."

1. Have you complained to the landlord yet? her friend asked.
2. Not yet, Jocelyn replied, although I know I should.
3. Jocelyn phoned the landlord and asked him to install a more secure lock on the front door.
4. The landlord said that "he believed that the lock was fine the way it was."
5. When Jocelyn phoned the landlord after the burglary, she said, I know this burglary would not have happened if that lock had been installed.
6. I am sorry, the landlord replied, but there is nothing I can do about it now.
7. Jocelyn asked a tenants' rights group whether she had grounds for a lawsuit.

8. The person she spoke to said that "she probably did."

9. If I were you, the person said, I would let your landlord know about your plans.

10. When Jocelyn told her landlord of the possible lawsuit, he said that he would reimburse her for the stolen items.

Quotation Marks for Certain Titles

When you refer to a short work such as a magazine or newspaper article, a chapter in a book, a short story, an essay, a song, or a poem, put quotation marks around the title of the work.

NEWSPAPER ARTICLE	"Volunteers Honored for Service"
SHORT STORY	"The Awakening"
ESSAY	"Why Are We So Angry?"

Usually, titles of longer works, such as novels, books, magazines, newspapers, movies, television programs, and CDs, are italicized. The titles of sacred books such as the Bible or the Koran are neither underlined nor surrounded by quotation marks.

| BOOK | *The Good Earth* |
| NEWSPAPER | *Washington Post* |

[Do not italicize or capitalize the word *the* before the name of a newspaper or magazine, even if it is part of the title: I saw that article in the *New York Times*. But do capitalize *The* when it is the first word in titles of books, movies, and other sources.]

TIP For more information on citing sources, see Chapter 18.

If you are writing a paper with many outside sources, your instructor will probably refer you to a particular system of citing sources. Follow that system's guidelines when you use titles in your paper.

NOTE: Do not enclose the title of a paragraph or an essay that you have written in quotation marks when it appears at the beginning of your paper. Do not italicize it either.

PRACTICE 3   Using Quotation Marks for Titles

Edit the following sentences by adding quotation marks around titles as needed. Underline any book, magazine, or newspaper titles.

EXAMPLE: After the terrorist attacks of September 11, 2001, the twelve hundred radio stations belonging to Clear Channel Communications were asked not to play songs with a political message, such as "Imagine" by John Lennon.

1. In 2002, Bruce Springsteen released his first new album in years, containing songs like Worlds Apart that dealt with the terrorist attacks on the United States.

2. The Missing, a review of the Springsteen album in the New Yorker magazine, found Springsteen's new songs unusual because they did not include many specific details about people, as older Springsteen songs like Born in the U.S.A. had done.

3. In 2011, Lady Gaga's song Judas was met with controversy for religious, rather than political, reasons.

4. In an article titled Lady Gaga's 'Judas' Upsets Religious Groups, the Hollywood Reporter described a Catholic leader's criticism of the song and Lady Gaga's video of it.

5. However, in an article in the British newspaper the Sun, Lady Gaga said how proud she was of the video.

Edit for Quotation Marks

PRACTICE 4 Editing Paragraphs for Quotation Marks

Edit the following paragraphs by adding twelve sets of quotation marks where needed and crossing out the two sets of incorrectly used quotation marks. Correct any errors in punctuation.

(1) When Ruiz first came into my office, he told me that he was a poor student. (2) I asked, What makes you think that?

(3) Ruiz answered, I have always gotten bad grades, and I do not know how to get any better. (4) He shook his head. (5) I have just about given up.

(6) I told him that "there were some resources on campus he could use and that we could work together to help him."

(7) "What kind of things are you talking about?" asked Ruiz. (8) What exactly will I learn?

(9) I said, There are plenty of programs to help you. (10) You really have no excuse to fail.

(11) Can you be a little more specific? he asked.

(12) Certainly, I said. (13) I told him about the survival skills program. (14) I also pulled out folders on study skills, such as managing time, improving memory, taking notes, and having a positive attitude. (15) Take a look at these, I said.

(16) Ruiz said, No, I am not interested in that. (17) And I do not have time.

(18) I replied, "That is your decision, Ruiz, but remember that education is one of the few things that people are willing to pay for and not get." (19) I paused and then added, It sounds to me like you are wasting the money you spent on tuition. (20) Why not try to get what you paid for?

(21) Ruiz thought for a moment, while he looked out the window, and finally told me that "he would try."

(22) Good, I said. (23) I am glad to hear it.

> **PRACTICE 5** Editing Your Own Writing for Quotation Marks
>
> Edit a piece of your own writing for quotation marks. It can be a paper for this course or another one, or something you have written for work or your everyday life.

Chapter Review

LEARNING JOURNAL Did you find quotation mark errors in your writing? How would you explain the use of quotation marks in direct and indirect quotes? What is unclear to you?

1. Quotation marks look like _____. They always appear in (pairs / threes).

2. A direct quotation exactly _____ what someone (or some outside source) said or wrote. (Use / Do not use) quotation marks around direct quotations.

3. An indirect quotation _____ _____.

   (Use / Do not use) quotation marks with indirect quotations.

4. To set off a quotation within a quotation, use _____.

5. Put quotation marks around the titles of short works such as (give four examples) _____ _____.

6. For longer works such as magazines, novels, books, newspapers, and so on, _____ the titles.

Chapter Test

Circle the correct choice for each of the following items.

1. If an underlined portion of this sentence is incorrect, select the revision that fixes it. If the sentence is correct as written, choose d.

   Do you think that <u>she was serious</u> when she <u>said, "Leave the</u>
                               A   B

   <u>building immediately?"</u>
             C

   a. "she"
   b. said "Leave
   c. immediately"?
   d. No change is necessary.

2. Choose the item that has no errors.
   a. "You need to strengthen that knee," Dr. Wheeler warned, "so be sure to do all your exercises".
   b. "You need to strengthen that knee," Dr. Wheeler warned, so be sure to do all your exercises.
   c. "You need to strengthen that knee," Dr. Wheeler warned, "so be sure to do all your exercises."

3. Choose the item that has no errors.
   a. Eric pointed at an article titled 'New Alternative Fuel in Your Backyard.'
   b. Eric pointed at an article titled New Alternative Fuel in Your Backyard.
   c. Eric pointed at an article titled "New Alternative Fuel in Your Backyard."

4. If an underlined portion of this sentence is incorrect, select the revision that fixes it. If the sentence is correct as written, choose d.

   The man said, "I'm sorry, <u>officer, but</u> did I hear you correctly
                                             A

   when you <u>said, "Drive</u> into that <u>ditch'?"</u>
                   B   C

   a. officer, "but
   b. said, 'Drive
   c. ditch?'"
   d. No change is necessary.

5. Choose the item that has no errors.
   a. Rachel told the security guard that she needed to enter the building for official business.
   b. Rachel told the security guard that "she needed to enter the building for official business."
   c. Rachel told the security guard that she "needed to enter the building for official business."

37

Other Punctuation

(; : ( ) -- -)

THIS CHAPTER
- explains what five other punctuation marks are and how they are used.
- gives you practice using punctuation correctly.

Understand What Punctuation Does

Punctuation helps readers understand your writing. If you use punctuation incorrectly, you send readers a confusing—or, even worse, a wrong—message. This chapter covers five punctuation marks that people sometimes use incorrectly because they are not quite sure what these marks are supposed to do.

Practice Using Punctuation Correctly

Semicolon ;

SEMICOLONS TO JOIN CLOSELY RELATED SENTENCES

Use a semicolon to join two closely related sentences into one sentence.

> In an interview, hold your head up and do not slouch; it is important to look alert.
>
> Make good eye contact; looking down is not appropriate in an interview.

> **LANGUAGE NOTE:** Using a comma instead of a semicolon to join two sentences would create a run-on (see Chapter 21).

SEMICOLONS WHEN ITEMS IN A LIST CONTAIN COMMAS

Use semicolons to separate items in a list that itself contains commas. Otherwise, it is difficult for readers to tell where one item ends and another begins.

For dinner, Bob ate an order of onion rings; a 16-ounce steak; a baked potato with sour cream, bacon bits, and cheese; a green salad; and a huge bowl of ice cream with fudge sauce.

Because one item, *a baked potato with sour cream, bacon bits, and cheese*, contains its own commas, all items need to be separated by semicolons.

Colon :

COLONS BEFORE LISTS

Use a colon after an independent clause to introduce a list. An independent clause contains a subject, a verb, and a complete thought. It can stand on its own as a sentence.

> The software conference fair featured a vast array of products: financial-management applications, games, educational CDs, college-application programs, and so on.

COLONS BEFORE EXPLANATIONS OR EXAMPLES

Use a colon after an independent clause to let readers know that you are about to provide an explanation or example of what you just wrote.

> The conference was overwhelming: too much hype about too many things.

One of the most common misuses of colons is to use them after a phrase instead of an independent clause. Watch out especially for colons following the phrases *such as* and *for example*.

INCORRECT	Tonya enjoys sports that are sometimes dangerous. For example: white-water rafting, wilderness skiing, rock climbing, and motorcycle racing.
CORRECT	Tonya enjoys sports that are sometimes dangerous: white-water rafting, wilderness skiing, rock climbing, and motorcycle racing.
INCORRECT	Jeff has many interests. They are: bicycle racing, sculpting, and building musical instruments.
CORRECT	Jeff has many interests: bicycle racing, sculpting, and building musical instruments.

TIP See Chapter 34 (Commas), Chapter 35 (Apostrophes), and Chapter 36 (Quotation Marks) for coverage of these punctuation marks. For more information on using semicolons to join sentences, see Chapter 27.

COLONS IN BUSINESS CORRESPONDENCE AND BEFORE SUBTITLES

Use a colon after a greeting (called a *salutation*) in a business letter and after the standard heading lines at the beginning of a memorandum.

Dear Mr. Hernandez:

To: Pat Toney
From: Susan Anker

Colons should also be used before subtitles—for example, "Running a Marathon: The Five Most Important Tips."

Parentheses ( )

Use parentheses to set off information that is not essential to the meaning of a sentence. Parentheses are always used in pairs and should be used sparingly.

My grandfather's most successful invention (and also his first) was the electric blanket.

When he died (at the age of ninety-six), he had more than 150 patents registered.

Dash --

Dashes can be used like parentheses to set off additional information, particularly information that you want to emphasize. Make a dash by writing or typing two hyphens together. Do not put extra spaces around a dash.

The final exam--worth 25 percent of your total grade--will be next Thursday.

A dash can also indicate a pause, much like a comma does.

My uncle went on long fishing trips--without my aunt and cousins.

Hyphen -

HYPHENS TO JOIN WORDS THAT FORM A SINGLE DESCRIPTION

Writers often join two or more words that together form a single description of a person, place, or thing. To join the words, use a hyphen.

Being a stockbroker is a high-risk career.

Jill is a lovely three-year-old girl.

When writing out two-word numbers from twenty-one to ninety-nine, put a hyphen between the two words.

Seventy-five people participated in the demonstration.

HYPHENS TO DIVIDE A WORD AT THE END OF A LINE

Use a hyphen to divide a word when part of the word must continue on the next line.

> Critics accused the tobacco industry of increasing the amounts of nico-tine in cigarettes to encourage addiction and boost sales.

If you are not sure where to break a word, look it up in a dictionary. The word's main entry will show you where you can break the word: *dic • tio • nary*. If you still are not confident that you are putting the hyphen in the correct place, do not break the word; write it all on the next line.

TIP Most word-processing programs automatically put an entire word on the next line rather than hyphenating it. When you write by hand, however, you need to hyphenate correctly.

Edit for Other Punctuation Marks

PRACTICE 1 Editing Paragraphs for Other Punctuation Marks

Edit the following paragraphs by adding semicolons, colons, parentheses, dashes, and hyphens when needed. In some places, more than one type of punctuation may be acceptable.

TIP For more practice using the types of punctuation covered in this chapter, visit *Exercise Central* at **bedfordstmartins.com/realwriting**.

(1) When John Wood was on a backpacking trip to Nepal in 1998, he discovered something he had not expected only a few books in the nation's schools. (2) He knew that if the students did not have the materials they needed, it would be much harder for them to learn. (3) They did not need high tech supplies as much as they needed old fashioned books. (4) Wood decided that he would find a way to get those books.

(5) Two years later, Wood founded Room to Read, an organization dedicated to shipping books to students who needed them. (6) Since then, the group has donated more than three million books. (7) One of Wood's first shipments was carried to students on the back of a yak. (8) Many others arrived in a Cathay Pacific Airlines plane.

(9) Along with the books, Room to Read has also built almost three hundred schools and has opened five thousand libraries. (10) Different companies donate books to the organization Scholastic, Inc., recently sent 400,000 books to Wood's group. (11) Money to fund all these efforts comes through various fund-raisers read-a-thons, auctions, and coin drives.

PRACTICE 2 Editing Your Own Writing for Punctuation

Edit a piece of your own writing for semicolons, colons, parentheses, dashes, and hyphens. It can be a paper for this course or another one, or something you have written for work or your everyday life. You may want to try more than one way to use these punctuation marks in your writing.

Chapter Review

1. Semicolons (;) can be used to _____
   _____ and to _____
   _____.

2. Colons (:) can be used in what three ways? _____
   _____
   _____
   _____

3. A colon in a sentence must always be used after an _____.

4. Parentheses ( ) set off information that is _____ to a sentence.

5. _____ also set off information in a sentence, usually information that you want to emphasize.

6. Hyphens (-) can be used to join two or more words that together _____ and to _____ a word at the end of a line.

LEARNING JOURNAL What is the main thing you have learned about the punctuation marks in this chapter? What is unclear to you?

Chapter Test

Circle the correct choice for each of the following items.

1. Choose the item that has no errors.
   a. Our car trip took us through Pittsburgh, Pennsylvania, Wheeling, West Virginia, and Bristol, Tennessee.
   b. Our car trip took us through Pittsburgh, Pennsylvania; Wheeling, West Virginia; and Bristol, Tennessee.
   c. Our car trip took us through Pittsburgh; Pennsylvania, Wheeling; West Virginia, and Bristol; Tennessee.

PUNCTUATION AND CAPITALIZATION
Chapter Test   603

2. If an underlined portion of this sentence is incorrect, select the revision that fixes it. If the sentence is correct as written, choose d.

    Gary's dog <u>(a seventeen-year-old</u> easily won first prize in the
    　　　　　　　　　　A

    Elderly Dog <u>Show;</u> she had the shiniest <u>coat and</u> the most
    　　　　　　　　B　　　　　　　　　　　　　　C

    youthful step.

    a. (a seventeen-year-old)   **c.** coat: and
    b. Show-she   **d.** No change is necessary.

3. Choose the item that has no errors.
    a. As our computer specialist, you have three tasks: fixing malfunctioning computers, teaching people to use their computers, and not making any problem worse.
    b. As our computer specialist: you have three tasks, fixing malfunctioning computers, teaching people to use their computers, and not making any problem worse.
    c. As our computer specialist, you have three tasks: fixing malfunctioning computers, teaching people to use their computers (and not making any problem worse).

4. Choose the item that has no errors.
    a. Is there such a thing as a low-stress-job?
    b. Is there such a thing as a low-stress job?
    c. Is there such a thing as a low stress-job?

5. If an underlined portion of this sentence is incorrect, select the revision that fixes it. If the sentence is correct as written, choose d.

    You will have <u>5 and only 5</u> minutes <u>to leave</u> the office <u>before the</u>
    　　　　　　　　　A　　　　　　　　　　B　　　　　　　　C

    alarm sounds.

    a. 5—and only 5—   **c.** before; the
    b. to: leave   **d.** No change is necessary.

38

Capitalization

Using Capital Letters

THIS CHAPTER
- explains three important rules of capitalization.
- gives you practice capitalizing correctly.

LearningCurve
Capitalization
bedfordstmartins.com/
realwriting/LC

Understand Three Rules of Capitalization

Capital letters (A, B, C) are generally bigger than lowercase letters (a, b, c), and they may have a different form. To avoid the most common errors of capitalization, follow these three rules:

Capitalize the first letter

- Of every new sentence.
- In names of specific people, places, dates, and things (also known as proper nouns).
- Of important words in titles.

Practice Capitalization

Capitalization of Sentences

Capitalize the first letter of each new sentence, including the first word of a direct quotation.

> **T**he superintendent was surprised.
>
> **H**e asked, "**W**hat is going on here?"

Capitalization of Names of Specific People, Places, Dates, and Things

The general rule is to capitalize the first letter in names of specific people, places, dates, and things. Do not capitalize a generic (common) name such as *college* as opposed to the specific name: *Carroll State College*. Look at the examples for each group.

PEOPLE

Capitalize the first letter in names of specific people and in titles used with names of specific people.

SPECIFIC	NOT SPECIFIC
Jean Heaton	my neighbor
Professor Fitzgerald	your math professor

SPECIFIC	NOT SPECIFIC
Dr. Cornog	the doctor
Aunt Pat, Mother	my aunt, your mother

The name of a family member is capitalized when the family member is being addressed directly: Happy Birthday, *Mother*. In other instances, do not capitalize: It is my *mother's* birthday.

The word *president* is not capitalized unless it comes directly before a name as part of that person's title: *President* Barack Obama.

PLACES

Capitalize the first letter in names of specific buildings, streets, cities, states, regions, and countries.

SPECIFIC	NOT SPECIFIC
Bolton Town Hall	the town hall
Arlington Street	our street
Dearborn Heights	my hometown
Arizona	this state
the South	the southern region
Spain	that country

Do not capitalize directions in a sentence.

Drive *south* for five blocks.

DATES

Capitalize the first letter in the names of days, months, and holidays. Do not capitalize the names of the seasons (winter, spring, summer, fall).

SPECIFIC	NOT SPECIFIC
Wednesday	tomorrow
June 25	summer
Thanksgiving	my birthday

LANGUAGE NOTE: Some languages, such as Spanish, French, and Italian, do not capitalize days, months, and languages. In English, such words must be capitalized.

INCORRECT	I study russian every monday, wednesday, and friday from january through may.
CORRECT	I study **Russian** every **Monday**, **Wednesday**, and **Friday** from **January** through **May**.

ORGANIZATIONS, COMPANIES, AND GROUPS

SPECIFIC	NOT SPECIFIC
Taft Community College	my college
Microsoft	that software company
Alcoholics Anonymous	the self-help group

LANGUAGES, NATIONALITIES, AND RELIGIONS

SPECIFIC	NOT SPECIFIC
English, Greek, Spanish	my first language
Christianity, Buddhism	your religion

The names of languages should be capitalized even if you aren't referring to a specific course.

I am taking psychology and *Spanish*.

COURSES

SPECIFIC	NOT SPECIFIC
Composition 101	a writing course
Introduction to Psychology	my psychology course

COMMERCIAL PRODUCTS

SPECIFIC	NOT SPECIFIC
Diet Pepsi	a diet cola
Skippy peanut butter	peanut butter

Capitalization of Titles

TIP For more on punctuating titles, see Chapter 36. For a list of common prepositions, see page 332.

When you write the title of a book, movie, television program, magazine, newspaper, article, story, song, paper, poem, and so on, capitalize the first word and all important words. The only words that do not need to be capitalized (unless they are the first word) are *the, a, an,* coordinating conjunctions (*and, but, for, nor, or, so, yet*), and prepositions.

I Love Lucy was a long-running television program.

Both *USA Today* and the *New York Times* are popular newspapers.

"Once More to the Lake" is one of Chuck's favorite essays.

Chapter Review

1. Capitalize the _____ of every new sentence.
2. Capitalize the first letter in names of specific _____, _____, _____, and _____.
3. Capitalize the first word and all _____ in titles.

LEARNING JOURNAL Did you find capitalization errors in your writing? What is the main thing you have learned about capitalization that will help you? What is unclear to you?

Chapter Test

Circle the correct choice for each of the following items.

1. Choose the item that has no errors.
   a. My daughter's school, Spitzer High School, no longer sells pepsi and other sodas in its vending machines.
   b. My daughter's school, Spitzer high school, no longer sells pepsi and other sodas in its vending machines.
   c. My daughter's school, Spitzer High School, no longer sells Pepsi and other sodas in its vending machines.

2. If an underlined portion of this sentence is incorrect, select the revision that fixes it. If the sentence is correct as written, choose d.

   Will our company <u>President</u> speak at the <u>annual meeting</u>, or will
                                A   B

   <u>Dr. Anders</u>?
     C

   a. president
   b. Annual Meeting
   c. doctor Anders
   d. No change is necessary.

3. Choose the item that has no errors.
   a. Which Library do you go to, Hill Library or Barry Township Library?
   b. Which library do you go to, Hill Library or Barry Township Library?
   c. Which library do you go to, Hill library or Barry Township library?

4. If an underlined portion of this sentence is incorrect, select the revision that fixes it. If the sentence is correct as written, choose d.

In my <u>english 99</u> class <u>last summer</u>, we read some interesting
   　　　　A　　　　　　　B

essays by <u>famous authors</u>.
　　　　　　　C

a. English 99
b. last Summer
c. Famous Authors
d. No change is necessary.

5. If an underlined portion of this sentence is incorrect, select the revision that fixes it. If the sentence is correct as written, choose d.

Of the states in the <u>East</u>, one can travel the farthest <u>North</u> in
　　　　　　　　　　　　A　　　　　　　　　　　　　　　　　　　　B

<u>Maine</u>.
　C

a. east
b. north
c. maine
d. No change is necessary.

Editing Review Test 1

The Four Most Serious Errors (Chapters 19–23)

DIRECTIONS: Each of the underlined word groups contains one or more errors. As you locate and identify each error, write its item number on the appropriate line below. Then, edit the underlined word groups to correct the errors. If you need help, turn back to the chapters indicated.

Two fragments _____   Two verb problems _____

Two run-ons _____   Four subject-verb
                                     agreement errors _____

1 Every time you step outside, you are under attack. **2** Which you may not know what is hitting you, but the attack is truly happening. **3** Invisible storms of sky dust rain down on you all the time. **4** It does not matter if the sun is shining and the sky are bright blue. **5** The dust is still there.

6 Sky dust consist of bug parts, specks of hair, pollen, and even tiny chunks of comets. **7** According to experts, 6 million pounds of space dust settle on the earth's surface every year. **8** You will never notice it, scientists, however, are collecting it in order to learn more about weather patterns and pollution. **9** Using sophisticated equipment like high-tech planes and sterile filters to collect dust samples.

10 Dan Murray, a geologist at the University of Rhode Island, has began a new project that invites students and teachers to help collect samples of cosmic dust. **11** Murray says that collecting the dust particles are quite simple. **12** It starts with a researcher setting up a small, inflatable swimming pool. **13** Next, this investigator leaves the pool out in the open for 48 hours. **14** Finally, the researcher uses a special type of tape to pick up whatever have settled over time. **15** The tape is put into a beaker of water to dissolve a microscope is used to analyze what comes off the tape. **16** The information finded there will help scientists predict insect seasons, measure meteor showers, or even catch signs of global warming.

609

Editing Review Test 2

The Four Most Serious Errors (Chapters 19–23)

DIRECTIONS: Each of the underlined word groups contains one or more errors. As you locate and identify each error, write its item number on the appropriate line below. Then, edit the underlined word groups to correct the errors. If you need help, turn back to the chapters indicated.

Two fragments _____   Two verb problems _____

Three run-ons _____   Three subject-verb agreement errors _____

1 Most people spend many hours a day indoors, so windows and natural light is important to their health. 2 Light helps people feel connected to the world around them. 3 However, traditional windows allow the loss of heat in winter and of cool air in summer; the result is high energy costs to maintain office buildings and homes at comfortable temperatures. 4 Architects and designers knowed this fact, so they have developed energy-efficient "smart windows." 5 Shifting from clear to dark and back again. 6 Some smart windows change from clear to dark with a touch of a button others change automatically in response to the intensity of the outside light.

7 Their design and engineering make smart windows *chromogenic*, or able to change colors. 8 Smart windows shifts to darker colors when they are given a small electrical charge. 9 The darker the room, the more it remains cool the sun does not warm it. 10 Smart windows take only a minute or so to darken.

11 Although these smart windows save energy, they may not be ready for the market. 12 For a few more years. 13 At present, designers face some resistance from potential customers who distrust the technology. 14 Another obstacle is the price tag, this new technology remains expensive. 15 To deal with both of these issues, developers are starting small. 16 They were creating motorcycle and ski helmets with face masks that switch between dark and clear. 17 They hopes that handy products like these helmets will help the new technology gain wide acceptance.

Editing Review Test 3

The Four Most Serious Errors (Chapters 19–23)
Other Grammar Concerns (Chapters 24–30)

DIRECTIONS: Each of the underlined word groups contains one or more errors. As you locate and identify each error, write its item number on the appropriate line below. Then, edit the underlined word groups to correct the errors. If you need help, turn back to the chapters indicated.

Two fragments _____   Two verb problems _____

One run-on _____   Two pronoun errors _____

One adjective error _____   One parallelism error _____

Two subject-verb
agreement errors _____

1 Flying an airplane across the Atlantic Ocean may have been a miracle almost a century ago, but today it be quite commonplace. **2** When a man named Maynard Hill decided to do it, however, most people told him that he simply could not be done. **3** Giving it a try despite everyone's doubts. **4** His persistence was rewarded when TAM-5, his 11-pound model airplane, flew from Canada to Ireland in approximately 39 hours. **5** TAM-5's flight sat world records not only for the longest distance but also for the longest time ever flown by this type of airplane. **6** Following the same path as the first nonstop flight across the ocean in 1919.

7 This successful trip was not Hill's first attempt, by any means. **8** He started its project a decade ago, and he lost several planes trying to complete the journey. **9** Finally, in August 2003, he made a fifth attempt. **10** He tossed the TAM-5 into the air once airborne, it was guided by remote control on the ground. **11** It was the most best version he had made. **12** It soared to a cruising altitude of almost 1,000 feet, and at that point a computerized autopilot took over.

13 For days, the flight crew watched the clock, followed the TAM-5's progress, and hopes for the best. **14** A crowd of fifty people waited on the shore in Ireland to watch the TAM-5's landing. **15** When the plane appeared on the horizon, a cheer went up. **16** Today, model plane enthusiasts remembers his feat. **17** Even though the plane were made out of nothing more than balsa wood, fiberglass, and plastic film, it flew right into history that August afternoon.

611

Editing Review Test 4

The Four Most Serious Errors (Chapters 19–23)
Other Grammar Concerns (Chapters 24–30)

DIRECTIONS: Each of the underlined word groups contains one or more errors. As you locate and identify each error, write its item number on the appropriate line below. Then, edit the underlined word groups to correct the errors. If you need help, turn back to the chapters indicated.

Two fragments _____   One run-on _____

One subject-verb agreement error _____   One pronoun error _____

One misplaced/dangling modifier _____   Two coordination/
                                           subordination errors _____
One use of inappropriately
informal or casual language _____

1 Early on May 1, 2011, Sohaib Athar, an IT consultant in Pakistan, was surprised to hear helicopters flying over his house. **2** Soon, he sent a Twitter message about it: "Helicopter hovering above Abbottabad at 1 AM (is a rare event)." **3** He continued to tweet about what he was hearing for the next half hour, attracting many Twitter followers.

4 Because he didn't know it at the time, Athar became the first person to publicize the raid in which Osama bin Laden was captured and assassinated. **5** For this reason, Athar also became one of the most famous of a growing number of so-called citizen journalists. **6** Unlike most traditional news gatherers, citizen journalists aren't trained in journalism. **7** They follow events and trends that interest them, but they send their observations to others through Facebook, Twitter, and other social media.

8 Certain media critics argue, however, that if someone tweets about something newsworthy, they don't necessarily deserve to be called a journalist. **9** That is the view of Dan Miller, a reporter who had the following reaction to Athar's famous reports: "Wondering on Twitter why there are helicopters flying around your neighborhood isn't journalism." **10** According to Miller, traditional media, not Athar, got the 411 about bin Laden's capture out to the whole world. **11** Not to just some Twitter followers.

12 Others say that Athar provided a more valuable service. **13** For example, he communicated with people who were following him and tried to answer their questions, he sought out other sources of information and shared them. **14** Also, tried to analyze what he observed himself and what he learned from other sources.

15 Whether or not Athar deserves to be called a journalist, one thing is clear: More people is feeling driven to tweet, text, or blog from their particular corners of the world.

Editing Review Test 5

The Four Most Serious Errors (Chapters 19–23)
Other Grammar Concerns (Chapters 24–30)
Word Use (Chapters 31–33)

DIRECTIONS: Each of the underlined word groups contains one or more errors. As you locate and identify each error, write its item number on the appropriate line below. Then, edit the underlined word groups to correct the errors. If you need help, turn back to the chapters indicated.

One run-on _____   One verb problem _____

One word-choice error _____   Two pronoun errors _____

One adjective error _____   One spelling error _____

One subject-verb agreement error ___   One misplaced/dangling modifier _____

Two commonly
confused word errors _____

1 How do you celebrate the New Year? **2** <u>Some people watch television on New Year's Eve so that he can see the glittering ball drop in New York's Times Square.</u> **3** Others invite friends and family over to celebrate with special foods or fireworks. **4** <u>The New Year are celebrated all over the world in a variety of ways.</u> **5** <u>For example, in Australia, people spended the day in fun, outdoor activities, such as picnics, trips to the beach, and rodeos.</u> **6** After all, it is summertime there in January. **7** In Spain, people eat a dozen grapes at midnight. **8** <u>They eat one each time the clock chimes because she believe that it will bring good luck for the New Year.</u> **9** <u>The people of Denmark have the unusualest tradition.</u> **10** On New Year's Eve, they throw old dishes at the doors of their friends' homes. **11** <u>If you find a lot of broken junk in front of your house in the morning, you are well-liked.</u> **12** Wearing all new clothes is the way many Koreans celebrate the start of the New Year. **13** <u>In Germany, people leave food on there plates, this practice is meant to ensure that their kitchens will be full of food for the coming New Year.</u> **14** Not all countries celebrate the New Year on January 1. **15** <u>Setting off firecrackers, the holiday is celebrated later by the Chinese people.</u> **16** <u>The date of the Chinese New Year depends on the lunar calander and usually falls somewhere between January 21 and February 20.</u> **17** The Chinese often have a big parade with colorful floats of dancing dragons. **18** <u>The mythical creatures are supposed to be cymbals of wealth and long life.</u>

613

Editing Review Test 6

The Four Most Serious Errors (Chapters 19–23)
Other Grammar Concerns (Chapters 24–30)
Word Use (Chapters 31–33)

DIRECTIONS: Each of the underlined word groups contains one or more errors. As you locate and identify each error, write its item number on the appropriate line below. Then, edit the underlined word groups to correct the errors. If you need help, turn back to the chapters indicated.

One run-on _____

One subject-verb agreement error _____

One parallelism error _____

Two commonly
confused word errors _____

One use of inappropriately
informal or casual language _____

One verb problem _____

One pronoun error _____

Two spelling errors _____

  1 The idea of being able to unlock your car, turn on a light, or starting your computer just by waving your hand sounds like something out of a science-fiction novel. **2** Thanks to advancements in technology, the futuristic idea has became a reality. **3** Some people are all ready able to accomplish routine actions in this unusual way. **4** They do not have special powers they have special computer chips embedded inside their bodies. **5** These high-tech chips help people do daily tasks with little or no effort.

  6 Known as RFIDs, which stands for "radio frequency identification devices," the chips are way small. **7** They are as tiny as a peice of rice, have small antennas that send signals, and can be painlessly implanted and worn under the skin. **8** Health-care workers uses the chips in a variety of life-saving ways. **9** For example, emergency medical workers can scan the chips in accident victims to determine his blood type or allergies.

  10 For security reasons, some parents have their children wear RFIDs on backpacks, bracelets, or ID tags. **11** Through a cell-phone signal, the chips automatically let the parents know when their children have reached and left school or other destinations. **12** Even some pets are now equipped with these computer chips. **13** If the pet runs away or gets lost, than its owners can track down their pet more easily by using the chip. **14** Although many people think that these chips have great potential, others worry that the government will eventually use them to spy on people.

614

Editing Review Test 7

The Four Most Serious Errors (Chapters 19–23)
Other Grammar Concerns (Chapters 24–30)
Word Use (Chapters 31–33)
Punctuation and Capitalization (Chapters 34–38)

DIRECTIONS: Each of the underlined word groups contains one or more errors. As you locate and identify each error, write its item number on the appropriate line below. Then, edit the underlined word groups to correct the errors. If you need help, turn back to the chapters indicated.

One run-on _____   One verb problem _____
One apostrophe error _____   One pronoun error _____
One adverb error _____   One quotation mark error _____
One subject-verb agreement error _____   One capitalization error _____
One comma error _____   One semicolon error _____

1 In response to the ongoing economic crisis, more high schools are teaching financial literacy: how to create a budget, save money, and stay out of debt. **2** Although most experts agree that teaching these skills is a good idea, some recommend that such education begin more earlier—even in preschool. **3** This way, young people have more time to learn good habit's, save money, and plan for their financial future.

4 The Moonjar is one Tool for teaching children good money skills. **5** It consists of three tin boxes; each of which is labeled "spend," "save," or "share." **6** Children are encouraged to divide allowances or gifts of money equally among the boxes. **7** As the weeks pass by, they watch their savings grow, helping them see the benefits of saving money over time, they also learn discipline about spending. **8** For example a child who is shopping with a parent might ask for a pack of candy or a small toy. **9** The parent can reply, "Do you have enough money in your spend box"? **10** Exchanges like that one help the child understand the consequences of financial decisions; if they spend money on one item now, less money will be available for other purchases in the future.

11 Mary Ryan Karges, who is in charge of sales for Moonjar LLC, recommend that financial skills be emphasized as much as other basic skills taught to young children. **12** She says, "If we teach save, spend, share with the same vigor that we teach stop, look, listen, we won't run into so many financial problems." **13** Once children have seed the benefits of good financial choices, they are on their way to a better future.

615

Editing Review Test 8

The Four Most Serious Errors (Chapters 19–23)
Other Grammar Concerns (Chapters 24–30)
Word Use (Chapters 31–33)
Punctuation and Capitalization (Chapters 34–38)

DIRECTIONS: Each of the underlined word groups contains one or more errors. As you locate and identify each error, write its item number on the appropriate line below. Then, edit the underlined word groups to correct the errors. If you need help, turn back to the chapters indicated.

One run-on _____
One pronoun error _____
One comma error _____
One apostrophe error _____
One use of inappropriately
informal or casual language _____
One capitalization error _____

One semicolon error _____
One verb problem _____
One adverb error _____
One spelling error _____
One parallelism error _____
One hyphen error _____

1 If it seems as though places in the United States are more crowded lately; it might be because the country's population recently hit 300 million. **2** The nation has the third-largest population in the world. **3** Only China and India have more people. **4** Experts belief that by 2043 there will be 400 million people in the United States.

5 The country is growing rapidly because people are having more babies more people are moving to the United States. **6** The northeast is the most populated area within the country. **7** It took fifty two years for the country's population to go from 100 million to 200 million. **8** It took only thirty-nine years to rise from 200 million to its current 300 million. **9** If experts statistics are correct, it will take even less time for the population of the United States to reach 400 million.

10 Some people worry that the United States is growing too quick. **11** Researchers predict some super scary possibilitys. **12** They state that if the population grows too large, it will stress available land, deplete water resources, and it can increase air pollution. **13** Its concerns are valid ones; in the meantime, the population just keeps growing. **14** Although this country is large future generations may be squeezed in more tightly than the present generation can imagine.

616

Editing Review Test 9

The Four Most Serious Errors (Chapters 19–23)
Other Grammar Concerns (Chapters 24–30)
Word Use (Chapters 31–33)
Punctuation and Capitalization (Chapters 34–38)

DIRECTIONS: Each of the underlined word groups contains one or more errors. As you locate and identify each error, write its item number on the appropriate line below. Then, edit the underlined word groups to correct the errors. If you need help, turn back to the chapters indicated.

One fragment _____
One run-on _____
One pronoun error _____
One parallelism error _____
One commonly confused word error _____

One spelling error _____
One hyphen error _____
One semicolon error _____
One parenthesis error _____
One word-choice error _____

1 Whenever you have to write a paper, a letter, or any other document for work or school, you probably head toward the computer. **2** <u>In this day and age, most people reach for keyboards faster than they pick up pens.</u> **3** <u>At one elementary school in Scotland, however, the principle, Bryan Lewis, is taking a different approach.</u> **4** <u>He believes that neat handwriting is still an important skill, so he has his students write not only by hand but also with old fashioned fountain pens.</u>

5 Fountain pens were used in schools long ago and lately have been regaining popularity because they are refillable. **6** A writer using a fountain pen dips the point into a little ink bottle. **7** <u>Drawing ink up into the barrel of the pen, as needed.</u> **8** <u>Today, a writer simply throws an empty pen away; and gets a new one.</u>

9 <u>So far, Principal Lewis is pleased with the results of his experimint.</u> **10** <u>He reports that students are taking more care with their work, their self-esteem has improved as well.</u> **11** He stresses to teachers all over the world that the ability to produce legible handwriting remains a necessary skill. **12** <u>Lewis is happy with the improvement he sees in his students' writing (and in his own writing, too.</u> **13** <u>He knows that computers are here to stay and that it will not disappear.</u> **14** <u>However, he believes that the practice with fountain pens helps students focus, write faster, and they can feel proud of themselves.</u>

617

Editing Review Test 10

The Four Most Serious Errors (Chapters 19–23)
Other Grammar Concerns (Chapters 24–30)
Word Use (Chapters 31–33)
Punctuation and Capitalization (Chapters 34–38)

DIRECTIONS: Each of the underlined word groups contains one or more errors. As you locate and identify each error, write its item number on the appropriate line below. Then, edit the underlined word groups to correct the errors. If you need help, turn back to the chapters indicated.

One subject-verb agreement error _____   One spelling error _____
One pronoun error _____   One comma error _____
One coordination/subordination error _____   One semicolon error _____
One colon error _____   One apostrophe error _____
One commonly confused word error _____

1 When Shaun Ellis decided that he wanted to learn more about wolves, he made a radical life change. **2** <u>He decided to live with the wolves yet imitate their wild lifestyle as closely as he possibly could.</u> **3** For eighteen months, he lived with three wolf pups that had been abandoned. **4** <u>He pretended to be its mother in many ways.</u> **5** He worked to teach them the skills they would need to survive in the wild. **6** It certainly was not an easy way to live. **7** <u>Ellis shared an outdoor pen with the pups, and it had no heat or beding.</u> **8** To keep warm on the cold nights, he had to snuggle with the young wolves.

9 <u>To communicate with them, Ellis learned how to: growl, snarl, and howl.</u> **10** He also learned how to use body positions and facial expressions in order to get a message across to the animals. **11** <u>While living with the wolves, he also try to eliminate any emotion because animals do not feel things as human beings do.</u> **12** <u>This mans transition back to regular life was quite difficult for him.</u>

13 <u>Ellis's unorthodox methods have earned him criticism from his colleagues; but he firmly believes that his techniques led to valuable knowledge about wolves.</u> **14** <u>He has founded, the Wolf Pack Management organization in England.</u> **15** <u>Its goal is to get captive wolves released back into the wild and than use what was learned to help the animals avoid future conflicts with humans.</u>

618

"I write to persuade and to make connections."
—John F., student

Part 8
Readings for Writers

39	Narration	621
40	Illustration	629
41	Description	638
42	Process Analysis	648
43	Classification	657
44	Definition	667
45	Comparison and Contrast	675
46	Cause and Effect	687
47	Argument	696

39

Narration

In this part of the book (this chapter through Chapter 47), you will find twenty-one essays that demonstrate the types of writing you studied in Part 2 of this book. In all cases but Chapter 47 (Argument), the first essay in each chapter is written by a student; the second one is by a professional writer. (Chapter 47 contains three student essays and two professional essays.)

In addition to serving as good models of writing, these essays can also provide you with ideas for your own writing, both in and out of school. Most important, they offer you a chance to become a better reader and to learn skills from other writers.

Each essay in this chapter uses narration to get its main point across to the reader. As you read these essays, consider how they achieve the Four Basics of Good Narration that are listed below and discussed in Chapter 8.

TIP As discussed in Chapter 3, it is a good idea to keep a journal to record and explore your thoughts and feelings and come up with ideas for writing. Throughout this part of the book, you will be asked to record information in an idea journal, which you may have started already. You might also want to keep a reading journal to record information about the essays in this chapter and your thoughts about them.

Four Basics of Good Narration

1. It reveals something of importance to the writer (the main point).
2. It includes all the major events of the story (primary support).
3. It brings the story to life with details about the major events (secondary support).
4. It presents the events in a clear order, usually according to when they happened.

Lauren Mack

Gel Pens

Lauren Mack expects to graduate from the University of Massachusetts Amherst in 2013 with a major in communications and a minor in film studies. Mack wrote "Gel Pens" for an English class when she was a senior in high school preparing to go to college. She was inspired to write this essay because it was a true story that had a strong effect on her. The fifth-grade incident made her realize the importance of kindness over popularity, and it showed her the true meaning of friendship. Mack's advice to other writers is to read a lot and to write what you know. "When something means a lot to you, the writing will come naturally," she said.

In this essay, Mack tells the story of a grade school experience that changed how she sees herself.

GUIDING QUESTION
Why are gel pens important in this essay?

1   I was in fifth grade. Everything was new and interesting; our elementary school had just been redone, I had a new teacher, and a whole new class. And more than anything, I wanted to be cool. The way I saw it, once I was cool, I'd be popular; and once I was popular, I'd have lots of friends which, of course, was the key to juvenile[1] happiness. So on the first day of school, I pulled the boldest move of my elementary career. Rather than sitting with my old friends who I knew were friendly and nice, I sat with the popular girls, Caitlin, Carly, and Maggie. It was my ticket to fame, I thought, because these girls could help me become the person I wanted to be. But I'd never been so wrong.

2   And so all year, I sat with Caitlin, Carly, and Maggie, and throughout that entire year, I was the odd girl out. What stands out more than anything from fifth grade were these gel pens. I remember the girls had this fantastic collection of gel pens in all different colors; sparkly greens and pinks and blues, and they were the greatest things that a fifth grader could fathom[2] and they were all right in front of me—except I couldn't use them. I wasn't cool enough to use these gel pens and, to me, this was absolutely heartbreaking.

3   Looking back, it's strange to think that, throughout an entire year of being shunned[3] and neglected by these girls, it was a collection of pens that made me come to my senses about what I was doing wrong. What was the logical[4] sense in being popular if, in the end, I was constantly feeling jealous, upset, and left out? To answer this, I turned to music and writing as my refuge.[5] After I graduated fifth grade, I began playing guitar and writing my own songs. And with that, it didn't take me long to realize

---

1. **juvenile:** an adjective referring to young people   2. **fathom:** to understand or discover   3. **shunned:** avoided   4. **logical:** based on reasoning   5. **refuge:** a place of escape or relief

that there is so much more to happiness than Caitlin, Carly, and Maggie and their silly gel pens. In breaking free from the disciples[6] of "cool," I felt that I not only set myself apart from others but also found something I hadn't found at all that year: happiness and satisfaction in myself.

These days, I refuse to adjust myself to meet the standards of others. Instead, I invest my time working on the things that have molded me into the person I am today. I am a musician: I write my songs about people, but not for them. I am an artist: I create my works from my own imagination, not from the person next to me. I am a writer: I express my ideas and opinions by crafting[7] words to my own liking. But above all, I am my own person: People can influence me, but they cannot change me, regardless of how many gel pens they may have.

4

IDENTIFY: Underline the definitions Mack gives of "an artist," "a writer," and "my own person."

SUMMARIZE AND RESPOND

In your reading journal or elsewhere, summarize the main point of "Gel Pens." Then, go back over the essay, and check off the support for this idea. Next, write a brief summary of the essay. Finally, write a brief response to the reading. How does the author rethink or build upon traditional definitions of "happiness"?

CHECK YOUR COMPREHENSION

1. An alternate title for this essay could be
   a. "Gel Pens Are Artists' Best Tools."
   b. "A Musician Joins the Cool Kids and Thrives."
   c. "Happiness Found in a Break with the Crowd."
   d. "The Most Popular Students Are Shallow."

2. The main point of this essay is that
   a. young people will find the most happiness if they take the time and effort to be accepted by the popular crowd.
   b. a person who develops into a talented artist may be shunned by others who are jealous.
   c. playing the guitar and writing songs is a better way to find happiness than drawing with gel pens.
   d. happiness comes from becoming one's own person, not from being accepted by the popular crowd.

3. How did the gel pens help the author "come to [her] senses about what [she] was doing wrong"?
   a. The pens helped the author see that her artistic talents were greater than any talents the popular girls possessed.
   b. The author realized that the pens, and the girls who used them, weren't as important as pursuing her own interests.

6. **disciples:** followers   7. **crafting:** to form skillfully

c. The pens helped the author see that visual art wasn't for her; instead, making music was what she loved most.

d. Because the "cool" girls didn't want to share their pens with the author, she saw that she was better off without the popular crowd.

4. Does this essay include the Four Basics of Good Narration? Why or why not?

5. Look back at the vocabulary you underlined, and write sentences using these words: *fathom* (para. 2); *refuge, disciples* (3); *crafting* (4).

TIP For tools to build your vocabulary, visit the *Student Site for Real Writing* at bedfordstmartins.com/realwriting.

READ CRITICALLY

1. The opening paragraph suggests different definitions of friendship. In your view, what are these different definitions, and what are the results of pursuing one type of friendship over another?

2. How did the author's idea of who she wanted to be (para. 1) change as a result of the experiences described in the essay?

3. Why do you suppose Mack chose to make the gel pens an important part of her essay? What appeal did they have for her apart from their "sparkly greens and pinks and blues" (2)?

4. Mack discusses how making music and writing helped her become a more satisfied and independent person. Would any further details about her music and writing have helped you better understand Mack and the changes she went through? If so, explain the types of details you would like her to have included.

5. In the final paragraph, Mack writes, "People can influence me, but they cannot change me." Based on this essay and your own experiences, what kind of things influence people (affect their beliefs or behaviors, often in subtle ways), and what kinds of things cause deep and lasting change? Give as many examples as you can.

WRITE

TIP For a sample narration paragraph, see page 124.

WRITE A PARAGRAPH: In a paragraph, tell the story of how finding a personal interest—in music, sports, or something else—has had a positive effect on your life. Make your story as specific and detailed as possible.

WRITE AN ESSAY: Write an essay about a time when an action you took to improve your life (such as Mack's joining in with the popular crowd) had unexpected results. What was the experience, and what did you learn from it?

Pat Conroy
Chili Cheese Dogs, My Father, and Me

The writing of Pat Conroy (b. 1945) draws heavily on his life experiences. *The Water Is Wide* (1972) recounts his days teaching at a one-room school in South Carolina. *The Great Santini* (1976) describes the difficulty of growing up with a strict military father. Several of Conroy's books have been made into movies. The most famous of these films is *The Prince of Tides* (1991), which was based on Conroy's 1986 novel of the same name. His most recent books include *The Pat Conroy Cookbook: Recipes of My Life* (2005), a mix of food writing and memoir; the novel *South of Broad* (2009); and *My Reading Life* (2010), in which Conroy explores the role of books in his life.

In the following essay, Conroy uses narration to tell a story about two important relationships—with food and with his father—and how they came together.

GUIDING QUESTION
What is the significance of chili cheese dogs in the narrator's relationship with his father?

When I was growing up and lived at my grandmother's house in Atlanta, my mother would take us after church to The Varsity, an institution with more religious significance to me than any cathedral in the city. Its food was celebratory, fresh, and cleansing to the soul. It still remains one of my favorite restaurants in the world.

I had then what I order now—a habit that has not deviated[1] since my sixth birthday in 1951, when my grandmother, Stanny, ordered for me what she considered the picture-perfect Varsity meal: a chili cheese hot dog, onion rings, and a soft drink called "The Big Orange."

On that occasion, when my family had finished the meal, my mother lit six candles on a cupcake she had made, and Stanny, Papa Jack, my mother, and my sister Carol sang "Happy Birthday" as I blushed with pleasure and surprise. I put together for the first time that the consumption[2] of food and celebration was a natural and fitting combination. It was also the first time I realized that no one in my family could carry a tune.

When my father returned home from the Korean War, he refused to believe that The Varsity—or the American South, for that matter—could produce a hot dog worthy of consumption. My Chicago-born father was a fierce partisan[3] of his hometown, and he promised me that he would take me to eat a real "red hot" after we attended my first White Sox game.

That summer, we stayed with my dad's parents on the South Side of Chicago. There, I met the South Side Irish for the first time on their own turf. My uncles spent the summer teasing me about being a southern hick as they played endless games of pinochle[4] with my father. Then, my father

IDEA JOURNAL Describe a relationship of yours that has changed over time.

CRITICAL READING
■ Preview
■ Read
■ Pause
■ Review

See pages 9–12.

VOCABULARY DEVELOPMENT Certain words in this essay are defined at the bottom of the page. Underline these words as you read them.

REFLECT: Based on paragraph 4, how would you describe the father's personality?

1. **deviated:** changed 2. **consumption:** using; eating (in the case of food)
3. **partisan:** one who takes sides 4. **pinochle:** a card game popular in the mid-1900s

took me for the sacramental⁵ rite of passage: my first major league baseball game. We watched the White Sox beat the despised Yankees.

After the game, my father drove my Uncle Willie and me to a place called Superdawg to get a red hot. He insisted that the Superdawg sold the best red hots in the city. When my father handed me the first red hot I had ever eaten, he said, "This will make you forget The Varsity for all time." That summer, I learned that geography itself was one of the great formative⁶ shapers of identity. The red hot was delicious, but in my lifetime I will never forsake⁷ the pleasure of The Varsity chili cheese dog.

When my father was dying of colon cancer in 1998, he would spend his days with me at home on Fripp Island, South Carolina, then go back to Beaufort at night to stay with my sister Kathy, who is a nurse and was in charge of his medications. Since I was responsible for his daily lunch, I told him I would cook him anything he wanted as long as I could find it in a South Carolina supermarket.

"Anything, pal?" my father asked.

"Anything," I said.

Thus, the last days between a hard-core Marine and his edgy son, who had spent his career writing about horrific father-son relationships, became our best days as we found ourselves united by the glorious subject of food.

My father was a simple man with simple tastes, but he was well-traveled, and he began telling me his life story as we spent our long hours together. The first meal he ordered was an egg sandwich, a meal I had never heard of but one that kept him alive during the Depression.⁸ He told me, "You put a fried egg on two slices of white bread which has been spread with ketchup."

"It sounds repulsive,"⁹ I said.

"It's delicious," he replied.

When Dad spoke of his service in Korea, I fixed him kimchi (spicy pickled vegetables), and when he talked about his yearlong duty on an aircraft carrier on the Mediterranean, I made spaghetti carbonara¹⁰ or gazpacho.¹¹ But most of the time, I made him elaborate sandwiches: salami or baloney tiered high with lettuce, tomatoes, and red onions. The more elaborate I made them, the more my father loved them.

He surprised me one day by asking me to make him some red hots, done "the Chicago way, pal." That day, I called Superdawg and was surprised that it was still in business. A very pleasant woman told me to dress the red hots with relish, mustard, onion, and hot peppers with a pickle on the side. "If you put ketchup on it, just throw it in the trash," she added.

The following week, he surprised me again by ordering up some chili cheese dogs, "just like they make at The Varsity in Atlanta." So I called The Varsity and learned step by step how to make one of their scrumptious chili cheese dogs.

PREDICT: What do you think will happen next?

5. **sacramental:** sacred   6. **formative:** giving form to   7. **forsake:** to give up
8. **Depression:** a serious economic downturn lasting from 1929 until the late 1930s
9. **repulsive:** disgusting   10. **spaghetti carbonara:** pasta with a sauce of cream, eggs, and bacon   11. **gazpacho:** a cold vegetable soup from Spain

When my father began his quick, slippery descent[12] into death, my brothers and sisters drove from all directions to sit six-hour shifts at his bedside. We learned that watching a fighter pilot die is not an easy thing. One morning, I arrived for my shift and heard screaming coming from the house. I raced inside and found Carol yelling at Dad: "Dad, you've got to tell me you're proud of me. You've got to do it before you die."

I walked Carol out of the bedroom and sat her down on the sofa. "That's Don Conroy in there, Carol—not Bill Cosby,"[13] I said. "You've got to learn how to translate Dad. He says it, but in his own way."

Two weeks before my father died, he presented me with a gift of infinite price. I made him the last chili cheese dog from The Varsity's recipe that he would ever eat. When he finished, I took the plate back to the kitchen and was shocked to hear him say, "I think the chili cheese dog is the best red hot I've ever eaten."

There is a translation to all of this, and here is how it reads: In the last days of his life, my father was telling me how much he loved me, his oldest son, and he was doing it with food.

17 **REFLECT:** Why does Carol act as she does here?

18

19

20 **SUMMARIZE:** How do the father's words show that he loves his son?

SUMMARIZE AND RESPOND

In your reading journal or elsewhere, summarize the main point of "Chili Cheese Dogs, My Father, and Me." Then, go back over the essay, and check off the support for this idea. Next, write a brief summary of the essay. Finally, write a brief response to the reading. What impression does Conroy create of his changing relationship with his father?

CHECK YOUR COMPREHENSION

1. An alternate title for this essay could be
   a. "My Father, the Fighter Pilot."
   b. "How My Father Told Me He Loved Me."
   c. "How I Learned to Love Chili Cheese Dogs."
   d. "The Varsity vs. Superdawg."

2. The main point of this essay is that
   a. chili cheese dogs are better tasting than red hots.
   b. men can learn to be excellent and creative cooks.
   c. people can communicate their affection for others in indirect ways.
   d. only when a parent is dying does a child learn what that parent is really like.

---

12. **descent:** a way down; a passage down to a wise, kind father in a 1980s TV comedy

13. **Bill Cosby:** the actor who played

3. What is Conroy's point in telling the story of his sister Carol's angry outburst toward their father (para. 17)?

   a. He wants readers to understand that he comes from a family in which yelling is common.
   b. He wants to show the kind of relationship he has with his sister.
   c. He wants readers to see that anger is not useful in dealing with parents.
   d. He wants to show how difficult it is for his father to express feelings for his children.

4. Look back at the vocabulary you underlined, and write sentences using the following words: *deviated* (2); *consumption* (3); *formative* (6); *repulsive* (12); *descent* (17).

READ CRITICALLY

1. What details show the change in Conroy's father's attitude toward The Varsity's chili cheese dogs? What is the significance of this change?

2. What three stories does Conroy narrate in this essay? When does he shift to telling about his father's last days? How do you know?

3. Based on details from the essay, describe the ways in which father and son are "united by the glorious subject of food"?

4. Beginning in paragraph 8, Conroy includes a number of direct quotations from himself and his father. What is the effect of Conroy's presenting this dialogue?

5. Although this essay tells a sad story overall, it has some humorous moments. What are they, and how did they affect you?

WRITE

WRITE A PARAGRAPH: Write a paragraph that tells about a time when a particular food played a special role during a family celebration, such as a birthday or a holiday. Like Conroy, include details about family members and your own response to the occasion.

WRITE AN ESSAY: In an essay, trace the history of your relationship with an older family member or someone else who has played a significant role in your life. As Conroy does in writing about his relationship with his father, tell specific stories about your times with this person, and suggest ways in which your relationship changed over time.

40

Illustration

Each essay in this chapter uses illustration to get its main point across to the reader. As you read these essays, consider how they achieve the Four Basics of Good Illustration that are listed below and discussed in Chapter 9 of this book.

Four Basics of Good Illustration

1. It has a point.
2. It gives specific examples that show, explain, or prove the point.
3. It gives details to support the examples.
4. It uses enough examples to get the point across to the reader.

True Shields
To Stand in Giants' Shadows

True Shields wrote the following essay for the *Daily Californian,* an independent student newspaper at the University of California, Berkeley, where he majored in English and graduated in the spring of 2012. Shields also writes short fiction, and he hopes to enter an M.F.A. program in writing.

Of "To Stand in Giants' Shadows" Shields writes, "The piece is about the first time I really got interested in games as something with a competitive ladder—that is, I found out that competition is fun, even when you know you're a poor athlete/gamer, because you can always learn from someone. I enjoyed writing this column because it gave me an opportunity to think about people to whom I really owe a lot of thanks."

Shields's advice to other aspiring writers is to "find a routine and stick with it. There's no greater enemy to writers than a lack of discipline. Also, make sure your computer isn't connected to the Internet, if you're using one to write."

GUIDING QUESTION
Who are the "giants" in this essay?

CRITICAL READING
- Preview
- Read
- Pause
- Review

See pages 9–12.

VOCABULARY DEVELOPMENT Certain words in this essay are defined at the bottom of the page. Underline these words as you read them.

IDEA JOURNAL Write about a game you like to play and why you enjoy it.

IDENTIFY: Underline the examples of the grandfather's skills in this paragraph.

1. Imagine being guided by an old yet firm hand into a living room and then sat before a growling fire and a bowl of ice cream. The hand pats you on the back after sitting you down and leaves momentarily to retrieve something: a circular wooden board, with semi-spherical divots[1] bored out of it in a first-aid symbol pattern. The marbles—some quartz, some amethyst,[2] and others minerals you don't recognize—rest like clay soldiers awaiting a general's hand in the grooves. The hand removes one marble from the center and then leapfrogs another marble over an adjacent[3] one, removing the hopped-over crystal sphere. It motions for you to do the same. Bewildered,[4] you look down and reach, uncertain, while the hand guides yours.

2. This was my first introduction to games.

3. I remember childhood visits to my grandparents' house in the Pacific Palisades as opportunities for my brother and me to stuff our faces and fall asleep in front of the fire after going for a swim. This was all fine and good, but the real meat and potatoes of our visits, our *raisons d'être*,[5] were the times spent hunched over the marble solitaire[6] board like miniature Rodin[7] sculptures.

4. I never knew much about my grandfather—he was tall, handsome in his youth and was stationed in Southeast Asia during World War II—but I did know he was a master of this particular game. He would ceaselessly[8] eliminate the marbles, one by one, without mercy or hesitation. He seemed to just know how it worked. I recall picking more difficult starting points (normally the center marble is removed), and he still managed to decimate[9] the poor things like they were disobedient legionnaires.[10]

5. Like most solitaire games, patience and planning are key to winning. One can't expect to pick marbles out willy-nilly[11] like a heron[12] at a sardine farm and succeed—that is a recipe for disaster. The few times I have

1. **divots:** indentations   2. **amethyst:** a purple-colored quartz stone
3. **adjacent:** nearby   4. **bewildered:** confused; puzzled   5. ***raisons d'être*:** reasons for being (French)   6. **solitaire:** in this case, a game somewhat similar to chess in that the player tries to eliminate marbles from the playing board by jumping them with another marble. The goal is to have just one marble left on the board at the end of the game.   7. **Rodin:** Auguste Rodin, a French sculptor best known for *The Thinker*, a marble-and-bronze statue of a man shown in deep thought
8. **ceaselessly:** without pause   9. **decimate:** to get rid of; destroy. The word is based on the Latin root *decimus,* meaning *tenth,* and is said to relate to Roman military leaders' practice of punishing disobedient troops by killing every tenth man.
10. **legionnaires:** soldiers   11. **willy-nilly:** carelessly   12. **heron:** a bird whose diet consists largely of fish

managed to get down to three or four marbles have been the result of carefully calculated moves and persistence.[13] A healthy dose of dumb luck never hurts, either.

I myself never managed to reach the one-marble end zone before my grandfather passed away, but the game remains with my grandmother, who often chides[14] me playfully when I insist that this time, I've got it. I never do. But the importance of the game is that it is something passed on, something I am beholden[15] to as a token of my grandfather's influence on my early life.

Older people seem to have an uncanny[16] ability to dominate games of skill. Whether it is the pith[17]-helmeted man playing chess and shouting nonsense or the crusty old veteran of the beach volleyball courts, often the most expert competitors are those who have seen all the moves.

My grandfather was surely one of these people. But these people do not simply punish you for losing by kicking sand in your face or jamming bishops up your nose—many masters of games are more than willing to pass on their wisdom to young upstarts.[18]

These days the closest thing I have to a mentor is Cal's[19] club volleyball coach. At first glance Omar might not seem a font of wisdom—he is strong but chubby, smart but physically slow due to his age, and he speaks with a nearly indecipherable[20] Cuban accent.

"Jou godda flotate de serf, adawaise de atha team, dey can pass de boll more eassier."

"When jou are blocking, turn de ousside han into de cour and ge ih frrron ohf dem."

Yet he remains well loved because of his willingness to take the youngest players aside during practice and show them what he learned playing for the Cuban national team years ago. Even off the court, he has demonstrated knowledge that helps a bunch of lanky[21] boys become men; to date, he has instructed us on how best to compliment women, taught us how to salsa dance, and given marriage advice to prospective[22] husbands.

Mentors can teach us fundamental lessons about winning and losing that we often take for granted. They teach us that life has certain rules and that to succeed in this world we must play by them yet use them to their fullest advantage. Especially in the realm[23] of gaming, the advice mentors give is often applicable[24] beyond the game.

When the gentleman across from you warns you not to bring your queen out too early, he's really telling you not to be so impetuous.[25] When the beach player tells you to float serve because the wind will make it difficult to pass, he's telling you to watch your surroundings. The lessons we glean from mentors transcend[26] games themselves, if we pay close enough attention.

---

13. **persistence:** continual/dedicated effort   14. **chides:** scolds   15. **beholden:** indebted   16. **uncanny:** mysterious; supernatural   17. **pith:** plant tissue often used in protective helmets   18. **upstarts:** people who are rising up quickly in a certain skill area or social group   19. **Cal's:** belonging to the University of California, Berkeley   20: **indecipherable:** not understandable   21. **lanky:** skinny   22. **prospective:** potential; future   23. **realm:** world   24. **applicable:** relevant   25. **impetuous:** impulsive; careless   26. **transcend:** go beyond

Without them, we would just pick marbles at random and hope to succeed. Instead, I will endeavor to choose my moves in life carefully and imagine a guiding hand helping me pick the best move.

It just gets a little weirder when I imagine a phantom Omar helping me suavely[27] talk about babies while salsa dancing.

SUMMARIZE AND RESPOND

In your reading journal or elsewhere, summarize the main point of "To Stand in Giants' Shadows." Then, go back over the essay, and check off the support for this idea. Next, write a brief summary of the essay. Finally, write a brief response to the reading. What kind of life skills can we learn from others—skills that are not necessarily taught at school?

CHECK YOUR COMPREHENSION

1. An alternate title for this essay could be
   a. "Games Are Essential to Forming Family Bonds."
   b. "With the Right Skills, Game Players Achieve Regular Success."
   c. "Mentors in Game Playing Can Teach Lasting Lessons."
   d. "Older People Are the Best Teachers."

2. The main point of this essay is that
   a. the importance of game playing to happiness and personal success should be recognized more widely.
   b. under the guidance of a good mentor, a game player can learn skills that are relevant not only to the game but also to life.
   c. patience and persistence are the most important requirements for succeeding in games—and in life in general.
   d. no one can truly achieve success in life without game-playing experience.

3. Why does the game that Shields used to play with his grandfather have lasting importance to him?
   a. It taught Shields that he could beat anyone at this game if he tried hard enough.
   b. It represents a major influence that the grandfather had during Shields's childhood.
   c. It proved to him that cheating at a game is useless if the opponent is highly skilled.
   d. It showed Shields that the best players do not show any emotion while they are winning or losing.

27. **suavely:** in a sophisticated way

4. Does this essay include the Four Basics of Good Illustration? Why or why not?

5. Look back at the vocabulary you underlined, and write sentences using these words: *bewildered* (para. 1); *persistence* (5); *uncanny* (7); *impetuous, transcend* (14).

TIP For tools to build your vocabulary, visit the *Student Site for Real Writing* at bedfordstmartins.com/ realwriting.

READ CRITICALLY

1. Shields weaves personal stories into his essay to make his point about the importance of mentors. How would the essay have been different if he had left out such stories and used only information from psychologists or other experts about the benefits that mentors provide? Would the essay have been more interesting and informative or less so? Why?

2. Shields focuses on mentors who help others become better game players — and more. In what other situations might he have come in contact with and benefited from mentors? Are there any other points about mentors that could be made?

3. Shields appears to be an experienced game player, but instead of bragging about his expertise, he modestly describes what he has learned — and continues to learn — from others. How does this perspective affect you as a reader? Would a more prideful tone impress you, or would it put you off? Why?

4. In a few places, Shields uses very short paragraphs. (See, for instance, paras. 2 and 16.) What might be the reason for including such short paragraphs? What effect(s) do they produce?

5. Do the last two paragraphs provide a satisfying conclusion? Why or why not?

WRITE

WRITE A PARAGRAPH: In a paragraph, write about one of your own mentors, giving examples and details that will make it clear to readers why this person is important to you.

TIP For a sample illustration paragraph, see page 142.

WRITE AN ESSAY: Write an essay about at least two mentors who have played an important role in your life. Give as many examples and details as you can so that readers will understand these mentors' significance to you. Also, provide clear transitions from one example to the next.

Dianne Hales
Why Are We So Angry?

Dianne Hales specializes in writing about mental health, fitness, and other issues related to the body and mind. A former contributing editor for *Parade* magazine, she has also written several college-level health textbooks. In her critically acclaimed book *Just Like a Woman* (2000), she examined assumptions about the biological differences between women and men. Most recently, she authored *La Bella Lingua: My Love Affair with Italian, the World's Most Enchanting Language* (2009). Both the American Psychiatric Association and the American Psychological Association have presented Hales with awards for excellence in writing. In addition, she has earned an Exceptional Media Merit Award (EMMA) from the National Women's Political Caucus for health reporting. She lives in Marin County, California.

In the following article, Hales uses vivid examples to illustrate the "rage" phenomenon. She reports on the causes and results of the apparent increase in out-of-control anger—and explains what can be done to relieve the problem.

GUIDING QUESTION
Does the author present specific and plentiful examples to answer the question that she poses in her title?

Something snapped inside Jerry Sola during his evening commute through the Chicago suburbs two years ago. When the driver in front of the fifty-one-year-old salesman suddenly slammed on his brakes, Sola got so incensed[1] that he gunned his engine to cut in front of the man. Still steaming when both cars stopped at a red light, Sola grabbed a golf club from the backseat and got out.

"I was just about to smash his windshield or do him some damage," the brawny, 6-foot-1 former police officer recalls. "Then it hit me: 'What in God's name am I doing? I'm really a nice, helpful guy. What if I killed a man, went to jail, and destroyed two families over a crazy, trivial thing?' I got back into my car and drove away."

Like Sola, more and more Americans are feeling pushed to the breaking point. The American Automobile Association's Foundation for Traffic Safety says incidents of violently aggressive driving—which some dub[2] "mad driver disease"—rose 7 percent a year in the 1990s. Airlines are reporting more outbursts of sky rage. And sideline rage has become widespread: A Pennsylvania kids' football game ended in a brawl involving more than one hundred coaches, players, parents, and fans. In a particularly tragic incident that captured national attention, a Massachusetts father—angered over rough play during his son's hockey practice—beat another father to death as their children watched.

No one seems immune[3] to the anger epidemic. Women fly off the handle just as often as men, though they're less likely to get physical. The young and the infamous, such as musicians Sean "Puffy" Combs

---
1. **incensed:** angered   2. **dub:** to call   3. **immune:** protected against

and Courtney Love—both sentenced to anger-management classes for violent outbursts—may seem more volatile,[4] but even senior citizens have erupted into "line rage" and pushed ahead of others simply because they felt they had "waited long enough" in their lives.

"People no longer hold themselves accountable[5] for their bad behavior," says Doris Wilde Helmering, a therapist and author of *Sense Ability*. "They blame anyone and everything for their anger."

It's a mad, mad world. Violent outbursts are just as likely to occur in leafy suburbs as in crowded cities, and even idyllic[6] vacation spots are not immune. "Everyone everywhere seems to be hotter under the collar these days," observes Sybil Evans, a conflict-resolution expert in New York City, who singles out three primary culprits[7]: time, technology, and tension. "Americans are working longer hours than anyone else in the world. The cell phones and pagers that were supposed to make our lives easier have put us on call 24/7/365. Since we're always running, we're tense and low on patience. And the less patience we have, the less we monitor what we say to people and how we treat them."

Ironically,[8] the recent boom times may have brought out the worst in some people. "Never have so many with so much been so unhappy," observes Leslie Charles, author of *Why Is Everyone So Cranky?* "There are more of us than ever, all wanting the same space, goods, services, or attention. Everyone thinks, 'Me first. I don't have time to be polite.' We've lost not only our civility but our tolerance for inconvenience."

The sheer complexity of our lives also has shortened our collective fuse. We rely on computers that crash, drive on roads that gridlock, place calls to machines that put us on endless hold. "It's not any one thing but lots of little things that make people feel like they don't have control of their lives," says Jane Middleton-Moz, a therapist and author. "A sense of helplessness is what triggers rage. It's why people end up kicking ATM machines."

Getting a grip. When his lawn mower wouldn't start, a St. Louis man got so angry that he picked it up by the handle, smashed it against the patio, and tore off each of its wheels. Playing golf, he sometimes became so enraged that he threw his clubs 50 feet up the fairway and into the trees and had to get someone to retrieve them. In anger-therapy sessions with Doris Wilde Helmering, he learned that such outbursts accomplish nothing. "Venting" may make you feel better—but only for a moment.

"Catharsis[9] is worse than useless," says Brad Bushman, a psychology professor at Iowa State University whose research has shown that letting anger out makes people more aggressive, not less. "Many people think of anger as the psychological equivalent of the steam in a pressure cooker: It has to be released, or it will explode. That's not true. The people who react by hitting, kicking, screaming, and swearing just feel more angry."

Over time, temper tantrums sabotage physical health as well as psychological equanimity.[10] By churning out stress hormones like adrenaline,

PREDICT: Pick one of the culprits; how do you think Hales in subsequent paragraphs will show it to be a cause of anger?

IDENTIFY: According to this paragraph, what triggers rage?

SUMMARIZE: In your own words, summarize how letting anger out creates problems.

---

4. **volatile:** explosive   5. **accountable:** responsible   6. **idyllic:** peaceful
7. **culprits:** guilty ones   8. **ironically:** opposite to what is or might be expected
9. **catharsis:** release of emotional tension   10. **equanimity:** balance

chronic[11] anger revs the body into a state of combat readiness, multiplying the risk for stroke and heart attack—even in healthy individuals. In one study by Duke University researchers, young women with "*Jerry Springer Show*–type anger," who tended to slam doors, curse, and throw things in a fury, had higher cholesterol levels than those who reacted more calmly.

How do you tame a toxic temper? The first step is to figure out what's really making you angry. Usually the rude sales clerk is the final straw that unleashes bottled-up fury over a more difficult issue, such as a divorce or a domineering boss. Next, monitor yourself for early signs of exhaustion or overload. While stress alone doesn't cause a blow-up, it makes you more vulnerable[12] to overreacting.

When you feel yourself getting angry, control your tongue and your brain. "Like any feeling, anger lasts only about three seconds," says Doris Wilde Helmering. "What keeps it going is your negative thinking." As long as you focus on who or what irritated you—like the oaf who rammed that grocery cart into your heels—you'll stay angry. "Once you come to understand that you're driving your own anger with your thoughts," adds Helmering, "you can stop it."

Since his roadside epiphany,[13] Jerry Sola has conscientiously worked to rein in his rage. "I am a changed person," he says, "especially behind the wheel. I don't listen to the news on the car radio. Instead, I put on nice, soothing music. I force myself to smile at rude drivers. And if I feel myself getting angry, I ask a simple question: 'Why should I let a person I'm never going to see again control my mood and ruin my whole day?'"

IDENTIFY: Underline the sentence that presents a solution to releasing anger.

SUMMARIZE AND RESPOND

In your reading journal or elsewhere, summarize the main point of "Why Are We So Angry?" Then, go back over the essay, and check off the support for this idea. Next, write a brief summary of the essay. Finally, write a brief response to the reading. Can you identify with the angry people Hales writes about in this essay? Have you ever been one of them?

CHECK YOUR COMPREHENSION

1. An alternate title for this essay could be
   a. "Anger Management."
   b. "Road Rage."
   c. "Investigating the Anger Epidemic."
   d. "The Breaking Point."

---

11. **chronic:** habitual   12. **vulnerable:** open to damage or attack
13. **epiphany:** a sudden understanding of something

2. The main point of this essay is that
   a. anger is a widespread occurrence in today's society.
   b. anger is most common in sports.
   c. people should enroll in anger-management courses.
   d. road rage must stop.

3. What do experts say about releasing anger?
   a. Releasing anger reduces frustration.
   b. Hitting a pillow is a simple way to release anger.
   c. Releasing anger is not productive.
   d. People in the suburbs are most likely to release anger.

4. Look back at the vocabulary you underlined, and write sentences using the following words: *immune* (para. 4); *accountable* (5); *chronic* (11); *vulnerable* (12).

READ CRITICALLY

1. Based on your personal experience and observations, do the examples presented in this essay seem realistic?

2. Throughout the essay, Hales presents information gained from therapists and experts. Does this information strengthen Hales's main point? Would the essay be just as effective without it?

3. What role does technology play in creating anger?

4. Do the steps presented under "How do you tame a toxic temper?" (paras. 12 and 13) seem like a workable solution? Why or why not?

5. Hales begins her essay with the example of Jerry Sola and ends with it. Why do you suppose she uses this technique?

WRITE

WRITE A PARAGRAPH: Write a paragraph about a location where you have seen people exhibit their anger. Identify the location, and provide concrete examples of the way people show their anger.

WRITE AN ESSAY: Write an essay about a time when either you or someone you knew lost control. What happened? Give concrete examples of the loss of control. What were the consequences? Did you learn anything from the experience about expressing anger? Feel free to include the ideas you wrote about in your reading journal for Summarize and Respond.

41

Description

Each essay in this chapter uses description to get its main point across to the reader. As you read these essays, consider how they achieve the Four Basics of Good Description that are listed below and discussed in Chapter 10 of this book.

> **Four Basics of Good Description**
>
> 1. It creates a main impression—an overall effect, feeling, or image—about the topic.
> 2. It uses specific examples to support the main impression.
> 3. It supports those examples with details that appeal to the five senses: sight, hearing, smell, taste, and touch.
> 4. It brings a person, place, or physical object to life for the reader.

Brian Healy
First Day in Fallujah

Brian Healy served in Iraq and later pursued a degree in business management at Florida Community College. Although a typical writing process includes submitting a piece to several rounds of revision, Healy decided to "revise this essay as little as possible." He says, "I felt that given the topic, I should go with what I first wrote so that it would show more dirty truth than be polished to perfection." He values the role of emotion in writing and exhorts others not to "write for the sake of writing, [but to] write because you are passionate about it."

GUIDING QUESTION
What events affected Healy?

The year was 2004, and I was a young, 21-year-old Marine Corporal on my second tour of Iraq. I had been in the country for five months and was not enjoying it any more than the first time. From the first time I had set foot in Iraq, I perceived it as a foul-smelling wasteland[1] where my youth and, as I would soon find out, my innocence were being squandered.[2] I had been in a number of firefights, roadside bomb attacks, and mortar and rocket attacks; therefore, I had thought I had seen it all. So when the word came down that my battalion[3] was going to Fallujah to drive through the center of the city, I was as naïve[4] as a child on the first day of school. The lesson of that first day would be taught with blood, sweat, and tears, learned through pain and suffering, and never forgotten.

At 2:00 in the morning on November 10, the voice of my commander pierced the night: "Mount up!" Upon hearing these words, I boarded the amtrack transport. I heard a loud "clank, clank," the sound of metal hitting metal as the ramp closed and sealed us in. Sitting shoulder to shoulder, we had no more room to move than sardines in a very dark can. The diesel fumes choked our lungs and burned our throats. There was a sudden jolt as the metal beast began to move, and with each bump and each turn, I was thrown from side to side inside the beast's belly with only the invisible bodies of my comrades to steady myself. I thought back to my childhood, to a time of carefree youth. I thought how my father would tell me how I was the cleanest of his sons. I chuckled as I thought, "If only he could see me now, covered in sweat and dirt and five days away from my last shower."

I was violently jerked back into the present with three thunderous explosions on the right side of the amtrack vehicle. We continued to move faster and faster with more intensity and urgency than before. My heart was racing, pounding as if it were trying to escape from my chest when we came to a screeching halt.

With the same clank that sealed us in, the ramp dropped and released us from our can. I ran out of the amtrack nearly tripping on the ramp. There was no moon, no street light, nothing to pierce the blanket of night. Therefore, seeing was almost completely out of the question. However, what was visible was a scene that I will never forget. The massive craters[5] from our bombs made it seem as if we were running on the surface of the moon. More disturbing were the dead bodies of those enemies hit with the bombs. Their bodies were strewn about in a frenzied manner: a leg or arm here, torso[6] there, a head severed[7] from its body. Trying to avoid stepping on them was impossible. Amidst all this and the natural "fog of war,"[8] we managed to get our bearings and move toward our objective.[9]

CRITICAL READING
- Preview
- Read
- Pause
- Review

See pages 9–12.

VOCABULARY DEVELOPMENT Certain words in this essay are defined at the bottom of the page. Underline these words as you read them.

IDEA JOURNAL Write about a time when you were very frightened.

PREDICT: What do you think the next paragraph will be about?

IDENTIFY: Underline some of the vivid images.

---

1. **wasteland:** an area that is uncultivated and barren, or devastated by natural disasters or war   2. **squandered:** wasted; not used to good advantage   3. **battalion:** an army unit   4. **naïve:** unsophisticated; lacking experience, judgment, or information   5. **craters:** shallow, bowl-shaped depressions on a surface, caused by an impact or explosion   6. **torso:** the trunk of a human body   7. **severed:** cut or divided   8. **fog of war:** a term describing the general uncertainty that soldiers experience during military operations   9. **objective:** a goal or target

We were able to take the entrance to a government complex located at the center of the city, and we did so in fine style. "Not so tough," we all thought. We would not have to wait long until we would find out how insanely foolish we were.

As the sun began to rise, there were no morning prayers, no loudspeakers, and no noise at all. This, of course, was odd since we had become accustomed to the sounds of Iraq in the morning. However, this silence did not last long and was shattered as the enemy released hell's wrath[10] upon us. The enemy was relentless[11] in its initial assault but was unable to gain the advantage and was slowly pushed back.

As the day dragged on, the enemy fought us in an endless cycle of attack and retreat. There was no time to relax as rocket-propelled grenades[12] whistled by our heads time and time again. Snipers' bullets skipped off the surface of the roof we were on. While some bullets tore through packs, radios, and boots and clothing, a lucky few found their mark and ripped through flesh like a hot knife through butter.

Suddenly, there was a deafening crack as three 82-millimeter mortars rained upon us, throwing me to the ground. The dust blacked out the sun and choked my lungs. I began to rise only to be thrown back down by a rocket-propelled grenade whizzing just overhead, narrowly missing my face. At this point, it seemed clear to me that there was no end to this enemy. In the windows, out the doorways, through alleyways, and down streets, they would run. We would kill one, and another would pop up in his stead, as if some factory just out of sight was producing more and more men to fight us.

As the sun fell behind the horizon, the battle, which had so suddenly started, ended just as swiftly. The enemy, like moths to light, were nowhere to be seen. The rifles of the Marines, which were so active that day, were silent now. We were puzzled as to why it was so quiet. My ears were still ringing from that day's events when the order came down to hole up for the night. There was no sleep for me that night; the events of the day made sure of that. I sat there that cold November night not really thinking of anything. I just sat in a trance,[13] listening to small firefights of the battle that were still raging: a blast of machine gun fire, tracer rounds,[14] and air strikes. Artillery[15] flying through the air gave the appearance of a laser light show. Explosions rattling the earth lit my comrades' faces. As I looked over at them, I did not see my friends from earlier in the day; instead, I was looking at old men who were wondering what the next day would bring. I wondered if I would survive the next day.

The battle for Fallujah would rage on for another three weeks. The Marines of the First Battalion Eighth Marine Regiment would continue to fight with courage and honor. As each day of the battle passed, I witnessed new horrors and acts of bravery, of which normal men are not

IDENTIFY: What senses has Healy used in his description?

---

10. **wrath:** strong, fierce anger; angry vengeance 11. **relentless:** steady; persistent; unyielding 12. **grenades:** handheld explosives 13. **trance:** a dazed or bewildered condition; a state seemingly between sleeping and waking 14. **tracer rounds:** ammunition containing a substance that causes bullets or rounds to trail smoke or fire so as to make their path visible and show a target for other shooters 15. **artillery:** large, crew-operated weapons

capable. However, none of those days would have the impact[16] on me that that first day did.

The battle is over, but for the men who were there, it will never end. It is fought every day in their heads and in voices of friends long gone, all the while listening to the screams and taunts[17] of people who know nothing of war but would call these men terrorists.

10 REFLECT: What effect does this essay have on you?

SUMMARIZE AND RESPOND

In your reading journal or elsewhere, summarize the main point of "First Day in Fallujah." Then, go back over the essay, and check off the support for this idea. Next, write a brief summary of the essay. Finally, write a brief response to the reading. Although Healy writes about the chaotic and violent aspects of war, does he also make his battle experience meaningful?

CHECK YOUR COMPREHENSION

1. An alternate title for this essay could be
   a. "The United States at War in the Middle East."
   b. "Changed Forever in the Fog of War."
   c. "Liberating Fallujah and Iraq."
   d. "A News Update from Iraq."

2. The main point of this essay is that
   a. the United States should make military service a requirement for all citizens.
   b. the writer has maintained his innocence, despite having experienced combat.
   c. combat is intense, frightening, and confusing, and its effects change soldiers.
   d. the war in Iraq was unwinnable because the number of enemies there is infinite.

3. Why does Healy recall his father's remark that Healy was "the cleanest of his sons"?
   a. Healy wants the reader to know how infrequently soldiers bathe.
   b. This memory shows Healy's change from the child he once was.
   c. Healy wants to show how well he adapted to conditions in Iraq.
   d. Healy thinks his father would be disappointed at how dirty he has become.

4. Does this essay include the Four Basics of Good Description? Why or why not?

---

16. impact: influence; an effect; a collision   **17. taunts:** scornful insults, jeering, or ridicule

TIP For tools to build your vocabulary, visit the *Student Site for Real Writing* at **bedfordstmartins.com/ realwriting**.

5. Look back at the vocabulary you underlined, and write sentences using these words: *squandered, naïve* (para. 1); *severed* (4); *relentless* (5); *impact* (9).

READ CRITICALLY

1. In giving his description of combat, how does Healy appeal to his readers' different senses? Provide specific examples.

2. How would you characterize the tone of "First Day in Fallujah," and why?

3. Healy opens his essay by describing himself as "a young, 21-year-old Marine Corporal." How does he change during the course of his account? What is the difference between "lost" innocence and "squandered" innocence?

4. In paragraph 9, Healy says that his battalion fought with "courage and honor" and that he witnessed "new horrors and acts of bravery, of which normal men are not capable." What does he mean by "normal"?

5. In the conclusion of his essay, Healy writes that the battle is still fought every day in the heads of these soldiers and "in voices of friends long gone." What experience is he writing about here?

WRITE

TIP For a sample description paragraph, see page 163.

WRITE A PARAGRAPH: Write a descriptive paragraph that recounts a personal experience that transformed you and made you less innocent or naïve.

WRITE AN ESSAY: At the very end of his narrative, Healy refers to people who "know nothing of war but would call these men terrorists." Write an essay that considers the value of reading accounts such as Healy's: Do they help us "know" war? Did his essay change the way you understand soldiers, combat, and war, generally?

Eric Liu
Po-Po in Chinatown

Eric Liu, a graduate of Yale University and Harvard Law School, is a former speechwriter for President Bill Clinton and also served as the president's Deputy Domestic Policy Advisor. Liu has written several books on a range of subjects and edited the Norton anthology *Next: Young American Writers on the New Generation* (1994). His book *The Accidental Asian: Notes of a Native Speaker* (1999) was selected as a *New York Times* Notable Book and was also featured in the PBS documentary *Matters of Race*. His most recent book is *Imagination First: Unlocking the Power of Possibility*, which he coauthored with Scott Noppe-Brandon.

GUIDING QUESTION
What picture do you form of Po-Po and the author's attitude toward her?

For more than two decades, my mother's mother, Po-Po, lived in a cinder-block[1] one-bedroom apartment on the edge of New York's Chinatown.[2] She was twenty floors up, so if you looked straight out of the main room, which faced north, one block appeared to melt into the next, all the way to the spire of the Empire State Building[3] off in the distance. This was a saving grace, the view, since her own block down below was not much to look at. Her building, one of those interchangeable towers of 1970s public housing, was on the lower east side of the Lower East Side,[4] at the corner of South and Clinton Streets. It was, as the Realtors say, only minutes from the Brooklyn Bridge and the South Street Seaport, although those landmarks,[5] for all she cared, might as well have been in Nebraska. They weren't part of the world Po-Po inhabited, which was the world that I visited every few months during the last years of her life.

My visits followed a certain pattern. I'd get to her apartment around noon, and when I knocked on the door, I could hear her scurrying[6] with excitement. When she opened the door, I'd be struck always as if for the first time, by how tiny she was: four feet nine and shrinking. She wore loose, baggy clothes, nylons, and ill-fitting old glasses that covered her soft, wrinkled face. It was a face I recognized from my own second-grade class photo. *Eh, Po-Po, ni hao maaa?* She offered a giggle as I bent to embrace her. With an impish smile, she proclaimed my American name in her Yoda-like[7] voice: *Areek.* She got a kick out of that. As she shuffled to the kitchen where Li Tai Tai, her caregiver, was preparing lunch, I would head to the bathroom, trained to wash my hands upon entering Po-Po's home.

In the small bath were the accessories of her everyday life: a frayed[8] toothbrush in a plastic Star Trek mug I'd given her in 1979, stiff washrags and aged pantyhose hanging from a clothesline, medicine bottles and hair dye cluttered on the sinktop. I often paused for a moment there, looking for my reflection in the filmy, clouded mirror, taking a deep breath or two. Then I would walk back into the main room. The place was neat but basically grimy. Some of the furniture — the lumpy couch, the coffee table with old magazines and congealed[9] candies, the lawn chair where she read her Chinese newspaper through a magnifying glass — had been there as long as I could remember. The windowsill was crammed with plants and flowers. The only thing on the thickly painted white wall was a calendar. *Your house looks so nice*, I'd say in a tender tone of Mandarin[10] that I used only with her. On a tray beside me, also surveying the scene, was a faded black-and-white portrait of Po-Po as a beautiful young woman, dressed in Chinese costume. *Lai chi ba*, Po-Po would say, inviting me to eat.

---

1. **cinder-block:** a concrete block 2. **Chinatown:** a section of New York City with a large population of Chinese immigrants 3. **Empire State Building:** a famous skyscraper in New York City 4. **Lower East Side:** a neighborhood in New York City traditionally known for its immigrant population 5. **landmarks:** buildings with historical importance 6. **scurrying:** moving quickly 7. **Yoda:** a small, elderly creature from the *Star Wars* movies 8. **frayed:** worn out, with threads raveling 9. **congealed:** jelled or hardened 10. **Mandarin:** the official language of China

Invariably,[11] there was a banquet's worth of food awaiting me on the small kitchen table: *hongshao* stewed beef, a broiled fish with scallions and ginger, a leafy green called *jielan*, a soup with chicken and winter melon and radishes, tofu with ground pork, stir-fried shrimp still in their salty shells. Po-Po ate sparingly, and Li Tai Tai, in her mannerly Chinese way, adamantly[12] refused to dine with us, so it was up to me to attack this meal. I gorged[13] myself, loosening my belt within the half hour and sitting back dazed and short of breath by the end. No matter how much I put down, Po-Po would express disappointment at my meager[14] appetite.

As I ate, she chattered excitedly, pouring forth a torrent[15] of opinions about politics in China, Hong Kong pop singers, the latest developments in Taiwan. After a while, she'd move into stories about people I'd never met, distant relations, half-brothers killed by the Communists, my grandfather, who had died when I was a toddler. Then she'd talk about her friends who lived down the "F" train in Flushing[16] or on the other side of Chinatown and who were dying one by one, and she'd tell me about seeing Jesus after she'd had a cancer operation in 1988, and how this blond Jesus had materialized and said to her in Chinese, *You are a good person, too good to die now. Nobody knows how good you are. Nobody appreciates you as much as I do.* I would sit quietly then, not sure whether to smile. But just as she approached the brink,[17] she would take a sip of 7-Up and swerve back to something in the news, perhaps something about her heroine, the Burmese dissident[18] aunt Aung San Kyi.[19] She was an incredible talker, Po-Po, using her hands and her eyes like a performer. She built up a tidal momentum, relentless, imaginative, spiteful[20] like a child.

I generally didn't have much to say in response to Po-Po's commentary, save the occasional Chinese-inflected[21] *Oh?* and *Wah!* I took in the lilt[22] of her Sichuan[23] accent and relied on context to figure out what she was saying. In fact, it wasn't until I brought my girlfriend to meet Po-Po that I realized just how vague my comprehension was. *What did she say?* Carroll would ask. *Um, something about, something, I think, about the president of Taiwan.* Of course, I'm not sure Po-Po even cared whether I understood. If I interrupted, she'd cut me off with a hasty *bushide—no, it's not that*—a habit I found endearing in small doses but that my mother, over a lifetime, had found maddening.

If there was a lull, I might ask Po-Po about her health, which would prompt her to spring up from her chair and, bracing herself on the counter, kick her leg up in the air: *I do this ten times every morning at five*, she would proudly say in Chinese. *Then this*, she'd add, and she would stretch her arms out like little wings, making circles with her fingertips. *And last week, I had a headache, so I rubbed each eye like this thirty-six times.* Pretty soon, I was out of my chair, too, laughing, rubbing, kicking, as Po-Po

REFLECT: Why do you think that the author finds Po-Po endearing, whereas his mother found her maddening?

11. **invariably:** always; without exception   12. **adamantly:** in a stubborn or unyielding manner   13. **gorged:** ate a huge amount   14. **meager:** deficient; of a very small amount   15. **torrent:** a violently flowing stream, river, or downpour of rain   16. **Flushing:** a neighborhood in New York City   17. **brink:** the edge, as of a cliff   18. **dissident:** a protester; one who disagrees with a political establishment   19. **Aung San [Suu] Kyi:** a Nobel Peace Prize–winning human rights activist from Burma   20. **spiteful:** mean-spirited   21. **inflected:** accented in a certain way   22. **lilt:** a pleasant varation in the pitch of one's speech   23. **Sichuan:** a province of south-central China

schooled me in her system of exercises and home remedies. We did this every visit, like a ritual.

Time moved so slowly when I was at Po-Po's. After lunch, we might sit on the couch next to each other or go to her room so she could tell me things that she didn't want Li Tai Tai to hear. We would rest there, digesting, our conversation turning more mellow. I might pull out of my bag a small keepsake[24] for her, a picture of Carroll and me, or a souvenir from a recent vacation. She would show me a bundle of poems she had written in classical Chinese, scribbled on the backs of small cardboard rectangles that come with travel packs of Kleenex. She would recount how she'd been inspired to write this poem or that one. Then she would open a spiral notebook that she kept, stuffed with news clippings and filled with idioms[25] and sentences she had copied out of the Chinese newspaper's daily English lesson: *Let's get a move on. I don't like the looks of this.* At my urging, she'd read the sentences aloud, tentatively.[26] I would praise her warmly, she would chuckle, and then she might show me something else, a photo album, a book about qigong.[27]

One day, she revealed to me her own way of prayer, demonstrating how she sat on the side of her bed at night, and clasped her hands, bowing as if before Buddha, repeating in fragile English, *God bless me? God bless me? God bless me?* Another time, she urgently recited to me a short story that had moved her to tears, but I understood hardly a word of it. On another visit, she fell asleep beside me, her glasses still on, her chin tucked into itself. And so the hours would pass, until it was time for me to go—until, that is, I decided it was time to go, for she would have wanted me to stay forever—and I would hold her close and stroke her knotted back and tell her that I loved her and that I would miss her, and Po-Po, too modest to declare her heart so openly, would nod and press a little red envelope of money into my hand and say to me quietly in Chinese, *How I wish I had wings so I could come to see you where you live.*

SUMMARIZE AND RESPOND

In your reading journal or elsewhere, summarize the main point of "Po-Po in Chinatown." Then, go back over the essay, and check off the support for the idea. Next, write a brief summary of the essay. Finally, write a brief response to the reading. Do you think Liu enjoyed these visits with his grandmother? Why or why not?

CHECK YOUR COMPREHENSION

1. An alternate title for this essay could be
    a. "Memories of My Chinese Grandmother."
    b. "My Grandmother's Dirty Apartment."

---

24. keepsake: a reminder of something past **25. idioms:** words or sayings specific to a region **26. tentatively:** uncertainly; hesitantly **27. qigong:** a traditional Chinese practice of meditation and self-healing

c. "Confessions of a Chinese American Grandmother."

d. "An Immigrant Story."

2. The main point of this essay is that

   a. the language barrier between Liu and his Chinese grandmother made their relationship nearly impossible.

   b. New York is a city full of immigrant neighborhoods, such as Chinatown.

   c. Liu's grandmother liked to talk, but her anger and inability to learn English made it impossible for her to feel at home in America.

   d. Liu's grandmother was a complex, funny, and opinionated woman, and his memories of visiting her remain with him.

3. Why does Liu mention the 1979 plastic Star Trek mug in his grandmother's bathroom?

   a. It shows how his grandmother had abandoned her Chinese heritage.

   b. His grandmother loved watching American television.

   c. It shows how time stood still in her apartment.

   d. It shows that his grandmother had good health habits.

4. Look back at the vocabulary you underlined, and write sentences using these words: *adamantly, meager* (para. 4); *torrent, spiteful* (5); *tentatively* (8).

READ CRITICALLY

1. In paragraph 3, Liu writes that his grandmother's apartment was "neat but basically grimy." What do you think that distinction means? How do the details in the essay support this claim?

2. Liu appeals to his reader's senses throughout the essay. Find specific examples in the text where he appeals to at least three of the five senses (sound, sight, taste, touch, and smell). How do they contribute to the overall impression of "Po-Po in Chinatown"?

3. Liu writes in paragraph 5 that his grandmother "built up a tidal momentum" when she talked. In what specific ways does Liu's writing evoke her excited chatter for the reader?

4. In paragraph 6, Liu writes that he's not sure if his grandmother even cared if he understood what she said to him. What does this sentence say about their relationship, and how is it related to the larger point of the essay?

5. At the conclusion of the essay, Liu writes that he would tell his grandmother he loved her but that she was "too modest to declare her heart so openly." How does he give an impression of his grandmother's love, even though she never tells him explicitly?

WRITE

WRITE A PARAGRAPH: Write a paragraph that vividly describes the home, apartment, or living space of a close friend or relative. Like Liu, include details that show how the person's home reflects his or her personality, life, and relationships.

WRITE AN ESSAY: Liu writes that his visits to his grandmother "followed a certain pattern," which he then recounts in the essay. Write an essay in which you describe the pattern of your own regular visits or meetings with a friend, relative, or group of people. Try to show how this order of events reveals important aspects of your relationship with the person or people you visit.

42

Process Analysis

Each essay in this chapter uses process analysis to get its main point across to the reader. As you read these essays, consider how they achieve the Four Basics of Good Process Analysis that are listed below and discussed in Chapter 11 of this book.

Four Basics of Good Process Analysis

1. It tells readers what process the writer wants them to know about and makes a point about it.
2. It presents the essential steps in the process.
3. It explains the steps in detail.
4. It presents the steps in a logical order (usually time order).

Jasen Beverly
My Pilgrimage

Jasen Beverly is the author of the essay "My Pilgrimage," a piece he began for an introductory college English class. Although publication was not an original goal of his, he was later encouraged to seek a larger audience beyond his class. Before submitting the essay, Beverly spent two weeks editing his work, working through several drafts and aiming each time "to make it better with every draft." In addition to a series of revisions, he also looks to his friends for editorial support with his writing and "to make sure it is never too wordy or sugar-coated."

GUIDING QUESTION
Why does Beverly title his essay "My Pilgrimage"?

I'm tired and scared as hell. I've been running from this thing for who knows how long, but now I'm trapped. I crouch into a fetal position as the monster approaches me. With a closer look, I realize it's my best friend trying to kill me. He lifts his arm and cocks the gun back. Without words, he pulls the trigger.

The sound of a newly received instant message wakes me up. It's only 6:30 in the morning, so I'm hesitant to check the instant message. Minutes later, I roll over and reach for my phone. I slowly wipe the crust from my eyes and begin to read, "Wakey, wakey, eggs and bakey . . . skoo time!" reads the IM from my Mexican friend. I slide my phone open and reply with a quick "aiight," before I proceed to pass out again. Just as I begin to reconnect with my dream, at about 6:45, I'm interrupted once more. This time, it is a loud repeated banging at my bedroom door.

Without thoughts or words, I roll out of bed, grab my cloth and towel, and head for the bathroom. Upon reaching the bathroom, I hop into the shower. When my shower ends, I am forced to rush through both the grooming and dressing processes because there is a massive cold front sweeping through my apartment. This cold front is caused by a lack of heat in the apartment. This, in turn, is caused by what I like to call "hard times."

By 7:20, all is well, and I am ready to begin my pilgrimage[1] to Bunker Hill Community College for my first day of college. I leave my apartment with my hoodie unzipped, backpack half on, while trying fast to detangle my headphones for use. As I walk down the street, the frigid air begins to take its toll. My whole face is stinging as if it was being poked, the air circulating inside my shirt. I immediately slip my headphones into my pocket and zip my hoodie. I tie my hood tightly around my eyes. My hood cuts off my peripheral[2] vision but keeps all unwanted air off my face. Now I finish untangling my headphones and plug them into my phone. I quickly browse my list of albums before choosing one to listen to. This morning, I choose John Legend's *Once Again*. The music is soothing; it puts me in the zone as I continue the short trek to the bus stop.

While waiting patiently at the bus stop, I begin to ponder.[3] My first thought is, "How much longer will I be here waiting for the bus?" Next, I ask myself, "Am I even going to be able to sit when I get on the bus?" As this thought leaves my head, I see a bus coming down Columbia Road.

I enter the bus, tap my Charlie Card[4] on the target area, and begin to walk away. Shortly after, a stranger taps me on my leg as I walk by. When I look back, he is pointing to the fare box. I walk back and notice the driver saying something. I'm not able to make out what he is saying because I have my headphones on. My card must not have been processed

---

1. **pilgrimage:** a long journey, often made to some sacred place as an act of religious devotion   2. **peripheral:** to the sides of a person's main line of sight   3. **ponder:** to think about   4. **Charlie Card:** a plastic pass card used to pay fares on Boston's public transportation

correctly. I re-tap my card on the target area. This time, I wait for it to register before walking away. I spot a seat in the back of the bus, so I fill it. Once I sit, I look around at the other people on the bus. I feel as if everyone is looking at me, so I close my eyes and let the music soothe my mind. When the bus pulls into Andrews Station, I stand and exit the bus. I walk down the stairs and wait for the train to arrive.

When it arrives, it is packed with an uncountable number of businesspeople taking a trip to the Financial District. In fact, it is so packed that I prefer to wait for the next train. While waiting, I begin to think about all of the businesspeople. I ask myself, "How long did they have to attend college to put themselves into the position they're in now?" As the next train pulls into the station, I notice it is much like the last, but this time I squeeze myself into the middle of the car. Luckily for me, Downtown Crossing, my stop, is only three stops away.

Upon reaching Downtown Crossing at 7:45, I exit the train and begin to watch as people dart down the long corridor in hopes of catching the train. This becomes the highlight of the morning as I watch the doors slam in people's faces. There's no explaining the humor of watching people who have tried so hard, panting angrily as the train leaves without them. After this joyous moment, I proceed to transfer from the Red Line to the Orange Line.

Standing on the Orange Line platform, I recognize a few familiar faces. They belong to students of Charlestown High School. I laugh, knowing that school for them began at 7:20. Then I begin to reminisce[5] about my own CHS experiences. I think about all my suspension hearings, the work I refused to do, and how easy it was to get by doing the bare minimum. Only the cold draft of the approaching train brings me back to reality.

I step on the train and position myself against the door. I could sit, but I figure it is too short a ride to get comfortable. One by one, the stops come and go: State, Haymarket, and then North Station. The train seems to be on an effortless glide as it starts to move toward Community College.

My stomach begins to churn[6] as I start the last phase of my pilgrimage. The last phase consists of walking out of the train station, down the walkway, and into Bunker Hill Community College. I compare this walk to the walk death row inmates take before they are executed. As I take this walk, I begin to ask myself, "What the ---- are you doing here?" Within seconds, my sensible half answers, "You're here so that you don't have to live like the rest of your family. The rest of your friends are in school, and Lord knows half of them aren't half as smart as you. Lastly, we already paid for this, so get it done." With BHCC right in front of me, I take a deep breath and end this pilgrimage by entering the Mecca[7] that will start me on the path of reaching my pinnacle.[8]

REFLECT: Why does Beverly think about the businesspeople?

SUMMARIZE: What kind of student was Beverly in high school?

5. **reminisce:** to think back or recollect   6. **churn:** to stir powerfully   7. **Mecca:** a place that many people want to visit; a center of activity (Mecca is an Islamic holy city in Saudi Arabia)   8. **pinnacle:** the highest point or achievement

SUMMARIZE AND RESPOND

In your reading journal or elsewhere, summarize the main point of "My Pilgrimage." Then go back over the essay, and check off the support for this idea. Next, write a brief summary of the essay. Finally, write a brief response to the reading. How would you describe Beverly's attitude toward his education?

CHECK YOUR COMPREHENSION

1. An alternate title for this essay could be
   a. "First Steps on My Path to Success."
   b. "Why I Hate School-Day Mornings."
   c. "How Music Gets Me through My Day."
   d. "Public Transportation Is a Good Option for Students."

2. The main point of this essay is that
   a. the first day of college can be exciting and a little scary.
   b. the writer does not take his education seriously enough.
   c. people must make the most of their educational opportunities.
   d. college is not much different than high school.

3. What memories of high school does Beverly recall?
   a. He remembers his athletic success and popularity.
   b. He recalls how he enjoyed traveling to high school in the mornings more than he enjoys his college commute.
   c. He remembers how he got in trouble and did not work hard.
   d. He recalls that his teachers encouraged him to go to college.

4. Does this essay include the Four Basics of Good Process Analysis? Why or why not?

5. Look back at the vocabulary you underlined, and write sentences using these words: *peripheral* (para. 4); *ponder* (5); *reminisce* (9); *pinnacle* (11).

TIP For tools to build your vocabulary, visit the *Student Site for Real Writing* at **bedfordstmartins.com/realwriting**.

READ CRITICALLY

1. What do you think is the author's main point or purpose in writing this essay?

2. This essay opens with the author's having a nightmare. What effect does this introduction have? How do you think the bad dream is related to the rest of the essay?

3. According to Beverly, his apartment does not have heat because of what he refers to as "hard times." What do you think those words mean, and why would he put them in quotation marks?

4. Beverly gives almost a step-by-step account of his morning commute and "pilgrimage." What details stand out the most for you?

5. What motivates Beverly to go on this pilgrimage? What do we learn about his fears, hopes, and goals from this essay?

WRITE

WRITE A PARAGRAPH: Write a paragraph about a short, everyday kind of trip you often take. As Beverly does in "My Pilgrimage," give a description of every step of the trip.

TIP For a sample process analysis paragraph, see page 178.

WRITE AN ESSAY: Write an essay analyzing the process of your own current commute to work or school, or any other trip you make regularly that seems meaningful or memorable. What do you see, think about, or feel during the journey?

Sherman Alexie

The Joy of Reading and Writing: Superman and Me

Acclaimed author Sherman Alexie was born in 1966 and raised on the Spokane Indian Reservation, northwest of Spokane, Washington. An avid reader from an early age, he graduated from Washington State University with a B.A. in American studies. Soon after, Alexie published two books of poetry, *The Business of Fancydancing* (1992), which inspired a later screenplay by Alexie, and *I Would Steal Horses* (also 1992). He is best known, however, for his works of fiction, which include *The Lone Ranger and Tonto Fistfight in Heaven* (1993), a winner of the PEN/Hemingway Award for the Best First Book of Fiction; *Reservation Blues* (1995); *Flight* (2007); and, most recently, *War Dances* (2009), winner of the 2010 PEN Faulkner Award. Alexie also wrote the screenplay for the award-winning film *Smoke Signals* (1998).

In the following essay, Alexie explores the process of becoming a reader and of transforming his life through the power of words.

GUIDING QUESTION
What do you think "the joy of reading and writing" might be?

CRITICAL READING
- Preview
- Read
- Pause
- Review

See pages 9–12.

1   I learned to read with a Superman comic book. Simple enough, I suppose. I cannot recall which particular Superman comic book I read, nor can I remember which villain he fought in that issue. I cannot remember the plot, nor the means by which I obtained the comic book. What I can remember is this: I was 3 years old, a Spokane Indian boy living with his family on the Spokane Indian Reservation in eastern Washington state. We were poor by most standards, but one of my parents usually managed to

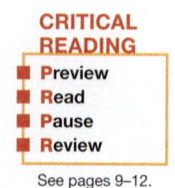

find some minimum-wage job or another, which made us middle-class by reservation standards. I had a brother and three sisters. We lived on a combination of irregular paychecks, hope, fear, and government surplus food.

My father, who is one of the few Indians who went to Catholic school on purpose, was an avid reader of westerns, spy thrillers, murder mysteries, gangster epics, basketball player biographies, and anything else he could find. He bought his books by the pound at Dutch's Pawn Shop, Goodwill, Salvation Army, and Value Village. When he had extra money, he bought new novels at supermarkets, covenience stores, and hospital gift shops. Our house was filled with books. They were stacked in crazy piles in the bathroom, bedrooms, and living room. In a fit of unemployment-inspired creative energy, my father built a set of bookshelves and soon filled them with a random assortment of books about the Kennedy assassination,[1] Watergate,[2] the Vietnam War, and the entire 23-book series of the Apache westerns. My father loved books, and since I loved my father with an aching devotion,[3] I decided to love books as well.

I can remember picking up my father's books before I could read. The words themselves were mostly foreign, but I still remember the exact moment when I first understood, with a sudden clarity,[4] the purpose of a paragraph. I didn't have the vocabulary to say "paragraph," but I realized that a paragraph was a fence that held words. The words inside a paragraph worked together for a common purpose. They had some specific reason for being inside the same fence. This knowledge delighted me. I began to think of everything in terms of paragraphs. Our reservation was a small paragraph within the United States. My family's house was a paragraph, distinct from the other paragraphs of the LeBrets to the north, the Fords to our south, and the Tribal School to the west. Inside our house, each family member existed as a separate paragraph but still had genetics[5] and common experiences to link us. Now, using this logic, I can see my changed family as an essay of seven paragraphs: mother, father, older brother, the deceased sister, my younger twin sisters, and our adopted little brother.

At the same time I was seeing the world in paragraphs, I also picked up that Superman comic book. Each panel, complete with picture, dialogue, and narrative was a three-dimensional[6] paragraph. In one panel, Superman breaks through a door. His suit is red, blue, and yellow. The brown door shatters into many pieces. I look at the narrative above the picture. I cannot read the words, but I assume it tells me that "Superman is breaking down the door." Aloud, I pretend to read the words and say, "Superman is breaking down the door." Words, dialogue, also float out of Superman's mouth. Because he is breaking down the door, I assume he says, "I am breaking down the door." Once again, I pretend to read the words and say aloud, "I am breaking down the door." In this way, I learned to read.

---

1. **Kennedy assassination:** the assassination of President John F. Kennedy on November 22, 1963   2. **Watergate:** a series of political scandals that led to the resignation of President Richard M. Nixon in August 1974   3. **aching devotion:** deep dedication or loyalty   4. **clarity:** clearness   5. **genetics:** inherited biological traits   6. **three-dimensional:** having the illusion of depth or variations in distance

5   This might be an interesting story all by itself. A little Indian boy teaches himself to read at an early age and advances quickly. He reads *Grapes of Wrath*[7] in kindergarten when other children are struggling through "Dick and Jane."[8] If he'd been anything but an Indian boy living on the reservation, he might have been called a prodigy.[9] But he is an Indian boy living on the reservation and is simply an oddity. He grows into a man who often speaks of his childhood in the third person, as if it will somehow dull the pain and make him sound more modest about his talents.

SUMMARIZE: In your own words, summarize the main point of this paragraph.

6   A smart Indian is a dangerous person, widely feared and ridiculed by Indians and non-Indians alike. I fought with my classmates on a daily basis. They wanted me to stay quiet when the non-Indian teacher asked for answers, for volunteers, for help. We were Indian children who were expected to be stupid. Most lived up to those expectations inside the classroom but subverted[10] them on the outside. They struggled with basic reading in school but could remember how to sing a few dozen powwow[11] songs. They were monosyllabic[12] in front of their non-Indian teachers but could tell complicated stories and jokes at the dinner table. They submissively[13] ducked their heads when confronted by a non-Indian adult but would slug it out with the Indian bully who was 10 years older. As Indian children, we were expected to fail in the non-Indian world. Those who failed were ceremonially[14] accepted by other Indians and appropriately pitied by non-Indians.

7   I refused to fail. I was smart. I was arrogant.[15] I was lucky. I read books late into the night, until I could barely keep my eyes open. I read books at recess, then during lunch, and in the few minutes left after I had finished my classroom assignments. I read books in the car when my family traveled to powwows or basketball games. In shopping malls, I ran to the bookstores and read bits and pieces of as many books as I could. I read the books my father brought home from the pawnshops and secondhand. I read the books I borrowed from the library. I read the backs of cereal boxes. I read the newspaper. I read the bulletins posted on the walls of the school, the clinic, the tribal offices, the post office. I read junk mail. I read auto-repair manuals. I read magazines. I read anything that had words and paragraphs. I read with equal parts joy and desperation. I loved those books, but I also knew that love had only one purpose. I was trying to save my life.

8   Despite all the books I read, I am still surprised I became a writer. I was going to be a pediatrician. These days, I write novels, short stories, and poems. I visit schools and teach creative writing to Indian kids. In all my years in the reservation school system, I was never taught how to write

---

7. *Grapes of Wrath*: an award-winning 1939 novel by John Steinbeck (1902–1968) about the difficulties faced by migrant workers in California   8. **"Dick and Jane":** a series of books, popular from the 1930s through the 1960s, that was used to teach children how to read   9. **prodigy:** an unusually talented young person
10. **subverted:** overthrew; defied   11. **powwow:** a Native American ceremony
12. **monosyllabic:** speaking few words; literally, "consisting of one syllable"
13. **submissively:** obediently   14. **ceremonially:** ritually   15. **arrogant:** proud; assuming a superior attitude toward others

poetry, short stories, or novels. I was certainly never taught that Indians wrote poetry, short stories, and novels. Writing was something beyond Indians. I cannot recall a single time that a guest teacher visited the reservation. There must have been visiting teachers. Who were they? Where are they now? Do they exist? I visit the schools as often as possible. The Indian kids crowd the classroom. Many are writing their own poems, short stories, and novels. They have read my books. They have read many other books. They look at me with bright eyes and arrogant wonder. They are trying to save their lives. Then there are the sullen[16] and already defeated Indian kids who sit in the back rows and ignore me with theatrical precision.[17] The pages of their notebooks are empty. They carry neither pencil nor pen. They stare out the window. They refuse and resist. "Books," I say to them. "Books," I say. I throw my weight against their locked doors. The door holds. I am smart. I am arrogant. I am lucky. I am trying to save our lives.

SUMMARIZE AND RESPOND

In your reading journal or elsewhere, summarize the main point of "The Joy of Reading and Writing: Superman and Me." Then, go back over the essay, and check off the support for this idea. Next, write a brief summary of the essay. Finally, write a brief response to the reading. Why has reading been so important to Alexie? What importance does it have in your own life?

CHECK YOUR COMPREHENSION

1. An alternate title for this essay could be
   a. "Defying Others' Low Expectations through a Love of Books."
   b. "The Importance of Reading in Children's Lives."
   c. "Parents Who Read Make Their Children Lifelong Readers."
   d. "Schools on Indian Reservations Must Place a Greater Emphasis on Reading."

2. The main point of this essay is that
   a. some children read at an unusually early age.
   b. comic books are a good tool for teaching kids to read.
   c. reading has the power to change lives.
   d. smart kids are often subject to bullying.

3. After learning what the word *paragraph* meant, Alexie
   a. couldn't stop repeating this definition.
   b. started circling paragraphs in everything he read.
   c. started writing paragraph-length stories.
   d. started to think of everything in terms of paragraphs.

16. **sullen:** gloomy; quiet manner
17. **theatrical precision:** an exaggerated or dramatic

4. Look back at the vocabulary you underlined, and write sentences using these words: *clarity* (para. 3); *prodigy* (5); *submissively* (6); *arrogant* (7); *sullen* (8).

READ CRITICALLY

1. Why do you suppose that Alexie opens the essay with his memory of the Superman comic book? Why does that memory—and the comic book itself—have so much significance to him?

2. In parts of the essay, Alexie suggests that his love of reading and learning didn't always have positive results. What were some of the drawbacks of this love?

3. In paragraph 7, Alexie describes the wide variety of the things he read. What might be the purpose of mentioning even junk mail and the writing on cereal boxes?

4. In paragraphs 7 and 8, Alexie makes repeated references to reading as a life saver. What do you think he means by this word choice? Are you convinced by the point he is making? Why or why not?

5. Notice how, at the end of paragraph 8, Alexie mentions throwing his weight against the "locked doors" of students who are resistant to books. Now, look back at paragraph 4. How are these paragraphs connected in wording and meaning? What is Alexie trying to say about the power of reading?

WRITE

WRITE A PARAGRAPH: Identify something you like to do that you think others would also enjoy or benefit from. Then, write a paragraph describing the steps you would take to get friends interested in this activity.

WRITE AN ESSAY: Alexie writes about "trying to save [his] life" through reading. Think about an activity or hobby that changed your life or helped make you the person you are today. Then, write an essay that introduces readers to this activity or hobby and describes—step by step, if possible—how it changed you. Like Alexie, you might also discuss others' reactions to this change or to your interests.

43

Classification

Each essay in this chapter uses classification to get its main point across to the reader. As you read these essays, consider how they achieve the Four Basics of Good Classification that are listed below and discussed in Chapter 12 of this book.

Four Basics of Good Classification

1. It makes sense of a group of people or items by organizing them into categories.
2. It has a purpose for sorting the people or items.
3. It categorizes using a single organizing principle.
4. It gives detailed explanations or examples of what fits into each category.

Kelly Hultgren

Pick Up the Phone to Call, Not Text

Kelly Hultgren is studying journalism, communication, and anthropology at the University of Arizona and plans to graduate in the spring of 2013. In addition to contributing articles to the *Arizona Daily Wildcat,* the student newspaper in which the following essay first appeared, Hultgren also enjoys writing creative nonfiction.

In this essay, Hultgren writes about the different types of texters and the limitations of texting. She says, "Nowadays, people get to know one another through technology rather than face to face. We're attempting to get personal through impersonal methods, and subsequently judging potential partners' characters through technology."

CRITICAL READING
- **P**review
- **R**ead
- **P**ause
- **R**eview

See pages 9–12.

VOCABULARY DEVELOPMENT Certain words in this essay are defined at the bottom of the page. Underline these words as you read them.

IDEA JOURNAL When do you think it is better to call rather than text someone?

REFLECT: Have you ever made an incorrect assumption about a texter based on his or her message or a lack of response to one of your own texts?

IDENTIFY: Underline the different types of texters Hultgren describes.

GUIDING QUESTION
What are the different types of texters?

1 "So, I met this guy last week and I thought he really liked me, because he was texting me all the time, and then suddenly he started taking longer to respond. I think he's not interested anymore. You better believe I am not texting him until he texts me first. I can't believe he led me on like that."

2 Does that sound familiar? That's because you've probably heard someone say it or have said it yourself. Perhaps not word for word, but please raise your hand if you've ever made assumptions at the beginning of a relationship, based solely on texts. My hand just hit the ceiling.

3 Once upon a time, people pursuing potential mates evaluated each other on personality, looks, lifestyle, and how the person felt he or she was being treated. People always will base their opinions on the categories listed above, but now, a more relevant and scrutinized[1] trait is a person's texting habits. People, especially we college students, rely on texting to get to know someone. Both men and women are equally guilty of this. We are all busy, and texting is quick and convenient and facilitates[2] communication throughout the day. I've used those arguments too. But instead of spending three hours on Facebook or watching TV, pick up the damn phone, call, and meet in person.

4 For budding relationships, texting is used not only as a screening device but also as a deal-breaker. It sounds absolutely ridiculous because it is. From simply looking to get some action to embarking[3] on a long-lasting romantic journey, cellular discourse[4] is now crucial in the process. Take my starting quote, for example. The hypothetical[5] girl first assumed the hypothetical guy liked her and then assumed he didn't based only on his texting frequency. What if the poor guy was having phone issues or was working? You're just getting started; don't expect him to drop the whole world just to send back a response to your simple "hey" text message.

5 This example addresses some aspects of texting: You don't know what the person is physically doing, and you cannot tell the person's mood (emoticons[6] do not count). Therefore, one of every student's favorite forms of interaction is inherently[7] deceiving. At the start of a relationship, why do we communicate and subsequently[8] put so much emphasis on texting, when it's not a reliable way to get to know someone?

6 As I mentioned before, texting can be a deal-breaker. Let's classify some different types of texters and how they can create problems.

7 First up, we have Lazy Texters. Lazy Texters often initiate the conversation and then leave the responsibility of carrying on the conversation with the other person, rarely asking questions and usually responding with one-word answers.

---

1. **scrutinized:** closely observed or studied   2. **facilitates:** makes something easier
3. **embarking:** starting out on   4. **discourse:** communication; discussion
5. **hypothetical:** theoretical; supposed or imagined   6. **emoticons:** tiny electronic images or punctuation groupings meant to imitate facial expressions and thus to convey emotions   7. **inherently:** by its very nature   8. **subsequently:** afterward

Then we have the Minimalists. Minimalists make their texts short and concise, and they often take longer to respond. They are also notorious[9] for ignoring people, but you would never know this, because you didn't call. This leads us to another bittersweet characteristic of texting: You really don't know if someone has seen your text or not (unless you have Blackberry Messenger; then, your cover is blown).

The next type is the Stage Five Clinger, who will constantly blow up your phone wanting to know what you're doing, where you're going, and where you live. This texter sometimes sends text after text, even when you're not responding. Creepy.

A less creepy yet still consistent type of texter is the Text-a-holic. They are constantly texting, and they experience separation anxiety[10] when away from their phones.

The use of texting to get acquainted with someone is really just a small portion of humanity's increasing problem of becoming socially inept.[11] I said socially inept, not social-networking inept, as in not being able to communicate with someone face to face. The next time you meet someone and get that warm and fuzzy feeling in your tummy, break through the technological barricade[12] and get to know the person in person. And, please refrain[13] from sending the emoticon with hearts for its eyes.

REFLECT: Do you plan to take any of Hultgren's advice? Why or why not?

SUMMARIZE AND RESPOND

In your reading journal or elsewhere, summarize the main point of "Pick Up the Phone to Call, Not Text." Then, go back over the essay and check off the support for this idea. Next, write a brief summary of the essay. Finally, write a brief response to the reading. Did Hultgren's essay change your view of texting in any way? If so, how?

CHECK YOUR COMPREHENSION

1. An alternate title for this essay could be
   a. "Talking over the Phone Is a Better Way to Communicate Than Texting."
   b. "To Really Get to Know Someone, Meet in Person Instead of Texting."
   c. ~~"People Who Call Instead of Text Are More Successful in Dating."~~
   d. ~~"The More Texts You Send Each Day, the More You Will Annoy Others."~~

---

9. **notorious:** well known   10. **separation anxiety:** emotional upset caused by being separated from someone or something   11. **inept:** clumsy or lacking in skill   12. **barricade:** barrier   13. **refrain:** to resist a temptation; to avoid doing something

2. The main point of the essay is that
   a. before the days of texting, people had more successful personal relationships.
   b. people are becoming more and more socially inept.
   c. people are more likely to be dishonest in text messages than in person.
   d. if you really want to get to know someone, meet him or her face to face.

3. What is one characteristic of Minimalists?
   a. They respond quickly but with few words.
   b. They text only once or twice a day.
   c. They may ignore texts sent to them.
   d. They carry a phone but few other gadgets.

4. Does this essay include the Four Basics of Good Classification? Why or why not?

5. Look back at the vocabulary you underlined, and write sentences using these words: *scrutinized* (para. 3); *hypothetical* (4); *inherently* (5); *notorious* (8); *inept* (11).

TIP For tools to build your vocabulary, visit the *Student Site for Real Writing* at bedfordstmartins.com/realwriting.

READ CRITICALLY

1. Hultgren begins her essay with a quotation from a hypothetical texter. What might be the reasons for starting the essay this way? What other approaches might have been used?

2. In paragraph 3, Hultgren writes, "People, especially we college students, rely on texting to get to know someone." Do you agree or disagree with this statement? Give examples from your own experiences to support your answer.

3. Is there any way in which you would revise the categories of texters as presented by Hultgren? What other categories might you add?

4. In paragraph 11, Hultgren says that an overreliance on texting in personal relationships "is really just a small portion of humanity's increasing problem of becoming socially inept." Do you agree with this statement? Why or why not?

5. Hultgren refers to situations in which it is better to call someone and meet him or her in person rather than sending a text. Are there any situations in which you think it is better to text instead of call or meet face to face? Provide examples of these situations.

WRITE

WRITE A PARAGRAPH: Write a paragraph that describes one type of behavior that you find either annoying or admirable. Give specific examples of actions that fit into this category.

WRITE AN ESSAY: Think of a group of people (such as students, drivers, or shoppers) who might be categorized according to their varying behaviors, habits, or preferences. Then, using Hultgren's essay as a model, write an essay that breaks the group into categories, giving reasons and examples for your subgroupings.

TIP For a sample classification paragraph, see page 198.

Stephanie Ericsson
The Ways We Lie

Stephanie Ericsson was born in 1953 and raised in San Francisco. She has lived in a variety of places, including New York, Los Angeles, London, Mexico, the Spanish island of Ibiza, and Minnesota, where she currently resides. Ericsson's life took a major turn when her husband died suddenly, when she was two months pregnant. She began a journal to help her cope with the grief and loss, and she later used her writing to help others with similar struggles. An excerpt from her journal appeared in the *Utne Reader,* and her writings were later published in a book entitled *Companion through the Darkness: Inner Dialogues on Grief* (1993). About her book, Ericsson writes, "It belongs to those who have had the blinders ripped from their eyes, who suddenly see the lies of our lives and the truths of existence for what they are."

In "The Ways We Lie," which also appeared in the *Utne Reader* and is taken from her follow-up work, *Companion into the Dawn: Inner Dialogues on Loving* (1994), Ericsson continues her search for truth by examining and classifying our daily lies.

GUIDING QUESTION
As you read this essay, pay attention to the examples Ericsson provides. What examples of lying can you think of from your own experience?

1   The bank called today, and I told them my deposit was in the mail, even though I hadn't written a check yet. It'd been a rough day. The baby I'm pregnant with decided to do aerobics on my lungs for two hours, our three-year-old daughter painted the living-room couch with lipstick, the IRS put me on hold for an hour, and I was late to a business meeting because I was tired.

2   I told my client that the traffic had been bad. When my partner came home, his haggard[1] face told me his day hadn't gone any better than mine, so when he asked, "How was your day?" I said, "Oh, fine," knowing that

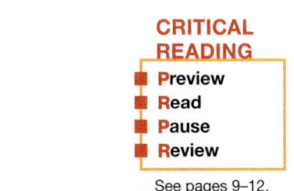

CRITICAL READING
- Preview
- Read
- Pause
- Review

See pages 9–12.

VOCABULARY DEVELOPMENT Certain words in this essay are defined at the bottom of the page. Underline these words as you read them.

---
1. **haggard:** drawn, worn out

IDEA JOURNAL Think of another common human behavior. Break it into categories, and give examples for each category.

IDENTIFY: In the first two paragraphs, the author provides four examples of lies she has told. Put an X by these examples.

REFLECT: Do you agree that there "must be some merit to lying"? Why or why not?

one more straw might break his back. A friend called and wanted to take me to lunch. I said I was busy. Four lies in the course of a day, none of which I felt the least bit guilty about.

3 We lie. We all do. We exaggerate, we minimize,[2] we avoid confrontation,[3] we spare people's feelings, we conveniently forget, we keep secrets, we justify lying to the big-guy institutions. Like most people, I indulge[4] in small falsehoods and still think of myself as an honest person. Sure I lie, but it doesn't hurt anything. Or does it?

4 I once tried going a whole week without telling a lie, and it was paralyzing. I discovered that telling the truth all the time is nearly impossible. It means living with some serious consequences: The bank charges me $60 in overdraft fees, my partner keels[5] over when I tell him about my travails,[6] my client fires me for telling her I didn't feel like being on time, and my friend takes it personally when I say I'm not hungry. There must be some merit to lying.

5 But if I justify lying, what makes me any different from slick politicians or the corporate robbers who raided the S&L industry? Saying it's OK to lie one way and not another is hedging.[7] I cannot seem to escape the voice deep inside me that tells me: When someone lies, someone loses.

6 What far-reaching consequences will I, or others, pay as a result of my lie? Will someone's trust be destroyed? Will someone else pay *my* penance[8] because I ducked out? We must consider the *meaning of our actions*. Deception, lies, capital crimes, and misdemeanors[9] all carry meanings. *Webster's* definition of *lie* is specific:

1. a false statement or action especially made with the intent to deceive;
2. anything that gives or is meant to give a false impression.

7 A definition like this implies that there are many, many ways to tell a lie. Here are just a few.

The White Lie

8 The white lie assumes that the truth will cause more damage than a simple, harmless untruth. Telling a friend he looks great when he looks like hell can be based on a decision that the friend needs a compliment more than a frank[10] opinion. But, in effect, it is the liar deciding what is best for the lied to. Ultimately, it is a vote of no confidence. It is an act of subtle arrogance[11] for anyone to decide what is best for someone else.

9 Yet not all circumstances are quite so cut and dried. Take, for instance, the sergeant in Vietnam who knew one of his men was killed in action but listed him as missing so that the man's family would receive

---

2. **minimize:** to reduce   3. **confrontation:** an argumentative meeting
4. **indulge:** to become involved in   5. **keels:** falls over   6. **travails:** painful efforts; tribulations   7. **hedging:** avoiding the question   8. **penance:** a penalty to make up for an action   9. **misdemeanors:** minor violations of rules   10. **frank:** honest; direct   11. **arrogance:** belief in one's superiority

indefinite compensation instead of the lump-sum pittance[12] the military gives widows and children. His intent was honorable. Yet for twenty years this family kept their hopes alive, unable to move on to a new life.

Facades

We all put up facades[13] to one degree or another. When I put on a suit to go to see a client, I feel as though I am putting on another face, obeying the expectation that serious businesspeople wear suits rather than sweatpants. But I'm a writer. Normally, I get up, get the kid off to school, and sit at my computer in my pajamas until four in the afternoon. When I answer the phone, the caller thinks I'm wearing a suit (although the UPS man knows better).

But facades can be destructive because they are used to seduce others into an illusion. For instance, I recently realized that a former friend was a liar. He presented himself with all the right looks and the right words and offered lots of new consciousness theories, fabulous books to read, and fascinating insights. Then I did some business with him, and the time came for him to pay me. He turned out to be all talk and no walk. I heard a plethora[14] of reasonable excuses, including in-depth descriptions of the big break around the corner. In six months of work, I saw less than a hundred bucks. When I confronted him, he raised both eyebrows and tried to convince me that I'd heard him wrong, that he'd made no commitment to me. A simple investigation into his past revealed a crowded graveyard of disenchanted former friends.

Ignoring the Plain Facts

In the sixties, the Catholic Church in Massachusetts began hearing complaints that Father James Porter was sexually molesting children. Rather than relieving him of his duties, the ecclesiastical[15] authorities simply moved him from one parish to another between 1960 and 1967, actually providing him with a fresh supply of unsuspecting families and innocent children to abuse. After treatment in 1967 for pedophilia,[16] he went back to work, this time in Minnesota. The new diocese[17] was aware of Father Porter's obsession with children, but they needed priests and recklessly believed treatment had cured him. More children were abused until he was relieved of his duties a year later. By his own admission, Porter may have abused as many as a hundred children.

Ignoring the facts may not in and of itself be a form of lying, but consider the context[18] of this situation. If a lie is *a false action done with the intent to deceive,* then the Catholic Church's conscious covering for Porter created irreparable consequences. The church became a coperpetrator[19] with Porter.

10

11 **IDENTIFY:** Underline the main point of this paragraph. What example does Ericsson use to support it?

12 **SUMMARIZE:** In your own words, summarize the example in this paragraph in one or two sentences.

13

---

12. **pittance:** a small amount   13. **facades:** masks   14. **plethora:** excess
15. **ecclesiastical:** relating to a church   16. **pedophilia:** sexual abuse of children
17. **diocese:** a district or churches under the guidance of a bishop   18. **context:** a surrounding situation   19. **coperpetrator:** the helper of a person who commits an action

Stereotypes and Clichés

Stereotype and cliché serve a purpose as a form of shorthand. Our need for vast amounts of information in nanoseconds[20] has made the stereotype vital to modern communication. Unfortunately, it often shuts down original thinking, giving those hungry for truth a candy bar of misinformation instead of a balanced meal. The stereotype explains a situation with just enough truth to seem unquestionable.

All the *isms*—racism, sexism, ageism, et al.—are founded on and fueled by the stereotype and the cliché, which are lies of exaggeration, omission, and ignorance. They are always dangerous. They take a single tree and make it a landscape. They destroy curiosity. They close minds and separate people. The single mother on welfare is assumed to be cheating. Any black male could tell you how much of his identity is obliterated[21] daily by stereotypes. Fat people, ugly people, beautiful people, old people, large-breasted women, short men, the mentally ill, and the homeless all could tell you how much more they are like us than we want to think. I once admitted to a group of people that I had a mouth like a truck driver. Much to my surprise, a man stood up and said, "I'm a truck driver, and I never cuss." Needless to say, I was humbled.

Out-and-Out Lies

Of all the ways to lie, I like this one the best, probably because I get tired of trying to figure out the real meanings behind things. At least I can trust the bald-faced lie. I once asked my five-year-old nephew, "Who broke the fence?" (I had seen him do it.) He answered, "The murderers." Who could argue?

At least when this sort of lie is told it can be easily confronted. As the person who is lied to, I know where I stand. The bald-faced lie doesn't toy with my perceptions—it argues with them. It doesn't try to refashion reality; it tries to refute[22] it. *Read my lips* . . . No sleight[23] of hand. No guessing. If this were the only form of lying, there would be no such thing as floating anxiety or the adult-children of alcoholics movement.

These are only a few of the ways we lie. Or are lied to. As I said earlier, it's not easy to entirely eliminate lies from our lives. No matter how pious[24] we may try to be, we will still embellish,[25] hedge, and omit to lubricate the daily machinery of living. But there is a world of difference between telling functional lies and living a lie. Martin Buber once said, "The lie is the spirit committing treason against itself." Our acceptance of lies becomes a cultural cancer that eventually shrouds[26] and reorders reality until moral garbage becomes as invisible to us as water is to a fish.

How much do we tolerate before we become sick and tired of being sick and tired? When will we stand up and declare our *right* to trust? When do we stop accepting that the real truth is in the fine print? Whose lips do we read this year when we vote for president? When will we stop being so

---

20. nanoseconds: billionths of a second   **21. obliterated:** wiped out   **22. refute:** to deny   **23. sleight:** a skillful trick   **24. pious:** religious   **25. embellish:** to decorate   **26. shrouds:** covers, conceals

---

PREDICT: Pause just as you start the "Out-and-Out Lies" section. How do you think Ericsson might define such lies?

REFLECT: Think back on your answer to the question on page 662 about whether lying ever has any merit. Have your views on this issue changed? Why or why not?

reticent[27] about making judgments? When do we stop turning over our personal power and responsibility to liars?

Maybe if I don't tell the bank the check's in the mail I'll be less toler- 20 ant of the lies told to me every day. A country song I once heard said it all for me: "You've got to stand for something or you'll fall for anything."

SUMMARIZE AND RESPOND

In your reading journal or elsewhere, summarize the main point of "The Ways We Lie." Then, go back over the essay, and check off the support for this idea. Next, write a brief summary of the essay. Finally, write a brief response to the reading. What did it make you think about or feel? Do you agree with Ericsson's claim that we all tell lies every day? Provide examples from your own experience that support your answer.

CHECK YOUR COMPREHENSION

1. An alternate title for this essay could be
   a. "Lying Never Hurt Anyone."
   b. "The Check's in the Mail: The Greatest Lie of All."
   c. "Justification for Lying."
   d. "Lies in Our Lives."

2. The main point of this essay is that
   a. small lies are OK because everyone lies.
   b. we should reevaluate the role that lies play in our lives.
   c. lies told by someone you trust are the worst kind of lies.
   d. to trust and be trusted, we must refuse to lie.

3. What distinction does Ericsson make between telling a functional lie and living a lie?
   a. Telling a functional lie makes someone feel bad, and living a lie cheats big institutions.
   b. Telling a functional lie is relatively harmless, but living a lie can have serious consequences.
   c. Telling a functional lie has no merit, and living a lie is a good idea.
   d. Telling a functional lie is honest, and living a lie is dishonest.

4. Look back at the vocabulary you underlined, and write sentences using these words: *confrontation* (para. 3); *penance* (6); *obliterated* (15); *embellish* (18); *reticent* (19).

27. **reticent:** reserved; silent; reluctant

READ CRITICALLY

1. Describe Ericsson's tone in this essay. For example, what is her tone in paragraph 1 when she tells us that "the baby I'm pregnant with decided to do aerobics on my lungs for two hours"?

2. How does Ericsson organize her essay? How does she classify the ways we tell lies?

3. What images does Ericsson associate with telling lies? Select one that you like, and explain why.

4. What is Ericsson's attitude toward lying? What examples in the essay support your answer?

5. In paragraph 16, Ericsson writes, "At least I can trust the bald-faced lie." What do you think she means by trusting a lie?

WRITE

WRITE A PARAGRAPH: Write a paragraph that describes another category of lies. Be sure to provide examples for your readers.

WRITE AN ESSAY: Write an essay that continues Ericsson's classification of the ways we lie. Provide detailed examples from your experiences—or the experiences of people you know—for at least two of the categories she provides. Develop two new categories of your own. Feel free to include the ideas you wrote about in your reading journal for Summarize and Respond.

44

Definition

Each essay in this chapter uses definition to get its main point across to the reader. As you read these essays, consider how they achieve the Four Basics of Good Definition that are listed below and discussed in Chapter 13 of this book.

Four Basics of Good Definition

1. It tells readers what is being defined.
2. It presents a clear definition.
3. It uses examples to show what the writer means.
4. It gives details to support the examples.

John Around Him

Free Money

John Around Him grew up on a reservation in South Dakota. He wrote the following essay for a writing class he took when he was a student at Bunker Hill Community College (BHCC) in Boston. Before enrolling at BHCC, John had served as a Marine in Iraq, so he qualified for financial aid. In 2008, he transferred from BHCC to Dartmouth College, from which he graduated in 2012. As a writer, Around Him is interested in education and Native American issues, and he plans to pursue a career in education, which he knows will require a lot of writing. Before beginning an essay, he says that he

667

often looks to his friends as a sounding board for his ideas and potential topics because "they give a different window in which to see my ideas." When offering advice to fellow student writers, Around Him writes, "Through writing you may discover who you are, so have fun while doing it."

GUIDING QUESTION
How does a student get financial aid for college?

CRITICAL READING
- Preview
- Read
- Pause
- Review

See pages 9–12.

VOCABULARY DEVELOPMENT Certain words in this essay are defined at the bottom of the page. Underline these words as you read them.

IDEA JOURNAL Have you ever received something for free?

PREDICT: What do you think the essay will be about?

IDENTIFY: Underline the eligibility criteria.

1   **F**ree money: The words almost take your breath away. For the average college student, the idea is especially appealing. The weight of college tuition, in combination with the cost of food, rent, and other living expenses, makes the climb toward educational success appear almost impossible. However, assistance in the form of financial aid is available to help lighten the load.

2   Financial aid is money to help pay for college tuition or other expenses while going to college. Financial aid comes in an array[1] of programs, from federal and state funding to scholarships. Federal financial aid is the source most students use. It is available in the form of grants, student loans, and the Federal Work-Study Program. A grant really is free money, while a student loan has to be repaid when a student either completes college or stops going. The Federal Work-Study Program allows students to earn money while attending college. In 2008, the budget for Federal Pell Grants was about $15 billion. In that same year, the student loan budget was $72.8 billion, and the work-study program's budget was $980 million.

3   To apply for federal financial aid, students must fill out the Free Application for Federal Student Aid (FAFSA), available at your college's financial aid office or online (Google FAFSA). In order to receive aid, a student must meet the following criteria:[2] be a U.S. citizen or eligible non-citizen of the United States with a valid social security number; have a high school diploma or have passed the General Education Development (GED) test; and be enrolled in a degree program, taking a minimum of six credits. Men between the ages of eighteen and twenty-six must have registered in the selective service.[3]

4   Using the information provided in the FAFSA, the federal government calculates each applicant's Expected Family Contribution (EFC). The EFC is calculated with a formula based on the student's income or, if the student is a dependent,[4] the family's income and assets.[5] For students who are dependents but do not receive financial support from their parents, the EFC can be a problem because counting family income might

---

1. array: a large range of a particular kind of thing   **2. criteria:** standards by which something is judged or decided   **3. selective service:** a system that requires all men between the ages of eighteen and twenty-six to register so that the federal government has information available about potential soldiers in case of war   **4. dependent:** a person who relies on someone for money or other support   **5. assets:** total financial resources, such as cash and property

make the student ineligible. However, that is the formula. Other factors[6] include the number of family members in the household and number of family members in college. Last year, I applied for financial aid but did not qualify because, according to the financial aid office at my college, I made too much money. Nevertheless, I will continue to apply for financial aid.

Students should always apply for financial aid, but many do not. Much of the money available is not used because students do not know about it or fill out the proper forms. Looking around and going to your college's financial aid office is worth the time required because there really is free money. For example, there are scholarships for health-care programs, for business programs, for graduate programs, to name just a few. My goal is to finish my two-year degree and transfer to a four-year college. In order to do this, I need to have a plan and prepare myself by researching schools to find out which ones are suitable for me. Then, I can find out what courses I need to take to graduate and to transfer with as many credits as possible. I won't do this alone: I will take advantage of the various services available at my college, including meeting with my adviser. I will apply to many sources of financial aid, because getting my degree will be very expensive.

5 **REFLECT:** Have you visited your college's financial aid office?

Clearly, the price tag for higher education is very high, and most students cannot afford it without assistance. I know that the money is available, and some of it is free. However, as the saying goes, "Nothing in life is free," and that means that getting what I need requires effort. It is my responsibility to work hard to find that money, along with working hard to get good grades.

6 **REFLECT:** What services does your college offer?

SUMMARIZE AND RESPOND

In your reading journal or elsewhere, summarize the main point of "Free Money." Then, go back over the essay, and check off the support for this idea. Next, write a brief summary of the essay. Finally, write a brief response to the reading. Do you think federal and state governments do enough to help college students financially?

CHECK YOUR COMPREHENSION

1. An alternate title for this essay could be
    a. "Nothing in Life Is Free."
    b. "Wealthy Students Should Not Receive Financial Aid."
    c. "Students Need to Learn to Save Money."
    d. "Students Should Take Advantage of Financial Aid."

---

6. factors: elements that contribute to a process, a result, or an accomplishment

2. The main point of this essay is that
    a. many financial resources are available to students.
    b. the federal government should increase aid to college students.
    c. the selective service is a requirement for financial aid.
    d. students should be less financially dependent on their families.

3. In the past, the writer was denied financial aid for college because
    a. he had not registered for selective service.
    b. he was not a U.S. citizen.
    c. he made too much money.
    d. he missed the deadline for applying.

4. Does this essay include the Four Basics of Good Definition? Why or why not?

5. Look back at the vocabulary you underlined, and write sentences using these words: *array* (para. 2); *criteria* (3); *dependent, assets, factors* (4).

TIP For tools to build your vocabulary, visit the *Student Site for Real Writing* at **bedfordstmartins.com/realwriting**.

READ CRITICALLY

1. What do you think Around Him wants his readers to do with the information in this essay?

2. In paragraph 1, the writer says that college tuition and expenses can make getting an education "appear almost impossible." Do you agree, and do you think higher education is too expensive?

3. Around Him lists and explains the requirements students must meet to receive federal or state financial aid. Do these requirements seem reasonable? Why or why not?

4. Do you think it is fair that some students are ineligible for financial aid because their parents have too much money?

5. Although this essay encourages students to seek financial support, how does it also suggest that they take responsibility for their education?

WRITE

TIP For a sample definition paragraph, see page 216.

WRITE A PARAGRAPH: Around Him refers to the saying "Nothing in life is free." Write a paragraph that either supports this saying or argues against it. You may draw on a personal experience to make your point.

WRITE AN ESSAY: Around Him argues that students "should always apply for financial aid." Who do you think should receive "free money" to go to college? In an essay, define the kinds of students who should receive the most financial assistance for college expenses.

Michael Thompson
Passage into Manhood

Michael Thompson is a consultant, child psychologist, and author. His 1999 book *Raising Cain: Protecting the Emotional Life of Boys* (1999), cowritten with Dan Kindlon, was the inspiration for a PBS documentary of the same name. Both the book and the documentary, which was hosted by Thompson, explore boys' emotional development and the negative consequences of common misunderstandings about them. Thompson's other books include *Speaking of Boys: Answers to the Most-Asked Questions about Raising Sons* (2000), *Mom, They're Teasing Me: Helping Your Child Solve Social Problems* (2002), *The Pressured Child: Helping Your Child Achieve Success in School and in Life* (with Teresa Barker, 2004), and *It's a Boy! Your Son's Development from Birth to Age 18* (2008).

In "Passage into Manhood," which appeared in the *Boston Globe* in 2005, Thompson gets one young man's definition of manhood, raising questions about what our society does—and, more important, does not do—to prepare boys to become men.

GUIDING QUESTION
What is necessary for the passage into manhood, according to the author?

1 The boy sitting next to me on the plane from Toronto to North Bay was seventeen years old, a rising high school senior with a slight beard. He had the misfortune[1] to sit next to a child psychologist, a so-called expert on boys, who would pester him with questions for the entire trip about how he was spending his summer, and why. "This is kind of like a final exam," he observed, trying to get me to relent,[2] but I wouldn't let go.

2 After he had gamely[3] answered a number of my questions about the summer camp to which he was headed, I sprang the big one on him, the question I have asked many boys his age. "Do you consider yourself to be a man?"

3 "Yes," he replied immediately. Then he caught himself, hesitating momentarily before declaring with conviction:[4] "Well, no. But I will be in August!"

4 What could a seventeen-year-old boy do between the last week of June and August that he could anticipate[5] would make him a man? American culture doesn't have any universal ritual[6] that sees a boy through that psychologically difficult passage from boyhood to manhood. Many boys, actually, almost every boy, struggles with what it means to become a man. Boys (or young men, if you prefer) of seventeen, nineteen, and into their early twenties wrestle with the riddle: What test do I have to pass to become a man, and who will be able to recognize that I have reached that point? My young companion thought he had found an answer.

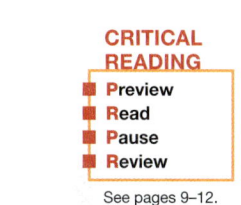

VOCABULARY DEVELOPMENT Certain words in this essay are defined at the bottom of the page. Underline these words as you read them.

REFLECT: In paragraph 3, why do you suppose the boy answered "yes" and then changed his mind?

IDEA JOURNAL Write about a personal experience that you believe marked a passage from youth to adulthood. What happened, and how did the experience change you?

---

1. **misfortune:** bad luck   2. **relent:** to give up; to stop   3. **gamely:** enthusiastically   4. **conviction:** a strong belief or feeling   5. **anticipate:** to expect   6. **ritual:** a ceremony or rite of passage

IDENTIFY: Paragraph 5 provides several examples. Check off the experiences that the boy expects to have.

IDENTIFY: In paragraphs 6 and 7, underline the boy's definitions of manhood.

SUMMARIZE: In a sentence or two (in your own words), sum up the point that the author makes in paragraph 10.

5   It turned out that he was going to embark[7] the next morning on a fifty-day canoeing trip that would take him and nine companions through lakes, rivers, rapids, mud, and ferocious[8] mosquitoes, all the way up to Hudson's Bay, a distance of six hundred miles. He and his friends had been preparing for this by developing wilderness skills for the last four years at their camp. They would carry all of their own food, they would take risks, and they would suffer. Toward the end of their journey they would see the Northern lights[9] and would visit an Inuit[10] settlement. They might see moose and wolves, but, he told me, they were not going to be tourists. "This isn't about seeing wild animals," he asserted.

6   What was his definition of manhood? "It's taking responsibility," he said. "At the end of the day, it's taking responsibility and taking things you've learned from others and creating your own self."

7   "It's about finishing a grueling portage,"[11] he said. "It's about doing work and getting a result."

8   Didn't he get that from school and varsity athletics? No. Though he did well in school and had bright college prospects, school didn't address his hunger to be a man, not even playing sports. "After sports you go home, take a shower, and watch TV." When he was canoe tripping, he felt as if he made a sustained[12] effort that connected him to all the men who had canoed before him at that camp for more than one hundred years.

9   Could he find the experience he sought among his friends back home? What were they doing this summer? "Hanging out. They're playing video games," he said. They didn't get it. "It's frustrating. You try to explain to them how great it is. You tell them about paddling all day, and cooking your own food, about the mosquitoes, and carrying a wood canoe, and they say, 'What, are you crazy?'"

10   This young about-to-be man described his father as a "good guy," his mother as a hardworking professional, and his step-father as financially successful, but none of them seemed to hold the key to helping him become a man. American culture has no universal ritual for helping boys move from boyhood to manhood. Jewish boys have their bar mitzvahs,[13] Mormon boys have their year of missionary service, other boys sign up for the military. Yet every boy yearns[14] to be a man, and traditional societies always took boys away from their parents to pass an initiation rite. We no longer have such rituals, but boys still wonder: What is the test, where do I find it, how do I pass it, and who will recognize that moment when I pass from boyhood to manhood? We fail to provide a meaningful, challenging path that speaks to the souls of a majority of boys.

11   The key to his manhood lay with the counselors who accompany him on the journey and with his companions whose lives he would protect and who would, in turn, look out for him. Past the rain, the bugs, the smelling

---

7. **embark:** to go on board; to make a start
8. **ferocious:** fierce; menacing
9. **Northern lights:** a colorful display of lights in the sky, caused by solar winds
10. **Inuit:** a native people of North America
11. **grueling portage:** a difficult journey that requires the carrying of supplies
12. **sustained:** continuous; ongoing
13. **bar mitzvahs:** ceremonies marking Jewish boys' thirteenth birthdays and the beginning of their religious responsibilities
14. **yearns:** wants, desires

bad, he would discover his manhood in community and in the kind of challenge that only nature offers up.

Our plane journey over, I wished him luck. And then I couldn't get our conversation out of my mind. While a demanding canoe trip is not for every boy, I'm certain that every boy is searching for a test. You can find the test by taking on anything that requires commitment and courage. However, there is something that happens out-of-doors that strips you down to the essentials: safety, companionship, a shared sense of mission. You set aside the busyness and crap of daily life, and then you can think about what it actually means to be a man.

SUMMARIZE AND RESPOND

In your reading journal or elsewhere, summarize the main point of "Passage into Manhood." Then, go back over the essay, and check off support for this idea. Next, write a brief summary of the essay. Finally, write a brief response to the reading. Do you agree with the author about what is needed for boys to make the passage into manhood?

CHECK YOUR COMPREHENSION

1. An alternate title for this essay could be
   a. "American Boys Overwhelmed by Adult Responsibilities."
   b. "One Teen's Story of His Passage into Manhood."
   c. "The Path to Manhood: A Difficult Journey for Most Boys."
   d. "American Boys Need a Meaningful Path to Manhood."

2. The main point of this essay is that
   a. undergoing a wilderness challenge is the only real way to become a man.
   b. young men should be able to define for themselves what it means to be a man, even if most people would disagree.
   c. going through a significant ritual or test makes boys feel like men, but American culture fails to provide such paths.
   d. American boys should be given a bar mitzvah or be required to perform missionary service.

3. What challenge was the boy Thompson spoke with about to take on?
   a. A boating competition
   b. A fifty-day canoeing trip
   c. A hiking and biking tour
   d. A Canadian triathalon

4. Look back at the vocabulary you underlined, and write sentences using the following words: *relent* (para. 1); *conviction* (3); *anticipate* (4); *sustained* (8); *yearns* (10).

READ CRITICALLY

1. In paragraph 2, the author asks the boy what he considers to be a "big" question: Does the boy consider himself to be a man? Why does the author consider it to be a big question, and do you agree? Why or why not?

2. How do you define manhood or womanhood? How is your definition similar to or different from that provided by the boy Thompson speaks to?

3. In paragraph 10, Thompson argues, "We fail to provide a meaningful, challenging path [to adulthood] that speaks to the souls of a majority of boys." Do you agree? Why or why not? What other possible paths to manhood are not mentioned by Thompson?

4. Why, according to Thompson, are outdoor challenges especially useful for boys making the passage toward manhood? Do you share his view?

5. Why do you suppose Thompson is interested in the opinions of one young person he meets on a plane? How do the quotations from the boy contribute to the point of Thompson's essay?

WRITE

WRITE A PARAGRAPH: Write a paragraph that gives at least two pieces of advice to a boy who is about to become a man or to a girl who is about to become a woman. The person could be a brother or sister, a son or daughter, or a friend. Or you could imagine a boy or girl to address the advice to. Be sure to explain why each piece of advice is important, and give examples to show what you mean.

WRITE AN ESSAY: Write an essay that defines what it is to be a man or a woman. Use examples from your personal experience to help define the concept. If you answered question 2 under Read Critically, you might want to use some of the insights from that question to develop your essay. Explain why you think Thompson, or the boy he interviewed, might agree or disagree with your definition.

45

Comparison and Contrast

Each essay in this chapter uses comparison and contrast to get its main point across to the reader. As you read these essays, consider how they achieve the Four Basics of Good Comparison and Contrast that are listed below and discussed in Chapter 14 of this book.

Four Basics of Good Comparison and Contrast

1. It uses subjects that have enough in common to be compared/contrasted in a useful way.
2. It serves a purpose—to help readers make a decision, to help them understand the subjects, or to show your understanding of the subjects.
3. It presents several important, parallel points of comparison/contrast.
4. It arranges points in a logical order.

Courtney Stoker
The Great Debate: Essentialism vs. Dominance

Courtney Stoker wrote the following essay while pursuing an accounting degree at the University of North Carolina at Pembroke, where she was a member of the Sigma Alpha Pi and Alpha Chi honor societies and a university marshal. She also served as vice president of the Accounting Students Association and as secretary of the Honors Council, and she was a member of the student chapter of the Society of Human Resource Management.

This essay was published in *ReVisions: Best Student Essays of the University of North Carolina at Pembroke*. In it, Stoker examines researchers' claims about the differing communication styles of men and women, and she comes to some thoughtful conclusions.

GUIDING QUESTION
What perceived differences between men and women are behind the "great debate"?

In an episode of the popular television show *Friends*, Rachel kisses Ross and then they each go home and tell their friends about their experience. Rachel's girlfriends, Phoebe and Monica, get very excited and have to get out the wine and unplug the phone before she tells the story so that they do not miss any details. They giggle and clap as they ask all sorts of questions like where his hands were and what kind of kiss it was. On the other hand, Ross simply tells his friends, Chandler and Joey, that he kissed her. The boys do not even stop eating to hear about the kiss, and the only question they have is whether or not tongue was involved ("Difference Between Men and Women"). Clearly, this episode demonstrates and exaggerates the existence of communication differences between men and women recognized by many linguists[1] today. While a pretty solid consensus[2] exists among scholars and the general public that differences in communication purposes and styles exist, the conflict lies in why these differences are present.

There are two prominent[3] explanations available for the discrepancies[4] in communication between the sexes—the essentialism theory and the dominance theory. Essentialism is the original theory and found strength in the 1950s and 1960s as feminists began to embrace and celebrate the qualities of a female. According to the essentialism school of thought, women and men are innately[5] different, and women are more polite and nurturing[6] from birth because they are women (Bucholtz 416). According to the essentialist school of thought, Rachel is giddy[7] because she is a woman, and it is part of her natural instincts to react in that way. Furthermore, Dr. Louann Brizendine, a professor of neuropsychiatry,[8] would attribute[9] Rachel's and her girlfriends' chatty[10] tendencies to a rush of oxytocin—a hormone related to emotions—which women presumably[11] get while gossiping (Solomon). In essence, the essentialism theory claims that by exhibiting differences in communication, men and women are simply conveying their natural selves.

As time progressed, many found the essentialism theory to be too limited in defining gender; thus, the dominance theory was born. According to the dominance theory, the differences in communication between the sexes are a learned behavior that can be blamed on men's historical dominance in society over women. According to the dominance theory, a woman is polite and does not say much because she fears punishment

---

1. **linguists:** those who study language or its use 2. **consensus:** general agreement
3. **prominent:** leading; well-known 4. **discrepancies:** differences; inconsistencies
5. **innately:** by nature 6. **nurturing:** supportive; protective; motherly 7. **giddy:** dizzy with joy 8. **neuropsychiatry:** a field of psychiatry that considers neurological (nervous system) factors behind mental states and disorders 9. **attribute:** to assign
10. **chatty:** talkative 11. **presumably:** probably; likely

for overstepping her bounds in society. In Rachel's case, the dominance theory would suggest that she was simply living up to the giddy, gabby[12] girl that society would want a woman to be and that Ross was simply being the cool guy who is only concerned about the sexual aspect of their relationship because society has defined men as unemotional creatures. But dominance theory fails to explain why women continue to communicate differently than men among a group of all females; it would seem that in the absence of sexual diversity, there would be no subservient[13] group that would feel the need to live up to stereotypes. While it is easy to simply take a side in the great debate, the fact is that neither side has enough empirical[14] data or an effective way of measuring the data to be declared victorious.

Two major figures in the debate of essentialism and dominance are essentialist theorist[15] Deborah Tannen and dominance theorist Deborah Cameron. According to Tannen, men communicate to solve problems, whereas women communicate to establish emotional connections. Additionally, women find intimacy through conversation, and men find it through actions. Tannen claims a man's need to solve problems leads to disputes because a woman feels her heterosexual mate does not understand her problems or is belittling[16] them by constantly offering solutions while the woman is actually seeking support (Kelly and Cotter). This theory gained popularity because it is relatable to everyday life. For example, when my mother complained to my father about being worn out and tired after a long day at work, he suggested she start taking a multivitamin in order to keep her energy up. My mother became annoyed because she felt that my father's suggestion of a multivitamin was belittling her stress and partly blaming her for not taking better care of her body; additionally, he had failed to give her the emotional recognition and understanding she craved. On the other hand, my father was upset that my mother did not appreciate his helpful advice. My parents' misunderstanding is a typical case of a communication problem between men and women. Essentialists would argue that we must learn about these innate differences so that men and women can better understand one another.

Both essentialists and dominance theorists recognize a woman's tendency to be suggestive[17] and indirect with language. This claim may be finding some validity[18] today with many studies claiming that women use language more indirectly by making suggestions rather than giving orders. On the other hand, these studies claim that men are more likely to bark out orders, clearly conveying their wants. This use of suggestions versus orders can often leave men confused as to what women actually mean or want, and women are left annoyed that men are not more perceptive.[19] Many women feel that if their mate truly loves and cares about them, then they will be able to know what they want and understand exactly what

5 **SUMMARIZE:** In your own words, summarize the start of this paragraph (up to the story of Amanda and Christopher).

---

12. **gabby:** talkative   13. **subservient:** submissive or subordinate to others; in a serving position rather than a leading one   14. **empirical:** based on experiments or close observation   15. **theorist:** one who develops or applies theories
16. **belittling:** insulting; talking down to   17. **suggestive:** hinting at or subtly suggesting something instead of stating it directly   18. **validity:** acceptance based on reason   19. **perceptive:** insightful; understanding

they are thinking without clear verbalization[20] (Cotter and Kelly). For example, my friend Amanda told her boyfriend of nine months, Christopher, that she did not want to celebrate Valentine's Day because it was a "greeting card company holiday." When February fourteenth rolled around, Amanda got exactly what she asked for—nothing, not even a card. Enraged, Amanda called me to vent[21] about how unloving, unromantic, and emotionally handicapped Christopher was. In Christopher's eyes when Amanda said "no Valentine's Day," she meant no Valentine's Day. But what Amanda actually meant was "I want you to think that I do not want anything, but I really do care about Valentine's Day, and no matter what I say, you should get me something because you love me, and on top of that you should know me well enough to know that deep down I really do care about Valentine's Day." Clearly it is easy to understand why Christopher would be confused. According to essentialist thinkers, Amanda and Christopher need to learn about and accept their communication differences in order to communicate more effectively. To them, Amanda cannot help that she wants Christopher to be able to read between the lines and do exactly what she wants even if she does not verbalize it. However, according to dominance theorists, Amanda and Christopher need to stop living up to the stereotypes set for them by society and openly communicate. Amanda need not fear seeming clingy and needy by wanting a Valentine's Day gift. It is easy to see both sides of the debate and how they play a role in everyday relationship and communication problems.

IDENTIFY: Underline the main point of paragraph 6.

6   The main problem with the essentialist school of thought is that it is outdated and even insulting in today's world. Essentialism taken to the extreme would define both men and women as having the ability to hold only certain roles or occupations in our society. Clearly, this is not the case today with male nurses, Nancy Pelosi[22] as the speaker of the House, Sarah Palin[23] running for vice president, men being stay-at-home dads, women working as CEOs, etc. Our society is redefining the gender roles and stereotypes that have been in place for hundreds of years. According to dominance theorists, women were put into their subservient and nurturing roles because of a lack of birth control; in the past, prior to effective contraceptives, a woman could have been pregnant as many as fifteen or twenty times in a lifetime. Thus, a woman was easily forced into the nurturing role, but, as birth control developed and women's rights emerged, women were able to begin to redefine themselves as more than the baby-making machines of society (Solomon). The possibilities for women and men are not defined merely by their gender, and for that reason their language cannot be either. Many of the opponents of essentialism feel that essentialism as a school of thought boxes the genders into stereotypical roles, actions, and ways of communicating that cannot be condoned[24] in today's "equal opportunity" society.

20. **verbalization:** the use of words   21. **vent:** to express feelings; to complain
22. **Nancy Pelosi:** minority leader of the U.S. House of Representatives; from 2007 to 2011, speaker of the House   23. **Sarah Palin:** former Alaska governor who was the Republican nominee for vice president during the 2008 U.S. presidential race
24. **condoned:** allowed; approved of

Cameron blatantly[25] condemns the work of Tannen and other "self help" authors as being nothing more than a string of fallacies[26] and stereotypes taken as scientific fact. While condemning the work of others, Cameron argues that the issue of gender and language is so complex that it cannot be correctly analyzed or studied without isolating all of the factors besides gender that may affect language, an obviously impossible task to accomplish (Cameron 578–80). While Cameron still maintains that language differences are created by society, she seems to admit that the research is still impossible. Furthermore, Cameron attacks scientists and intellectuals who blindly quote the trumped-up[27] data from self help books in their academic work (578)....

Regarding the differences in communication between men and women, I acknowledge and accept some aspects of both the essentialist school of thought (men and women are simply different in some ways) and the dominance theory (some behaviors and tendencies in men and women become magnified by stereotypes). But I also condemn some aspects of both. In reference to the essentialist school of thought, I do not feel that we are completely predestined[28] or predetermined[29] by gender. Nor do I feel that history and society can be fully blamed for the differences between men and women as presented by the dominance theory. Presently, there is not sufficient evidence to support either side of the debate. I believe the true answer may be some sort of a blend of the two, with some tendencies and habits being more prevalent in men or women at birth and yet others simply the product of the society that we live in and historical injustices. But once again, I do not feel as if there is enough evidence to consciously declare one theory correct. Before any accurate judgments can be made, the field of gender language studies is going to have to be revised to create uniform standards of experimentation. Furthermore, if scientists and linguists are going to apply the results of their studies to the population as a whole, a more accurate representation of society must be represented in the studies. Middle-class white suburbia[30] cannot be used to represent the population as a whole by any account. Studies must include samples from a diverse group of economic, educational, social, religious, cultural, and ethnic groups; by not acknowledging the role of all of these factors, the human experience is being oversimplified. It is irresponsible and impossible to expect accurate and reproducible results while measuring such subjective[31] data in such haphazard[32] and biased ways. While creating the standards for research will address the issue of whether or not differences exist and what exactly they are, it still will not answer the question of why these differences exist. Honestly, we may never be able to confidently and empirically show the root of differences between men and women; the human experience may simply be too complex and multidimensional to pinpoint the cause. However, it is important to continue to look for the answers in determining how and

---

25. blatantly: strongly **26. fallacies:** statements that are false, misleading, or logically unsound **27. trumped-up:** heavily praised or promoted despite faults
28.–29. predestined, predetermined: following a preset, unchangeable course
30. suburbia: the suburbs, collectively **31. subjective:** based on personal opinions or reactions **32. haphazard:** disorganized; careless

why men and women are different so that future generations can communicate more effectively. But for now, in my book, the argument over dominance theory versus essentialism goes down as yet another stalemate[33] taking us back once again to one of the great questions of life: nature or nurture?[34]

Works Cited

Bucholtz, Mary. "Language, Gender, and Sexuality." *Language in the USA: Themes for the Twenty-First Century*. Ed. Edward Finegan and John R. Rickford. Cambridge: Cambridge UP, 2004. 410–29. Print.

Cameron, Deborah. "A Language in Common." *Psychologist* 22.7 (2009): 578–80. *Academic Search Complete*. EBSCO. Web. 24 Feb. 2010.

"Difference between Men and Women." *YouTube*. Web. 31 Mar. 2010.

Kelly, K., and M. Cotter. "In the Name of Domestic Glasnost, Deborah Tannen Tries to Bridge the Linguistic Gap between the Sexes." *People* 34.10 (1990): 133. *Academic Search Complete*. EBSCO. Web. 24 Feb. 2010.

Solomon, Deborah. "Questions for Dr. Louann Brizendine: He Thought, She Thought." *Nytimes.com*. New York Times, 10 Dec. 2006. Web. 30 Mar. 2010.

SUMMARIZE AND RESPOND

In your reading journal or elsewhere, summarize the main point of "Essentialism vs. Dominance." Then, go back over the essay, and check off the support for this idea. Next, write a brief summary of the essay. Finally, write a brief response to the reading. To what extent does your own experience match Stoker's observations? Do you agree with her conclusions about the "great debate"?

CHECK YOUR COMPREHENSION

1. An alternate title for this essay could be
   a. "Better Research Would Prove that Men's and Women's Communication Styles Are More Alike than Different."
   b. "Researchers Will Never Fully Understand Communication Differences between Men and Women."
   c. "Dominance Theory Insults Women and Oversimplifies Their Behavior."
   d. "Better Research Needed to Understand Communication Differences between Men and Women."

---

33. **stalemate:** a situation in which two opposing sides have come to a standstill on an issue or argument   34. **nature or nurture:** the longstanding debate over whether nature (our genetic inheritance) or nurture (how we are raised and under what conditions) plays a greater part in shaping who we are

2. The main point of this essay is that
   a. the dominance theory, although imperfect, is the best and most fair explanation of the communication differences between men and women.
   b. the two main theories about why men and women communicate differently are flawed.
   c. because most behavioral researchers are biased, they should base their findings on numerical data instead of personal observations.
   d. essentialism does a better job than dominance of showing how social factors influence men's and women's communication styles.

3. According to the author, both essentialist and dominance theorists agree that
   a. women can be indirect in their use of language.
   b. women express more understanding of others than men do.
   c. women's use of language is becoming more like men's.
   d. men need to be more understanding of how women communicate.

4. Does this essay include the Four Basics of Good Comparison and Contrast? Why or why not?

5. Look back at the vocabulary you underlined, and write sentences using these words: *consensus* (para. 1); *discrepancies* (2); *subservient* (3); *blatantly* (7); *predestined* (8).

TIP For tools to build your vocabulary, visit the *Student Site for Real Writing* at bedfordstmartins.com/ realwriting.

READ CRITICALLY

1. What do you suppose Stoker wants general readers, as opposed to researchers, to take away from this essay? Specifically, how does she want us to think about the communication differences between women and men, and about what experts have previously said about these differences?

2. In paragraphs 4 and 5, Stoker provides personal examples illustrating communication differences between women and men. Why do you suppose she chose personal stories instead of examples from academic sources?

3. Stoker has applied some of the basics of critical thinking (see p. 7) and of argument (see p. 696). Which basics do you notice, and where? In general, do you think she makes an effective argument? Why or why not?

4. This essay also has elements of cause and effect (see Chapters 15 and 46). Where do you notice these elements, and why do you think the author included them?

5. Stoker cites several sources to support her main point. Think of a question that you still have about her topic. Then, with this question

WRITE

WRITE A PARAGRAPH: Write a paragraph describing another difference in behavior between women and men. Be sure to describe this differing behavior clearly and in detail.

WRITE AN ESSAY: Stoker focuses mainly on differences between women and men. Write an essay on the behavior of men and women in a particular situation (or in various situations), but try not to limit yourself to contrasts; consider similarities as well. Develop a clear thesis that makes a general point about the behavior of women and men, and support this point using specific examples from your own observations and experiences.

TIP For a sample comparison-and-contrast paragraph, see page 237.

Judith Ortiz Cofer
Don't Misread My Signals

Judith Ortiz Cofer is a Puerto Rican author and the Regents' and Franklin Professor of English and Creative Writing at the University of Georgia, where she has taught since 1984. She earned a B.A. in English from Augusta College and an M.A. in English from Florida Atlantic University. In 2007, she was awarded an honorary doctorate in human letters from Lehman University in New York City. Cofer's works span across literary genres, including books of poetry, novels, autobiographical writing, and collections of short stories and essays. Her work has appeared in numerous literary journals, and it is often anthologized and included in textbooks.

GUIDING QUESTION
How do people's assumptions about Cofer, based on her appearance, differ from who she is?

CRITICAL READING
- Preview
- Read
- Pause
- Review

See pages 9–12.

1 On a bus to London from Oxford University, where I was earning some graduate credits one summer, a young man, obviously fresh from a pub, approached my seat. With both hands over his heart, he went down on his knees in the aisle and broke into an Irish tenor's[1] rendition[2] of "Maria"[3] from *West Side Story*.[4] I was not amused. "Maria" had followed me to London, reminding me of a prime fact of my life: You can leave the island of Puerto Rico, master the English language, and travel as far as

---
1. **tenor:** the highest range of the adult male voice   2. **rendition:** a performance
3. **"Maria":** a song from *West Side Story* about one of the main Puerto Rican characters
4. ***West Side Story*:** a 1957 Broadway musical, made into a film in 1961

you can, but if you're a Latina,[5] especially one who so clearly belongs to Rita Moreno's[6] gene pool, the island travels with you.

Growing up in New Jersey and wanting most of all to belong, I lived in two completely different worlds. My parents designed our life as a microcosm[7] of their casas[8] on the island—we spoke Spanish, ate Puerto Rican food bought at the bodega,[9] and practiced strict Catholicism complete with Sunday mass in Spanish.

I was kept under tight surveillance[10] by my parents, since my virtue and modesty were, by their cultural equation, the same as their honor. As teenagers, my friends and I were lectured constantly on how to behave as proper senoritas. But it was a conflicting message we received, since our Puerto Rican mothers also encouraged us to look and act like women by dressing us in clothes our Anglo schoolmates and their mothers found too "mature" and flashy.[11] I often felt humiliated when I appeared at an American friend's birthday party wearing a dress more suitable for a semiformal. At Puerto Rican festivities, neither the music nor the colors we wore could be too loud.

I remember Career Day in high school, when our teachers told us to come dressed as if for a job interview. That morning, I agonized[12] in front of my closet, trying to figure out what a "career girl" would wear, because the only model I had was Marlo Thomas[13] on TV. To me and my Puerto Rican girlfriends, dressing up meant wearing our mothers' ornate[14] jewelry and clothing.

At school that day, the teachers assailed[15] us for wearing "everything at once"—meaning too much jewelry and too many accessories. And it was painfully obvious that the other students in their tailored skirts and silk blouses thought we were hopeless and vulgar.[16] The way they looked at us was a taste of the cultural clash that awaited us in the real world, where prospective[17] employers and men on the street would often misinterpret our tight skirts and bright colors as a come-on.[18]

It is custom, not chromosomes,[19] that leads us to choose scarlet over pale pink. Our mothers had grown up on a tropical island where the natural environment was a riot of primary colors, where showing your skin was one way to keep cool as well as to look sexy. On the island, women felt free to dress and move provocatively[20] since they were protected by the traditions and laws of a Spanish Catholic system of morality and machismo,[21] the main rule of which was, "You may look at my sister, but if

---

5. **Latina:** a female Latin American living in the United States   6. **Rita Moreno:** a Puerto Rican actress who played in *West Side Story*   7. **microcosm:** a world in miniature   8. **casas:** Spanish for "houses"   9. **bodega:** Spanish for "small grocery store"   10. **surveillance:** a watch kept over a person or group of people   11. **flashy:** showy   12. **agonized/worried:** to worry about   13. **Marlo Thomas:** an American actress who played a modern single woman on the television show *That Girl*, which ran from 1966 to 1971   14. **ornate:** decorated with complex patterns   15. **assailed:** attacked   16. **vulgar:** common; crude; lacking in good taste   17. **prospective:** likely to become; expected   18. **come-on:** flirting   19. **chromosomes:** material that carries genes or biological traits from parent to child   20. **provocatively:** in a way that causes a response or calls forth feelings, thoughts, or actions   21. **machismo:** a strong or exaggerated sense of manliness or power

you touch her, I will kill you." The extended family and church structure provided them with a circle of safety on the island; if a man "wronged" a girl, everyone would close in to save her family honor.

Off-island, signals often get mixed. When a Puerto Rican girl who is dressed in her idea of what is attractive meets a man from mainstream[22] culture who has been trained to react to certain types of clothing as a sexual signal, a clash is likely to take place. She is seen as a Hot Tamale, a sexual firebrand.[23] I learned this lesson at my first formal dance when my date leaned over and painfully planted a sloppy, overeager kiss on my mouth. When I didn't respond with sufficient passion, he said in a resentful tone, "I thought you Latin girls were supposed to mature early." It was the first time I would feel like a fruit or vegetable—I was supposed to ripen, not just grow into womanhood like other girls.

These stereotypes,[24] though rarer, still surface in my life. I recently stayed at a classy metropolitan hotel. After having dinner with a friend, I was returning to my room when a middle-aged man in a tuxedo stepped directly into my path. With his champagne glass extended toward me, he exclaimed, "*Evita!*"[25]

REFLECT: Have you ever been stereotyped? How?

Blocking my way, he bellowed the song "Don't Cry for Me, Argentina." Playing to the gathering crowd, he began to sing loudly, a ditty[26] to the tune of "La Bamba"—except the lyrics were about a girl named Maria whose exploits[27] all rhymed with her name and gonorrhea.[28]

I knew that this same man—probably a corporate executive, even worldly by most standards—would never have regaled[29] a white woman with a dirty song in public. But to him, I was just a character in his universe of "others," all cartoons.

Still, I am one of the lucky ones. There are thousands of Latinas without the privilege of the education that my parents gave me. For them, every day is a struggle against the misconceptions[30] perpetuated[31] by the myth of the Latina as a whore, domestic worker, or criminal.

Rather than fight these pervasive[32] stereotypes, I try to replace them with a more interesting set of realities. I travel around the United States reading from my books of poetry and my novel. With the stories I tell, the dreams and fears I examine in my work, I try to get my audience past the particulars of my skin color, my accent, or my clothes.

I once wrote a poem in which I called Latinas "God's brown daughters." It is really a prayer of sorts, for communication and respect. In it, Latin women pray "in Spanish to an Anglo God with a Jewish heritage," and they are "fervently[33] hoping that if not omnipotent,[34] at least He be bilingual."

22. **mainstream:** ideas and behaviors considered to be normal   23. **firebrand:** a person who is passionate about a particular cause   24. **stereotypes:** conventional and oversimplified ideas, opinions, or images   25. *Evita*: a musical and film about Eva Perón, Argentina's first lady from 1946 to 1952   26. **ditty:** a short, simple song   27. **exploits:** bold and daring actions   28. **gonorrhea:** a sexually transmitted disease   29. **regaled:** entertained   30. **misconceptions:** false opinions based on lack of understanding   31. **perpetuated:** preserved   32. **pervasive:** widespread   33. **fervently:** passionately   34. **omnipotent:** all-powerful

SUMMARIZE AND RESPOND

In your reading journal or elsewhere, summarize the main point of "Don't Misread My Signals." Then, go back over the essay, and check off the support for this idea. Next, write a brief summary of the essay. Finally, write a brief response to the reading. Have you ever misread signals, stereotyped someone, or gotten the wrong impression of someone? How did it occur?

CHECK YOUR COMPREHENSION

1. An alternate title for this essay could be
   a. "My Name Is Not 'Maria.'"
   b. "Learning to Embrace Stereotypes."
   c. "The Struggles of Immigrant Life."
   d. "The Benefits of a Good Education."

2. The main point of this essay is that
   a. young Puerto Rican women often dress in a flashy, provocative way.
   b. Cofer dislikes musicals like *West Side Story* and *Evita*.
   c. Cofer has faced common misunderstandings about Latinas.
   d. Cofer's parents kept a strict watch over their daughters.

3. Cofer includes accounts of strangers singing to her because
   a. she likes getting attention from men.
   b. the stories are good examples of stereotyping.
   c. these men show a strict morality and machismo.
   d. in Puerto Rico, it is common for men to sing in public.

4. Look back at the vocabulary you underlined, and write sentences using these words: *prospective* (para. 5); *misconceptions, perpetuated* (11); *pervasive* (12); *fervently* (13).

READ CRITICALLY

1. Who do you suppose is Cofer's intended audience for this essay? Why?

2. The title of the essay is "Don't Misread My Signals." What specific examples does Cofer provide of people misreading her?

3. In paragraph 3, Cofer refers to receiving a "conflicting message." What is it, and how does it cause difficulties?

4. Cofer is writing about stereotypes of Latinas. Where do these images and ideas seem to come from? How do they distort reality?

5. According to Cofer, she has a "privilege" that many other Latinas do not have. What is her privilege, and what does this advantage allow her to do?

WRITE

WRITE A PARAGRAPH: Cofer is writing, in part, about being misunderstood. Write a paragraph in which you recall a time when people have misunderstood you or have gotten the wrong idea about your behavior, background, appearance, or words. Contrast the misunderstanding with the reality of the situation, and try to understand the source of the mistake.

WRITE AN ESSAY: Cofer focuses primarily on misunderstandings or myths about Latinas, but there are many other stereotypes in our culture as well. Choose and describe a common stereotype that you think is mistaken; then, compare and contrast those stereotypical images or ideas with a more accurate portrait of reality. For example, you might write about the way women are portrayed in some rap songs versus how they really are.

46

Cause and Effect

Each essay in this chapter uses cause and effect to get its main point across to the reader. As you read these essays, consider how they achieve the Four Basics of Good Cause and Effect that are listed below and discussed in Chapter 15 of this book.

Four Basics of Good Cause and Effect

1. The main point reflects the writer's purpose: to explain causes, effects, or both.
2. If the purpose is to explain causes, the writing presents real causes.
3. If the purpose is to explain effects, it presents real effects.
4. It gives readers detailed examples or explanations of the causes or effects.

Holly Moeller
Say, Don't Spray

Holly Moeller received a bachelor's degree in chemistry and biology from Rutgers University in 2008. In 2010, she received a master's degree in biological oceanography jointly from the Massachusetts Institute of Technology and the Woods Hole Oceanographic Institution. Currently, she is pursuing a doctorate at Stanford University, where she plans to finish her studies in 2014.

Her essay "Say, Don't Spray," about the effects of agricultural pesticides, is an entry from Moeller's Seeing Green column for the *Stanford Daily,* Stanford's student newspaper. Moeller says of her column, "I write Seeing Green because I believe in the importance of scientific communication. If I can write one piece a week and teach just one person about an environmental issue that had never before crossed his or her radar, then I feel like I'm doing part of my job as an environmental scientist."

Moeller offers this writing advice: "Be disciplined. Find a strategy for breaking writer's block that works for you, and use it. For me, that sometimes means shutting the door, turning off phones and computers (yes, I still write all my columns out by hand before revising!), and not leaving my desk until a column is written. And, it's just like exercise: if you consistently manage to drag yourself out the door for a morning run, it will get easier, and even become a habit."

GUIDING QUESTION
What are the effects of pesticides used in agriculture?

CRITICAL READING
- Preview
- Read
- Pause
- Review

See pages 9–12.

VOCABULARY DEVELOPMENT Certain words in this essay are defined at the bottom of the page. Underline these words as you read them.

IDEA JOURNAL Write about an event or situation that strongly affected you.

REFLECT: Why do you suppose the agriculture industry uses such a large share of pesticides in the United States?

PREDICT: Why do you think we became so chemically dependent?

1 The news finally broke last week, months after the first anxious reports of browning and dying trees near lawns and golf courses across America: unlike their wild cousins in the Rockies and British Columbia, these conifers[1] aren't dying of pest outbreaks—they're suffering from pesticides.[2]

2 It seems that Imprelis, a recently released DuPont herbicide[3] marketed for environmental friendliness, is poisoning ornamentals[4] like Norway spruce and eastern white pine. Now, DuPont is promising new labeling for Imprelis; the Environmental Protection Agency is reevaluating its approval, and New York and California are congratulating themselves for never approving it in the first place. Add Imprelis to the list of pesticides whose ultimate toxicity[5] took us by surprise. At least this time we noticed the signs within six months, not 25 years, as was the case with DDT.[6]

3 The herbicides, fungicides,[7] and insecticides[8] applied to lawns each year may seem the most gratuitous[9]—at least to those of us who don't mind a dandelion or clover here and there. But it's actually agriculture that applies 80 percent of the 1.1 billion pounds of pesticides used in the U.S. each year, quelling[10] insect outbreaks, smothering weeds, and ensuring[11] un-nibbled produce.

4 Of course, when we nibble that produce—or eat animals who've nibbled it—any residues[12] and leftover toxins transfer to us.

5 How did we become so chemically dependent?

6 Most of the story should be familiar: it's the tale of the Green Revolution, which tripled our agricultural yields.[13] By growing hybrid[14] crops with shallow root systems and short stalks, farmers ensure that their plants dedicate the majority of their energy to producing big yields. But these varieties also need babying: lots of water to keep shallow roots moist, fertilizer to support increased fruiting, and pesticide applications to knock out wilder, tougher neighbors and natural enemies.

1. **conifers:** evergreen trees or shrubs   2. **pesticides:** chemicals used to kill pests, such as weeds, insects, or funguses   3. **herbicide:** a pesticide used to kill weeds specifically   4. **ornamentals:** decorative trees or shrubs   5. **toxicity:** the quality of being toxic or poisonous   6. **DDT:** a powerful insect-killing chemical that was found to harm humans and animals. In 1972, the U.S. government banned it for most uses.   7. **fungicides:** pesticides used to kill funguses specifically   8. **insecticides:** pesticides used to kill insects specifically   9. **gratuitous:** without a good reason   10. **quelling:** stopping   11. **ensuring:** making possible   12. **residues:** remaining materials   13. **yields:** goods produced   14. **hybrid:** in this case, a genetic combination of different plants

Of course, pesticide application is not without consequences. In sufficiently high doses, some pesticides are acutely[15] toxic to humans as well as their intended victims. Low-level, long-term exposures can cause cancer, reduce fertility, and disrupt endocrine signaling.[16] And many of the compounds don't break down right away, so they're washed into waterways and may accumulate[17] downstream—persistent[18] pollutants acting in unintended ways on unintended targets.

Some new technologies have been developed to reduce this spillover (and, of course, make immense profits for their patent[19] holders).

In 1996, Monsanto began marketing its Roundup Ready line—crop varieties resistant to the herbicide glyphosate (Roundup). Glyphosate is believed to break down quickly on fields, theoretically[20] providing a localized, targeted attack on weeds. But beyond campaigns against genetically modified crops (nicknamed "Frankenfoods" by protestors), there are real fears that glyphosate resistance could "escape" (through genetic reshuffling by cross-pollination) and take off in the wild weeds. Repeated application of glyphosate on acre after rolling acre creates strong selection pressure in favor of any plant that evolves to tolerate the chemical. Like antibiotic resistance, pesticide resistance can spread rapidly through populations, devastating food supplies and livelihoods.

To minimize such risks, Roundup Ready's sister seed, Bt-corn, comes with a mandate[21] that other corn strains be planted alongside it. Bt-corn has been genetically modified to produce a toxin normally manufactured by the soil bacterium *Bacillus thuringiensis* (Bt). This Bt toxin is noxious[22] to insects that would normally attack the corn—in fact, farmers sometimes spray the bacterium itself on crops.

Of course, any bug that developed a tolerance for Bt toxin would have exclusive[23] rights to a field full of juicy, fat ears of corn. Its reproductive fitness would skyrocket, and that field, and its neighbors, would be demolished by the lucky arthropod's[24] offspring. In theory, though, any toxin-free corn nearby would harbor[25] an abundance[26] of the same species, but without resistant traits. Hopefully, that first resistant bug would choose a mate from among the susceptible[27] population, and the resistance trait would be lost in the genetic shuffle. (Note: this only works if resistance arises from a recessive mutation, i.e., one in which two copies of the gene are needed—one from each parent.)

IDENTIFY: Check the effects described in this paragraph.

But who wants to plant an offering for the enemy when Bt-corn is so profitable and successful? At least one in four farmers was willing to dodge[28] the law back in 2008, when the EPA surveyed U.S. corn plantings. With reports of resistance spreading in China and India, our time bomb could explode at any moment.

---

15. **acutely:** severely   16. **endocrine signaling:** the process by which hormones are released from endocrine glands to regulate functions in the body   17. **accumulate:** to build up   18. **persistent:** lasting   19. **patent:** the right to make, use, or sell an invented or discovered item for a limited period   20: **theoretically:** in theory; supposedly   21. **mandate:** requirement   22. **noxious:** poisonous   23. **exclusive:** sole; not extended to others   24. **arthropod:** a category of invertebrates that includes insects   25. **harbor:** to provide shelter for   26. **abundance:** a large amount   27. **susceptible:** at risk—in this case to death by toxins   28. **dodge:** to avoid

13   And so we find ourselves locked into another arms race with evolution, pitting our chemical engineering against the random[29] luck of millions of mutating, adapting plants, insects, and fungi. To fail is to surrender a huge and critical segment of our food supply. But to prevail is to release more and more toxins deliberately into our environment, some of which will have side effects far deadlier than DuPont's Imprelis.

14   Some people are bowing gracefully out of the dance, turning to the traditional methods of "Integrated Pest Management." They rotate crops, use mechanical pest traps, breed pest predators,[30] and plant a range of plant varieties. These are the tools organic farmers use—with the delicious success you can witness at weekend farmers' markets or in your own backyard garden.

15   Join me for a bite.

SUMMARIZE AND RESPOND

In your reading journal or elsewhere, summarize the main point of "Say, Don't Spray." Then, go back over the essay, and check off the support for this idea. Next, write a brief summary of the essay. Finally, write a brief response to the reading. Did it change your view or understanding of how pesticides affect the environment and human health? If so, how?

CHECK YOUR COMPREHENSION

1. An alternate title for this essay could be
   a. "Agricultural Pesticides Create More Problems than Solutions."
   b. "Most People Remain Unaware of Pesticides' Dangers."
   c. "Corn Crops Are Especially Susceptible to Weeds and Insects."
   d. "Organic Farming Is the Best Alternative to Chemical-Based Agriculture."

2. The main point of this essay is that
   a. chemical- and gene-based efforts to fight pests are creating a more toxic environment in the long run.
   b. because of a growing awareness of pesticides' dangers, more and more U.S. farmers are turning to organic-farming techniques.
   c. gene-based approaches to pest control are safer than chemical-based methods and should be more widely adopted.
   d. the growing use of pesticides is affecting the mating patterns of insects.

3. What is one of the drawbacks of higher-yield hybrid crops?
   a. They are too expensive for the average farmer and do not always produce the yields promised by the seed industry.

---

29. random: unpredictable; not following a pattern   **30. predators:** killers

b. They rely on the use of pesticides to combat natural enemies and tougher plants nearby.

  c. They are especially susceptible to damage by agricultural chemicals

  d. They have been bred to contain toxins that can harm humans as well as pests.

4. Does this essay include the Four Basics of Good Cause and Effect? Why?

5. Look back at the vocabulary you underlined, and write sentences using these words: *toxicity* (para. 2); *gratuitous* (3); *yields* (6); *persistent* (7); *susceptible* (11).

TIP For tools to build your vocabulary, visit the *Student Site for Real Writing* at bedfordstmartins.com/realwriting.

READ CRITICALLY

1. According to Moeller, why did the agriculture industry become so dependent on chemicals? What have been the effects of this dependency?

2. What is Moeller's opinion of one attempt to reduce the effect of herbicides—the Roundup Ready product line? What facts does she present to support this opinion?

3. This essay describes some complicated biological processes (see para. 11, for example). In your opinion, are these processes clearly explained? What questions, if any, do you have about this material?

4. What would be the benefits of using the "Integrated Pest Management" strategies Moeller describes in paragraph 14?

5. What larger argument is Moeller making in the last sentence of her essay? Are you convinced that you should join her? Why or why not?

WRITE

WRITE A PARAGRAPH: Sometimes, actions we take to improve a situation have unexpected and undesired results. Write a paragraph in which you describe a situation in which your actions, or someone else's, had a different effect than what was planned or desired.

TIP For a sample cause-and-effect paragraph, see page 257.

WRITE AN ESSAY: Humans' negative effect on the environment has been the subject of much discussion in the media and elsewhere. At the same time, efforts are being made to reduce this effect or in some cases to reverse it. Identify one type of negative environmental effect (such as air pollution, water pollution, or improper waste disposal). Then, in a brief research essay that draws on at least two sources, discuss the causes and effects of this effect, and describe efforts being made to reduce it.

TIP The Web site for the Environmental Protection Agency, www.epa.gov, might be a good place to start your research. For more information on the research essay, see Chapter 18.

John Tierney

Yes, Money Can Buy Happiness

A well-known columnist for the *New York Times* since 1990, John Tierney has an extensive background in news writing. After graduating with a degree in American studies from Yale University, Tierney reported for a series of publications, including the *Bergen Record,* the *Washington Star,* and *Science* magazine. He then worked for several years as a freelance writer, reporting on six continents and publishing articles in more than fifteen national newspapers and magazines. His 2011 book, *Willpower: Rediscovering the Greatest Human Strength,* written with Roy Baumeister, was named one of Amazon's Best Books of that year.

GUIDING QUESTION
In the essay, how does money buy happiness?

1 Yes, money can buy happiness, but probably not in the way you imagined. Spending it on yourself may not do much for your spirits, but spending it on others will make you happier, according to a report from a team of social psychologists in the new issue of *Science*.

2 The researchers confirmed[1] the joys of giving in three separate ways. First, by surveying a national sample of more than 600 Americans, they found that spending more on gifts and charity correlated[2] with greater happiness, whereas spending more money on oneself did not. Second, by tracking sixteen workers before and after they received profit-sharing bonuses, the researchers found that the workers who gave more of the money to others ended up happier than the ones who spent more of it on themselves. In fact, how the bonus was spent was a better predictor of happiness than the size of the bonus.

3 The final bit of evidence came from an experiment in which forty-six students were given either $5 or $20 to spend by the end of the day. The ones who were instructed to spend the money on others — they bought toys for siblings, treated friends to meals, and made donations to the homeless — were happier at the end of the day than the ones who were instructed to spend the money on themselves.

4 "These experimental results," the researchers conclude, "provide direct support for our causal argument that spending money on others promotes happiness more than spending money on oneself." The social psychologists — Elizabeth Dunn and Lara Aknin of the University of British Columbia, Vancouver, and Michael Norton of Harvard Business School — also conclude that "how people choose to spend their money is at least as important as how much money they make."

5 I asked Dr. Dunn if she had any advice for readers on how much to spend on others. Her reply was, "I think even minor changes in spending habits can make a difference. In our experiment with college students,

---

1. **confirmed:** proved the truth   2. **correlated:** had a connection with

we found that spending just $5 prosocially[3] had a substantial[4] effect on happiness at the end of the day. But I wouldn't say that there's some fixed amount that everyone should spend on others. Rather, the best bet might be for people to think about whether they can push themselves to devote just a little more of their money to helping others."

But why wouldn't people be doing that already? Because most people don't realize the personal benefits of charity, according to Dr. Dunn and her colleagues. When the researchers surveyed another group of students, they found that most of the respondents predicted that personal spending would make them happier than spending the money on other people.

Perhaps that will change as word of these experiments circulates — although that prospect raises another question, which I put to Dr. Dunn: If people started giving away money chiefly in the hope of making themselves happier, as opposed to wanting to help others, would they still derive[5] the same happiness from it?

"This is a fascinating question," she replied. "I certainly hope that telling people about the emotional benefits of prosocial spending doesn't completely erase these benefits; I would hate to be responsible for the downfall[6] of joyful prosocial behavior."

Do you have any theories on the joys of giving? Any reports of your own experiments? Or any questions you'd like to ask the researchers? Dr. Dunn, in keeping with the results of her experiments, has generously offered to provide some answers free of charge.

REFLECT: Do you agree that charity always makes people feel better?

REFLECT: Answer the questions in paragraph 9.

SUMMARIZE AND RESPOND

In your reading journal or elsewhere, summarize the main point of "Yes, Money Can Buy Happiness." Then, go back over the essay, and check off the support for this idea. Next, write a brief summary of the essay. Finally, write a brief response to the reading. How do you see the relationship between money and happiness in your own life, both now and as you look toward the future?

CHECK YOUR COMPREHENSION

1. An alternate title for this essay could be
   a. "Profit-Sharing Proves Profitable for Employees and Employers."
   b. "Spending Money on Others Can Increase Your Happiness."
   c. "Charity Should Begin and End at Home."
   d. "Study Finds that Money Is the Key to Happiness."

---

3. **prosocially:** in a manner that is intended to benefit another person, as in cases of helping or sharing   4. **substantial:** significant   5. **derive:** to get something from   6. **downfall:** a loss of power or status

2. The main point of this essay is that
   a. people are often happier when they spend money on others than on themselves.
   b. people are beginning to give more money to charity because they realize that such generosity is a source of happiness.
   c. scientists are fascinated by the spending habits of the American people.
   d. even in a bad economy, people should continue their charitable giving.

3. According to the article, why don't people spend more money on others than they already do?
   a. Human beings are selfish and therefore do not like giving.
   b. People mostly like to be charitable during the holiday season.
   c. College students do not make a good sample for a scientific study.
   d. Most people do not realize the personal benefits of charity.

4. Look back at the vocabulary you underlined, and write sentences using these words: *confirmed* (para. 2); *substantial* (5); *derive* (7); *downfall* (8).

READ CRITICALLY

1. Tierney suggests in his opening paragraph that money can buy happiness, "but probably not in the way you imagined." Do you find the results of these studies surprising? Why or why not?

2. Tierney writes that spending money "on yourself may not do much for your spirits." How do people generally spend money to change their mood or lift their "spirits"?

3. Social psychologists in the article conclude that "how people spend their money is at least as important as how much money they make" (para. 4). Does this statement seem true to you? What other factors might social psychologists take into account as far as discovering the relationship between money and happiness?

4. How does Tierney structure this essay in terms of explaining the experiments, the conclusions, and their implications?

5. What apparently common human flaw or flaws does this article highlight in paragraph 8?

WRITE

WRITE A PARAGRAPH: The scientist in the article says she hopes that people will "think about whether they can push themselves to devote just a little more of their money to helping others." Will this article change your attitude about charity or cause you to alter your behavior in any way? Write a paragraph explaining your answer.

WRITE AN ESSAY: Tierney's article explores "the emotional benefits of prosocial spending." Have you ever experienced these "benefits"? Write an essay in which you examine an experience when you spent money on or helped others. Did the action cause the effects that scientists found in their studies?

47

Argument

The essays in this chapter use argument to make clear their positions on two different topics: (1) snitching and (2) the granting of certain rights to illegal immigrants. As you read these essays, consider how the writers achieve the Four Basics of Good Argument listed below and discussed in Chapter 16 of this book.

Four Basics of Good Argument

1. It takes a strong and definite position.
2. It gives good reasons and supporting evidence to defend the position.
3. It considers opposing views.
4. It has enthusiasm and energy from start to finish.

Also, keep in mind the basics of critical thinking discussed in Chapter 1 and reviewed in Chapter 16. In particular, pay attention to the assumptions being made by the writers, and be sure to question them. Such questioning will help you form your own position on the two topics, as you will be asked to do in the writing assignments on pages 708 and 716.

SNITCHING

Each of the following essays—the first one by a student and the next two by professional writers—offers a different viewpoint on the subject of snitching. As you read them, pay close attention to how each writer interprets what snitching is.

Robert Phansalkar
Stop Snitchin' Won't Stop Crime

Robert Phansalkar graduated from the University of Wisconsin (UW) in 2007 with degrees in languages and cultures of Asia and political science, and he later received a law degree from Fordham Law School. He wrote the essay "Stop Snitchin' Won't Stop Crime" when he was a student at UW, and it first appeared in the UW student newspaper, the *Badger Herald Weekly*. Of the piece, he says he explores "issues facing minorities in law enforcement," a topic that connects to his overall concerns as a writer: "Law and social justice issues interest me the most because these play off of fundamental issues of fairness. It is rare to find someone who does not have an opinion, developed or not, on these issues."

GUIDING QUESTION
How would Phansalkar define snitching, and what is his position on the Stop Snitchin' movement?

1   The "Stop Snitchin'" movement is a reaction to racial profiling and racism in police actions. Now widespread and promoted by many, it began with a homemade DVD called *Stop Snitching*, hosted by a rapper known as Skinny Suge. It featured a number of rappers and others who threatened violence against people who gave the police any information about crimes. Among the people in the DVD was Carmelo Anthony, an NBA star, whose participation helped the DVD gain media attention. Now there are Web sites, T-shirts, and lots of other items that promote the Stop Snitchin' campaign. The movement maintains[1] that until the system reflects real justice, minorities should willfully avoid helping police with ongoing investigations, regardless of circumstance or crime. While many support the movement, maintaining that silence in the face of injustice is more honorable than cooperation, the cities suffer as witnesses fail to give any information they have about crimes. Stop Snitchin' does not stop crime.

2   While the movement has developed into rappers' sales and perceived "street cred,"[2] it has also blossomed into an unfortunate force that hinders[3] crime prevention. For example, Cameron Giles, known as Cam'ron or Killa Cam, was shot multiple times during an attempted carjacking, but he refused to give police information about the suspects. Avoiding the police encourages the very kind of lawlessness that is all too common in cities riddled[4] with gang violence. At the movement's Web site, stopsnitchin.com, rappers and others complain about their experiences in rough, violent neighborhoods, but they promote it with Stop Snitchin'.

3   It is difficult to connect how refusing to contribute to investigations helps the problem. Even if the Stop Snitchin' movement isn't aiming to lower crime rates, not cooperating with police certainly does not help the neighborhoods that these rappers grew up in, which makes their support

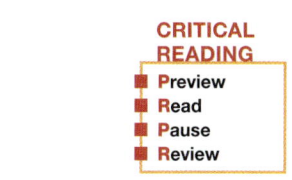

CRITICAL READING
- Preview
- Read
- Pause
- Review

See pages 9–12.

VOCABULARY DEVELOPMENT Certain words in this essay are defined at the bottom of the page. Underline these words as you read them.

IDEA JOURNAL Write about a time you "snitched" on someone.

IDENTIFY: Where does the author acknowledge the opposing view?

---

1. maintains: believes; states   **2. street cred:** trustworthiness and value as seen by young, urban people, especially in hip-hop culture   **3. hinders:** causes difficulties or delays   **4. riddled:** spread throughout

of the movement all the more confusing. If people actually want to reduce gang violence in the neighborhoods and have a shot at breaking boundaries and moving beyond poverty and violence, why allow criminals to run wild? Why not work to promote successful and peaceful neighborhoods? Most of the rappers and other supporters of Stop Snitchin' believe that the justice system is based on racism and that cooperating with the police actually threatens innocent people because snitchers lie to save themselves.

Certainly, racism in law enforcement practices is a legitimate[5] issue that needs to be addressed, but simply not cooperating with the institutions that exist to protect people is a ludicrous[6] solution. Turning your back on the system ensures one thing: The system will continue to not work for you. Expecting change to happen when you look away is precisely the kind of mentality[7] that rarely accomplishes anything and draws more heat than if you were working positively to effect change in your community.

Instead of rapping about not snitching on real criminals, why not rap about not committing crimes? Why not rap about improving the systems of inequality and injustice through positive action? Stop Snitchin' doesn't answer any of these questions, and even though the movement defies[8] the logic of self-preservation, it continues because nobody has the courage to stand up and say what really happened.

SUMMARIZE: What is the author's basic argument? Do his reasons support his position?

SUMMARIZE AND RESPOND

In your writing journal or elsewhere, summarize the main point of "Stop Snitchin' Won't Stop Crime." Then, go back over the essay, and check off the support for this idea. Next, write a brief summary of the essay. Finally, write a brief response to the reading. Why would a campaign like "Stop Snitchin'" be popular or persuasive?

CHECK YOUR COMPREHENSION

1. An alternate title for this essay could be
   a. "Turning Your Back on the System Ensures More Crime and Injustice."
   b. "High-Crime Communities Need Jobs and Schools, Not Snitches."
   c. "Hip-Hop Stars and Athletes Must Strive to Be Better Role Models."
   d. "Silence in the Face of Injustice Is More Honorable than Cooperation."

---

5. **legitimate:** real; valid 6. **ludicrous:** laughable 7. **mentality:** a way of thinking 8. **defies:** goes against; disagrees with

2. The main point of this essay is that

   a. too many people are using the Internet to promote illegal behavior.

   b. racism is not a problem in the United States, although many people claim that it still exists.

   c. refusing to cooperate with the police will not change the legal system or prevent crime.

   d. snitches threaten innocent people because they often lie to save themselves.

3. According to the writer, rappers might have a more positive effect if they would

   a. rap about fixing inequalities and work to create peaceful neighborhoods.

   b. discourage people from snitching, even though it will make cities less safe.

   c. join with professional athletes to speak out against carjacking.

   d. stop complaining about racism.

4. Does this essay include the Four Basics of Good Argument? Why or why not?

5. Look back at the vocabulary you underlined, and write sentences using these words: *maintains* (para. 1); *hinders* (2); *legitimate, mentality* (4); *defies* (5).

TIP For tools to build your vocabulary, visit the *Student Site for Real Writing* at bedfordstmartins.com/realwriting.

READ CRITICALLY

1. How would you state the thesis of Phansalkar's essay in your own words?

2. Where and how does the writer acknowledge and address views other than his own?

3. Who is the audience for this essay? What readers does the writer want to persuade? How do you know?

4. Why does Phansalkar include the example of rapper Cameron Giles (para. 2), who was shot during a carjacking? What point does it make?

5. Phansalkar ends his essay by questioning the "courage" of those who participate in or support the Stop Snitchin' campaign. Why does he do so? What effect does it have?

WRITE

As Phansalkar writes, NBA player Carmelo Anthony participated in the Stop Snitchin' campaign. Do you think star athletes and other celebrities have an obligation to be law-abiding role models? Should society hold them to a higher standard than private citizens? Write a paragraph or an essay that takes a position on this issue.

Bill Maxwell
Start Snitching

Bill Maxwell is an internationally syndicated columnist and editorial writer for the *Tampa Bay Times* (formerly the *St. Petersburg Times*) in Florida. After receiving a B.A. from Bethune-Cookman College, he went on to earn a master's and a doctoral degree from the University of Chicago before he began teaching in 1973. His diverse background as an educator and a writer is evident in the many publications for which he has written, including the *Fort Pierce Tribune,* the *Gainesville Sun,* and the *Tampa Bay Times*. He wrote the essay "Start Snitching" in September 2007 for the *Times* in response to the deaths of several black men from the community.

GUIDING QUESTION
What does Maxwell's Wall of Black Death represent to him, and how does it relate to snitching?

CRITICAL READING
- **P**review
- **R**ead
- **P**ause
- **R**eview

See pages 9–12.

VOCABULARY DEVELOPMENT Certain words in this essay are defined at the bottom of the page. Underline these words as you read them.

REFLECT: What effect does the list of names that starts the essay have?

IDEA JOURNAL Are you surprised when you read about gang murders? Why or why not?

IDENTIFY: What kinds of evidence does the author use?

1   Cedric "C. J." Mills. Isaiah Brooks. Tedric Maynor. Felicia Hines. Vinson Phillips. Kurt Anthony Bryant. Amuel Murph. Alfonso Williams. These names are forever inscribed[1] on my private "Wall of Black Death." My wall contains the names of black people killed by other black people, along with those believed to have been killed by fellow blacks, in the Tampa Bay area since May. I will update the roster[2] as soon as new deaths are reported. More are sure to follow. I do not have answers as to how to stop blacks from killing their brethren.[3] But I do have an answer for catching some, if not all, of these murderers. Snitch.

2   Nationwide, too many blacks refuse to help the police identify, find, and arrest killers in their communities. To enjoy a decent quality of life in their communities, blacks must begin to help the police. Studies show that homicides,[4] especially unsolved homicides, destabilize[5] low-income communities. Needless to say, many of the nation's black communities have individuals and families with low incomes. Businesses that can provide jobs for unemployed residents and provide the amenities[6] that other areas take for granted are wary[7] of locating in black communities where homicide rates are high.

3   A recent *St. Petersburg Times* article reported that a group of Tampa black residents have organized an effort to stop the "don't snitch" culture that permits killers to remain free. Many of the organizers are related in some way to a youngster killed by a fellow black. Consider this sobering portrait of blacks and homicide and other serious crimes from a recent U.S. Bureau of Justice Statistics report: Although blacks comprised only 13 percent of the population in 2005, they were victims of about 49 percent of all homicides. The bureau estimated that 16,400 murders

---

1. **inscribed:** listed; written   2. **roster:** a list of people   3. **brethren:** brothers; men within the same race, nationality, or group   4. **homicides:** murders
5. **destabilize:** to make unsteady or cause something to fail   6. **amenities:** comforts, conveniences, or pleasures   7. **wary:** cautious

occurred in the United States in 2005. Of that number, 8,000 victims were black, 93 percent of those victims were killed by other blacks, and 77 percent of those murders involved firearms. Most black victims were between ages 17 and 29.

Many people, including police officials I have spoken with, say that fear prevents most blacks from snitching. I agree that some residents remain silent out of fear, but I suspect that the fear factor receives too much weight. I have come to believe that an untold number of blacks have grown as insensitive to black-on-black murders as they have to other black-on-black crimes. For one thing, the high number of homicides in their communities has made many blacks inured[8] to all but the most sensational killings that receive a lot of press.

"I expect somebody to shoot somebody every week around here," a St. Petersburg woman who lives in a predominantly[9] black neighborhood said a few weeks ago when I asked if she had known a man who had been killed recently. "I don't go near my windows at night. They shoot guns around here all the time. I don't pay attention when they say somebody got shot. I just try to make sure it won't be me one of these days."

I am not a sociologist,[10] but I suspect that many blacks in high-crime communities have all the symptoms of the abused person syndrome:[11] We have been cruel toward one another for so long we have internalized[12] the belief that such cruelty is normal. Those of us who have internalized the cruelty think nothing of treating other blacks likewise, thus perpetuating[13] the cycle without apparent[14] end. Each day I open the newspaper and switch on TV news, I brace[15] myself for yet another murder. With each killing, I feel sadness, regret, helplessness, anger, and shame—shame of being associated with such people in any way.

Because I regularly write about this issue, I receive a lot of hate mail from both whites and blacks. White letter-writers remind me that blacks are "animals" and "cause all of America's social problems." Black letter-writers see me as the "enemy of the people" and a "sell-out" because I condemn blacks for killing one another without taking into account the nation's history of racism. To whites, I have nothing to say. To blacks, I have one message: We need to start snitching. Only we can stop black-on-black murders. Until then, I will be adding names to the Wall of Black Death.

5 **REFLECT:** Does the information in paragraphs 4 and 5 surprise you?

7 **REFLECT:** Does the race of the author have an effect on the way you read this essay? Why or why not?

SUMMARIZE AND RESPOND

In your reading journal or elsewhere, summarize the main point of "Start Snitching." Then, go back over the essay, and check off the support for this idea. Next, write a brief summary of the essay. Finally, write a brief response to the reading. Maxwell speculates that "an untold number of blacks" have

---

8. **inured:** accustomed to or used to   9. **predominantly:** mainly
10. **sociologist:** a person who studies the origin, development, and other aspects of human society   11. **syndrome:** a disorder or an illness   12. **internalized:** made something part of your core beliefs or attitudes   13. **perpetuating:** continuing
14. **apparent:** obvious   15. **brace:** to prepare for

become "insensitive to black-on-black murders." As a result, they refuse to snitch. What other reasons would you suggest account for this reluctance to work with the police?

CHECK YOUR COMPREHENSION

1. An alternate title for this essay could be
   a. "Snitching and the 'Wall of Black Death.'"
   b. "Black Communities Must Provide More Jobs and Amenities."
   c. "Stop Racist Hate Mail."
   d. "Most Black Murder Victims Are between 17 and 29."

2. The main point of this essay is that
   a. only the most sensational killings now capture the attention of African Americans.
   b. Maxwell lives in fear of speaking out about snitching because he gets so much angry mail.
   c. white people have become indifferent to the crime and violence in America's black communities.
   d. African Americans must cooperate with police to help reduce black-on-black violence.

3. According to Maxwell, what is one of the reasons African Americans do not snitch?
   a. They have been persuaded by calls from black celebrities and athletes to avoid speaking to the police about black-on-black crime.
   b. The police do not listen to the concerns of people living in predominantly black neighborhoods.
   c. People in black communities prefer to enforce their own justice when they catch suspected criminals and do not wish to bother the police.
   d. Many blacks are insensitive to black-on-black murders, having internalized the belief that such behavior is "normal."

4. Look back at the vocabulary you underlined, and write sentences using these words: *wary* (para. 2); *predominantly* (5); *syndrome, perpetuating, apparent* (6).

READ CRITICALLY

1. Why does Maxwell open his essay with this list of names? Do you find the introduction effective? Why or why not?

2. What effects does black-on-black violence have on communities, according to Maxwell?

3. How does the quotation in paragraph 5 help Maxwell's argument? Which of his claims does it support?

4. Does the writer acknowledge or address competing points of view in his essay?

5. In the concluding paragraph, Maxwell refers to his hate mail and claims that he has "nothing to say" to the whites who write him hate mail. Why do you think he refuses to address these letter writers?

WRITE

In the conclusion of his essay, Maxwell refers to the "hate mail" he receives from two general categories of letter writers. Write a paragraph or essay that addresses and responds to the claims of either one of these groups. How would you engage them in a civil and meaningful discussion?

Alexandra Natapoff

Bait and Snitch: The High Cost of Snitching for Law Enforcement

Alexandra Natapoff is a law professor at Loyola Law School in Los Angeles, California, where she teaches criminal law and criminal procedure. She graduated cum laude with a B.A. from Yale University and earned her J.D. with distinction at Stanford Law School. Before becoming a professor, Natapoff worked as an assistant federal public defender in Baltimore, Maryland; while there, she founded the Urban Law & Advocacy Project. As a scholar and writer, Natapoff is interested in the criminal justice system, as well as race and the law and administrative law. Her book, *Snitching: Criminal Informants and the Erosion of American Justice,* was published in 2009.

GUIDING QUESTION
How does Natapoff define snitching?

From Baltimore to Boston to New York; in Pittsburgh, Denver, and Milwaukee, kids are sporting the ominous[1] fashion statement, "Stop Snitchin'," prompting local fear, outrage, and fierce arguments over crime. Several trials have been disrupted by the T-shirts; some witnesses refuse to testify. With cameo appearances in the growing controversy[2] by NBA star Carmelo Anthony of the Denver Nuggets and the rapper Lil Kim, snitching is making urban culture headlines.

CRITICAL READING
- Preview
- Read
- Pause
- Review

See pages 9–12.

VOCABULARY DEVELOPMENT Certain words in this essay are defined at the bottom of the page. Underline these words as you read them.

1. ominous: threatening   **2. controversy:** an argument; a conflict of opinion

IDEA JOURNAL Write about a law or practice that you think is unfair.

IDENTIFY: Check the reasons the author gives to show that snitching is a bad practice.

The "Stop Snitchin'" T-shirt drama looks, at first, like a dust-up[3] over a simple counterculture[4] message launched by some urban criminal entrepreneurs;[5] that friends don't snitch on friends. But it is, in fact, a symptom of a more insidious[6] reality that has largely escaped public notice.

For the last 20 years, state and federal governments have been creating criminal snitches and setting them loose in poor, high-crime communities. The backlash[7] against snitches reflects a growing national recognition that snitching is dangerous public policy—producing bad information, endangering innocent people, letting dangerous criminals off the hook, compromising the integrity[8] of police work, and inciting[9] violence and distrust in socially vulnerable[10] neighborhoods.

The heart of the snitching problem lies in the secret deals that police and prosecutors make with criminals. In investigating drug offenses, police and prosecutors rely heavily—and sometimes exclusively—on criminals willing to trade information about other criminals in exchange for leniency.[11] Many snitches avoid arrest altogether, thus continuing to use and deal drugs and commit other crimes in their neighborhoods, while providing information to the police. As drug dockets[12] swell and police and prosecutors become increasingly dependent on snitches, high-crime communities are filling up with these active criminals who will turn in friends, family, and neighbors in order to "work off" their own crimes.

Critics of the T-shirts tend to dismiss the "stop snitching" sentiment as pro-criminal and antisocial, a subcultural expression of misplaced loyalty. But the T-shirts should be heeded[13] as evidence of a failed public policy. Snitching is an entrenched[14] law-enforcement practice that has become pervasive[15] due to its crucial role in the war on drugs. This practice is favored not only by police and prosecutors, but by legislatures: Mandatory[16] minimum sentences and restrictions on judges make snitching one of the only means for defendants to negotiate in the face of rigid and drastic[17] sentences. But the policy has turned out to be a double-edged sword.[18] Nearly every drug offense involves a snitch, and snitching is increasingly displacing more traditional police work, such as undercover operations and independent investigation.

According to some agents and prosecutors, snitching is also slowly crippling law enforcement: "Informers are running today's drug investigations, not the agents," says veteran DEA [Drug Enforcement Administration] agent Celerino Castillo. "Agents have become so dependent on informers that the agents are at their mercy."

The government's traditional justification for creating criminal snitches—"we-need-to-flip-little-fishes-to-get-to-the-Big-Fish"—is at best

3. **dust-up:** a fight   4. **counterculture:** opposed to established culture
5. **entrepreneurs:** people who start or manage businesses   6. **insidious:** dangerous while appearing harmless   7. **backlash:** a strong or sudden violent reaction toward something   8. **integrity:** morality, honesty, and legality   9. **inciting:** urging on; encouraging   10. **vulnerable:** easily harmed   11. **leniency:** mildness; softness; tolerance   12. **dockets:** lists of legal cases to be tried   13. **heeded:** paid attention to   14. **entrenched:** deeply dug in; secure   15. **pervasive:** widespread
16. **mandatory:** required   17. **drastic:** extreme   18. **double-edged sword:** something that can have both good and bad consequences

an ideal and mostly the remnant[19] of one. Today, the government lets all sorts of criminals, both big and little, trade information to escape punishment for nearly every kind of crime, and often the snitches are more dangerous than the targets.

Snitching thus puts us right through the looking glass:[20] Criminals direct police investigations while avoiding arrest and punishment. Nevertheless, snitching is ever more popular with law enforcement: It is easier to "flip" defendants and turn them into snitches than it is to fight over their cases. For a criminal system that has more cases than it can prosecute, and more defendants than it can incarcerate,[21] snitching has become a convenient case-management tool for an institution that has bitten off more than it can chew.

And while the government's snitching policy has gone mostly unchallenged, it is both damaging to the justice system and socially expensive. Snitches are famously unreliable: A 2004 study by the Northwestern University Law School's Center on Wrongful Convictions reveals that 46 percent of wrongful death penalty convictions are due to snitch misinformation—making snitches the leading cause of wrongful conviction in capital cases. Jailhouse snitches routinely concoct[22] information; the system gives them every incentive[23] to do so. Los Angeles snitch Leslie White infamously avoided punishment for his crimes for years by fabricating[24] confessions and attributing[25] them to his cellmates.

Snitches also undermine law-enforcement legitimacy—police who rely on and protect their informants are often perceived as favoring criminals. In a growing number of public fiascos,[26] snitches actually invent crimes and criminals in order to provide the government with the information it demands. In Dallas, for example, in the so-called "fake drug scandal," paid informants set up innocent Mexican immigrants with fake drugs (gypsum) while police falsified drug field tests in order to inflate their drug-bust statistics.

10 REFLECT: Why is this paragraph's evidence persuasive?

Finally, as the T-shirt controversy illustrates, snitching worsens crime, violence, and distrust in some of the nation's most socially vulnerable communities. In the poorest neighborhoods, vast numbers of young people are in contact with the criminal justice system. Nearly every family contains someone who is in prison, under supervision, or has a criminal record. In these communities, the law-enforcement policy of pressuring everyone to snitch can have the devastating[27] effect of tearing families and social networks apart. Ironically,[28] these are the communities most in need of positive role models, strong social institutions, and good police-community relations. Snitching undermines these important goals by setting criminals loose, creating distrust, and compromising police integrity.

---

19. **remnant:** a piece or part of   20. **through the looking glass:** a place or situation where things happen in a way that is the opposite of expectations   21. **incarcerate:** to put in jail   22. **concoct:** to make up or invent   23. **incentive:** a reason to do something   24. **fabricating:** making up or inventing   25. **attributing:** giving credit to someone   26. **fiascos:** complete failures   27. **devastating:** overwhelming; destructive   28. **ironically:** in a way that goes against expectations or a desired outcome

ANALYZE: How are the author's opinions different from Phansalkar's (pp. 697–98)?

The "Stop Snitchin'" T-shirts have drawn local fire for their perceived threat to law-abiding citizens who call the police. But in the outrage over that perceived threat, the larger message of the shirts has been missed: Government policies that favor criminal snitching harm the communities most in need of law-enforcement protection. 12

While snitching will never be abolished,[29] the practice could be substantially improved, mostly by lifting the veil of secrecy that shields law-enforcement practices from public scrutiny. As things stand, police and prosecutors can cut a deal with a criminal; turn him into a snitch or cut him loose; forgive his crimes or resurrect them later; release him into the community; or decide to pick him up. They do all this at their discretion, without legal rules, in complete secrecy, with no judicial or public accountability. As a result, we have no idea whether snitching even reduces crime or actually increases it, and we can only guess at the collateral harms it imposes on high-crime communities. 13

REFLECT: Does the author present a good argument? Has she changed your mind?

The government should reveal snitching's real costs, including data on how many snitches are released into high-crime neighborhoods and what sorts of snitch crimes are forgiven. The government should also be required to establish the concrete benefit of a policy that releases some criminals to catch others, by accounting for how much crime actually gets stopped or solved by snitch information. Only then can we rationally evaluate how much government-sponsored snitching makes sense. Until we can know the real value of snitching, the T-shirts remain an important reminder that this particular cure for crime may be as bad as the disease. 14

SUMMARIZE AND RESPOND

In your reading journal or elsewhere, summarize the main point of "Bait and Snitch: The High Cost of Snitching for Law Enforcement." Then, go back over the essay, and check off the support for this idea. Next, write a brief summary of the essay. Finally, write a brief response to the reading. The writer discusses the popularity of "Stop Snitchin'" T-shirts, which some say are procriminal and antisocial. Why do you think crime and criminals—whether organized crime, "urban criminal entrepreneurs," or even western outlaws—have had such a lasting appeal in American popular culture?

CHECK YOUR COMPREHENSION

1. An alternate title for this essay could be
    a. "The United States Needs to Build More Prisons."
    b. "Snitching Undermines Law Enforcement and Harms Communities."
    c. "Law Enforcement Authorities Must Take Steps to Ban 'Stop Snitchin'' T-Shirts."
    d. "Too Many Snitches Cut Deals with the Police and Escape Justice."

29. **abolished:** ended

2. The main point of this essay is that
   a. the U.S. justice system is weak, which means that too many criminals go unpunished.
   b. the police and other legal authorities are overwhelmed by the number of drug offenders.
   c. policies that favor criminal snitching harm the legal system and do damage to many communities.
   d. snitching is an unfortunate but necessary part of our justice system.

3. According to Natapoff, the heart of the snitching problem lies in
   a. the communities that choose to protect criminals rather than bring them to justice.
   b. American prisons, which are overcrowded.
   c. police officers, judges, and politicians who incarcerate too many innocent people.
   d. the secret deals that police and prosecutors make with criminals.

4. Look back at the vocabulary you underlined, and write sentences using these words: *controversy* (para. 1); *integrity* (3); *mandatory* (5); *concoct* (9); *abolished* (13).

READ CRITICALLY

1. Natapoff argues that critics of the "Stop Snitchin'" T-shirts misunderstand their meaning. What is the misunderstanding? What do the T-shirts actually represent, according to Natapoff?

2. In paragraph 3, the writer claims that the practice of using "criminal snitches" hurts the "integrity of police work." What do you think that phrase means?

3. The writer argues that the reliance on snitches has led to "public fiascos" (para. 10). How does she support this claim?

4. How does Natapoff use statistics in this essay, and how do they support her argument?

5. What practical steps does Natapoff propose at the conclusion of this essay? Does the essay convince you that they are necessary? Why or why not?

WRITE

The immediate focus of this essay is the role of snitching in law enforcement, but the figure of the "snitch," "rat," informant, or even "tattletale" has almost always been one that many people dislike. Why do you think that is the case, even if such informants and snitches can help bring criminals to justice or, more generally, stop bad things from happening? Write a paragraph or essay that addresses these issues.

WRITE USING READINGS

TIP For more on quoting and paraphrasing, see Chapter 18.

Write an essay either in favor of or against snitching, drawing on the opinions and evidence given in the essays by Phansalkar, Maxwell, and Natapoff. You may want to quote directly from any of the three essays or paraphrase their arguments. Whichever position you take, you should take the opposing position into consideration by referring to one of the authors who disagrees with your opinion. In your concluding paragraph, review the reasons you have given to support your position.

RIGHTS FOR ILLEGAL IMMIGRANTS

The next two essays, both by students, take positions on legislation aimed at granting more rights, in limited cases, to illegal immigrants. The first essay describes a law, passed in California in 2011, that gives eligible members of this population access to state-funded financial aid. The second essay describes the federal DREAM Act, which would grant U.S. citizenship rights to illegal immigrants who meet certain requirements.

Heather Rushall
Dream Act Is Finance Fantasy

Heather Rushall wrote the following essay for the *Daily Aztec,* the student newspaper at San Diego State University, where she is studying journalism and political science and expects to graduate in June 2013. Rushall, also the author of the blog "Heather Writes," says that she has enjoyed writing as far back as she can remember, and in the past she's produced poetry, short stories, and many journal entries. Her advice to other student writers is, "Just write. Don't think about it, don't try to plan it. Just sit down and write. You will be amazed with what you can produce, and there is always room to improve upon it afterwards." This essay was published on October 17, 2011.

GUIDING QUESTION
What issues does the author take with California's Dream Act?

1   **A**s of July 1 next year [July 1, 2012], just weeks before the start of a new school year, illegal immigrants will be eligible to receive state-funded financial aid in California. The new opportunity has been coined[1] the

CRITICAL READING
- Preview
- Read
- Pause
- Review

See pages 9–12.

1. **coined:** named

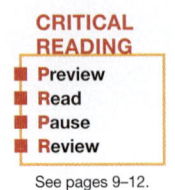

California Dream Act—Development, Relief and Education of Alien Minors—also known as Assembly Bill 131. Acting with unmatched time management abilities, Gov. Jerry Brown waited until the last minute to sign the bill, which was proposed by Assemblyman Gil Cedillo of Los Angeles earlier this year.

Requirements to reap[2] the benefits of the act are simple: Applicants must have attended a California high school for at least three years, graduated from said high school or have received a GED diploma, and must show proof they are either actively seeking citizenship or will seek it once they are eligible to do so.

Those seem like some ridiculously easy and unfair requirements compared to the standards needed to be filled by applicants who are already U.S. citizens living in California. Cal Grant—the program the new Dream Act would make undocumented immigrants eligible for—requires traditional applicants to first prove, through the Free Application for Student Aid system, that they are "independent."

Independent students can be 25 years of age or older, a parent of a child who receives at least half of his or her income, or married. If the student is not considered independent, they must file using their parents' tax information and come from a poverty-level home based on income. That requirement alone makes a very large portion of financial aid applicants ineligible right off the bat.

The Cal Grant issuance is split into two sections—Cal Grant A and Cal Grant B. Most applicants will receive only one of the sections based on the difference in eligibility requirements. Part A is based entirely on grade point average and financial need, whereas part B considers GPA, the highest level of school completed by the applicant's parents, and marital[3] status. Unmarried applicants will not receive part B, and students with average or less-than-average grades will not receive either portion.

A "Competitive Cal Grant" is money available to students with exceptional[4] need or otherwise special circumstances. These grants will only be available to Dream Act applicants if there is additional funding available after the grants have been awarded.

The other program the Dream Act will make available to non-citizen applicants living in California is the Board of Governors Fee Waiver.[5] The fee waiver allows students of low-income backgrounds to pay little or no money for enrollment in community college, waives health and other service fees, and decreases the cost of parking permits. The waiver is based solely on financial necessity, and few other requirements need to be met.

In general, the act is unfair to citizens. Because of the lesser eligibility requirements imposed[6] upon the undocumented applicants, they will be able to garner[7] more funding in a quicker, easier manner with less paperwork to process than resident students. According to the California Department of Finance, about 2,500 students are projected[8] to receive Cal Grants totaling $14.5 million, averaging $5,800 per student. While our state government is struggling to balance a budget, the governor adds

---

2. **reap:** receive   3. **marital:** marriage   4. **exceptional:** unusual   5. **waiver:** a document that releases or relieves someone from something   6. **imposed:** placed   7. **garner:** get   8. **projected:** predicted; expected

REFLECT: What do you think would be a fair approach to illegal immigrants who want to go to college in the United States?

more debt to the list. We cannot afford to extend these comforts to people not paying into the funds they are receiving or hoping to receive.

Like simple parenting, rewarding a child for poor behavior is counterproductive.[9] Similarly, rewarding illegal immigrants for successfully defying[10] the system is hardly fair to anyone. I am by no means against immigration, but the "illegal" part of the immigration gives absolutely no means for compensation.[11] Having eager and willing people wanting to come to our free and beautiful country is an honor, but issuing government money from taxpayer dollars to accommodate[12] someone who chose not to immigrate legally is disgraceful. Perhaps allowing additional financial funding to successfully immigrated persons as a reward for coming here with legitimate papers and going through the necessary steps to become a U.S. citizen would be more fair.

Education is vital to anyone's future. Paying to educate people who cannot work because they do not have a Social Security number and therefore cannot pay taxes is a backward system with no real benefit. I personally would be more inclined[13] to assist a person openly willing to come to America the "right way" than I would to assist someone who cheated the system long enough to have completed high school without documentation.

GOP Assemblyman Tim Donnelly has a similar view. Donnelly had previously vowed[14] to file a referendum[15] prior to the act being passed, and with a total of 505,000 signatures (5 percent of last year's gubernatorial[16] votes), the bill could be frozen before being implemented.[17] Donnelly has only 90 days to collect the signatures, but practically before the ink dried from Brown's signature hitting the bill, he already had 5,000 volunteers ready to collect the community's John Hancocks.[18]

"Brown chose to fund illegals' dreams over funding our schools, pub safety & veterans," Donnelly tweeted just days after the bill was signed.

Whether the Dream Act is implemented next year or not, in the end someone is going to be left unhappy. But who should be the priority:[19] American citizens or illegal immigrants?

SUMMARIZE AND RESPOND

In your reading journal or elsewhere, summarize the main point of "Dream Act Is Finance Fantasy." Then, go back over the essay, and check off the support for this idea. Next, write a brief summary of the essay. Finally, write a brief response to the reading. Do you think the law it describes should be kept or repealed? Why?

9. **counterproductive:** working against advancement or improvement   10. **defying:** challenging; going against   11. **compensation:** benefits—usually, financial ones   12. **accommodate:** make way for   13. **inclined:** in favor of   14. **vowed:** promised   15. **referendum:** a means of setting up a vote on whether a proposed or existing law should be passed or rejected   16. **gubernatorial:** related to a governor—in this case, the election of a governor   17. **implemented:** carried out   18. **John Hancocks:** signatures; refers to the American statesman who was the first signer of the Declaration of Independence   19. **priority:** something placed ahead of other things

CHECK YOUR COMPREHENSION

1. An alternate title for this essay could be
   a. "California Dream Act Likely to Be Repealed."
   b. "California Dream Act Will Leave the State in Financial Ruin."
   c. "California Dream Act Unfair to Legal Residents."
   d. "New Dream Act Will Cause Illegal Immigrants to Flood to California."

2. The main point of this essay is that
   a. the California Dream Act makes it easy for illegal immigrants to get financial aid and push legal residents out of college enrollment slots.
   b. the California Dream Act rewards illegal immigrants for breaking the law while putting legal residents at a disadvantage.
   c. States should impose tougher financial aid restrictions on illegal immigrants who want to attend college.
   d. Some changes to the California Dream Act would make it more acceptable to all residents of the state.

3. According to Rushall, when it comes to the Cal Grant program, what is one requirement imposed on legal residents that is not imposed on illegal immigrants?
   a. Legal residents must file a much longer financial aid application with copies of past tax returns—their own or those of their parents.
   b. Legal residents must file a much longer financial aid application and include a copy of their birth certificate.
   c. Legal residents must prove that they are independent and provide tax information to show that they are receiving poverty-level wages.
   d. Legal residents must prove that they are independent, or they must provide their parents' tax information and prove that they come from a poverty-level household.

4. Does this essay include the Four Basics of Good Argument? Why or why not?

5. Look back at the vocabulary you underlined, and write sentences using these words: *reap* (para. 2); *imposed, garner* (8); *defying* (9); *vowed* (11).

TIP For tools to build your vocabulary, visit the *Student Site for Real Writing* at bedfordstmartins.com/realwriting.

READ CRITICALLY

1. What seems to be the purpose of the essay? How do you know?
2. Does Rushall do enough to address opposing views? Why or why not?

3. In paragraph 9, Rushall says, "Like simple parenting, rewarding a child for poor behavior is counterproductive. Similarly, rewarding illegal immigrants for successfully defying the system is hardly fair to anyone." Do you think this comparison is just and accurate? Why or why not?

4. What evidence does Rushall provide to support her claim that the new law is unfair?

5. The quotation from Assemblyman Tim Donnelly in paragraph 12 makes a point that goes beyond the law's perceived unfairness to legal residents. What is this point, and why do you think Rushall included it?

WRITE

Rushall describes financial aid requirements for both legal citizens and illegal immigrants in California. If you applied for financial aid, think back on all the steps you had to take and all the information you had to provide to complete your application. Can you identify any ways in which the process could be simplified or otherwise improved for all types of applicants, regardless of their legal status? Write a paragraph or essay that outlines your proposed changes and explains their benefits.

Dominic Deiro

I Have a DREAM

Dominic Deiro (1990–2011) wrote the following essay for an English course at San Joaquin Delta College, where he had been expecting to graduate with an associate's degree in 2012. The piece was published in *Delta Winds,* a collection of writings by students at the college. Deiro said of his essay, "After completing some research on the DREAM Act, I saw how it encompassed the idea of 'freedom of opportunity' that America stands for, and how it would benefit the youth of our nation and the overall goodwill of our society if passed by Congress." Deiro recommended that student writers who are assigned an argument paper research their topic thoroughly. Also, he suggested that they get other students to review their work "to eliminate any careless mistakes or to clear up any misunderstandings." (For more on peer review, see Chapter 7.)

GUIDING QUESTION
What is the "dream," as the author defines it?

1   Imagine being in high school all four years, making friends, joining clubs, playing sports, and bettering your education. What if that were ripped away from you in one second because you were an illegal alien about to be deported?[1] I, along with many other Americans, believe this

1. **deported:** forced to leave the country

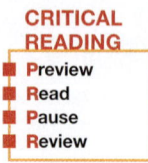

type of treatment to be inhumane.[2] In order to combat the issue of deporting young illegal aliens, Senator Dick Durbin and Senator Richard Lugar drew up the DREAM Act, which would allow illegal alien students who graduated from high school, who have good moral character, who arrived in the U.S. as minors, and who have been in the country for at least five years the opportunity to earn permanent residency if they complete two years in the military or two years in college. Even though proponents[3] of the act drew many supporters in 2007, with 52 senators voting in favor of it, they still could not break the filibuster,[4] and thus the DREAM Act was not considered. However, in December of 2010, the act may come up for vote again.* If it were proposed in Congress today, I would vote for the DREAM Act because it would increase the number of active duty soldiers, it would raise the amount of money in circulation, and it would allow young individuals the opportunity to get an education and to further benefit the community.

After considering the pros and cons of the DREAM Act, I have decided that I should support this bill because it would increase the number of active duty soldiers in our various military branches. The DREAM Act states that illegal aliens who want to gain citizenship must either attend college or join the military for two years. I believe many immigrants would sign up for the military since some of them are not good in school. They would rather take their chances in the military. Despite our active participation in the wars in Iraq and Afghanistan, our American military units are in need of people to serve. Essentially, if this act were to be passed, then our number of service personnel would increase, and our armed forces would be stronger and more unstoppable. My brother is in the National Guard, and when I asked him how he felt about having outsiders enlist in the Army, he smiled and said the following: "All of us in the Army feel like a big family, and we gladly accept anyone who is willing to join. If some people who want to be Americans want to join the Army, we would all accept them without doubts or hesitations." If the people who are risking their lives for this country are willing to accept immigrants into their family, I think we should too. I believe that we should support the DREAM Act due to its potential to increase the number of active duty soldiers.

Besides increasing the number of participants in the armed forces, the DREAM Act would improve the economy. If the illegal immigrants were granted U.S. citizenships, they would also become law-abiding[5] taxpayers. Currently, in many of our cities and states, we have illegal immigrants working under poor conditions: They are paid low wages "under the table." This money is not taxed. Even though the workers eventually do spend their money to buy products, there could potentially be more money in our economy from taxes on their wages. At my first job, I was paid under the table, and I was not taxed at all. Nowadays, however, with

VOCABULARY DEVELOPMENT Certain words in this essay are defined at the bottom of the page. Underline these words as you read them.

IDEA JOURNAL In your opinion, how can education create better citizens?

2 **IDENTIFY:** Underline the reasons it would be helpful to have immigrants join the military.

3 **SUMMARIZE:** In your own words, summarize the main point of this paragraph.

---

2. **inhumane:** cruel; lacking humanity   3. **proponents:** supporters   4. **filibuster:** an effort to block passage of a piece of legislation   5. **abiding:** following
*The version of the DREAM Act described in this essay did not pass into law. At the time of this writing, a revised version of the act, introduced in 2011, was still pending in Congress.

my current job, I am taxed every time I receive a paycheck, and I am often astonished[6] at how much is taken out. America is in a depression, and there is no sign of us getting out. If the DREAM act were passed, wages would increase for those individuals who qualify. Essentially, not only would the DREAM Act open up more opportunities for individuals in continuing their education and finding jobs, but it could potentially provide the chance for us to boost the economy.

4   Lastly, the DREAM Act should be passed because it would allow young individuals the opportunity to get an education and to further benefit the community. The act states that in order to become an American citizen, the individual must either join the military or enroll in a college. With those extra years of schooling, these individuals would increase their knowledge and would be in a position to benefit society. Throughout the history of America, there have been many immigrants who have made a strong and long-lasting impact. Albert Einstein,[7] who emigrated from Germany, was critical in World War II when he advised President Roosevelt of a bomb the Nazis were developing. John Muir,[8] who emigrated from Scotland, helped to create Yosemite National Park to benefit our environment. More personally, my mother, who worked at St. Joseph's Hospital, learned about an immigrant doctor from Iraq. She told me that he was one of the most skilled doctors at the hospital: "He was very attentive,[9] always focused in surgery. I've seen him save more lives than any other doctor I have worked with." In all of these examples, the immigrants who had an opportunity to become American citizens were able to benefit society—giving back to the nation that allowed them to work toward their goals. Under the DREAM Act, young immigrants would have the same chance.

REFLECT: In your opinion, what is the most important part of the American Dream?

5   I believe that America, its citizens, and those around the world would benefit from the DREAM Act. By increasing the number of active duty soldiers, improving the economy, and allowing young individuals the opportunity to get an education, the DREAM Act builds on our forefathers'[10] idea of life, liberty, and the pursuit of happiness. Increasing the number of individuals in our military not only strengthens our stance[11] as an international power but also builds on a sense of family and camaraderie.[12] Taxes on paychecks would increase the amount of money in circulation and would aid the U.S. in its quest to get out of debt. Finally, more individuals would be granted the opportunity to get an education, which would allow them to further benefit the community. Overall, these three reasons promote strength and support for the DREAM Act. I believe that it should be passed so that everyone can be a part of the American Dream.

---

6. astonished: shocked or surprised   **7. Albert Einstein** (1879–1955): Nobel Prize–winning physicist who formulated the theory of relativity   **8. John Muir** (1838–1914): a naturalist and conservationist who has been called the "Father of Our National Parks"   **9. attentive:** observant; focused   **10. forefathers:** ancestors; in this case, the signers of the U.S. Declaration of Independence   **11. stance:** position   **12. camaraderie:** companionship; alliance

SUMMARIZE AND RESPOND

In your reading journal or elsewhere, summarize the main point of "I Have a DREAM." Then, go back over the essay, and check off the support for this idea. Next, write a brief summary of the essay. Finally, write a brief response to the reading. Do you think passage of the federal DREAM Act would lead to all the benefits Deiro describes? Why or why not?

CHECK YOUR COMPREHENSION

1. An alternate title for this essay could be
   a. "Passage of the DREAM Act Would Benefit Immigrants and Society as a Whole."
   b. "Passage of the DREAM Act Is Essential to Maintaining U.S. Military Strength."
   c. "Passage of the DREAM Act Would Double the Growth of the U.S. Economy."
   d. "Passage of the DREAM Act Would Make the United States More Respected Internationally."

2. The main point of this essay is that
   a. immigrants will be more of a burden to society than a benefit to it if they are not given a chance to become legal citizens.
   b. passage of the DREAM Act, and the increased tax base it would provide, might be the only way to get the United States out of debt within a decade.
   c. passage of the DREAM Act would benefit the military, strengthen the U.S. economy, and give immigrants more opportunity to get an education and improve their communities.
   d. granting citizenship rights to educated illegal immigrants will produce more geniuses like Albert Einstein.

3. According to the author's brother, what would soldiers think of illegal immigrants who want to join the Army?
   a. They would accept the immigrants reluctantly because the Army is in need of recruits.
   b. They would accept the immigrants without hesitation.
   c. They would prefer that the immigrants join the Navy, Air Force, or Marines instead.
   d. They would accept the immigrants slowly, after getting to know them.

4. Does this essay include the Four Basics of Good Argument? Why or why not?

TIP For tools to build your vocabulary, visit the *Student Site for Real Writing* at **bedfordstmartins.com/realwriting**.

5. Look back at the vocabulary you underlined, and write sentences using these words: *inhumane* (para. 1); *astonished* (3); *attentive* (4); *camaraderie* (5).

READ CRITICALLY

1. In the first two sentences of his essay, Deiro asks readers to put themselves in the shoes of illegal immigrants. How did this opening affect you? Do you think it is a good way to begin the essay? Why or why not?

2. Does Deiro acknowledge and address views other than his own? If so, where?

3. Deiro includes quotations from two sources he interviewed. Which parts of his argument do these quotations support?

4. Why, according to the author, is the current status of illegal immigrants problematic from an economic point of view? Are you convinced by the argument being made here?

5. In paragraph 4, Deiro mentions the famous immigrants Albert Einstein and John Muir. How do these examples contribute to his argument?

WRITE

In the final paragraph of his essay, Deiro says that passage of the DREAM Act would help more U.S. residents achieve the "American Dream." How would you define the American Dream, and, in your opinion, what specific opportunities and achievements does it include? In a paragraph or essay, explain your views, using examples from Deiro's essay and including examples and observations of your own.

WRITE USING READINGS

Drawing on opinions and evidence from the essays by Rushall and Deiro, write an essay either in favor of or against extending more rights — including financial aid and citizenship — to illegal immigrants. You may quote directly from Rushall's and Deiro's writings or paraphrase their arguments. Whichever position you take, you should include opposing views by referring to the author who disagrees with your opinion. In your concluding paragraph, review the reasons you have given to support your position.

Acknowledgments

Susan Adams. "The Weirdest Job Interview Questions and How to Handle Them." Forbes.com, June 16, 2011. Reprinted by permission of Forbes Media LLC © 2011.

Sherman Alexie. "Superman and Me," from *The Most Wonderful Books: Writers on Discovering the Pleasures of Reading*, ed. Michael Dorris and Emilie Buchwald.

Janice Castro with Dan Cook and Cristina Garcia, "Spanglish Spoken Here." From *Time*, July 11, 1988. Copyright TIME INC. Reprinted by permission. TIME is a registered trademark of Time Inc. All rights reserved.

Judith Ortiz Cofer. "Don't Misread My Signals." From *The Latin Deli: Prose and Poetry*. Copyright © 1993 by Judith Ortiz Cofer. Reprinted by permission of the University of Georgia Press.

Patrick Conroy. "Chili Cheese Dogs, My Father and Me." From *Parade Magazine*, November 4, 2004, pp. 4–5. © Pat Conroy. Initially published in *Parade Magazine*. All rights reserved. Used by permission of Parade Magazine and Marly Rusoff & Associates, Inc.

Dominic Deiro. "I Have a Dream." *Delta Winds: A Magazine of Student Essays 2011*. San Joaquin Delta College. Reprinted by permission.

Ericsson, Stephanie. "The Ways We Lie." Copyright © 1992 by Stephanie Ericsson. Originally published by The Utne Reader. Reprinted by permission of Dunham Literary as agents for the author.

Ian Frazier. "How to Operate the Shower Curtain." *The New Yorker*, January 8, 2007. Reprinted by permission of the author.

Dianne Hales. "Why Are We So Angry?" © 2001 by Dianne Hales. Originally published in *Parade Magazine*, September 2, 2001. All rights reserved.

Oscar Hijuelos. "Memories of New York City Snow" from *Metropolis Found: New York Is Book Country 25th Anniversary Collection* (New York: New York Is Book Country, 2003). Copyright © 2003 by Oscar Hijuelos. Reprinted with the permission of The Jennifer Lyons Literary Agency, LLC for the author.

Kelly Hultgren. "Pick Up the Phone to Call, Not Text." Dailywildcat.com, August 31, 2011. Reprinted by permission of the author.

Amanda Jacobowitz. "A Ban on Water Bottles: A Way to Bolster the University's Image." *Student Life* newspaper. Posted by Amanda Jacobowitz on April 28, 2010. Forum Staff Columnists. Reprinted by permission of the author.

Frances Cole Jones. "Don't Work in a Goat's Stomach," from *The Wow Factor: The 33 Things You Must (and Must Not) Do to Guarantee Your Edge in Today's Business World* by Frances Cole Jones, copyright © 2009, 2010 by Frances Cole Jones. Used by permission of Ballantine Books, a division of Random House, Inc.

Eric Liu. Excerpt from "The Chinatown Idea," from *The Accidental Asian: Notes of a Native Speaker* by Eric Liu, copyright © 1998 by Eric Liu. Used by permission of Random House, Inc.

Lauren Mack. "Gel Pens." Reprinted by permission of the author.

Heather [Rushall] Mathis. "Dream Act Is Finance Fantasy." *The Daily Aztec*, October 17, 2011.

Bill Maxwell. "Start Snitching." *St. Petersburg Times*, September 30, 2007. Reprinted by permission of the author.

Holly Moeller. "Seeing Green: Say, Don't Spray." *The Stanford Daily*, July 21, 2011. Reprinted by permission of the author.

Alexandra Natapoff. "Bait and Snitch." Used by permission of Alexandra Natapoff.

Robert Phansalkar. "Stop Snitchin' Won't Stop Crime." From the *Badger Herald*, March 1, 2007. Used by permission of the Badger Herald.

Caroline Bunker Rosdahl and Mary T. Kowalski. Excerpt from *Textbook of Basic Nursing* 9th. © 2008 Wolters Kluwer Health/Lippincott Williams & Wilkins.

Shields, True. "The Daily Californian—To Stand in Giants' Shadows." Reprinted by permission of the author.

Courtney Stoker. "The Great Debate." From *ReVisions: Best Student Essays of the University of North Carolina at Pembroke*, Vol. 11, Spring 2011, p. 22. Reprinted by permission of the author.

Amy Tan. "Fish Cheeks." First appeared in *Seventeen* magazine. Reprinted by permission of the author and the Sandra Dijkstra Literary Agency.

Michael Thompson. "Passage into Manhood." Used by permission of Michael Thompson.

John Tierney. "Yes, Money Can Buy Happiness." From *The New York Times*, March 20, 2008. © 2008 The New York Times. All rights reserved. Used by permission and protected by the laws of the United States. The printing, copying redistribution, or transmission of the material without express permission is prohibited.

Commander Kristen Ziman. "Bad Attitudes and Glowworms." Originally appeared in the *Sun-Times Beacon News*, May 8, 2011. Reprinted by permission of the author.

Photo/Art Credits

Part photos by Joel Beaman.
Page 4: Courtesy of DIGO (DiMassimo Goldstein).
Page 6: ADB Photography.
Page 20: Ryan McVay/Getty Images.
Page 25: Tim Boyle/Getty Images.
Page 52: Chapters 3–7 Chelsea Wilson/Nick Brown photographs: Pelle Cass.
Page 114: Markku Lahdesmaki/Lightroom Inc.
Page 122: Getty Images.
Page 126: WireImage/Getty Images.
Page 129: Steve Davis Photography.
Page 133: Honey Lazar.
Page 140: The Art Archive/Tate Gallery London/Eileen Tweedy/Art Resource, NY.
Page 144: Photo by Seth David Cohen.
Page 149: Martin Kirchner/laif/Redux.
Page 153: Timm Suess.
Page 164: Taylor Hill/Getty Images.
Page 168: AP Photo/Khalid Mohammed.
Page 171: Yamakov/Shutterstock.
Page 179: Lawrence Lucier/Getty Images.
Page 185: Photos from the film ERASING HATE, courtesy of Bill Brummel, erasinghatethemovie.com.
Page 189: Javier Larrea/Getty Images.
Page 194: mart/Shutterstock.
Page 199: ©2007 Cosimo Scianna.
Page 204: Razorlight Media/waltonportfolio.com.
Page 208: Stan Honda/Getty Images.
Page 211: ADB Photography.
Page 218: Courtesy Janice E. Castro.
Page 222: Reuters/STR/Landov.
Page 226: (Frog) David Maitland/Getty Images. (Toad) Joel Sartore/Getty Images.
Page 227: Asia Kepka.

Page 238: Library of Congress.
Pages 242–43: (1973 phone) AP Photo/Eric Risberg. (1985 phone) ©Science and Society/SuperStock. (4 phones) Martin Shields/Photo Researchers, Inc. (new phone) AP Photo/Steve Senne.
Pages 248–49: (Tornado survivors in Brimfield, MA, June 2011.) AP Photo/Worcester Telegram & Gazette. (Tornado survivors, who had previously survived Hurricane Katrina, in Joplin, MO, May 2011.) AP Photo/Tulsa World, Adam Wisneski. (Prayer circle outside destroyed church in Tuscaloosa, AL, May 2011.) AP Photo/Dave Martin. (Volunteers from another town help clear rubble in Joplin, MO, June 2011.) Reuters/STR/Landov.
Page 259: Daniel White/Daily Herald.
Page 263: Ken Fisher/Getty Images.
Page 266: Courtesy of adbusters.org.
Page 286: AP Photo/Maya Hitij.
Page 308: Jason Stitt/Shutterstock.
Page 309: Mayo Foundation for Medical Education and Research.
Page 321: Photo by Jennifer Caprioli/Courtesy of U.S. Army.
Page 343: iofoto/Shutterstock.
Page 364: Arun Joseph.
Page 408: The New York Times/Redux.
Page 409: Jon Gilbert Leavitt.
Page 547: Matt Devine/Alamy.
Page 549: AP Photo/The Daily Comet, Abb Tabor.
Page 563: Janet Fekete/Getty Images.
Page 584: (Heroes sign) Martin Sasse/laif/Redux. (Restroom sign) Jeff Deck.
Page 625: AP Photo/Lou Krasky.
Page 629: The Daily Californian.
Page 634: Robert E. Hales.
Page 642: © Barbara Kinney.
Page 652: Ulf Andersen/Getty Images.
Page 661: Copyright ©2009 by Stephanie Ericsson. Reprinted by the permission of Dunham Literary as agents for the author.
Page 671: Ming Louie.
Page 682: University of Georgia Photographic Services. All rights reserved.
Page 687: Photograph by Daniel Karp.
Page 692: Fred R. Conrad/The New York Times/Redux.
Page 700: Michelle Gray/StPetePhotos.com.
Page 703: Courtesy Alexandra Natapoff.

Index

A

a
  versus *an*/*and*, 546
  basics of, 524–27
  capitalization of, 607
Abbreviations, possessive of, 582
Abstract words, avoiding, 536–38
accept/*except*, 546
Action verbs, 334
Active voice, 414–15
Adams, Susan, "The Weirdest Job Interview Questions and How to Handle Them," 144–47
Additions, transitional words/phrases for, 104
Addresses, commas in, 577
Adjective clauses
  commas around, 574–76
  joining ideas with, 494–96
Adjectives, 448–57
  basics of, 330
  coordinate, commas between, 568–69
  cumulative, 568
  prepositions after, 527
  sentence patterns and, 338
Adverbs, 448–57
  basics of, 330
  conjunctive; *see* Conjunctive adverbs
  sentence patterns and, 338
  starting sentences with, 487–88
advice/*advise*, 546
affect/*effect*, 546
Alexie, Sherman, "The Joy of Reading and Writing: Superman and Me," 652–55
  introduction of, 87
"All My Music" (Mattazi), 198–99
almost, 458–59
Altschiller, Donald, "Animal-Assisted Therapy," 312
am, 405; *see also be*, forms of
Ambiguous pronoun reference, 431–33
an
  basics of, 524–27
  capitalization of, 607

Analysis
  in problem solving, 24–25
  of reading, 18
  of visual image, 23
and
  versus *a*/*an*, 546
  in compound sentences, 569
  for coordination, 465–66
  correcting run-ons with, 365–66
  parallelism and, 479
  subject-verb agreement and, 384–87
"Animal-Assisted Therapy" (Altschiller), 312
Antecedent, 425
Anthology
  in-text citations of, 316
  Works Cited documentation of, 317
Apostrophes
  basics of, 582–89
  possessive pronouns and, 435
Appositives
  commas around, 572–74
  joining ideas with, 492–94
Appropriate degree forms, 568; *see also* Cumulative adjectives
are; *see also be*, forms of
  versus *our*, 547
  present tense and, 405
Argument, 265–88
  reading and analyzing, 278–84
  readings for, 696–716
  understanding, 265–78
  writing, 284–87
Around Him, John, "Free Money," 667–69
Articles, running bibliography for, 310
Articles (*a*, *an*, *the*), basics of, 524–27; *see also a*; *an*; *the*
as
  in comparisons, 438
  parallelism and, 480
Assumptions, questioning
  in argument, 271–76
  critical thinking and, 7–8
  narrowing topic by, 44–45

Audience, understanding, 27–33
Audio recording, Works Cited documentation of, 319

B

"Bad Attitudes and Glowworms" (Ziman), 259–60
bad/*badly*, 452–54
"Bait and Snitch: The High Cost of Snitching for Law Enforcement" (Natapoff), 703–06
"Ban on Water Bottles: A Way to Bolster the University's Image, A" (Jacobowitz), 12–14
Base form (of verb), 397
be, forms of
  as helping verbs, 335
  as linking verbs, 334
  passive voice and, 413–15
  past participles and, 401–02
  in past progressive tense, 513
  in past tense, 379, 406–07
  in present progressive tense, 512
  in present tense, 379, 405–06
  questions and, 503
  subject-verb agreement and, 379–81
Beck, Shari, "A Classroom Distraction—and Worse," 282–83
become
  forms of, 334
  as linking verb, 334
Bedford Research Room, 307
been, after *have* or *has*, 511
"Benefits of Getting a College Degree, The" (Wilson), 93, 107–08
Beverly, Jasen, "My Pilgrimage," 648–50
Biases, avoiding, 8–9
Bible, 594
Bibliography, running, 310–11
"Bird Rescue" (Cepeda), 163
Blogs, Works Cited documentation of, 319

I-1

Body of essay
    compared to paragraph, 31–33, 55–57
    drafting, 85–86
    purpose of, 31
Body of paragraph
    compared to essay, 32–33, 55–57
    purpose of, 30–31
Boldface terms, previewing, 9
Booker, Mary LaCue, 247, 256–57, 360
Books
    in-text citation of, 314–15
    italicizing title of, 594
    running bibliography for, 310
    Works Cited documentation of, 316–17
both . . . and, 481
Brainstorming, 47
"'A Brother's Murder': A Painful Story That Is As True as Ever," 296
Brown, Charlton, "Buying a Car at an Auction," 178–79
Brown, Nick, 42, 47, 51, 52, 67
Business correspondence, colons in, 599–600
but
    in compound sentences, 569
    for coordination, 465–66
    correcting run-ons with, 365–66
buy/by/bye, 547–48
"Buying a Car at an Auction" (Brown), 178–79

C
Call number, library, 305
can, as helping verb, 516, 519
Capitalization
    basics of, 604–08
    of direct quotations, 591
    of specific (proper) nouns, 604
Castro, Janice E., "Spanglish," 218–20
Cause and effect, 246–64
    reading and analyzing, 266–61
    readings for, 687–95
    understanding, 246–55
    writing, 261–64
Causes, transitional words/phrases for, 104
CDs
    italicizing title of, 594
    Works Cited documentation of, 319
Cepeda, Alessandra
    "Bird Rescue," 163
    community involvement of, 167

Chapter in book, quotation marks for title of, 594
Chapter reviews, previewing, 10
Checklists
    for evaluating draft essay, 94
    for evaluating draft paragraph, 92
    for evaluating main point, 66
    for evaluating revised essay, 109
    for evaluating revised paragraph, 107
    for evaluating support, 75
    for peer reviewing, 98
    for previewing, 10
    for responding to essay exam questions, 301
    for revising, 97
    for topic choice, 50
    for writing argument, 287
    for writing cause and effect, 264
    for writing classification, 205
    for writing comparison and contrast, 244
    for writing definition, 223–24
    for writing description, 169
    for writing illustration, 150
    for writing narration, 130
    for writing process analysis, 186
    for writing report, 297–98
    for writing research essay, 325–26
    for writing summary, 294–95
"Chili Cheese Dogs, My Father, and Me" (Conroy), 625–27
Chronological order
    in narration, 121
    transitional words/phrases for, 104
    using, 78
Citing Electronic Information, 307
Citing sources, 313–18
Classification, 188–206
    reading and analyzing, 197–202
    readings for, 657–66
    understanding, 188–97
    writing, 202–05
"Classroom Distraction—and Worse, A" (Beck), 282–83
Clause, 344
Clichés, avoiding, 540–41
Clustering, 48
Cofer, Judith Ortiz, "Don't Misread My Signals," 682–84
Coherence, revising for, 103–05
Collective nouns, pronouns for, 429–31
Colons, 599–600
Commas, 567–81
    in addresses, 577
    for adverbs at start of sentence, 487

after introductory words, 571–72
around adjective clauses, 574–76
around appositives and interrupters, 572–74
in compound sentences, 569–71
for conjunctive adverbs, 467–68
between coordinate adjectives, 568–69
for coordination, 465–66
correcting run-ons with, 361, 362, 365–66
in dates, 577
for dependent clauses, 368
in direct quotations, 591
editing for, 578–79
for fragments as examples or explanations, 352
for fragments starting with dependent words, 345, 346
for fragments starting with -ing verb forms, 348
for fragments starting with prepositions, 343
for fragments starting with to plus verb, 350
between items in series, 567–68
for joining ideas with adjective clauses, 494
for joining ideas with appositives, 493
for joining ideas with -ing verbs, 488
for joining ideas with past participles, 491
with names, 577
with quotation marks, 576–77
with semicolons, 598–99
for subordination, 471–72
then and, 370
with yes or no, 577
Comma splice
    correcting with comma and coordinating conjunction, 365
    correcting with dependent word, 368
    correcting with period, 361
    correcting with semicolon, 362
    as run-on, 359
Commercial products, capitalization of, 606
Common (generic) nouns, 604
Commonly confused words, 545–56, 558
Commonly misspelled words, 562
Community Connections
    Cepeda, Alessandra, 167
    Costas, Corin, 221
    Elswick, Shawn, 262

Haun, Jenny, 128
Powers, Caroline, 203
Rankins, Evelka, 147
Roque, Jorge, 285
Schiller, Lynze, 241
Wyant, Robin, 183
Companies, capitalization of, 606
Comparatives, 450–54
Comparison and contrast, 225–45
  reading and analyzing, 235–40
  readings for, 675–86
  understanding, 225–35
  writing, 240–44
Comparisons
  adjectives and adverbs in, 450–52
  parallelism in, 480–81
  pronouns used in, 438–40
Complete sentences, drafting in, 82–83
Complete thoughts, sentences as, 336–37
Complete verbs, helping verbs and, 335
Compound nouns, plurals of, 561
Compound objects, pronouns used with, 436–38
Compound sentences, commas in, 569–71
Compound subjects
  basics of, 332
  pronouns used with, 436–38
  subject-verb agreement and, 384–87
Concluding sentence
  in argument, 270
  in cause and effect, 253
  in classification, 194
  compared to essay conclusion, 31–33, 55–57
  in comparison and contrast, 229
  in definition, 212
  in description, 158
  drafting, 83
  in illustration, 136
  in narration, 118
  in outline, 80
  in process analysis, 174
  purpose of, 30
Conclusion of essay
  in argument, 269, 271, 276
  in cause and effect, 253
  in classification, 195
  compared to concluding sentence, 31–33, 55–57
  in comparison and contrast, 231
  in definition, 213
  in description, 159
  drafting, 89–90

in illustration, 137
in narration, 119
previewing, 10
in process analysis, 175
purpose of, 31
Concrete words, using, 536–37
Confused words, commonly, 545–56, 558
Conjunctions
  basics of, 330
  coordinating; *see* Coordinating conjunctions
  correlative, 481–83
  subordinating; *see* Dependent words
Conjunctive adverbs
  for coordination, 467–68
  correcting run-ons with, 361, 362
  list of common, 362
Conroy, Pat, "Chili Cheese Dogs, My Father, and Me," 625–27
conscience/conscious, 548
Consonants
  doubling final, spelling rules for, 560
  list of, 559
Contractions, apostrophes in, 585–86
Contrast; *see also* Comparison and contrast
  definition of, 225
  transitional words/phrases for, 104
Cook, Dan, "Spanglish," 218–20
Coordinate adjectives, commas between, 568–69
Coordinating conjunctions
  capitalization of, 607
  for coordination, 465–67
  correcting run-ons with, 361, 365–66
Coordination, 465–70, 473–77
Correlative conjunctions, 481–83
Costas, Corin
  community involvement of, 221
  "What Community Involvement Means to Me," 216–17
could
  as helping verb, 516, 519
  using *of* or *have* after, 550
Count nouns, using *a, an* or *the* with, 524–27
Courses, capitalization of, 606
Critical reading, 9–16
Critical thinking
  in argument, 271
  understanding, 3–9
Cumulative adjectives, 568

D

-d
  for past tense, 400
  for simple past tense, 508, 509
Dangling modifiers, 460–64
Dashes, 600
Database articles, Works Cited documentation of, 318
Databases, library, 306
Dates
  capitalization of, 604, 605–06
  commas in, 577
Deck, Jeff, *The Great Typo Hunt: Two Friends Changing the World, One Correction at a Time*, 584
Definite articles, 524; *see also the*
Definition, 207–24
  reading and analyzing, 214–20
  readings for, 667–74
  understanding, 207–14
  writing, 220–24
Definition of terms, previewing, 9
Deiro, Dominic, "I Have a DREAM," 712–14
Demonstrative pronouns, 436
Dependent clauses
  subject-verb agreement and, 383–84
  for subordination, 471–72
Dependent words
  correcting run-ons with, 361, 367–69
  fragments starting with, 344–47
  list of common, 345
  for subordination, 471–72
Description, 152–69
  reading and analyzing, 161–66
  readings for, 638–47
  understanding, 152–61
  writing, 166–69
Detail; *see* Support
Dictionaries
  for spelling, 557
  for word choice, 535
Differences; *see* Comparison and contrast
"Difficult Decision with a Positive Outcome, A" (Prokop), 257–58
Digital files, Works Cited documentation of, 319
Direct objects, sentence patterns and, 338, 500
Direct quotations
  avoiding plagiarism and, 313
  in-text citation of, 314
  quotation marks for, 590–93
Discussing, as prewriting technique, 47
do, forms of

as helping verbs, 335
  negative statements and, 502
  in present tense, 380
  questions and, 503
  subject-verb agreement and, 379–81
Documenting sources, 313–18
"Don't Misread My Signals" (Cofer), 682–84
"Don't Work in a Goat's Stomach" (Jones), 199–201
Double negatives, 502, 509
Drafting, 77–95
  arranging ideas in, 78–79
  of essay, 84–91
  making plan in, 80–82
  of paragraph, 82–84
  understanding, 77–78
  writing process and, 34
"Dream Act Is Finance Fantasy" (Rushall), 708–10
DVD, Works Cited documentation of, 319

E

-e, dropping final, spelling rules for, 559
-ed
  adjectives ending in, 449
  past participles and, 401–02
  past tense and, 400–01
  simple past tense and, 508, 509
Editing
  versus revising, 96–97
  writing process and, 34
Editing review tests, 609–18
Editorials, Works Cited documentation of, 317
.edu, 309
Effect, 246; see also Cause and effect
effect/affect, 546
either . . . or, 481
ei versus ie, spelling rules for, 559
Electronic sources, Works Cited documentation of, 317–19
Elswick, Shawn, 262
E-mail
  in-text citation of, 316
  Works Cited documentation of, 317
Emerson, Ralph Waldo, 273
Encyclopedia articles
  in-text citation of, 315
  Works Cited documentation of, 317
Energy, in argument, 267

English, formal, audience and, 29–30
English as Second Language; see English basics
English basics, 499–532
  articles (*a, an, the*) and, 524–27
  making direct points and, 53
  prepositions and, 527–29
  pronouns and, 505–07
  sentence patterns and, 499–504
  verbs and, 507–23; see also Verbs
Enthusiasm, in argument, 267
-er, 450–51
Ericsson, Stephanie, "The Ways We Lie," 661–65
-es
  adding, spelling rules for, 560–61
  count nouns and, 524
  for simple present tense, 508, 509
ESL; see English basics
Essays; see also Essays versus paragraphs; Research essay
  drafting, 84–91
  exam questions and, 298–301
  outlining, 81–82
  quotation marks for title of, 594
  revising, 107–09; see also Revising
  topic for, 45
  understanding form of, 30–33
Essays versus paragraphs
  in argument, 270–71
  in cause and effect, 252–53
  in classification, 194–95
  in comparison and contrast, 230–31
  comparison of forms in, 31–33, 55–57
  in definition, 212–13
  in description, 158–59
  in illustration, 136–37
  in narration, 118–19
  in process analysis, 174–75
  support in, 69–70
-est
  adjectives ending in, 449
  superlatives and, 450–51
et al., 317
Evaluating Web sites, 307–09
Evaluation
  in problem solving, 25–26
  of reading, 20–21
  of visual images, 24
Events, time order for, 78
Evidence, in argument, 268–76
Examples; see also Illustration
  in argument, 272–73
  colons before, 599
  fragments as, 351–53

opening essay with, 87
  transitional words/phrases for, 104
Exam questions, 298–301
except/accept, 546
Exclamation points, in direct quotations, 591
Expert opinion, in argument, 272–73
Explanations
  colons before, 599
  fragments as, 351–53
"Eyeglasses vs. Laser Surgery: Benefits and Drawbacks" (Ibrahim), 237

F

Facts, in argument, 272–73
Fana, Mayerlin, 377
FANBOYS, 330, 365, 465, 569
Feminine pronouns
  basics of, 505, 506
  pronoun agreement and, 427
Figures in visual images, 22
Film, Works Cited documentation of, 319
fine/find, 548
"First Day in Fallujah" (Healy), 638–41
First person pronouns, 441–42
"Fish Cheeks" (Tan), 126–27
Flowcharts
  for adjectives and adverbs, 457
  for coordination, 469, 477
  for dangling modifiers, 464
  for fragments, 358
  for misplaced modifiers, 464
  for parallelism, 485
  for pronouns, 447
  for run-ons, 376
  for sentence variety, 498
  for subject-verb agreement errors, 396
  for subordination, 477
  for verb tense errors, 421
  for word choice, 544
for
  in compound sentences, 569
  for coordination, 465–66
  correcting run-ons with, 365–66
Forecasts, in argument, 272–73
Formal English
  basics of; see English basics
  formal audience and, 29–30
Fragments, 341–58
  editing for, 353–55
  as examples or explanations, 351–53

flowchart for finding and fixing, 358
starting with dependent words, 344–47
starting with -ing verb forms, 348–49
starting with prepositions, 343–44
starting with *to* plus verb, 349–51
understanding, 341–42
Frazier, Ian, "How to Operate the Shower Curtain," 179–82
"Free Money" (Around Him), 667–69
Freewriting, 46
Fused sentences
correcting with comma and coordinating conjunction, 365
correcting with dependent word, 368
correcting with period, 361
correcting with semicolon, 362
as run-on, 359
Future tenses
perfect, 510–11
progressive, 513–14
simple, 508–9

G

Garcia, Cristina, "Spanglish," 218–20
"Gel Pens" (Mack), 622–23
Gender
of pronouns, 427–31, 505, 506
sexist language and, 541
Generating ideas, writing process and, 34
Generic (common) nouns, 604
Gerunds, 521–23; *see also* -ing verb forms
"Gifts from the Heart" (Palmer), 142–43
good, versus *well*, 452–54
Government publications
in-text citation of, 315
Works Cited documentation of, 318
Grading criteria, 35–40
Graham, Jeremy, 172, 177–78
"Great Debate, The: Essentialism vs. Dominance" (Stoker), 675–80
Great Typo Hunt: Two Friends Changing the World, One Correction at a Time, The (Deck), 584
Groups, capitalization of, 606
Guiding question
asking, before reading, 10
for research, 304

H

had, for past perfect tense, 412–13, 510, 511
had to, versus *must*, 519
Hales, Dianne, "Why Are We So Angry?," 634–36
introduction of, 87
reference of conclusion to introduction in, 89–90
hardly, 458–59
Hargreaves, Ken, 397
has, for present perfect tense, 410–12, 510, 511
Haun, Jenny, 128
have, forms of
with *could/should/would*, 519
as helping verb, 335
versus *of*, 550
past participles and, 401–02
in present perfect tense, 410–12, 510, 511
in present tense, 379, 405–06
subject-verb agreement and, 379–81
he, sexist use of, 428
Headings, previewing, 9
Headnotes, previewing, 9
Healy, Brian, "First Day in Fallujah," 638–41
Helping verbs, 335–36
list of common, 501
in negative statements, 501–02
past participles and, 410–15
questions and, 503
here, subject-verb agreement and, 389–91
Hijuelos, Oscar, "Memories of New York City Snow," 164–65
his or her, 427, 428
"How to Operate the Shower Curtain" (Frazier), 179–82
Hultgren, Kelly, "Pick Up the Phone to Call, Not Text," 657–59
Hyde, Celia, 154
Hyphenating words, 601
Hyphens, 600–01

I

-i, changing -y to
adding -ed to, 400
before adding -er or -est, 450–51
spelling rules for, 559–60
I, versus *me*, 436
Ibrahim, Said, "Eyeglasses vs. Laser Surgery: Benefits and Drawbacks," 237
Ideas, arranging, 78–79
ie versus *ei*, spelling rules for, 559
"I Have a DREAM" (Deiro), 712–14
Illustration, 132–51
reading and analyzing, 140–47
readings for, 629–37
understanding, 132–40
writing, 147–50
Importance, order of; *see* Order of importance
Incomplete sentences; *see* Fragments
Incomplete thoughts, 336–37
Indefinite articles, 524; *see also a; an*
Indefinite pronouns
basics of, 428–29
list of common, 367, 426
subject-verb agreement and, 387–89
Independent clauses, 359; *see also* Sentences
Indirect objects, sentence patterns and, 338, 500
Indirect quotations
avoiding plagiarism and, 311–13
in-text citation of, 314
quotation marks and, 593–94
Infinitives
basics of, 521–23
fragments starting with, 349–51
-ing, adding to word ending in -y, 560
-ing verb forms
fragments starting with, 348–49
for future progressive tense, 513–14
joining ideas with, 488–90
as misplaced modifiers, 459
for past progressive tense, 513
for present progressive tense, 511–12
Intensive pronouns, 436
Interjections, 331
Internet
address extensions on, 309
evaluating sources from, 307–09
finding sources on, 306–07
prewriting and, 48–49
Interrogative pronouns, 436
Interrupters, commas around, 572–74
Interviews
conducting, 307
in-text citation of, 314, 316
Works Cited documentation of, 319
In-text citations, 313, 314–16
Introduction of essay
conclusion referring to, 89–90
drafting, 86–89

Introduction of essay (cont.)
  previewing, 9
  purpose of, 31
Introductory words, commas after, 571–72
Invisible writing, 46
Irregular plurals, 561
Irregular verbs
  subject-verb agreement and, 379–81
  verb tense and, 402–10
is, 405; *see also* *be*, forms of
Items in series, commas for, 567–68
its, versus *it's*, 548, 583

J

Jacobowitz, Amanda, "A Ban on Water Bottles: A Way to Bolster the University's Image," 12–14
Jones, Frances Cole, "Don't Work in a Goat's Stomach," 199–201
Journal, prewriting and, 49
Journal articles, running bibliography for, 310
"Joy of Reading and Writing: Superman and Me, The" (Alexie), 652–55
  introduction of, 87
just, 458–59

K

Key words
  previewing, 9
  repeating for coherence, 105
  searching with, 306
King, Leigh, 190, 197–98, 342
knew/new/know/no, 549
know/no/knew/new, 549
Koran, 594
Kowalski, Mary T., *Textbook of Basic Nursing*, 17

L

Language notes
  on adjectives as singular or plural, 448
  on articles (*a/an/the*), 333
  on *be*, 335
  on capitalization, 606
  on complete sentences, 341
  on *-ed* and *-ing* forms of adjectives, 449
  on forming questions, 389
  on *in* and *on*, 332
  on present perfect tense, 411
  on progressive tenses, 399
  on pronoun gender, 435
  on *that*, 350
  on verb endings, 397
Languages, capitalization of, 606
Layland, Kelly, 115, 123–24
"Learning Tool Whose Time Has Come, A" (Yilmaz), 281–82
Leibov, Brad, 228, 236–37
Lester, Jimmy, 359
Letters, apostrophes with, 587
Librarian, consulting, 304–05
Library, finding sources at, 304–06
Linking verbs, 334–35, 338
Listing
  for generating support, 73
  as prewriting technique, 47
Lists
  colons before, 599
  parallelism in, 479
  semicolons for, 598–99
Liu, Eric, "Po-Po in Chinatown," 642–45
lose/loose, 550
Lowercase, 604
-ly, forming adverbs with, 449
Lynch, Jelani, "My Turnaround," 124–25

M

Mack, Lauren, "Gel Pens," 622–23
Magazine articles
  quotation marks for title of, 594
  running bibliography for, 310
  Works Cited documentation of, 317, 318
Magazines, italicizing title of, 594
Main point; *see also* Thesis statement; Topic sentence
  in argument, 267–68, 269–71
  in cause and effect, 250–53
  in classification, 190–95
  in comparison and contrast, 228–31
  in definition, 209–10, 212–13
  in description, 154–56, 157–59
  of essay, 31
  finding while reading, 10–11
  forceful, 64
  as idea to show, explain, or prove, 62–63
  in illustration, 134–37
  in narration, 115–16, 117–19
  of paragraph, 30
  of paragraph versus essay, 32–33
  in process analysis, 172, 173–75
  single versus multiple, 60–61
  specific versus general, 61–62
Main verb, 334; *see also* Verbs
Mancuso, Tony, 329
Mapping, 48
Masculine pronouns
  basics of, 505, 506
  pronoun agreement and, 427, 428
Mattazi, Lorenza, "All My Music," 198–99
Maxwell, Bill, "Start Snitching," 700–02
  introduction of, 87–88
  reference of conclusion to introduction in, 90
may, as helping verb, 516
me, versus *I*, 436
Melancon, Diane, 266, 279–81
"Memories of New York City Snow" (Hijuelos), 164–65
might
  as helping verb, 517
  using *of* or *have* after, 550
mind/mine, 550
Misplaced modifiers, 458–60, 461–64
Misspelled words, commonly, 562
MLA documentation, 313–18
Modal verbs (modal auxiliaries), 401, 515–19; *see also* Helping verbs
Modifiers
  dangling, 460–64
  misplaced, 458–60, 461–64
Moeller, Holly, "Say, Don't Spray," 687–90
more, 450–51
most, 450–51
Movies
  italicizing title of, 594
  Works Cited documentation of, 319
must, as helping verb, 517, 519
"My Career Goal" (Wilson), 91–92, 106
"My Home Exercise Program" (Wood), 88
"My Pilgrimage" (Beverly), 648–50
"My Turnaround" (Lynch), 124–25

N

Names
  capitalization of, 604–06
  commas with, 577
Narration, 113–31
  opening essay with, 87
  reading and analyzing, 123–27
  readings for, 621–28

understanding, 113–22
writing, 128–30
Natapoff, Alexandra, "Bait and Snitch: The High Cost of Snitching for Law Enforcement," 703–06
Nationalities, capitalization of, 606
n.d., 317
nearly, 458–59
Negative statements
basics of, 501–02
in future progressive tense, 513
helping verbs for, 515–18
in past progressive tense, 513
in present progressive tense, 512
in simple tense, 509
neither . . . nor, 481
.net, 309
new/knew/know/no, 549
Newspaper articles
quotation marks for title of, 594
running bibliography for, 310
Works Cited documentation of, 317, 318
Newspapers, italicizing title of, 594
no
commas with, 577
versus *know/knew/new*, 549
Noncount nouns, using *a, an, the* with, 524–27
nor
in compound sentences, 569
for coordination, 465–66
correcting run-ons with, 365–66
subject-verb agreement and, 384–87
not, negative statements and, 501–02
not only . . . but also, 481
Noun phrase, 329, 493
Nouns; *see also* Pronouns
basics of, 329
sentence patterns and, 338
Novels, italicizing title of, 594
Numbers
apostrophes with, 587
writing out with hyphens, 600

O

Object of preposition, subject of sentence and, 332
Object pronouns
basics of, 505–06
in comparisons, 438–40
compound objects and, 436–38
correct use of, 434–35
whom as, 440–41

Objects
sentence patterns and, 499–500
space order for, 79
in visual images, 22
of/have, 550
Online databases, library, 306
Online dictionaries, 535, 557
Online library catalog, 305
Online thesaurus, 536
only, 458–59
Opinion, opening essay with, 87–88
or
in compound sentences, 569
for coordination, 465–66
correcting run-ons with, 365–66
parallelism and, 479
subject-verb agreement and, 384–87
Order of ideas, 78–79
Order of importance
in argument, 276–77
in cause and effect, 254
in classification, 196
in comparison and contrast, 234
in definition, 214
in description, 160
in illustration, 139
transitional words/phrases for, 104
using, 78, 79
.org, 309
Organization
in argument, 276–78
in cause and effect, 254–55
in classification, 196–97
in comparison and contrast, 232–35
in definition, 214
in description, 160–61
in illustration, 139
in narration, 121–22
in process analysis, 176
Organizations, capitalization of, 606
Organizing principle, in classification, 188, 190–92
our/are, 547
Outlining, 80–82
Ownership, apostrophes for, 582–85

P

Pairs, parallelism in, 479
Palmer, Casandra, "Gifts from the Heart," 142–43
"Parabens: Widely Used Chemicals Spark New Cautions," 82–83
Paragraphs; *see also* Paragraphs versus essays
drafting, 82–84
outlining, 80

revising, 105–07; *see also* Revising
titling, 84
topics for, 45
understanding form of, 30–33
Paragraphs versus essays
in argument, 270–71
in cause and effect, 252–53
in classification, 194–95
in comparison and contrast, 230–31
comparison of forms in, 31–33, 55–57
in definition, 212–13
in description, 158–59
in illustration, 136–37
in narration, 118–19
in process analysis, 174–75
support in, 69–70
Parallelism, 478–85
Paraphrases, avoiding plagiarism in, 311, 312–13
Parentheses, 600
Participle, 330
"Passage into Manhood" (Thompson), 671–73
passed/past, 550–51
Passive voice, 413–15
Past participles
for future perfect tense, 511
irregular verbs as, 402–05, 409–10
joining ideas with, 490–92
for past perfect tense, 510, 511
for present perfect tense, 510, 511
regular verbs as, 401–02
verb tense and, 410–15
Past tenses
forms of *be* in, 379, 406–07
irregular verbs in, 402–05
perfect, 412–13, 510
progressive, 511–12, 513
regular verbs in, 400–01
simple, 502, 508, 509
peace/piece, 551
Peer review, 97–98
People
capitalization of, 604–05
space order for, 79
Periodicals
indexes/databases for, 306
in-text citation of, 314
running bibliography for, 310
Works Cited documentation of, 317
Periods
correcting run-ons with, 361, 363
in direct quotations, 591

Personal interviews
  conducting, 307
  in-text citation of, 314
  Works Cited documentation of, 319
Personal pronouns, list of common, 426
Personal spelling list, 558
Person of pronouns, 441–42
Persuasion; *see* Argument
Phansalkar, Robert, "Stop Snitchin' Won't Stop Crime," 697–98
"Pick Up the Phone to Call, Not Text" (Hultgren), 657–59
piece/peace, 551
Places
  capitalization of, 604, 605
  space order for, 79
Plagiarism, avoiding, 35, 310–13
Plural nouns/pronouns, 427–31, 561
Plural subject/verb, 377; *see also* Subject-verb agreement
Plurals, irregular, 561
Podcast, Works Cited documentation of, 319
Poems, quotation marks for title of, 594
Point-by-point comparison, 232–34
"Po-Po in Chinatown" (Liu), 642–45
Position, opening essay with, 87–88
Possessive pronouns
  apostrophes and, 583
  basics of, 505
  correct use of, 434–35, 436
  list of common, 426
Powers, Caroline, 203
Predictions, in argument, 272–73
Prepositional phrases
  as misplaced modifiers, 459
  pronouns in, 436
  sentence patterns and, 500
  subject of sentence and, 332–33
  subject-verb agreement and, 381–83
Prepositions
  basics of, 330, 527–29
  capitalization of, 607
  fragments starting with, 343–44
  list of common, 332, 344
Present tenses
  forms of *be* in, 379, 405–06
  forms of *do* in, 380
  forms of *have* in, 379, 405–06
  irregular verbs in, 402–05
  perfect, 410–12, 509–10, 511
  progressive, 399

regular verbs in, 377–78, 398–400
  simple, 399, 508, 509
Previewing, before reading, 9–10
Prewriting techniques
  for exploring topic, 46–49
  for generating support, 71
Primary support
  in argument, 269–71
  in cause and effect, 251–53
  in classification, 194–95
  in comparison and contrast, 229–31
  in definition, 212–13
  in description, 158–59
  drafting, 85–86
  in essays, 70
  in illustration, 136–37
  in narration, 116–19
  in outlines, 80, 81
  in paragraphs, 69–70
  in process analysis, 174–75
  selecting best, 71–72
  student example of, 74
  understanding, 68
principal/principle, 551
Problem solving, 24–26
Process analysis, 170–87
  reading and analyzing, 176–82
  readings for, 648–56
  understanding, 170–76
  writing, 183–86
Profiles of Success
  Booker, Mary LaCue, 256–57
  Graham, Jeremy, 177–78
  Hyde, Celia, 161–62
  King, Leigh, 197–98
  Layland, Kelly, 123–24
  Leibov, Brad, 236–37
  Melancon, Diane, 279–81
  Scanlon, Walter, 215–16
  Upright, Karen, 140–42
Prokop, Caitlin, "A Difficult Decision with a Positive Outcome," 257–58
Pronouns, 425–47
  basics of, 330, 505–07
  checking for agreement of, 427–31
  editing, 442–44
  flowchart for errors with, 447
  identifying, 425–27
  indefinite; *see* Indefinite pronouns
  list of common, 426
  making clear reference of, 431–34
  making consistent in person, 441–42
  relative; *see* Relative pronouns

understanding, 425
  using right type of, 434–41
Proofreading, for spelling, 558
Proper (specific) nouns, 604
Punctuation
  apostrophes, 435, 582–89
  colons, 599–600
  commas; *see* Commas
  dashes, 600
  hyphens, 600–01
  parentheses, 600
  question marks, 503, 591
  quotation marks; *see* Quotation marks
  semicolons; *see* Semicolons
Purpose for writing
  finding while reading, 10
  understanding, 27–33

Q

qtd. in, 313
Question marks
  basics of, 503
  in direct quotations, 591
Questions
  asking, to narrow topic, 45
  basics of, 503
  in future progressive tense, 514
  guiding, asking before reading, 10
  helping verbs for, 515–18
  opening essay with, 88
  in past progressive tense, 513
  in present progressive tense, 512
  subject-verb agreement and, 389, 390–91
quiet/quite/quit, 551
Quotation marks
  basics of, 590–97
  commas with, 576–77
  for direct quotations, 313
  single, 592
Quotations
  avoiding plagiarism and, 35, 311–13
  direct, 590–93
  indirect, 593–94
  in-text citation of, 314
  opening essay with, 86–87
  with quotations, 592

R

Radio program, Works Cited documentation of, 319
Random House Webster's College Dictionary, 535
Rankins, Evelka, 147

rather . . . than, 481
Reading
  critically, 9–17
  to report, 297
  to summarize, 292–94
  writing critically about, 16–21
Real-world documents, reading critically, 14–16
Reasons, in argument, 268–76
Reciprocal pronouns, 436
Recording, Works Cited documentation of, 319
Reference librarian, consulting, 304–05
Reflexive pronouns, 436
Regular verbs; *see also* Verbs
  in present tense, 377–78
  verb tense and, 398–402
Relative pronouns
  basics of, 436, 505, 506–07
  correcting run-ons with, 367
Religions, capitalization of, 606
Repetitious pronoun reference, 433–34
Reports, 295–98
Research essay, 302–25
  avoiding plagiarism in, 310–13
  choosing topic for, 303–04
  citing and documenting sources for, 313–18
  evaluating sources for, 307–09
  finding sources for, 304–07
  making schedule for, 302–03
  student example of, 319–24
Results, transitional words/phrases for, 104
Review tests for editing, 609–18
Revising, 96–110
  for coherence, 103–05
  for detail and support, 101–02
  of essay, 107–09
  of paragraph, 105–07
  peer review and, 97–98
  understanding, 96–97
  for unity, 99–101
  writing process and, 34
Riesler, Dara (student writer)
  research steps of, 304, 305
  "Service Dogs Help Heal the Mental Wounds of War," 320–24
right/write, 552
Rodale, J. I., *The Synonym Finder*, 536
Roman, Naomi, 341
Roque, Jorge, 277–78, 285
Rosdahl, Caroline Bunker, *Textbook of Basic Nursing*, 17

Rubric, 35–40
Running bibliography, 310–11
Run-ons, 359–76
  editing for, 371–73
  finding and correcting, 361–70
  flowchart for, 376
  understanding, 359–60
Rushall, Heather, "Dream Act Is Finance Fantasy," 708–10

S

-s
  adding, spelling rules for, 560–61
  count nouns and, 524
  present tense and, 377–78, 398–400
  simple present tense and, 508, 509
-'s
  for plural letters and numbers, 587
  to show ownership, 582–85
  with time, 587
"Say, Don't Spray" (Moeller), 687–90
Scanlon, Walter, 208, 215–16, 378
Schedule, for research essay, 302–03
Schiller, Lynze, 241
Search engines, 306
Secondary support
  adding, 72–73
  in argument, 268–71
  in cause and effect, 251–53
  in classification, 194–95
  in comparison and contrast, 229–31
  in definition, 212–13
  in description, 157–59
  in essays, 70
  in illustration, 135–37
  in narration, 116–18
  in outlines, 80, 81
  in paragraphs, 69–70
  in process analysis, 174–75
  student example of, 74
  understanding, 68
Second person pronouns, 441–42
seem, 334
Semicolons
  basics of, 598–99
  for coordination, 467–69
  correcting run-ons with, 361, 362–63
Senses, in description, 156
Sentences, 329–40
  basic patterns of, 337–39, 499–504

  capitalization of, 604
  complete thoughts and, 336–37
  incomplete; *see* Fragments
  joining with semicolons, 598
  parts of speech and, 329–31
  run-ons and, 359
  subjects of, 331–33
  verbs in, 334–36
Sentence variety, 486–98
  editing for, 496–97
  joining ideas with adjective clauses for, 494–96
  joining ideas with appositives for, 492–94
  joining ideas with *-ing* verbs for, 488–90
  joining ideas with past participles for, 490–92
  starting sentences with adverbs for, 487–88
  understanding, 486–87
Series, items in, commas for, 567–68
"Service Dogs Help Heal the Mental Wounds of War" (Riesler), 320–24
set/sit, 552
Sexist language
  avoiding, 541
  pronouns and, 428
Shields, True, "To Stand in Giants' Shadows," 629–32
Short stories, quotation marks for title of, 594
should
  as helping verb, 517, 519
  using *of* or *have* after, 550
Sight, in description, 156
Similarities; *see* Comparison and contrast
Simple future tense, 508–09
Simple past tense
  basics of, 508, 509
  negatives in, 502
Simple present tense
  basics of, 508, 509
  versus present progressive, 399
Singular nouns/pronouns, 427–31
Singular subject/verb, 377; *see also* Subject-verb agreement
sit/set, 552
Slang, avoiding, 538
Smell, in description, 156
so
  in compound sentences, 569
  for coordination, 465–66
  correcting run-ons with, 365–66

Songs, quotation marks for title of, 594
Sound, in description, 156
Soundalike words, 545–56
Sources
  avoiding plagiarism and, 35
  citing and documenting, 313–18
  evaluating, for research essay, 307–09
  finding, for research essay, 304–07
Space order
  in cause and effect, 254
  in classification, 196
  in description, 160
  transitional words/phrases for, 103
  using, 78, 79
"Spanglish" (Castro et al), 218–20
Specific (proper) nouns, 604
Specific words, using, 536–37
Speech, parts of, 329–31
Spell checker, 557
Spelling, 557–63
"Start Snitching" (Maxwell), 700–02
  introduction of, 87–88
  reference of conclusion to introduction in, 90
Statements, basics of, 499–501
Stoker, Courtney, "The Great Debate: Essentialism vs. Dominance," 675–80
"Stop Snitchin' Won't Stop Crime" (Phansalkar), 697–98
Subject of sentence
  basics of, 331–33, 341
  sentence patterns and, 338, 499–500
  verbs before, 389–91
  words between verb and, 381–84
Subject pronouns
  basics of, 505–06
  in comparisons, 438–40
  compound subjects and, 436–38
  correct use of, 434–35
  who as, 440–41
Subject-verb agreement, 377–96
  compound subject and, 384–87
  editing for, 391–93
  flowchart for, 396
  forms of *be, have, do* and, 379–81
  indefinite pronouns and, 387–89
  understanding, 377–78
  verb before subject and, 389–91
  words between subject and verb and, 381–84

Subordinating conjunctions; *see* Dependent words
Subordination, 471–77
Subtitles, colons before, 599–600
Summary
  avoiding plagiarism in, 311
  previewing, 10
  in problem solving, 24
  of readings, 17–18
  of visual images, 21–22
  writing, 291–95
Superlatives, 450–54
"Supersize It" (Verini), 86–87
Support, 68–76
  in argument, 268–76
  in cause and effect, 251–53
  in classification, 193–95
  in comparison and contrast, 229–31
  in definition, 210–13
  in description, 156–59
  finding while reading, 10, 11–12
  in illustration, 135–37
  in narration, 116–20
  in process analysis, 172–75
  revising for, 101–02
Support paragraphs, 31–33, 55–57
Support sentences, 30–33, 55–57
suppose/supposed, 552
Surprise, opening essay with, 87
Synonym Finder, The (Rodale), 536
Synonyms, thesaurus for, 536
Synthesis
  in problem solving, 25
  of readings, 18–20
  of visual images, 23–24

T

Tan, Amy, "Fish Cheeks," 126–27
Tappening advertisement, 4–5
Taste, in description, 156
Television programs
  italicizing title of, 594
  Works Cited documentation of, 319
Tests, editing review, 609–18
Textbook of Basic Nursing (Rosdahl and Kowalski), 17
than
  in comparisons, 438
  parallelism and, 480
  versus *then*, 552–53
that
  adjective clauses and, 494
  basics of, 506–07
  commas and, 574–75

  as misplaced modifier, 459
  subject-verb agreement and, 383
the
  basics of, 524–27
  capitalization of, 607
  italicizing or capitalizing, 594
their
  versus *his or her*, 428
  versus *there/they're*, 553
then
  run-ons caused by, 370
  versus *than*, 552–53
there, subject-verb agreement and, 389–91
there is/there are, 504
Thesaurus, 536
Thesis statement, 52–67; *see also* Main point
  in argument, 267–68, 270–71
  in cause and effect, 250, 251, 252–53
  in classification, 192, 193–95
  compared to topic sentence, 31–33, 55–57
  in comparison and contrast, 228–29, 230–31
  in definition, 209–10, 212–13
  in description, 155, 157, 158–159
  developing, 55–64
  drafting, 85
  in illustration, 134, 135, 136–37
  in narration, 115, 116, 118–19
  in outline, 80, 81
  in process analysis, 172, 174–75
  purpose of, 31
  supporting, 68–76
  understanding, 52–55
  writing, 64–66
Thinking critically, 3–9
Third person pronouns, 441–42
Thompson, Michael, "Passage into Manhood," 671–73
though/through/threw, 553
through/threw/though, 553
Tierney, John, "Yes, Money Can Buy Happiness," 692–93
Time, apostrophes with, 587
Time order
  in cause and effect, 254
  in classification, 196
  in description, 160
  in illustration, 139
  in narration, 121
  in process analysis, 176
  transitional words/phrases for, 104
  using, 78

Titles
    capitalization of, 606–07
    of paragraph, 84
    previewing, 9
    quotation marks for, 590, 594–95
to
    helping verbs and, 518
    versus *too* and *two*, 553–54
Topic, 42–51
    choosing for research essay, 303–04
    exploring, 46–49
    finding, 43
    narrowing, 43–45
    understanding, 42–43
Topic sentence, 52–67; *see also* Main point
    in argument, 267–68, 269, 270
    in cause and effect, 250, 251, 252
    in classification, 192, 193, 194
    compared to thesis statement, 31–33, 55–57
    in comparison and contrast, 228–29, 230
    concluding sentence referring to, 83
    in definition, 209, 210–11, 212
    in description, 155, 157–58
    developing, 55–64
    drafting for essay, 85–86
    in illustration, 134, 135–36
    in narration, 115, 116–19
    in outline, 80, 81
    in process analysis, 172, 173–74
    purpose of, 30
    revising for unity with, 99–100
    supporting, 68–76
    of support paragraphs in essay, 31–33
    understanding, 52–55
    writing, 64–66
to plus verb
    basics of, 521–23
    fragments starting with, 349–51
"To Stand in Giants' Shadows" (Shields), 629–32
Touch, in description, 156
Transitions
    in argument, 276–77
    in cause and effect, 254
    in classification, 196
    for coherence, 103–05
    in comparison and contrast, 234
    in definition, 214
    in description, 160
    in illustration, 139
    in narration, 121
    in process analysis, 176

Twain, Mark, "Two Ways of Seeing a River," 238–39
two/too/to, 553–54
"Two Ways of Seeing a River" (Twain), 238–39

U
Unity, revising for, 99–101
Upright, Karen, 134, 140–42, 398
use/used, 554

V
Vague pronoun reference, 431–33
Vague words, avoiding, 536–38
Verb phrase, 335
Verbs
    base form of, 397
    basics of, 330, 334–36
    followed by gerunds and infinitives, 521–23
    helping verbs and, 515–19
    prepositions after, 527–29
    sentence patterns and, 338, 499–500
    before subjects, 389–91
    words between subjects and, 381–84
Verb tense, 397–421; *see also* Future tenses; Past tenses; Present tenses
    basics of, 507–23
    consistency of, 415–16
    editing for, 416–18
    flowchart for, 421
    irregular verbs and, 402–10
    past participles and, 410–15
    regular verbs and, 398–402
    understanding, 397–98
Verini, James, "Supersize It," 86–87
Visual images
    of apostrophe errors, 584
    of argument, 266, 286
    of cause and effect, 248–49, 263
    of classification, 189, 204
    of commonly confused words, 547, 549
    of comparison and contrast, 227, 242–43
    of definition, 208, 222–23
    of description, 153, 167–68
    of fragments, 343
    of illustration, 133, 149
    of narration, 114, 129–30
    of process analysis, 171, 184–85
    of run-ons, 364
    of spelling errors, 563

    of subject-verb agreement errors, 386
    writing critically about, 21–24
Vowels, list of, 559

W
was, 406–07; *see also be*, forms of
"Ways We Lie, The" (Ericsson), 661–65
Weblogs, Works Cited documentation of, 318
Web sites
    evaluating reliability of, 308–09
    in-text citation of, 314
    library, 306
    running bibliography for, 310
    Works Cited documentation of, 318
"Weirdest Job Interview Questions and How to Handle Them, The" (Adams), 144–47
well, versus *good*, 452–54
were, 406–07; *see also be*, forms of
"What Community Involvement Means to Me" (Costas), 216–17
which
    adjective clauses and, 494
    basics of, 506–07
    commas and, 574–75
    fragments starting with, 345
    as misplaced modifier, 459
    subject-verb agreement and, 383
who
    adjective clauses and, 494
    basics of, 506–07
    commas and, 574–75
    fragments starting with, 345
    as misplaced modifier, 459
    subject-verb agreement and, 383
    versus *whom*, 440–41
whoever, 440
Whole-to-whole comparison, 232–34
whom
    subject-verb agreement and, 383
    versus *who*, 440–41
whomever, 440
whose
    fragments starting with, 345
    as misplaced modifier, 459
    subject-verb agreement and, 383
    versus *who's*, 554
who's/whose, 554
"Why Are We So Angry?" (Hales), 634–36
    introduction of, 87
    reference of conclusion to introduction in, 89–90

Wikipedia, 307
Wilde, Oscar, 285
will
  as helping verb, 518, 519
  for simple future tense, 509
will be, 513–14
will have, 511
Wilson, Chelsea
  "The Benefits of Getting a College Degree," 93, 107–08
  "My Career Goal," 91–92, 106
  outlining by, 80
  prewriting techniques by, 46–48
  primary and secondary support by, 73–74
  topic sentence by, 65
Wood, Michele, "My Home Exercise Program," 88
Words
  choice of, 535–44
  commonly confused, 545–56, 558
  commonly misspelled, 562
Wordy language, avoiding, 538–40
Works Cited
  guidelines for, 313, 314–18
  running bibliography for, 310
  student example of, 322–23

would
  as helping verb, 518, 519
  using *of* or *have* after, 550
write/*right*, 552
Writers at Work
  Booker, Mary LaCue, 247, 360
  Graham, Jeremy, 172
  Hyde, Celia, 154
  King, Leigh, 190, 342
  Layland, Kelly, 115
  Leibov, Brad, 228
  Melancon, Diane, 266
  Scanlon, Walter, 208, 378
  Upright, Karen, 134, 398
Writing basics, 27–41
  audience and, 27–33
  grading criteria and, 35–40
  purpose for writing and, 27–33
  writing process and, 34–35
Writing critically
  about readings, 16–21
  about visual images, 21–24
Writing process, understanding, 34–35
Wyant, Robin, 183

Y

-y
  adding *-ing* to, 560
  changing to *-i*, adding *-ed* to, 400
  changing to *-i*, before adding *-er* or *-est*, 450–51
  changing to *-i*, spelling rules for, 559–60
  as vowel or consonant, 559
yes, commas with, 577
"Yes, Money Can Buy Happiness" (Tierney), 692–93
yet
  in compound sentences, 569
  for coordination, 465–66
  correcting run-ons with, 365–66
Yilmaz, Jason, "A Learning Tool Whose Time Has Come," 281–82
your/*you're*, 554

Z

Ziman, Kristen, "Bad Attitudes and Glowworms," 259–60
Z pattern of visuals, 22

Real Take-Away Points

Four Basics of Good Writing

1. It considers what the audience knows and needs.
2. It fulfills the writer's purpose.
3. It includes a clear, definite point.
4. It provides support that shows, explains, or proves the main point.

For more on the elements of good writing, see Chapter 2.

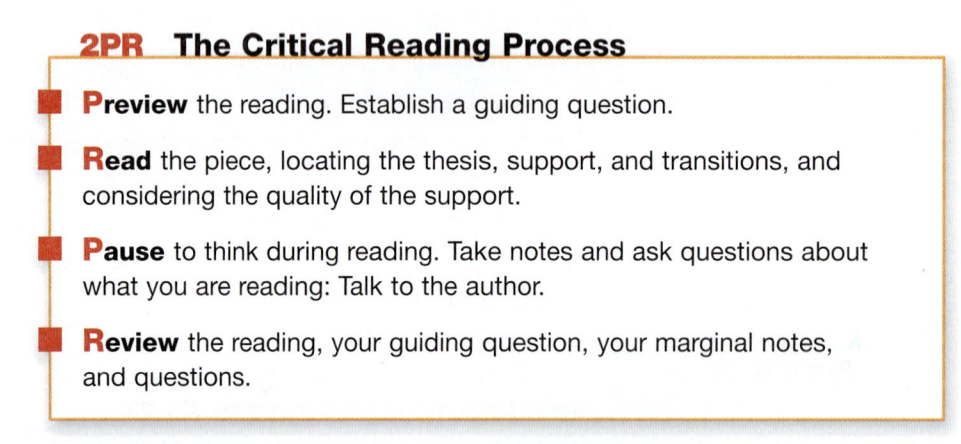

2PR The Critical Reading Process

- **Preview** the reading. Establish a guiding question.
- **Read** the piece, locating the thesis, support, and transitions, and considering the quality of the support.
- **Pause** to think during reading. Take notes and ask questions about what you are reading: Talk to the author.
- **Review** the reading, your guiding question, your marginal notes, and questions.

For more on the critical reading process, see pages 9–12.

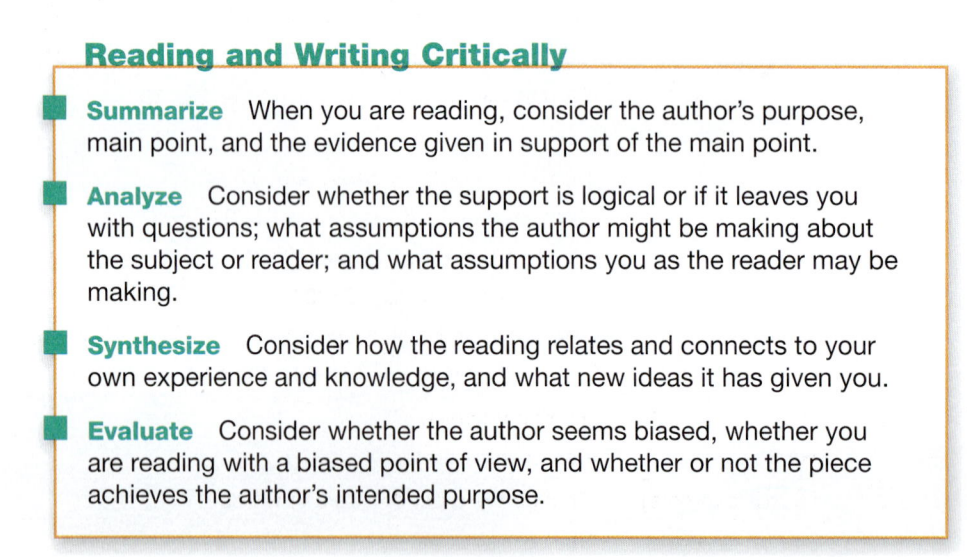

Reading and Writing Critically

- **Summarize** When you are reading, consider the author's purpose, main point, and the evidence given in support of the main point.
- **Analyze** Consider whether the support is logical or if it leaves you with questions; what assumptions the author might be making about the subject or reader; and what assumptions you as the reader may be making.
- **Synthesize** Consider how the reading relates and connects to your own experience and knowledge, and what new ideas it has given you.
- **Evaluate** Consider whether the author seems biased, whether you are reading with a biased point of view, and whether or not the piece achieves the author's intended purpose.

For more on reading and writing critically, see pages 16–21.

Editing and Proofreading Marks

The marks and abbreviations below are those typically used by instructors when marking papers (add any alternate marks used by your instructor in the left-hand column), but you can also mark your own work or that of your peers with these helpful symbols.

ALTERNATE SYMBOL	STANDARD SYMBOL	HOW TO REVISE OR EDIT (numbers in boldface are chapters where you can find help)
	adj	Use correct adjective form Ch. 25
	adv	Use correct adverb form Ch. 25
	agr	Correct subject-verb agreement or pronoun agreement Chs. 22 and 24
	awk	Awkward expression: edit for clarity Ch. 22
	cap or triple underline [example]	Use capital letter correctly Ch. 38
	case	Use correct pronoun case Ch. 24
	cliché	Replace overused phrase with fresh words Ch. 31
	coh	Revise paragraph or essay for coherence Ch. 7
	coord	Use coordination correctly Ch. 27
	cs	Comma splice: join the sentences correctly Ch. 21
	dev	Develop your paragraph or essay more completely Chs. 3 and 5
	dm	Revise to avoid a dangling modifier Ch. 26
	frag	Attach the fragment to a sentence or make it a sentence Ch. 20
	fs	Fused sentence: join the two sentences correctly Ch. 21
	ital	Use italics Ch. 36
	lc or diagonal slash [Example]	Use lowercase Ch. 38
	mm	Revise to avoid a misplaced modifier Ch. 26
	pl	Use the correct plural form of the verb Ch. 23
	ref	Make pronoun reference clear Ch. 24
	ro	Run-on sentence; join the two sentences correctly Ch. 21
	sp	Correct the spelling error Ch. 33
	sub	Use subordination correctly Ch. 27
	sup	Support your point with details, examples, or facts Ch. 5
	tense	Correct the problem with verb tense Ch. 23
	trans	Add a transition Ch. 7
	w	Delete unnecessary words Ch. 31
	wc	Reconsider your word choice Ch. 31
	?	Make your meaning clearer Ch. 7
	^,	Use comma correctly Ch. 34
	; : ( ) - —	Use semicolon / colon / parentheses / hyphen / dash correctly Ch. 37
	" "	Use quotation marks correctly Ch. 36
	^	Insert something
	⸺ [exaample]	Delete something
	⁀ [words example]	Change the order of letters or words
	¶	Start a new paragraph
	# [examplewords]	Add a space
	⌒ [ex ample]	Close up a space

For Easy Reference: Selected Lists and Charts

Critical Reading and Thinking Help

Four Basics of Critical Thinking 7
Questioning Assumptions 8
2PR The Critical Reading Process 9
Reading and Writing Critically 16

Four Basics of Good . . .

Writing 27
Narration 113
Illustration 132
Description 152
Process Analysis 170
Classification 188
Definition 207
Comparison and Contrast 225
Cause and Effect 246
Argument 265
Summaries 291
Reports 295
Responses to Essay Questions 299

Writing Help

Audience and Purpose 28
The Writing Process 34
Questions for Finding a Good Topic 43
Prewriting Techniques 46
Basics of a Good Topic Sentence or Thesis Statement 53
Basics of Good Support 69
Three Quick Strategies for Generating Support 71
Basics of a Good Draft 77
Basics of a Good Introduction 86
Basics of a Good Essay Conclusion 89
Basics of a Good Essay Title 91
Tips for Revising Your Writing 97
Basics of Useful Feedback 98
Questions for Peer Reviewers 98
Reading to Summarize 292
Sample Research Essay Schedule 303
Questions for the Librarian 304
Questions for Evaluating a Print or Electronic Source 308

Guide to Internet Address Extensions 309

Directory of MLA In-Text Citations 314
Directory of MLA Works Cited 316

Sample Student Research Paper 320

Grammar Help: How to . . .

Use Common Transitional Words and Phrases 103
Find and Fix Fragments 358
Find and Fix Run-Ons 376
Find and Fix Problems with Subject-Verb Agreement 396
Use Irregular Verb Forms 402
Find and Fix Verb-Tense Errors 421
Find and Fix Pronoun Problems 447
Edit for Correct Usage of Adjectives and Adverbs 457
Edit for Misplaced and Dangling Modifiers 464
Edit for Coordination and Subordination 477
Edit for Parallelism 485
Edit for Sentence Variety 498
Use Articles with Count and Noncount Nouns 525
Avoid Vague and Abstract Words 536
Avoid Common Wordy Expressions 539
Avoid Common Clichés 540
Edit for Word Choice 544
Avoid Commonly Misspelled Words 562

Profiles of Success

Kelly Layland, Registered Nurse 123
Karen Upright, Systems Manager 140
Celia Hyde, Chief of Police 161
Jeremy Graham, Youth Pastor and Motivational Speaker 177
Leigh King, Fashion Writer / Blogger 197
Walter Scanlon, Program and Workplace Consultant 215
Brad Leibov, President, New Chicago Fund, Inc. 236
Mary LaCue Booker, Singer, Actor 256
Diane Melancon, Oncologist 279